Data Structures And Algorithmic Thinking With Go

Narasimha Karumanchi

Concepts Problems Interview Questions

Designed by *Narasimha Karumanchi*

Acknowledgements

This book would not have been possible without the help of many people. I would like to express my gratitude to all of the people who provided support, talked things over, read, wrote, offered comments, allowed me to quote their remarks and assisted in the editing, proofreading and design. In particular, I would like to thank the following individuals:

- *Mohan Mullapudi*, IIT Bombay, Architect, dataRPM Pvt. Ltd.
- *Navin Kumar Jaiswal*, Senior Consultant, Juniper Networks Inc.

–Narasimha Karumanchi

M-Tech, *IIT Bombay*

Founder, *CareerMonk Publications*

- By all means to my wife, *Swathi*, for being patient and understanding.
- To my children, *Aryan*, and *Sri Saila Anika*.
- To my sisters, *Leela*, *Vijaya*, and *Prameela*. They spend so much time wishing my every action.
- *Mother* (*Laxmi*) and *Father* (*Modaiah*), it is impossible to thank you adequately for everything you have done, from loving me unconditionally to raising me in a stable household, where your persistent efforts and traditional values taught your children to celebrate and embrace life. I could not have asked for better parents or role-models. You showed me that anything is possible with faith, hard work and determination.

Preface

Dear Reader,

Please hold on! I know many people typically do not read the Preface of a book. But I strongly recommend that you read this particular Preface.

The study of algorithms and data structures is central to understanding what computer science is all about. Learning computer science is not unlike learning any other type of difficult subject matter. The only way to be successful is through deliberate and incremental exposure to the fundamental ideas. A beginning computer scientist needs practice so that there is a thorough understanding before continuing on to the more complex parts of the curriculum. In addition, a beginner needs to be given the opportunity to be successful and gain confidence. This textbook is designed to serve as a text for a first course on data structures and algorithms. In this book, we cover abstract data types and data structures, writing algorithms, and solving problems. We look at a number of data structures and solve classic problems that arise. The tools and techniques that you learn here will be applied over and over as you continue your study of computer science.

It is not the main objective of this book to present you with the theorems and proofs on *data structures* and *algorithms*. I have followed a pattern of improving the problem solutions with different complexities (for each problem, you will find multiple solutions with different, and reduced, complexities). Basically, it's an enumeration of possible solutions. With this approach, even if you get a new question, it will show you a way to *think* about the possible solutions. You will find this book useful for interview preparation, competitive exams preparation, and campus interview preparations.

As a *job seeker*, if you read the complete book, I am sure you will be able to challenge the interviewers. If you read it as an *instructor*, it will help you to deliver lectures with an approach that is easy to follow, and as a result your students will appreciate the fact that they have opted for Computer Science / Information Technology as their degree.

This book is also useful for *Engineering degree students* and *Masters degree students* during their academic preparations. In all the chapters you will see that there is more emphasis on problems and their analysis rather than on theory. In each chapter, you will first read about the basic required theory, which is then followed by a section on problem sets.

If you read the book as a *student* preparing for competitive exams for Computer Science / Information Technology, the content covers *all the required topics* in full detail. While writing this book, my main focus was to help students who are preparing for these exams.

In all the chapters you will see more emphasis on problems and analysis rather than on theory. In each chapter, you will first see the basic required theory followed by various problems.

For many problems, *multiple* solutions are provided with different levels of complexity. We start with the *brute force* solution and slowly move toward the *best solution* possible for that problem. For each problem, we endeavor to understand how much time the algorithm takes and how much memory the algorithm uses.

It is recommended that the reader does at least one *complete* reading of this book to gain a full understanding of all the topics that are covered. Then, in subsequent readings you can skip directly to any chapter to refer to a specific topic. Even though many readings have been done for the purpose of correcting errors, there could still be some minor typos in the book. If any are found, they will be updated at *www.CareerMonk.com*. You can monitor this site for any corrections and also for new problems and solutions. If any are found, they will be updated at *CareerMonk.com*. You can monitor this site for any corrections and also for new problems and solutions. Also, please provide your valuable suggestions at: *Info@CareerMonk.com*.

I wish you all the best and I am confident that you will find this book useful.

–*Narasimha Karumanchi*
M-Tech, *IIT Bombay*
Founder, *CareerMonk Publications*

Source code: https://github.com/careermonk/data-structures-and-algorithmic-thinking-with-go.git

Other Books by Narasimha Karumanchi

- Data Structures and Algorithms Made Easy
- IT Interview Questions
- Data Structures and Algorithms for GATE
- Data Structures and Algorithms Made Easy in Java
- Coding Interview Questions
- Peeling Design Patterns
- Elements of Computer Networking
- Data Structures and Algorithmic Thinking with Python
- Algorithm Design Techniques

Table of Contents

Data Structure Operations Cheat Sheet

Data Structure Name	Average Case Time Complexity				Worst Case Time Complexity				Space Complexity
	Accessing n^{th} element	Search	Insertion	Deletion	Accessing n^{th} element	Search	Insertion	Deletion	Worst Case
Arrays	O(1)	$O(n)$	$O(n)$	$O(n)$	O(1)	$O(n)$	$O(n)$	$O(n)$	$O(n)$
Stacks	$O(n)$	$O(n)$	O(1)	O(1)	$O(n)$	$O(n)$	O(1)	O(1)	$O(n)$
Queues	$O(n)$	$O(n)$	O(1)	O(1)	$O(n)$	$O(n)$	O(1)	O(1)	$O(n)$
Binary Trees	$O(n)$	$O(n)$	$O(n)$	$O(n)$	$O(n)$	$O(n)$	$O(n)$	$O(n)$	$O(n)$
Binary Search Trees	$O(logn)$	$O(logn)$	$O(logn)$	$O(logn)$	$O(n)$	$O(n)$	$O(n)$	$O(n)$	$O(n)$
Balanced Binary Search Trees	$O(logn)$	$O(logn)$	$O(logn)$	$O(logn)$	$O(logn)$	$O(logn)$	$O(logn)$	$O(logn)$	$O(logn)$
Hash Tables	N/A	O(1)	O(1)	O(1)	N/A	$O(n)$	$O(n)$	$O(n)$	$O(n)$

Note: For best case operations, the time complexities are O(1).

Sorting Algorithms Cheat Sheet

Sorting Algorithm Name	Time Complexity			Space Complexity	Is Stable?	Sorting Class Type	Remarks
	Best Case	Average Case	Worst Case	Worst Case			
Bubble Sort	$O(n)$	$O(n^2)$	$O(n^2)$	O(1)	Yes	Comparison	Not a preferred sorting algorithm.
Insertion Sort	$O(n)$	$O(n^2)$	$O(n^2)$	O(1)	Yes	Comparison	In the best case (already sorted), every insert requires constant time
Selection Sort	$O(n^2)$	$O(n^2)$	$O(n^2)$	O(1)	Yes	Comparison	Even a perfectly sorted array requires scanning the entire array
Merge Sort	$O(nlogn)$	$O(nlogn)$	$O(nlogn)$	$O(n)$	Yes	Comparison	On arrays, it requires $O(n)$ space; and on linked lists, it requires constant space
Heap Sort	$O(nlogn)$	$O(nlogn)$	$O(nlogn)$	O(1)	No	Comparison	By using input array as storage for the heap, it is possible to achieve constant space
Quick Sort	$O(nlogn)$	$O(nlogn)$	$O(n^2)$	$O(logn)$	No	Comparison	Randomly picking a pivot value can help avoid worst case scenarios such as a perfectly sorted array.
Tree Sort	$O(nlogn)$	$O(nlogn)$	$O(n^2)$	$O(n)$	Yes	Comparison	Performing inorder traversal on the balanced binary search tree.
Counting Sort	$O(n + k)$	$O(n + k)$	$O(n + k)$	$O(k)$	Yes	Linear	Where k is the range of the non-negative key values.
Bucket Sort	$O(n + k)$	$O(n + k)$	$O(n^2)$	$O(n)$	Yes	Linear	Bucket sort is stable, if the underlying sorting algorithm is stable.
Radix Sort	$O(dn)$	$O(dn)$	$O(dn)$	$O(d + n)$	Yes	Linear	Radix sort is stable, if the underlying sorting algorithm is stable.

ORGANIZATION OF CHAPTERS

CHAPTER

0

0.1 What Is This Book About?

This book is about the fundamentals of data structures and algorithms – the basic elements from which large and complex software projects are built. To develop a good understanding of a data structure requires three things: first, you must learn how the information is arranged in the memory of the computer; second, you must become familiar with the algorithms for manipulating the information contained in the data structure; and third, you must understand the performance characteristics of the data structure so that when called upon to select a suitable data structure for a particular application, you are able to make an appropriate decision.

The algorithms and data structures in this book are presented in the *Go* programming language. A unique feature of this book, when compared to the available books on the subject, is that it offers a balance of theory, practical concepts, problem solving, and interview questions.

Concepts + Problems + Interview Questions

The book deals with some of the most important and challenging areas of programming and computer science in a highly readable manner. It covers both algorithmic theory and programming practice, demonstrating how theory is reflected in real *Go* programs. Well-known algorithms and data structures that are built into the *Go* language is explained, and the user is shown how to implement and evaluate others.

The book offers a large number of questions, with detailed answers, so you can practice and assess your knowledge before you take the exam or are interviewed.

Salient features of the book are:

- Basic principles of algorithm design
- How to represent well-known data structures in *Go* language
- How to implement well-known algorithms in *Go* language
- How to transform new problems into well-known algorithmic problems with efficient solutions
- How to analyze algorithms and *Go* programs using both mathematical tools and basic experiments and benchmarks
- How to understand several classical algorithms and data structures in depth, and be able to implement these efficiently in *Go*

0.2 Should I Buy This Book?

The book is intended for Go programmers who need to learn about algorithmic problem-solving or who need a refresher. However, others will also find it useful, including data and computational scientists employed to do cloud computing; big data analytic analysis; game programmers and financial analysts/engineers; and students of computer science or programming-related subjects such as bioinformatics.

Although this book is more precise and analytical than many other data structure and algorithm books, it rarely uses mathematical concepts that are more advanced than those taught in high school. I have made an effort to avoid using any advanced calculus, probability, or stochastic process concepts. The book is therefore appropriate for undergraduate students preparing for interviews.

0.3 Organization of Chapters

Data structures and algorithms are important aspects of computer science as they form the fundamental building blocks of developing logical solutions to problems, as well as creating efficient programs that perform tasks optimally. This book covers the topics required for a thorough understanding of the subjects such concepts as Linked Lists, Stacks, Queues, Trees, Priority Queues, Searching, Sorting, Hashing, Algorithm Design Techniques, Greedy, Divide and Conquer, Dynamic Programming and Symbol Tables.

The chapters are arranged as follows:

1. ***Introduction***: This chapter provides an overview of algorithms and their place in modern computing systems. It considers the general motivations for algorithmic analysis and the various approaches to studying the performance characteristics of algorithms.
2. ***Recursion and Backtracking***: *Recursion* is a programming technique that allows the programmer to express operations in terms of themselves. In other words, it is the process of defining a function or calculating a number by the repeated application of an algorithm.

   For many real-world problems, the solution process consists of working your way through a sequence of decision points in which each choice leads you further along some path (for example problems in the Trees and Graphs domain). If you make the correct set of choices, you end up at the solution. On the other hand, if you reach a dead end or otherwise discover that you have made an incorrect choice somewhere along the way, you have to backtrack to a previous decision point and try a different path.

   Algorithms that use this approach are called *backtracking* algorithms, and backtracking is a form of recursion. Also, some problems can be solved by combining recursion with backtracking.
3. ***Linked Lists***: A *linked list* is a dynamic data structure. The number of nodes in a list is not fixed and can grow and shrink on demand. Any application which has to deal with an unknown number of objects will need to use a linked list. It is a very common data structure that is used to create other data structures like trees, graphs, hashing. etc.
4. ***Stacks***: A *stack* abstract type is a container of objects that are inserted and removed according to the last-in-first-out (LIFO) principle. There are many applications of stacks, including:
   a. Space for function parameters and local variables is created internally using a stack.
   b. Compiler's syntax check for matching braces is implemented by using stack.
   c. Support for recursion.
   d. It can act as an auxiliary data structure for other abstract data types.
5. ***Queues***: *Queue* is also an abstract data structure or a linear data structure, in which the first element is inserted from one end called as *rear* (also called *tail*), and the deletion of the existing element takes place from the other end, called as *front* (also called *head*). This makes queue as FIFO data structure, which means that element inserted first will also be removed first. There are many applications of stacks, including:
   a. In operating systems, for controlling access to shared system resources such as printers, files, communication lines, disks and tapes.
   b. Computer systems must often provide a *holding area* for messages between two processes, two programs, or even two systems. This holding area is usually called a *buffer* and is often implemented as a queue.
   c. It can act as an auxiliary data structure for other abstract data types.
6. ***Trees***: A *tree* is an abstract data structure used to organize the data in a tree format so as to make the data insertion or deletion or search faster. Trees are one of the most useful data structures in computer science. Some of the common applications of trees are:

   a. The library database in a library, a student database in a school or college, an employee database in a company, a patient database in a hospital, or basically any database would be implemented using trees.
   b. The file system in your computer, i.e. folders and all files, would be stored as a tree.
   c. And a tree can act as an auxiliary data structure for other abstract data types.

   A tree is an example of a non-linear data structure. There are many variants in trees, classified by the number of children and the way of interconnecting them. This chapter focuses on some of these variants, including Generic Trees, Binary Trees, Binary Search Trees, Balanced Binary Trees, etc.
7. ***Priority Queues***: The *priority queue* abstract data type is designed for systems that maintain a collection of prioritized elements, where elements are removed from the collection in order of their priority. Priority queues turn up in various applications, for example, processing jobs, where we process each job based on how urgent it is. For example, operating systems often use a priority queue for the ready queue of processes to run on the CPU.
8. ***Graph Algorithms***: Graphs are a fundamental data structure in the world of programming. A graph abstract data type is a collection of nodes called *vertices*, and the connections between them called *edges*. Graphs are an example of a non-linear data structure. This chapter focuses on representations of graphs (adjacency list and matrix representations), shortest path algorithms, etc. Graphs can be used to model many types of relations and processes in physical, biological, social and information systems, and many practical problems can be represented by graphs.
9. ***Disjoint Set ADT***: A disjoint set abstract data type represents a collection of sets that are disjoint: that is, no item is found in more than one set. The collection of disjoint sets is called a partition, because the items are partitioned among the sets. As an example, suppose the items in our universe are companies that still exist today or were acquired by other corporations. Our sets are companies that still exist under their own name. For instance, "*Motorola*," "*YouTube*," and "*Android*" are all members of the "*Google*" set.

   This chapter is limited to two operations. The first is called a *union* operation, in which we merge two sets into one. The second is called a *find* query, in which we ask a question like, "What corporation does Android belong to today?" More generally, a $find$ query takes an item and tells us which set it is in. Data structures designed to support these operations are called $union/find$ data structures. Applications of $union/find$ data structures include maze generation and Kruskal's algorithm for computing the minimum spanning tree of a graph.

10. ***Sorting Algorithms***: *Sorting* is an algorithm that arranges the elements of a list in a certain order [either ascending or descending]. The output is a permutation or reordering of the input, and sorting is one of the important categories of algorithms in computer science. Sometimes sorting significantly reduces the complexity of the problem, and we can use sorting as a technique to reduce search complexity. Much research has gone into this category of algorithms because of its importance. These algorithms are used in many computer algorithms, for example, searching elements and database algorithms. In this chapter, we examine both comparison-based sorting algorithms and linear sorting algorithms.
11. ***Searching Algorithms***: In computer science, *searching* is the process of finding an item with specified properties from a collection of items. The items may be stored as records in a database, simple data elements in arrays, text in files, nodes in trees, vertices and edges in graphs, or elements of other search spaces.

    Searching is one of the core computer science algorithms. We know that today's computers store a lot of information, and to retrieve this information we need highly efficient searching algorithms. There are certain ways of organizing the data which improves the searching process. That means, if we keep the data in proper order, it is easy to search the required element. Sorting is one of the techniques for making the elements ordered. In this chapter we will see different searching algorithms.
12. ***Selection Algorithms***: A *selection algorithm* is an algorithm for finding the kth smallest/largest number in a list (also called as k^{th} order statistic). This includes finding the minimum, maximum, and median elements. For finding k^{th} order statistic, there are multiple solutions which provide different complexities, and in this chapter, we will enumerate those possibilities. We will also look at a linear algorithm for finding the kth element in a given list.
13. ***Symbol Tables*** (*Dictionaries*): Since childhood, we all have used a dictionary, and many of us have a word processor (say, Microsoft Word), which comes with a spell checker. The spell checker is also a dictionary but limited in scope. There are many real time examples for dictionaries and a few of them are:
    a. Spell checker
    b. The data dictionary found in database management applications
    c. Symbol tables generated by loaders, assemblers, and compilers
    d. Routing tables in networking components (DNS lookup)

    In computer science, we generally use the term 'symbol' table rather than dictionary, when referring to the abstract data type (ADT).
14. ***Hashing***: *Hashing* is a technique used for storing and retrieving information as fast as possible. It is used to perform optimal search and is useful in implementing symbol tables. From the *Trees* chapter we understand that balanced binary search trees support operations such as insert, delete and search in O($logn$) time. In applications, if we need these operations in O(1), then *hashing* provides a way. Remember that the worst-case complexity of hashing is still O(n), but it gives O(1) on the average. In this chapter, we will take a detailed look at the hashing process and problems which can be solved with this technique.
15. ***String Algorithms***: To understand the importance of string algorithms, let us consider the case of entering the URL (Uniform Resource Locator) in any browser (say, Internet Explorer, Firefox, or Google Chrome). You will observe that after typing the prefix of the URL, a list of all possible URLs is displayed. That means, the browsers are doing some internal processing and giving us the list of matching URLs. This technique is sometimes called *auto-completion*. Similarly, consider the case of entering the directory name in a command line interface (in both Windows and UNIX). After typing the prefix of the directory name, if we press tab button, we then get a list of all matched directory names available. This is another example of auto completion.

    In order to support these kinds of operations, we need a data structure which stores the string data efficiently. In this chapter, we will look at the data structures that are useful for implementing string algorithms. We start our discussion with the basic problem of strings: given a string, how do we search a substring (pattern)? This is called *string matching problem*. After discussing various string-matching algorithms, we will see different data structures for storing strings.
16. ***Algorithms Design Techniques***: In the previous chapters, we have seen many algorithms for solving different kinds of problems. Before solving a new problem, the general tendency is to look for the similarity of the current problem to other problems for which we have solutions. This helps us to get the solution easily. In this chapter, we see different ways of classifying the algorithms, and in subsequent chapters we will focus on a few of them (e.g., Greedy, Divide and Conquer, and Dynamic Programming).
17. ***Greedy Algorithms***: A greedy algorithm is also called a *single-minded* algorithm. A greedy algorithm is a process that looks for simple, easy-to-implement solutions to complex, multi-step problems by deciding which next step will provide the most obvious benefit. The idea behind a greedy algorithm is to perform a single procedure in the recipe over and over again until it can't be done any more, and see what kind of results it will produce. It may not completely solve the problem, or, if it produces a solution, it may not be the very best one, but it is one way of approaching the problem and sometimes yields very good (or even the best possible) results. Examples of greedy algorithms include selection sort, Prim's algorithms, Kruskal's algorithms, Dijkstra algorithm, Huffman coding algorithm etc.
18. ***Divide And Conquer***: These algorithms work based on the principles described below.

a. *Divide* - break the problem into several subproblems that are similar to the original problem but smaller in size
b. *Conquer* - solve the subproblems recursively.
c. *Base case*: If the subproblem size is small enough (i.e., the base case has been reached) then solve the subproblem directly without more recursion.
d. *Combine* - the solutions to create a solution for the original problem

Examples of divide and conquer algorithms include Binary Search, Merge Sort etc....

19. ***Dynamic Programming***: In this chapter we will try to solve the problems for which we failed to get the optimal solutions using other techniques (say, Divide & Conquer and Greedy methods). Dynamic Programming (DP) is a simple technique but it can be difficult to master. One easy way to identify and solve DP problems is by solving as many problems as possible. The term Programming is not related to coding; it is from literature, and it means filling tables (similar to Linear Programming).
20. ***Complexity Classes***: In previous chapters we solved problems of different complexities. Some algorithms have lower rates of growth while others have higher rates of growth. The problems with lower rates of growth are called easy problems (or easy solved problems) and the problems with higher rates of growth are called hard problems (or hard solved problems). This classification is done based on the running time (or memory) that an algorithm takes for solving the problem. There are lots of problems for which we do not know the solutions.

    In computer science, in order to understand the problems for which solutions are not there, the problems are divided into classes, and we call them *complexity classes*. In complexity theory, a complexity class is a set of problems with related complexity. It is the branch of theory of computation that studies the resources required during computation to solve a given problem. The most common resources are time (how much time the algorithm takes to solve a problem) and space (how much memory it takes). This chapter classifies the problems into different types based on their complexity class.
21. ***Miscellaneous Concepts*: *Bit – wise Hacking***: The commonality or applicability depends on the problem in hand. Some real-life projects do benefit from bit-wise operations.

    Some examples:
    - You're setting individual pixels on the screen by directly manipulating the video memory, in which every pixel's color is represented by 1 or 4 bits. So, in every byte you can have packed 8 or 2 pixels and you need to separate them. Basically, your hardware dictates the use of bit-wise operations.
    - You're dealing with some kind of file format (e.g. GIF) or network protocol that uses individual bits or groups of bits to represent pieces of information.
    - Your data dictates the use of bit-wise operations. You need to compute some kind of checksum (possibly, parity or CRC) or hash value, and some of the most applicable algorithms do this by manipulating with bits.

    In this chapter, we discuss a few tips and tricks with a focus on bitwise operators. Also, it covers a few other uncovered and general problems.

At the end of each chapter, a set of problems/questions is provided for you to improve/check your understanding of the concepts. The examples in this book are kept simple for easy understanding. The objective is to enhance the explanation of each concept with examples for a better understanding.

0.4 Some Prerequisites

This book is intended for two groups of people: *Go* programmers who want to beef up their algorithmics, and students taking algorithm courses who want a supplement to their algorithm's textbook. Even if you belong to the latter group, I'm assuming you have a familiarity with programming in general and with *Go* in particular. If you don't, the *Go* web site also has a lot of useful material. *Go* is a really easy language to learn. There is some math in the pages ahead, but you don't have to be a math prodigy to follow the text. We'll be dealing with some simple sums and nifty concepts such as polynomials, exponentials, and logarithms, but I'll explain it all as we go along.

0.5 GoLang Cheat Sheet

Go (also referred to as GoLang) is an open source and lower level progra-mming language designed and created at Google in 2009 by Robert Griesemer, Rob Pike and Ken Thompson, to enable users to easily write simple, reliable, and highly efficient computer programs. Golang is better known for its built-in concurrency and garbage collection features. Also, GoLang is a statically typed language.

0.5.1 Go in a Nutshell

- Go is a statically typed language
- Syntax similar to Java/C/C++, but less parentheses and no semicolons
- Compiles to native code (no JVM)
- Go does not have classes, but it has structs with methods
- Go has interfaces
- No implementation inheritance. There's type embedding, though.
- Functions are first class citizens

- Go functions can return multiple values
- Go has closures
- Go support pointers, but not pointer arithmetic
- Go has built-in concurrency support: Goroutines and Channels

0.5.2 Basic Syntax

```
package main
import "fmt"
func main() {
  message := sayHello("Simha")
  fmt.Println(message)
}
func sayHello(name string) string {
  return "Hello, " + name + "!"
}
```

0.5.3 Packages

- Package declaration is required at top of every source go file
- Executables are in *main* package
- Convention: package name == last name of import path (import path math/rand => package rand)
- Upper case identifier: exported (visible to other packages)
- Lower case identifier: private (not visible to other packages)

0.5.4 Operators

Arithmetic Operators

- + addition
- - subtraction
- multiplication
- / quotient
- % remainder

Bitwise Operators

- & bitwise and
- | bitwise or
- ^ bitwise xor
- &^ bit clear (and not)
- << left shift
- >> right shift

Comparison Operators

- == equal
- != not equal
- < less than
- <= less than or equal
- > greater than
- >= greater than or equal

Logical Operators

- && logical and
- || logical or
- ! logical not

Other Operators

- & address of / create pointer
- dereference pointer
- <- send / receive operator

0.5.5 Functions

A simple function

```
func functionName() {}
```

Function with parameters

```
func functionName(param1 string, param2 int) {}
```

Multiple parameters of the same type

```
func functionName(param1, param2 int) {}
```

Return type declaration

```
func functionName() int {
   return 19
}
```

Return multiple

```
func returnMultiple() (int, string) {
   return 19, "string value"
}
var x, str = returnMultiple()
```

Return multiple named results simply by return

```
func returnMultiple() (n int, s string) {
   n = 19
   s = "value1"
   // n and s will be returned
   return
}
var x, str = returnMultiple()
```

Functions as Values and Closures

```
func main() {
    // assign a function to a name
    sub := func(a, b int) int {
        return a - b
    }
    // use the name to call the function
    fmt.Println(sub(6, 3))
}
// Closures, lexically scoped: Functions can access values that were in scope when defining the function
func scope() func() int{
     outer_var := 2
    foo := func() int { return outer_var}
    return foo
}
func another_scope() func() int{
    // won't compile because outer_var and foo not defined in this scope
    outer_var = 999
    return foo
}
// Closures: don't mutate outer vars, instead redefine them!
func outer() (func() int, int) {
    outer_var := 2
     inner := func() int {
        outer_var += 99 // attempt to mutate outer_var from outer scope
        return outer_var // => 101 (but outer_var is a newly redefined variable visible only inside inner)
    }
    return inner, outer_var // => 101, 2 (outer_var is still 2, not mutated by foo!)
}
```

Variadic Functions

```
func main() {
    fmt.Println(adder(1, 2, 3))     // 6
    fmt.Println(adder(9, 9))        // 18

    nums := []int{10, 20, 30}
    fmt.Println(adder(nums...))  // 60
}
```

```
    // By using ... before the type name of the last parameter we can indicate that
    // it takes zero or more of those parameters. The function is invoked like any
    // other function except we can pass as many arguments as we want.
func adder(args ...int) int {
        total := 0
        for _, v := range args { // Iterates over the arguments whatever the number.
            total += v
        }
        return total
    }
```

0.5.6 Declarations

```
var foo int                        // declare without initial
var foo int = 19                   // declare with initial
var foo, bar int = 19, 1302        // declare and init
var a, b int = 12, 13              // declare and init
a, b := 12, 13                     // declare and init
var foo = 19                       // type omitted, will be inferred
foo := 9                           // shorthand
const constant = "This is a constant"
const Phi = 1.618                  // another constant of float type
```

0.5.7 Type Conversions

The expression T(v) converts the value v to the type T.

Some numeric conversions:

```
var i int = 19
var f float64 = float64(i)
var u uint = uint(f)
```

Or, we can put more simply as:

```
i := 19
f := float64(i)
u := uint(f)
```

Unlike in C, in Go assignment between items of different type requires an explicit conversion. Try removing the float64 or uint conversions in the example and see what happens.

```
var x, y int = 2, 3
var f float64 = math.Sqrt(float64(x*x + y*y))
var z uint = uint(f)
fmt.Println(x, y, z)          // prints-> 2 3 3
```

0.5.8 Type assertions

A type assertion provides access to an interface value's underlying concrete value.

```
t := i.(T)
```

This statement asserts that the interface value i holds the concrete type T and assigns the underlying T value to the variable t. If i does not hold a T, the statement will trigger a panic. To test whether an interface value holds a specific type, a type assertion can return two values: the underlying value and a boolean value that reports whether the assertion succeeded.

```
t, ok := i.(T)
```

If i holds a T, then t will be the underlying value and ok will be true. If not, ok will be false and t will be the zero value of type T, and no panic occurs. Note the similarity between this syntax and that of reading from a map.

```
var i interface{} = "CareerMonk"

s := i.(string)
fmt.Println(s)          // prints-> CareerMonk

s, ok := i.(string)
fmt.Println(s, ok)      // prints-> CareerMonk true

f, ok := i.(float64)
fmt.Println(f, ok)      // prints-> 0 false

f = i.(float64)         // panic
```

```
fmt.Println(f)
```

0.5.9 Arrays, Slices, and Ranges

Arrays

```
var A [10]int
// declare an int array with length 10. Array length is part of the type!
A[5] = 19                    // set elements
i := A[35]                   // read elements
// declare and initialize
var A = [3]int{1, 2, 10}
A := [3]int{1, 2}            //shorthand
A := [...]int{1, 2}          // ellipsis -> Compiler figures out array length
```

Slices

```
var A []int                  // declare a slice - similar to an array, but length is unspecified
var A = []int {1, 2, 3, 4} // declare and initialize a slice (backed by the array given implicitly)
A := []int{1, 2, 3, 4}       // shorthand
chars := []string{0:"a", 2:"c", 1: "b"} // ["a", "b", "c"]
var B = A[low: high]           // creates a slice (view of the array) from index low to high-1
var B = A[1:4]               // slice from index 1 to 3
var B = A[:3]                // missing low index implies 0
var B = A[3:]                // missing high index implies len(a)

// create a slice with make
A = make([]byte, 5, 5)  // first arg length, second capacity
A = make([]byte, 5)          // capacity is optional

// create a slice from an array
X := [6]string{"Aditi", "Adi", "Ammu", "Aryan", "Dubbu", "Anika"}
S := X[:]                    // a slice referencing the storage of X
```

Operations on Arrays and Slices

```
len(A) gives you the length of an array/A slice. It's a built-in function, not an attribute/method on the array.
// loop over an array/a slice
for i, e := range A {
   // i is the index, e the element
}
// if you only need e:
for _, e := range A {
   // e is the element
}
// ...and if you only need the index
for i := range A {
}
// In Go pre-1.4, you'll get a compiler error if you're not using i and e.
// Go 1.4 introduced a variable-free form, so that you can do this
for range time.Tick(time.Second) {
   // do it once a sec
}
```

0.5.10 Built-In Types

- bool
- string
- int int8 int16 int32 int64
- uint uint8 uint16 uint32 uint64 uintptr
- byte // alias for uint8
- rune // alias for int32 ~= a character (Unicode code point) - very Viking
- float32 float64
- complex64 complex128

0.5.11 Control Structures

If

```
func main() {
```

```
// Basic one
  if x > 0 {
   return x
  } else {
   return -x
 }
 // We can put one statement before the condition
if a := b + c; a < 5 {
    return a
} else {
    return a - 5
 }
 // Type assertion inside if
 var val interface{}
  val = "foo"
  if str, ok := val.(string); ok {
   fmt.Println(str)
 }
}
```

Example-2

```
if day == "Sunday" || day == "Saturday" {
    rest()
} else if day == "Monday" && isTired() {
groan()
} else {
    work()
}
```

Loops

```
// There only for, no while, no until
for i := 1; i < 10; i++ {
    fmt.Println("My counter is at", i)
}
for i < 10 { // while - loop
    fmt.Println("My counter is at", i)
}
for i < 10 { // omit semicolons
    fmt.Println("My counter is at", i)
}
for { //omit the condition ~ while (true); indefinite loop need exit condition inside the loop
}
for i := 0; i <= 10; i++ {
    fmt.Println("My counter is at", i)
}
```

Switch

```
switch operatingSystem {
case "mac":
   fmt.Println("Mac OS Geek")
   // cases break automatically
case "windows":
   fmt.Println("Windows Geek")
default:
   // Windows, BSD, ...
   fmt.Println("Other")
}
// as with for and if, you can have an assignment statement before the switch value
switch os := runtime.GOOS; os {
case "mac": ...
}
```

0.5.12 Maps

```
// Creating a map
var m = make(map[string]string)
```

```
// Adding (key,value) to a map
m["one"] = "1"    // Assigns the value "Angelina" to the key "Rajeev"
m["two"] = "2"
m["three"] = "3"

// Reading map value with key
var value = m["two"]

// Creation and initialization of maps
var m = map[string]int{
    "one":  1,
    "two":  2,
    "three": 3,
    "four": 4,
    "five": 5, // Comma is necessary
}
fmt.Println(m)

// Checking if a key exists in a map
```

When we retrieve the value assigned to a given key using the syntax map[key], it returns an additional boolean value as well which is true if the key exists in the map, and false if it doesn't exist. So, we can check for the existence of a key in a map by using the following two-value assignment -

```
value, ok := m[key]
```

The boolean variable ok will be true if the key exists, and false otherwise.

0.5.13 Structs

There are no classes, only structs. Structs can have methods.

```
// A struct is a type. It's also a collection of fields.

// Declaration
type Edge struct {
   From, To int
}

// Creating
var e = Edge{1, 2}
var e = Edge{From: 1, To: 2} // Creates a struct by defining values with keys

// Accessing members
e.From = 4

// You can declare methods on structs. The struct you want to declare the
// method on (the receiving type) comes between the func keyword and
// the method name. The struct is copied on each method call(!)
func (e Edge) Abs() float64 {
   return math.Sqrt(e.From*e.From + e.To*e.To)
}

// Call method
e.Abs()

// For mutating methods, you need to use a pointer (see below) to the Struct
// as the type. With this, the struct value is not copied for the method call.
func (e *Edge) add(n float64) {
   e.From += n
   e.To += n
}
```

0.5.14 Pointers

```
p := Edge1, 2}        // p is an Edge
q := &p               // q is a pointer to an Edge
r := &Edge{1, 2}      // r is also a pointer to an Edge

// The type of a pointer to an Edge is *Edge

var s *Edge = new(Edge) // new creates a pointer to a new struct instance
```

0.5.15 Interfaces

```
// interface declaration
type Awesomizer interface {
   Awesomize() string
```

```
}
// types do *not* declare to implement interfaces
type Foo struct {}
// instead, types implicitly satisfy an interface if they implement all required methods
func (foo Foo) Awesomize() string {
    return "Awesome!!"
}
```

0.5.16 Concurrency

Goroutines

Goroutines are lightweight threads (managed by Go, not OS threads). go f(a, b) starts a new goroutine which runs f (given f is a function).

```
// just a function (which can be later started as a goroutine)
func doStuff(s string) {
}
func main() {
    // using a named function in a goroutine
    go doStuff("foobar")
    // using an anonymous inner function in a goroutine
    go func (x int) {
        // function body goes here
    }(19)
}
```

Channels

```
ch := make(chan int)    // create a channel of type int
ch <- 42                // Send a value to the channel ch.
v := <-ch               // Receive a value from ch
// Non-buffered channels block. Read blocks when no value is available, write blocks if a value already has been written but not read.
// Create a buffered channel. Writing to a buffered channel does not block if less than <buffer size> unread values have been written.
ch := make(chan int, 100)
close(c) // closes the channel (only sender should close)
// read from channel and test if it has been closed
v, ok := <-ch
// if ok is false, channel has been closed
// Read from channel until it is closed
for i := range ch {
    fmt.Println(i)
}
// select blocks on multiple channel operations, if one unblocks, the corresponding case is executed
func doStuff(channelOut, channelIn chan int) {
    select {
    case channelOut <- 19:
        fmt.Println("We could write to channelOut!")
    case x := <- channelIn:
        fmt.Println("We could read from channelIn")
    }
}
```

CHAPTER

INTRODUCTION 1

The objective of this chapter is to explain the importance of the analysis of algorithms, their notations, relationships and solving as many problems as possible. Let us first focus on understanding the basic elements of algorithms, the importance of algorithm analysis, and then slowly move toward the other topics as mentioned above. After completing this chapter, you should be able to find the complexity of any given algorithm (especially recursive functions).

1.1 Variables

Before going to the definition of variables, let us relate them to old mathematical equations. All of us have solved many mathematical equations since childhood. As an example, consider the below equation:

$$x^2 + 2y - 2 = 1$$

We don't have to worry about the use of this equation. The important thing that we need to understand is that the equation has names (x and y), which hold values (data). That means the *names* (x and y) are placeholders for representing data. Similarly, in computer science programming we need something for holding data, and *variables* is the way to do that.

1.2 Data Types

In the above-mentioned equation, the variables x and y can take any values such as integral numbers (10, 20), real numbers (0.23, 5.5), or just 0 and 1. To solve the equation, we need to relate them to the kind of values they can take, and *data type* is the name used in computer science programming for this purpose. A *data type* in a programming language is a set of data with predefined values. Examples of data types are: integer, floating point, unit number, character, string, etc.

Computer memory is all filled with zeros and ones. If we have a problem and we want to code it, it's very difficult to provide the solution in terms of zeros and ones. To help users, programming languages and compilers provide us with data types. For example, *integer* takes 2 bytes (actual value depends on compiler), *float* takes 4 bytes, etc. This says that in memory we are combining 2 bytes (16 bits) and calling it an *integer*. Similarly, combining 4 bytes (32 bits) and calling it a *float*. A data type reduces the coding effort. At the top level, there are two types of data types:

- System-defined data types (also called *Primitive* data types)
- User-defined data types

System-defined data types (Primitive data types)

Data types that are defined by system are called *primitive* data types. The primitive data types provided by *Go* programming language are: int (platform dependent, int32, int64,float32, float64, byte, bool, etc. The number of bits allocated for each primitive data type depends on the programming languages, the compiler and the operating system. For the same primitive data type, different languages may use different sizes. Depending on the size of the data types, the total available values (domain) will also change.

The int, uint, and uintptr types are usually 32 bits wide on 32-bit systems and 64 bits wide on 64-bit systems. When you need an integer value you should use int unless you have a specific reason to use a sized or unsigned integer type. For example, "*int*" may take 4 bytes or 8 bytes. If it takes 4 bytes (32 bits), then the total possible values are from -2^{31} *to* $2^{31}-1$. If it takes 8 bytes (64 bits), then the possible values are between -2^{64} *to* $2^{64}-1$. The same is the case with other data types.

User defined data types

If the system-defined data types are not enough, then most programming languages allow the users to define their own data types, called *user – defined data types*. Good examples of user defined data types are: structures in *Go language* and classes in *Java, C + +,* and *Python*. For example, in the snippet below, we are combining many system-defined data types and calling the user defined data type by the name "*NewType*". This gives more flexibility and comfort in dealing with computer memory.

```
type NewType struct {
        data1 int   // platform dependent 32 bits wide on a 32-bit system and 64-bits wide on a 64-bit system
        float32 data2
        ...
        data interface{} // generic data type
};
```

1.3 Data Structures

Based on the discussion above, once we have data in variables, we need some mechanism for manipulating that data to solve problems. *Data structure* is a particular way of storing and organizing data in a computer so that it can be used efficiently. A *data structure* is a special format for organizing and storing data. General data structure types include arrays, files, linked lists, stacks, queues, trees, graphs and so on.

Depending on the organization of the elements, data structures are classified into two types:

1) *Linear data structures*: Elements are accessed in a sequential order but it is not compulsory to store all elements sequentially. *Examples*: Linked Lists, Stacks and Queues.
2) *Non – linear data structures*: Elements of this data structure are stored/accessed in a non-linear order. *Examples*: Trees and graphs.

1.4 Abstract Data Types (ADTs)

Before defining abstract data types, let us consider the different view of system-defined data types. We all know that, by default, all primitive data types (int, float, etc.) support basic operations such as addition and subtraction. The system provides the implementations for the primitive data types. For user-defined data types we also need to define operations. The implementation for these operations can be done when we want to actually use them. That means, in general, user defined data types are defined along with their operations.

To simplify the process of solving problems, we combine the data structures with their operations and we call this *Abstract Data Types* (ADTs). An ADT consists of *two parts*:

1. Declaration of data
2. Declaration of operations

Commonly used ADTs *include*: Linked Lists, Stacks, Queues, Priority Queues, Binary Trees, Dictionaries, Disjoint Sets (Union and Find), Hash Tables, Graphs, and many others. For example, stack uses LIFO (Last-In-First-Out) mechanism while storing the data in data structures. The last element inserted into the stack is the first element that gets deleted. Common operations of it are: creating the stack, pushing an element onto the stack, popping an element from stack, finding the current top of the stack, finding number of elements in the stack, etc.

While defining the ADTs do not worry about the implementation details. They come into the picture only when we want to use them. Different kinds of ADTs are suited to different kinds of applications, and some are highly specialized to specific tasks. By the end of this book, we will go through many of them and you will be in a position to relate the data structures to the kind of problems they solve.

1.5 What is an Algorithm?

Let us consider the problem of preparing an *omelette*. To prepare an omelette, we follow the steps given below:

1) Get the frying pan.
2) Get the oil.
    a. Do we have oil?
        i. If yes, put it in the pan.
        ii. If no, do we want to buy oil?
            1. If yes, then go out and buy.
            2. If no, we can terminate.
3) Turn on the stove, etc...

What we are doing is, for a given problem (preparing an omelet), we are providing a step-by-step procedure for solving it. The formal definition of an algorithm can be stated as:

An algorithm is the step-by-step unambiguous instructions to solve a given problem.

In the traditional study of algorithms, there are two main criteria for judging the merits of algorithms: correctness (does the algorithm give solution to the problem in a finite number of steps?) and efficiency (how much resources (in terms of memory and time) does it take to execute the).

Note: We do not have to prove each step of the algorithm.

1.6 Why the Analysis of Algorithms?

To go from city "*A*" to city "*B*", there can be many ways of accomplishing this: by flight, by bus, by train and also by bicycle. Depending on the availability and convenience, we choose the one that suits us. Similarly, in computer science, multiple algorithms are available for solving the same problem (for example, a sorting problem has many algorithms, like insertion sort, selection sort, quick sort and many more). Algorithm analysis helps us to determine which algorithm is most efficient in terms of time and space consumed.

1.7 Goal of the Analysis of Algorithms

The analysis of an algorithm can help us understand it better and can suggest informed improvements. The main and important role of analysis of algorithm is to predict the performance of different algorithms in order to guide design decisions. The goal of the *analysis of algorithms* is to compare algorithms (or solutions) mainly in terms of running time but also in terms of other factors (e.g., memory, developer effort, etc.).

In theoretical analysis of algorithms, it is common to estimate their complexity in the asymptotic sense, i.e., to estimate the complexity function for arbitrarily large input. The term "analysis of algorithms" was coined by Donald Knuth.

Algorithm analysis is an important part of computational complexity theory, which provides theoretical estimation for the required resources of an algorithm to solve a specific computational problem. Most algorithms are designed to work with inputs of arbitrary length. Analysis of algorithms is the determination of the amount of time and space resources required to execute it.

Usually, the efficiency or running time of an algorithm is stated as a function relating the input length to the number of steps, known as time complexity, or volume of memory, known as space complexity.

1.8 What is Running Time Analysis?

It is the process of determining how processing time increases as the size of the problem (input size) increases. Input size is the number of elements in the input, and depending on the problem type, the input may be of different types. The following are the common types of inputs.

- Size of an array
- Polynomial degree
- Number of elements in a matrix
- Number of bits in the binary representation of the input
- Vertices and edges in a graph.

1.9 How to Compare Algorithms

To compare algorithms, let us define a few *objective measures*:

Execution times? *Not a good measure* as execution times are specific to a particular computer.

Number of statements executed? *Not a good measure*, since the number of statements varies with the programming language as well as the style of the individual programmer.

Ideal solution? Let us assume that we express the running time of a given algorithm as a function of the input size n (i.e., $f(n)$) and compare these different functions corresponding to running times. This kind of comparison is independent of machine time, programming style, etc.

1.10 What is Rate of Growth?

The rate at which the running time increases as a function of input is called *rate of growth*. Let us assume that you go to a shop to buy a car and a bicycle. If your friend sees you there and asks what you are buying, then in general you say *buying a car*. This is because the cost of the car is high compared to the cost of the bicycle (approximating the cost of the bicycle to the cost of the car).

$$Total\ Cost = cost\_of\_car + cost\_of\_bicycle$$
$$Total\ Cost \approx cost\_of\_car\ (approximation)$$

For the above-mentioned example, we can represent the cost of the car and the cost of the bicycle in terms of function, and for a given function ignore the low order terms that are relatively insignificant (for large value of input size, n). As an example, in the case below, n^4, $2n^2$, $100n$ and 500 are the individual costs of some function and approximate to n^4 since n^4 is the highest rate of growth.

$$n^4 + 2n^2 + 100n + 500 \approx n^4$$

1.11 Commonly Used Rates of Growth

Below is the list of growth rates you will come across in the following chapters.

Time Complexity	Name	Description
1	Constant	Whatever is the input size n, these functions take a constant amount of time.
$logn$	Logarithmic	These are slower growing than even linear functions.
n	Linear	These functions grow linearly with the input size n.
$nlogn$	Linear Logarithmic	Faster growing than linear but slower than quadratic.
n^2	Quadratic	These functions grow faster than the linear logarithmic functions.
n^3	Cubic	Faster growing than quadratic but slower than exponential.
2^n	Exponential	Faster than all of the functions mentioned here except the factorial functions.
$n!$	Factorial	Fastest growing than all these functions mentioned here.

The diagram below shows the relationship between different rates of growth.

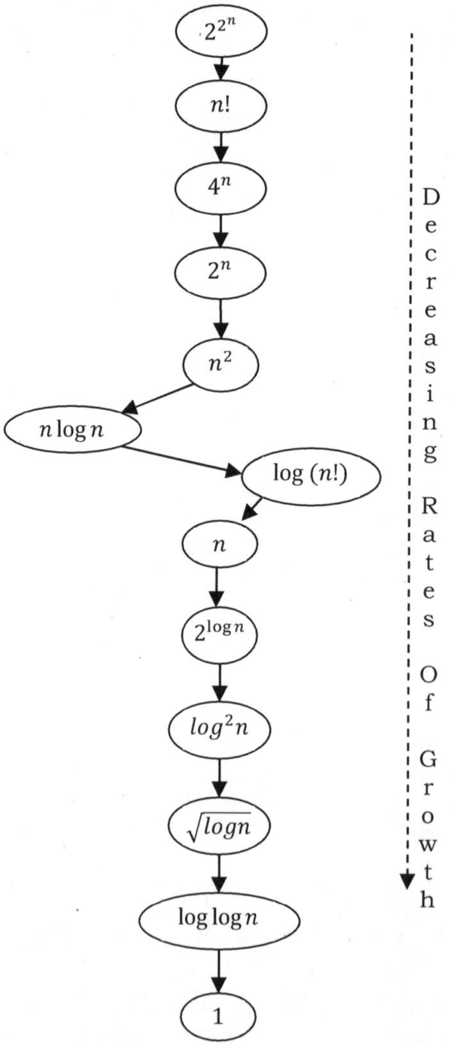

1.12 Types of Analysis

To analyze the given algorithm, we need to know with which inputs the algorithm takes less time (performing well) and with which inputs the algorithm takes a long time. We have already seen that an algorithm can be represented in the form of an expression. That means we represent the algorithm with multiple expressions: one for the case where it takes less time and another for the case where it takes more time.

In general, the first case is called the *best case* and the second case is called the *worst case* for the algorithm. To analyze an algorithm, we need some kind of syntax, and that forms the base for asymptotic analysis/notation. There are three types of analysis:

- Worst case
    - Defines the input for which the algorithm takes a long time (slowest time to complete).
    - Input is the one for which the algorithm runs the slowest.
- Best case
    - Defines the input for which the algorithm takes the least time (fastest time to complete).
    - Input is the one for which the algorithm runs the fastest.
- Average case
    - Provides a prediction about the running time of the algorithm.
    - Run the algorithm many times, using many different inputs that come from some distribution that generates these inputs, compute the total running time (by adding the individual times), and divide by the number of trials.
    - Assumes that the input is random.

Lower Bound <= Average Time <= Upper Bound

For a given algorithm, we can represent the best, worst and average cases in the form of expressions. As an example, let $f(n)$ be the function which represents the given algorithm.

$$f(n) = n^2 + 500, \text{ for worst case}$$
$$f(n) = n + 100n + 500, \text{ for best case}$$

Similarly, for the average case. The expression defines the inputs with which the algorithm takes the average running time (or memory).

1.13 Asymptotic Notation

Having the expressions for the best, average and worst cases, for all three cases we need to identify the upper and lower bounds. To represent these upper and lower bounds, we need some kind of syntax, and that is the subject of the following discussion. Let us assume that the given algorithm is represented in the form of function $f(n)$.

1.14 Big-O Notation

This notation gives the *tight* upper bound of the given function. Generally, it is represented as $f(n) = O(g(n))$. That means, at larger values of n, the upper bound of $f(n)$ is $g(n)$. For example, if $f(n) = n^4 + 100n^2 + 10n + 50$ is the given algorithm, then n^4 is $g(n)$. That means $g(n)$ gives the maximum rate of growth for $f(n)$ at larger values of n.

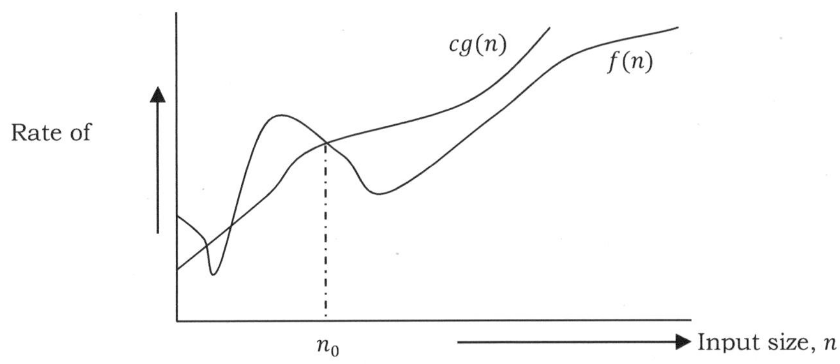

Let us see the O–notation with a little more detail. O–notation defined as $O(g(n)) = \{f(n)$: there exist positive constants c and n_0 such that $0 \le f(n) \le cg(n)$ for all $n \ge n_0\}$. $g(n)$ is an asymptotic tight upper bound for $f(n)$. Our objective is to give the smallest rate of growth $g(n)$ which is greater than or equal to the given algorithms' rate of growth $f(n)$.

Generally, we discard lower values of n. That means the rate of growth at lower values of n is not important. In the figure, n_0 is the point from which we need to consider the rate of growth for a given algorithm. Below n_0, the rate of growth could be different. n_0 is called threshold for the given function.

Big-O Visualization

$O(g(n))$ is the set of functions with smaller or the same order of growth as $g(n)$. For example; $O(n^2)$ includes $O(1), O(n), O(nlogn)$, etc.

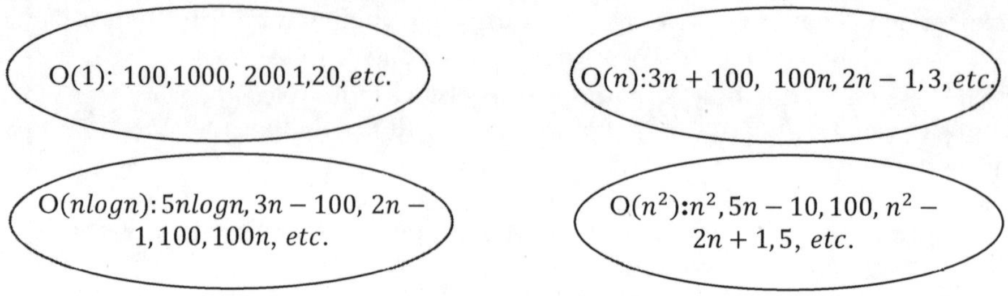

Note: Analyze the algorithms at larger values of n only. What this means is, below n_0 we do not care about the rate of growth.

Big-O Examples

Example-1 Find upper bound for $f(n) = 3n + 8$

Solution: $3n + 8 \leq 4n$, for all $n \geq 8$
$\therefore 3n + 8 = O(n)$ with c = 4 and $n_0 = 8$

Example-2 Find upper bound for $f(n) = n^2 + 1$

Solution: $n^2 + 1 \leq 2n^2$, for all $n \geq 1$
$\therefore n^2 + 1 = O(n^2)$ with $c = 2$ and $n_0 = 1$

Example-3 Find upper bound for $f(n) = n^4 + 100n^2 + 50$

Solution: $n^4 + 100n^2 + 50 \leq 2n^4$, for all $n \geq 11$
$\therefore n^4 + 100n^2 + 50 = O(n^4)$ with $c = 2$ and $n_0 = 11$

Example-4 Find upper bound for $f(n) = 2n^3 - 2n^2$

Solution: $2n^3 - 2n^2 \leq 2n^3$, for all $n \geq 1$
$\therefore 2n^3 - 2n^2 = O(n^3)$ with $c = 2$ and $n_0 = 1$

Example-5 Find upper bound for $f(n) = n$

Solution: $n \leq n$, for all $n \geq 1$
$\therefore n = O(n)$ with $c = 1$ and $n_0 = 1$

Example-6 Find upper bound for $f(n) = 410$

Solution: $410 \leq 410$, for all $n \geq 1$
$\therefore 410 = O(1)$ with $c = 1$ and $n_0 = 1$

No Uniqueness?

There is no unique set of values for n_0 and c in proving the asymptotic bounds. Let us consider, $100n + 5 = O(n)$. For this function there are multiple n_0 and c values possible.

Solution1: $100n + 5 \leq 100n + n = 101n \leq 101n$, for all $n \geq 5$, $n_0 = 5$ and $c = 101$ is a solution.

Solution2: $100n + 5 \leq 100n + 5n = 105n \leq 105n$, for all $n \geq 1$, $n_0 = 1$ and $c = 105$ is also a solution.

1.15 Omega-Ω Notation [Lower Bounding Function]

Similar to the O discussion, this notation gives the tighter lower bound of the given algorithm and we represent it as $f(n) = \Omega(g(n))$. That means, at larger values of n, the tighter lower bound of $f(n)$ is $g(n)$. For example, if $f(n) = 100n^2 + 10n + 50$, $g(n)$ is $\Omega(n^2)$.

The Ω notation can be defined as $\Omega(g(n)) = \{f(n)$: there exist positive constants c and n_0 such that $0 \leq cg(n) \leq f(n)$ for all $n \geq n_0\}$. $g(n)$ is an asymptotic tight lower bound for $f(n)$. Our objective is to give the largest rate of growth $g(n)$ which is less than or equal to the given algorithm's rate of growth $f(n)$.

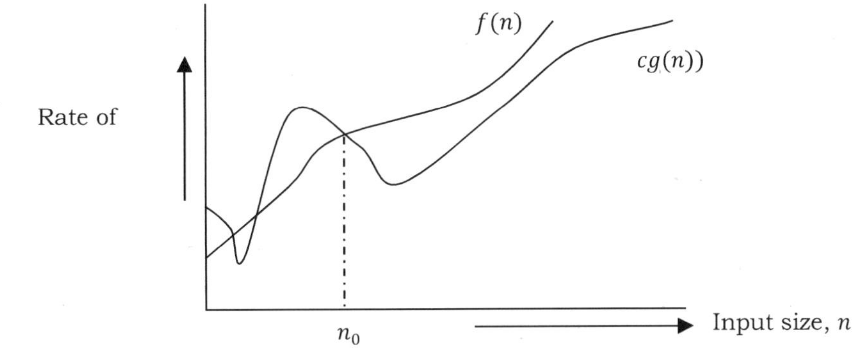

Ω Examples

Example-1 Find lower bound for $f(n) = 5n^2$.

Solution: $\exists\, c,\ n_0$ Such that: $0 \le cn^2 \le 5n^2 \Rightarrow cn^2 \le 5n^2 \Rightarrow c = 5$ and $n_0 = 1$

$\therefore 5n^2 = \Omega(n^2)$ with $c = 5$ and $n_0 = 1$

Example-2 Prove $f(n) = 100n + 5 \neq \Omega(n^2)$.

Solution: $\exists$ c, n_0 Such that: $0 \le cn^2 \le 100n + 5$

$100n + 5 \le 100n + 5n\ (\forall n \ge 1) = 105n$

$cn^2 \le 105n \Rightarrow n(cn - 105) \le 0$

Since n is positive $\Rightarrow cn - 105 \le 0 \Rightarrow n \le 105/c$

$\Rightarrow$ Contradiction: n cannot be smaller than a constant

Example-3 $2n = \Omega(n)$, $n^3 = \Omega(n^3)$, $logn = \Omega(logn)$.

1.16 Theta-Θ Notation

This notation decides whether the upper and lower bounds of a given function (algorithm) are the same. The average running time of an algorithm is always between the lower bound and the upper bound. If the upper bound (O) and lower bound (Ω) give the same result, then the Θ notation will also have the same rate of growth. As an example, let us assume that $f(n) = 10n + n$ is the expression. Then, its tight upper bound $g(n)$ is $O(n)$. The rate of growth in the best case is $g(n) = O(n)$.

In this case, the rates of growth in the best case and worst case are the same. As a result, the average case will also be the same. For a given function (algorithm), if the rates of growth (bounds) for O and Ω are not the same, then the rate of growth for the Θ case may not be the same. In this case, we need to consider all possible time complexities and take the average of those (for example, for a quick sort average case, refer to the *Sorting* chapter).

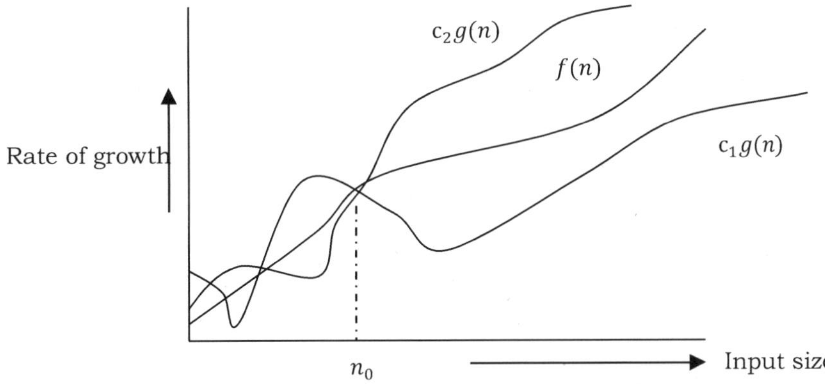

Now consider the definition *of* Θ notation. It is defined as $\Theta(g(n)) = \{f(n)$: there exist positive constants c_1, c_2 and n_0 such that $0 \le c_1 g(n) \le f(n) \le c_2 g(n)$ for all $n \ge n_0\}$. $g(n)$ is an asymptotic tight bound for $f(n)$. $\Theta(g(n))$ is the set of functions with the same order of growth as $g(n)$.

Θ Examples

Example 1 Find Θ bound for $f(n) = \frac{n^2}{2} - \frac{n}{2}$

Solution: $\frac{n^2}{5} \le \frac{n^2}{2} - \frac{n}{2} \le n^2$, for all, $n \ge 2$

$\therefore \frac{n^2}{2} - \frac{n}{2} = \Theta(n^2)$ with $c_1 = 1/5, c_2 = 1$ and $n_0 = 2$

Example 2 Prove $n \neq \Theta(n^2)$

Solution: $c_1 n^2 \le n \le c_2 n^2 \Rightarrow$ only holds for: $n \le 1/c_1$
$\therefore n \ne \Theta(n^2)$

Example 3 Prove $6n^3 \ne \Theta(n^2)$

Solution: $c_1 n^2 \le 6n^3 \le c_2 n^2 \Rightarrow$ only holds for: $n \le c_2/6$
$\therefore 6n^3 \ne \Theta(n^2)$

Example 4 Prove $n \ne \Theta(logn)$

Solution: $c_1 logn \le n \le c_2 logn \Rightarrow c_2 \ge \frac{n}{\log n}, \forall n \ge n_0$ – Impossible

Important Notes

For analysis (best case, worst case and average), we try to give the upper bound (O) and lower bound (Ω) and average running time (Θ). From the above examples, it should also be clear that, for a given function (algorithm), getting the upper bound (O) and lower bound (Ω) and average running time (Θ) may not always be possible. For example, if we are discussing the best case of an algorithm, we try to give the upper bound (O) and lower bound (Ω) and average running time (Θ).

In the remaining chapters, we generally focus on the upper bound (O) because knowing the lower bound (Ω) of an algorithm is of no practical importance, and we use the Θ notation if the upper bound (O) and lower bound (Ω) are the same.

1.17 Why is it called Asymptotic Analysis?

From the discussion above (for all three notations: worst case, best case, and average case), we can easily understand that, in every case for a given function $f(n)$ we are trying to find another function $g(n)$ which approximates $f(n)$ at higher values of n. That means $g(n)$ is also a curve which approximates $f(n)$ at higher values of n.

In mathematics we call such a curve an *asymptotic curve*. In other terms, $g(n)$ is the asymptotic curve for $f(n)$. For this reason, we call algorithm analysis *asymptotic analysis*.

1.18 Guidelines for Asymptotic Analysis

There are some general rules to help us determine the running time of an algorithm.

1) **Loops:** The running time of a loop is, at most, the running time of the statements inside the loop (including tests) multiplied by the number of iterations.

```
for i := 1; i <= n; i++ {          // executes n times
    m = m + 2                      // constant time, c
}
```

Total time = a constant $c \times n = c\,n = O(n)$.

2) **Nested loops:** Analyze from the inside out. Total running time is the product of the sizes of all the loops.

```
for i := 1; i <= n; i++ {          // outer loop executed n times
    for j := 1; j <= n; j++ {      // inner loop executes n times
        k = k+1                    // constant time
    }
}
```

Total time = $c \times n \times n = cn^2 = O(n^2)$.

3) **Consecutive statements:** Add the time complexities of each statement.

```
x = x +1; //constant time
for i := 1; i <= n; i++ {          // executes n times
    m = m + 2                      // constant time
}
for i := 1; i <= n; i++ {          // outer loop executes n times
    for j := 1; j <= n; j++ {      // inner loop executed n times
        k = k+1 //constant time
    }
}
```

Total time = $c_0 + c_1 n + c_2 n^2 = O(n^2)$.

4) **If-then-else statements:** Worst-case running time: the test, plus *either* the *then* part *or* the *else* part (whichever is the larger).

```
if length( ) == 0 {                //constant time
    return false                   //then part: constant
} else {                           // else part: (constant + constant) * n
```

```
        for j := 1; j <= len(A); j++ {
            k = k+1                          //constant time
        }
        for n := 0; n < length( ); n++ {
            if !list[n].equals(otherList.list[n]) {        // another if : constant + constant (no else part)
                return false                               //constant time
            }
        }
    }
```

Total time $= c_0 + (c_1 + c_2) * n = O(n)$.

5) **Logarithmic complexity:** An algorithm is $O(logn)$ if it takes a constant time to cut the problem size by a fraction (usually by ½). As an example, let us consider the following program:

```
    for i := 1; i <= n; {
        i = i*2
    }
```

If we observe carefully, the value of i is doubling every time. Initially $i = 1$, in next step $i = 2$, and in subsequent steps $i = 4, 8$ and so on. Let us assume that the loop is executing some k times. At k^{th} step $2^k = n$, and at $(k+1)^{th}$ step we come out of the *loop*. Taking logarithm on both sides, gives

$$log(2^k) = logn$$
$$klog2 = logn$$
$$k = logn \quad //\text{if we assume base-2}$$

Total time $= O(logn)$.

Note: Similarly, for the case below, the worst-case rate of growth is $O(logn)$ [discussion holds good for the decreasing sequence as well].

```
    for i := n; i >= 1; {
        i = i/2
    }
```

Another example: binary search (finding a word in a dictionary of n pages)

- Look at the center point in the dictionary
- Is the word towards the left or right of center?
- Repeat the process with the left or right part of the dictionary until the word is found.

1.20 Simplifying properties of asymptotic notations

- Transitivity: $f(n) = \Theta(g(n))$ and $g(n) = \Theta(h(n)) \Rightarrow f(n) = \Theta(h(n))$. Valid for O and Ω as well.
- Reflexivity: $f(n) = \Theta(f(n))$. Valid for O and Ω.
- Symmetry: $f(n) = \Theta(g(n))$ if and only if $g(n) = \Theta(f(n))$.
- Transpose symmetry: $f(n) = O(g(n))$ if and only if $g(n) = \Omega(f(n))$.
- If $f(n)$ is in $O(kg(n))$ for any constant $k > 0$, then $f(n)$ is in $O(g(n))$.
- If $f_1(n)$ is in $O(g_1(n))$ and $f_2(n)$ is in $O(g_2(n))$, then $(f_1 + f_2)(n)$ is in $O(\max(g_1(n), g_1(n)))$.
- If $f_1(n)$ is in $O(g_1(n))$ and $f_2(n)$ is in $O(g_2(n))$ then $f_1(n)\, f_2(n)$ is in $O(g_1(n)\, g_1(n))$.

1.21 Commonly used Logarithms and Summations

Logarithms

$log\, x^y = y\, log\, x$	$logn = log_{10}^{n}$
$log\, xy = logx + logy$	$log^k n = (logn)^k$
$log\, logn = log(logn)$	$log\frac{x}{y} = logx - logy$
$a^{log_b^x} = x^{log_b^a}$	$log_b^x = \frac{log_a^x}{log_a^b}$

Arithmetic series

$$\sum_{K=1}^{n} k = 1 + 2 + \cdots + n = \frac{n(n+1)}{2}$$

Geometric series

$$\sum_{k=0}^{n} x^k = 1 + x + x^2 \ldots + x^n = \frac{x^{n+1} - 1}{x - 1} (x \neq 1)$$

Harmonic series

$$\sum_{k=1}^{n} \frac{1}{k} = 1 + \frac{1}{2} + \ldots + \frac{1}{n} \approx \log n$$

Other important formulae

$$\sum_{k=1}^{n} \log k \approx n\log n$$

$$\sum_{k=1}^{n} k^p = 1^p + 2^p + \cdots + n^p \approx \frac{1}{p+1} n^{p+1}$$

1.22 Master Theorem for Divide and Conquer Recurrences

All divide and conquer algorithms (also discussed in detail in the *Divide and Conquer* chapter) divide the problem into sub-problems, each of which is part of the original problem, and then perform some additional work to compute the final answer. As an example, a merge sort algorithm [for details, refer to *Sorting* chapter] operates on two sub-problems, each of which is half the size of the original, and then performs $O(n)$ additional work for merging. This gives the running time equation:

$$T(n) = 2T\left(\frac{n}{2}\right) + O(n)$$

The following theorem can be used to determine the running time of divide and conquer algorithms. For a given program (algorithm), first we try to find the recurrence relation for the problem. If the recurrence is of the below form then we can directly give the answer without fully solving it. If the recurrence is of the form $T(n) = aT(\frac{n}{b}) + \Theta(n^k \log^p n)$, where $a \geq 1, b > 1, k \geq 0$ and p is a real number, then:

1) If $a > b^k$, then $T(n) = \Theta(n^{\log_b^a})$
2) If $a = b^k$
   a. If $p > -1$, then $T(n) = \Theta(n^{\log_b^a} \log^{p+1} n)$
   b. If $p = -1$, then $T(n) = \Theta(n^{\log_b^a} \log\log n)$
   c. If $p < -1$, then $T(n) = \Theta(n^{\log_b^a})$
3) If $a < b^k$
   a. If $p \geq 0$, then $T(n) = \Theta(n^k \log^p n)$
   b. If $p < 0$, then $T(n) = O(n^k)$

1.23 Divide and Conquer Master Theorem: Problems & Solutions

For each of the following recurrences, give an expression for the runtime $T(n)$ if the recurrence can be solved with the Master Theorem. Otherwise, indicate that the Master Theorem does not apply.

Problem-1 $T(n) = 3T(n/2) + n^2$
Solution: $T(n) = 3T(n/2) + n^2 \Rightarrow T(n) = \Theta(n^2)$ (Master Theorem Case 3.a)

Problem-2 $T(n) = 4T(n/2) + n^2$
Solution: $T(n) = 4T(n/2) + n^2 \Rightarrow T(n) = \Theta(n^2 \log n)$ (Master Theorem Case 2.a)

Problem-3 $T(n) = T(n/2) + n^2$
Solution: $T(n) = T(n/2) + n^2 \Rightarrow \Theta(n^2)$ (Master Theorem Case 3.a)

Problem-4 $T(n) = 2^n T(n/2) + n^n$
Solution: $T(n) = 2^n T(n/2) + n^n \Rightarrow$ Does not apply (a is not constant)

Problem-5 $T(n) = 16T(n/4) + n$
Solution: $T(n) = 16T(n/4) + n \Rightarrow T(n) = \Theta(n^2)$ (Master Theorem Case 1)

Problem-6 $T(n) = 2T(n/2) + n\log n$
Solution: $T(n) = 2T(n/2) + n\log n \Rightarrow T(n) = \Theta(n\log^2 n)$ (Master Theorem Case 2.a)

Problem-7 $T(n) = 2T(n/2) + n/\log n$
Solution: $T(n) = 2T(n/2) + n/\log n \Rightarrow T(n) = \Theta(n\log\log n)$ (Master Theorem Case 2.b)

Problem-8 $T(n) = 2T(n/4) + n^{0.51}$
Solution: $T(n) = 2T(n/4) + n^{0.51} \Rightarrow T(n) = \Theta(n^{0.51})$ (Master Theorem Case 3.b)

Problem-9 $T(n) = 0.5T(n/2) + 1/n$

Solution: $T(n) = 0.5T(n/2) + 1/n$ => Does not apply ($a < 1$)

Problem-10 $T(n) = 6T(n/3) + n^2 logn$
Solution: $T(n) = 6T(n/3) + n^2 logn$ => $T(n) = \Theta(n^2 logn)$ (Master Theorem Case 3.a)

Problem-11 $T(n) = 64T(n/8) - n^2 logn$
Solution: $T(n) = 64T(n/8) - n^2 logn$ => Does not apply (function is not positive)

Problem-12 $T(n) = 7T(n/3) + n^2$
Solution: $T(n) = 7T(n/3) + n^2$ => $T(n) = \Theta(n^2)$ (Master Theorem Case 3.as)

Problem-13 $T(n) = 4T(n/2) + logn$
Solution: $T(n) = 4T(n/2) + logn$ => $T(n) = \Theta(n^2)$ (Master Theorem Case 1)

Problem-14 $T(n) = 16T(n/4) + n!$
Solution: $T(n) = 16T(n/4) + n!$ => $T(n) = \Theta(n!)$ (Master Theorem Case 3.a)

Problem-15 $T(n) = \sqrt{2}T(n/2) + logn$
Solution: $T(n) = \sqrt{2}T(n/2) + logn$ => $T(n) = \Theta(\sqrt{n})$ (Master Theorem Case 1)

Problem-16 $T(n) = 3T(n/2) + n$
Solution: $T(n) = 3T(n/2) + n$ => $T(n) = \Theta(n^{log3})$ (Master Theorem Case 1)

Problem-17 $T(n) = 3T(n/3) + \sqrt{n}$
Solution: $T(n) = 3T(n/3) + \sqrt{n}$ => $T(n) = \Theta(n)$ (Master Theorem Case 1)

Problem-18 $T(n) = 4T(n/2) + cn$
Solution: $T(n) = 4T(n/2) + cn$ => $T(n) = \Theta(n^2)$ (Master Theorem Case 1)

Problem-19 $T(n) = 3T(n/4) + nlogn$
Solution: $T(n) = 3T(n/4) + nlogn$ => $T(n) = \Theta(nlogn)$ (Master Theorem Case 3.a)

Problem-20 $T(n) = 3T(n/3) + n/2$
Solution: $T(n) = 3T(n/3) + n/2$ => $T(n) = \Theta(nlogn)$ (Master Theorem Case 2.a)

1.24 Master Theorem for Subtract and Conquer Recurrences

Let $T(n)$ be a function defined on positive n, and having the property

$$T(n) = \begin{cases} c, & \text{if } n \le 1 \\ aT(n-b) + f(n), & \text{if } n > 1 \end{cases}$$

for some constants $c, a > 0, b > 0, k \ge 0$, and function $f(n)$. If $f(n)$ is in $O(n^k)$, then

$$T(n) = \begin{cases} O(n^k), & \text{if a} < 1 \\ O(n^{k+1}), & \text{if a} = 1 \\ O\left(n^k a^{\frac{n}{b}}\right), & \text{if a} > 1 \end{cases}$$

1.25 Variant of Subtraction and Conquer Master Theorem

The solution to the equation $T(n) = T(\alpha\, n) + T((1-\alpha)n) + \beta n$, where $0 < \alpha < 1$ and $\beta > 0$ are constants, is $O(nlogn)$.

1.26 Method of Guessing and Confirming

Now, let us discuss a method which can be used to solve any recurrence. The basic idea behind this method is:

guess the answer; and then *prove* it correct by induction.

In other words, it addresses the question: What if the given recurrence doesn't seem to match with any of these (master theorem) methods? If we guess a solution and then try to verify our guess inductively, usually either the proof will succeed (in which case we are done), or the proof will fail (in which case the failure will help us refine our guess).

As an example, consider the recurrence $T(n) = \sqrt{n}\, T(\sqrt{n}) + n$. This doesn't fit into the form required by the Master Theorems. Carefully observing the recurrence gives us the impression that it is similar to the divide and conquer method (dividing the problem into $\sqrt{n}$ subproblems each with size $\sqrt{n}$). As we can see, the size of the subproblems at the first level of recursion is n. So, let us guess that $T(n) = O(nlogn)$, and then try to prove that our guess is correct.

Let's start by trying to prove an *upper* bound $T(n) \le cnlogn$:

$$\begin{aligned} T(n) &= \sqrt{n}\, T(\sqrt{n}) + n \\ &\le \sqrt{n}.\, c\sqrt{n}\, log\sqrt{n} + n \\ &= n.\, c\, log\sqrt{n} + n \\ &= n.c.\tfrac{1}{2}.logn + n \\ &\le cnlogn \end{aligned}$$

The last inequality assumes only that $1 \le c.\frac{1}{2}.logn$. This is correct if n is sufficiently large and for any constant c, no matter how small. From the above proof, we can see that our guess is correct for the upper bound. Now, let us prove the *lower* bound for this recurrence.

$$\begin{aligned} T(n) &= \sqrt{n}\, T(\sqrt{n}) + n \\ &\ge \sqrt{n}.\, k\, \sqrt{n}\, log\sqrt{n} + n \\ &= n.\, k\, log\sqrt{n} + n \\ &= n.k.\tfrac{1}{2}.logn + n \\ &\ge knlogn \end{aligned}$$

The last inequality assumes only that $1 \ge k.\frac{1}{2}.logn$. This is incorrect if n is sufficiently large and for any constant k. From the above proof, we can see that our guess is incorrect for the lower bound.

From the above discussion, we understood that $\Theta(nlogn)$ is too big. How about $\Theta(n)$? The lower bound is easy to prove directly:

$$T(n) = \sqrt{n}\, T(\sqrt{n}) + n \quad \ge n$$

Now, let us prove the upper bound for this $\Theta(n)$.

$$\begin{aligned} T(n) &= \sqrt{n}\, T(\sqrt{n}) + n \\ &\le \sqrt{n}.c.\sqrt{n} + n \\ &= n.\, c + n \\ &= n\,(c + 1) \\ &\nleq cn \end{aligned}$$

From the above induction, we understood that $\Theta(n)$ is too small and $\Theta(nlogn)$ is too big. So, we need something bigger than n and smaller than $nlogn$. How about $n\sqrt{logn}$?

Proving the upper bound for $n\sqrt{logn}$:

$$\begin{aligned} T(n) &= \sqrt{n}\, T(\sqrt{n}) + n \\ &\le \sqrt{n}.c.\sqrt{n}\sqrt{log\sqrt{n}} + n \\ &= n.\, c.\tfrac{1}{\sqrt{2}}\, log\sqrt{n} + n \\ &\le cnlog\sqrt{n} \end{aligned}$$

Proving the lower bound for $n\sqrt{logn}$:

$$\begin{aligned} T(n) &= \sqrt{n}\, T(\sqrt{n}) + n \\ &\ge \sqrt{n}.k.\sqrt{n}\sqrt{log\sqrt{n}} + n \\ &= n.\, k.\tfrac{1}{\sqrt{2}}\, log\sqrt{n} + n \\ &\ngeq knlog\sqrt{n} \end{aligned}$$

The last step doesn't work. So, $\Theta(n\sqrt{logn})$ doesn't work. What else is between n and $nlogn$? How about $nloglogn$?

Proving upper bound for $nloglogn$:

$$\begin{aligned} T(n) &= \sqrt{n}\, T(\sqrt{n}) + n \\ &\le \sqrt{n}.c.\sqrt{n}loglog\sqrt{n} + n \\ &= n.\, c.loglogn\text{-}c.n + n \\ &\le cnloglogn, \text{ if } c \ge 1 \end{aligned}$$

Proving lower bound for $nloglogn$:

$$\begin{aligned} T(n) &= \sqrt{n}\, T(\sqrt{n}) + n \\ &\ge \sqrt{n}.k.\sqrt{n}loglog\sqrt{n} + n \\ &= n.\, k.loglogn\text{-}k.n + n \\ &\ge knloglogn, \text{ if } k \le 1 \end{aligned}$$

From the above proofs, we can see that $T(n) \le cnloglogn$, if $c \ge 1$ and $T(n) \ge knloglogn$, if $k \le 1$. Technically, we're still missing the base cases in both proofs, but we can be fairly confident at this point that $T(n) = \Theta(nloglogn)$.

1.27 Amortized Analysis

Amortized analysis refers to determining the time-averaged running time for a sequence of operations. It is different from average case analysis, because amortized analysis does not make any assumption about the distribution of the data values, whereas average case analysis assumes the data are not "bad" (e.g., some sorting algorithms do well *on average* over all input orderings but very badly on certain input orderings). That is, amortized analysis is a worst-case analysis, but for a sequence of operations rather than for individual operations.

The motivation for amortized analysis is to better understand the running time of certain techniques, where standard worst-case analysis provides an overly pessimistic bound. Amortized analysis generally applies to a method that consists of a sequence of operations, where the vast majority of the operations are cheap, but some of the operations are expensive. If we can show that the expensive operations are particularly rare, we can *change them* to the cheap operations, and only bound the cheap operations.

The general approach is to assign an artificial cost to each operation in the sequence, such that the total of the artificial costs for the sequence of operations bounds the total of the real costs for the sequence. This artificial cost is called the amortized cost of an operation. To analyze the running time, the amortized cost thus is a correct way of understanding the overall running time — but note that particular operations can still take longer so it is not a way of bounding the running time of any individual operation in the sequence.

When one event in a sequence affects the cost of later events:

- One particular task may be expensive.
- But it may leave data structure in a state that the next few operations become easier.

Example: Let us consider an array of elements from which we want to find the kth smallest element. We can solve this problem using sorting. After sorting the given array, we just need to return the kth element from it. The cost of performing the sort (assuming comparison-based sorting algorithm) is O($nlogn$). If we perform n such selections then the average cost of each selection is O($nlogn/n$) = O($logn$). This clearly indicates that sorting once is reducing the complexity of subsequent operations.

1.28 Algorithms Analysis: Problems & Solutions

Note: From the following problems, try to understand the cases which have different complexities (O(n), O($logn$), O($loglogn$) etc.).

Problem-21 Find the complexity of the below recurrence:

$$T(n) = \begin{cases} 3T(n-1), if\ n > 0, \\ 1, \quad otherwise \end{cases}$$

Solution: Let us try solving this function with substitution.

$$T(n) = 3T(n-1)$$
$$T(n) = 3\big(3T(n-2)\big) = 3^2T(n-2)$$
$$T(n) = 3^2(3T(n-3))$$
$$T(n) = 3^nT(n-n) = 3^nT(0) = 3^n$$

This clearly shows that the complexity of this function is O(3^n).

Note: We can use the *Subtraction and Conquer* master theorem for this problem.

Problem-22 Find the complexity of the below recurrence:

$$T(n) = \begin{cases} 2T(n-1) - 1, if\ n > 0, \\ 1, \quad otherwise \end{cases}$$

Solution: Let us try solving this function with substitution.

$$T(n) = 2T(n-1) - 1$$
$$T(n) = 2(2T(n-2) - 1) - 1 = 2^2T(n-2) - 2 - 1$$
$$T(n) = 2^2(2T(n-3) - 2 - 1) - 1 = 2^3T(n-4) - 2^2 - 2^1 - 2^0$$
$$T(n) = 2^nT(n-n) - 2^{n-1} - 2^{n-2} - 2^{n-3} \ldots .2^2 - 2^1 - 2^0$$
$$T(n) = 2^n - 2^{n-1} - 2^{n-2} - 2^{n-3} \ldots .2^2 - 2^1 - 2^0$$
$$T(n) = 2^n - (2^n - 1)\ [note: 2^{n-1} + 2^{n-2} + \cdots + 2^0 = 2^n]$$
$$T(n) = 1$$

∴ Time Complexity is O(1). Note that while the recurrence relation looks exponential, the solution to the recurrence relation here gives a different result.

Problem-23 What is the running time of the following function?

```
func function(n int) {
  i := 1
  s := 1
  for s <= n {
     i++
     s = s + i
```

```
            fmt.Print("*")
        }
    }
```

Solution: Consider the comments in the below function:

```
func function(n int) {
    i := 1
    s := 1
    for s <= n {  // s is increasing not at rate 1 but i
        i++
        s = s + i
        fmt.Print("*")
    }
}
```

We can define the 's' terms according to the relation $s_i = s_{i-1} + i$. The value of 'i' increases by 1 for each iteration. The value contained in 's' at the ith iteration is the sum of the first 'i' positive integers. If k is the total number of iterations taken by the program, then the *while* loop terminates if:

$$1 + 2 + \ldots + k = \frac{k(k+1)}{2} > n \Rightarrow k = O(\sqrt{n}).$$

Problem-24 Find the complexity of the function given below.

```
func function(n int) {
    count := 0
    for i := 1; i*i <= n; i++ {
        count++
    }
    fmt.Print(count)
}
```

Solution:

```
func function(n int) {
    count := 0
    for i := 1; i*i <= n; i++ {
        count++
    }
    fmt.Print(count)
}
```

The function the loop will end, if $i^2 > n \Rightarrow T(n) = O(\sqrt{n})$. This is similar to Problem-23.

Problem-25 What is the complexity of the program given below:

```
func function(n int) {
    count := 0
    for i := n / 2; i <= n; i++ {
        for j := 1; j+n/2 <= n; j = j + 1 {
            for k := 1; k <= n; k = k * 2 {
                count++
            }
        }
    }
    fmt.Print(count)
}
```

Solution: Consider the comments in the following function.

```
func function(n int) {
    count := 0
    for i := n / 2; i <= n; i++ {
        for j := 1; j+n/2 <= n; j = j + 1 {
            for k := 1; k <= n; k = k * 2 {
                count++
            }
        }
    }
    fmt.Print(count)
}
```

The complexity of the above function is $O(n^2 logn)$.

Problem-26 What is the complexity of the program given below:

```
func function(n int) {
```

```
    count := 0
    for i := n / 2; i <= n; i++ {
        for j := 1; j <= n; j = 2 * j {
            for k := 1; k <= n; k = k * 2 {
                count++
            }
        }
    }
    fmt.Print(count)
}
```

Solution: Consider the comments in the following function.

```
func function(n int) {
    count := 0
    for i := n / 2; i <= n; i++ {
        for j := 1; j <= n; j = 2 * j {
            for k := 1; k <= n; k = k * 2 {
                count++
            }
        }
    }
    fmt.Print(count)
}
```

The complexity of the above function is O($nlog^2n$).

Problem-27 Find the complexity of the program below.

```
func function(n int) {
    if n == 1 {
        return
    }
    for i := 1; i <= n; i++ {
        for j := 1; j <= n; j++ {
            fmt.Print("*")
            break
        }
    }
}
```

Solution: Consider the comments in the function below.

```
func function(n int) {
    if n == 1 {                     //constant time
        return
    }
    for i := 1; i <= n; i++ {       //outer loop execute n times
        for j := 1; j <= n; j++ {   // inner loop executes only time due to break statement.
            fmt.Print("*")
            break
        }
    }
}
```

The complexity of the above function is O(n). Even though the inner loop is bounded by n, due to the break statement it is executing only once.

Problem-28 Write a recursive function for the running time $T(n)$ of the function given below. Prove using the iterative method that $T(n) = \Theta(n^3)$.

```
func function(n int) {
    if n == 1 {
        return
    }
    for i := 1; i <= n; i++ {
        for j := 1; j <= n; j++ {
            fmt.Print("*")
        }
    }
    function(n - 3)
}
```

Solution: Consider the comments in the function below:

```
func function(n int) {
    if n == 1 {                        //constant time
        return
    }
    for i := 1; i <= n; i++ {          //outer loop execute n times
        for j := 1; j <= n; j++ {      //inner loop executes n times
            fmt.Print("*")             //constant time
        }
    }
    function(n - 3)
}
```

The recurrence for this code is clearly $T(n) = T(n-3) + cn^2$ for some constant $c > 0$ since each call prints out n^2 asterisks and calls itself recursively on n - 3. Using the iterative method we get: $T(n) = T(n-3) + cn^2$. Using the *Subtraction and Conquer* master theorem, we get $T(n) = \Theta(n^3)$.

Problem-29 Determine Θ bounds for the recurrence relation: $T(n) = 2T\left(\frac{n}{2}\right) + nlogn$.

Solution: Using Divide and Conquer master theorem, we get $O(nlog^2n)$.

Problem-30 Determine Θ bounds for the recurrence: $T(n) = T\left(\frac{n}{2}\right) + T\left(\frac{n}{4}\right) + T\left(\frac{n}{8}\right) + n.$

Solution: Substituting in the recurrence equation, we get: $T(n) \leq c1 * \frac{n}{2} + c2 * \frac{n}{4} + c3 * \frac{n}{8} + cn \leq k * n$, where k is a constant. This clearly says $\Theta(n)$.

Problem-31 Determine Θ bounds for the recurrence relation: $T(n) = T(\lceil n/2 \rceil) + 7$.

Solution: Using Master Theorem we get: $\Theta(logn)$.

Problem-32 Prove that the running time of the code below is $\Omega(logn)$.

```
void Read(int n) {
        int k = 1;
        while( k < n )
                k = 3*k;
}
```

Solution: The *while* loop will terminate once the value of 'k' is greater than or equal to the value of 'n'. In each iteration the value of 'k' is multiplied by 3. If i is the number of iterations, then 'k' has the value of 3^i after i iterations. The loop is terminated upon reaching i iterations when $3^i \geq n \leftrightarrow i \geq \log_3 n$, which shows that $i = \Omega\,(logn)$.

Problem-33 Solve the following recurrence.

$$T(n) = \begin{cases} 1, & if\ n = 1 \\ T(n-1) + n(n-1), & if\ n \geq 2 \end{cases}$$

Solution: By iteration:

$$T(n) = T(n-2) + (n-1)(n-2) + n(n-1)$$

...

$$T(n) = T(1) + \sum_{i=1}^{n} i(i-1)$$

$$T(n) = T(1) + \sum_{i=1}^{n} i^2 - \sum_{i=1}^{n} i$$

$$T(n) = 1 + \frac{n((n+1)(2n+1)}{6} - \frac{n(n+1)}{2}$$

$$T(n) = \Theta(n^3)$$

Note: We can use the *Subtraction and Conquer* master theorem for this problem.

Problem-34 Consider the following pseudocode:

```
Fib[n]
if(n==0) then return 0
else if(n==1) then return 1
else return Fib[n-1]+Fib[n-2]
```

Solution: The recurrence relation for the running time of this program is: $T(n) = T(n-1) + T(n-2) + c$. Note $T(n)$ has two recurrence calls indicating a binary tree. Each step recursively calls the program for n reduced by 1 and 2, so the depth of the recurrence tree is O(n). The number of leaves at depth n is 2^n since this is a full binary tree, and each leaf takes at least O(1) computations for the constant factor. Running time is clearly exponential in n and it is O(2^n).

Problem-35 Running time of following program?

```
func function(n int) {
  for i := 1; i <= n; i++ {
      for j := 1; j <= n; j += i {
          fmt.Print("*")
      }
  }
}
```

Solution: Consider the comments in the function below:

```
func function(n int) {
  for i := 1; i <= n; i++ {          //outer loop execute n times
      for j := 1; j <= n; j += i {   //this loop executes j times with j increase by the rate of i
          fmt.Print("*")             //constant time
      }
  }
}
```

In the above code, inner loop executes n/i times for each value of i. Its running time is $n \times (\sum_{i=1}^{n} n/i) = O(nlogn)$.

Problem-36 What is the complexity of $\sum_{i=1}^{n} log\, i$?

Solution: Using the logarithmic property, $logxy = logx + logy$, we can see that this problem is equivalent to

$$\sum_{i=1}^{n} logi = log\ 1 + log\ 2 + \cdots + log\ n = log\,(1 \times 2 \times \ldots \times n) = log\,(n!) \ \leq log\,(n^n) \leq nlogn$$

This shows that the time complexity = $O(nlogn)$.

Problem-37 What is the running time of the following recursive function (specified as a function of the input value n)? First write the recurrence formula and then find its complexity.

```
func function(n int) {
  if n <= 1 {
      return
  }
  for i := 1; i <= 3; i++ {
      fmt.Print("*")
      function(int(math.Ceil((float64)(n / 3))))
  }
}
```

Solution: Consider the comments in the below function:

```
func function(n int) {
  if n <= 1 {                  // constant time
      return
  }
  for i := 1; i <= 3; i++ {    // this loop executes with recursive loop of n/3 value
      fmt.Print("*")
      function(int(math.Ceil((float64)(n / 3))))
  }
}
```

We can assume that for asymptotical analysis $k = \lceil k \rceil$ for every integer $k \geq 1$. The recurrence for this code is $T(n) = 3T(\frac{n}{3}) + \Theta(1)$. Using master theorem, we get $T(n) = \Theta(n)$.

Problem-38 What is the running time of the following recursive function (specified as a function of the input value n)? First write a recurrence formula, and show its solution using induction.

```
func function(n int) {
  if n <= 1 {
      return
  }
  for i := 1; i <= 3; i++ {
      function(n - 1)
  }
}
```

Solution: Consider the comments in the function below:

```
func function(n int) {
  if n <= 1 {                 // constant time
      return
  }
  for i := 1; i <= 3; i++ {   // this loop executes 3 times with recursive call of n-1 value
```

```
        function(n - 1)
    }
}
```

The *if* statement requires constant time [O(1)]. With the *for* loop, we neglect the loop overhead and only count three times that the function is called recursively. This implies a time complexity recurrence:

$$T(n) = c, if\ n \le 1;$$
$$= c + 3T(n-1), if\ n > 1.$$

Using the *Subtraction and Conquer* master theorem, we get $T(n) = \Theta(3^n)$.

Problem-39 Write a recursion formula for the running time $T(n)$ of the function whose code is below.

```
func function(n float32) {
    if n <= 1 {
        return
    }
    for i := 1; i <= int(n); i++ {
        function(0.8 * n)
    }
}
```

Solution: Consider the comments in the function below:

```
func function(n float32) {
    if n <= 1 {                      //constant time
        return
    }
    for i := 1; i <= int(n); i++ {       // this loop executes n times with constant time loop
        function(0.8 * n)                //recursive call with 0.8n
    }
}
```

The recurrence for this piece of code is $T(n) = T(.8n) + O(n) = T(4/5n) + O(n) = 4/5\ T(n) + O(n)$. Applying master theorem, we get $T(n) = O(n)$.

Problem-40 Find the complexity of the recurrence: $T(n) = 2T(\sqrt{n}) + logn$

Solution: The given recurrence is not in the master theorem format. Let us try to convert this to the master theorem format by assuming $n = 2^m$. Applying the logarithm on both sides gives, $logn = mlog2 \Rightarrow m = logn$. Now, the given function becomes:

$$T(n) = T(2^m) = 2T(\sqrt{2^m}) + m = 2T\left(2^{\frac{m}{2}}\right) + m.$$

To make it simple we assume $S(m) = T(2^m) \Rightarrow S(\frac{m}{2}) = T(2^{\frac{m}{2}}) \Rightarrow S(m) = 2S\left(\frac{m}{2}\right) + m.$
Applying the master theorem format would result in $S(m) = O(mlogm)$.
If we substitute $m = logn$ back, $T(n) = S(logn) = O((logn)\ loglogn)$.

Problem-41 Find the complexity of the recurrence: $T(n) = T(\sqrt{n}) + 1$

Solution: Applying the logic of Problem-40 gives $S(m) = S\left(\frac{m}{2}\right) + 1$. Applying the master theorem would result in $S(m) = O(logm)$. Substituting $m = logn$, gives $T(n) = S(logn) = O(loglogn)$.

Problem-42 Find the complexity of the recurrence: $T(n) = 2T(\sqrt{n}) + 1$

Solution: Applying the logic of Problem-40 gives: $S(m) = 2S\left(\frac{m}{2}\right) + 1$. Using the master theorem results $S(m) = O\left(m^{log_2^2}\right) = O(m)$. Substituting $m = logn$ gives $T(n) = O(logn)$.

Problem-43 Find the complexity of the below function.

```
func function(n float64) float32 {
    if n <= 2 {
        return 1
    } else {
        return function(math.Floor(math.Sqrt(n))) + 1
    }
}
```

Solution: Consider the comments in the function below:

```
func function(n float64) float32 {
    if n <= 2 {                                         //constant time
        return 1
    } else {
        return function(math.Floor(math.Sqrt(n))) + 1     // executes √n + 1 times
```

```
        }
    }
```

For the above code, the recurrence function can be given as: $T(n) = T(\sqrt{n}) + 1$. This is same as that of Problem-41.

Problem-44 Analyze the running time of the following recursive pseudo-code as a function of n.

```
func function(n int) int {
    counter := 0
    if n < 2 {
        return counter
    }
    for i := 1; i <= 8; i++ {
        function(int(math.Floor( float64(n) / 2)))
        for i := 1; i <= int(math.Pow(float64(n), 3)); i++ {
            counter = counter + 1
        }
    }
    return counter
}
```

Solution: Consider the comments in below pseudo-code and call running time of function(n) as $T(n)$.

```
func function(n int) int {
    counter := 0
    if n < 2 {                                   //constant time
        return counter                           //constant time
    }
    for i := 1; i <= 8; i++ {                    // this loop executes 8 times with n value half in every call
        function(int(math.Floor( float64(n) / 2)))
        for i := 1; i <= int(math.Pow(float64(n), 3)); i++ { // this loop executes n^3 times
            counter = counter + 1                //constant time
        }
    }
    return counter
}
```

$T(n)$ can be defined as follows:

$$T(n) = 1 \; if \; n < 2,$$
$$= 8T(\frac{n}{2}) + n^3 + 1 \; otherwise.$$

Using the master theorem gives: $T(n) = \Theta(n^{log_2^8} logn) = \Theta(n^3 logn)$.

Problem-45 Find the complexity of the below pseudocode:

```
temp = 1
repeat
    for i z 1 to n
        temp = temp + 1;
        n = n/2;
until n <= 1
```

Solution: Consider the comments in the pseudocode below:

```
temp = 1                        //constant time
repeat                          // this loop executes n times
  for i = 1 to n
    temp = temp + 1;
    n = n/2;                    //recursive call with n/2 value
until n <= 1
```

The recurrence for this function is $T(n) = T(n/2) + n$. Using master theorem, we get $T(n) = O(n)$.

Problem-46 Running time of the following program?

```
func function(n int) int {
    count := 0
    for i := 1; i <= n; i++ {
        for j := 1; j <= n; j = 2 * j {
            count++
        }
    }
    return count
```

```
}
```

Solution: Consider the comments in the below function:

```
func function(n int) int {
    count := 0
    for i := 1; i <= n; i++ {           // this loop executes n times
        for j := 1; j <= n; j = 2 * j {   // this loop executes logn times from our logarithm's guideline
            count++
        }
    }
    return count
}
```

Complexity of above program is: O($nlogn$).

Problem-47 Running time of the following program?

```
func function(n int) int {
    count := 0
    for i := 1; i <= n/3; i++ {
        for j := 1; j <= n; j += 4 {
            count++
        }
    }
    return count
}
```

Solution: Consider the comments in the below function:

```
func function(n int) int {
    count := 0
    for i := 1; i <= n/3; i++ {       // this loop executes n/3 times
        for j := 1; j <= n; j += 4 {   // this loop executes n/4 times
            count++
        }
    }
    return count
}
```

The time complexity of this program is: O(n^2).

Problem-48 Find the complexity of the below function:

```
func function(n float32) {
    if n <= 1 {
        return
    }
    fmt.Print("*")
    function(n / 2)
    function(n / 2)
}
```

Solution: Consider the comments in the below function:

```
func function(n float32) {
    if n <= 1 {             //constant time
        return
    }
    fmt.Print("*")
    function(n / 2)         //recursion with n/2 value
    function(n / 2)         //recursion with n/2 value
}
```

The recurrence for this function is: $T(n) = 2T\left(\frac{n}{2}\right) + 1$. Using master theorem, we get $T(n) = O(n)$.

Problem-49 Find the complexity of the below function:

```
func function(n int) {
    i := 1
    for i < n {
        j := n
        for j > 0 {
            j = j / 2
        }
        i = 2 * i
```

```
        }
    }
```

Solution:

```
func function(n int) {
    i := 1
    for i < n {
        j := n
        for j > 0 {            //logn code
            j = j / 2
        }
        i = 2 * i              //logn code
    }
}
```

Time Complexity: $O(logn * logn) = O(log^2n)$.

Problem-50 $\sum_{1\le k\le n} O(n)$, where O(n) stands for order n is:
(A) $O(n)$ (B) $O(n^2)$ (C) $O(n^3)$ (D) $O(3n^2)$ (E) $O(1.5n^2)$

Solution: (**B**). $\sum_{1\le k\le n} O(n) = O(n)\sum_{1\le k\le n} 1 = O(n^2)$.

Problem-51 Which of the following three claims are correct?
I $(n + k)^m = \Theta(n^m)$, where k and m are constants II $2^{n+1} = O(2^n)$ III $2^{2n+1} = O(2^n)$
(A) I and II (B) I and III (C) II and III (D) I, II and III

Solution: (**A**). (I) $(n + k)^m = n^k + c1*n^{k-1} + \ldots k^m = \Theta(n^k)$ and (II) $2^{n+1} = 2*2^n = O(2^n)$

Problem-52 Consider the following functions:
f(n) $= 2^n$ g(n) $= n!$ h(n) $= n^{logn}$
Which of the following statements about the asymptotic behavior of f(n), g(n), and h(n) is true?
(A) f(n) = O(g(n)); g(n) = O(h(n)) (B) f(n) = Ω (g(n)); g(n) = O(h(n)
(C) g(n) = O(f(n)); h(n) = O(f(n)) (D) h(n) = O(f(n)); g(n) = Ω (f(n))

Solution: (**D**). According to the rate of growth: h(n) < f(n) < g(n) (g(n) is asymptotically greater than f(n), and f(n) is asymptotically greater than h(n)). We can easily see the above order by taking logarithms of the given 3 functions: $lognlogn < n < log(n!)$. Note that, $log(n!) = O(nlogn)$.

Problem-53 Consider the following segment of C-code:

```
int j=1, n;
while (j <=n)
    j = j*2;
```

The number of comparisons made in the execution of the loop for any $n > 0$ is:
(A) ceil(log_2^n)+ 1 (B) n (C) ceil(log_2^n) (D) floor(log_2^n) + 1

Solution: (**a**). Let us assume that the loop executes k times. After k^{th} step the value of j is 2^k. Taking logarithms on both sides gives $k = log_2^n$. Since we are doing one more comparison for exiting from the loop, the answer is ceil(log_2^n)+ 1.

Problem-54 Consider the following C code segment. Let T(n) denote the number of times the for loop is executed by the program on input n. Which of the following is true?

```
func isPrime(n int) bool {
  for i := 2; i <= int(math.Sqrt(float64(n))); i++ {
      if n%i == 0 {
          return false
      }
  }
  return true
}
```

(A) T(n) = $O(\sqrt{n})$ and T(n) = $\Omega(\sqrt{n})$ (B) T(n) = $O(\sqrt{n})$ and T(n) = $\Omega(1)$ (C) T(n) = $O(n)$ and T(n) =$\Omega(\sqrt{n})$ (D) None of the above

Solution: (**B**). Big O notation describes the tight upper bound and Big Omega notation describes the tight lower bound for an algorithm. The for loop in the question is run maximum $\sqrt{n}$ times and minimum 1 time. Therefore, T(n) = $O(\sqrt{n})$ and T(n) = $\Omega(1)$.

Problem-55 In the following C function, let $n \ge m$. How many recursive calls are made by this function?

```
func gcd(n, m int) int {
  if n%m == 0 {
      return m
  }
  n = n % m
```

```
        return gcd(m, n)
    }
```

(A) $\Theta(log_2^n)$ (B) $\Omega(n)$ (C) $\Theta(log_2 log_2^n)$ (D) $\Theta(n)$

Solution: No option is correct. Big O notation describes the tight upper bound and Big Omega notation describes the tight lower bound for an algorithm. For $m = 2$ and for all $n = 2^i$, the running time is O(1) which contradicts every option.

Problem-56 Suppose $T(n) = 2T(n/2) + n$, T(0)=T(1)=1. Which one of the following is false?

(A) $T(n) = O(n^2)$ (B) $T(n) = \Theta(nlogn)$ (C) $T(n) = \Omega(n^2)$ (D) $T(n) = O(nlogn)$

Solution: **(C)**. Big O notation describes the tight upper bound and Big Omega notation describes the tight lower bound for an algorithm. Based on master theorem, we get $T(n) = \Theta(nlogn)$. This indicates that tight lower bound and tight upper bound are the same. That means, $O(nlogn)$ and $\Omega(nlogn)$ are correct for given recurrence. So, option (C) is wrong.

Problem-57 Find the complexity of the below function:

```
func function(n int) {
 for i := 0; i < n; i++ {
     for j := i; j < i*i; j++ {
         if j%i == 0 {
             for k := 0; k < j; k++ {
                 fmt.Print(" * ")
             }
         }
     }
 }
}
```

Solution:

```
func function(n int) {
    for i := 0; i < n; i++ {                     // Executes n times
        for j := i; j < i*i; j++ {               // Executes n*n times
            if j%i == 0 {
                for k := 0; k < j; k++ {  // Executes j times = (n*n) times
                    fmt.Print(" * ")
                }
            }
        }
    }
}
```

Time Complexity: $O(n^5)$.

Problem-58 To calculate 9^n, give an algorithm and discuss its complexity.

Solution: Start with 1 and multiply by 9 until reaching 9^n.

Time Complexity: There are $n - 1$ multiplications and each takes constant time giving a $\Theta(n)$ algorithm.

Problem-59 For Problem-58, can we improve the time complexity?

Solution: Refer to the *Divide and Conquer* chapter.

Problem-60 Find the time complexity of recurrence $T(n) = T(\frac{n}{2}) + T(\frac{n}{4}) + T(\frac{n}{8}) + n$.

Solution: Let us solve this problem by method of guessing. The total size on each level of the recurrence tree is less than n, so we guess that $f(n) = n$ will dominate. Assume for all $i < n$ that $c_1 n \le T(i) \le c_2 n$. Then,

$$c_1\frac{n}{2} + c_1\frac{n}{4} + c_1\frac{n}{8} + kn \le T(n) \le c_2\frac{n}{2} + c_2\frac{n}{4} + c_2\frac{n}{8} + kn$$

$$c_1 n(\frac{1}{2} + \frac{1}{4} + \frac{1}{8} + \frac{k}{c_1}) \le T(n) \le c_2 n(\frac{1}{2} + \frac{1}{4} + \frac{1}{8} + \frac{k}{c_2})$$

$$c_1 n(\frac{7}{8} + \frac{k}{c_1}) \le T(n) \le c_2 n(\frac{7}{8} + \frac{k}{c_2})$$

If $c_1 \ge 8k$ and $c_2 \le 8k$, then $c_1 n = T(n) = c_2 n$. So, $T(n) = \Theta(n)$. In general, if you have multiple recursive calls, the sum of the arguments to those calls is less than n (in this case $\frac{n}{2} + \frac{n}{4} + \frac{n}{8} < n$), and $f(n)$ is reasonably large, a good guess is $T(n) = \Theta(f(n))$.

Problem-61 Rank the following functions by order of growth: $(n+1)!$, $n!$, 4^n, $n \times 3^n$, $3^n + n^2 + 20n$, $(\frac{3}{2})^n$, $4n^2$, 4^{lgn}, $n^2 + 200$, $20n + 500$, 2^{lgn}, $n^{2/3}$, 1.

Solution:

Function	Rate of Growth	
$(n+1)!$	$O(n!)$	
$n!$	$O(n!)$	
4^n	$O(4^n)$	
$n \times 3^n$	$O(n3^n)$	
$3^n + n^2 + 20n$	$O(3^n)$	
$(\frac{3}{2})^n$	$O((\frac{3}{2})^n)$	Decreasing rate of growths
$4n^2$	$O(n^2)$	
4^{lgn}	$O(n^2)$	
$n^2 + 200$	$O(n^2)$	
$20n + 500$	$O(n)$	
2^{lgn}	$O(n)$	
$n^{2/3}$	$O(n^{2/3})$	
1	$O(1)$	

Problem-62 Can we say $3^{n^{0.75}} = O(3^n)$?

Solution: Yes: because $3^{n^{0.75}} < 3^{n^1}$.

Problem-63 Can we say $2^{3n} = O(2^n)$?

Solution: No: because $2^{3n} = (2^3)^n = 8^n$ not less than 2^n.

Problem-64 Solve the following recurrence relation using the recursion tree method: $T(n)=T(\frac{n}{2}) + T(\frac{2n}{3}) + n^2$.

Solution: How much work do we do in each level of the recursion tree?

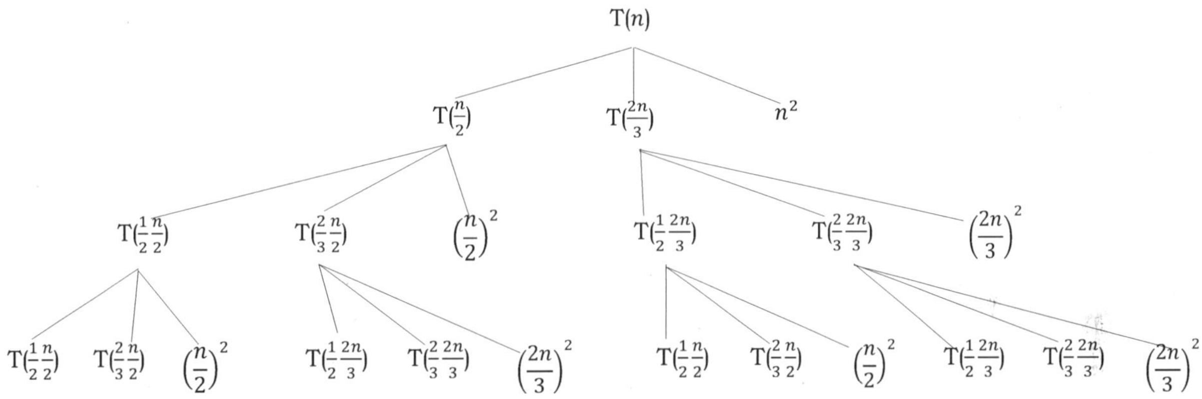

In level 0, we take n^2 time. At level 1, the two subproblems take time:

$$\left(\frac{1}{2}n\right)^2 + \left(\frac{2}{3}n\right)^2 = \left(\frac{1}{4}+\frac{4}{9}\right)n^2 = \left(\frac{25}{36}\right)n^2$$

At level 2 the four subproblems are of size $\frac{1}{2}\frac{n}{2}$, $\frac{2}{3}\frac{n}{2}$, $\frac{1}{2}\frac{2n}{3}$, and $\frac{2}{3}\frac{2n}{3}$ respectively. These two subproblems take time:

$$\left(\frac{1}{4}n\right)^2 + \left(\frac{1}{3}n\right)^2 + \left(\frac{1}{3}\right)n^2 + \left(\frac{4}{9}\right)n^2 = \frac{625}{1296}n^2 = \left(\frac{25}{36}\right)^2 n^2$$

Similarly, the amount of work at level k is at most $\left(\frac{25}{36}\right)^k n^2$.

Let $\alpha = \frac{25}{36}$, the total runtime is then:

$$\begin{aligned} T(n) &\leq \sum_{k=0}^{\infty} \alpha^k n^2 \\ &= \frac{1}{1-\alpha} n^2 \\ &= \frac{1}{1-\frac{25}{36}} n^2 \\ &= \frac{1}{\frac{11}{36}} n^2 \\ &= \frac{36}{11} n^2 \\ &= O(n^2) \end{aligned}$$

That is, the first level provides a constant fraction of the total runtime.

CHAPTER

RECURSION AND BACKTRACKING

2

2.1 Introduction

In this chapter, we will look at one of the important topics, "*recursion*", which will be used in almost every chapter, and also its relative "*backtracking*".

2.2 What is Recursion?

Any function which calls itself is called *recursive*. A recursive method solves a problem by calling a copy of itself to work on a smaller problem. This is called the recursion step. The recursion step can result in many more such recursive calls.

It is important to ensure that the recursion terminates. Each time the function calls itself with a slightly simpler version of the original problem. The sequence of smaller problems must eventually converge on the base case.

2.3 Why Recursion?

Recursion is a useful technique borrowed from mathematics. Recursive code is generally shorter and easier to write than iterative code. Generally, loops are turned into recursive functions when they are compiled or interpreted.

Recursion is most useful for tasks that can be defined in terms of similar subtasks. For example, sort, search, and traversal problems often have simple recursive solutions.

2.4 Format of a Recursive Function

A recursive function performs a task in part by calling itself to perform the subtasks. At some point, the function encounters a subtask that it can perform without calling itself. This case, where the function does not recur, is called the ***base case***. The former, where the function calls itself to perform a subtask, is referred to as the ***recursive case***. We can write all recursive functions using the format:

```
if(test for the base case) {
    return some base case value
}
else if(test for another base case) {
    return some other base case value
}
// the recursive case
return (some work and then a recursive call)
```

As an example, consider the factorial function: $n!$ is the product of all integers between n and 1. The definition of recursive factorial looks like:

$$n! = 1, \quad \text{if } n = 0$$
$$n! = n * (n-1)! \quad \text{if } n > 0$$

This definition can easily be converted to recursive implementation. Here the problem is determining the value of $n!$, and the subproblem is determining the value of $(n - l)!$. In the recursive case, when n is greater than 1, the function calls itself to determine the value of $(n - l)!$ and multiplies that with n. In the base case, when n is 0 or 1, the function simply returns 1. This looks like the following:

```
var factVal uint64 = 1 // uint64 is the set of all unsigned 64-bit integers.
// calculates factorial of a positive integer
func factorial(n int) int {
```

```
        if(n == 0) {                            // base case: fact of 0
            return 1
        }
        // recursive case: multiply n by (n – 1) factorial
        return n* factorial(n-1)
    }
    // factorial iterative algorithm
    func factorialIterative(n int) uint64 {
        var factVal uint64 = 1                  // uint64 is the set of all unsigned 64-bit integers.
        if n < 0 {
            fmt.Print("Factorial of negative number doesn't exist.")
        } else {
            for i := 1; i <= n; i++ {
                factVal *= uint64(i)            // mismatched types int64 and int
            }
        }
        return factVal                          // return from function
    }
```

2.5 Recursion and Memory (Visualization)

Each recursive call makes a new copy of that method (actually only the variables) in memory. Once a method ends (that is, returns some data), the copy of that returning method is removed from memory. The recursive solutions look simple but visualization and tracing takes time. For better understanding, let us consider the following example.

```
package main
import "fmt"
// print numbers 1 to n backward
func print(n int) int {
    if n == 0 {
        return 0                    // this is the terminating base case
    }
    fmt.Println(n)
    return print(n - 1)             // recursive call to itself again
}
func main() {
    fmt.Println(print(5))
}
```

For this example, if we call the print function with n=4, visually our memory assignments may look like:

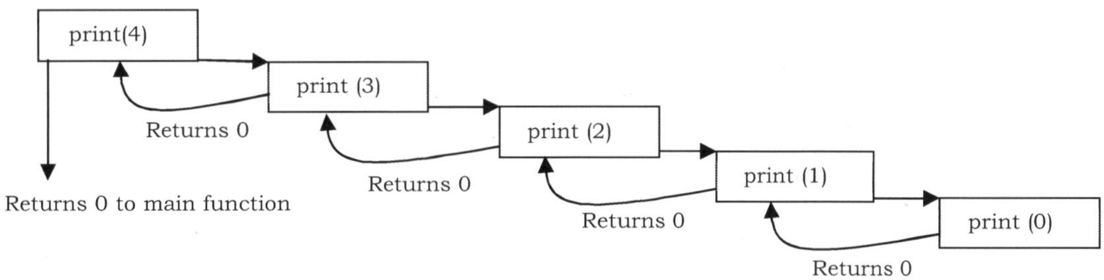

Now, let us consider our factorial function. The visualization of factorial function with n=4 will look like:

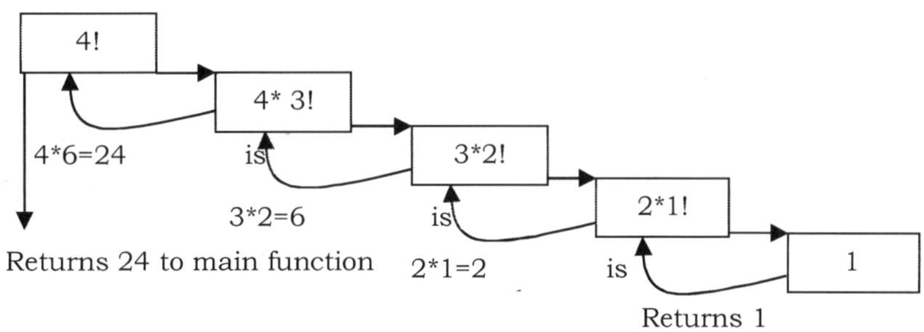

2.6 Recursion versus Iteration

While discussing recursion, the basic question that comes to mind is: which way is better? – iteration or recursion? The answer to this question depends on what we are trying to do. A recursive approach mirrors the problem that we are trying to solve. A recursive approach makes it simpler to solve a problem that may not have the most obvious of answers. But recursion adds overhead for each recursive call (needs space on the stack frame).

Recursion

- Terminates when a base case is reached.
- Each recursive call requires extra space on the stack frame (memory).
- If we get infinite recursion, the program may run out of memory and result in stack overflow.
- Solutions to some problems are easier to formulate recursively.

Iteration

- Terminates when a condition is proven to be false.
- Each iteration does not require extra space.
- An infinite loop could loop forever since there is no extra memory being created.
- Iterative solutions to a problem may not always be as obvious as a recursive solution.

2.7 Notes on Recursion

- Recursive algorithms have two types of cases, recursive cases and base cases.
- Every recursive function case must terminate at a base case.
- Generally, iterative solutions are more efficient than recursive solutions [due to the overhead of function calls].
- A recursive algorithm can be implemented without recursive function calls using a stack, but it's usually more trouble than its worth. That means any problem that can be solved recursively can also be solved iteratively.
- For some problems, there are no obvious iterative algorithms.
- Some problems are best suited for recursive solutions while others are not.

2.8 Example Algorithms of Recursion

- Fibonacci Series, Factorial Finding
- Merge Sort, Quick Sort
- Binary Search
- Tree Traversals and many Tree Problems: InOrder, PreOrder PostOrder
- Graph Traversals: DFS [Depth First Search] and BFS [Breadth First Search]
- Dynamic Programming Examples
- Divide and Conquer Algorithms
- Towers of Hanoi
- Backtracking Algorithms [we will discuss in next section]

2.9 Recursion: Problems & Solutions

In this chapter we cover a few problems with recursion and we will discuss the rest in other chapters. By the time you complete reading the entire book, you will encounter many recursion problems.

Problem-1 Discuss Towers of Hanoi puzzle.

Solution: The Towers of Hanoi is a mathematical puzzle. It consists of three rods (or pegs or towers), and a number of disks of different sizes which can slide onto any rod. The puzzle starts with the disks on one rod in ascending order of size, the smallest at the top, thus making a conical shape. The objective of the puzzle is to move the entire stack to another rod, satisfying the following rules:

- Only one disk may be moved at a time.
- Each move consists of taking the upper disk from one of the rods and sliding it onto another rod, on top of the other disks that may already be present on that rod.
- No disk may be placed on top of a smaller disk.

Algorithm:

- Move the top $n - 1$ disks from $Source$ to $Auxiliary$ tower,
- Move the nth disk from $Source$ to $Destination$ tower,
- Move the $n - 1$disks from $Auxiliary$ tower to $Destination$ tower.

- Transferring the top $n-1$ disks from *Source* to *Auxiliary* tower can again be thought of as a fresh problem and can be solved in the same manner. Once we solve *Towers of Hanoi* with three disks, we can solve it with any number of disks with the above algorithm.

```
package main
import "fmt"

func TOHUtil(n int, from, to, temp string) {
	/* If only 1 disk, make the move and return */
	if n == 1 {
	  fmt.Println("Move disk ", n, " from peg ", from, " to peg ", to)
		return
	}
	/* Move top n-1 disks from A to B, using C as auxiliary */
	TOHUtil(n-1, from, temp, to)

	/* Move remaining disks from A to C */
	fmt.Println("Move disk ", n, " from peg ", from, " to peg ", to)

	/* Move n-1 disks from B to C using A as auxiliary */
	TOHUtil(n-1, temp, to, from)
}
func TowersOfHanoi(n int) {
	TOHUtil(n, "A", "C", "B")
}
func main() {
	TowersOfHanoi(3)
}
```

Problem-2 Given an array, check whether the array is in sorted order with recursion.

Solution:

```
package main
import "fmt"
func isSorted(A []int) bool {
		n := len(A)
		if n == 1 {
		return true
		}
		if A[n-1] < A[n-2] {
		return false
		}
		return isSorted(A[:n-1])
}

func main() {
		A := []int{10, 20, 23, 23, 45, 78, 88}
		fmt.Println(isSorted(A))
		A = []int{10, 20, 3, 23, 45, 78, 88}
		fmt.Println(isSorted(A))
}
```

Time Complexity: O(n). Space Complexity: O(n) for recursive stack space.

2.10 What is Backtracking?

Backtracking is an improvement of the brute force approach. It systematically searches for a solution to a problem among all available options. In backtracking, we start with one possible option out of many available options and try to solve the problem if we are able to solve the problem with the selected move then we will print the solution else we will backtrack and select some other option and try to solve it. If none if the options work out, we will claim that there is no solution for the problem.

Backtracking is a form of recursion. The usual scenario is that you are faced with a number of options, and you must choose one of these. After you make your choice you will get a new set of options; just what set of options you get depends on what choice you made. This procedure is repeated over and over until you reach a final state. If you made a good sequence of choices, your final state is a goal state; if you didn't, it isn't.

Backtracking can be thought of as a selective tree/graph traversal method. The tree is a way of representing some initial starting position (the root node) and a final goal state (one of the leaves). Backtracking allows us to deal with situations in which a raw brute-force approach would explode into an impossible number of options to consider. Backtracking is a sort of refined brute force. At each node, we eliminate choices that are obviously not possible and proceed to recursively check only those that have potential.

What's interesting about backtracking is that we back up only as far as needed to reach a previous decision point with an as-yet-unexplored alternative. In general, that will be at the most recent decision point. Eventually, more and more of these decision points will have been fully explored, and we will have to backtrack further and further. If we backtrack all the way to our initial state and have explored all alternatives from there, we can conclude the particular problem is unsolvable. In such a case, we will have done all the work of the exhaustive recursion and known that there is no viable solution possible.

- Sometimes the best algorithm for a problem is to try all possibilities.
- This is always slow, but there are standard tools that can be used to help.
- Tools: algorithms for generating basic objects, such as binary strings [2^n possibilities for n-bit string], permutations [$n!$], combinations [$n!/r!(n-r)!$], general strings [k −ary strings of length n has k^n possibilities], etc...
- Backtracking speeds the exhaustive search by pruning.

2.11 Example Algorithms of Backtracking

- Binary Strings: generating all binary strings
- Generating k −ary Strings
- N-Queens Problem
- The Knapsack Problem
- Generalized Strings
- Hamiltonian Cycles [refer to *Graphs* chapter]
- Graph Coloring Problem

2.12 Backtracking: Problems & Solutions

Problem-3 Generate all the strings of n bits. Assume $A[0..n-1]$ is an array of size n.

Solution:

```
func printResult(A []int, n int) {
    var i int
    for ; i < n; i++ {
        // Function to print the output
        fmt.Print(A[i])
    }
    fmt.Printf("\n")
}
// Function to generate all binary strings
func generateBinaryStrings(n int, A []int, i int) {
    if i == n {
        printResult(A, n)
        return
    }
    // assign "0" at ith position and try for all other permutations for remaining positions
    A[i] = 0
    generateBinaryStrings(n, A, i+1)
    // assign "1" at ith position and try for all other permutations for remaining positions
    A[i] = 1
    generateBinaryStrings(n, A, i+1)
}
```

Let $T(n)$ be the running time of $binary(n)$. Assume function $printf$ takes time O(1).

$$T(n) = \begin{cases} c, & \text{if } n < 0 \\ 2T(n-1) + d, & \text{otherwise} \end{cases}$$

Using Subtraction and Conquer Master theorem we get: $T(n) = O(2^n)$. This means the algorithm for generating bit-strings is optimal.

Problem-4 Generate all the strings of length n drawn from $0...k-1$.

Solution: Let us assume we keep current k-ary string in an array $A[0..n-1]$. Call function $k\text{-}string$(n, k):

```
// Function to generate all k-ary strings
func generateK_aryStrings(n int, A []int, i int, k int) {
    if i == n {
        printResult(A, n)
        return
    }
    for j := 0; j < k; j++ {
        // assign j at ith position and try for all other permutations for remaining positions
        A[i] = j
        generateK_aryStrings(n, A, i+1, k)
    }
}
```

Let $T(n)$ be the running time of $k - string(n)$. Then,

$$T(n) = \begin{cases} c, & if\ n < 0 \\ kT(n-1) + d, & otherwise \end{cases}$$

Using Subtraction and Conquer Master theorem we get: $T(n) = O(k^n)$.

Note: For more problems, refer to *String Algorithms* chapter.

Problem-5 **Finding the length of connected cells of 1s (regions) in a matrix of 0s and 1s**: Given a matrix, each of which may be 1 or 0. The filled cells that are connected form a region. Two cells are said to be connected if they are adjacent to each other horizontally, vertically or diagonally. There may be several regions in the matrix. How do you find the largest region (in terms of number of cells) in the matrix?

Sample Input: 11000 Sample Output: 5
01100
00101
10001
01011

Solution: The simplest idea is: for each location traverse in all 8 directions and in each of those directions keep track of maximum region found.

```
func findConnects(matrix [][]int, M, N, r, c int) int {
    answer := 0
    if r < 0 || c < 0 || r >= M || c >= N {
        answer = 0

    } else if matrix[r][c] == 1 {
        matrix[r][c] = 0
        answer = 1 +
            findConnects(matrix, M, N, r-1, c) +
            findConnects(matrix, M, N, r+1, c) +
            findConnects(matrix, M, N, r, c-1) +
            findConnects(matrix, M, N, r, c+1) +
            findConnects(matrix, M, N, r-1, c-1) +
            findConnects(matrix, M, N, r-1, c+1) +
            findConnects(matrix, M, N, r+1, c-1) +
            findConnects(matrix, M, N, r+1, c+1)
    }
    return answer
}
func findMaxConnects(matrix [][]int, M, N int) int {
    maxConnects := 0
    for r := 0; r < M; r++ {
        for c := 0; c < N; c++ {
            maxConnects = max(maxConnects, findConnects(matrix, M, N, r, c))
        }
    }
    return maxConnects
}
```

Test Call:

```
func main() {
    scanner := bufio.NewScanner(os.Stdin)
    scanner.Split(bufio.ScanWords)
```

```
        scanner.Scan()
        M, _ := strconv.Atoi(scanner.Text())
        scanner.Scan()
        N, _ := strconv.Atoi(scanner.Text())
        matrix := make([][]int, M)
        for i := 0; i < M; i++ {
            matrix[i] = make([]int, N)
            for j := 0; j < N; j++ {
                scanner.Scan()
                v, _ := strconv.Atoi(scanner.Text())
                matrix[i][j] = v
            }
        }
        maxConnects := 0
        for r := 0; r < M; r++ {
            for c := 0; c < N; c++ {
                maxConnects = max(maxConnects, findConnects(matrix, M, N, r, c))
            }
        }
        fmt.Println(findMaxConnects(matrix, M, N))
}
```

Problem-6 Solve the recurrence $T(n) = 2T(n - 1) + 2^n$.

Solution: At each level of the recurrence tree, the number of problems is double from the previous level, while the amount of work being done in each problem is half from the previous level. Formally, the ith level has 2^i problems, each requiring 2^{n-i} work. Thus the ith level requires exactly 2^n work. The depth of this tree is n, because at the ith level, the originating call will be $T(n - i)$. Thus, the total complexity for $T(n)$ is $T(n2^n)$.

CHAPTER

LINKED LISTS 3

3.1 What is a Linked List?

One disadvantage of using arrays to store data is that arrays are static structures and therefore cannot be easily extended or reduced to fit the data set. Arrays are also expensive to maintain new insertions and deletions. In this chapter we consider another data structure called Linked Lists that addresses some of the limitations of arrays. A linked list is a data structure used for storing collections of data. A linked list has the following properties. A linked list is a linear dynamic data structure. The number of nodes in a list is not fixed and can grow and shrink on demand. Each node of a linked list is made up of two items - the data and a reference to the next node. The last node has a reference to *nil*. The entry point into a linked list is called the head of the list. It should be noted that head is not a separate node, but the reference to the first node. If the list is empty then the head is a null reference.

- Successive elements are connected by pointers.
- The last element points to *nil*.
- Can grow or shrink in size during execution of a program.
- Can be made just as long as required (until systems memory exhausts).
- Does not waste memory space (but takes some extra memory for pointers). It allocates memory as list grows.

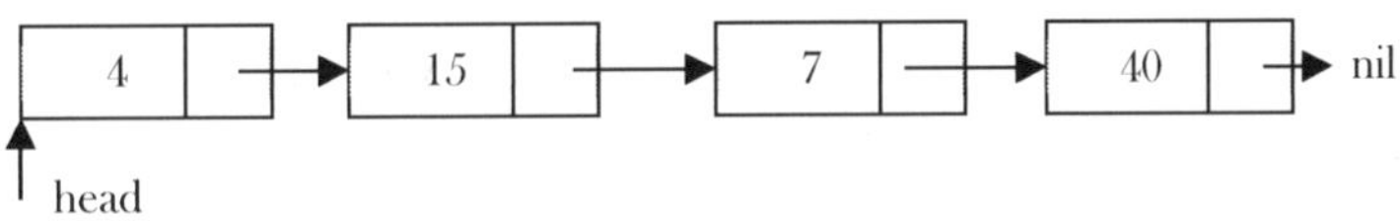

3.2 Linked Lists ADT

The following operations make linked lists an ADT:

Main Linked Lists Operations

- Insert: inserts an element into the list
- Delete: removes and returns the specified position element from the list

Auxiliary Linked Lists Operations

- Delete List: removes all elements of the list (disposes the list)
- Count: returns the number of elements in the list
- Find n^{th} node from the end of the list

3.3 Why Linked Lists?

There are many other data structures that do the same thing as linked lists. Before discussing linked lists, it is important to understand the difference between linked lists and arrays. Both linked lists and arrays are used to store collections of data, and since both are used for the same purpose, we need to differentiate their usage. That means in which cases *arrays* are suitable and in which cases *linked lists* are suitable.

3.4 Arrays Overview

One memory block is allocated for the entire array to hold the elements of the array. The array elements can be accessed in constant time by using the index of the particular element as the subscript.

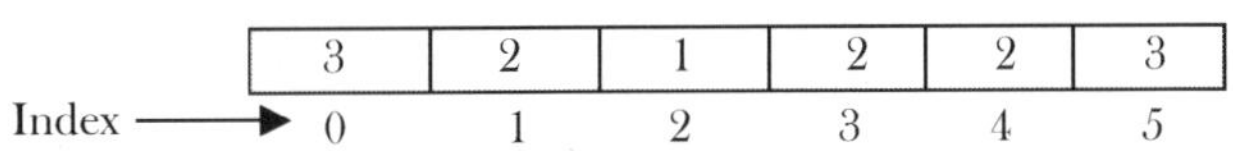

Why Constant Time for Accessing Array Elements?

To access an array element, the address of an element is computed as an offset from the base address of the array and one multiplication is needed to compute what is supposed to be added to the base address to get the memory address of the element. First the size of an element of that data type is calculated and then it is multiplied with the index of the element to get the value to be added to the base address. This process takes one multiplication and one addition. Since these two operations take constant time, we can say the array access can be performed in constant time.

Advantages of Arrays

- Simple and easy to use
- Faster access to the elements (constant access)

Disadvantages of Arrays

- Preallocates all needed memory up front and wastes memory space for indices in the array that are empty.
- **Fixed size:** The size of the array is static (specify the array size before using it).
- **One block allocation**: To allocate the array itself at the beginning, sometimes it may not be possible to get the memory for the complete array (if the array size is big).
- **Complex position-based insertion**: To insert an element at a given position, we may need to shift the existing elements. This will create a position for us to insert the new element at the desired position. If the position at which we want to add an element is at the beginning, then the shifting operation is more expensive.

Dynamic Arrays

Dynamic array (also called as *growable array*, *resizable array*, *dynamic table*, or *array list*) is a random access, variable-size list data structure that allows elements to be added or removed.

One simple way of implementing dynamic arrays is to initially start with some fixed size array. As soon as that array becomes full, create the new array double the size of the original array. Similarly, reduce the array size to half if the elements in the array are less than half.

Note: We will see the implementation for *dynamic arrays* in the *Stacks*, *Queues* and *Hashing* chapters.

Advantages of Linked Lists

Linked lists have both advantages and disadvantages. The advantage of linked lists is that they can be *expanded* in constant time. To create an array, we must allocate memory for a certain number of elements. To add more elements to the array when full, we must create a new array and copy the old array into the new array. This can take a lot of time.

We can prevent this by allocating lots of space initially but then we might allocate more than we need and waste memory. With a linked list, we can start with space for just one allocated element and *add* on new elements easily without the need to do any copying and reallocating.

Issues with Linked Lists (Disadvantages)

There are a number of issues with linked lists. The main disadvantage of linked lists is *access time* to individual elements. Array is random-access, which means it takes O(1) to access any element in the array. Linked lists take O(n) for access to an element in the list in the worst case. Another advantage of arrays in access time is *spacial locality* in memory. Arrays are defined as contiguous blocks of memory, and so any array element will be physically near its neighbors. This greatly benefits from modern CPU caching methods.

Although the dynamic allocation of storage is a great advantage, the *overhead* with storing and retrieving data can make a big difference. Sometimes linked lists are *hard to manipulate*. If the last item is deleted, the last but one must then have its pointer changed to hold a *nil* reference. This requires that the list is traversed to find the last but one link, and its pointer set to a *nil* reference.

Finally, linked lists waste memory in terms of extra reference points.

3.5 Comparison of Linked Lists with Arrays and Dynamic Arrays

As with most choices in computer programming and design, no method is well suited to all circumstances. A linked list data structure might work well in one case, but cause problems in another. This is a list of some of the common tradeoffs involving linked list structures. In general, if you have a dynamic collection, where elements are frequently being added and deleted, and the location of new elements added to the list is significant, then benefits of a linked list increase.

Parameter	Linked list	Array	Dynamic array
Indexing	O(*n*)	O(1)	O(1)
Insertion/deletion at beginning	O(1)	O(*n*), if array is not full (for shifting the elements)	O(*n*)
Insertion at ending	O(*n*)	O(1), if array is not full	O(1), if array is not full O(*n*), if array is full
Deletion at ending	O(*n*)	O(1)	O(*n*)
Insertion in middle	O(*n*)	O(*n*), if array is not full (for shifting the elements)	O(*n*)
Deletion in middle	O(*n*)	O(*n*), if array is not full (for shifting the elements)	O(*n*)
Wasted space	O(*n*) (for pointers)	0	O(*n*)

3.6 Singly Linked Lists

The linked list consists of a series of structures called nodes. We can think of each node as a record. The first part of the record is a field that stores the data, and the second part of the record is a field that stores a pointer to a node. So, each node contains two fields: a *data* field and a *next* field which is a pointer used to link one node to the next node. Generally, "linked list" means a singly linked list. This list consists of a number of nodes in which each node has a *next* pointer to the following element. The link of the last node in the list is *nil*, which indicates the end of the list.

Each node is allocated in the heap with a call to *new*(), so the node memory continues to exist until it is explicitly deallocated with a call to *free*(). The node called a *head* is the first node in the list. The last node's next pointer points to *nil* value.

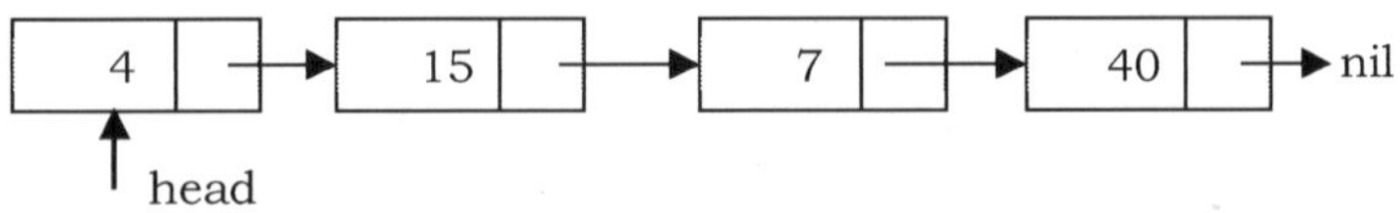

A linked list node contains a pointer to the next node as well the data. This generic behavior is achieved by marking the data field as type interface{}:

```
type ListNode struct {          // defines a ListNode in a singly linked list
    data interface{}            // the datum
    next *ListNode              // pointer to the next ListNode
}
```

A linked list contains pointer to first node in the list and its size. The *size* field in the linked list structure stores the length of the linked list. The *head* field of ListNode type stores the memory address of the head or the first node of the linked list.

```
type LinkedList struct {
    head *ListNode
    size  int
}
```

Basic Operations on a List

- Traversing the list
- Inserting an item in the list
- Deleting an item from the list

Traversing the Linked List

Let us assume that the *head* points to the first node of the list. To traverse the list, we do the following.

- Follow the pointers.
- Display the contents of the nodes (or count) as they are traversed.
- Stop when the next pointer points to *nil*.

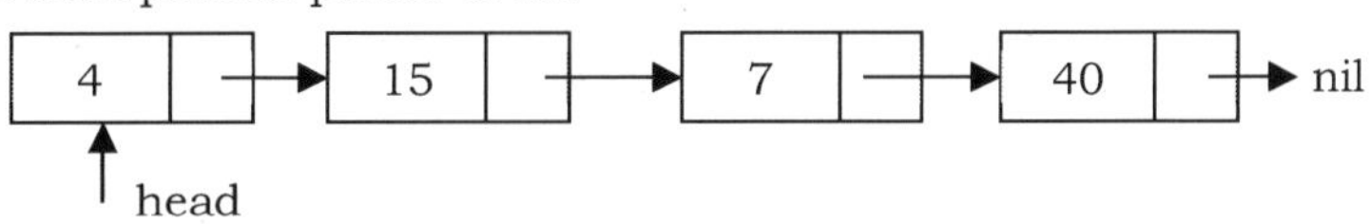

The function given below can be used for printing the list data with extra print function.

```
func (ll *LinkedList) Display() error {
    if ll.head == nil {
        return fmt.Errorf("display: List is empty")
    }
    current := ll.head
    for current != nil {
        fmt.Printf("%v -> ", current.data)
        current = current.next
    }
    fmt.Println()
    return nil
}
```

The length() function takes a linked list as input and counts the number of nodes in the list. To find the length of a linked list, one would normally have to traverse all nodes, and count them. This operation takes O(*n*) time. In order to have this operation done in constant time, we can add the size field in linked list structure definition. Hence, finding the list size is trivial:

```
// with extra size field
func (ll *LinkedList) Length() int {
    return ll.size
}

// length returns the linked list size
func (ll *LinkedList) Length() int {
    size := 0
    current := ll.head
    for current!= nil {
        size++
        current = current.next
    }
    return size
}
```

Time Complexity: O(*n*), for scanning the list of size *n*. Space Complexity: O(1), for creating a temporary variable.

Singly Linked List Insertion

Insertion into a singly-linked list has three cases:

- Inserting a new node before the head (at the beginning)
- Inserting a new node after the tail (at the end of the list)
- Inserting a new node at the middle of the list (random location)

Note: To insert an element in the linked list at some position *p*, assume that after inserting the element the position of this new node is *p*.

Inserting a Node at the Beginning

In this case, a new node is inserted before the current head node. *Only one next pointer* needs to be modified (new node's next pointer) and it can be done in two steps:

- Update the next pointer of new node, to point to the current head.

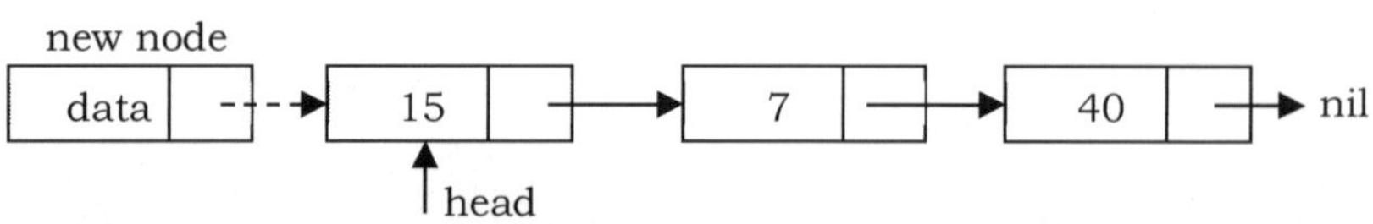

- Update head pointer to point to the new node.

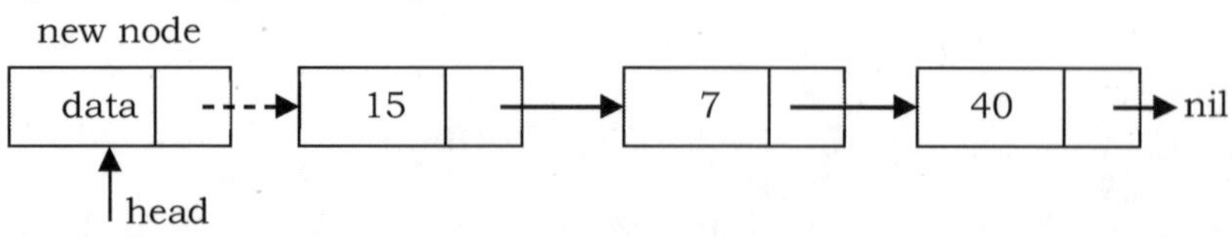


```
func (ll *LinkedList) InsertBeginning(data interface{}) {
    node := &ListNode{
```

```
            data: data,
        }
        if ll.head == nil {
            ll.head = node
        } else {
            node.next = ll.head
            ll.head = node
        }
        ll.size++
        return
    }
```

Time Complexity: O(1). Space Complexity: O(1).

Inserting a Node at the Ending

In this case, we need to modify *two next pointers* (last nodes next pointer and new nodes next pointer).

- New nodes next pointer points to *nil*.

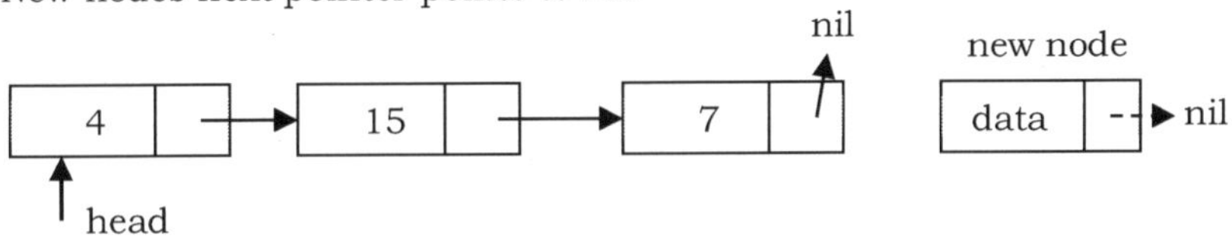

- Last nodes next pointer points to the new node.

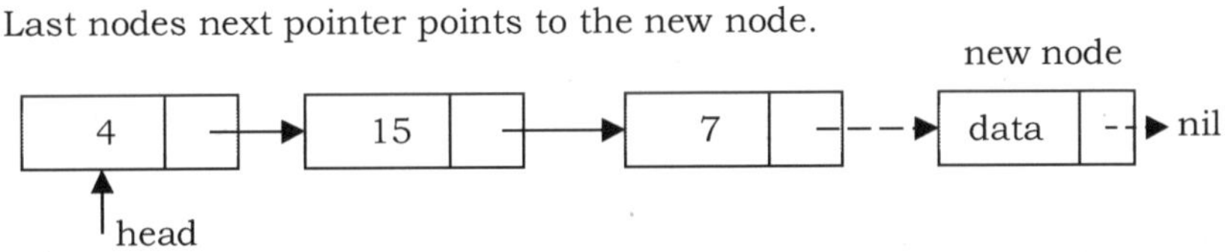


```
    func (ll *LinkedList) InsertEnd(data interface{}) {
        node := &ListNode{
            data: data,
        }
        if ll.head == nil {
            ll.head = node
        } else {
            current := ll.head
            for current.next != nil {
                current = current.next
            }
            current.next = node
        }
        ll.size++
        return
    }
```

Time Complexity: O(n), for scanning the list of size n. Space Complexity: O(1).

Inserting a Node at the Given Position

Let us assume that we are given a position where we want to insert the new node. In this case also, we need to modify two next pointers.

- To add an element at position 3 then we stop at position 2. That means, traverse 2 nodes and insert the new node. For simplicity let us assume that *prev* will point to the predecessor of new node. The next pointer of new node points to the next node of the *prev* node.

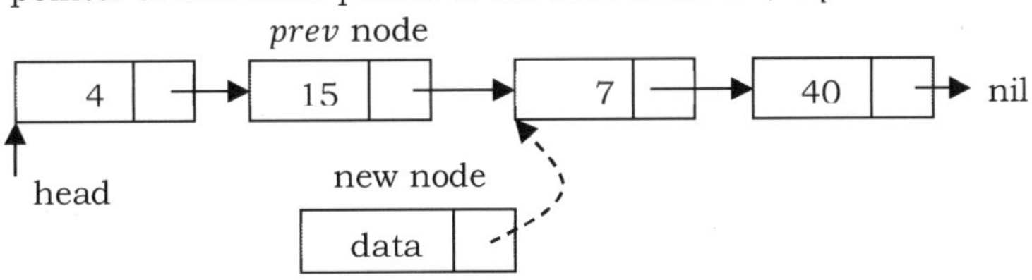

- *prev* node's next pointer now points to the new node.

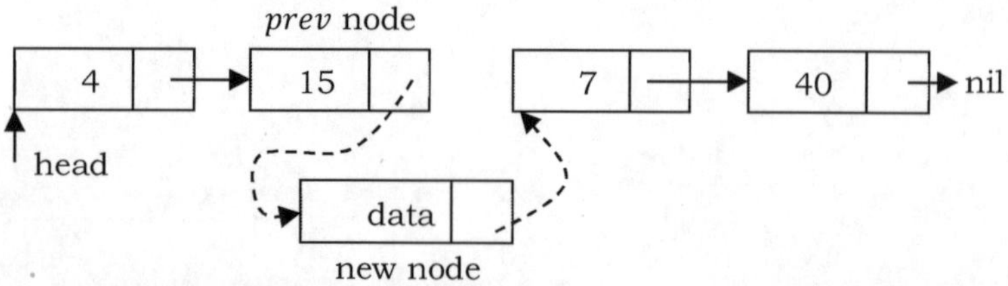

Let us write the code for all three cases. We must update the first element pointer in the calling function, not just in the called function. The following code inserts a node in the singly linked list.

```
// Insert adds an item at position i
func (ll *LinkedList) Insert(position int, data interface{}) error {
    // This condition to check whether the position given is valid or not.
    if position < 1 || position > ll.size+1 {
        return fmt.Errorf("insert: Index out of bounds")
    }
    newNode := &ListNode{data, nil}
    var prev, current *ListNode
    prev = nil
    current = ll.head
    for position > 1 {
        prev = current
        current = current.next
        position = position - 1
    }
    if prev != nil {
        prev.next = newNode
        newNode.next = current
    } else {
        newNode.next = current
        ll.head = newNode
    }
    ll.size++
    return nil
}
```

Time Complexity: O(n). In the worst case, we may need to insert an element at the end of the linked list.
Space Complexity: O(1).

Note: We can implement the three variations of the *insert* operation separately.

Singly Linked List Deletion

Similar to insertion, here also have three cases.

- Deleting the first node
- Deleting the last node
- Deleting an intermediate node

Deleting the First Node

First node (current head node) is removed from the list. It can be done in two steps:

- Create a temporary node which will point to the same node as that of head.

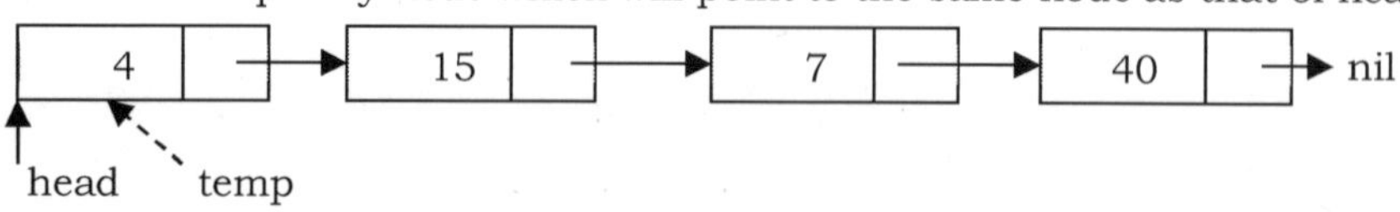

- Now, move the head nodes pointer to the next node and dispose of the temporary node.

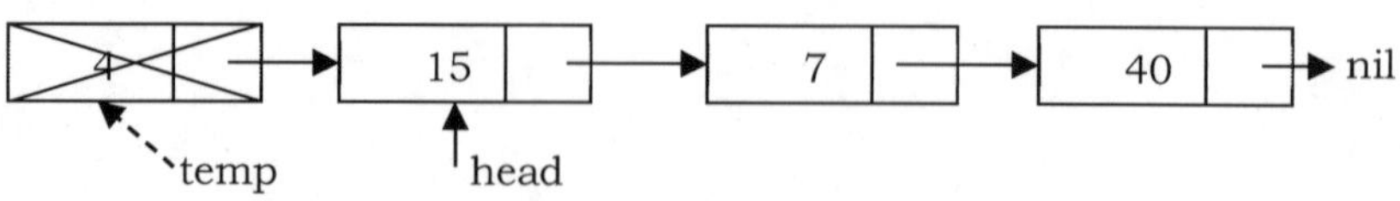


```
func (ll *LinkedList) DeleteFirst() (interface{}, error) {
```

```
    if ll.head == nil {
        return nil, fmt.Errorf("deleteFront: List is empty")
    }
    data := ll.head.data
    ll.head = ll.head.next
    ll.size--
    return data, nil
}
```

Time Complexity: $O(n)$, for scanning the list of size n. Space Complexity: $O(1)$.

Deleting the Last Node

In this case, the last node is removed from the list. This operation is a bit trickier than removing the first node, because the algorithm should find a node, which is previous to the tail. It can be done in three steps:

- Traverse the list and while traversing maintain the previous node address also. By the time we reach the end of the list, we will have two pointers, one pointing to the *tail* node and the other pointing to the node *before* the tail node.

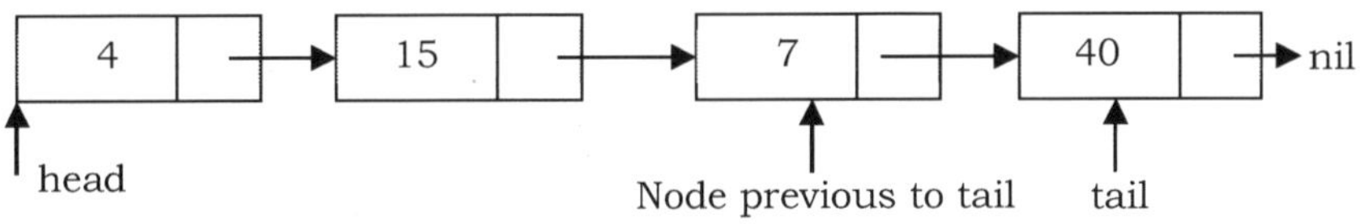

- Update previous node's next pointer with *nil*.

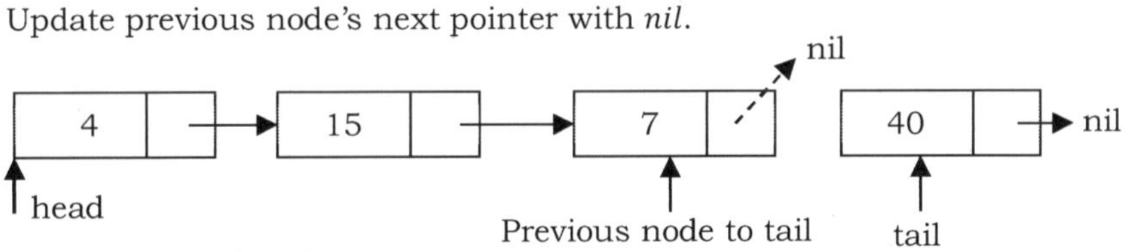

- Dispose the tail node.

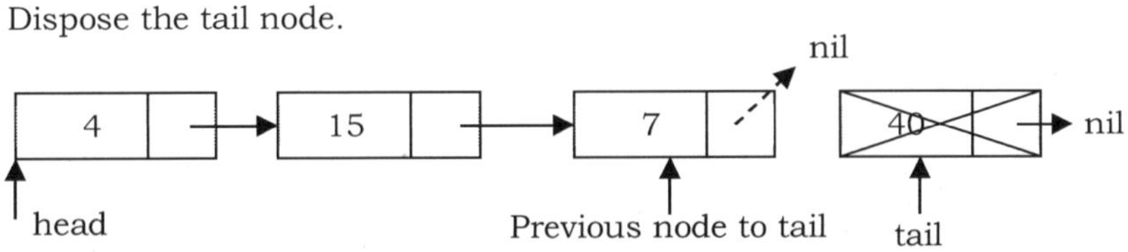


```
func (ll *LinkedList) DeleteLast() (interface{}, error) {
    if ll.head == nil {
        return nil, fmt.Errorf("deleteLast: List is empty")
    }
    var prev *ListNode
    current := ll.head
    for current.next != nil {
        prev = current
        current = current.next
    }
    if prev != nil {
        prev.next = nil
    } else {
        ll.head = nil
    }
    ll.size--
    return current.data, nil
}
```

Time Complexity: $O(n)$, for scanning the list of size n. Space Complexity: $O(1)$.

Deleting an Intermediate Node

In this case, the node to be removed is *always located between* two nodes. Head and tail links are not updated in this case. Such a removal can be done in two steps:

- Similar to the previous case, maintain the previous node while traversing the list. Once we find the node to be deleted, change the previous node's next pointer to the next pointer of the node to be deleted.

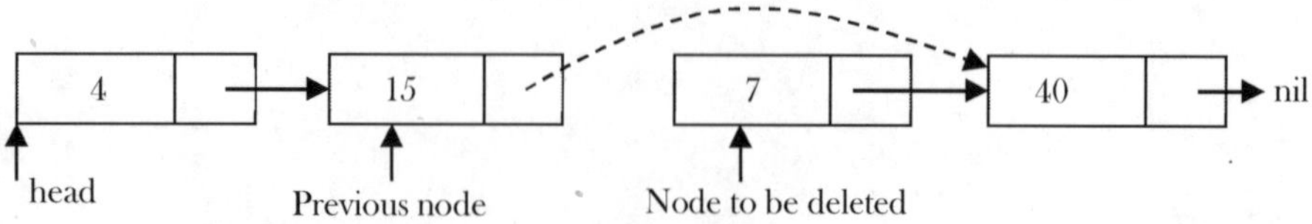

- Dispose of the current node to be deleted.

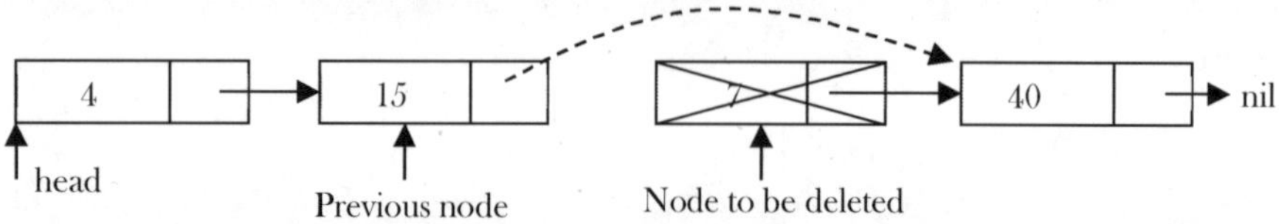

```
// delete removes an element at position i
func (ll *LinkedList) Delete(position int) (interface{}, error) {
    // This condition to check whether the position given is valid or not.
    if position < 1 || position > ll.size+1 {
        return nil, fmt.Errorf("insert: Index out of bounds")
    }
    var prev, current *ListNode
    prev = nil
    current = ll.head
    pos := 0
    if position == 1 {
        ll.head = ll.head.next
    } else {
        for pos != position - 1 {
            pos = pos + 1
            prev = current
            current = current.next
        }
        if current != nil {
            prev.next = current.next
        }
    }
    ll.size--
    return current.data, nil
}
```

Time Complexity: O(n). In the worst case, we may need to delete the node from the end of the linked list.
Space Complexity: O(1).

3.7 Doubly Linked Lists

A doubly linked list is a linked list in which a node contains a pointer to the previous as well as the next node in the sequence. Therefore, in a doubly linked list (also called *two – way linked list*), a node consists of three parts: data, a pointer to the next node in sequence (next pointer), a pointer to the previous node (previous pointer). Each node has two links: one point to the previous node, or points to a *nil* value or empty list if it is the first node, and one point to the next, or points to a *nil* value or empty list if it is the final node.

The *advantage* of a doubly linked list is that given a node in the list, we can navigate in both directions. A node in a singly linked list cannot be removed unless we have the pointer to its predecessor. But in a doubly linked list, we can delete a node even if we don't have the previous node's address (since each node has a left pointer pointing to the previous node and can move backward).

The primary *disadvantages* of doubly linked lists are:

- Each node requires an extra pointer, requiring more space.
- The insertion or deletion of a node takes a bit longer (more pointer operations).

Similar to a singly linked list, let us implement the operations of a doubly linked list. If you understand the singly linked list operations, then doubly linked list operations are obvious. Following is a type declaration for a doubly linked list node:

```
type DLLNode struct { // defines a DLLNode in a doubly linked list
```

```
    data interface{} // the datum
    prev *DLLNode    // pointer to the previous DLLNode
    next *DLLNode    // pointer to the next DLLNode
}
```

A doubly linked list contains pointer to first and last node in the list and its size. The *size* field in the doubly linked list structure stores the length of the linked list. The *head* field of DLL type stores the memory address of the head or the first node of the doubly linked list. The *tail* field of DLL type stores the memory address of the head or the first node of the doubly linked list.

```
type DLL struct {
    head *DLLNode
    tail *DLLNode
    size int
}
```

Doubly Linked List Insertion

Insertion into a doubly-linked list has three cases (same as singly linked list):

- Inserting a new node before the head (at beginning).
- Inserting a new node after the tail (at the end of the list).
- Inserting a new node at the given position.

Inserting a Node at the Beginning

In this case, the new node is inserted before the head node. Previous and next pointers need to be updated and it can be done with the following steps:

- Create a new node and initialize both previous and next pointers to nil.

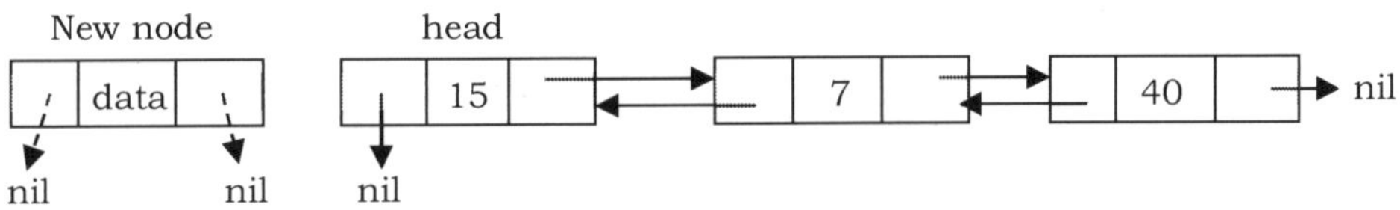

- Update the right pointer of the new node to point to the current head node (dotted link in below figure).

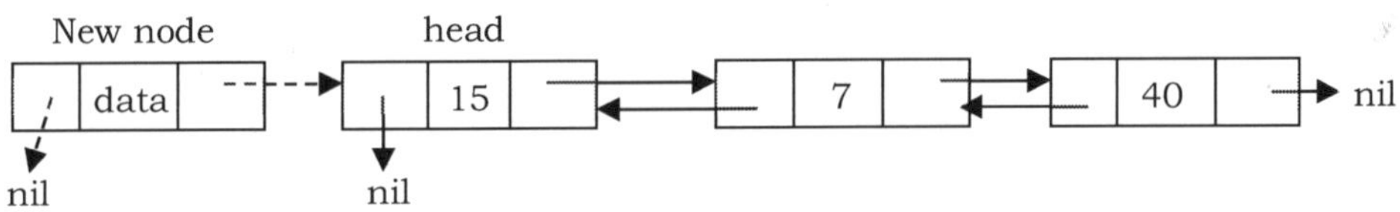

- Update head node's left pointer to point to the new node and make new node as head.

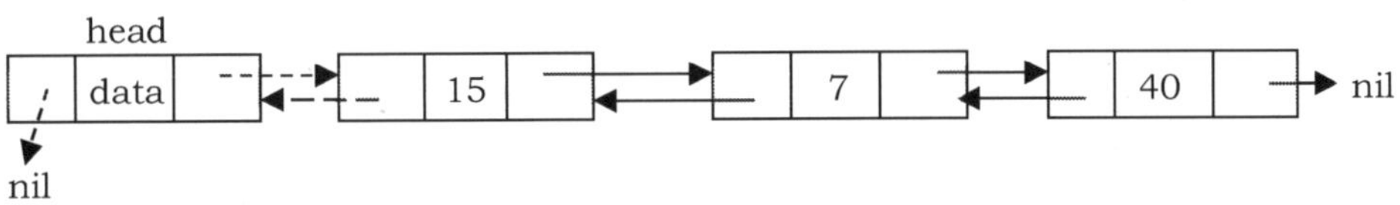


```
// CheckIfEmptyAndAdd ... check if doubly link list is empty
func (dll *DLL) CheckIfEmptyAndAdd(newNode *DLLNode) bool {
    // check if list is empty
    if dll.size == 0 {
        // insert first node in doubly linked list
        dll.head = newNode
        dll.tail = newNode
        dll.size++
        return true
    }
    return false
}
// InsertBeginning ... insert in the beginning of doubly linked list
func (dll *DLL) InsertBeginning(data int) {
    newNode := &DLLNode{
        data: data,
```

```
        prev: nil,
        next: nil,
    }
    if !(dll.CheckIfEmptyAndAdd(newNode)) {
        head := dll.head
        // update newnode links - prev and next
        newNode.next = head
        newNode.prev = nil

        // update head node
        head.prev = newNode

        // update dll start and length
        dll.head = newNode
        dll.size++
        return
    }
    return
}
```

Time Complexity: O(1). Space Complexity: O(1).

Inserting a Node at the Ending

In this case, traverse the list till the end and insert the new node.

- Create a new node and initialize both previous and next pointers to *nil*.

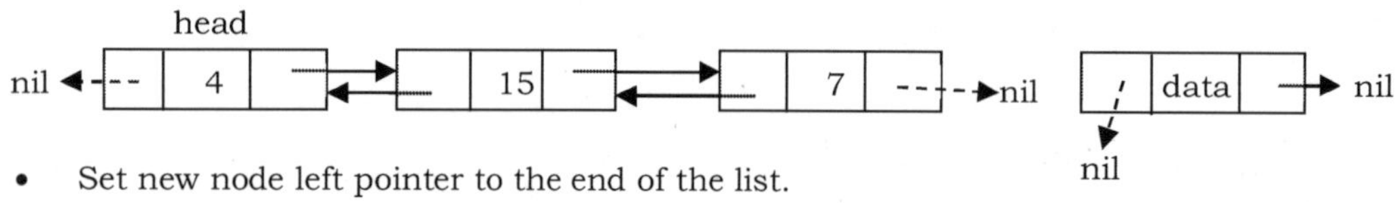

- Set new node left pointer to the end of the list.

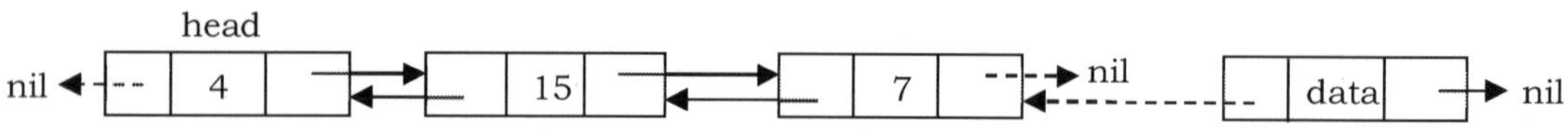

- Update right pointer of last node to point to new node.

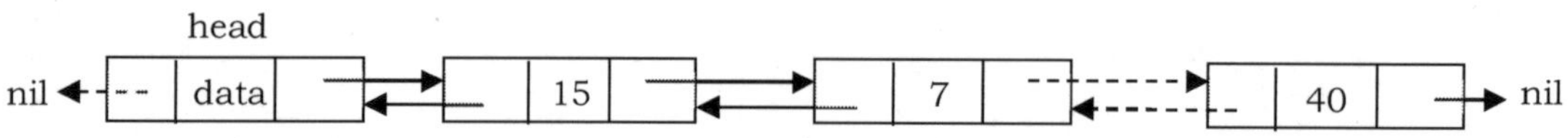


```
// InsertEnd ... inserts a node in the end of doubly linked list
func (dll *DLL) InsertEnd(data int) {
    newNode := &DLLNode{
        data: data,
        prev: nil,
        next: nil,
    }
    if !(dll.CheckIfEmptyAndAdd(newNode)) {
        head := dll.head
        for i := 0; i < dll.size; i++ {
            if head.next == nil {
                // update newnode links - prev and next
                newNode.prev = head
                newNode.next = nil

                //update head node
                head.next = newNode

                // update dll end and size
                dll.tail = newNode
                dll.size++
                break
            }
```

```
            head = head.next
        }
    }
    return
}
```

Time Complexity: $O(n)$. Space Complexity: $O(1)$.

Inserting a Node at the Given Position

As discussed in singly linked lists, traverse the list to the position node and insert the new node.

- *New node* right pointer points to the next node of the *position node* where we want to insert the new node. Also, *new node* left pointer points to the *position node.*

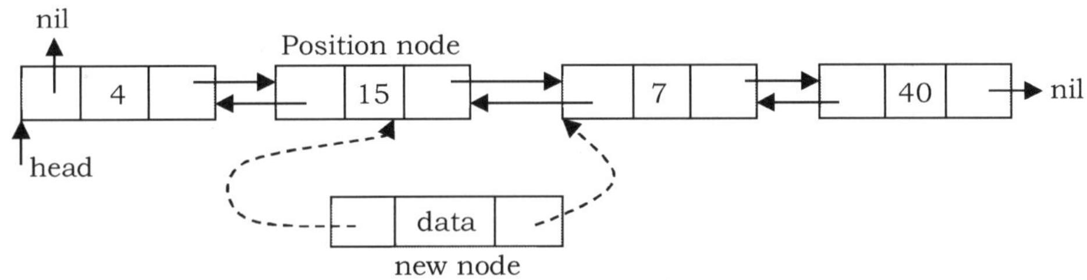

- Position node's right pointer points to the new node and the *left* of position nodes' *next node* points to new node.

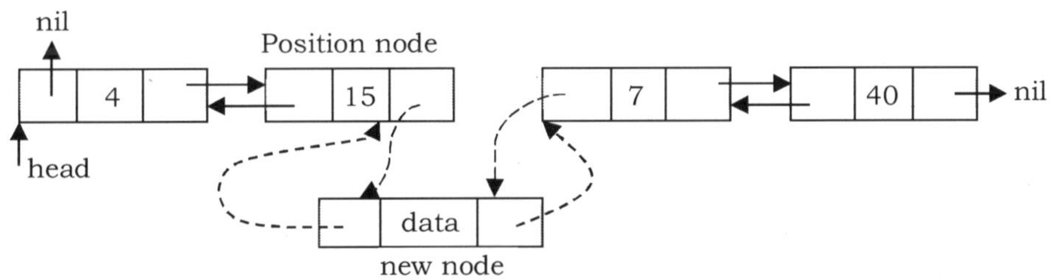

Now, let us write the code for all of these three cases. We must update the first element pointer in the calling function, not just in the called function. The following code inserts a node in the doubly linked list.

```
// Insert ... insert between two nodes in doubly linkedlist
func (dll *DLL) Insert (data int, loc int) {
    newNode := &DLLNode{
        data: data,
        prev: nil,
        next: nil,
    }
    if !(dll.CheckIfEmptyAndAdd(newNode)) {
        head := dll.head
        for i := 1; i < dll.size; i++ {
            if i == loc {
                // update newnode links - prev and next
                newNode.prev = head.prev
                newNode.next = head
                // update head node
                head.prev.next = newNode
                head.prev = newNode
                //keep traversing till we find the location
                dll.size++
                return
            }
            head = head.next
        }
    }
    return
}
```

Time Complexity: $O(n)$. In the worst case, we may need to insert the item at the end of the list. Space Complexity: $O(1)$.

Doubly Linked List Deletion

Similar to singly linked list deletion, here we have three cases:

- Deleting the first node
- Deleting the last node
- Deleting an intermediate node

Deleting the First Node

In this case, the first node (current head node) is removed from the list. It can be done in two steps:

- Create a temporary node which will point to the same node as that of head.

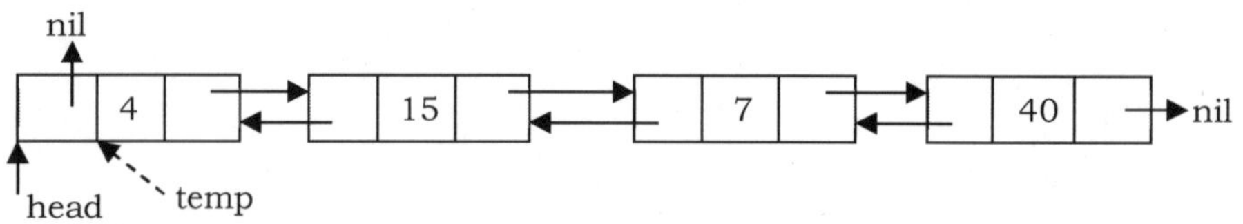

- Now, move the head nodes pointer to the next node and change the heads previous pointer to *nil*. Then, dispose of the temporary node.

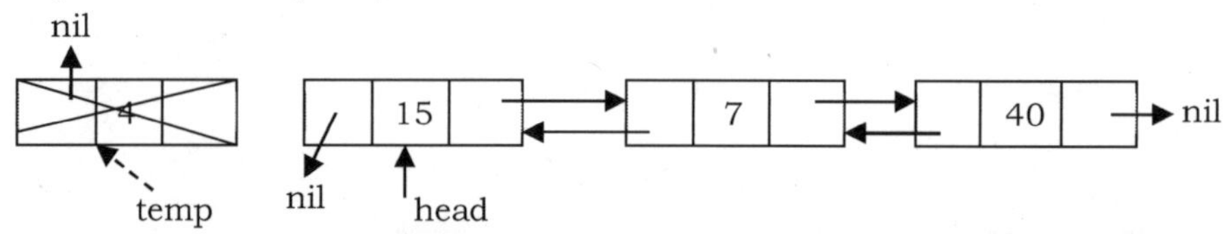


```
func (dll *DLL) DeleteFirst() int {      // DeleteFirst ... Delete last element
    if !(dll.CheckIfEmpty()) {
        head := dll.head
        if head.prev == nil {
            deletedNode := head.data
            dll.head = head.next          // update doubly linked list
            dll.head.prev = nil
            dll.size--
            return deletedNode
        }
    }
    return -1
}
```

Time Complexity: O(1). Space Complexity: O(1).

Deleting the Last Node

This operation is a bit trickier than removing the first node, because the algorithm should find a node, which is previous to the tail first. This can be done in three steps:

- Traverse the list, and while traversing maintain the previous node address. By the time we reach the end of the list, we will have two pointers, one pointing to the tail and the other pointing to the node before the tail.

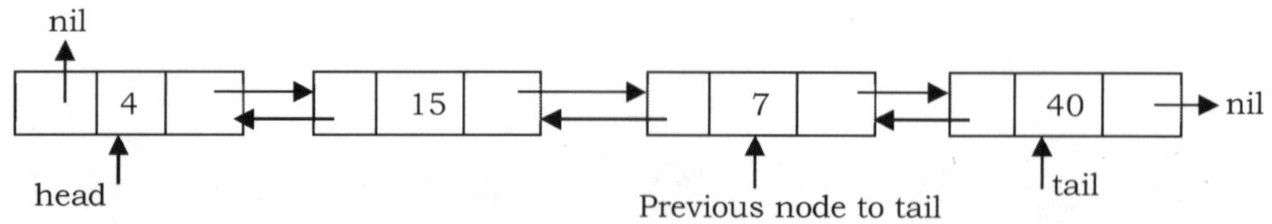

- Update the next pointer of previous node to the tail node with *nil*.

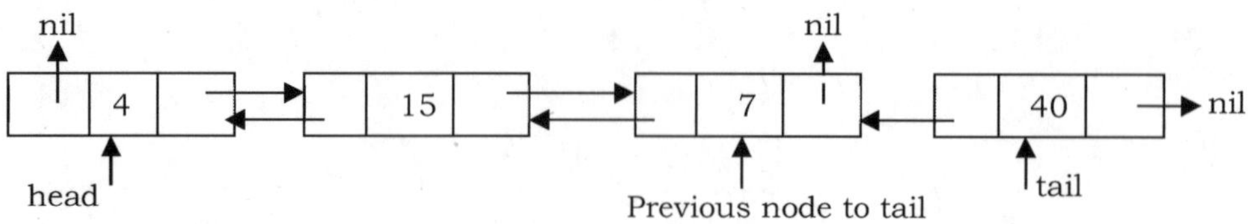

- Dispose the tail node.

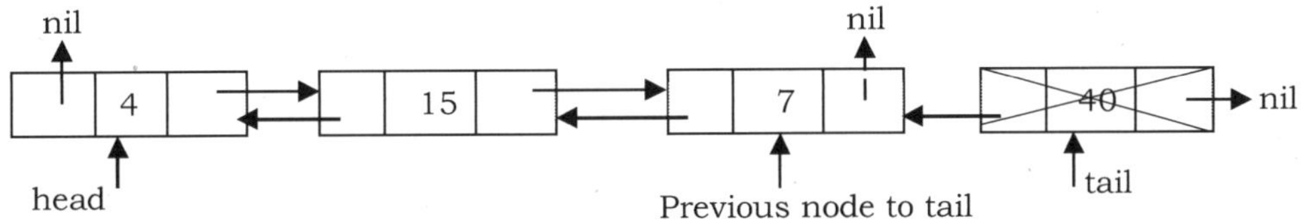


```
// DeleteLast ... deletes last element from doubly linked list
func (dll *DLL) DeleteLast() int {
    if !(dll.CheckIfEmpty()) {
        // delete from last
        head := dll.head
        for {
            if head.next == nil {
                break
            }
            head = head.next
        }
        // update doubly linked list
        dll.tail = head.prev
        dll.tail.next = nil
        dll.size--
        return head.data
    }
    return -1
}
```

Time Complexity: O(n). Space Complexity: O(1).

Deleting an Intermediate Node

In this case, the node to be removed is *always located between* two nodes, and the head and tail links are not updated. The removal can be done in two steps:

- Similar to the previous case, maintain the previous node while also traversing the list. Upon locating the node to be deleted, change the *previous node's* next pointer to the *next node* of the *node to be deleted*. Also, change the *previous* pointer of the *next node* to the *node to be deleted* to point to the *previous* node of the *node to be deleted*.

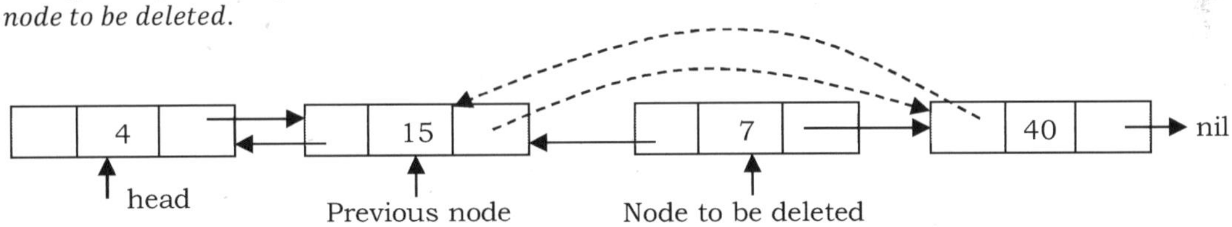

- Dispose the current node to be deleted.

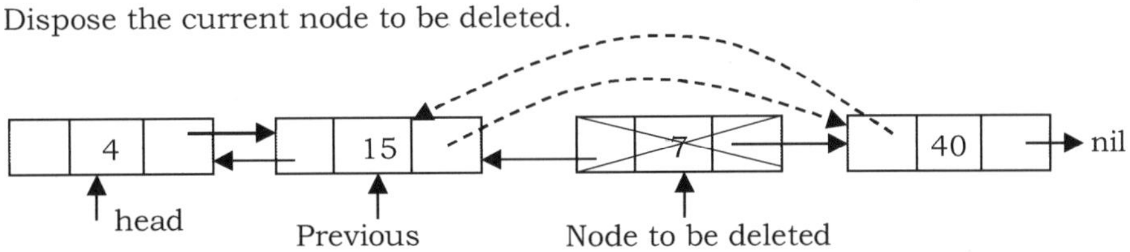


```
// Delete .. delete from any location
func (dll *DLL) Delete(pos int) int {
    if !(dll.CheckIfEmpty()) {
        //delete from any position
        head := dll.head
        for i := 1; i <= pos; i++ {
            if head.next == nil && pos > i {
                //list is lesser than given position
                return -1
            } else if i == pos {
                // delete from this location
                head.prev.next = head.next
```

```
                head.next.prev = head.prev
                dll.size--
                return head.data
            }
            head = head.next
        }
    }
    return -1
}
```

Time Complexity: O(n), for scanning the complete list of size n. Space Complexity: O(1).

3.8 Circular Linked Lists

In a singly-circularly-linked list, each node has one link, similar to an ordinary singly-linked list, except that the next link of the last node points back to the first node. In singly linked lists and doubly linked lists, the end of lists are indicated with nil value. But, circular linked lists do not have ends. While traversing the circular linked lists we should be careful; otherwise we will be traversing the list indefinitely.

In circular linked lists, each node has a successor. In a circular linked list, every node point to its next node in the sequence but the last node points to the first node in the list.

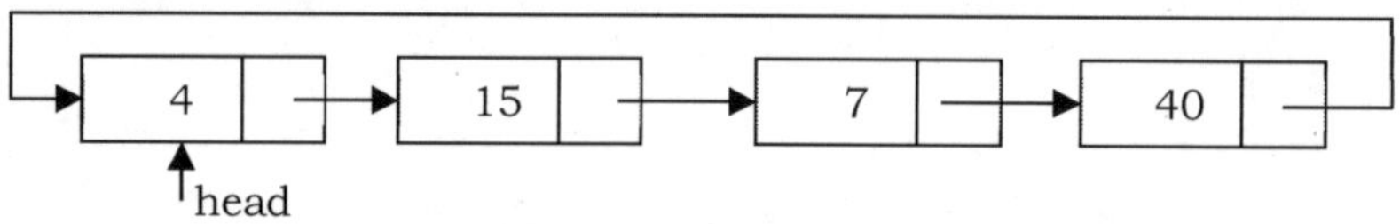

In some situations, circular linked lists are useful. For example, when several processes are using the same computer resource (say, CPU) for the same amount of time, we have to assure that no process accesses the resource before all other processes do (round robin algorithm). The following is a type declaration for a circular linked list of integers:

```
// CLLNode ... newNode of circular linked list
type CLLNode struct {
    data int
    next *CLLNode
}
```

In a circular linked list, we access the elements using the *head or start* node (similar to *head* node in singly linked list and doubly linked lists).

```
// CLL ... A linked list with len, start/head
type CLL struct {
    size  int
    head *CLLNode
}
```

Counting Nodes in a Circular Linked List

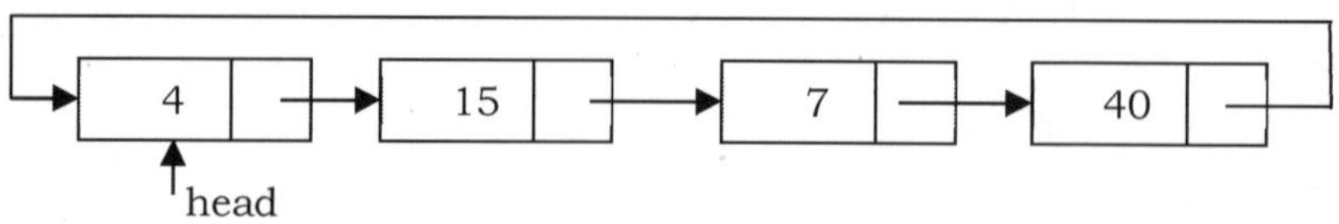

The circular list is accessible through the node marked *head*. To count the nodes, the list has to be traversed from the node marked *head*, with the help of a dummy node *current*, and stop the counting when *current* reaches the starting node *head*. If the list is empty, *head* will be nil, and in that case set *count* = 0. Otherwise, set the current pointer to the first node, and keep on counting till the current pointer reaches the starting node.

```
// Since we have size property in CLL, we can access the length directly, but following is an alternative
func (cll *CLL) Length() int {
    current := cll.head
    count := 1
    if current == nil {
        return 0
    }
    current = current.next
    for current != cll.start {
        current = current.next
```

```
        count++
    }
    return count
}
```

Time Complexity: $O(n)$, for scanning the complete list of size n. Space Complexity: $O(1)$, for creating one temporary variable.

Printing the Contents of a Circular Linked List

We assume here that the list is being accessed by its *head* node. Since all the nodes are arranged in a circular fashion, the *tail* node of the list will be the node previous to the *head* node. Let us assume we want to print the contents of the nodes starting with the *head* node. Print its contents, move to the next node and continue printing till we reach the *head* node again.

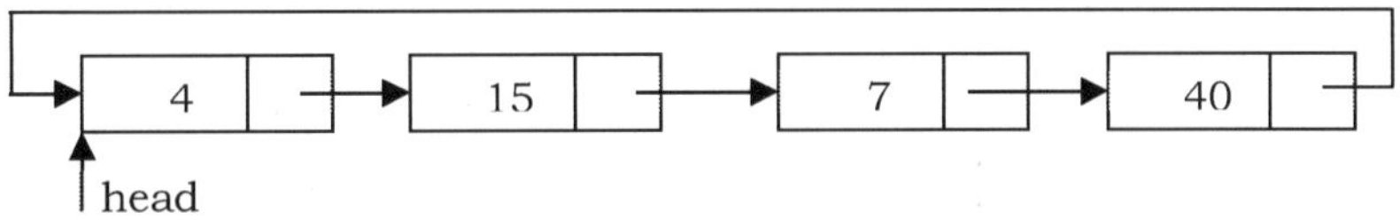


```
func (cll *CLL) Display() {        // Display ... Print Circular list
    head := cll.head
    for i := 0; i < cll.size; i++ {
        fmt.Print(head.data)
        fmt.Print("-->")
        head = head.next
    }
    fmt.Println()
}
```

Time Complexity: $O(n)$, for scanning the complete list of size n. Space Complexity: $O(1)$, for the temporary variable.

Inserting a Node at the Front

The only difference between inserting a node at the beginning and at the end is that, after inserting the new node, we just need to update the pointer. The steps for doing this are given below:

- Create a new node and initially keep its next pointer pointing to itself.

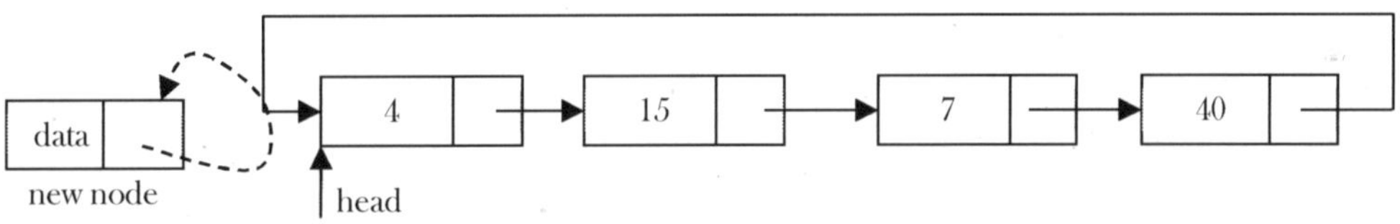

- Update the next pointer of the new node with the head node and also traverse the list until the tail node (node with data 40).

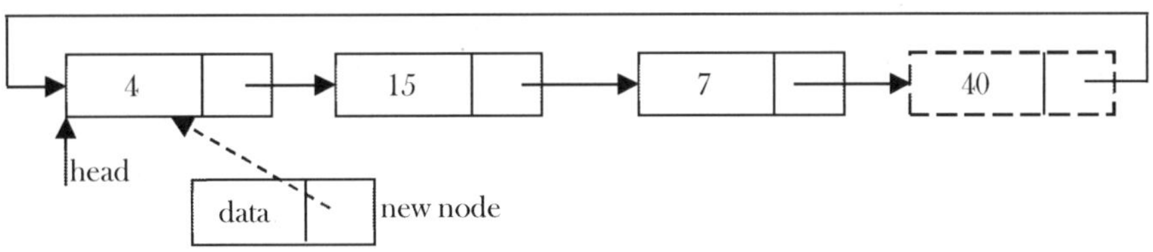

- Update the tail node in the list to point to the new node.

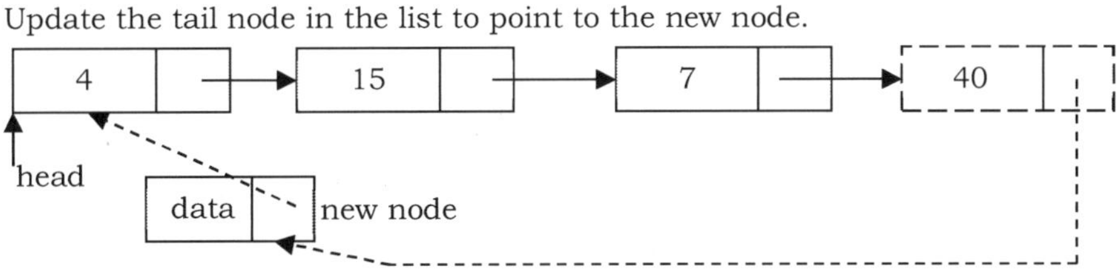

- Make the new node as the head.

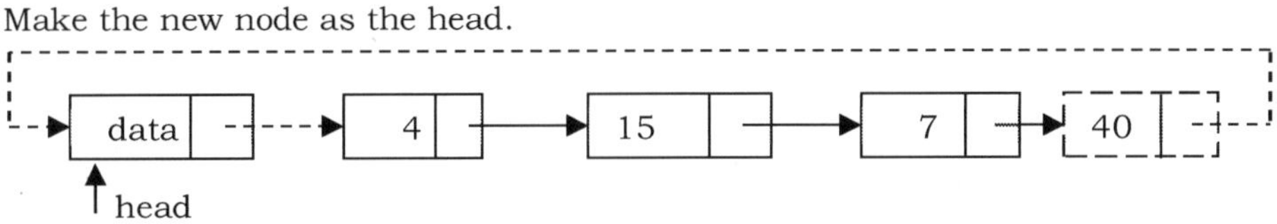

```
// CheckIfEmptyAndAdd ... check if doubly link list is empty
func (cll *CLL) CheckIfEmptyAndAdd(data int) bool {
    newNode := &CLLNode{
        data: data,
        next: nil,
    }
    if cll.size == 0 {                  // check if list is empty
        cll.head = newNode          // insert first node in doubly linked list
        cll.head.next = newNode
        cll.size++
        return true
    }
    return false
}
// InsertBeginning ... insert in the beginning
func (cll *CLL) InsertBeginning(data int) {
    if !(cll.CheckIfEmptyAndAdd(data)) {
        newNode := &CLLNode{
            data: data,
            next: nil,
        }
        current := cll.head
        newNode.next = current          // insert on current
        for {                                   // traverse this list until we find it's end
            if current.next == cll.head {
                break
            }
            current = current.next
        }
        current.next = newNode
        cll.head = newNode
        cll.size++
    }
}
```

Time Complexity: $O(n)$, for scanning the complete list of size n. Space Complexity: $O(1)$, for temporary variable.

Inserting a Node at the End

Let us add a node containing *data*, at the end of a list (circular list) headed by *head*. The new node will be placed just after the tail node (which is the last node of the list), which means it will have to be inserted in between the tail node and the first node.

- Create a new node and initially keep its next pointer pointing to itself.

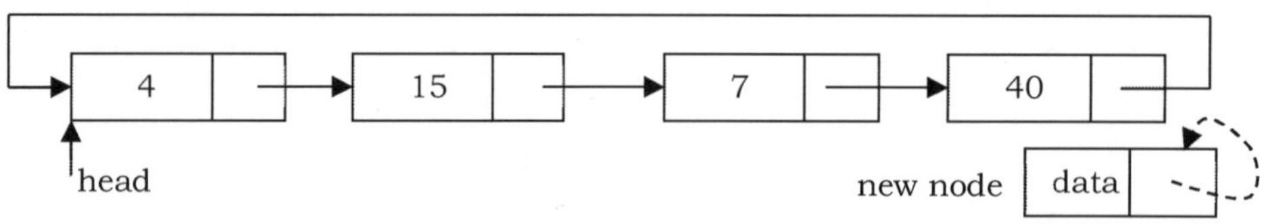

- Update the next pointer of the new node with the head node and also traverse the list to the tail. That means, in a circular list we should stop at the node whose next node is head.

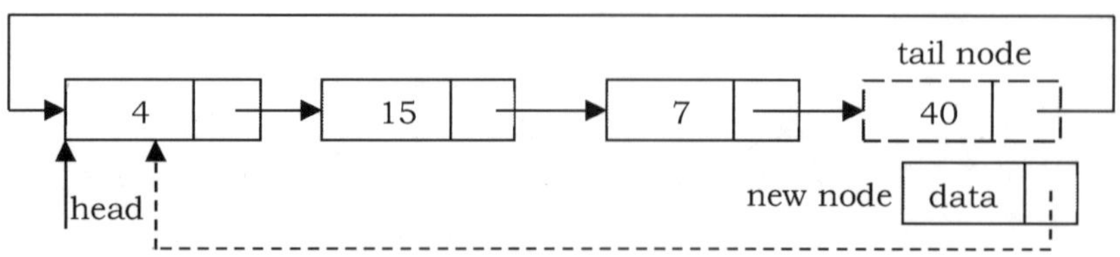

- Update the next pointer of the tail node to point to the new node and we get the list as shown below.

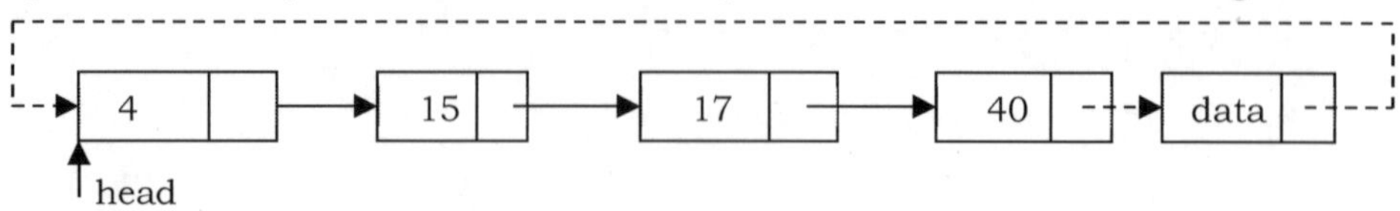

```
// InsertEnd ... insert in the end
func (cll *CLL) InsertEnd(data int) {
    if !(cll.CheckIfEmptyAndAdd(data)) {
        newNode := &CLLNode{
            data: data,
            next: nil,
        }
        current := cll.head
        for {
            if current.next == cll.head {
                break
            }
            current = current.next
        }
        current.next = newNode
        newNode.next = cll.head
        cll.size++
    }
}
```

Time Complexity: $O(n)$, for scanning the complete list of size n. Space Complexity: $O(1)$, for temporary variable.

Inserting a Node at the given Position

As discussed in singly and doubly linked lists, traverse the list to the position node and insert the new node.

- *New node's* right pointer points to the next node of the *position node* where we want to insert the new node. Also, *new node's* left pointer points to the *position node.*

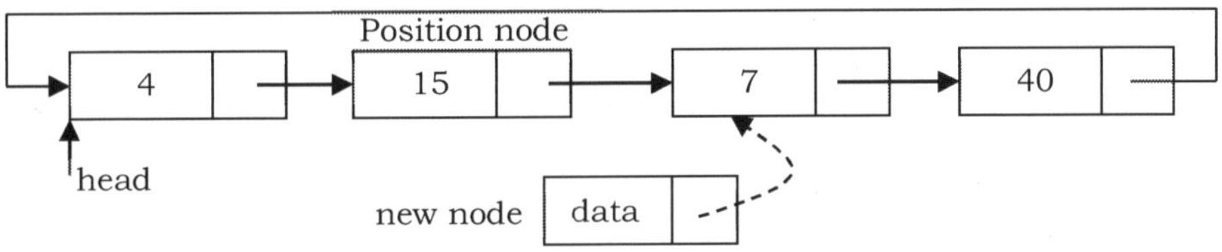

- Point the position node's next pointer to the new node.

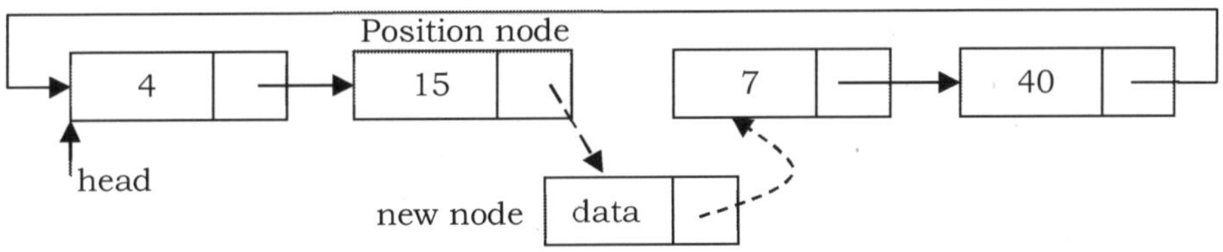

Now, let us write the code for all of these three cases. We must update the first element pointer in the calling function, not just in the called function. The following code inserts a node in the doubly linked list.

```
// Insert ... Insert in the list on a specific location
func (cll *CLL) Insert(data int, pos int) {
    if !(cll.CheckIfEmptyAndAdd(data)) {
        current := cll.head
        count := 1
        if pos == 1 {
            cll.InsertBeginning(data)
            return
        }
        newNode := &CLLNode{
            data: data,
            next: nil,
        }
        for {
            if current.next == nil && pos-1 > count {
                break
            }
            if count == pos-1 {
                newNode.next = current.next
```

```
            current.next = newNode
            cll.size++
            break
        }
        current = current.next
        count++
    }
  }
}
```

Deleting the First Node

The first node can be deleted by simply replacing the next field of the tail node with the next field of the first node.

- Find the tail node of the linked list by traversing the list. Tail node is the previous node to the head node which we want to delete.

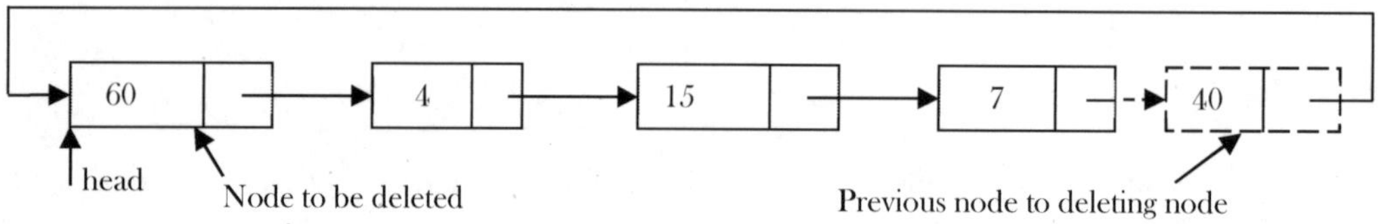

- Create a temporary node which will point to the head. Also, update the tail nodes next pointer to point to next node of head (as shown below).

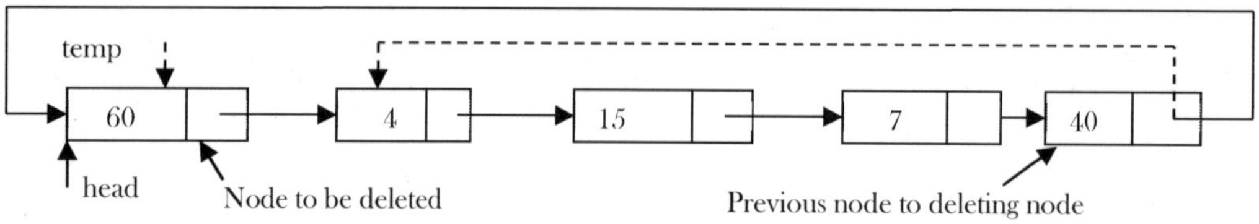

- Now, move the head pointer to next node and dispose the temporary node (as shown below).

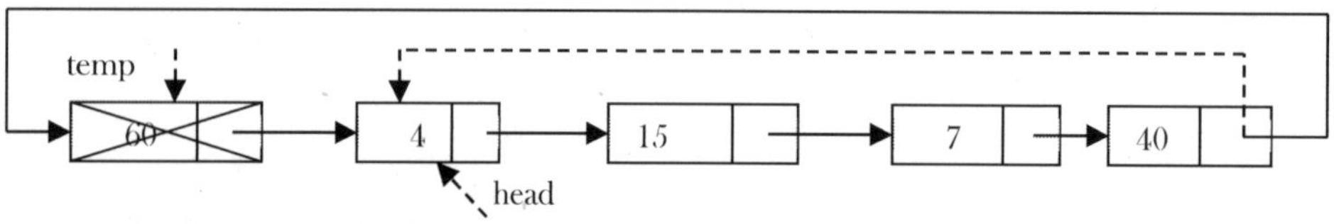


```
// CheckIfEmpty ... check if empty
func (cll *CLL) CheckIfEmpty() bool {
    if cll.size == 0 {
        return true
    }
    return false
}
// DeleteBeginning ... Delete from the head of the list
func (cll *CLL) DeleteBeginning() int {
    if !(cll.CheckIfEmpty()) {          //check if list if empty
        current := cll.head
        deletedElem := current.data
        if cll.size == 1 {
            cll.head = nil
            cll.size--
            return deletedElem
        }
        prevStart := cll.head
        cll.head = current.next
        for {                           // traverse till end and update last node's next to updated head
            if current.next == prevStart {
                break
            }
            current = current.next
        }
```

```
            current.next = cll.head
            cll.size--
            return deletedElem
        }
        return -1
    }
```

Time Complexity: O(n), for scanning the complete list of size n. Space Complexity: O(1), for a temporary variable.

Deleting the Last Node

The list has to be traversed to reach the last but one node. This has to be named as the tail node, and its next field has to point to the first node. Consider the following list. To delete the last node 40, the list has to be traversed till you reach 7. The next field of 7 has to be changed to point to 60, and this node must be renamed *pTail*.

- Traverse the list and find the tail node and its previous node.

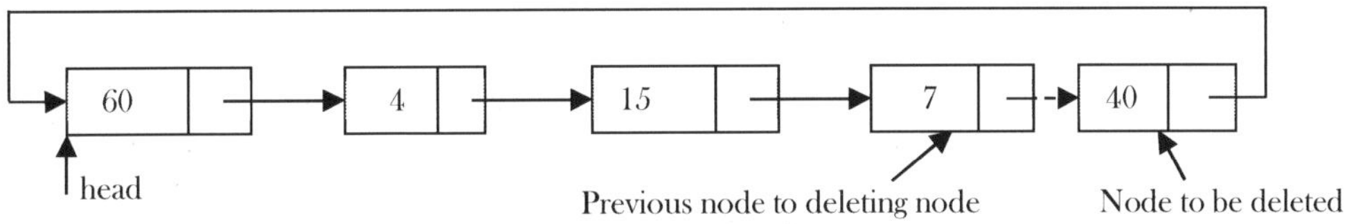

- Update the next pointer of tail node's previous node to point to head.

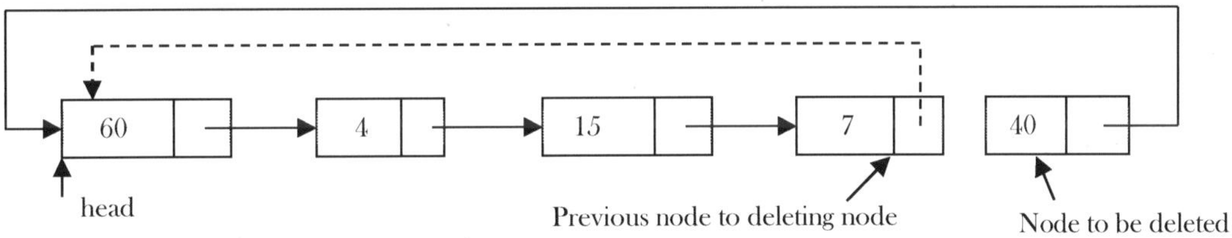

- Dispose the tail node.

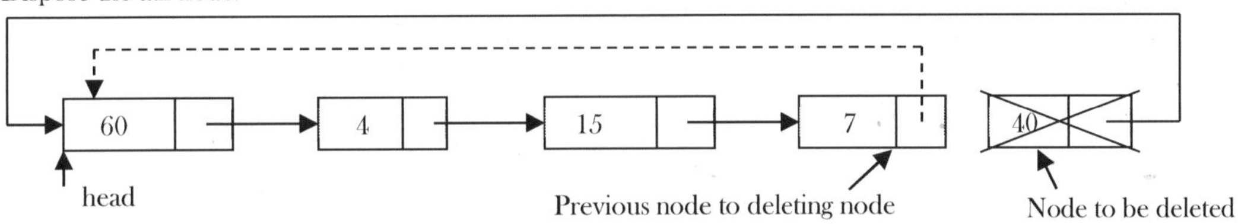


```
// DeleteEnd ... Delete the last element from circular list
func (cll *CLL) DeleteEnd() int {
    if !(cll.CheckIfEmpty()) {
        current := cll.head
        deletedEle := current.data
        if cll.size == 1 {
            // delete from beginning
            deletedEle = cll.DeleteBeginning()
            return deletedEle
        }
        //traverse till end
        for {
            if current.next.next == cll.head {
                deletedEle = current.next.data
                break
            }
            current = current.next
        }
        // update last element's next pointer
        current.next = cll.head
        cll.size--
        return deletedEle
    }
    return -1
}
```

Time Complexity: O(*n*), for scanning the complete list of size *n*. Space Complexity: O(1), for a temporary variable.

Deleting an Intermediate Node

As discussed in singly and doubly linked lists, traverse the list to the position node and delete the node. In this case, the node to be removed is *always located between* two nodes, and the head and tail links are not updated. The removal can be done in two steps:

- Similar to the previous case, maintain the previous node while also traversing the list. Upon locating the node to be deleted, change the *previous node's* next pointer to the *next node* of the *node to be deleted*.

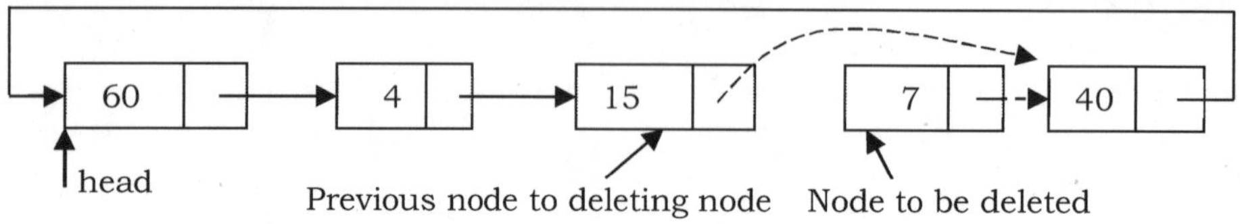

- Dispose of the current node to be deleted.

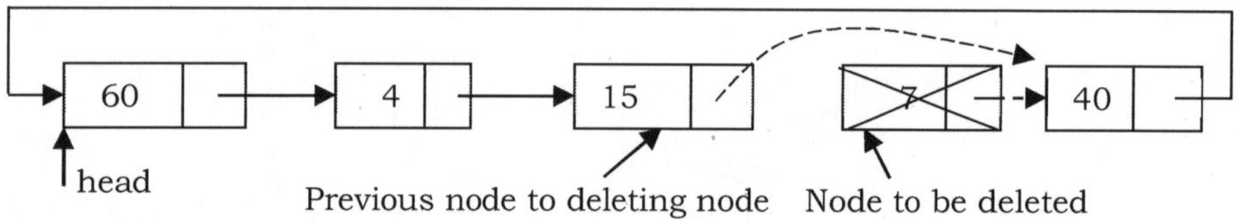


```
// Delete ... delete an element from circular list
func (cll *CLL) Delete(pos int) int {
    if !(cll.CheckIfEmpty()) {
        current := cll.head
        deletedEle := current.data
        if cll.size == 1 {
            // delete from beginning
            deletedEle = cll.DeleteBeginning()
            return deletedEle
        }
        if cll.size == pos {
            // delete from end
            deletedEle = cll.DeleteEnd()
            return deletedEle
        }
        // delete from middle
        count := 1
        for {                    // traverse till you find position
            if count == pos-1 {
                deletedEle = current.next.data
                break
            }
            current = current.next
        }
        current.next = current.next.next
        cll.size--
        return deletedEle
    }
    return -1
}
```

Applications of Circular List

Circular linked lists are used in managing the computing resources of a computer. We can use circular lists for implementing stacks and queues.

3.9 A Memory-efficient Doubly Linked Lists (XOR Linked Lists)

In conventional implementation, we need to keep a forward pointer to the next item on the list and a backward pointer to the previous item. That means elements in doubly linked list implementations consist of data, a pointer to the next node and a pointer to the previous node in the list as shown below.

Conventional Doubly Linked List Node Definition

```
type ListNode struct{
    data int
    prev *ListNode
    nextt *ListNode
}
```

A Linux journal (Sinha) presented an alternative implementation of the doubly linked list ADT, with insertion, traversal and deletion operations. This implementation is based on pointer difference. Each node uses only one pointer field to traverse the list back and forth.

New Node Definition

```
type ListNode struct{
    data int
    ptrdiff *ListNode
}
```

The *ptrdiff* pointer field contains the difference between the pointer to the next node and the pointer to the previous node. The pointer difference is calculated by using exclusive-or (⊕) operation.

$$ptrdiff = pointer\ to\ previous\ node \oplus pointer\ to\ next\ node.$$

The *ptrdiff* of the start node (head node) is the ⊕ of nil and *next* node (next node to head). Similarly, the *ptrdiff* of end node is the ⊕ of *previous* node (previous to end node) and nil. As an example, consider the following linked list.

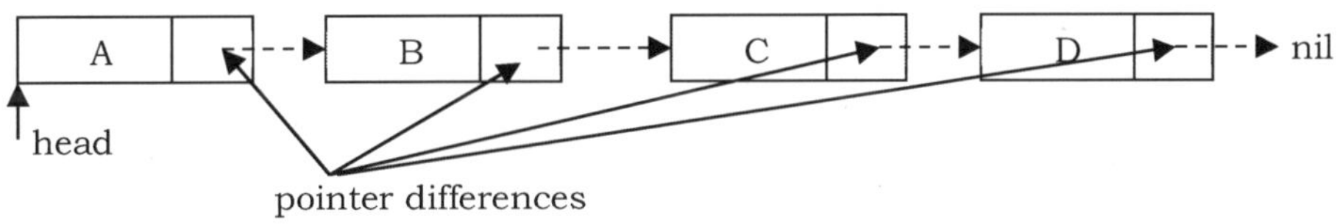

In the example above,

- The next pointer of A is: nil ⊕ B
- The next pointer of B is: A ⊕ C
- The next pointer of C is: B ⊕ D
- The next pointer of D is: C ⊕ nil

Why does it work?

To find the answer to this question let us consider the properties of ⊕:

X ⊕ X = 0
X ⊕ 0 = X
X ⊕ Y = Y ⊕ X (symmetric)
(X ⊕ Y) ⊕ Z = X ⊕ (Y ⊕ Z) (transitive)

For the example above, let us assume that we are at C node and want to move to B. We know that C's *ptrdiff* is defined as B ⊕ D. If we want to move to B, performing ⊕ on C's *ptrdiff* with D would give B. This is due to the fact that

(B ⊕ D) ⊕ D = B (since, D ⊕ D=0)

Similarly, if we want to move to D, then we have to apply ⊕ to C's *ptrdiff* with B to give D.

(B ⊕ D) ⊕ B = D (since, B ⊕ B=0)

From the above discussion we can see that just by using a single pointer, we can move back and forth. A memory-efficient implementation of a doubly linked list is possible with minimal compromising of timing efficiency.

3.10 Unrolled Linked Lists

One of the biggest advantages of linked lists over arrays is that inserting an element at any location takes only O(1) time. However, it takes O(*n*) to search for an element in a linked list. There is a simple variation of the singly linked list called *unrolled linked lists*.

An unrolled linked list stores multiple elements in each node (let us call it a block for our convenience). In each block, a circular linked list is used to connect all nodes.

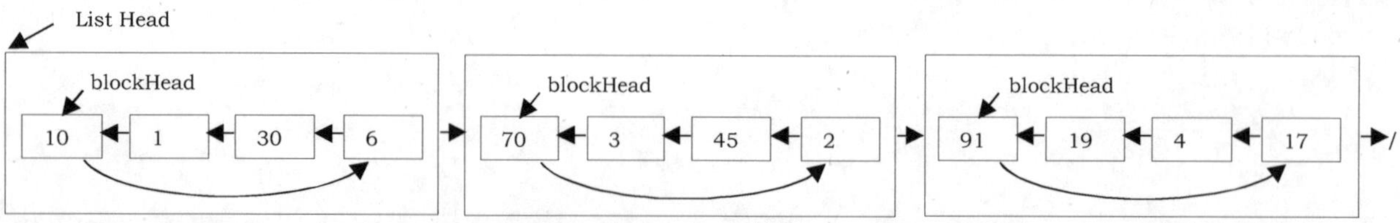

Assume that there will be no more than n elements in the unrolled linked list at any time. To simplify this problem, all blocks, except the last one, should contain exactly $\lceil\sqrt{n}\rceil$ elements. Thus, there will be no more than $\lfloor\sqrt{n}\rfloor$ blocks at any time.

Searching for an element in Unrolled Linked Lists

In unrolled linked lists, we can find the kth element in O($\sqrt{n}$):

1. Traverse the *list of blocks* to the one that contains the kth node, i.e., the $\left\lceil\frac{k}{\lceil\sqrt{n}\rceil}\right\rceil^{th}$ block. It takes O($\sqrt{n}$) since we may find it by going through no more than $\sqrt{n}$ blocks.
2. Find the (k mod $\lceil\sqrt{n}\rceil$)th node in the circular linked list of this block. It also takes O($\sqrt{n}$) since there are no more than $\lceil\sqrt{n}\rceil$ nodes in a single block.

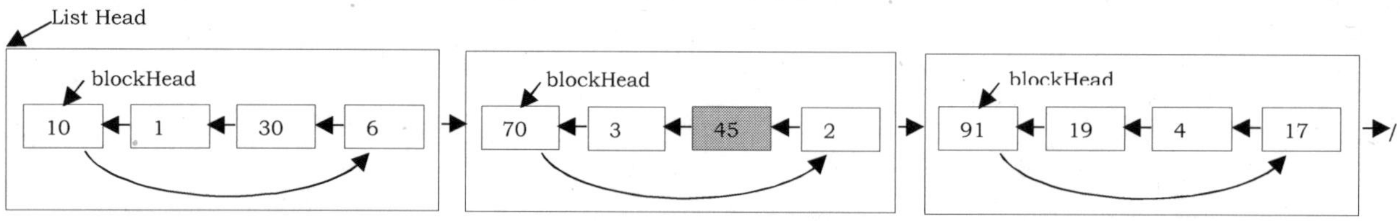

Inserting an element in Unrolled Linked Lists

When inserting a node, we have to re-arrange the nodes in the unrolled linked list to maintain the properties previously mentioned, that each block contains $\lceil\sqrt{n}\rceil$ nodes. Suppose that we insert a node x after the ith node, and x should be placed in the jth block. Nodes in the jth block and in the blocks after the jth block have to be shifted toward the tail of the list so that each of them still have $\lceil\sqrt{n}\rceil$ nodes. In addition, a new block needs to be added to the tail if the last block of the list is out of space, i.e., it has more than $\lceil\sqrt{n}\rceil$ nodes.

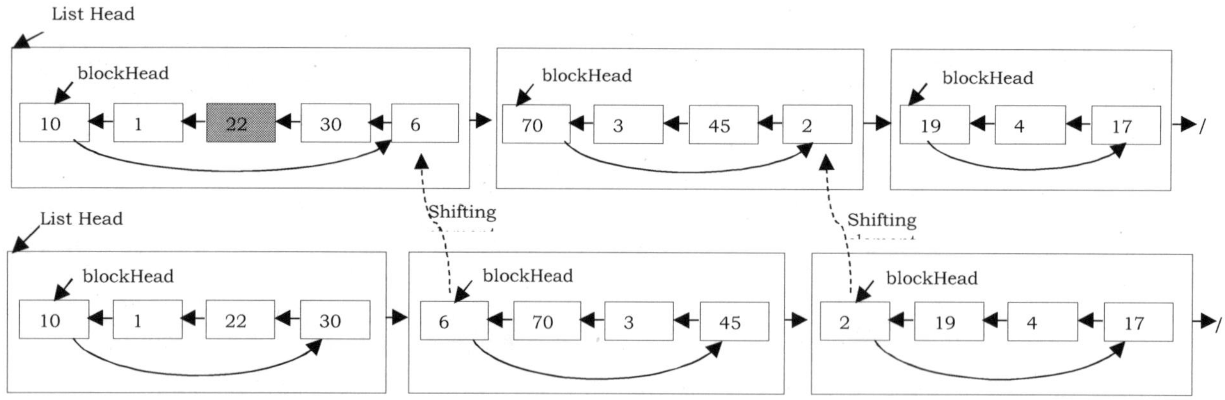

Performing Shift Operation

Note that each *shift* operation, which includes removing a node from the tail of the circular linked list in a block and inserting a node to the head of the circular linked list in the block after, takes only O(1). The total time complexity of an insertion operation for unrolled linked lists is therefore O($\sqrt{n}$); there are at most O($\sqrt{n}$) blocks and therefore at most O($\sqrt{n}$) shift operations.

1. A temporary pointer is needed to store the tail of A.

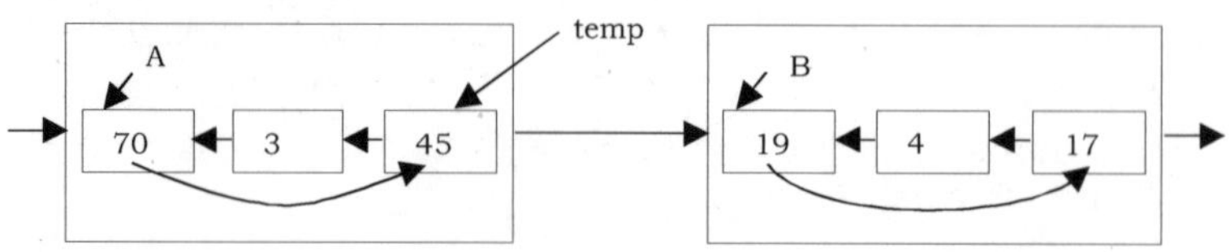

2. In block A, move the next pointer of the head node to point to the second-to-last node, so that the tail node of A can be removed.

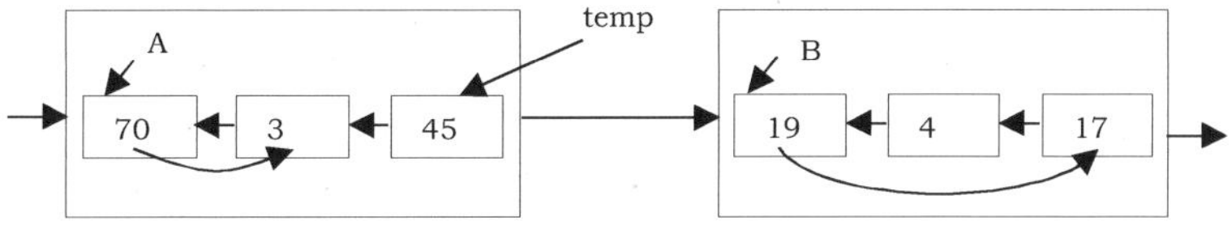

3. Let the next pointer of the node, which will be shifted (the tail node of A), point to the tail node of B.

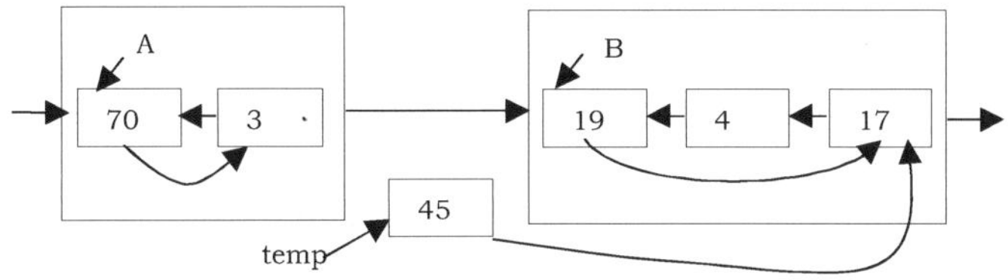

4. Let the next pointer of the head node of B point to the node *temp* points to.

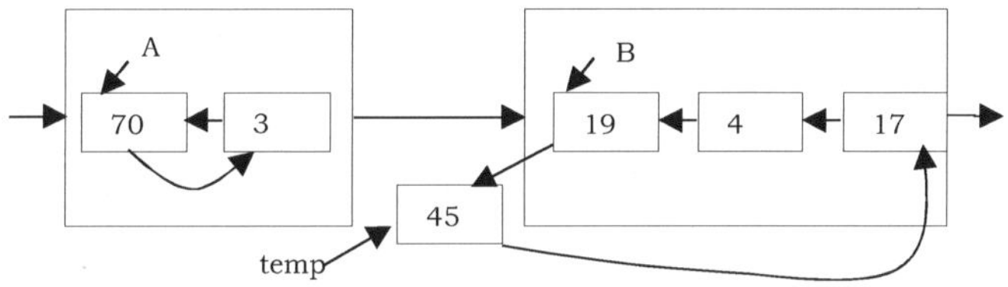

5. Finally, set the head pointer of B to point to the node *temp* points to. Now the node *temp* points to becomes the new head node of B.

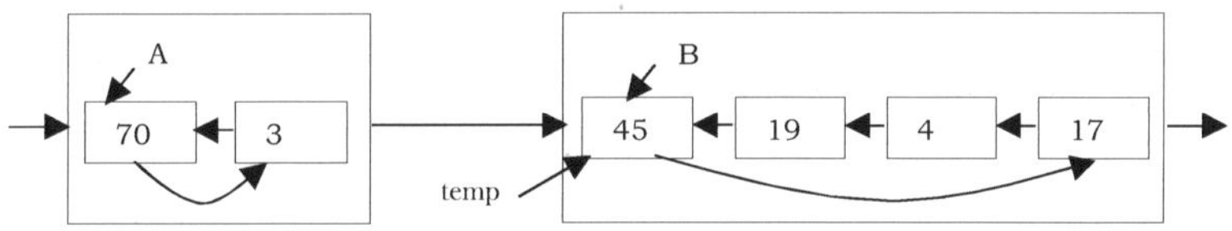

6. *temp* pointer can be thrown away. We have completed the shift operation to move the original tail node of A to become the new head node of B.

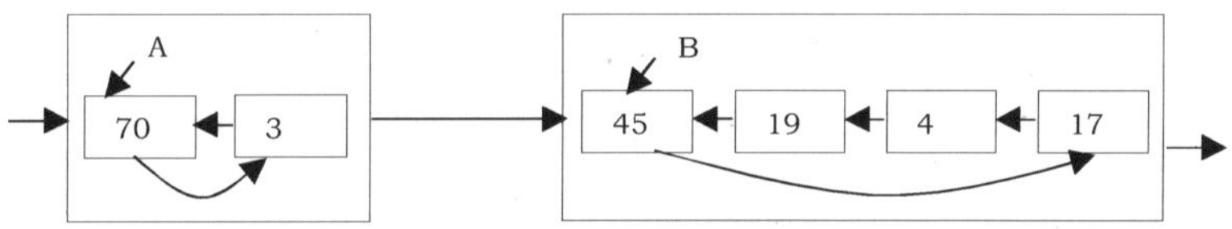

Performance

With unrolled linked lists, there are a couple of advantages, one in speed and one in space. First, if the number of elements in each block is appropriately sized (e.g., at most the size of one cache line), we get noticeably better cache performance from the improved memory locality. Second, since we have $O(n/m)$ links, where n is the number of elements in the unrolled linked list and m is the number of elements we can store in any block, we can also save an appreciable amount of space, which is particularly noticeable if each element is small.

Comparing Linked Lists and Unrolled Linked Lists

To compare the overhead for an unrolled list, elements in doubly linked list implementations consist of data, a pointer to the next node, and a pointer to the previous node in the list, as shown below.

```
type ListNode struct {
    data int
    next *ListNode
}
```

Assuming we have 4-byte pointers, each node is going to take 8 bytes. But the allocation overhead for the node could be anywhere between 8 and 16 bytes. Let's go with the best case and assume it will be 8 bytes. So, if we want to store 1K items in this list, we are going to have 16KB of overhead.

Now, let's think about an unrolled linked list node (let us call it *LinkedBlock*). It will look something like this:

```
type LinkedBlock struct {
    nodeCount int
    next     *LinkedBlock
    head      *ListNode
```

```
}
```

Therefore, allocating a single node (12 bytes + 8 bytes of overhead) with an array of 100 elements (400 bytes + 8 bytes of overhead) will now cost 428 bytes, or 4.28 bytes per element. Thinking about our 1K items from above, it would take about 4.2KB of overhead, which is close to 4x better than our original list. Even if the list becomes severely fragmented and the item arrays are only 1/2 full on average, this is still an improvement. Also, note that we can tune the array size to whatever gets us the best overhead for our application.

Implementation

```
package main
import "fmt"
var blockSize int //max number of nodes in a block
type ListNode struct {
    data int
    next *ListNode
}
type LinkedBlock struct {
    nodeCount int
    next      *LinkedBlock
    head      *ListNode
}
var blockHead *LinkedBlock
// create an empty block
func newLinkedBlock() *LinkedBlock {
    block := &LinkedBlock{}
    block.next = nil
    block.head = nil
    block.nodeCount = 0
    return block
}
// create a node
func newListNode(data int) *ListNode {
    newNode := &ListNode{}
    newNode.next = nil
    newNode.data = data
    return newNode
}
func searchElement(k int, fLinkedBlock **LinkedBlock, fListNode **ListNode) {
    // find the block
    j := (k + blockSize - 1) / blockSize // k-th node is in the j-th block
    p := blockHead
    j = j - 1
    for j > 0 {
        p = p.next
        j = j - 1
    }
    *fLinkedBlock = p
    // find the node
    q := p.head
    k = k % blockSize
    if k == 0 {
        k = blockSize
    }
    k = p.nodeCount + 1 - k
    for k > 0 {
        k = k - 1
        q = q.next
    }
    *fListNode = q
}
//start shift operation from block *p
```

```
func shift(A *LinkedBlock) {
    var B *LinkedBlock
    var temp *ListNode
    for A.nodeCount > blockSize { //if this block still have to shift
        if A.next == nil { //reach the end. A little different
            A.next = newLinkedBlock()
            B = A.next
            temp = A.head.next
            A.head.next = A.head.next.next
            B.head = temp
            temp.next = temp
            A.nodeCount--
            B.nodeCount++
        } else {
            B = A.next
            temp = A.head.next
            A.head.next = A.head.next.next
            temp.next = B.head.next
            B.head.next = temp
            B.head = temp
            A.nodeCount--
            B.nodeCount++
        }
        A = B
    }
}
func addElement(k, x int) {
    var p, q *ListNode
    var r *LinkedBlock
    if blockHead == nil { //initial, first node and block
        blockHead = newLinkedBlock()
        blockHead.head = newListNode(x)
        blockHead.head.next = blockHead.head
        blockHead.nodeCount++
    } else {
        if k == 0 { //special case for k=0.
            p = blockHead.head
            q = p.next
            p.next = newListNode(x)
            p.next.next = q
            blockHead.head = p.next
            blockHead.nodeCount++
            shift(blockHead)
        } else {
            searchElement(k, &r, &p)
            q = p
            for q.next != p {
                q = q.next
            }
            q.next = newListNode(x)
            q.next.next = p
            r.nodeCount++
            shift(r)
        }
    }
}
func search(k int) int {
    var p *ListNode
    var q *LinkedBlock
    searchElement(k, &q, &p)
    return p.data
}
```

```
// Test Code
func main() {
    blockSize = 3
    addElement(1, 15)
    addElement(2, 25)
    addElement(3, 35)
    addElement(0, 45)
    fmt.Println(search(1))        // prints 45
    fmt.Println(search(2))        // prints 15
    fmt.Println(search(3))        // prints 35
}
```

3.11 Skip Lists

Binary trees can be used for representing abstract data types such as dictionaries and ordered lists. They work well when the elements are inserted in a random order. Some sequences of operations, such as inserting the elements in order, produce degenerate data structures that give very poor performance. If it were possible to randomly permute the list of items to be inserted, trees would work well with high probability for any input sequence. In most cases queries must be answered on-line, so randomly permuting the input is impractical. Balanced tree algorithms re-arrange the tree as operations are performed to maintain certain balance conditions and assure good performance.

Skip lists are a probabilistic alternative to balanced trees. Skip list is a data structure that can be used as an alternative to balanced binary trees (refer to *Trees* chapter). As compared to a binary tree, skip lists allow quick search, insertion and deletion of elements. This is achieved by using probabilistic balancing rather than strictly enforce balancing. It is basically a linked list with additional pointers such that intermediate nodes can be skipped. It uses a random number generator to make some decisions.

In an ordinary sorted linked list, search, insert, and delete are in O(n) because the list must be scanned node-by-node from the head to find the relevant node. If somehow we could scan down the list in bigger steps (skip down, as it were), we would reduce the cost of scanning. This is the fundamental idea behind Skip Lists.

Skip Lists with One Level

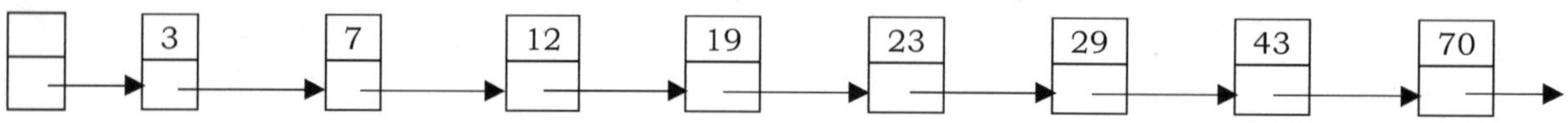

Skip Lists with Two Levels

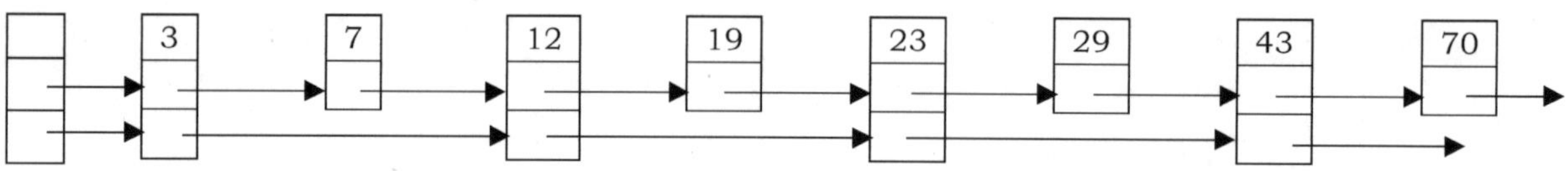

Skip Lists with Three Levels

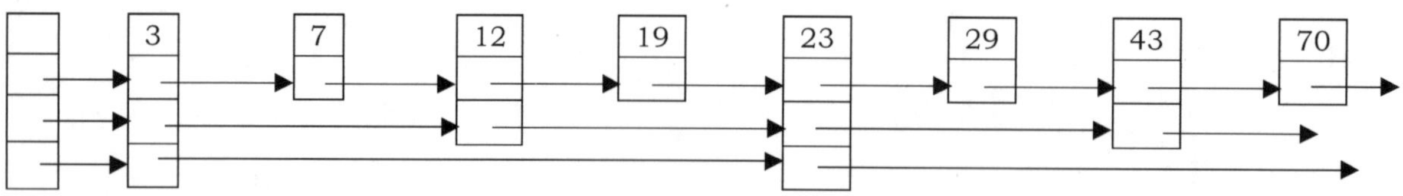

Performance

In a simple linked list that consists of n elements, to perform a search n comparisons are required in the worst case. If a second pointer pointing two nodes ahead is added to every node, the number of comparisons goes down to $n/2 + 1$ in the worst case.

Adding one more pointer to every fourth node and making them point to the fourth node ahead reduces the number of comparisons to $\lceil n/4 \rceil + 2$. If this strategy is continued so that every node with i pointers points to $2 * i - 1$ nodes ahead, O($logn$) performance is obtained and the number of pointers has only doubled ($n + n/2 + n/4 + n/8 + n/16 + ... = 2n$).

The find, insert, and remove operations on ordinary binary search trees are efficient, O($logn$), when the input data is random; but less efficient, O(n), when the input data is ordered. Skip List performance for these same operations and for any data set is about as good as that of randomly-built binary search trees - namely O($logn$).

Comparing Skip Lists and Unrolled Linked Lists

In simple terms, Skip Lists are sorted linked lists with two differences:

- The nodes in an ordinary list have one next reference. The nodes in a Skip List have many *next* references (also called *forward* references).
- The number of *forward* references for a given node is determined probabilistically.

We speak of a Skip List node having levels, one level per forward reference. The number of levels in a node is called the *size* of the node. In an ordinary sorted list, insert, remove, and find operations require sequential traversal of the list. This results in O(n) performance per operation. Skip Lists allow intermediate nodes in the list to be skipped during a traversal - resulting in an expected performance of O($logn$) per operation.

Implementation

```
package main
import (
    "fmt"
    "math/rand"
    "time"
)
const MAX_LEVEL = 32
type SkiplistNode struct {
    data  int
    level []*SkiplistNode
}
type Skiplist struct {
    head            *SkiplistNode
    currentMaxLevel int
    random          *rand.Rand
}
func createSkipList() Skiplist {
    skl := Skiplist{
        head:            new(SkiplistNode),
        currentMaxLevel: 0,
    }
    skl.head.level = make([]*SkiplistNode, MAX_LEVEL)
    source := rand.NewSource(time.Now().UnixNano())
    skl.random = rand.New(source)
    return skl
}
func (this *Skiplist) search(target int) bool {
    p := this.head
    for i := this.currentMaxLevel - 1; i >= 0; i-- {
        for p.level[i] != nil {
            if p.level[i].data == target {
                return true
            }
            if p.level[i].data > target {
                break
            }
            p = p.level[i]
        }
    }
    return false
}
func (this *Skiplist) add(num int) {
    update := make([]*SkiplistNode, MAX_LEVEL)
    p := this.head
    for i := this.currentMaxLevel - 1; i >= 0; i-- {
        for p.level[i] != nil && p.level[i].data < num {
            p = p.level[i]
```

```
        }
        update[i] = p
    }
    level := 1
    for this.random.Intn(2) == 1 {
        level++
    }
    if level > MAX_LEVEL {
        level = MAX_LEVEL
    }
    if level > this.currentMaxLevel {
        for i := this.currentMaxLevel; i < level; i++ {
            update[i] = this.head
        }
        this.currentMaxLevel = level
    }
    newNode := new(SkiplistNode)
    newNode.data = num
    newNode.level = make([]*SkiplistNode, level)
    for i := 0; i < level; i++ {
        newNode.level[i] = update[i].level[i]
        update[i].level[i] = newNode
    }
}
func (this *Skiplist) remove(num int) bool {
    if this.head.level[0] == nil { //Skiplist is null
        return false
    }
    update := make([]*SkiplistNode, MAX_LEVEL)
    p := this.head
    for i := this.currentMaxLevel - 1; i >= 0; i-- {
        for p.level[i] != nil && p.level[i].data < num {
            p = p.level[i]
        }
        update[i] = p
    }
    if update[0].level[0] == nil || update[0].level[0].data != num {
        return false
    }
    level := len(update[0].level[0].level)
    for i := 0; i < level; i++ {
        update[i].level[i] = update[i].level[i].level[i]
    }
    for i := this.currentMaxLevel - 1; this.head.level[i] == nil; i-- {
        this.currentMaxLevel--
    }
    return true
}
func main() {
    sl := createSkipList()
    sl.add(10)
    sl.add(3)
    sl.add(30)
    sl.add(11)
    sl.add(7)
    sl.add(89)
    sl.add(2)
    sl.add(19)
    sl.add(23)
    sl.add(3)
```

```
        sl.add(5)
        sl.add(4)
        sl.add(29)
        sl.add(33)
        sl.add(20)
        sl.add(9)
        sl.add(6)
        sl.add(14)
        fmt.Println(sl.search(66))
        sl.add(66)
        fmt.Println(sl.search(66))
        fmt.Println(sl.search(19))
        fmt.Println(sl.remove(19))
}
```

3.12 Linked Lists: Problems & Solutions

Problem-1 Implement Stack using Linked List.

Solution: Refer to *Stacks* chapter.

Problem-2 Find k^{th} node from the end of a Linked List.

Solution: Brute-Force Method: Start with the first node and count the number of nodes present after that node. If the number of nodes is $< k-1$ then return saying "fewer number of nodes in the list". If the number of nodes is $> k-1$ then go to next node. Continue this until the numbers of nodes after current node are $k-1$.

Time Complexity: $O(n^2)$, for scanning the remaining list (from current node) for each node. Space Complexity: O(1).

Problem-3 Can we improve the complexity of Problem-2?

Solution: Yes, using hash table. As an example, consider the following list.

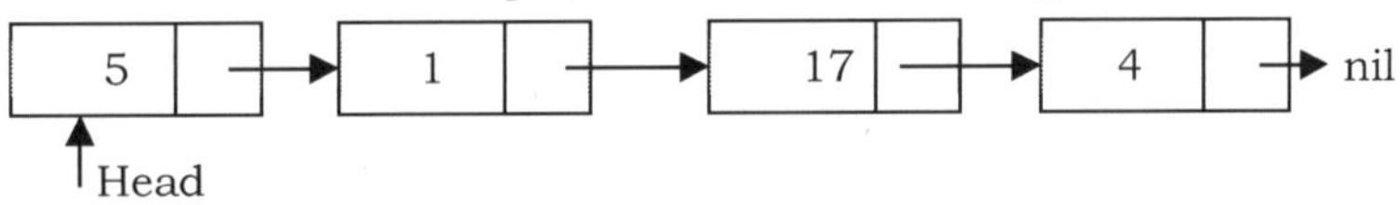

In this approach, create a hash table whose entries are $<$ *position of node, node address* $>$. That means, key is the position of the node in the list and value is the address of that node.

Position in List	Address of Node
1	Address of 5 node
2	Address of 1 node
3	Address of 17 node
4	Address of 4 node

By the time we traverse the complete list (for creating the hash table), we can find the list length. Let us say the list length is M. To find n^{th} from the end of linked list, we can convert this to $M\text{-}n+1^{th}$ from the beginning. Since we already know the length of the list, it is just a matter of returning $M\text{-}n+1^{th}$ key value from the hash table.

Time Complexity: Time for creating the hash table, $T(m) = O(m)$. Space Complexity: Since we need to create a hash table of size m, $O(m)$.

Problem-4 Can we use the Problem-3 approach for solving Problem-2 without creating the hash table?

Solution: Yes. If we observe the Problem-3 solution, what we are actually doing is finding the size of the linked list. That means we are using the hash table to find the size of the linked list. We can find the length of the linked list just by starting at the head node and traversing the list. So, we can find the length of the list without creating the hash table. After finding the length, compute $n-k+1$ and with one more scan we can get the $(n-k+1)^{th}$ node from the beginning. This solution needs two scans: one for finding the length of the list and the other for finding $(n-k+1)^{th}$ node from the beginning.

Time Complexity: Time for finding the length + Time for finding the $(n-k+1)^{th}$ node from the beginning. Therefore, $T(n) = O(n) + O(n) \approx O(n)$. Space Complexity: O(1). Hence, no need to create the hash table.

Problem-5 Can we solve Problem-2 in one scan?

Solution: Yes.

Efficient Approach: The above algorithm could be optimized to one pass. Instead of one pointer, we could use two pointers. The *first* pointer advances the list by $k+1$ steps from the beginning, while the *second* pointer starts from the beginning of the list. Now, both pointers are exactly separated by k nodes apart. We maintain this constant gap by advancing both pointers together until the $first$ pointer arrives past the last node. The *second* pointer will be pointing at the kth node counting from the last. We relink the next pointer of the node referenced by the *second* pointer to point to the node's next next node.

Note: Both pointers move one node at a time.

```
func kthFromEnd(head *ListNode, n int) *ListNode {
    first, second := head, head
    for ; n > 0; n-- {
        second = second.next
    }
    for ; second.next != nil; first, second = first.next, second.next {
    }
    first.next = first.next.next
    return first
}
```

Time Complexity: O(n). Space Complexity: O(1).

Problem-6 Check whether the given linked list is either *nil*-terminated or ends in a cycle (cyclic).

Solution: Brute-Force Approach. As an example, consider the following linked list which has a loop in it. The difference between this list and the regular list is that, in this list, there are two nodes whose next pointers are the same. In regular singly linked lists (without a loop) each node's next pointer is unique. That means the repetition of next pointers indicates the existence of a loop.

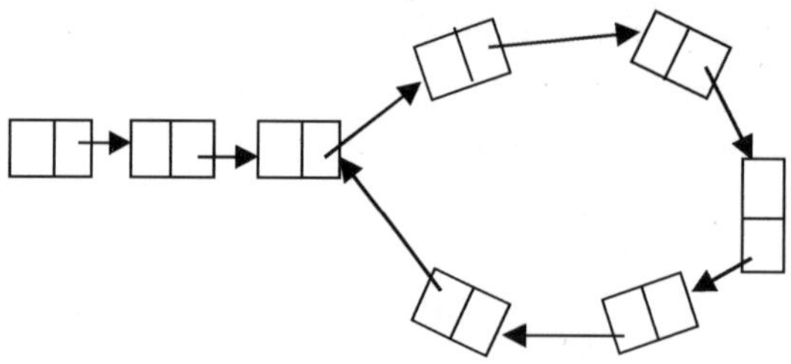

One simple and brute force way of solving this is, start with the first node and see whether there is any node whose next pointer is the current node's address. If there is a node with the same address then that indicates that some other node is pointing to the current node and we can say a loop exists. Continue this process for all the nodes of the linked list.

Does this method work? As per the algorithm, we are checking for the next pointer addresses, but how do we find the end of the linked list (otherwise we will end up in an infinite loop)?

Note: If we start with a node in a loop, this method may work depending on the size of the loop.

Problem-7 Can we use the hashing technique for solving Problem-6?

Solution: Yes. Using Hash Tables, we can solve this problem.

Algorithm:

- Traverse the linked list nodes one by one.
- Check if the address of the node is available in the hash table or not.
- If it is already available in the hash table, that indicates that we are visiting the node that was already visited. This is possible only if the given linked list has a loop in it.
- If the address of the node is not available in the hash table, insert that node's address into the hash table.
- Continue this process until we reach the end of the linked list *or* we find the loop.

Time Complexity*:* O(n) for scanning the linked list. Note that we are doing a scan of only the input.
Space Complexity*:* O(n) for hash table.

Problem-8 Can we solve Problem-6 using the sorting technique?

Solution: No. Consider the following algorithm which is based on sorting. Then we see why this algorithm fails.

Algorithm:

- Traverse the linked list nodes one by one and take all the next pointer values into an array.
- Sort the array that has the next node pointers.
- If there is a loop in the linked list, definitely two next node pointers will be pointing to the same node.
- After sorting if there is a loop in the list, the nodes whose next pointers are the same will end up adjacent in the sorted list.
- If any such pair exists in the sorted list then we say the linked list has a loop in it.

Time Complexity*:* $O(nlogn)$ for sorting the next pointers array. Space Complexity*:* O(n) for the next pointers array.

Problem with the above algorithm: The above algorithm works only if we can find the length of the list. But if the list has a loop then we may end up in an infinite loop. Due to this reason the algorithm fails.

Problem-9 Can we solve the Problem-6 in O(n)?

Solution: Yes. Efficient Approach (Memoryless Approach): The space complexity can be reduced to O(1) by considering two pointers at different speed - a slow pointer and a fast pointer. The slow pointer moves one step at a time while the fast pointer moves two steps at a time. This problem was solved by *Floyd*. The solution is named the Floyd cycle finding algorithm. It uses *two* pointers moving at different speeds to walk the linked list. If there is no cycle in the list, the fast pointer will eventually reach the end and we can return false in this case. Now consider a cyclic list and imagine the slow and fast pointers are two runners racing around a circle track. Once they enter the loop they are expected to meet, which denotes that there is a loop.

This works because the only way a faster moving pointer would point to the same location as a slower moving pointer is if somehow the entire list or a part of it is circular. Think of a tortoise and a hare running on a track. The faster running hare will catch up with the tortoise if they are running in a loop. As an example, consider the following example and trace out the Floyd algorithm. From the diagrams below we can see that after the final step they are meeting at some point in the loop which may not be the starting point of the loop.

Note: *slowPtr* (*tortoise*) moves one pointer at a time and *fastPtr* (*hare*) moves two pointers at a time.

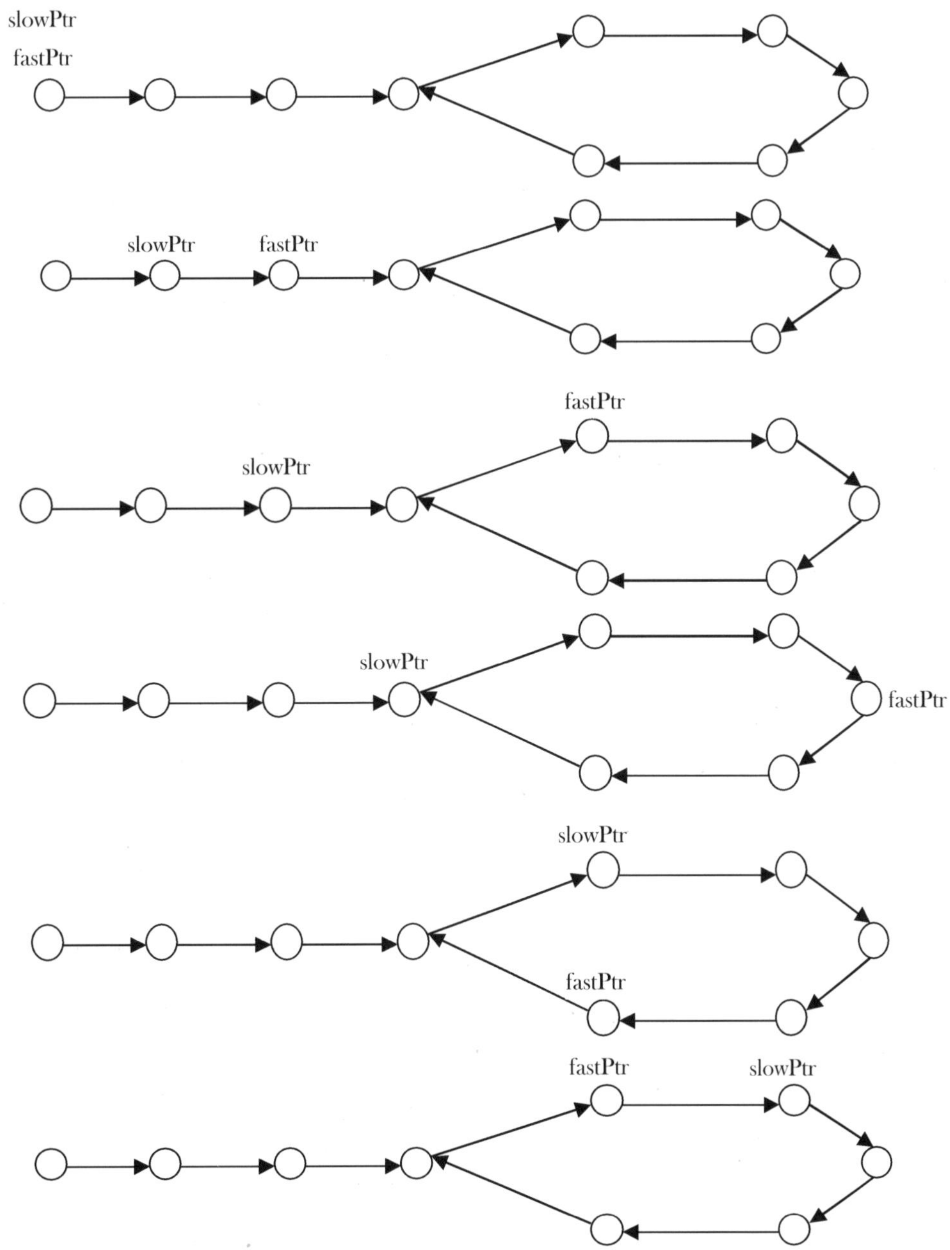

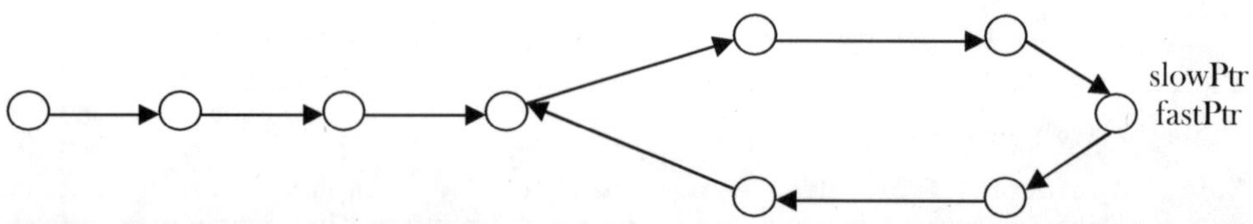


```
func hasCycle(head *ListNode) bool {
    fast, slow := head, head
    for fast != nil && fast.next != nil {
        fast = fast.next.next
        slow = slow.next
        if fast == slow {
            return true
        }
    }
    return false
}
```

Time Complexity: O(n). Space Complexity: O(1).

Problem-10 We are given a pointer to the first element of a linked list L. There are two possibilities for L: it either ends (snake) or its last element points back to one of the earlier elements in the list (snail). Give an algorithm that tests whether a given list L is a snake or a snail.

Solution: It is the same as Problem-6.

Problem-11 Check whether the given linked list is nil-terminated or not. If there is a cycle find the start node of the loop.

Solution: The solution is an extension to the solution in Problem-9. After finding the loop in the linked list, we initialize the *slow* to the head of the linked list. From that point onwards both *slow* and *fast* move only one node at a time. The point at which they meet is the start of the loop. Generally, we use this method for removing the loops.

```
func findLoopBeginning(head *ListNode) *ListNode {
    fast, slow := head, head
    loopExists := false
    for fast != nil && fast.next != nil {
        fast = fast.next.next
        slow = slow.next
        if fast == slow {
            loopExists = true
            break
        }
    }
    if loopExists {
        slow = head
        for slow != fast {
            fast = fast.next
            slow = slow.next
        }
        return slow
    }
    return nil
}
```

Time Complexity: O(n). Space Complexity: O(1).

Problem-12 From the previous discussion and problems we understand that the meeting of tortoise and hare concludes the existence of the loop, but how does moving the tortoise to the beginning of the linked list while keeping the hare at the meeting place, followed by moving both one step at a time, make them meet at the starting point of the cycle?

Solution: This problem is at the heart of number theory. In the Floyd cycle finding algorithm, notice that the tortoise and the hare will meet when they are $n \times L$, where L is the loop length. Furthermore, the tortoise is at the midpoint between the hare and the beginning of the sequence because of the way they move. Therefore, the tortoise is $n \times L$ away from the beginning of the sequence as well. If we move both one step at a time, from the position of the tortoise and from the start of the sequence, we know that they will meet as soon as both are in the loop, since they are $n \times L$, a multiple of the loop length, apart. One of them is already in the loop, so we just move the other one in single step until it enters the loop, keeping the other $n \times L$ away from it at all times.

Problem-13 In the Floyd cycle finding algorithm, does it work if we use steps 2 and 3 instead of 1 and 2?

Solution: Yes, but the complexity might be high. Trace out an example.

Problem-14 Check whether the given linked list is nil-terminated. If there is a cycle, find the length of the loop.

Solution: This solution is also an extension of the basic cycle detection problem. After finding the loop in the linked list, keep the *slow* as it is. The *fast* keeps on moving until it again comes back to *slow*. While moving *fast*, use a counter variable which increments at the rate of 1.

```
func findLoopLength(head *ListNode) int {
    fast, slow := head, head
    loopExists := false
    for fast != nil && fast.next != nil {
        fast = fast.next.next
        slow = slow.next
        if fast == slow {
            loopExists = true
            break
        }
    }
    if loopExists {
        counter := 1
        fast = fast.next
        for slow != fast {
            fast = fast.next
            counter++
        }
        return counter
    }
    return 0
}
```

Time Complexity: $O(n)$. Space Complexity: $O(1)$.

Problem-15 Insert a node in a sorted linked list.

Solution: Traverse the list and find a position for the element and insert it.

```
// Insert the given node into the correct sorted position in the given list sorted in increasing order
func (ll *LinkedList) sortedInsert(data int) {
    /* Create a new ListNode */
    newNode := &ListNode{
        data: data,
    }
    // Special case for the head end
    if ll.head == nil || ll.head.data.(int) >= data {
        newNode.next = ll.head
        ll.head = newNode
        return
    }
    // Locate the node before the point of insertion
    current := ll.head
    for current.next != nil && current.next.data.(int) < data {
        current = current.next
    }
    newNode.next = current.next
    current.next = newNode
}
```

Time Complexity: $O(n)$. Space Complexity: $O(1)$.

Problem-16 Reverse a singly linked list.

Solution: While traversing the list, change the current node's next pointer to point to its previous element. Since a node does not have reference to its previous node, we must store its previous element beforehand. We also need another pointer to store the next node before changing the reference. We will use three pointers "previous", "current" and "next" to keep track of previous, current and next node during linked list reversal.

```
func reverseList(head *ListNode) *ListNode {
    var prev, current *ListNode
    for current = head; current != nil {
        current.next, prev, current = prev, current, current.next
    }
    return prev
}
```

Time Complexity: $O(n)$. Space Complexity: $O(1)$.

Recursive version: The recursive version is slightly trickier and the key is to work backwards. We will find it easier to start from the bottom up, by asking and answering tiny questions:

- What is the reverse of nil (the empty list)? nil.
- What is the reverse of a one element list? The element itself.
- What is the reverse of an n element list? The reverse of the second element followed by the first element.

```
func reverseList(head *ListNode) *ListNode {
    if head == nil {
        return head
    }
    h := reverse(head)
    head.next = nil
    return h
}
func reverse(current *ListNode) *ListNode {
    if current == nil {
        return nil
    }
    temp := reverse(current.next)
    if temp == nil {
       return current
    }
    current.next.next = current
    return temp
}
```

Time Complexity: $O(n)$.
Space Complexity: $O(n)$. The extra space comes from implicit stack space due to recursion. The recursion could go up to n levels deep.

Problem-17 Suppose there are two singly linked lists both of which intersect at some point and become a single linked list. The head or start pointers of both the lists are known, but the intersecting node is not known. Also, the number of nodes in each of the lists before they intersect is unknown and may be different in each list. $List1$ may have n nodes before it reaches the intersection point, and $List2$ might have m nodes before it reaches the intersection point where m and n may be $m = n, m < n$ or $m > n$. Give an algorithm for finding the merging point.

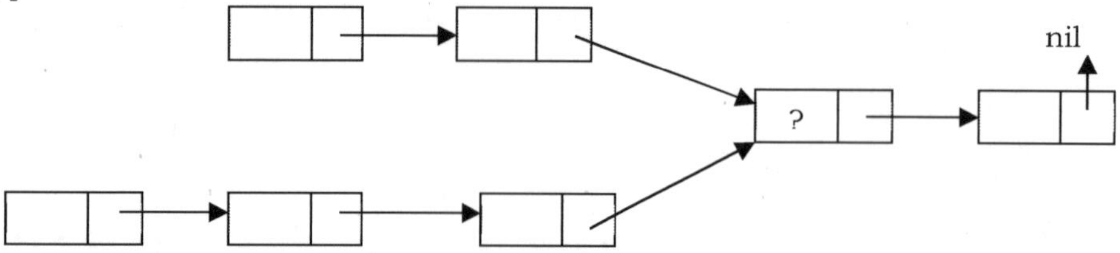

Solution: Brute-Force Approach: One easy solution is to compare every node pointer in the first list with every other node pointer in the second list by which the matching node pointers will lead us to the intersecting node. But, the time complexity in this case will be $O(mn)$ which will be high.

```
func getIntersectionNode(head1, head2 *ListNode) *ListNode {
    for head1 != nil {
        temp := head2
        for temp != nil {
            if temp == head1 {
                // found a matching node
```

```
                return head1
            }
            temp = temp.next
        }
        head1 = head1.next
    }
    return nil
}
```

Time Complexity: O(mn). Space Complexity: O(1).

Problem-18 Can we solve Problem-17 using the sorting technique?

Solution: No. Consider the following algorithm which is based on sorting and see why this algorithm fails.

Algorithm:

- Take first list node pointers and keep them in some array and sort them.
- Take second list node pointers and keep them in some array and sort them.
- After sorting, use two indexes: one for the first sorted array and the other for the second sorted array.
- Start comparing values at the indexes and increment the index according to whichever has the lower value (increment only if the values are not equal).
- At any point, if we are able to find two indexes whose values are the same, then that indicates that those two nodes are pointing to the same node and we return that node.

Time Complexity: Time for sorting lists + Time for scanning (for comparing)
= O($mlogm$) +O($nlogn$) +O($m + n$) We need to consider the one that gives the maximum value.

Space Complexity: O(1).

Any problem with the above algorithm? Yes. In the algorithm, we are storing all the node pointers of both the lists and sorting. But we are forgetting the fact that there can be many repeated elements. This is because after the merging point, all node pointers are the same for both the lists. The algorithm works fine only in one case and it is when both lists have the ending node at their merge point.

Problem-19 Can we solve Problem-17 using hash tables?

Solution: Yes.

Algorithm:

- Select a list which has a smaller number of nodes (If we do not know the lengths beforehand then select one list randomly).
- Now, traverse the other list and for each node pointer of this list check whether the same node pointer exists in the hash table.
- If there is a merge point for the given lists then we will definitely encounter the node pointer in the hash table.

Time Complexity: Time for creating the hash table + Time for scanning the second list = O(m) + O(n) (or O(n) + O(m), depending on which list we select for creating the hash table. But in both cases the time complexity is the same. Space Complexity: O(n) or O(m).

Problem-20 Can we use stacks for solving the Problem-17?

Solution: Yes.

Algorithm:

- Create two stacks: one for the first list and one for the second list.
- Traverse the first list and push all the node addresses onto the first stack.
- Traverse the second list and push all the node addresses onto the second stack.
- Now both stacks contain the node address of the corresponding lists.
- Now compare the top node address of both stacks.
- If they are the same, take the top elements from both the stacks and keep them in some temporary variable (since both node addresses are node, it is enough if we use one temporary variable).
- Continue this process until the top node addresses of the stacks are not the same.
- This point is the one where the lists merge into a single list.
- Return the value of the temporary variable.

Time Complexity: O($m + n$), for scanning both the lists.
Space Complexity: O($m + n$), for creating two stacks for both the lists.

Problem-21 Is there any other way of solving Problem-17?

Solution: **Yes**. Using "finding the first repeating number" approach in an array (for algorithm refer to *Searching* chapter).

Algorithm:

- Create an array A and keep all the next pointers of both the lists in the array.
- In the array find the first repeating element [Refer to *Searching* chapter for algorithm].
- The first repeating number indicates the merging point of both the lists.

Time Complexity: $O(m + n)$. Space Complexity: $O(m + n)$.

Problem-22 Can we still think of finding an alternative solution for Problem-17?

Solution: Yes. By combining sorting and search techniques we can reduce the complexity.

Algorithm:

- Create an array A and keep all the next pointers of the first list in the array.
- Sort these array elements.
- Then, for each of the second list elements, search in the sorted array (let us assume that we are using binary search which gives $O(logn)$).
- Since we are scanning the second list one by one, the first repeating element that appears in the array is nothing but the merging point.

Time Complexity: Time for sorting + Time for searching = $O(Max(mlogm, nlogn))$. Space Complexity: $O(Max(m,n))$.

Problem-23 Can we improve the complexity for Problem-17?

Solution: Yes. Maintain two pointers head1 and head2 initialized at the head of list1 and list2, respectively. Then let them both traverse through the lists, one node at a time. First calculate the length of two lists and find the difference. Then start from the longer list at the diff offset, iterate though 2 lists and find the node.

Efficient Approach:

- Find lengths (L1 and L2) of both lists -- $O(n) + O(m) = O(max(m,n))$.
- Take the difference d of the lengths -- $O(1)$.
- Make d steps in longer list -- $O(d)$.
- Step in both lists in parallel until links to next node match -- $O(min(m,n))$.
- Total time complexity = $O(max(m,n))$.
- Space Complexity = $O(1)$.

```
func getIntersectionNode(head1, head2 *ListNode) *ListNode {
    len1, len2 := findLen(head1), findLen(head2)
    if len1 > len2 {
        for ; len1 > len2; len1-- {
            head1 = head1.next
        }
    } else {
        for ; len2 > len1; len2-- {
            head2 = head2.next
        }
    }
    for head1 != head2 {
        head1, head2 = head1.next, head2.next
    }
    return head1
}
func findLen(head *ListNode) int {
    l := 0
    for ; head != nil; head = head.next {
        l++
    }
    return l
}
```

Problem-24 How will you find the middle of the linked list?

Solution: Brute-Force Approach: For each of the node, count how many nodes are there in the list, and see whether it is the middle node of the list.

Time Complexity: $O(n^2)$. Space Complexity: $O(1)$.

Problem-25 Can we improve the complexity of Problem-24?

Solution: Yes.

Algorithm:

- Traverse the list and find the length of the list.

- After finding the length, again scan the list and locate $n/2$ node from the beginning.

```
func middleNode(head *ListNode) *ListNode {
    l := length(head)
    count, target := 0, (l/2)+1
    for {
        count++
        if count == target {
            return head
        }
        head = head.Next
    }
}
func length(head *ListNode) int {
    current, count := head, 0
    for current != nil {
        count++
        current = current.Next
    }
    return count
}
```

Time Complexity: Time for finding the length of the list + Time for locating middle node = $O(n) + O(n) \approx O(n)$. Space Complexity: $O(1)$.

Problem-26 Can we use the hash table for solving Problem-24?

Solution: Yes. The reasoning is the same as that of Problem-3.

Time Complexity: Time for creating the hash table . Therefore, $T(n) = O(n)$.
Space Complexity: $O(n)$. Since we need to create a hash table of size n.

Problem-27 Can we solve Problem-24 just in one scan?

Solution: Efficient Approach: Use two pointers. Move one pointer at twice the speed of the second. When the first pointer reaches the end of the list, the second pointer will be pointing to the middle node. When traversing the list with a pointer *slow*, make another pointer *fast* that traverses twice as fast. When *fast* reaches the end of the list, *slow* must be in the middle.

Note: If the list has an even number of nodes, the middle node will be of $\lfloor n/2 \rfloor$.

```
func middleNode(head *ListNode) *ListNode {
    fast,slow := head, head
    for fast != nil && fast.next != nil {
        fast = fast.next.next
        slow = slow.next
    }
    return slow
}
```

Time Complexity: $O(n)$. Space Complexity: $O(1)$.

Problem-28 How will you display a Linked List from the end (in reverse)?

Solution: Traverse recursively till the end of the linked list. While coming back, start printing the elements.

```
func printListInReverse(head *ListNode) {
    if head == nil {
        return
    }
    printListInReverse(head.next)
    fmt.Print(head.data)
}
```

Time Complexity: $O(n)$. Space Complexity: $O(n)\rightarrow$ for Stack.

Problem-29 Check whether the given Linked List length is even or odd?

Solution: Use a $2x$ pointer. Take a pointer that moves at $2x$ [two nodes at a time]. At the end, if the length is even, then the pointer will be nil; otherwise it will point to the last node.

```
func (ll *LinkedList) IsLengthEven() bool {
    current := ll.head
```

```
    for current != nil && current.next != nil {
        current = current.next.next
    }
    if current != nil {
        return false
    }
    return true
}
```

Time Complexity: $O(\lfloor n/2 \rfloor) \approx O(n)$. Space Complexity: $O(1)$.

Problem-30 If the head of a Linked List is pointing to kth element, then how will you get the elements before kth element?

Solution: Use Memory Efficient Linked Lists [XOR Linked Lists].

Problem-31 Given two sorted Linked Lists, how to merge them into the third list in sorted order?

Solution: Assume the sizes of lists are m and n.

Recursive:

```
func mergeTwoLists(l1 *ListNode, l2 *ListNode) *ListNode {
    if l1 == nil {
        return l2
    }
    if l2 == nil {
        return l1
    }
    if l1.data < l2.data {
        l1.next = mergeTwoLists(l1.next, l2)
        return l1
    }
    l2.next = mergeTwoLists(l1, l2.next)
    return l2
}
```

Time Complexity: $O(n + m)$, where n and m are lengths of two lists.

Iterative:

```
func mergeTwoLists(l1 *ListNode, l2 *ListNode) *ListNode {
    dummy := new(ListNode)
    for node := dummy; l1 != nil || l2 != nil; node = node.next {
        if l1 == nil {
            node.next = l2
            break
        } else if l2 == nil {
            node.next = l1
            break
        } else if l1.data < l2.data {
            node.next = l1
            l1 = l1.next
        } else {
            node.next = l2
            l2 = l2.next
        }
    }
    return dummy.next
}
```

Time Complexity: $O(n + m)$, where n and m are lengths of two lists.

Problem-33 Merge k sorted linked lists and return it as one sorted list. Analyze and describe its complexity.

Solution: Once simplest way is to traverse all the linked lists and collect the values of the nodes into an array. Then, sort the array. After the sorting, iterate over this array to get the proper value of nodes.

Time Complexity: $O(nlogn)$. Space Complexity: $O(n)$, for sotring all the elements in an array.

As an alternative, we can compare every k nodes (head of every linked list) and get the node with the smallest value. We need to extend the final sorted linked list with the selected nodes.

Time Complexity: O(nk). Space Complexity: O(1).

As an improvement to the previous solution, we can use priority queue to get the minimum element among the k elements. Refer *Priority Queues* chapter for more details.

Time Complexity: O($nlogk$). Space Complexity: O(k), for creating a priority queue of size k.

As a final solution, we can convert the problem of merging k lists problem to merge 2 lists ($k - 1$) times. For this, we can use the solution of previous problem.

```
func mergeKLists(lists []*ListNode) *ListNode {
    if lists == nil || len(lists) == 0 {
        return nil
    }
    for len(lists) > 1 {
        l1 := lists[0]
        l2 := lists[1]
        lists = lists[2:]
        merged := mergeTwoLists(l1, l2)
        lists = append(lists, merged)
    }
    return lists[0]
}
```

Problem-34 Given a binary tree convert it to doubly linked list.

Solution: Refer *Trees* chapter.

Problem-35 How do we sort the Linked Lists?

Solution: The idea is simple, just recursively divide the list to the first half and the second half (using two pointers and delete the connection between the former and the latter).

After it's divided into single element, then apply "merge two sorted lists" method for each pair, back to the sorted one list. Refer *Sorting* chapter for more details about merge sort algorithm.

```
func sortList(head *ListNode) *ListNode {
    if head == nil || head.next == nil {
        return head
    }
    slow, fast := head, head
    for fast.next != nil && fast.next.next != nil {
        slow, fast = slow.next, fast.next.next
    }
    firstTail := slow
    slow = slow.next
    firstTail.next = nil          // divide the first list and the second
    first, second := sortList(head), sortList(slow)
    return merge(first, second)
}
func merge(head1 *ListNode, head2 *ListNode) *ListNode {
    curHead := &ListNode{}
    tmpHead := curHead
    for head1 != nil && head2 != nil {
        if head1.data < head2.data {
            curHead.next = head1
            head1 = head1.next
            curHead = curHead.next
        } else {
            curHead.next = head2
            head2 = head2.next
            curHead = curHead.next
        }
    }
    if head1 != nil {
        curHead.next = head1
    } else if head2 != nil {
```

```
            curHead.next = head2
        }
        return tmpHead.next
    }
```

Problem-36 Split a Circular Linked List into two equal parts. If the number of nodes in the list are odd then make first list one node extra than second list.

Alternative problem statement: Given a linked list, split it into two sublists — one for the front half, and one for the back half. If the number of elements is odd, the extra element should go in the front list. So, the algorithm on the list {2, 3, 5, 7, 11} should yield the two lists {2, 3, 5} and {7, 11}.

Solution:

Algorithm:

- Store the mid and last pointers of the circular linked list using Floyd cycle finding algorithm.
- Make the second half circular.
- Make the first half circular.
- Set head pointers of the two linked lists.

As an example, consider the following circular list.

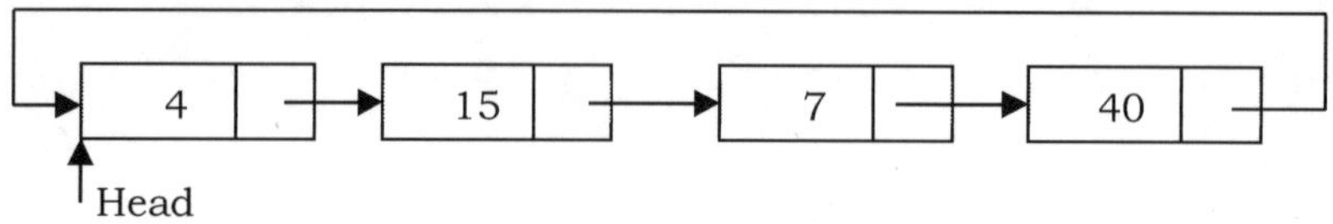

After the split, the above list will look like:

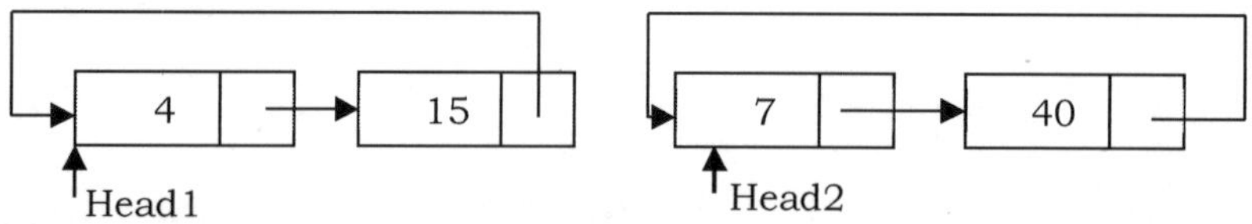


```
// Uses the fast/slow pointer strategy
func splitList(head *ListNode) (head1 *ListNode, head2 *ListNode) {
    var slow, fast *ListNode
    if head == nil || head.next == nil { // length < 2 cases
        head1 = head
        head2 = nil
    } else {
        slow = head
        fast = head.next
        // Advance 'fast' two nodes, and advance 'slow' one ListNode
        for fast != nil {
            fast = fast.next
            if fast != nil {
                slow = slow.next
                fast = fast.next
            }
        }
        // 'slow' is before the midpoint in the list, so split it in two at that point.
        head1 = head
        head2 = slow.next
        slow.next = nil
    }
    return head1, head2
}
```

Time Complexity: $O(n)$. Space Complexity: $O(1)$.

Problem-37 If we want to concatenate two linked lists which of the following gives O(1) complexity?
1) Singly linked lists 2) Doubly linked lists 3) Circular doubly linked lists

Solution: Circular Doubly Linked Lists. This is because for singly and doubly linked lists, we need to traverse the first list till the end and append the second list. But in the case of circular doubly linked lists we don't have to traverse the lists.

Problem-37 How will you check if the linked list is palindrome or not?

Solution:

Algorithm:

1. Get the middle of the linked list.
2. Reverse the second half of the linked list.
3. Compare the first half and second half.
4. Construct the original linked list by reversing the second half again and attaching it back to the first half.

Time Complexity: $O(n)$. Space Complexity: $O(1)$.

Problem-38 For a given K value $(K > 0)$ reverse blocks of K nodes in a list.

Example: Input: 1 2 3 4 5 6 7 8 9 10. Output for different K values:

For $K = 2$: 2 1 4 3 6 5 8 7 10 9   For $K = 3$: 3 2 1 6 5 4 9 8 7 10   For $K = 4$: 4 3 2 1 8 7 6 5 9 10

Solution:

Algorithm: This is an extension of swapping nodes in a linked list.

1) Check if remaining list has K nodes.
   a. If yes get the pointer of $K + 1^{th}$ node.
   b. Else return.
2) Reverse first K nodes.
3) Set next of last node (after reversal) to $K + 1^{th}$ node.
4) Move to $K + 1^{th}$ node.
5) Go to step 1.
6) $K - 1^{th}$ node of first K nodes becomes the new head if available. Otherwise, we can return the head.

```
func reverseBlockOfKNodes(head *ListNode, k int) *ListNode {
    // base check
    if (head == nil || k == 1 ) {
        return head
    }
    // get length
    length := 0
    node := head
    for node != nil {
        length++
        node = node.next
    }
    // result
    result := ListNode{0, head}
    previous := &result
    for step := 0; step + k <= length; step = step + k {
        // two things to keep, head and previous tail is the new last node previous is where need to link back
        // move head to the first element of the section (k section)
        tail := previous.next
        nextNode := tail.next
        // reverse k-1 pointers
        for i := 1; i < k; i++ {
            // point nextNode of 1 to 3; take out 2
            tail.next = nextNode.next
            // point nextNode of 2 to 1; link 2 to original first element in the group
            nextNode.next = previous.next
            // point nextNode of 0 to 2; link result head to the new first element
            previous.next = nextNode
            // now is 0 -> 2 -> 1 -> 3; linkage is done
            // move nextNode to 3; now we are working on 3
            nextNode = tail.next
            // so that nextNode round, we need to link 0 to 3. ( previous.next = nextNode )
        }
        // tail the is the new previous
        // previous is the result one, the one we shouldn't move
        previous = tail
    }
    return result.next
}
```

Problem-39 Is it possible to get O(1) access time for Linked Lists?

Solution: Yes. Create a linked list and at the same time keep it in a hash table. For n elements we have to keep all the elements in a hash table which gives a preprocessing time of O(n). To read any element we require only constant time O(1) and to read n elements we require $n * 1$ unit of time = n units. Hence by using amortized analysis we can say that element access can be performed within O(1) time.

Time Complexity – O(1) [Amortized]. Space Complexity - O(n) for Hash Table.

Problem-40 **Josephus Circle:** N people have decided to elect a leader by arranging themselves in a circle and eliminating every M^{th} person around the circle, closing ranks as each person drops out. Find which person will be the last one remaining (with rank 1).

Solution: Assume the input is a circular linked list with N nodes and each node has a number (range 1 to N) associated with it. The head node has number 1 as data.

```
package main
import "fmt"
type ListNode struct {          // defines a ListNode in a singly linked list
    data interface{}            // the datum
    next *ListNode              // pointer to the next ListNode
}
// Create a new node of circular linked list
func NewListNode(data int) *ListNode {
    temp := &ListNode{}
    temp.next = temp
    temp.data = data
    return temp
}
// Function to find the only person left after one in every m-th node is killed in a circle of n nodes
func getJosephusPosition(m, n int) {
    // Create a circular linked list of size N.
    head := NewListNode(1)
    prev := head
    for i := 2; i <= n; i++ {
        prev.next = newListNode(i)
        prev = prev.next
    }
    prev.next = head // Connect last node to first
    // while only one node is left in the linked list
    ptr1, ptr2 := head, head
    for ptr1.next != ptr1 {
        // Find m-th node
        count := 1
        for count != m {
            ptr2 = ptr1
            ptr1 = ptr1.next
            count++
        }
        // Remove the m-th node
        ptr2.next = ptr1.next
        ptr1 = ptr2.next
    }
    fmt.Println("Last person left standing ", "(Josephus Position) is ", ptr1.data)
}
// Driver program to test above functions
func main() {
    n, m := 14, 2
    getJosephusPosition(m, n)
}
```

Problem-41 Given a linked list consists of data, a next pointer and also a random pointer which points to a random node of the list. Give an algorithm for cloning the list.

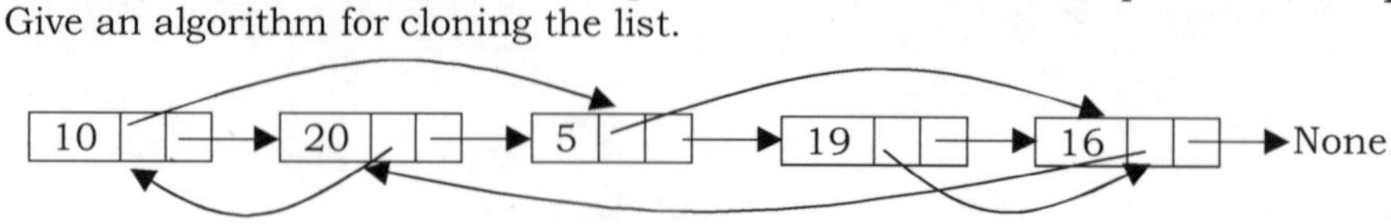

Solution: To clone a linked list with random pointers, the idea is to maintain a hash table for storing the mappings from an original linked list node to its clone. For each node in the original linked list, we create a new node with same data and set its next pointers. While doing so, we also create a mapping from the original node to the duplicate node in the hash table. Finally, we traverse the original linked list again and update random pointers of the duplicate nodes using the hash table.

Algorithm:

- Scan the original list and for each node X, create a new node Y with data of X, then store the pair (X, Y) in hash table using X as a key. Note that during this scan set $Y \to next$ with $X \to next$ and $Y \to random$ to nil and we will fix it in the next scan. Now for each node X in the original list we have a copy Y stored in our hash table.
- To update the random pointers, read random pointer of node X from original linked list and get the corresponding random node in cloned list from hash table created in previous step. Assign random pointer of node X from cloned list to corresponding node we got.

```
type ListNode struct {          // defines a ListNode in a singly linked list
    data   interface{}          // the datum
    next   *ListNode            // pointer to the next ListNode
    random *ListNode            // pointer to a random ListNode
}
func clone(head *ListNode) *ListNode {
    var (
        result *ListNode         = &ListNode{}
        Y                        = result
        X    *ListNode           = head
        HT   map[*ListNode]*ListNode = make(map[*ListNode]*ListNode, 0)
    )
    for X != nil {
        Y.next = &ListNode{data: X.data}
        HT[X] = Y.next
        Y = Y.next
        X = X.next
    }
    X = head
    Y = result.next
    for X != nil {
        if n, found := HT[X.random]; found {
            Y.random = n
        }
        Y = Y.next
        X = X.next
    }
    return result.next
}
```

Time Complexity: O(n). Space Complexity: O(n).

Problem-42 Can we solve Problem-41 without any extra space?

Solution: Yes. First, a new node is inserted after each node in the original linked list. The content of the new node is the same as the previous node. For example, in the figure, insert 10 after 10, insert 20 after 20, and so on.

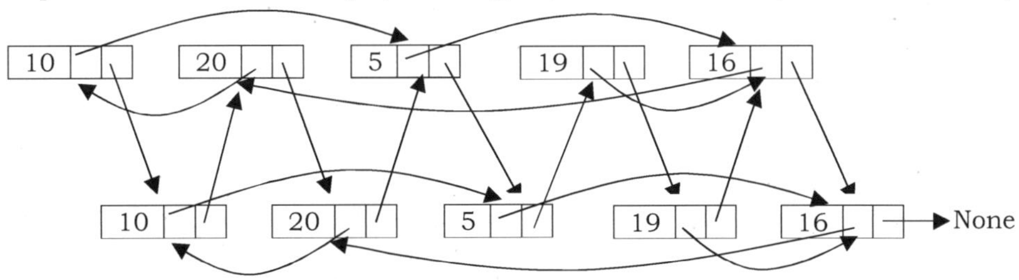

Second, how does the random pointer in the original linked list map? For example, in the figure above, the random pointer of 10 node points to 5, and the random pointer of 19 nodes points to 16. For every node X in the original list, the statement: X.next.random = X.random.next this problem can be solved. This works because $X \to next$ is nothing but copy of original and $X \to random \to next$ is nothing but copy of random.

The third step is to split the new linked list from the linked list.

```
func clone(head *ListNode) *ListNode {
    // Duplicate each node.
    X := head
    for X != nil {
        newNode := &ListNode{
            data: X.data,
            next: X.next,
            random: X.random,
        }
        X.next = newNode
        X = newNode.next
    }
    // Make the duplicated nodes point to the correct random.
    X = head
    for X != nil {
        X = X.next
        if X.random != nil {
            X.random = X.random.next
        }
        X = X.next
    }
    // Extract the duplicated nodes and recover the original list.
    result := &ListNode{}
    Y := result
    X = head
    for X != nil {
        n := X.next
        X.next = X.next.next
        X = X.next
        Y.next = n
        Y = Y.next
    }
    return result.next
}
```

Time Complexity: $O(3n) \approx O(n)$. Space Complexity: O(1).

Problem-43 We are given a pointer to a node (not the tail node) in a singly linked list. Delete that node from the linked list.

Solution: To delete a node, we have to adjust the next pointer of the previous node to point to the next node instead of the current one. Since we don't have a pointer to the previous node, we can't redirect its next pointer. So, what do we do? We can easily get away by moving the data from the next node into the current node and then deleting the next node.

```
func deleteNode(node *ListNode) {
    temp = node.next
    node.data = node.next.data
    node.next = temp.next
    temp = nil
}
```

Time Complexity: O(1). Space Complexity: O(1).

Problem-44 Given a linked list with even and odd numbers, create an algorithm for making changes to the list in such a way that all even numbers appear at the beginning.

Solution: To solve this problem, we can use the splitting logic. While traversing the list, split the linked list into two: one contains all even nodes and the other contains all odd nodes. Now, to get the final list, we can simply append the odd node linked list after the even node linked list.

To split the linked list, traverse the original linked list and move all odd nodes to a separate linked list of all odd nodes. At the end of the loop, the original list will have all the even nodes and the odd node list will have all the odd nodes. To keep the ordering of all nodes the same, we must insert all the odd nodes at the end of the odd node list.

Time Complexity: $O(n)$. Space Complexity: O(1).

Problem-45 In a linked list with n nodes, the time taken to insert an element after an element pointed by some pointer is

(A) O(1) (B) O($logn$) (C) O(n) (D) O($n1ogn$)

Solution: A.

Problem-46 **Find modular node:** Given a singly linked list, write a function to find the last element from the beginning whose $n\%k == 0$, where n is the number of elements in the list and k is an integer constant. For example, if $n = 19$ and $k = 3$ then we should return 18^{th}node.

Solution: For this problem the value of n is not known in advance.

```
func (ll *LinkedList) modularNodeFromBegin(k int) *ListNode {
    if k <= 0 {
        return nil
    }
    i := 1
    current, modularNode := ll.head, ll.head
    for ; current != nil; current = current.next {
        if i%k == 0 {
            modularNode = ll.head
        } else {
            modularNode = modularNode.next
        }
        current = current.next
        i++
    }
    return modularNode
}
```

Time Complexity: O(n). Space Complexity: O(1).

Problem-47 **Find modular node from the end:** Given a singly linked list, write a function to find the first from the end whose $n\%k == 0$, where n is the number of elements in the list and k is an integer constant. If $n = 19$ and $k = 3$ then we should return 16th node.

Solution: For this problem the value of n is not known in advance. To solve this problem, we are going to combine the solutions of finding the k^{th}element from the end of the the linked list, and finding the modular node from the beginning. Every time, whenever *current position mod k* becomes zero, we reinitialize the modular node to point to k^{th} node behind the current location.

```
func (ll *LinkedList) modularNodeFromEnd(k int) *ListNode {
    if k <= 0 {
        return nil
    }
    current, modularNode := ll.head, ll.head
    i := 0
    for i = 0; i < k; i++ {          // Move the head pointer for k steps so that,
        if current != nil {          // we get a difference of k nodes between the pointers
            current = current.next
        } else {
            break
        }
    }
    for current != nil {             // Maintain the k distance between the pointers, and move till the end
        modularNode = modularNode.next
        current = current.next
        i++
    }
    j := k - (i % k)
    for j > 0 && modularNode != nil { // Now, adjust the modularNode to point to the correct node
        modularNode = modularNode.next
        j--
    }
    return modularNode
}
```

Time Complexity: O(n). Space Complexity: O(1).

Problem-48 **Find fractional node:** Given a singly linked list, write a function to find the $\frac{n}{k}th$ element, where n is the number of elements in the list.

Solution: For this problem the value of n is not known in advance.

```
func (ll *LinkedList) fractionalNode(k int) *ListNode {
    if k <= 0 {
        return nil
    }
    i := 0
    current := ll.head
    var fractionalNode *ListNode
    for ; current != nil; current = current.next {
        if i%k == 0 {
            if fractionalNode == nil {
                fractionalNode = ll.head
            } else {
                fractionalNode = fractionalNode.next
            }
        }
        i++
    }
    return fractionalNode
}
```

Time Complexity: O(n). Space Complexity: O(1).

Problem-49 **Find $\sqrt{n}^{th}$ node:** Given a singly linked list, write a function to find the $\sqrt{n}^{th}$ element, where n is the number of elements in the list. Assume the value of n is not known in advance.

Solution: For this problem the value of n is not known in advance. Hence, we would increase the second pointer for every perfect square position.

```
func (ll *LinkedList) sqrtNode() *ListNode {
    current := ll.head
    var sqrtN *ListNode
    for i, j := 1, 1; current != nil; current = current.next {
        if i == j*j {
            if sqrtN == nil {
                sqrtN = ll.head
            } else {
                sqrtN = sqrtN.next
            }
            j++
        }
        i++
    }
    return sqrtN
}
```

Time Complexity: O(n). Space Complexity: O(1).

Problem-50 Given two lists List1 = $\{A_1, A_2, \ldots, A_n\}$ and List2 = $\{B_1, B_2, \ldots, B_m\}$ with data (both lists) in ascending order. Merge them into the third list in ascending order so that the merged list will be:

$$\{A_1, B_1, A_2, B_2 \ldots\ldots A_m, B_m, A_{m+1} \ldots\ldots A_n\} \text{ if } n >= m$$
$$\{A_1, B_1, A_2, B_2 \ldots\ldots A_n, B_n, B_{n+1} \ldots\ldots B_m\} \text{ if } m >= n$$

Solution: To merge two sorted linked lists, we need to pay attention to the order of their values. We iterate both lists at the same time, but go to next only on the list that has a current node value smaller than the one in the other current list. We have to handle the cases when one or the other list are empty.

```
func mergeTwoLists(head1 *ListNode, head2 *ListNode) *ListNode {
    h := ListNode{}
    l := &h

    for head1 != nil && head2 != nil {
        if head1.data.(int) <= head2.data.(int) {
            l.next = head1
```

```
                head1 = head1.next
            } else {
                l.next = head2
                head2 = head2.next
            }
            l = l.next
        }
        if head1 == nil {
            l.next = head2
        }
        if head2 == nil {
            l.next = head1
        }
        return h.next
    }
    func mergeTwoLists(head1 *ListNode, head2 *ListNode) *ListNode {
        if head1 == nil {
            return head2
        }
        if head2 == nil {
            return head1
        }
        if head1.data < head2.data {
            head1.next = mergeTwoLists(head1.next, head2)
            return head1
        }
        head2.next = mergeTwoLists(head1, head2.next)
        return head2
    }
```

Time Complexity: The *while* loop takes $O(min(n, m))$ time as it will run for $min(n, m)$ times. The other steps run in O(1). Therefore, the total time complexity is $O(min(n, m))$. Space Complexity: O(1).

Problem-51 Median in an infinite series of integers

Solution: Median is the middle number in a sorted list of numbers (if we have an odd number of elements). If we have an even number of elements, the median is the average of two middle numbers in a sorted list of numbers. We can solve this problem with linked lists (with both sorted and unsorted linked lists).

First, let us try with an *unsorted* linked list. In an unsorted linked list, we can insert the element either at the head or at the tail. The disadvantage with this approach is that finding the median takes $O(n)$. Also, the insertion operation takes O(1).

Now, let us try with a *sorted* linked list. We can find the median in O(1) time if we keep track of the middle elements. Insertion to a particular location is also O(1) in any linked list. But, finding the right location to insert is not $O(logn)$ as in a sorted array, it is instead $O(n)$ because we can't perform binary search in a linked list even if it is sorted. So, using a sorted linked list isn't worth the effort as insertion is $O(n)$ and finding median is O(1), the same as the sorted array. In the sorted array the insertion is linear due to shifting, but here it's linear because we can't do a binary search in a linked list.

Note: For an efficient algorithm refer to the *Priority Queues and Heaps* chapter.

Problem-52 Given a linked list, how do you modify it such that all the even numbers appear before all the odd numbers in the modified linked list?

Solution:

```
    type ListNode struct { // defines a ListNode in a singly linked list
        data int              // the datum
        next *ListNode        // pointer to the next ListNode
    }
    // Function to separate even and odd nodes
    func segregateEvenOdds(head *ListNode) *ListNode {
        var evensHead, evenEnd, oddsHead, oddEnd *ListNode
        evensHead, evenEnd, oddsHead, oddsHead = nil, nil, nil, nil
        // ListNode to traverse the list.
        currNode := head
```

```
    for currNode != nil {
        val := currNode.data
        // If current data is even, add it to evens list
        if val%2 == 0 {
            if evensHead == nil {
                evensHead = currNode
                evenEnd = evensHead
            } else {
                evenEnd.next = currNode
                evenEnd = evenEnd.next
            }
        } else { // If current data is odd, add it to odds list
            if oddsHead == nil {
                oddsHead = currNode
                oddEnd = oddsHead
            } else {
                oddEnd.next = currNode
                oddEnd = oddEnd.next
            }
        }
        // Move head pointer one step in forward direction
        currNode = currNode.next
    }
    // If either odd list or even list is empty, no change is required as all elements are either even or odd
    if oddsHead == nil || evensHead == nil {
        return head
    }
    // Add odd list after even list
    evenEnd.next = oddsHead
    oddEnd.next = nil
    return evensHead
}
```

Problem-53 Given a list, List1 = $\{A_1, A_2, \ldots A_{n-1}, A_n\}$ with data, reorder it to $\{A_1, A_n, A_2, A_{n-1} \ldots\ldots\}$ without using any extra space.

Solution: Find the middle of the linked list. We can do it by *slow* and *fast* pointer approach. After finding the middle node, we reverse the first (or second) half, then we do a in place merge of the two halves of the linked list.

```
func reorderList(head *ListNode) {
    if head == nil || head.next == nil {
        return
    }
    slow, fast := head, head
    for fast != nil && fast.next != nil {
        slow, fast = slow.next, fast.next.next
    }
    var prev *ListNode
    for slow != nil {
        slow.next, prev, slow = prev, slow, slow.next
    }
    first := head
    for prev.next != nil {
        first.next, first = prev, first.next
        prev.next, prev = first, prev.next
    }
}
```

Problem-54 Given a singly linked list, group all even nodes (based on position) together followed by the odd nodes. Please note here we are talking about the node number and not the value in the nodes.

Solution:

```
func oddEvenList(head *ListNode) *ListNode {
    if head == nil {
        return nil
```

```
    } else if head.next == nil {
        return head
    }
    oddsHead := head
    evensHead := head.next
    for current, temp := head, head.next; temp != nil; current, temp = temp, temp.next {
        current.next = temp.next
    }
    oddsTail := oddsHead
    for ; oddsTail.next != nil; oddsTail = oddsTail.next {
    }
    oddsTail.next = evensHead
    return oddsHead
}
```

Time Complexity: O(n). Space Complexity: O(1).

Problem-32 Reverse the linked list in pairs. If you have a linked list that holds $1 \to 2 \to 3 \to 4 \to X$, then after the function has been called the linked list would hold $2 \to 1 \to 4 \to 3 \to X$.

Solution:

Recursive:

```
func reversePairs(head *ListNode) *ListNode {
    if head == nil || head.next == nil {
        return head
    }
    result := head.next
    head.next = swapPairs(head.next.next)
    result.next = head
    return result
}
```

Iterative:

```
func reversePairs(head *ListNode) *ListNode {
    if head == nil || head.next == nil {
        return head
    }
    result := head.next
    var previousNode *ListNode
    for head != nil && head.next != nil {
        nextNode := head.next
        head.next = nextNode.next
        nextNode.next = head
        if previousNode != nil {
            previousNode.next = nextNode
        }
        previousNode = head
        head = head.next
    }
    return result
}
```

Time Complexity: O(n). Space Complexity: O(1).

Problem-55 **Partition list**: Given a linked list and a value X, partition it such that all nodes less than X come before nodes greater than or equal to X. Notice that, you should preserve the original relative order of the nodes in each of the two partitions.

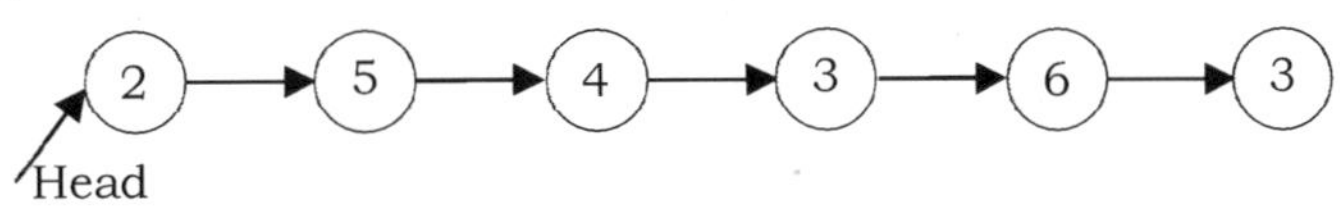

For example, the above linked list with X = 4 should return the following linked list.

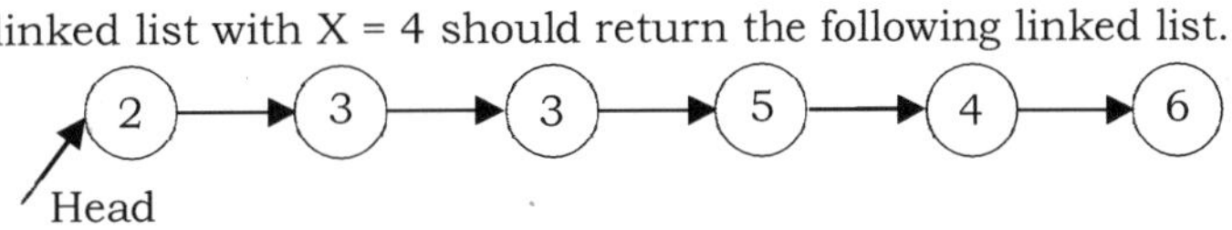

Solution: The problem wants us to rearrange the linked list elements, such that the elements lesser than value X, come before the elements greater or equal to X. This essentially means in this rearranged list, there would be a point in the linked list before which all the elements would be smaller than X and after which all the elements would be greater or equal to X. Let's call this point as the *pivot*. Careful observation tells us that if we break the rearranged list at the *pivot*, we will get two smaller linked lists, one with lesser elements and the other with elements greater or equal to X. In the solution, our main aim is to create these two linked lists and join them.

We can take two pointers lesser and greater to keep track of the two linked lists as described above. These two pointers could be used two create two separate lists and then these lists could be combined to form the desired rearranged list. We will traverse the original linked list as usual, and depending upon a node's value, we will append it into one of the partitions.

Algorithm:

1. Initialize two pointers lesser and greater with dummy linked list nodes.
2. Iterate the original linked list, using the head pointer. If the node's value pointed by head is lesser than X, the node should be part of the lesser list. So, we move it to lesser list. Else, the node should be part of greater list. So, we move it to greater list.
3. Once we are done with all the nodes in the original linked list, we would have two list lesser and greater. The original list nodes are either part of lesser list or greater list, depending on its value.
4. Now, these two lists lesser and greater can be combined to form the reformed list.

Since we traverse the original linked list from left to right, at no point would the order of nodes change relatively in the two lists. Another important thing to note here is that we show the original linked list intact in the above diagrams. However, in the implementation, we remove the nodes from the original linked list and attach them in the lesser or greater list. We don't utilize any additional space. We simply move the nodes from the original list around.

```
func partition(head *ListNode, X int) *ListNode {
    lesser, greater := &ListNode{}, &ListNode{}
    lesserHead, greaterHead := lesser, greater
    for head != nil {
        if head.data < X {
            lesser.next = head
            lesser = lesser.next
        } else {
            greater.next = head
            greater = greater.next
        }
        head = head.next
    }
    lesser.next, greater.next = nil, nil // cut the connection
    if greaterHead.next != nil {
        lesser.next = greaterHead.next
    }
    return lesserHead.next
}
```

Time complexity: O(n), where n is the number of nodes in the original linked list and we iterate the original list.
Space complexity: O(1), we have not utilized any extra space, the point to note is that we are reforming the original list, by moving the original nodes, we have not used any extra space as such.

Problem-56 Given two linked lists, each list node with one integer digit, add these two linked lists. The result should be stored in the third linked list. Also note that the head node contains the most significant digit of the number.

Solution: Since the integer addition starts from the least significant digit, we first need to visit the last node of both lists and add them up, create a new node to store the result, take care of the carry if any, and link the resulting node to the node which will be added to the second least significant node and continue.

First of all, we need to take into account the difference in the number of digits in the two numbers. So before starting recursion, we need to do some calculation and move the longer list pointer to the appropriate place so that we need the last node of both lists at the same time. The other thing we need to take care of is *carry*. If two digits add up to more than 10, we need to forward the *carry* to the next node and add it. If the most significant digit addition results in a *carry*, we need to create an extra node to store the *carry*.

The function below is actually a wrapper function which does all the housekeeping like calculating lengths of lists, calling recursive implementation, creating an extra node for the *carry* in the most significant digit, and adding any remaining nodes left in the longer list.

```
func addTwoNumbers(l1 *ListNode, l2 *ListNode) *ListNode {
    carry, result := 0, new(ListNode)
    for node := result; l1 != nil || l2 != nil || carry > 0; node = node.next {
        if l1 != nil {
            carry += l1.data
            l1 = l1.next
        }
        if l2 != nil {
            carry += l2.data
            l2 = l2.next
        }
        node.next = &ListNode{carry%10, nil}
        carry /= 10
    }
    return result.next
}
```

Time Complexity: O(max ($List1$ $length, List2$ $length$)).
Space Complexity: O(min ($List1$ $length, List2$ $length$)) for recursive stack.

Note: It can be solved using stacks as well.

Problem-57 Which sorting algorithm is easily adaptable to singly linked lists?

Solution: Simple Insertion sort is easily adaptable to singly linked lists. To insert an element, the linked list is traversed until the proper position is found, or until the end of the list is reached. It is inserted into the list by merely adjusting the pointers without shifting any elements, unlike in the array. This reduces the time required for insertion but not the time required for searching for the proper position.

```
func insertionSortList(head *ListNode) *ListNode {
    if head == nil || head.next == nil {
        return head
    }
    result := &ListNode{next: head}
    current := head.next
    head.next = nil
    for current != nil {
        pre := result
        target := result.next
        for target != nil && current.data > target.data {
            target = target.next
            pre = pre.next
        }
        temp := current
        current = current.next
        temp.next = target
        pre.next = temp
    }
    return result.next
}
```

Problem-58 Given two sorted linked lists, given an algorithm to return the common elements of them.

Solution: The easiest way to build up a list with common elements is by adding nodes at the beginning. The disadvantage is that the elements will appear in the list in the reverse order that they are added.

```
// Solution to give common elements in the reverse
func intersection(list1, list2 *ListNode) *ListNode {
    list := LinkedList{}
    for list1 != nil && list2 != nil {
        if list1.data == list2.data {
            list.insertAtBeginning(list1.data) // Copy common element.
            list1 = list1.next
            list2 = list2.next
        } else if list1.data.(int) > list2.data.(int) {
            list2 = list2.next
        } else { // list1.data < list2.data
            list1 = list1.next
```

```
        }
    }
    return list.head
}
```

Time complexity O(m + n), where m is the lengh of list1 and n is the length of list2. Space Complexity: O(1).

What if we want to get the common elements in the increasing order (or in the same order of their appearance)? i.e., What about adding nodes at the "tail end" of the list? Adding a node at the tail of a list most often involves locating the last node in the list, and then changing its .next field from nil to point to the new node, such as the tail variable in the following example of adding a "3" node to the end of the list {1, 2}...

This is just a special case of the general rule: to insert or delete a node inside a list, you need a pointer to the node just before that position, so you can change its .next field. Many list problems include the sub-problem of advancing a pointer to the node before the point of insertion or deletion. The one exception is if the operation falls on the first node in the list — in that case the head pointer itself must be changed.

Consider the problem of building up the list {1, 2, 3, 4, 5} by appending the nodes to the tail end. The difficulty is that the very first node must be added at the head pointer, but all the other nodes are inserted after the last node using a tail pointer. The simplest way to deal with both cases is to just have two separate cases in the code. Special case code first adds the head node {1}. Then there is a separate loop that uses a tail pointer to add all the other nodes. The tail pointer is kept pointing at the last node, and each new node is added at tail->next. The only "problem" with this solution is that writing separate special case code for the first node is a little unsatisfying. Nonetheless, this approach is a solid one for production code — it is simple and runs fast.

```
func intersection(list1, list2 *ListNode) *ListNode {
    headList := LinkedList{}
    tailList := LinkedList{}
    head, tail := headList.head, tailList.head
    for list1 != nil && list2 != nil {
        if list1.data == list2.data {
            if head == nil {
                headList.insertAtBeginning(list1.data)
                tailList = headList
            } else {
                tailList.insertAtBeginning(list1.data)
                tail = tail.next
            }
            list1 = list1.next
            list2 = list2.next
        } else if list1.data.(int) > list2.data.(int) {
            list2 = list2.next
        } else { // list1.data < list2.data
            list1 = list1.next
        }
    }
    return headList.head
}
```

There is a slightly unusual technique that can be used to shorten the code: The strategy here uses a temporary dummy node as the start of the result list. The trick is that with the dummy, every node appears to be added after the .next field of some other node. That way the code for the first node is the same as for the other nodes. The tail pointer plays the same role as in the previous example. The difference is that now it also handles the first node as well.

The pointer tail always points to the last node in the result list, so appending new nodes is easy. The dummy node gives tail something to point to initially when the result list is empty. This dummy node is efficient, since it is only temporary, and it is allocated in the stack. The loop proceeds, removing one node from either 'list1' or 'list2', and adding it to tail. When we are done, the result is in dummy.next.

```
// Solution uses the temporary dummy node to build up the result list
func intersection(list1, list2 *ListNode) *ListNode {
    dummy := &ListNode{}
    list := LinkedList{}
    list.head = dummy
    for list1 != nil && list2 != nil {
        if list1.data == list2.data {
            list.insertAtBeginning(list1.data)
```

```
            list1 = list1.next
            list2 = list2.next
        } else if list1.data.(int) > list2.data.(int) {
            list2 = list2.next
        } else { // list1.data < list2.data
            list1 = list1.next
        }
    }
    return list.head
}
```

Problem-59 Sort the linked list elements in O(*n*), where *n* is the number of elements in the linked list.

Solution: Refer *Sorting* chapter.

Problem-60 Give an algorithm to delete duplicate nodes from the sorted linked list. Ideally, the list should only be traversed once.

Solution: Since the list is sorted, we can proceed down the list and compare adjacent nodes. When adjacent nodes are the same, remove the second one. There's a tricky case where the node after the next node needs to be noted before the deletion.

```
func removeDuplicates(head *ListNode) *ListNode {
    current := head
    for current != nil {
        if current.next != nil && current.data == current.next.data {
            current.next = current.next.next
            continue
        }
        current = current.next
    }
    return head
}
```

Time Complexity: O(*n*). Space Complexity: O(1).

Problem-61 Give an algorithm that takes a list and divides up its nodes to make two smaller lists. The sublists should be made from alternating elements in the original list. So if the original list is {1, 2, 3, 4, 5}, then one sublist should be {1, 3, 5} and the other should be {2, 4}.

Solution: The simplest approach iterates over the given linked list and pull nodes off the list and alternately put them on lists 'a' and b'. The only strange part is that the nodes will be in the reverse order that they occurred in the source list.

```
func alternatingSplit(head *ListNode) (head1, head2 *ListNode) {
    var a *ListNode = nil // Split the nodes to these 'a' and 'b' lists
    var b *ListNode = nil
    current := head
    for current != nil {
        // Move a ListNode to 'a'
        newNode := current      // the front current node
        current = newNode.next // Advance the current pointer
        newNode.next = a       // Link the node with the head of list a
        a = newNode
        // Move a ListNode to 'b'
        if current != nil {
            newNode := current      // the front source node
            current = newNode.next // Advance the source pointer
            newNode.next = b       // Link the node with the head of list b
            b = newNode
        }
    }
    head1, head2 = a, b
    return head1, head2
}
```

Time Complexity: O(*n*). Space Complexity: O(1).

Problem-62 Given a pointer to head of a linked list, give an algorithm to repeatedly delete consecutive sequences of nodes that sum to 0 until there are no such sequences. **Input**: 1->2->-3->3->1 **Output**: 3->1

Solution: The basic idea of this problem is to record an accumulated sum from head to current position. If we define sum(i) = summation from index 0 to index i and we find sum(i) == sum(j) when i != j, then we can imply that the sum within index (i, j] is 0. So, we can use a map to record the first time this accumulated sum appears, and if we find the same accumulated sum, we discard all nodes between these two nodes. Although we may modify some discarded nodes' next pointer value, it has no impact on our answer.

```
func removeZeroSumSublists(head *ListNode) *ListNode {
    type SumNode struct {
        Node *ListNode
        Sum int
    }
    acc, sum, dummy := 0, make(map[int]SumNode), &ListNode{next: head}
    sum[0] = SumNode{dummy, 0}
    for curr := head; curr != nil; curr = curr.next {
        acc += curr.Val
        if p, ok := sum[acc]; ok {
            for node, subSum := p.Node.next, p.Sum; node != curr; node = node.next {
                subSum += node.Val
                delete(sum, subSum)
            }
            p.Node.next = curr.next
        } else {
            sum[acc] = SumNode{curr, acc}
        }
    }
    return dummy.next
}
```

Time Complexity: O(n). Space Complexity: O(n).

CHAPTER

STACKS

4

4.1 What is a Stack?

A stack is a simple data structure used for storing data (similar to Linked Lists). In a stack, the order in which the data arrives is important. A pile of plates in a cafeteria is a good example of a stack. The plates are added to the stack as they are cleaned and they are placed on the top. When a plate, is required it is taken from the top of the stack. The first plate placed on the stack is the last one to be used.

Definition: A *stack* is an ordered list in which insertion and deletion are done at one end, called *top*. The last element inserted is the first one to be deleted. Hence, it is called the Last in First out (LIFO) or First in Last out (FILO) list.

Special names are given to the two changes that can be made to a stack. When an element is inserted in a stack, the concept is called *push*, and when an element is removed from the stack, the concept is called *pop*. Trying to pop out an empty stack is called *underflow* and trying to push an element in a full stack is called *overflow*. Generally, we treat them as exceptions. As an example, consider the snapshots of the stack.

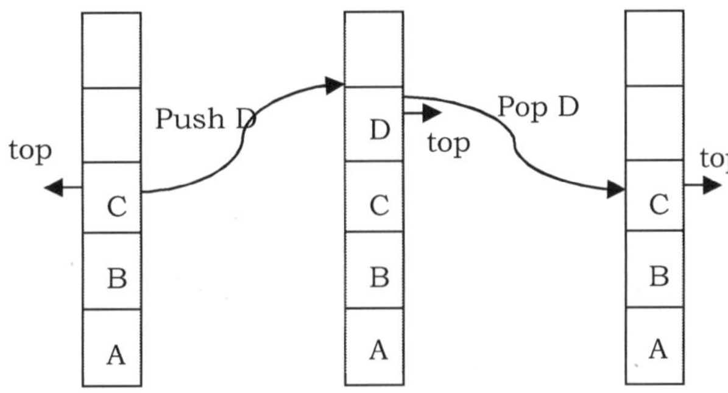

4.2 How Stacks are used

Consider a working day in the office. Let us assume a developer is working on a long-term project. The manager then gives the developer a new task which is more important. The developer puts the long-term project aside and begins work on the new task. The phone rings, and this is the highest priority as it must be answered immediately. The developer pushes the present task into the pending tray and answers the phone.

When the call is complete the task that was abandoned to answer the phone is retrieved from the pending tray and work progresses. To take another call, it may have to be handled in the same manner, but eventually the new task will be finished, and the developer can draw the long-term project from the pending tray and continue with that.

4.3 Stack ADT

The following operations make a stack an ADT. For simplicity, assume the data is an integer type.

Main stack operations

- func Push(data interface{}): Inserts *data* onto stack.
- func Pop() data interface{}: Removes and returns the last inserted element from the stack.

Auxiliary stack operations

- func Peek() int: Returns the last inserted element without removing it.

- func Size() int: Returns the number of elements stored in the stack.
- func IsEmpty() bool: Indicates whether any elements are stored in the stack or not.
- func IsFull() bool: Indicates whether the stack is full or not.

Exceptions

Attempting the execution of an operation may sometimes cause an error condition, called an exception. Exceptions are said to be "thrown" by an operation that cannot be executed. In the Stack ADT, operations pop and top cannot be performed if the stack is empty. Attempting the execution of pop (top) on an empty stack throws an exception. Trying to push an element in a full stack throws an exception.

4.4 Applications

Following are some of the applications in which stacks play an important role.

Direct applications

- Balancing of symbols
- Infix-to-postfix conversion
- Evaluation of postfix expression
- Implementing function calls (including recursion)
- Finding of spans (finding spans in stock markets, refer to *Problems* section)
- Page-visited history in a Web browser [Back Buttons]
- Undo sequence in a text editor
- Matching Tags in HTML and XML

Indirect applications

- Auxiliary data structure for other algorithms (Example: Tree traversal algorithms)
- Component of other data structures (Example: Simulating queues, refer *Queues* chapter)

4.5 Implementation

There are many ways of implementing stack ADT; below are the commonly used methods.

- Simple array-based implementation
- Dynamic array-based implementation
- Linked lists implementation

Simple Array Implementation

This implementation of stack ADT uses an array. In the array, we add elements from left to right and use a variable to keep track of the index of the top element.

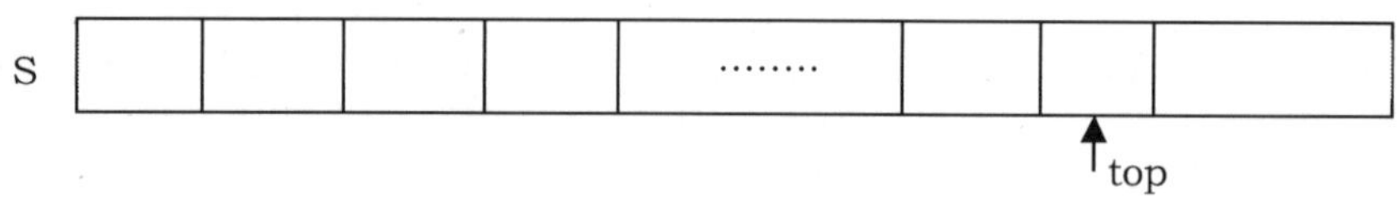

The array storing the stack elements may become full. A push operation will then throw a *full stack exception*. Similarly, if we try deleting an element from an empty stack it will throw *stack empty exception*.

```
package main
import (
    "errors"
    "fmt"
)
type Stack struct {
    top      int
    capacity uint
    array    []interface{}
}
// Returns an initialized stack
func (stack *Stack) Init(capacity uint) *Stack {
    stack.top = -1
    stack.capacity = capacity
    stack.array = make([]interface{}, capacity)
```

```
    return stack
}
// Returns a new stack
func NewStack(capacity uint) *Stack {
    return new(Stack).Init(capacity)
}
// Stack is full when top is equal to the last index
func (stack *Stack) IsFull() bool {
    return stack.top == int(stack.capacity)-1
}
// Stack is empty when top is equal to -1
func (stack *Stack) IsEmpty() bool {
    return stack.top == -1
}
// Returns the size of the size
func (stack *Stack) Size() uint {
    return uint(stack.top + 1)
}
func (stack *Stack) Push(data interface{}) error {
    if stack.IsFull() {
        return errors.New("stack is full")
    }
    stack.top++
    stack.array[stack.top] = data
    return nil
}
func (stack *Stack) Pop() (interface{}, error) {
    if stack.IsEmpty() {
        return nil, errors.New("stack is empty")
    }
    temp := stack.array[stack.top]
    stack.top--
    return temp, nil
}
func (stack *Stack) Peek() (interface{}, error) {
    if stack.IsEmpty() {
        return nil, errors.New("stack is empty")
    }
    temp := stack.array[stack.top]
    return temp, nil
}
// Drain removes all elements that are currently in the stack.
func (stack *Stack) Drain() {
    stack.array = nil
    stack.top = -1
}
func main() {
    stack := NewStack(100)
    stack.Push(10)
    fmt.Println("Pushed to stack : 10")
    stack.Push(20)
    fmt.Println("Pushed to stack : 20")
    stack.Push(30)
    fmt.Println("Pushed to stack : 30")
    data, _ := stack.Peek()
    fmt.Println("Top element : ", data)
    data, _ = stack.Pop()
    fmt.Println("Popped from stack : ", data)
    stack.Drain()
    fmt.Println("Stack size: ", stack.Size()) // prints 0 as stack size
```

```
}
```

Performance & Limitations

Performance

Let n be the number of elements in the stack. The complexities of stack operations with this representation can be given as:

Space complexity (for n push operations)	$O(n)$
Time complexity of Push()	O(1)
Time complexity of Pop()	O(1)
Time complexity of Size()	O(1)
Time complexity of IsEmpty()	O(1)
Time complexity of IsFull()	O(1)
Time complexity of Peek()	O(1)
Time complexity of Drain()	O(1)

Limitations

The maximum size of the stack must first be defined and it cannot be changed. Trying to push a new element into a full stack causes an implementation-specific exception.

Dynamic Array Implementation

First, let's consider how we implemented a simple array-based stack. We took one index variable *top* which points to the index of the most recently inserted element in the stack. To insert (or push) an element, we increment *top* index and then place the new element at that index.

Similarly, to delete (or pop) an element we take the element at *top* index and then decrement the *top* index. We represent an empty queue with *top* value equal to -1. The issue that still needs to be resolved is what we do when all the slots in the fixed size array stack are occupied?

First try: What if we increment the size of the array by 1 every time the stack is full?

- push(): increase size of S[] by 1
- pop(): decrease size of S[] by 1

Issues with this approach?

This way of incrementing the array size is too expensive. Let us see the reason for this. For example, at $n = 1$, to push an element create a new array of size 2 and copy all the old array elements to the new array, and at the end add the new element. At $n = 2$, to push an element create a new array of size 3 and copy all the old array elements to the new array, and at the end add the new element.

Similarly, at $n = n-1$, if we want to push an element create a new array of size n and copy all the old array elements to the new array and at the end add the new element. After n push operations the total time $T(n)$ (number of copy operations) is proportional to $1 + 2 + \ldots + n \approx O(n^2)$.

Alternative Approach: Repeated Doubling

Let us improve the complexity by using the array *doubling* technique. If the array is full, create a new array of twice the size, and copy the items. With this approach, pushing n items takes time proportional to n (not n^2).

For simplicity, let us assume that initially we started with $n = 1$ and moved up to $n = 32$. That means, we do the doubling at $1, 2, 4, 8, 16$. The other way of analyzing the same approach is: at $n = 1$, if we want to add (push) an element, double the current size of the array and copy all the elements of the old array to the new array.

At $n = 1$, we do 1 copy operation, at $n = 2$, we do 2 copy operations, and at $n = 4$, we do 4 copy operations and so on. By the time we reach $n = 32$, the total number of copy operations is $1 + 2 + 4 + 8 + 16 = 31$ which is approximately equal to $2n$ value (32). If we observe carefully, we are doing the doubling operation $logn$ times. Now, let us generalize the discussion. For n push operations we double the array size $logn$ times. That means, we will have $logn$ terms in the expression below. The total time $T(n)$ of a series of n push operations is proportional to

$$\begin{aligned}1 + 2 + 4 + 8 \ldots + \frac{n}{4} + \frac{n}{2} + n &= n + \frac{n}{2} + \frac{n}{4} + \frac{n}{8} \ldots + 4 + 2 + 1 \\ &= n\left(1 + \frac{1}{2} + \frac{1}{4} + \frac{1}{8} \ldots + \frac{4}{n} + \frac{2}{n} + \frac{1}{n}\right) \\ &= n(2) \approx 2n = O(n)\end{aligned}$$

$T(n)$ is $O(n)$ and the amortized time of a push operation is $O(1)$.

```
package main
import (
    "errors"
    "fmt"
)
type Stack struct {
    top      int
    capacity uint
    array    []interface{}
}
// Returns an initialized stack
func (stack *Stack) Init(capacity uint) *Stack {
    stack.top = -1
    stack.capacity = capacity
    stack.array = make([]interface{}, capacity)
    return stack
}
// Returns an new stack
func NewStack(capacity uint) *Stack {
    return new(Stack).Init(capacity)
}
// Returns the size of the size
func (stack *Stack) Size() uint {
    return uint(stack.top + 1)
}
// Stack is full when top is equal to the last index
func (stack *Stack) IsFull() bool {
    return stack.top == int(stack.capacity)-1
}
// Stack is empty when top is equal to -1
func (stack *Stack) IsEmpty() bool {
    return stack.top == -1
}
func (stack *Stack) Resize() {
    if stack.IsFull() {
        stack.capacity *= 2
    } else {
        stack.capacity /= 2
    }
    target := make([]interface{}, stack.capacity)
    copy(target, stack.array[:stack.top+1])
    stack.array = target
}
func (stack *Stack) Push(data interface{}) error {
    if stack.IsFull() {
        stack.Resize()
    }
    stack.top++
    stack.array[stack.top] = data
    return nil
}
func (stack *Stack) Pop() (interface{}, error) {
    if stack.IsEmpty() {
        return nil, errors.New("stack is empty")
    }
    temp := stack.array[stack.top]
    stack.top--
    if stack.Size() < stack.capacity/2 {
        stack.Resize()
```

```
	}
	return temp, nil
}
func (stack *Stack) Peek() (interface{}, error) {
	if stack.IsEmpty() {
		return nil, errors.New("stack is empty")
	}
	temp := stack.array[stack.top]
	return temp, nil
}
// Drain removes all elements that are currently in the stack.
func (stack *Stack) Drain() {
	stack.array = nil
	stack.top = -1
}
func main() {
	stack := NewStack(1)
	stack.Push(10)
	fmt.Println("Pushed to stack : 10")
	stack.Push(20)
	fmt.Println("Pushed to stack : 20")
	stack.Push(30)
	fmt.Println("Pushed to stack : 30")
	fmt.Println("Stack size: ", stack.Size())
	data, _ := stack.Peek()
	fmt.Println("Top element : ", data)
	data, _ = stack.Pop()
	data, _ = stack.Pop()
	data, _ = stack.Pop()
	fmt.Println("Popped from stack : ", data)
	fmt.Println("Stack size: ", stack.Size())
	stack.Drain()
	fmt.Println("Stack size: ", stack.Size())
}
```

Performance

Let n be the number of elements in the stack. The complexities for operations with this representation can be given as:

Space complexity (for n push operations)	$O(n)$
Time complexity of Push()	O(1) (on average)
Time complexity of Pop()	O(1)
Time complexity of Size()	O(1)
Time complexity of IsEmpty()	O(1)
Time complexity of IsFull()	O(1)
Time complexity of Peek()	O(1)
Time complexity of Drain()	O(1)

Note: Too many doublings may cause memory overflow exception.

Linked List Implementation

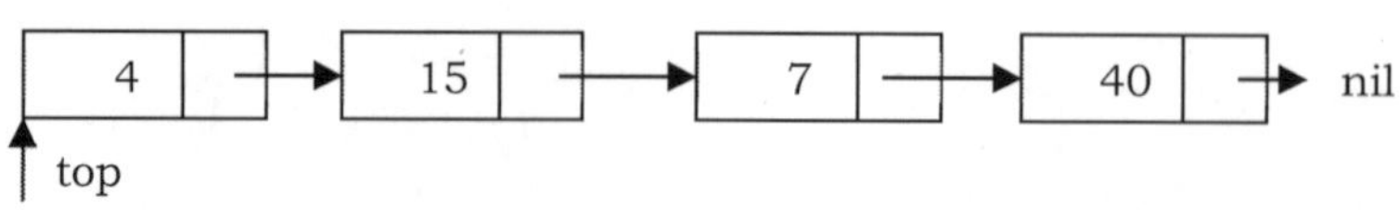

The other way of implementing stacks is by using Linked lists. Push operation is implemented by inserting element at the beginning of the list. Pop operation is implemented by deleting the node from the beginning (the header/top node).

```
package main
import "fmt"
```

```
type Stack struct {
    top  *ListNode
    size int
}
type ListNode struct {
    data interface{} // All types satisfy the empty interface, so we can store anything here.
    next *ListNode
}
// Return the stack's length
func (s *Stack) length() int {
    return s.size
}
// Return true if size of the stack is zero otherwise, false
func (s *Stack) isEmpty() bool{
    return s.size == 0
}
// Return false as it is a linked list implementation.
func (s *Stack) isFull() bool{
    return false
}
// push a new element onto the stack
func (s *Stack) push(data interface{}) {
    s.top = &ListNode{data, s.top}
    s.size++
}
// Remove the top element from the stack and return it's data. If the stack is empty, return nil
func (s *Stack) pop() (data interface{}) {
    if s.size > 0 {
        data, s.top = s.top.data, s.top.next
        s.size--
        return
    }
    return nil
}
// Return the top element's data. If the stack is empty, return nil
func (s *Stack) peek() (data interface{}) {
    if s.size > 0 {
        data = s.top.data
        return
    }
    return nil
}
func main() {
    stack := new(Stack)
    stack.push("Go")
    fmt.Println(stack.peek().(string))
    stack.push("Data")
    stack.push("Algorithms")
    fmt.Println(stack.peek().(string))
    for stack.length() > 0 {
        // We have to do a type assertion because we get back a variable of type
        // interface{} while the underlying type is a string.
        fmt.Printf("%s ", stack.pop().(string))
    }
    fmt.Println()
}
```

Performance

Let n be the number of elements in the stack. The complexities for operations with this representation can be given as:

Space complexity (for n push operations)	$O(n)$
Time complexity of createStack()	O(1)
Time complexity of push()	O(1) (Average)
Time complexity of pop()	O(1)
Time complexity of peek()	O(1)
Time complexity of isEmpty()	O(1)
Time complexity of isFull()	O(1)
Time complexity of deleteStack()	$O(n)$

4.6 Comparison of Implementations

Comparing Incremental Strategy and Doubling Strategy

We compare the incremental strategy and doubling strategy by analyzing the total time $T(n)$ needed to perform a series of n push operations. We start with an empty stack represented by an array of size 1. We call *amortized* time of a push operation is the average time taken by a push over the series of operations, that is, $\frac{T(n)}{n}$.

Incremental Strategy

The amortized time (average time per operation) of a push operation is $O(n)$ $[O(n^2)/n]$.

Doubling Strategy

In this method, the amortized time of a push operation is O(1) $[O(n)/n]$.

Note: For analysis, refer to the *Implementation* section.

Comparing Array Implementation and Linked List Implementation

Array Implementation

- Operations take constant time.
- Expensive doubling operation every once in a while.
- Any sequence of n operations (starting from empty stack) – "*amortized*" bound takes time proportional to n.

Linked List Implementation

- Grows and shrinks gracefully.
- Every operation takes constant time O(1).
- Every operation uses extra space and time to deal with references.

4.7 Stacks: Problems & Solutions

Problem-1 Discuss how stacks can be used for checking balancing of symbols/parentheses.

Solution: Stacks can be used to check whether the given expression has balanced symbols. This algorithm is very useful in compilers. Each time the parser reads one character at a time. If the character is an opening delimiter such as (, {, or [- then it is written to the stack. When a closing delimiter is encountered like), }, or]- the stack is popped. The opening and closing delimiters are then compared. If they match, the parsing of the string continues. If they do not match, the parser indicates that there is an error on the line. A linear-time $O(n)$ algorithm based on stack can be given as:

Algorithm:

a) Create a stack.
b) while (end of input is not reached) {
    1) If the character read is not a symbol to be balanced, ignore it.
    2) If the character is an opening symbol like (, [, {, push it onto the stack
    3) If it is a closing symbol like),],}, then if the stack is empty report an error. Otherwise pop the stack.
    4) If the symbol popped is not the corresponding opening symbol, report an error.
  }
c) At end of input, if the stack is not empty report an error

Examples:

Example	Valid?	Description
(A+B)+(C-D)	Yes	The expression has a balanced symbol

((A+B)+(C-D)	No	One closing brace is missing
((A+B)+[C-D])	Yes	Opening and immediate closing braces correspond
((A+B)+[C-D]}	No	The last closing brace does not correspond with the first opening parenthesis

For tracing the algorithm let us assume that the input is: () (() [()])

Input Symbol, A[i]	Operation	Stack	Output
(	Push (	(	
)	Pop (Test if (and A[i] match? YES		
(	Push (	(	
(	Push (	((	
)	Pop (Test if (and A[i] match? YES	(	
[	Push [	([	
(	Push (	([(	
)	Pop (Test if(and A[i] match? YES	([	
]	Pop [Test if [and A[i] match? YES	(	
)	Pop (Test if(and A[i] match? YES		
	Test if stack is Empty? YES		TRUE

```
type pair struct {
    open  rune
    close rune
}
var pairs = []pair{
    {'(', ')'},
    {'[', ']'},
    {'{', '}'},
}
func isValid(s string) bool {
    stack := NewStack(1)
    for _, r := range s {
        for _, p := range pairs {
            temp, _ := stack.Peek()
            if r == p.open {
                stack.Push(r)
                break
            } else if r == p.close && stack.IsEmpty() {
                return false
            } else if r == p.close && temp == p.open {
                stack.Pop()
                break
            } else if r == p.close && temp != p.open {
                return false
            }
        }
    }
    return stack.IsEmpty()
}
```

Time Complexity: O(n). Since we are scanning the input only once. Space Complexity: O(n) [for stack].

Problem-2 Discuss infix to postfix conversion algorithm using stack.

Solution: Before discussing the algorithm, first let us see the definitions of infix, prefix and postfix expressions.

Infix: An infix expression is a single letter, or an operator, proceeded by one infix string and followed by another Infix string.

A
A+B
(A+B)+ (C-D)

Prefix: A prefix expression is a single letter, or an operator, followed by two prefix strings. Every prefix string longer than a single variable contains an operator, first operand and second operand.

A
+AB
++AB-CD

Postfix: A postfix expression (also called Reverse Polish Notation) is a single letter or an operator, preceded by two postfix strings. Every postfix string longer than a single variable contains first and second operands followed by an operator.

A
AB+
AB+CD-+

Prefix and postfix notions are methods of writing mathematical expressions without parenthesis. Time to evaluate a postfix and prefix expression is $O(n)$, where n is the number of elements in the array.

Infix	Prefix	Postfix
A+B	+AB	AB+
A+B-C	-+ABC	AB+C-
(A+B)*C-D	-*+ABCD	AB+C*D-

Now, let us focus on the algorithm. In infix expressions, the operator precedence is implicit unless we use parentheses. Therefore, for the infix to postfix conversion algorithm we have to define the operator precedence (or priority) inside the algorithm.

The table shows the precedence and their associativity (order of evaluation) among operators.

Token	Operator	Precedence	Associativity
( ) [ ] → .	function call array element struct or union member	17	left-to-right
-- ++	increment, decrement	16	left-to-right
-- ++ ! - - + & * sizeof	decrement, increment logical not one's complement unary minus or plus address or indirection size (in bytes)	15	right-to-left
(type)	type cast	14	right-to-left
* / %	multiplicative	13	Left-to-right
+ -	binary add or subtract	12	left-to-right
<< >>	shift	11	left-to-right
> >= < <=	relational	10	left-to-right
== !=	equality	9	left-to-right
&	bitwise and	8	left-to-right
^	bitwise exclusive or	7	left-to-right
|	bitwise or	6	left-to-right
&&	logical and	5	left-to-right
||	logical or	4	left-to-right
?:	conditional	3	right-to-left
= += -= /= *= %= <<= >>= &= ^=	assignment	2	right-to-left
,	comma	1	left-to-right

Important Properties

- Let us consider the infix expression 2 + 3 * 4 and its postfix equivalent 2 3 4 * +. Notice that between infix and postfix the order of the numbers (or operands) is unchanged. It is 2 3 4 in both cases. But the order of the operators * and + is affected in the two expressions.

- Only one stack is enough to convert an infix expression to postfix expression. The stack that we use in the algorithm will be used to change the order of operators from infix to postfix. The stack we use will only contain operators and the open parentheses symbol '('.
  Postfix expressions do not contain parentheses. We shall not output the parentheses in the postfix output.

Algorithm:

```
a)  Create a stack
b)  for each character t in the input stream{
        if(t is an operand)
                output t
        else if(t is a right parenthesis){
                Pop and output tokens until a left parenthesis is popped (but not output)
        }
        else // t is an operator or left parenthesis{
                pop and output tokens until one of lower priority than t is encountered or a left parenthesis
                is encountered or the stack is empty
                Push t
        }
    }
c)  pop and output tokens until the stack is empty
```

For better understanding let us trace out an example: A * B- (C + D) + E

Input Character	Operation on Stack	Stack	Postfix Expression
A		Empty	A
*	Push	*	A
B		*	AB
-	Check and Push	-	AB*
(	Push	-(	AB*
C		-(	AB*C
+	Check and Push	-(+	AB*C
D			AB*CD
)	Pop and append to postfix till '('	-	AB*CD+
+	Check and Push	+	AB*CD+-
E		+	AB*CD+-E
End of input	Pop till empty		AB*CD+-E+

```
// Refer stack implementation from previous section
func IsOperator(c uint8) bool {
    return strings.ContainsAny(string(c), "+ & - & * & /")
}
func IsOperand(c uint8) bool {
    return c >= '0' && c <= '9'
}
func GetOperatorWeight(op string) int {
    switch op {
    case "+", "-":
        return 1
    case "*", "/":
        return 2
    }
    return -1
}
func HasHigherPrecedence(op1 string, op2 string) bool {
    op1Weight := GetOperatorWeight(op1)
    op2Weight := GetOperatorWeight(op2)
    return op1Weight >= op2Weight
}
func ToPostfix(s string) string {
    stack := NewStack(1)
    postfix := ""
    length := len(s)
```

```
        for i := 0; i < length; i++ {
            char := string(s[i])
            // Skip whitespaces
            if char == " " {
                continue
            }
            if char == "(" {
                stack.Push(char)
            } else if char == ")" {
                for !stack.IsEmpty() {
                    temp, _ := stack.Peek()
                    str := temp.(string)
                    if str == "(" {
                        break
                    }
                    postfix += " " + str
                    stack.Pop()
                }
                stack.Pop()
            } else if !IsOperator(s[i]) {
                // If character is not an operator
                // Keep in mind it's just an operand
                j := i
                number := ""
                for ; j < length && IsOperand(s[j]); j++ {
                    number = number + string(s[j])
                }
                postfix += " " + number
                i = j - 1
            } else {
                // If character is operator, pop two elements from stack,
                // perform operation and push the result back.
                for !stack.IsEmpty() {
                    temp, _ := stack.Peek()
                    top := temp.(string)
                    if top == "(" || !HasHigherPrecedence(top, char) {
                        break
                    }
                    postfix += " " + top
                    stack.Pop()
                }
                stack.Push(char)
            }
        }
        for !stack.IsEmpty() {
            temp, _ := stack.Peek()
            str := temp.(string)
            postfix += " " + str
        }
        return strings.TrimSpace(postfix)
    }
    func main() {
        fmt.Println(ToPostfix("(1 + 1)"))
        fmt.Println(ToPostfix(" ((2-1) + 2) "))
        fmt.Println(ToPostfix("((1+(4+5+2)-3)+(6+8))"))
    }
```

Problem-3 Discuss postfix evaluation using stacks?

Solution:

Algorithm:

1. Scan the Postfix string from left to right.
2. Initialize an empty stack.

3 Repeat steps 4 and 5 till all the characters are scanned.
4 If the scanned character is an operand, push it onto the stack.
5 If the scanned character is an operator, and if the operator is a unary operator, then pop an element from the stack. If the operator is a binary operator, then pop two elements from the stack. After popping the elements, apply the operator to those popped elements. Let the result of this operation be retVal onto the stack.
6 After all characters are scanned, we will have only one element in the stack.
7 Return top of the stack as result.

Example: Let us see how the above-mentioned algorithm works using an example. Assume that the postfix string is 123*+5-.

Initially the stack is empty. Now, the first three characters scanned are 1, 2 and 3, which are operands. They will be pushed into the stack in that order.

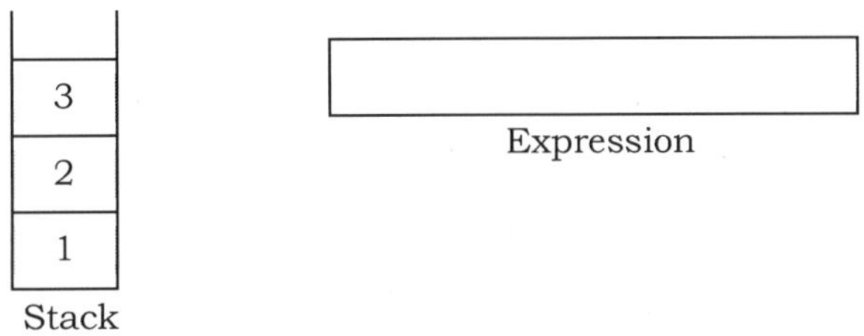

The next character scanned is "*", which is an operator. Thus, we pop the top two elements from the stack and perform the "*" operation with the two operands. The second operand will be the first element that is popped.

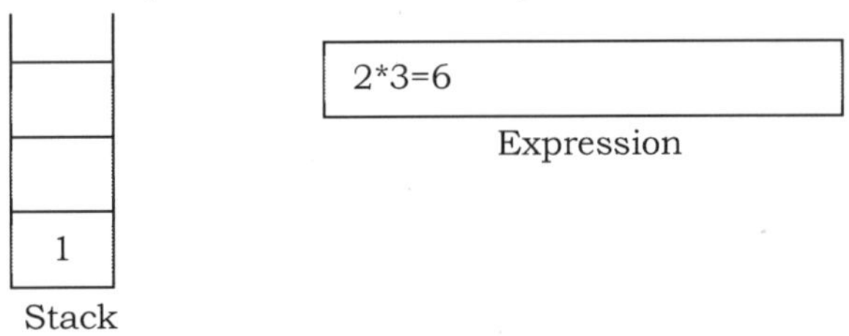

The value of the expression (2*3) that has been evaluated (6) is pushed into the stack.

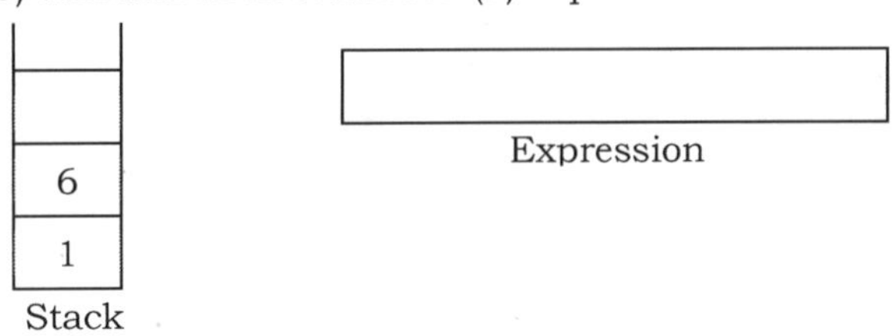

The next character scanned is "+", which is an operator. Thus, we pop the top two elements from the stack and perform the "+" operation with the two operands. The second operand will be the first element that is popped.

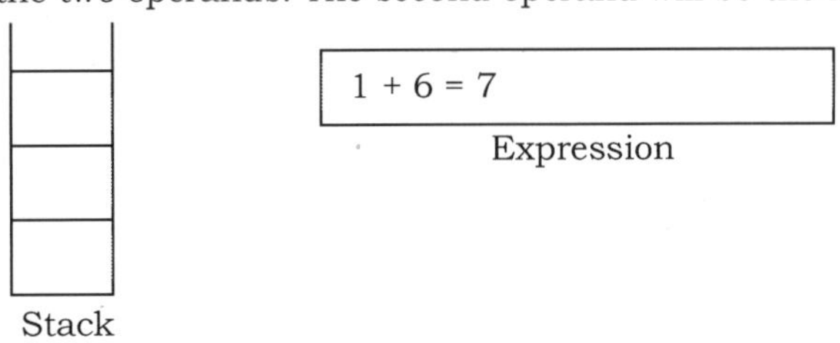

The value of the expression (1+6) that has been evaluated (7) is pushed into the stack.

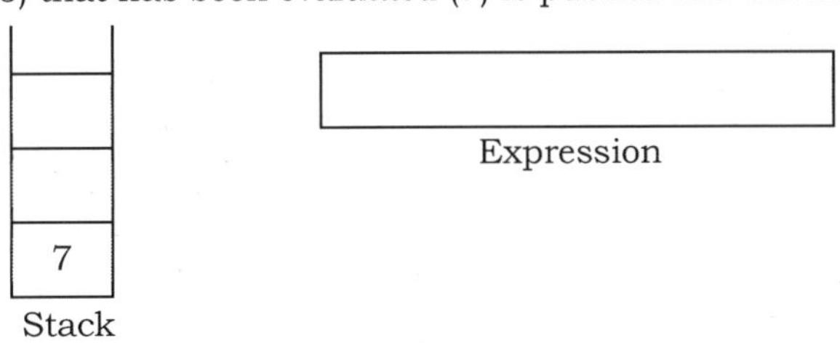

The next character scanned is "5", which is added to the stack.

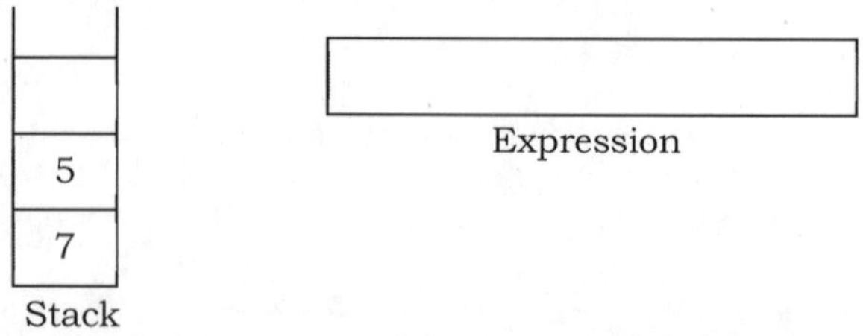

The next character scanned is "-", which is an operator. Thus, we pop the top two elements from the stack and perform the "-" operation with the two operands. The second operand will be the first element that is popped.

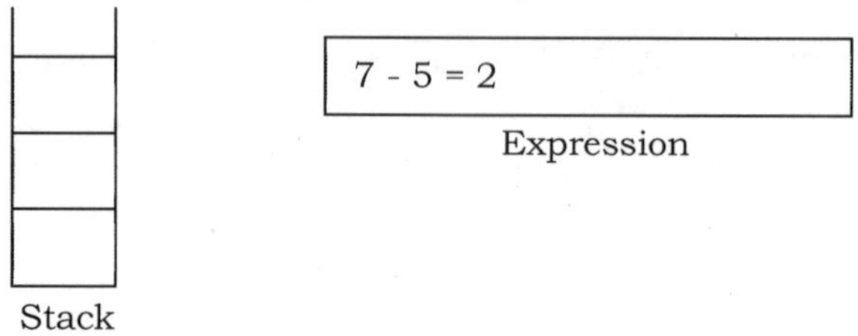

The value of the expression(7-5) that has been evaluated(23) is pushed into the stack.

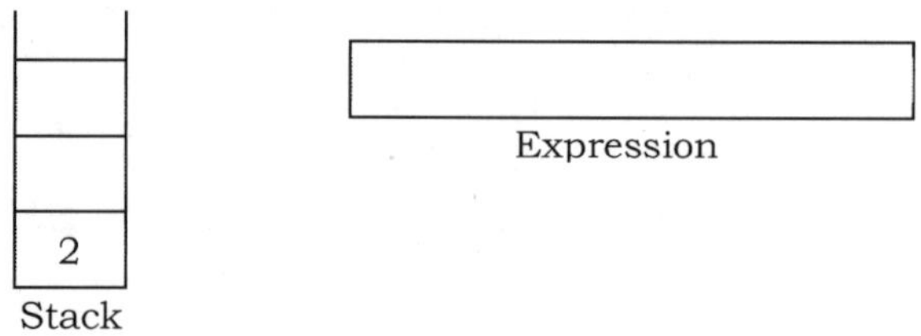

Now, since all the characters are scanned, the remaining element in the stack (there will be only one element in the stack) will be returned. End result:

- Postfix String : 123*+5-
- Result : 2

```
// Refer stack implementation from previous section
func isDigit(d uint8) bool {
    return (d >= 48 && d <= 57)
}
func calculate(s string) int {
    bs := 1             // bracket sign
    ls := 1             // local sign
    stack := NewStack(1) // we store sign on stack
    r := 0
    op := 0
    for i := 0; i < len(s); i++ {
        if s[i] == ' ' {
            continue
        }
        if s[i] == '(' {
            stack.Push(bs) // store bracket sign on stack
            bs = bs * ls
            ls = 1
        } else if s[i] == ')' {
            temp, _ := stack.Pop() // take last bracket sign
            bs = temp.(int)
            ls = 1
        } else if s[i] == '-' || s[i] == '+' {
            if s[i] == '-' {
                ls = -1
            }
        } else {
            if isDigit(s[i]) {
                end := i
                // extract here full number
```

```
                for d := i + 1; d < len(s); d++ {
                    if isDigit(s[d]) {
                        end = d
                    } else {
                        break
                    }
                }
                op, _ = strconv.Atoi(s[i : end+1])
                r += ls * bs * op
                i = end
                ls = 1
            }
        }
    }
    return r
}
func main() {
    fmt.Println(calculate("1 + 1"))
    fmt.Println(calculate(" 2-1 + 2 "))
    fmt.Println(calculate("(1+(4+5+2)-3)+(6+8)"))
}
```

Problem-4 Can we evaluate the infix expression with stacks in one pass?

Solution: Using 2 stacks we can evaluate an infix expression in 1 pass without converting to postfix.

Algorithm:

1) Create an empty operator stack
2) Create an empty operand stack
3) For each token in the input string
    a. Get the next token in the infix string
    b. If next token is an operand, place it on the operand stack
    c. If next token is an operator
        i. Evaluate the operator (next op)
4) While operator stack is not empty, pop operator and operands (left and right), evaluate left operator right and push result onto operand stack
5) Pop result from operator stack

Problem-5 How to design a stack such that getMinimum( ) should be O(1)?

Solution: Take an auxiliary stack that maintains the minimum of all values in the stack. Also, assume that each element of the stack is less than its below elements. For simplicity let us call the auxiliary stack *min stack*.

When we *pop* the main stack, *pop* the min stack too. When we push the main stack, push either the new element or the current minimum, whichever is lower. At any point, if we want to get the minimum, then we just need to return the top element from the min stack. Let us take an example and trace it out. Initially let us assume that we have pushed 2, 6, 4, 1 and 5. Based on the above-mentioned algorithm the *min stack* will look like:

Main stack	Min stack
5 → top	1 → top
1	1
4	2
6	2
2	2

After popping twice we get:

Main stack	Min stack
4 --→ top	2 → top
6	2
2	2

Based on the discussion above, now let us code the push, pop and getMinimum() operations.

```
// Refer basic stack implementation from previous section
type MinStack struct {
    elementStack  []int
    minimumsStack []int
}
```

```
func min(i, j int) int {
    if i < j {
        return i
    }
    return j
}
// initialize your data structure here.
func NewMinStack() MinStack {
    return MinStack{}
}
func (stack *MinStack) Push(data int) {
    stack.elementStack = append(stack.elementStack, data)
    if len(stack.minimumsStack) == 0 {
        stack.minimumsStack = append(stack.minimumsStack, data)
    } else {
        minimum := min(stack.minimumsStack[len(stack.minimumsStack)-1], data)
        stack.minimumsStack = append(stack.minimumsStack, minimum)
    }
}
func (stack *MinStack) Pop() int {
    if len(stack.elementStack) > 0 {
        popped := stack.elementStack[len(stack.elementStack)-1]
        stack.elementStack = stack.elementStack[:len(stack.elementStack)-1]
        stack.minimumsStack = stack.minimumsStack[:len(stack.minimumsStack)-1]
        return popped
    } else {
        return math.MaxInt32
    }
}
func (stack *MinStack) Peek() int {
    if len(stack.elementStack) > 0 {
        return stack.elementStack[len(stack.elementStack)-1]
    } else {
        return 0
    }
}
func (stack *MinStack) Size() int {
    return len(stack.elementStack)
}
func (stack *MinStack) GetMin() int {
    if len(stack.minimumsStack) > 0 {
        return stack.minimumsStack[len(stack.minimumsStack)-1]
    } else {
        return 0
    }
}
func (stack *MinStack) IsEmpty() bool {
    return len(stack.elementStack) == 0
}
func (stack *MinStack) Clear() {
    stack.elementStack = nil
    stack.minimumsStack = nil
}
func main() {
    minimumsStack := NewMinStack()
    minimumsStack.Push(-1)
    minimumsStack.Push(2)
    minimumsStack.Push(0)
    minimumsStack.Push(-4)
    // Stack Size() test
```

```
        if minimumsStack.Size() != 4 {
            fmt.Println("Test failed: Expected stack size = 4 from [-1, 2, 0, -4]")
        } else { //Just for printing
            fmt.Println("Test passed: Expected stack size = 4 from [-1, 2, 0, -4]")
        }
        // Stack GetMin() test
        if minimumsStack.GetMin() != -4 {
            fmt.Println("Test failed: Expected get minimum = -4 from [-1, 2, 0, -4]")
        } else { //Just for printing
            fmt.Println("Test passed: Expected get minimum = -4 from [-1, 2, 0, -4]")
        }
        // Stack Peek() test
        if minimumsStack.Peek() != -4 {
            fmt.Println("Test failed: Expected top of stack = -4 from [-1, 2, 0, -4]")
        } else { //Just for printing
            fmt.Println("Test passed: Expected top of stack = -4 from [-1, 2, 0, -4]")
        }
        // Pop() test
        minimumsStack.Pop() // [-1, 2, 0]
        if minimumsStack.Peek() != 0 {
            fmt.Println("Test failed: After pop, Expected top of stack = 0 from [-1, 2, 0]")
        } else { //Just for printing
            fmt.Println("Test passed: After pop, Expected top of stack = 0 from [-1, 2, 0]")
        }
        // Stack GetMin() test
        if minimumsStack.GetMin() != -1 {
            fmt.Println("Test failed: Expected get minimum = -1 from [-1, 2, 0]")
        } else { //Just for printing
            fmt.Println("Test passed: Expected get minimum = -1 from [-1, 2, 0]")
        }
        // Clear() and isEmpty() test
        minimumsStack.Clear()
        if minimumsStack.IsEmpty() != true {
            fmt.Println("Test failed: After Clear(), Stack is expected to be empty.")
        } else { //Just for printing
            fmt.Println("Test passed: After Clear(), Stack is expected to be empty.")
        }
    }
```

Time complexity: O(1).
Space complexity: O(n) [for Min stack]. This algorithm has much better space usage if we rarely get a "new minimum or equal".

Problem-6 For Problem-5 is it possible to improve the space complexity?

Solution: Yes. The main problem of the previous approach is, for each push operation we are pushing the element on to min stack also (either the new element or existing minimum element). That means, we are pushing the duplicate minimum elements on to the stack.

Now, let us change the algorithm to improve the space complexity. We still have the min stack, but we only pop from it when the value we pop from the main stack is equal to the one on the min stack. We only *push* to the min stack when the value being pushed onto the main stack is less than *or equal* to the current min value. In this modified algorithm also, if we want to get the minimum then we just need to return the top element from the min stack. For example, taking the original version and pushing 1 again, we'd get:

Main stack	Min stack
1 → top	
5	
1	
4	1 → top
6	1
2	2

Popping from the above pops from both stacks because 1 == 1, leaving:

Main stack	Min stack
5 → top	
1	
4	
6	1 → top
2	2

Popping again *only* pops from the main stack, because 5 > 1:

Main stack	Min stack
1 → top	
4	
6	1 → top
2	2

Popping again pops both stacks because 1 == 1:

Main stack	Min stack
4 → top	
6	
2	2 → top

Note: The difference is only in push & pop operations.

```
// No change in other functions
func (stack *MinStack) Push(data int) {
    stack.elementStack = append(stack.elementStack, data)
    if len(stack.minimumsStack) == 0 || stack.Peek() >= data {
        stack.minimumsStack = append(stack.minimumsStack, data)
    }
}
func (stack *MinStack) Pop() int {
    if len(stack.elementStack) > 0 {
        popped := stack.elementStack[len(stack.elementStack)-1]
        stack.elementStack = stack.elementStack[:len(stack.elementStack)-1]
        if stack.Peek() == popped {
            stack.minimumsStack = stack.minimumsStack[:len(stack.minimumsStack)-1]
        }
        return popped
    } else {
        return math.MinInt32
    }
}
```

Time complexity: O(1).
Space complexity: O(n) [for Min stack]. But this algorithm has much better space usage if we rarely get a "new minimum or equal".

Problem-7 For a given array with n symbols how many stack permutations are possible?

Solution: The number of stack permutations with n symbols is represented by Catalan number and we will discuss this in the *Dynamic Programming* chapter.

Problem-8 Given an array of characters formed with a's and b's. The string is marked with special character X which represents the middle of the list (for example: ababa...ababXbabab.....baaa). Check whether the string is palindrome.

Solution: A simple solution would be to reverse the string and compare if the original string is equal to the reversed string or not. If they are found to be equal, we can say that the given string is a palindrome. This solution, though simple and concise, is not in-place. Also, the comparison function might end up iterating all the way till end of the string. This is linear on paper but we still can do better.

```
func reverse(str string) string {
    result := []rune(str)          // Create a slice of runes.
    var beg int                    // Beginning index of rune slice.
    end := len(result) - 1         // Ending index of the rune slice.
    for beg < end {       // Loop until bd and end meet in the middle of the slice.
        // Swap rune
        result[beg], result[end] = result[end], result[beg]
        beg = beg + 1
```

```
            end = end - 1
        }
        return string(result)
    }
    func isPalindrome(testString string) bool {
        if reverse(testString) == testString {
            return true
        }
        return false
    }
```

This is one of the simplest algorithms. What we do is, start two indexes, one at the beginning of the string and the other at the end of the string. Each time compare whether the values at both the indexes are the same or not. If the values are not the same then we say that the given string is not a palindrome.

If the values are the same then increment the left index and decrement the right index. Continue this process until both the indexes meet at the middle (at X) or if the string is not palindrome.

```
func isPalindrome(input string) bool {
    for i := 0; i < len(input)/2; i++ {
        if input[i] != input[len(input)-i-1] {
            return false
        }
    }
    return true
}
```

Time Complexity: $O(n)$. Space Complexity: $O(1)$.

Problem-9 For Problem-8, if the input is in singly linked list then how do we check whether the list elements form a palindrome (That means, moving backward is not possible).

Solution: Refer Linked Lists chapter.

Problem-10 Can we solve Problem-8 using stacks?

Solution: Yes.

Algorithm:

- Traverse the list till we encounter X as input element.
- During the traversal push all the elements (until X) on to the stack.
- For the second half of the list, compare each element's content with top of the stack. If they are the same then pop the stack and go to the next element in the input list.
- If they are not the same then the given string is not a palindrome.
- Continue this process until the stack is empty or the string is not a palindrome.

```
// Refer basic stack implementation from previous section
func isPalindrome(str string) bool {
    stack := NewStack(1)        // Dynamic array implementation of stack
    i, n := 0, len(str)
    for i < n/2 {
        stack.Push(str[i])
        i++
    }
    if n%2 == 1 {               // To skip the middle character if the string length is empty
        i++
    }
    for i < len(str) {
        if stack.IsEmpty() || str[i] != stack.Pop() {
            return false
        }
        i++
    }
    return true
}
```

Time Complexity: $O(n)$. Space Complexity: $O(n/2) \approx O(n)$.

Problem-11 Given a stack, how to reverse the elements of the stack using only stack operations (push & pop)?

Solution:

Algorithm:

- First pop all the elements of the stack till it becomes empty.
- For each upward step in recursion, insert the element at the bottom of the stack.

```
// Refer basic stack implementation from previous section
func (stack *Stack) reverseStack() {
    if stack.IsEmpty() {
        return
    }
    data := stack.Pop()
    stack.reverseStack()
    stack.insertAtBottom(data)
}
func (stack *Stack) insertAtBottom(data interface{}) {
    if stack.IsEmpty() {
        stack.Push(data)
        return
    }
    temp := stack.Pop()
    stack.insertAtBottom(data)
    stack.Push(temp)
}
func main() {
    stack := NewStack(1)
    stack.Push(10)
    stack.Push(20)
    stack.Push(30)
    fmt.Println("Stack size: ", stack.Size())
    fmt.Println("Top element : ", stack.Peek())
    stack.reverseStack()
    fmt.Println("Top element : ", stack.Peek())
}
```

Time Complexity: $O(n^2)$. Space Complexity: $O(n)$, for recursive stack.

Problem-12 Show how to implement one queue efficiently using two stacks. Analyze the running time of the queue operations.

Solution: Refer Queues chapter.

Problem-13 Show how to implement one stack efficiently using two queues. Analyze the running time of the stack operations.

Solution: Refer Queues chapter.

Problem-14 How do we implement *two* stacks using only one array? Our stack routines should not indicate an exception unless every slot in the array is used?

Solution:

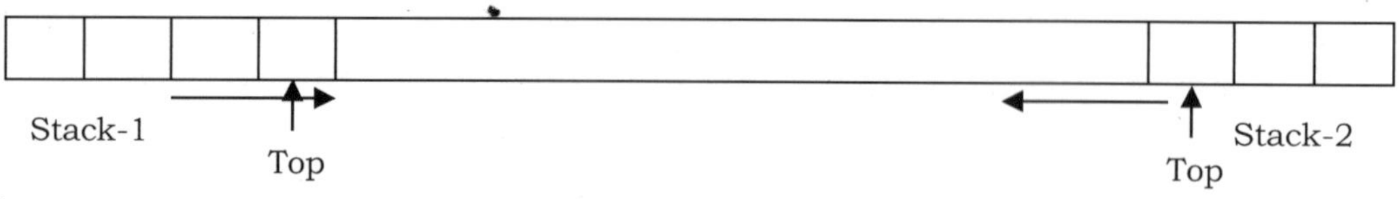

Algorithm:

- Start two indexes one at the left end and the other at the right end.
- The left index simulates the first stack and the right index simulates the second stack.
- If we want to push an element into the first stack then put the element at the left index.
- Similarly, if we want to push an element into the second stack then put the element at the right index.
- The first stack grows towards the right, and the second stack grows towards the left.

```
package main
import (
    "errors"
    "fmt"
    "math"
```

```
)
type MultiStacks struct {
    top1, top2 int
    capacity  int
    array     []int
}
// Returns an initialized stacks
func (stacks *MultiStacks) Init(capacity int) *MultiStacks {
    stacks.top1 = -1
    stacks.top2 = capacity
    stacks.capacity = capacity
    stacks.array = make([]int, capacity)
    return stacks
}
// Returns an new stacks
func NewStack(capacity int) *MultiStacks {
    return new(MultiStacks).Init(capacity)
}
// Returns the size of the size
func (stacks *MultiStacks) Size(stackNumber int) int {
    if stackNumber == 1 {
        return stacks.top1 + 1
    } else {
        return stacks.capacity - stacks.top2
    }
}
// MultiStacks is full when top is equal to the last index
func (stacks *MultiStacks) IsFull() bool {
    return (stacks.Size(1) + stacks.Size(1)) == stacks.capacity
}
// MultiStacks is empty when top is equal to -1
func (stacks *MultiStacks) IsEmpty(stackNumber int) bool {
    if stackNumber == 1 {
        return stacks.top1 == -1
    } else {
        return stacks.top2 == stacks.capacity
    }
}
func (stacks *MultiStacks) Push(stackNumber int, data int) error {
    if stacks.IsFull() {
        return errors.New("stacks is full")
    }
    if stackNumber == 1 {
        stacks.top1++
        stacks.array[stacks.top1] = data
    } else {
        stacks.top2 = stacks.top2 - 1
        stacks.array[stacks.top2] = data
    }
    return nil
}
func (stacks *MultiStacks) Pop(stackNumber int) int {
    var result int
    if stacks.IsEmpty(stackNumber) {
        return math.MinInt32
    }
    if stackNumber == 1 {
        result = stacks.array[stacks.top1]
        stacks.top1--
    } else {
        result = stacks.array[stacks.top2]
```

```
        stacks.top2++
    }
    return result
}
func (stacks *MultiStacks) Peek(stackNumber int) int {
    var result int
    if stacks.IsEmpty(stackNumber) {
        return math.MinInt32
    }
    if stackNumber == 1 {
        result = stacks.array[stacks.top1]
    } else {
        result = stacks.array[stacks.top2]
    }
    return result
}
// Drain removes all elements that are currently in the stacks.
func (stacks *MultiStacks) Drain() {
    stacks.array = nil
    stacks.top1 = -1
    stacks.top2 = stacks.capacity
}
func main() {
    stacks := NewStack(100)
    stacks.Push(1, 10)
    stacks.Push(1, 20)
    stacks.Push(2, 30)
    stacks.Push(2, 40)
    fmt.Println("Pushed to stacks : 40")
    fmt.Println("MultiStacks size: ", stacks.Size(1), stacks.Size(2))
    fmt.Println("Top elements : ", stacks.Peek(1), stacks.Peek(2))
    stacks.Drain()
    fmt.Println("MultiStacks size: ", stacks.Size(1))
    fmt.Println("MultiStacks size: ", stacks.Size(1), stacks.Size(2))
}
```

Time Complexity of push and pop for both stacks is O(1). Space Complexity is O(1).

Problem-15 3 stacks in one array: How to implement 3 stacks in one array?

Solution: For this problem, there could be other ways of solving it. Given below is one possibility and it works as long as there is an empty space in the array.

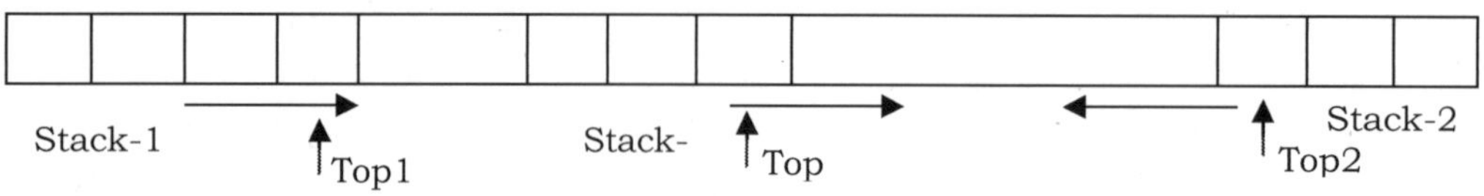

To implement 3 stacks we keep the following information.

- The index of the first stack (Top1): this indicates the size of the first stack.
- The index of the second stack (Top2): this indicates the size of the second stack.
- Starting index of the third stack (base address of third stack).
- Top index of the third stack.

Now, let us define the push and pop operations for this implementation.

Pushing:

- For pushing on to the first stack, we need to see if adding a new element causes it to bump into the third stack. If so, try to shift the third stack upwards. Insert the new element at (start1 + Top1).
- For pushing to the second stack, we need to see if adding a new element causes it to bump into the third stack. If so, try to shift the third stack downward. Insert the new element at (start2 – Top2).
- When pushing to the third stack, see if it bumps into the second stack. If so, try to shift the third stack downward and try pushing again. Insert the new element at (start3 + Top3).

Time Complexity: $O(n)$. Since we may need to adjust the third stack. Space Complexity: O(1).

Popping: For popping, we don't need to shift, just decrement the size of the appropriate stack.

Time Complexity: O(1). Space Complexity: O(1).

Problem-16 For Problem-15, is there any other way implementing the middle stack?

Solution: Yes. When either the left stack (which grows to the right) or the right stack (which grows to the left) bumps into the middle stack, we need to shift the entire middle stack to make room. The same happens if a push on the middle stack causes it to bump into the right stack.

To solve the above-mentioned problem (number of shifts) what we can do is: alternating pushes can be added at alternating sides of the middle list (For example, even elements are pushed to the left, odd elements are pushed to the right). This would keep the middle stack balanced in the center of the array but it would still need to be shifted when it bumps into the left or right stack, whether by growing on its own or by the growth of a neighboring stack. We can optimize the initial locations of the three stacks if they grow/shrink at different rates and if they have different average sizes. For example, suppose one stack doesn't change much. If we put it at the left, then the middle stack will eventually get pushed against it and leave a gap between the middle and right stacks, which grow toward each other. If they collide, then it's likely we've run out of space in the array. There is no change in the time complexity but the average number of shifts will get reduced.

Problem-17 Multiple (m) stacks in one array: Similar to Problem-15, what if we want to implement m stacks in one array?

Solution: Let us assume that array indexes are from 1 to n. Similar to the discussion in Problem-15, to implement m stacks in one array, we divide the array into m parts (as shown below). The size of each part is $\frac{n}{m}$.

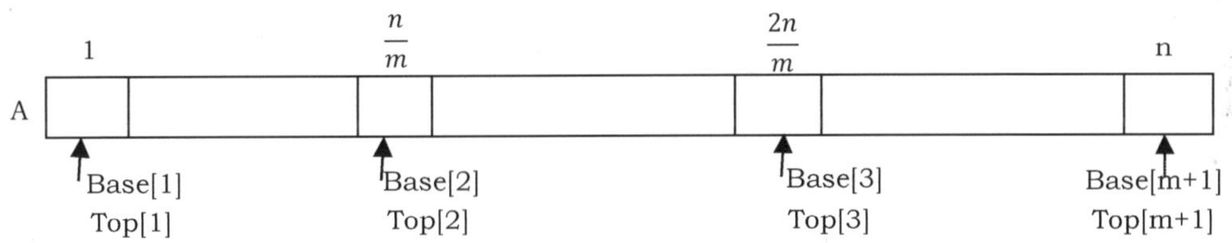

From the above representation we can see that, first stack is starting at index 1 (starting index is stored in Base[1]), second stack is starting at index $\frac{n}{m}$ (starting index is stored in Base[2]), third stack is starting at index $\frac{2n}{m}$ (starting index is stored in Base[3]), and so on. Similar to *Base* array, let us assume that *Top* array stores the top indexes for each of the stack. Consider the following terminology for the discussion.

- Top[i], for $1 \leq i \leq m$ will point to the topmost element of the stack i.
- If Base[i] == Top[i], then we can say the stack i is empty.
- If Top[i] == Base[i+1], then we can say the stack i is full.
  Initially Base[i] = Top[i] = $\frac{n}{m}(i-1)$, for $1 \leq i \leq m$.
- The i^{th}stack grows from Base[i]+1 to Base[i+1].

Pushing on to i^{th} stack:

1) For pushing on to the ith stack, we check whether the top of ith stack is pointing to Base[i+1] (this case defines that i^{th} stack is full). That means, we need to see if adding a new element causes it to bump into the $i+1^{th}$ stack. If so, try to shift the stacks from $i+1^{th}$ stack to m^{th} stack toward the right. Insert the new element at (Base[i] + Top[i]).
2) If right shifting is not possible then try shifting the stacks from 1 to $i-1^{th}$ stack toward the left.
3) If both of them are not possible then we can say that all stacks are full.

Time Complexity: O(n). Since we may need to adjust the stacks. Space Complexity: O(1).

Popping from i^{th} stack: For popping, we don't need to shift, just decrement the size of the appropriate stack. The only case to check is stack empty case.

Time Complexity: O(1). Space Complexity: O(1).

Problem-18 Consider an empty stack of integers. Let the numbers $1, 2, 3, 4, 5, 6$ be pushed on to this stack in the order they appear from left to right. Let S indicate a push and X indicate a pop operation. Can they be permuted in to the order 325641(output) and order 154623?

Solution: SSSXXSSXSXXX outputs 325641. 154623 cannot be output as 2 is pushed much before 3 so can appear only after 3 is output.

Problem-19 Earlier in this chapter, we discussed that for dynamic array implementation of stacks, the 'repeated doubling' approach is used. For the same problem, what is the complexity if we create a new array whose size is $n + K$ instead of doubling?

Solution: Let us assume that the initial stack size is 0. For simplicity let us assume that $K = 10$. For inserting the element we create a new array whose size is $0 + 10 = 10$. Similarly, after 10 elements we again create a new array whose size is $10 + 10 = 20$ and this process continues at values: 30, 40 ... That means, for a given n value, we are creating the new arrays at: $\frac{n}{10}, \frac{n}{20}, \frac{n}{30}, \frac{n}{40}$ ... The total number of copy operations is:

$$= \frac{n}{10} + \frac{n}{20} + \frac{n}{30} + \cdots 1 = \frac{n}{10}\left(\frac{1}{1} + \frac{1}{2} + \frac{1}{3} + \cdots \frac{1}{n}\right) = \frac{n}{10} logn \approx O(nlogn)$$

If we are performing n push operations, the cost per operation is $O(logn)$.

Problem-20 Given a string containing n $S's$ and n $X's$ where S indicates a push operation and X indicates a pop operation, and with the stack initially empty, formulate a rule to check whether a given string S of operations is admissible or not?

Solution: Given a string of length $2n$, we wish to check whether the given string of operations is permissible or not with respect to its functioning on a stack. The only restricted operation is pop whose prior requirement is that the stack should not be empty. So while traversing the string from left to right, prior to any pop the stack shouldn't be empty, which means the number of $S's$ is always greater than or equal to that of $X's$. Hence the condition is at any stage of processing of the string, the number of push operations (S) should be greater than the number of pop operations (X).

Problem-21 **Finding Spans:** Given an array A, the span $S[i]$ of $A[i]$ is the maximum number of consecutive elements $A[j]$ immediately preceding $A[i]$ and such that $A[j] \leq A[i]$?

Other way of asking: Given an array A of integers, find the maximum of $j - i$ subjected to the constraint of $A[i] < A[j]$.

Solution:

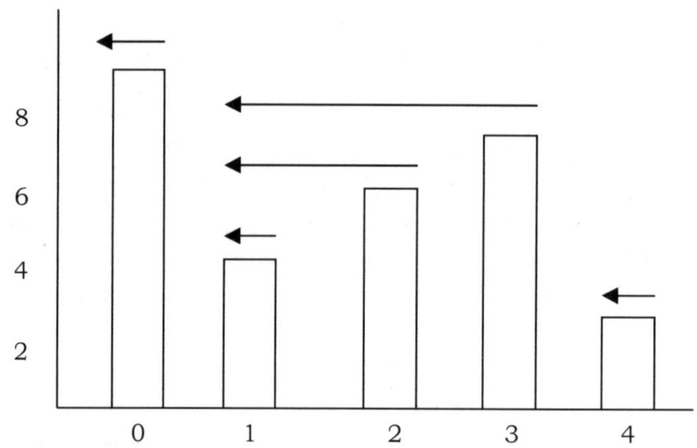

Day: Index i	Input Array A[i]	S[i]: Span of A[i]
0	6	1
1	3	1
2	4	2
3	5	3
4	2	1

This is a very common problem in stock markets to find the peaks. Spans are used in financial analysis (E.g., stock at 52-week high). The span of a stock price on a certain day, i, is the maximum number of consecutive days (up to the current day) the price of the stock has been less than or equal to its price on i.

As an example, let us consider the table and the corresponding spans diagram. In the figure the arrows indicate the length of the spans. Now, let us concentrate on the algorithm for finding the spans. One simple way is, each day, check how many contiguous days have a stock price that is less than the current price.

```
func findingSpans(A []int) []int {
    n := len(A)
    result := make([]int, n)
    for i := 0; i < n; i++ {
        j := 1
        for j <= i && A[i] > A[i-j] {
            j = j + 1
        }
        result[i] = j
    }
```

```
    return result
}
```

Time Complexity: $O(n^2)$. Space Complexity: O(1).

Problem-22 Can we improve the complexity of Problem-21?

Solution: From the example above, we can see that span $S[i]$ on day i can be easily calculated if we know the closest day preceding i, such that the price is greater on that day than the price on day i. Let us call such a day as P. If such a day exists then the span is now defined as $S[i] = i - P$.

```
func findingSpans2(A []int) []int {
    n := len(A)
    result := make([]int, n)
    stack := NewStack(1)
    var P int
    for i := 0; i < n; i++ {
        for !stack.IsEmpty() && A[i] > A[stack.Peek()] {
            stack.Pop()
        }
        if stack.IsEmpty() {
            P = -1
        } else {
            P = stack.Peek()
        }
        result[i] = i - P
        stack.Push(i)
    }
    return result
}
```

Time Complexity: Each index of the array is pushed into the stack exactly once and also popped from the stack at most once. The statements in the while loop are executed at most n times. Even though the algorithm has nested loops, the complexity is $O(n)$ as the inner loop is executing only n times during the course of the algorithm (trace out an example and see how many times the inner loop becomes successful). Space Complexity: $O(n)$ [for stack].

Problem-23 **Largest rectangle under histogram:** A histogram is a polygon composed of a sequence of rectangles aligned at a common base line. For simplicity, assume that the rectangles have equal widths but may have different heights. For example, the figure on the left shows a histogram that consists of rectangles with the heights 3, 2 , 5, 6, 1, 4, 4, measured in units where 1 is the width of the rectangles. Here our problem is: given an array with heights of rectangles (assuming width is 1), we need to find the largest rectangle possible. For the given example, the largest rectangle is the shared part.

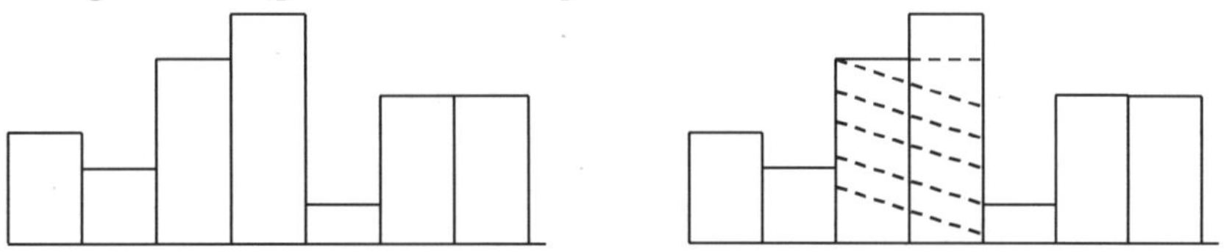

Solution: The first insight is to identify which rectangles to be considered for the solution: those which cover a contiguous range of the input histogram and whose height equals the minimum bar height in the range (rectangle height cannot exceed the minimum height in the range and there's no point in considering a height less than the minimum height because we can just increase the height to the minimum height in the range and get a better solution). This greatly constrains the set of rectangles we need to consider. Formally, we need to consider only those rectangles with $width = j - i + 1$ $(0 = i = j < n)$ and $height = min(A[i..j])$.

At this point, we can directly implement this solution.

```
func findMin(A []int, i, j int) int {
    min := A[i]
    for i <= j {
        if min > A[i] {
            min = A[i]
        }
        i++
    }
    return min
```

```
}
func largestRectangleArea(heights []int) int {
    maxArea := 0
    for i := 0; i < len(heights); i++ {
        for j, minimum_height := i, heights[i]; j < len(heights); j++ {
            minimum_height = findMin(heights, i, j)
            maxArea = findMax(maxArea, (j-i+1)*minimum_height)
        }
    }
    return maxArea
}
```

There are only n^2 choices for i and j. If we naively calculate the minimum height in the range [i..j], this will have time complexity $O(n^3)$.

Instead, we can keep track of the minimum height in the inner loop for j, leading to the following implementation with $O(n^2)$ time complexity and O(1) auxiliary space complexity.

```
func largestRectangleArea(heights []int) int {
    maxArea := 0
    for i := 0; i < len(heights); i++ {
        for j, minimum_height := i, heights[i]; j < len(heights); j++ {
            minimum_height = findMini(minimum_height, heights[j])
            maxArea = findMax(maxArea, (j-i+1)*minimum_height)
        }
    }
    return maxArea
}
```

Problem-24 For Problem-23, can we improve the time complexity?

Solution: We are still doing a lot of repeated work by considering all n^2 rectangles. There are only n possible heights. For each position j, we need to consider only 1 rectangle: the one with height = A[j] and width = k-i+1, where 0=i<=j<=k<n, A[i..k] >= A[j], A[i-1] < A[j] and A[k+1] < A[j].

Linear search using a stack of incomplete sub problems: There are many ways of solving this problem. *Judge* has given a nice algorithm for this problem which is based on stack. Process the elements in left-to-right order and maintain a stack of information about started but yet unfinished sub histograms. At each step we need the information of previously seen "candidate" bars - bars which give us hope. These are the bars of increasing heights. And since they'll need to be put in the order of their occurrence, stack should come to your mind.

If the stack is empty, open a new sub problem by pushing the element onto the stack. Otherwise compare it to the element on top of the stack. If the new one is greater we again push it. If the new one is equal we skip it. In all these cases, we continue with the next new element. If the new one is less, we finish the topmost sub problem by updating the maximum area with respect to the element at the top of the stack. Then, we discard the element at the top, and repeat the procedure keeping the current new element.

This way, all sub problems are finished when the stack becomes empty, or its top element is less than or equal to the new element, leading to the actions described above. If all elements have been processed, and the stack is not yet empty, we finish the remaining sub problems by updating the maximum area with respect to the elements at the top.

```
func largestRectangleArea(heights []int) int {
    i, max := 0, 0
    stack := make([]int, 0)
    for i < len(heights) {
        if len(stack) == 0 || heights[i] > heights[stack[len(stack)-1]] {
            stack = append(stack, i)
            i++
        } else {
            pop := stack[len(stack)-1]
            stack = stack[:len(stack)-1]
            h := heights[pop]
            var w int
            if len(stack) == 0 {
                w = i
            } else {
                w = i - stack[len(stack)-1] - 1
```

```
            }
            max = findMax(max, h*w)
        }
    }
    for len(stack) != 0 {
        pop := stack[len(stack)-1]
        stack = stack[:len(stack)-1]
        h := heights[pop]
        var w int
        if len(stack) == 0 {
            w = i
        } else {
            w = i - stack[len(stack)-1] - 1
        }
        max = findMax(max, h*w)
    }
    return max
}
func findMax(a, b int) int {
    if a > b {
        return a
    }
    return b
}
```

At the first impression, this solution seems to be having $O(n^2)$ complexity. But if we look carefully, every element is pushed and popped at most once, and in every step of the function at least one element is pushed or popped. Since the amount of work for the decisions and the update is constant, the complexity of the algorithm is $O(n)$ by amortized analysis. Space Complexity: $O(n)$ [for stack].

Problem-25 Suppose there are two singly linked lists which intersect at some point and become a single linked list. The head or start pointers of both the lists are known, but the intersecting node is not known. Also, the number of nodes in each of the lists before they intersect are unknown and both lists may have a different number. *List*1 may have n nodes before it reaches the intersection point and *List*2 may have m nodes before it reaches the intersection point where m and n may be $m = n, m < n$ or $m > n$. Can we find the merging point using stacks?

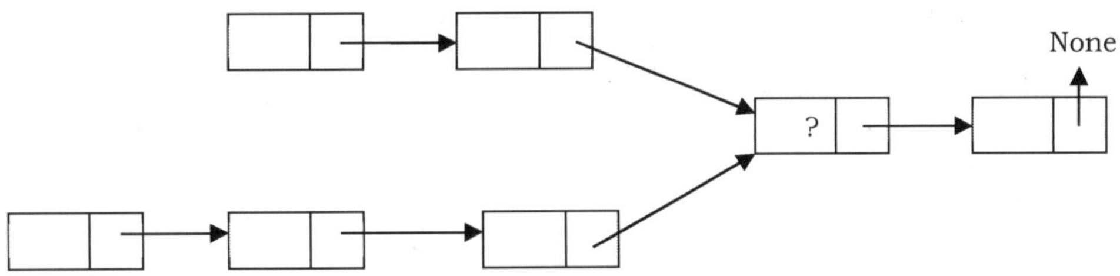

Solution: Yes. For algorithm refer to *Linked Lists* chapter.

Problem-26 Given a stack of integers, how do you check whether each successive pair of numbers in the stack is consecutive or not. The pairs can be increasing or decreasing, and if the stack has an odd number of elements, the element at the top is left out of a pair. For example, if the stack of elements are [4, 5, -2, -3, 11, 10, 5, 6, 20], then the output should be true because each of the pairs (4, 5), (-2, -3), (11, 10), and (5, 6) consists of consecutive numbers.

Solution:

```
func abs(x int) int {
    if x < 0 {
        return -x
    }
    return x
}
func pairWiseConsecutive(stack *Stack) bool {
    // Transfer elements of stack to auxStack
    auxStack := NewStack(1)
    for !stack.IsEmpty() {
```

```
            auxStack.Push(stack.Peek())
            stack.Pop()
        }
        // Traverse auxStack and see if elements are pairwise consecutive
        // or not. We also need to make sure that original content is retained.
        result := true
        for auxStack.Size() > 1 {
            // Fetch current top two elements of aux and check if they are consecutive.
            x := auxStack.Peek()
            auxStack.Pop()
            y := auxStack.Peek()
            auxStack.Pop()
            if abs(x-y) != 1 {
                result = false
            }
            // Push the elements to original stack
            stack.Push(x)
            stack.Push(y)
        }
        if auxStack.Size() == 1 {
            stack.Push(auxStack.Peek())
        }
        return result
    }
```

Problem-27 Recursively remove all adjacent duplicates: Given a string of characters, recursively remove adjacent duplicate characters from string. The output string should not have any adjacent duplicates.

Input: careermonk	*Input*: mississippi
Output: camonk	*Output*: m

Solution: This solution runs with the concept of in-place stack. When element on stack doesn't match the current character, we add it to stack. When it matches to stack top, we skip characters until the element matches the top of stack and remove the element from stack.

```
func removeDuplicates(S string) string {
    stack := make([]byte, 0, len(S))
    for i := range S {
        if len(stack) > 0 && stack[len(stack)-1] == S[i] {
            stack = stack[:len(stack)-1]
        } else {
            stack = append(stack, S[i])
        }
    }
    return string(stack)
}
```

Time Complexity: O(n). Space Complexity: O(n).

Note: We can solve this problem without stacks too. Refer *String Algorithms* chapter for solution.

Problem-28 How to implement a stack which will support following operations in O(1) time complexity?

- Push which adds an element to the top of stack.
- Pop which removes an element from top of stack.
- Find middle which will return middle element of the stack.
- Delete middle which will delete the middle element.

Solution: We can use a LinkedList data structure with an extra pointer to the middle element. Also, we need another variable to store whether the LinkedList has an even or odd number of elements.

- *Push*: Add the element to the head of the LinkedList. Update the pointer to the middle element according to variable.
- *Pop*: Remove the head of the LinkedList. Update the pointer to the middle element according to variable.
- *Find middle*: Find middle which will return middle element of the stack.
- *Delete middle*: Delete middle which will delete the middle element use the logic of Problem-43 from *Linked Lists* chapter.

CHAPTER

QUEUES

5

5.1 What is a Queue?

A queue is a data structure used for storing data (similar to Linked Lists and Stacks). In queue, the order in which data arrives is important. In general, a queue is a line of people or things waiting to be served in sequential order starting at the beginning of the line or sequence.

Definition: A *queue* is an ordered list in which insertions are done at one end (*rear*) and deletions are done at other end (*front*). The first element to be inserted is the first one to be deleted. Hence, it is called First in First out (FIFO) or Last in Last out (LILO) list.

Similar to *Stacks*, special names are given to the two changes that can be made to a queue. When an element is inserted in a queue, the concept is called *EnQueue*, and when an element is removed from the queue, the concept is called *DeQueue*.

DeQueueing an empty queue is called *underflow* and *EnQueuing* an element in a full queue is called *overflow*. Generally, we treat them as exceptions. As an example, consider the snapshot of the queue.

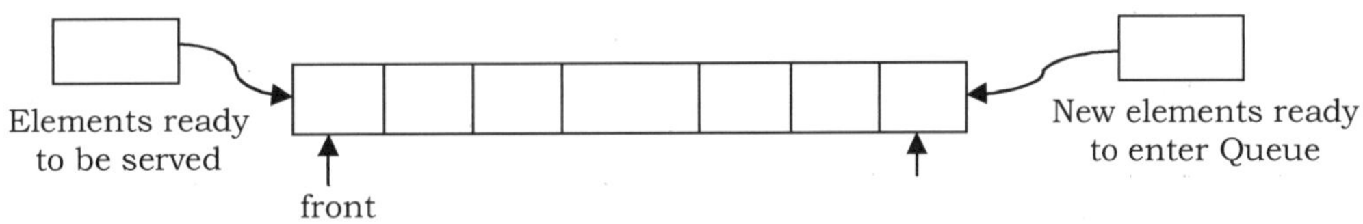

5.2 How are Queues Used?

The concept of a queue can be explained by observing a line at a reservation counter. When we enter the line we stand at the end of the line and the person who is at the front of the line is the one who will be served next. He will exit the queue and be served.

As this happens, the next person will come at the head of the line, will exit the queue and will be served. As each person at the head of the line keeps exiting the queue, we move towards the head of the line. Finally we will reach the head of the line and we will exit the queue and be served. This behavior is very useful in cases where there is a need to maintain the order of arrival.

5.3 Queue ADT

The following operations make a queue an ADT. Insertions and deletions in the queue must follow the FIFO scheme. For simplicity we assume the elements are integers.

Main Queue Operations

- func EnQueue(data interface{}): Inserts an element (data) at the end of the queue (at rear)
- func DeQueue() (data interface{}): Removes and returns the element (data) from the front of the queue

Auxiliary Queue Operations

- func Front() (data interface{}): Returns the element at the front without removing it
- func Rear() (data interface{}): Returns the element at the rear without removing it
- func Size() int: Returns the number of elements stored in the queue
- func IsEmpty() bool: Indicates whether no elements are stored in the queue or not

5.4 Exceptions

Similar to other ADTs, executing *DeQueue* on an empty queue throws an "*Empty Queue Exception*" and executing *EnQueue* on a full queue throws "*Full Queue Exception*".

5.5 Applications

Following are some of the applications that use queues.

Direct Applications

- Operating systems schedule jobs (with equal priority) in the order of arrival (e.g., a print queue).
- Simulation of real-world queues such as lines at a ticket counter or any other first-come first-served scenario requires a queue.
- Multiprogramming.
- Asynchronous data transfer (file IO, pipes, sockets).
- Waiting times of customers at call center.
- Determining number of cashiers to have at a supermarket.

Indirect Applications

- Auxiliary data structure for algorithms
- Component of other data structures

5.6 Implementation

There are many ways (similar to Stacks) of implementing queue operations and some of the commonly used methods are listed below.

- Simple circular array-based implementation
- Dynamic circular array-based implementation
- Linked list implementation

Why Circular Arrays?

First, let us see whether we can use simple arrays for implementing queues as we have done for stacks. We know that, in queues, the insertions are performed at one end and deletions are performed at the other end. After performing some insertions and deletions the process becomes easy to understand.

In the example shown below, it can be seen clearly that the initial slots of the array are getting wasted. So, simple array implementation for queue is not efficient. To solve this problem we assume the arrays as circular arrays. That means, we treat the last element and the first array elements as contiguous. With this representation, if there are any free slots at the beginning, the rear pointer can easily go to its next free slot.

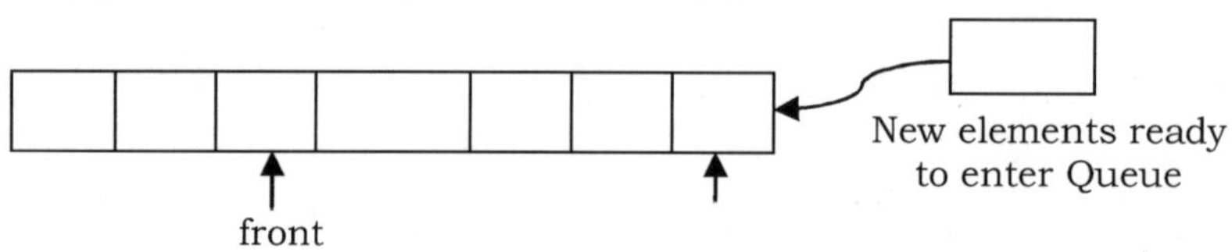

Note: The simple circular array and dynamic circular array implementations are very similar to stack array implementations. Refer to *Stacks* chapter for analysis of these implementations.

Simple Circular Array Implementation

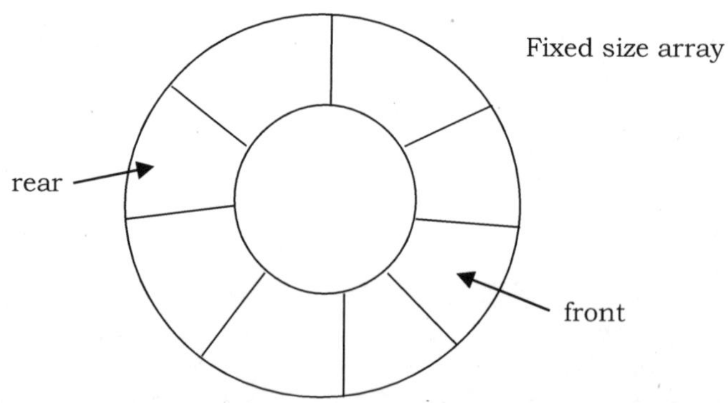

This simple implementation of Queue ADT uses an array. In the array, we add elements circularly and use two variables to keep track of the start element and end element. Generally, *front* is used to indicate the start element and *rear* is used to indicate the end element in the queue. The array storing the queue elements may become full. An *EnQueue* operation will then throw a *full queue exception*. Similarly, if we try deleting an element from an empty queue it will throw *empty queue exception*.

With stacks, the push method caused the single index field count to be increased by one, while the method pop caused it to be decreased by one. With queues, however, the two index fields, *front* and *rear*, can each only be increased by one. The field *front* is increased by one by the deQueue method, while the field rear is increased by one by the *enQueue* method. So as items leave and join the queue, the section of the array used to store the queue items will gradually shift along the array and will eventually reach its end. This is different from stacks, where the section of the array used to store the items in a stack only reaches the end of the array if the size of the stack goes beyond the size of the array.

To deal with this problem, a "wraparound" technique is used with queues implemented with arrays. When either the front or rear field is increased to the point where it would index past the end of the array, it is set *rear* to 0. Thus the state is reached where the front section of the queue is in the higher indexed section of the array and the rear section of the queue in the lower indexed section of the array.

Note: Initially, both front and rear points to -1 which indicates that the queue is empty.

```
package main
import (
    "bytes"
    "fmt"
)
const MaxInt = int(^uint(0) >> 1)
const MinInt = -MaxInt - 1
type Queue struct {
    // enQueue increments rear then writes to array[rear] ; enQueue writes to array[front] then
    // decrements front; len(array) is a power of two; unused slots are nil and not garbage.
    array    []interface{}
    front    int
    rear     int
    capacity int
    size     int
}
// New returns an initialized isEmpty queue.
func New(capacity int) *Queue {
    return new(Queue).Init(capacity)
}
// Init initializes with capacity
func (q *Queue) Init(capacity int) *Queue {
    q.array = make([]interface{}, capacity)
    q.front, q.rear, q.size, q.capacity = -1, -1, 0, capacity
    return q
}
// size returns the number of elements of queue q.
func (q *Queue) length() int {
    return q.size
}
// isEmpty returns true if the queue q has no elements.
func (q *Queue) isEmpty() bool {
    return q.size == 0
}
// isFull returns true if the queue q is at capacity.
func (q *Queue) isFull() bool {
    return q.size == q.capacity
}
// String returns a string representation of queue q formatted from front to rear.
func (q *Queue) String() string {
    var result bytes.Buffer
    result.WriteByte('[')
    j := q.front
    for i := 0; i < q.size; i++ {
        result.WriteString(fmt.Sprintf("%v", q.array[j]))
        if i < q.size-1 {
            result.WriteByte(' ')
```

```
		}
		j = (j + 1) % q.capacity
	}
	result.WriteByte(']')
	return result.String()
}
// Front returns the first element of queue q or nil.
func (q *Queue) Front() interface{} {
	// no need to check q.isEmpty(), unused slots are nil
	return q.array[q.front]
}
// Back returns the last element of queue q or nil.
func (q *Queue) Back() interface{} {
	return q.array[q.rear]
}
// enQueue inserts a new value v at the rear of queue q.
func (q *Queue) enQueue(v interface{}) {
	if q.isFull() {
		return
	}
	q.rear = (q.rear + 1) % q.capacity
	q.array[q.rear] = v
	if q.front == -1 {
		q.front = q.rear
	}
	q.size++
}
// deQueue removes and returns the first element of queue q or MinInt.
func (q *Queue) deQueue() interface{} {
	if q.isEmpty() {
		return MinInt
	}
	data := q.array[q.front]
	if q.front == q.rear {
		q.front = -1
		q.rear = -1
		q.size = 0
	} else {
		q.front = (q.front + 1) % q.capacity
		q.size -= 1
	}
	return data
}
func main() {
	var q Queue
	q.Init(10)
	q.enQueue(1)
	q.enQueue(6)
	q.enQueue(7)
	q.enQueue(8)
	q.enQueue(9)
	q.enQueue(2)
	q.enQueue(3)
	q.enQueue(4)
	q.enQueue(5)
	q.enQueue(6)
	q.enQueue(7)
	q.enQueue(8)
	q.enQueue(9)
	fmt.Println(q.String())
	want := "[1 6 7 8 9 2 3 4 5 6]"
	if s := q.String(); s != want {
```

```
        fmt.Println("q.String() = ", s, "want = ", want)
    }
    fmt.Println(q.deQueue())
    fmt.Println(q.deQueue())
    fmt.Println(q.deQueue())
    fmt.Println(q.deQueue())
    fmt.Println(q.deQueue())
    fmt.Println(q.deQueue())
    fmt.Println(q.deQueue())
    fmt.Println(q.deQueue())
    fmt.Println(q.deQueue())
    fmt.Println(q.deQueue())
    fmt.Println(q.deQueue())
    fmt.Println(q.deQueue())
    fmt.Println(q.deQueue())
    want = "[]"
    fmt.Println(q.String())
    if s := q.String(); s != want {
        fmt.Println("q.String() = ", s, "want = ", want)
    }
}
```

Performance and Limitations

Performance: Let n be the number of elements in the queue:

Space Complexity (for n enQueue operations)	O(n)
Time Complexity of enQueue()	O(1)
Time Complexity of deQueue()	O(1)
Time Complexity of isEmpty()	O(1)
Time Complexity of isFull()	O(1)
Time Complexity of length()	O(1)
Time Complexity of deleteQueue()	O(1)

Limitations: The maximum size of the queue must be defined as prior and cannot be changed. Trying to *EnQueue* a new element into a full queue causes an implementation-specific exception.

Dynamic Circular Array Implementation

```
package main
import (
    "bytes"
    "fmt"
)
const MaxInt = int(^uint(0) >> 1)
const MinInt = -MaxInt - 1
type Queue struct {
    array    []interface{}
    front    int
    rear     int
    capacity int
    size     int
}
// New returns an initialized isEmpty queue.
func New(capacity int) *Queue {
    return new(Queue).Init(capacity)
}
// Init initializes with capacity
func (q *Queue) Init(capacity int) *Queue {
    q.array = make([]interface{}, capacity)
    q.front, q.rear, q.size, q.capacity = -1, -1, 0, capacity
    return q
}
```

```
// size returns the number of elements of queue q.
func (q *Queue) length() int {
    return q.size
}
// isEmpty returns true if the queue q has no elements.
func (q *Queue) isEmpty() bool {
    return q.size == 0
}
// isFull returns true if the queue q is at capacity.
func (q *Queue) isFull() bool {
    return q.size == q.capacity
}
// String returns a string representation of queue q formatted
// from front to rear.
func (q *Queue) String() string {
    var result bytes.Buffer
    result.WriteByte('[')
    j := q.front
    for i := 0; i < q.size; i++ {
        result.WriteString(fmt.Sprintf("%v", q.array[j]))
        if i < q.size-1 {
            result.WriteByte(' ')
        }
        j = (j + 1) % q.capacity
    }
    result.WriteByte(']')
    return result.String()
}
// Front returns the first element of queue q or nil.
func (q *Queue) Front() interface{} {
    // no need to check q.isEmpty(), unused slots are nil
    return q.array[q.front]
}
// Back returns the last element of queue q or nil.
func (q *Queue) Back() interface{} {
    return q.array[q.rear]
}
// resize adjusts the size of queue q's underlying slice.
func (q *Queue) resize() {
    size := q.capacity
    q.capacity = q.capacity * 2
    adjusted := make([]interface{}, q.capacity)
    if q.front < q.rear {
        // array not "wrapped" around, one copy suffices
        copy(adjusted, q.array[q.front:q.rear+1])
    } else {
        // array is "wrapped" around, need two copies
        n := copy(adjusted, q.array[q.front:])
        copy(adjusted[n:], q.array[:q.rear+1])
    }
    q.array = adjusted
    q.front = 0
    q.rear = size-1
}
// enQueue inserts a new value v at the rear of queue q.
func (q *Queue) enQueue(v interface{}) {
    if q.isFull() {
        q.resize()
    }
    q.rear = (q.rear + 1) % q.capacity
    q.array[q.rear] = v
```

```
	if q.front == -1 {
		q.front = q.rear
	}
	q.size++
}
// deQueue removes and returns the first element of queue q or MinInt.
func (q *Queue) deQueue() interface{} {
	if q.isEmpty() {
		return MinInt
	}
	data := q.array[q.front]
	if q.front == q.rear {
		q.front = -1
		q.rear = -1
		q.size = 0
	} else {
		q.front = (q.front + 1) % q.capacity
		q.size -= 1
	}
	return data
}
func main() {
	var q Queue
	q.Init(1)
	q.enQueue(1)
	q.enQueue(2)
	q.enQueue(3)
	q.enQueue(4)
	q.enQueue(5)
	q.enQueue(6)
	q.enQueue(7)
	q.enQueue(8)
	q.enQueue(9)
	q.enQueue(10)
	q.enQueue(11)
	want := "[1 2 3 4 5 6 7 8 9 10 11]"
	if s := q.String(); s != want {
		fmt.Println("q.String() = ", s, "want = ", want)
	}
}
```

Performance

Let n be the number of elements in the queue.

Space Complexity (for n enQueue operations)	$O(n)$
Time Complexity of enQueue()	O(1) (Average)
Time Complexity of deQueue()	O(1)
Time Complexity of Size()	O(1)
Time Complexity of IsEmpty()	O(1)
Time Complexity of IsFull ()	O(1)
Time Complexity of deleteQueue()	O(1)

Linked List Implementation

Another way of implementing queues is by using Linked lists. *EnQueue* operation is implemented by inserting an element at the end of the list. *DeQueue* operation is implemented by deleting an element from the beginning of the list.

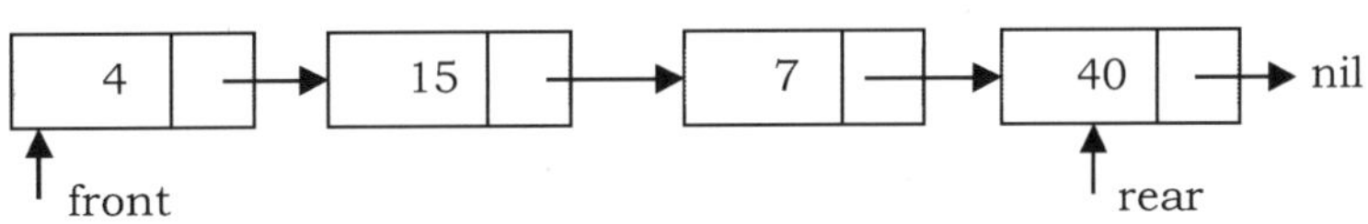

```
package main
import (
    "bytes"
    "errors"
    "fmt"
)
type ListNode struct {
    data interface{}
    next *ListNode
}
// Queue implements a queue backed by a linked list
type Queue struct {
    front *ListNode
    rear  *ListNode
    size  int
}
// enQueue adds an element to the end of the queue.
func (q *Queue) enQueue(data interface{}) {
    rear := new(ListNode)
    rear.data = data
    if q.isEmpty() {
        q.front = rear
    } else {
        oldLast := q.rear
        oldLast.next = rear
    }
    q.rear = rear
    q.size++
}
// deQueue removes the front element from the queue.
func (q *Queue) deQueue() (interface{}, error) {
    if q.isEmpty() {
        q.rear = nil
        return nil, errors.New("unable to dequeue element, queue is empty")
    }
    data := q.front.data
    q.front = q.front.next
    q.size--
    return data, nil
}
// front returns the front element in the queue without removing it.
func (q *Queue) frontElement() (interface{}, error) {
    if q.isEmpty() {
        return nil, errors.New("unable to peek element, queue is empty")
    }
    return q.front.data, nil
}
// isEmpty returns whether the queue is empty or not.
func (q *Queue) isEmpty() bool {
    return q.front == nil
}
// size returns the number of elements in the queue.
func (q *Queue) length() int{
    return q.size
}
// String returns a string representation of queue q formatted
// from front to rear.
func (q *Queue) String() string {
    var result bytes.Buffer
    result.WriteByte('[')
```

```
    j := q.front
    for i := 0; i < q.size; i++ {
        result.WriteString(fmt.Sprintf("%v", j.data))
        if i < q.size-1 {
            result.WriteByte(' ')
        }
        j = j.next
    }
    result.WriteByte(']')
    return result.String()
}
func main() {
    q := new(Queue)
    q.enQueue(1)
    q.enQueue(6)
    q.enQueue(7)
    q.enQueue(8)
    q.enQueue(9)
    q.enQueue(2)
    q.enQueue(3)
    q.enQueue(4)
    q.enQueue(5)
    q.enQueue(6)
    q.enQueue(7)
    q.enQueue(8)
    q.enQueue(9)
    fmt.Println(q.String())
    want := "[1 6 7 8 9 2 3 4 5 6 7 8 9]"
    if s := q.String(); s != want {
        fmt.Println("q.String() = ", s, "want = ", want)
    }
    fmt.Println(q.deQueue())
    fmt.Println(q.deQueue())
    fmt.Println(q.deQueue())
    fmt.Println(q.deQueue())
    fmt.Println(q.deQueue())
    fmt.Println(q.deQueue())
    fmt.Println(q.deQueue())
    fmt.Println(q.deQueue())
    fmt.Println(q.deQueue())
    fmt.Println(q.deQueue())
    fmt.Println(q.deQueue())
    fmt.Println(q.deQueue())
    fmt.Println(q.deQueue())
    want = "[]"
    fmt.Println(q.String())
    if s := q.String(); s != want {
        fmt.Println("q.String() = ", s, "want = ", want)
    }
}
```

Performance

Let n be the number of elements in the queue, then

Space Complexity (for n enQueue operations)	O(n)
Time Complexity of enQueue()	O(1) (Average)
Time Complexity of deQueue()	O(1)
Time Complexity of isEmpty()	O(1)
Time Complexity of deleteQueue()	O(1)

Comparison of Implementations

Note: Comparison is very similar to stack implementations and refer *Stacks* chapter.

5.7 Queues: Problems & Solutions

Problem-1 Give an algorithm for reversing a queue Q. To access the queue, we are only allowed to use the methods of queue ADT.

Solution: To solve this question will take the help of an auxiliary stack. The steps involved will be:-

- Create an auxiliary stack S.
- Until the queue Q is not empty, deQueue all the elements of the queue Q and push on to the stack S.
- Now we have a stack in which the last element of the queue Q is at the top in the stack S.
- Until the stack is empty pop(S), pop all the elements of the stack S and enQueue to the queue Q.

```
void reverseQueue(struct Queue *Q) {
   struct Stack *S = createStack(5);
   while (!isEmptyQueue(Q))
      push(S, deQueue(Q));
   while (!isEmptyStack(S))
      enQueue(Q, pop(S));
}
```

Time Complexity: $O(n)$.

Problem-2 How can you implement a queue using two stacks?

Solution: Let S1 and S2 be the two stacks to be used in the implementation of queue. All we have to do is to define the enQueue and deQueue operations for the queue.

EnQueue Algorithm

- Just push on to stack S1

Time Complexity: O(1).

DeQueue Algorithm

- If stack S2 is not empty then pop from S2 and return that element.
- If stack is empty, then transfer all elements from S1 to S2 and pop the top element from S2 and return that popped element [we can optimize the code a little by transferring only $n - 1$ elements from S1 to S2 and pop the nth element from S1 and return that popped element].
- If stack S1 is also empty then throw error.

```
package main
import (
   "fmt"
)
type Queue struct {
   stack1 []int
   stack2 []int
}
func NewQueue() Queue {
   return Queue{}
}
// Push element data to the back of queue.
func (q *Queue) EnQueue(data int) {
   q.stack1 = append(q.stack1, data)
}
// Removes the element from in front of queue and returns that element.
func (q *Queue) DeQueue() int {
   if len(q.stack2) == 0 {
      for len(q.stack1) > 0 {
         item := q.stack1[len(q.stack1)-1]
         q.stack1 = q.stack1[:len(q.stack1)-1]
         q.stack2 = append(q.stack2, item)
      }
   }
   item := q.stack2[len(q.stack2)-1]
   q.stack2 = q.stack2[:len(q.stack2)-1]
```

```
        return item
    }
    // Get the front element.
    func (q *Queue) Front() int {
        if len(q.stack2) < 1 {
            for len(q.stack1) > 0 {
                item := q.stack1[len(q.stack1)-1]
                q.stack1 = q.stack1[:len(q.stack1)-1]
                q.stack2 = append(q.stack2, item)
            }
        }
        return q.stack2[len(q.stack2)-1]
    }
    // Returns whether the queue is empty.
    func (q *Queue) IsEmpty() bool {
        return len(q.stack1) == 0 && len(q.stack2) == 0
    }
    func main() {
        obj := NewQueue()
        obj.EnQueue(10)
        obj.EnQueue(20)
        fmt.Println(obj.DeQueue())
        fmt.Println(obj.Front()) // prints 20
        fmt.Println(obj.IsEmpty())
        obj.EnQueue(30)
        obj.EnQueue(40)
        fmt.Println(obj.DeQueue())
        fmt.Println(obj.Front()) // prints 30
        fmt.Println(obj.IsEmpty())
    }
```

Time Complexity: From the algorithm, if the stack S2 is not empty then the complexity is O(1). If the stack S2 is empty, then we need to transfer the elements from S1 to S2. But if we carefully observe, the number of transferred elements and the number of popped elements from S2 are equal. Due to this the average complexity of pop operation in this case is O(1). The amortized complexity of pop operation is O(1).

Problem-3 Show how you can efficiently implement one stack using two queues. Analyze the running time of the stack operations.

Solution: Yes, it is possible to implement the Stack ADT using 2 implementations of the Queue ADT. One of the queues will be used to store the elements and the other to hold them temporarily during the *pop* and *top* methods. The *push* method would *enqueue* the given element onto the storage queue. The *top* method would transfer all but the last element from the storage queue onto the temporary queue, save the front element of the storage queue to be returned, transfer the last element to the temporary queue, then transfer all elements back to the storage queue. The *pop* method would do the same as top, except instead of transferring the last element onto the temporary queue after saving it for return, that last element would be discarded. Let Q1 and Q2 be the two queues to be used in the implementation of stack. All we have to do is to define the *push* and *pop* operations for the stack.

In the algorithms below, we make sure that one queue is always empty.

Push Operation Algorithm: Insert the element in whichever queue is not empty.

- Check whether queue Q1 is empty or not. If Q1 is empty then Enqueue the element into Q2.
- Otherwise enQueue the element into Q1.

Time Complexity: O(1).

Pop Operation Algorithm: Transfer $n - 1$ elements to the other queue and delete last from queue for performing pop operation.

- If queue Q1 is not empty then transfer $n - 1$ elements from Q1 to Q2 and then, deQueue the last element of Q1 and return it.
- If queue Q2 is not empty then transfer $n - 1$ elements from Q2 to Q1 and then, deQueue the last element of Q2 and return it.

Time Complexity: Running time of pop operation is $O(n)$ as each time pop is called, we are transferring all the elements from one queue to the other.

```
type Stack struct {
    Q1 Queue
    Q2 Queue
}
// Initialize your data structure here.
func NewStack() Stack {
    return Stack{}
}
// Push element data onto stack.
func (stack *Stack) Push(data int) {
    if stack.Q1.IsEmpty() { // Insert to queue whichever is not empty
        stack.Q2.EnQueue(data)
    } else {
        stack.Q1.EnQueue(data)
    }
}
// Removes the element on top of the stack and returns that element.
func (stack *Stack) Pop() int {
    if stack.Q2.IsEmpty() {
        i, n := 1, stack.Q1.Size()
        for i < n && !stack.Q1.IsEmpty() { // Transfer n-1 elements
            stack.Q2.EnQueue(stack.Q1.DeQueue())
            i++
        }
        return stack.Q1.DeQueue() // Delete the front element
    }
    i, n := 1, stack.Q2.Size()
    for i < n && !stack.Q2.IsEmpty() { // Transfer n-1 elements
        stack.Q1.EnQueue(stack.Q2.DeQueue()) // Delete the front element
        i++
    }
    return stack.Q2.DeQueue()
}
// Get the top element.
func (stack *Stack) Peek() int {
    if stack.Q2.IsEmpty() {
        i, n := 1, stack.Q1.Size()
        for i < n && !stack.Q1.IsEmpty() {
            stack.Q2.EnQueue(stack.Q1.DeQueue())
            i++
        }
        temp := stack.Q1.DeQueue() // The last element is the top element in the stack
        stack.Q2.EnQueue(temp)
        return temp
    }
    i, n := 1, stack.Q2.Size()
    for i < n && !stack.Q2.IsEmpty() {
        stack.Q1.EnQueue(stack.Q2.DeQueue())
        i++
    }
    temp := stack.Q2.DeQueue() // The last element is the top element in the stack
    stack.Q1.EnQueue(temp)
    return temp
}
// Returns whether the stack is empty.
func (stack *Stack) IsEmpty() bool {
    return stack.Q1.IsEmpty() && stack.Q2.IsEmpty()
}
type Queue struct {
    Data []int
}
```

```
func (queue *Queue) EnQueue(data int) {
    queue.Data = append(queue.Data, data)
}
func (queue *Queue) Front() int {
    if len(queue.Data) > 0 {
        return queue.Data[0]
    }
    return 0
}
func (queue *Queue) DeQueue() int {
    if len(queue.Data) > 0 {
        data := queue.Data[0]
        queue.Data = queue.Data[1:]
        return data
    }
    return 0
}
func (queue *Queue) Size() int {
    return len(queue.Data)
}
func (queue *Queue) IsEmpty() bool {
    return len(queue.Data) == 0
}
func main() {
    obj := NewStack()
    obj.Push(10)
    obj.Push(20)
    obj.Push(30)
    fmt.Println(obj.Peek())          // prints 30
    fmt.Println(obj.Pop())
    fmt.Println(obj.Peek())          // prints 20
    fmt.Println(obj.Pop())
    fmt.Println(obj.Peek())          // prints 20
    fmt.Println(obj.Pop())
}
```

Problem-4 **Maximum sum in sliding window:** Given array A[] with sliding window of size *w* which is moving from the very left of the array to the very right. Assume that we can only see the *w* numbers in the window. Each time the sliding window moves rightwards by one position. For example: The array is [1 3 -1 -3 5 3 6 7], and *w* is 3.

Window position	Max
[1 3 -1] -3 5 3 6 7	3
1 [3 -1 -3] 5 3 6 7	3
1 3 [-1 -3 5] 3 6 7	5
1 3 -1 [-3 5 3] 6 7	5
1 3 -1 -3 [5 3 6] 7	6
1 3 -1 -3 5 [3 6 7]	7

Input: A long array A[], and a window width *w*. **Output**: An array B[], B[i] is the maximum value from A[i] to A[i+w-1].

Requirement: Find a good optimal way to get B[i]

Solution: This problem can be solved with doubly ended queue (which supports insertion and deletion at both ends). Refer *Priority Queues* chapter for algorithms.

Problem-5 Given a queue Q containing n elements, transfer these items on to a stack S (initially empty) so that front element of Q appears at the top of the stack and the order of all other items is preserved. Using enQueue and deQueue operations for the queue, and push and pop operations for the stack, outline an efficient O(n) algorithm to accomplish the above task, using only a constant amount of additional storage.

Solution: Assume the elements of queue Q are $a_1, a_2 \dots a_n$. Dequeuing all elements and pushing them onto the stack will result in a stack with a_n at the top and a_1 at the bottom. This is done in O(n) time as deQueue and each push require constant time per operation. The queue is now empty. By popping all elements and pushing them on the queue we will get a_1 at the top of the stack. This is done again in O(*n*) time.

As in big-oh arithmetic we can ignore constant factors. The process is carried out in O(*n*) time. The amount of additional storage needed here has to be big enough to temporarily hold one item.

Problem-6 A queue is set up in a circular array A[0..n - 1] with front and rear defined as usual. Assume that $n - 1$ locations in the array are available for storing the elements (with the other element being used to detect full/empty condition). Give a formula for the number of elements in the queue in terms of *rear, front*, and *n*.

Solution: Consider the following figure to get a clear idea of the queue.

- Rear of the queue is somewhere clockwise from the front.
- To enQueue an element, we move *rear* one position clockwise and write the element in that position.
- To deQueue, we simply move *front* one position clockwise.
- Queue migrates in a clockwise direction as we enQueue and deQueue.
- Emptiness and fullness to be checked carefully.
- Analyze the possible situations (make some drawings to see where *front* and *rear* are when the queue is empty, and partially and totally filled). We will get this:

$$Number\ Of\ Elements = \begin{cases} rear - front + 1 & \text{if rear == front} \\ rear - front + n & \text{otherwise} \end{cases}$$

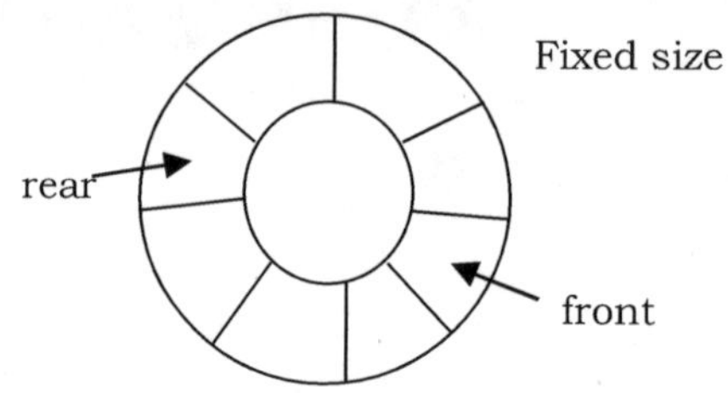

Problem-7 What is the most appropriate data structure to print elements of queue in reverse order?

Solution: Stack.

Problem-8 Implement doubly ended queues. A double-ended queue is an abstract data structure that implements a queue for which elements can only be added to or removed from the front (head) or back (tail).

Solution: A double ended queue also called as deque is a list in which the elements can be inserted or deleted at either end in constant time. It is also known as a head-tail linked list because elements can be added to or removed from either the front (head) or the back (tail) end. However, no element can be added and deleted from the middle. In the computer's memory, a deque is implemented using either a circular array or a circular doubly linked list. In a deque, two pointers are maintained, head and tail, which point to either end of the deque. The elements in a deque extend from the head end to the tail end and since it is circular, in a deque of n elements, nth element of deque is followed by the first element of the deque.

```
// minCapacity is the smallest capacity that deque may have.
// Must be power of 2 for bitwise modulus: x % n == x & (n - 1).
const minCapacity = 16

// DeQueue represents a single instance of the deque data structure.
type DeQueue struct {
    buffer   []interface{}
    head     int
    tail     int
    size     int
    capacity int
}
```

The following *Size* function returns the number of elements currently stored in the queue.

```
func (q *DeQueue) Size() int {
    return q.size
}
```

The *PushBack* function appends an element to the back of the queue. It implements FIFO when elements are removed with *PopFront*(), and LIFO when elements are removed with *PopBack*().

```
func (q *DeQueue) PushBack(elem interface{}) {
    q.growIfFull()
    q.buffer[q.tail] = elem
```

```
        // Calculate new tail position.
        q.tail = q.next(q.tail)
        q.size++
    }
```

The *PushFront* function prepends an element to the front of the queue.

```
    func (q *DeQueue) PushFront(elem interface{}) {
        q.growIfFull()
        // Calculate new head position.
        q.head = q.prev(q.head)
        q.buffer[q.head] = elem
        q.size++
    }
```

The *PopFront* function removes and returns the element from the front of the queue. It implements FIFO when used with *PushBack*(). If the queue is empty, it will give an exception.

```
    func (q *DeQueue) PopFront() interface{} {
        if q.size <= 0 {
            panic("deque: PopFront() called on empty queue")
        }
        ret := q.buffer[q.head]
        q.buffer[q.head] = nil
        // Calculate new head position.
        q.head = q.next(q.head)
        q.size--
        q.shrinkIfExcess()
        return ret
    }
    // next returns the next buffer position wrapping around buffer.
    func (q *DeQueue) next(i int) int {
        return (i + 1) & (len(q.buffer) - 1) // bitwise modulus
    }
```

The *PopBack* function removes and returns the element from the back of the queue. It implements LIFO when used with *PushBack*(). If the queue is empty, it will give an exception.

```
    func (q *DeQueue) PopBack() interface{} {
        if q.size <= 0 {
            panic("deque: PopBack() called on empty queue")
        }
        // Calculate new tail position
        q.tail = q.prev(q.tail)
        // Remove value at tail.
        ret := q.buffer[q.tail]
        q.buffer[q.tail] = nil
        q.size--
        q.shrinkIfExcess()
        return ret
    }
    // prev returns the previous buffer position wrapping around buffer.
    func (q *DeQueue) prev(i int) int {
        return (i - 1) & (len(q.buffer) - 1) // bitwise modulus
    }
```

The *Front* function returns the element at the front of the queue. This is the element that would be returned by PopFront(). This would call panics if the queue is empty.

```
    func (q *DeQueue) Front() interface{} {
        if q.size <= 0 {
            panic("deque: Front() called when empty")
        }
        return q.buffer[q.head]
    }
```

The *Back* function returns the element at the back of the queue. This is the element that would be returned by *PopBack*(). This call panics if the queue is empty.

```
func (q *DeQueue) Back() interface{} {
    if q.size <= 0 {
        panic("deque: Back() called when empty")
    }
    return q.buffer[q.prev(q.tail)]
}
```

The *At* returns the element at index i in the queue without removing the element from the queue. This method accepts only non-negative index values. *At*(0) refers to the first element and is the same as Front() and *At*(*Size*()-1) refers to the last element and is the same as *Back*(). If the index is invalid, the call panics.

The purpose of At is to allow DeQueue to serve as a more general-purpose circular buffer, where items are only added to and removed from the ends of the deque, but may be read from any place within the deque. Consider the case of a fixed-size circular log buffer: A new entry is pushed onto one end and when full the oldest is popped from the other end. All the log entries in the buffer must be readable without altering the buffer contents.

```
func (q *DeQueue) At(i int) interface{} {
    if i < 0 || i >= q.size {
        panic("deque: At() called with index out of range")
    }
    // bitwise modulus
    return q.buffer[(q.head+i)&(len(q.buffer)-1)]
}
```

The *Set* function puts the element at index *i* in the queue. Also, *Set* function shares the same purpose than At() but perform the opposite operation. The index i is the same index defined by *At*(). If the index is invalid, the call panics.

```
func (q *DeQueue) Set(i int, elem interface{}) {
    if i < 0 || i >= q.size {
        panic("deque: Set() called with index out of range")
    }
    // bitwise modulus
    q.buffer[(q.head+i)&(len(q.buffer)-1)] = elem
}
```

The *Clear* removes all elements from the queue, but retains the current capacity. This is useful when repeatedly reusing the queue at high frequency to avoid garbage collection during reuse. The queue will not be resized smaller as long as items are only added. Only when items are removed is the queue subject to getting resized smaller.

```
func (q *DeQueue) Clear() {
    // bitwise modulus
    modBits := len(q.buffer) - 1
    for h := q.head; h != q.tail; h = (h + 1) & modBits {
        q.buffer[h] = nil
    }
    q.head = 0
    q.tail = 0
    q.size = 0
}
```

The *SetMinCapacity* function sets a minimum capacity of $2^{minCapacityExp}$. If the value of the minimum capacity is less than or equal to the minimum allowed, then capacity is set to the minimum allowed. This may be called at anytime to set a new minimum capacity. Setting a larger minimum capacity may be used to prevent resizing when the number of stored items changes frequently across a wide range.

```
func (q *DeQueue) SetMinCapacity(minCapacityExp uint) {
    if 1<<minCapacityExp > minCapacity {
        q.capacity = 1 << minCapacityExp
    } else {
        q.capacity = minCapacity
    }
}
```

```
// growIfFull resizes up if the buffer is full.
func (q *DeQueue) growIfFull() {
```

```
        if len(q.buffer) == 0 {
            if q.capacity == 0 {
                q.capacity = minCapacity
            }
            q.buffer = make([]interface{}, q.capacity)
            return
        }
        if q.size == len(q.buffer) {
            q.resize()
        }
    }
```

```
    // shrinkIfExcess resize down if the buffer 1/4 full.
    func (q *DeQueue) shrinkIfExcess() {
        if len(q.buffer) > q.capacity && (q.size<<2) == len(q.buffer) {
            q.resize()
        }
    }
```

The *resize* function resizes the deque to fit exactly twice its current contents. This is used to grow the queue when it is full, and also to shrink it when it is only a quarter full.

```
    func (q *DeQueue) resize() {
        newBuf := make([]interface{}, q.size<<1)
        if q.tail > q.head {
            copy(newBuf, q.buffer[q.head:q.tail])
        } else {
            n := copy(newBuf, q.buffer[q.head:])
            copy(newBuf[n:], q.buffer[:q.tail])
        }
        q.head = 0
        q.tail = q.size
        q.buffer = newBuf
    }
```

Problem-9 Given a stack of integers, how do you check whether each successive pair of numbers in the stack is consecutive or not. The pairs can be increasing or decreasing, and if the stack has an odd number of elements, the element at the top is left out of a pair. For example, if the stack of elements are [4, 5, -2, -3, 11, 10, 5, 6, 20], then the output should be true because each of the pairs (4, 5), (-2, -3), (11, 10), and (5, 6) consists of consecutive numbers.

Solution:

```
    func checkStackPairwiseOrder(stack *Stack) bool {
        var q Queue
        q.Init(1)
        pairwiseOrdered := true
        for !stack.IsEmpty() {
            q.EnQueue(stack.Pop())
        }
        for !q.IsEmpty() {
            stack.Push(q.DeQueue())
        }
        for !stack.IsEmpty() {
            n := stack.Pop().(int)
            q.EnQueue(n)
            if !stack.IsEmpty() {
                m := stack.Pop().(int)
                q.EnQueue(m)
                if abs(n-m) != 1 {
                    pairwiseOrdered = false
                }
            }
        }
        for !q.IsEmpty() {
            stack.Push(q.DeQueue())
```

```
    }
    return pairwiseOrdered
}
```

Time Complexity: O(n). Space Complexity: O(n).

Problem-10 Given a queue of integers, rearrange the elements by interleaving the first half of the list with the second half of the list. For example, suppose a queue stores the following sequence of values: [11, 12, 13, 14, 15, 16, 17, 18, 19, 20]. Consider the two halves of this list: first half: [11, 12, 13, 14, 15] second half: [16, 17, 18, 19, 20]. These are combined in an alternating fashion to form a sequence of interleave pairs: the first values from each half (11 and 16), then the second values from each half (12 and 17), then the third values from each half (13 and 18), and so on. In each pair, the value from the first half appears before the value from the second half. Thus, after the call, the queue stores the following values: [11, 16, 12, 17, 13, 18, 14, 19, 15, 20].

Solution:

```
func interLeavingQueue(q *Queue) {
    if q.Size()%2 != 0 {
        return
    }
    stack := NewStack(1)
    halfSize := q.Size() / 2
    for i := 0; i < halfSize; i++ {
        stack.Push(q.DeQueue())
    }
    for !stack.IsEmpty() {
        q.EnQueue(stack.Pop())
    }
    for i := 0; i < halfSize; i++ {
        q.EnQueue(q.DeQueue())
    }
    for i := 0; i < halfSize; i++ {
        stack.Push(q.DeQueue())
    }
    for !stack.IsEmpty() {
        q.EnQueue(stack.Pop())
        q.EnQueue(q.DeQueue())
    }
}
```

Time Complexity: O(n). Space Complexity: O(n).

Problem-11 Given an integer k and a queue of integers, how do you reverse the order of the first k elements of the queue, leaving the other elements in the same relative order? For example, if k=4 and queue has the elements [10, 20, 30, 40, 50, 60, 70, 80, 90]; the output should be [40, 30, 20, 10, 50, 60, 70, 80, 90].

Solution:

```
func reverseQueueFirstKElements(q *Queue, k int) {
    if q == nil || k > q.Size() {
        return
    } else if k > 0 {
        stack := NewStack(1)
        for i := 0; i < k; i++ {
            stack.Push(q.DeQueue())
        }
        for !stack.IsEmpty() {
            q.EnQueue(stack.Pop())
        }
        for i := 0; i < q.Size()-k; i++ { // wrap around rest of elements
            q.EnQueue(q.DeQueue())
        }
    }
}
```

Time Complexity: O(n). Space Complexity: O(n).

CHAPTER

TREES

6

6.1 What is a Tree?

A *tree* is a data structure similar to a linked list but instead of each node pointing simply to the next node in a linear fashion, each node points to a number of nodes. Tree is an example of a non-linear data structure. A *tree* structure is a way of representing the hierarchical nature of a structure in a graphical form.

In trees ADT (Abstract Data Type), the order of the elements is not important. If we need ordering information, linear data structures like linked lists, stacks, queues, etc. can be used.

6.2 Glossary

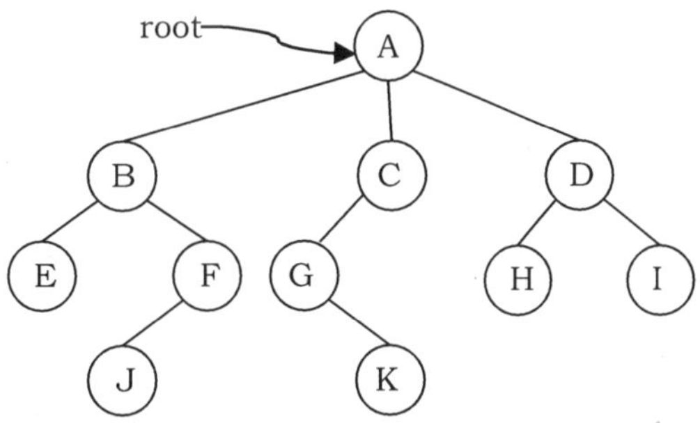

- The *root* of a tree is the node with no parents. There can be at most one root node in a tree (node A in the above example).
- An *edge* refers to the link from parent to child (all links in the figure).
- A node with no children is called *leaf* node (E, J, K, H and I).
- Children of same parent are called *siblings* (B, C, D are siblings of A, and E, F are the siblings of B).
- A node p is an *ancestor* of node q if there exists a path from *root* to q and p appears on the path. The node q is called a *descendant* of p. For example, A, C and G are the ancestors of K.
- The set of all nodes at a given depth is called the *level* of the tree (B, C and D are the same level). The root node is at level zero.

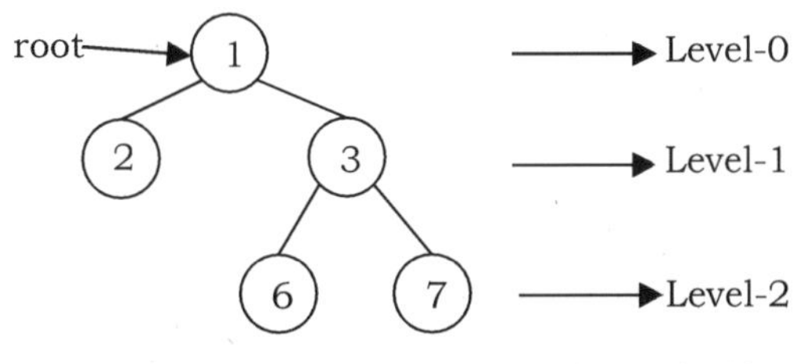

- The *depth* of a node is the length of the path from the root to the node (depth of G is 2, $A - C - G$).
- The *height* of a node is the length of the path from that node to the deepest node. The height of a tree is the length of the path from the root to the deepest node in the tree. A (rooted) tree with only one node (the root) has a height of zero. In the previous example, the height of B is 2 ($B - F - J$).
- *Height of the tree* is the maximum height among all the nodes in the tree and *depth of the tree* is the maximum depth among all the nodes in the tree. For a given tree, depth and height returns the same value. But for individual nodes we may get different results.

- The size of a node is the number of descendants it has including itself (the size of the subtree C is 3).
- If every node in a tree has only one child (except leaf nodes) then we call such trees *skew trees*. If every node has only left child then we call them *left skew trees*. Similarly, if every node has only right child then we call them *right skew trees*.

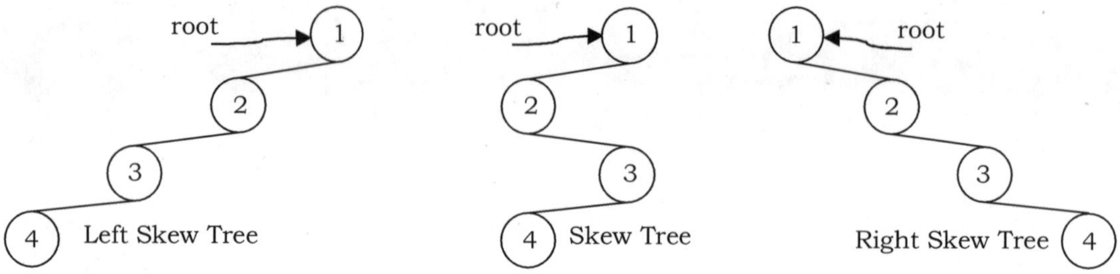

6.3 Binary Trees

A tree is called *binary tree* if each node has zero child, one child or two children. Empty tree is also a valid binary tree. We can visualize a binary tree as consisting of a root and two disjoint binary trees, called the left and right subtrees of the root.

Generic Binary Tree

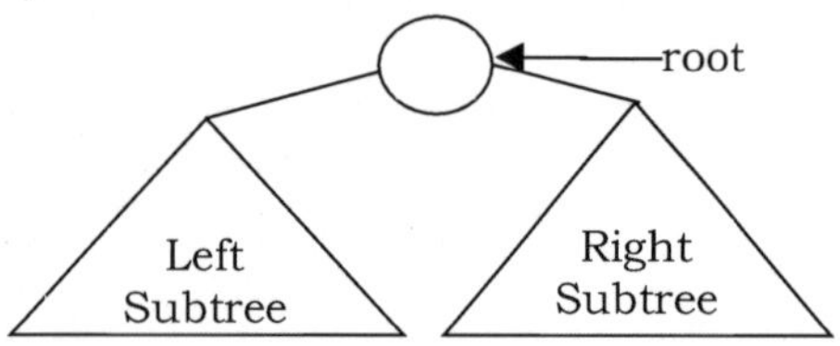

Example

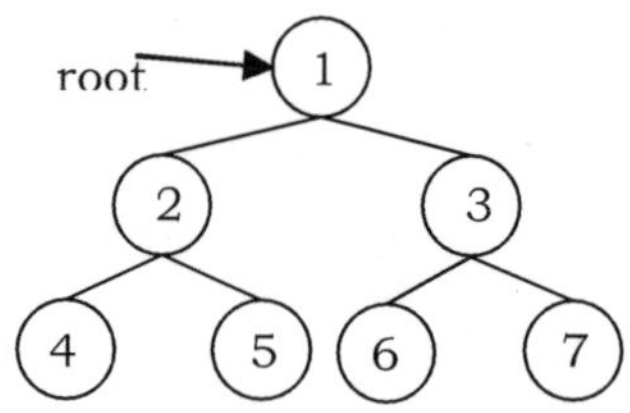

6.4 Types of Binary Trees

Strict Binary Tree: A binary tree is called *strict binary tree* if each node has exactly two children or no children.

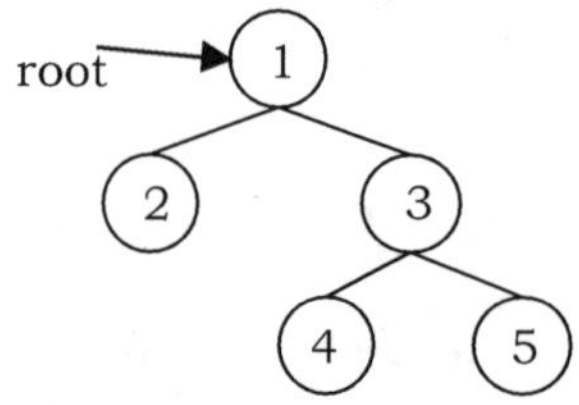

Full Binary Tree: A binary tree is called *full binary tree* if each node has exactly two children and all leaf nodes are at the same level.

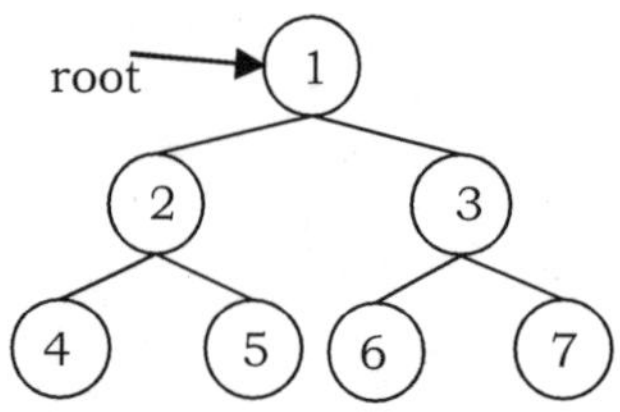

Complete Binary Tree: Before defining the *complete binary tree*, let us assume that the height of the binary tree is h. In complete binary trees, if we give numbering for the nodes by starting at the root (let us say the root node has 1) then we get a complete sequence from 1 to the number of nodes in the tree. While traversing we should give numbering for nil pointers also. A binary tree is called *complete binary tree* if all leaf nodes are at height h or $h - 1$ and also without any missing number in the sequence.

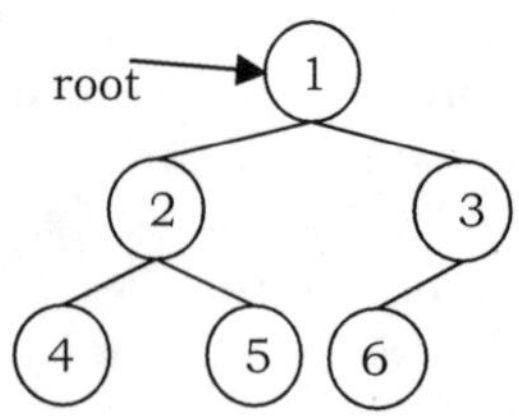

6.5 Properties of Binary Trees

For the following properties, let us assume that the height of the tree is h. Also, assume that root node is at height zero.

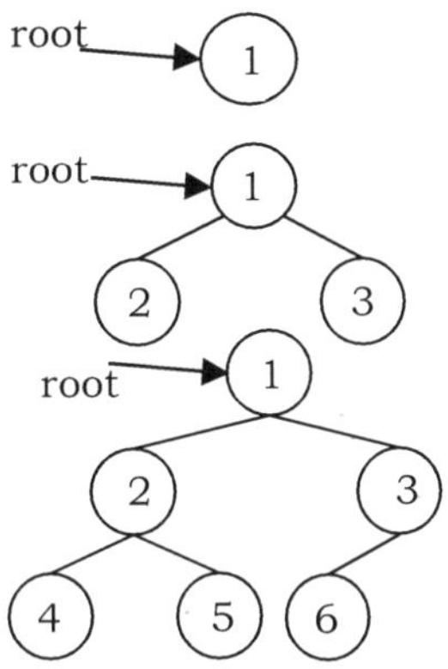

Height	Number of nodes at level h
$h = 0$	$2^0 = 1$
$h = 1$	$2^1 = 2$
$h = 2$	$2^2 = 4$

From the diagram we can infer the following properties:

- The number of nodes n in a full binary tree is $2^{h+1} - 1$. Since, there are h levels we need to add all nodes at each level $[2^0 + 2^1 + 2^2 + \cdots + 2^h = 2^{h+1} - 1]$.
- The number of nodes n in a complete binary tree is between 2^h (minimum) and $2^{h+1} - 1$ (maximum). For more information on this, refer to *Priority Queues* chapter.
- The number of leaf nodes in a full binary tree is 2^h.
- The number of None links (wasted pointers) in a complete binary tree of n nodes is $n + 1$.

Structure of Binary Trees

Now let us define structure of the binary tree. For simplicity, assume that the data of the nodes are integers. One way to represent a node (which contains data) is to have two links which point to left and right children along with data fields as shown below:

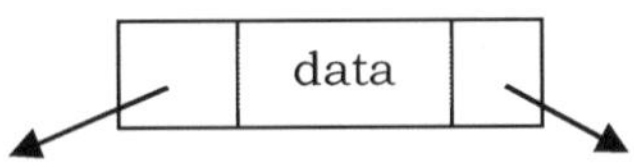

Or

```
// A BinaryTreeNode is a binary tree with integer values.
type BinaryTreeNode struct {
    left  *BinaryTreeNode
    data int
    right *BinaryTreeNode
}
```

Note: In trees, the default flow is from parent to children and it is not mandatory to show directed branches. For our discussion, we assume both the representations shown below are the same.

Operations on Binary Trees

Basic Operations

- Inserting an element into a tree
- Deleting an element from a tree
- Searching for an element
- Traversing the tree

Auxiliary Operations

- Finding the size of the tree
- Finding the height of the tree
- Finding the level which has maximum sum
- Finding the least common ancestor (LCA) for a given pair of nodes, and many more.

Applications of Binary Trees

Following are the some of the applications where *binary trees* play an important role:

- Expression trees are used in compilers.
- Huffman coding trees that are used in data compression algorithms.
- Binary Search Tree (BST), which supports search, insertion and deletion on a collection of items in $O(logn)$ (average).
- Priority Queue (PQ), which supports search and deletion of minimum (or maximum) on a collection of items in logarithmic time (in worst case).

6.6 Binary Tree Traversals

In order to process trees, we need a mechanism for traversing them, and that forms the subject of this section. The process of visiting all nodes of a tree is called *tree traversal*. Each node is processed only once but it may be visited more than once. As we have already seen in linear data structures (like linked lists, stacks, queues, etc.), the elements are visited in sequential order. But, in tree structures there are many different ways.

Tree traversal is like searching the tree, except that in traversal the goal is to move through the tree in a particular order. In addition, all nodes are processed in the *traversal but searching* stops when the required node is found.

Traversal Possibilities

Starting at the root of a binary tree, there are three main steps that can be performed and the order in which they are performed defines the traversal type. These steps are: performing an action on the current node (referred to as "visiting" the node and denoted with "D"), traversing to the left child node (denoted with "L"), and traversing to the right child node (denoted with "R"). This process can be easily described through recursion. Based on the above definition there are 6 possibilities:

1. LDR: Process left subtree, process the current node data and then process right subtree
2. LRD: Process left subtree, process right subtree and then process the current node data
3. DLR: Process the current node data, process left subtree and then process right subtree
4. DRL: Process the current node data, process right subtree and then process left subtree
5. RDL: Process right subtree, process the current node data and then process left subtree
6. RLD: Process right subtree, process left subtree and then process the current node data

Classifying the Traversals

The sequence in which these entities (nodes) are processed defines a particular traversal method. The classification is based on the order in which current node is processed. That means, if we are classifying based on current node (D) and if D comes in the middle then it does not matter whether L is on left side of D or R is on left side of D.

Similarly, it does not matter whether L is on right side of D or R is on right side of D. Due to this, the total 6 possibilities are reduced to 3 and these are:

- PreOrder (DLR) Traversal
- InOrder (LDR) Traversal
- PostOrder (LRD) Traversal

There is another traversal method which does not depend on the above orders and it is:

- Level Order Traversal: This method is inspired from Breadth First Traversal (BFS of Graph algorithms).

Let us use the diagram below for the remaining discussion.

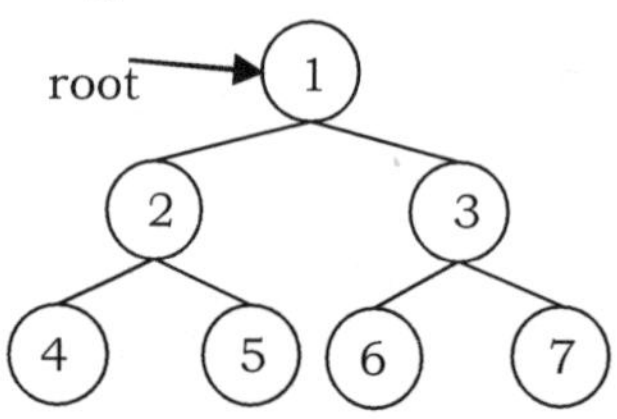

PreOrder Traversal

In preorder traversal, each node is processed before (pre) either of its subtrees. This is the simplest traversal to understand. However, even though each node is processed before the subtrees, it still requires that some information must be maintained while moving down the tree. In the example above, 1 is processed first, then the left subtree, and this is followed by the right subtree.

Therefore, processing must return to the right subtree after finishing the processing of the left subtree. To move to the right subtree after processing the left subtree, we must maintain the root information. The obvious ADT for such information is a stack. Because of its LIFO structure, it is possible to get the information about the right subtrees back in the reverse order.

Preorder traversal is defined as follows:

- Visit the root.
- Traverse the left subtree in Preorder.
- Traverse the right subtree in Preorder.

The nodes of tree would be visited in the order: 1 2 4 5 3 6 7

```
// PreOrder traverses a tree in pre-order
func PreOrder(root *BinaryTreeNode) {
    if root == nil {
        return
    }
    fmt.Printf("%d ", root.data)
    PreOrder(root.left)
    PreOrder(root.right)
}
```

```
// PreOrderWalk traverses a tree in pre-order, sending each data on a channel.
func PreOrderWalk(root *BinaryTreeNode, ch chan int) {
    if root == nil {
        return
    }
    ch <- root.data
    PreOrderWalk(root.left, ch)
    PreOrderWalk(root.right, ch)
}

// PreOrderWalker launches Walk in a new goroutine, and returns a read-only channel of values.
func PreOrderWalker(root *BinaryTreeNode) <-chan int {
    ch := make(chan int)
    go func() {
        PreOrderWalk(root, ch)
        close(ch)
    }()
    return ch
}
```

```
// NewBinaryTree returns a new, random binary tree holding the values 1k, 2k, ..., nk.
func NewBinaryTree(n, k int) *BinaryTreeNode {
    var root *BinaryTreeNode
    for _, v := range rand.Perm(n) {
        root = insert(root, (1+v)*k)
    }
    return root
}
func insert(root *BinaryTreeNode, v int) *BinaryTreeNode {
    if root == nil {
        return &BinaryTreeNode{nil, v, nil}
    }
    if v < root.data {
        root.left = insert(root.left, v)
        return root
    }
    root.right = insert(root.right, v)
    return root
}
func main() {
    t1 := NewBinaryTree(10, 1)
    // Pre-Order walk with print statements
    PreOrder(t1)
    fmt.Println()
```

```
    // Pre-Order walk with channel
    c := PreOrderWalker(t1)
    for {
        v, ok := <-c
        if !ok {
            break
        }
        fmt.Printf("%d ", v)
    }
}
```

Time Complexity: O(n). Space Complexity: O(n).

Non-Recursive PreOrder Traversal

In the recursive version, a stack is required as we need to remember the current node so that after completing the left subtree we can go to the right subtree. To simulate the same, first we process the current node and before going to the left subtree, we store the current node on stack. After completing the left subtree processing, *pop* the element and go to its right subtree. Continue this process until stack is nonempty.

```
func PreOrder(root *BinaryTreeNode) {
    if root == nil {
        return
    }
    current := root
    stack := NewStack(1)        // Refer Stacks chapter for implementation of dynamic stack
    stack.Push(current)
    for stack.Size() > 0 {
        temp := stack.Pop()
        current = temp.(*BinaryTreeNode)
        fmt.Printf("%d ", current.data)
        if current.right != nil {
            stack.Push(current.right)
        }
        if current.left != nil {
            stack.Push(current.left)
        }
    }
}
```

Time Complexity: O(n). Space Complexity: O(n).

InOrder Traversal

In Inorder Traversal the root is visited between the subtrees. Inorder traversal is defined as follows:

- Traverse the left subtree in Inorder.
- Visit the root.
- Traverse the right subtree in Inorder.

The nodes of tree would be visited in the order: 4 2 5 1 6 3 7

```
// InOrder traverses a tree in pre-order
func InOrder(root *BinaryTreeNode) {
    if root == nil {
        return
    }
    InOrder(root.left)
    fmt.Printf("%d ", root.data)
    InOrder(root.right)
}
```

```
// InOrderWalk traverses a tree in in-order, sending each data on a channel.
func InOrderWalk(root *BinaryTreeNode, ch chan int) {
    if root == nil {
        return
    }
```

```
        InOrderWalk(root.left, ch)
        ch <- root.data
        InOrderWalk(root.right, ch)
    }
    // InOrderWalker launches Walk in a new goroutine, and returns a read-only channel of values.
    func InOrderWalker(root *BinaryTreeNode) <-chan int {
        ch := make(chan int)
        go func() {
            InOrderWalk(root, ch)
            close(ch)
        }()
        return ch
    }
```

Time Complexity: O(n). Space Complexity: O(n).

Non-Recursive Inorder Traversal

The Non-recursive version of Inorder traversal is similar to Preorder. The only change is, instead of processing the node before going to left subtree, process it after popping (which is indicated after completion of left subtree processing).

```
    func InOrder(root *BinaryTreeNode) {
        if root == nil {
            return
        }
        temp := root
        stack := NewStack(1)        // Refer Stacks chapter for implementation of dynamic stack
        for stack.Size() > 0 || temp != nil {
            if temp != nil {
                stack.Push(temp)
                temp = temp.left
            } else {
                obj := stack.Pop()
                temp = obj.(*BinaryTreeNode)
                fmt.Printf("%d ", temp.data)
                temp = temp.right
            }
        }
    }
```

Time Complexity: O(n). Space Complexity: O(n).

PostOrder Traversal

In post order traversal, the root is visited after both subtrees. PostOrder traversal is defined as follows:

- Traverse the left subtree in PostOrder.
- Traverse the right subtree in PostOrder.
- Visit the root.

The nodes of the tree would be visited in the order: 4 5 2 6 7 3 1

```
    // PostOrder traverses a tree in pre-order
    func PostOrder(root *BinaryTreeNode) {
        if root == nil {
            return
        }
        PostOrder(root.left)
        PostOrder(root.right)
        fmt.Printf("%d ", root.data)
    }
    // PostOrderWalk traverses a tree in in-order, sending each data on a channel.
    func PostOrderWalk(root *BinaryTreeNode, ch chan int) {
        if root == nil {
            return
        }
```

```
        PostOrderWalk(root.left, ch)
        PostOrderWalk(root.right, ch)
        ch <- root.data
    }
    // PostOrderWalker launches Walk in a new goroutine, and returns a read-only channel of values.
    func PostOrderWalker(root *BinaryTreeNode) <-chan int {
        ch := make(chan int)
        go func() {
            PostOrderWalk(root, ch)
            close(ch)
        }()
        return ch
    }
```

Time Complexity: O(n). Space Complexity: O(n).

Non-Recursive PostOrder Traversal

In preorder and inorder traversals, after popping the stack element we do not need to visit the same vertex again. But in post order traversal, each node is visited twice. That means, after processing the left subtree we will visit the current node and after processing the right subtree we will visit the same current node. But we should be processing the node during the second visit. Here the problem is how to differentiate whether we are returning from the left subtree or the right subtree.

We use a *previous* variable to keep track of the earlier traversed node. Let's assume *current* is the current node that is on top of the stack. When *previous* is *current's* parent, we are traversing down the tree. In this case, we try to traverse to *current's* left child if available (i.e., push left child to the stack). If it is not available, we look at *current's* right child. If both left and right child do not exist (ie, *current* is a leaf node), we print *current's* value and pop it off the stack.

If prev is *current's* left child, we are traversing up the tree from the left. We look at *current's* right child. If it is available, then traverse down the right child (i.e., push right child to the stack); otherwise print *current's* value and pop it off the stack. If *previous* is *current's* right child, we are traversing up the tree from the right. In this case, we print *current's* value and pop it off the stack.

```
    func PostOrder(root *BinaryTreeNode) []int {
        var result []int
        stack := NewStack(1)        // Refer Stacks chapter for implementation of dynamic stack
        stack.Push(root)
        for !stack.IsEmpty() {
            temp := stack.Pop().(*BinaryTreeNode)
            result = append(result, temp.data)
            if temp.left != nil {
                stack.Push(temp.left)
            }
            if temp.right != nil {
                stack.Push(temp.right)
            }
        }
        n := len(result)
        for i := 0; i < n/2; i++ {
            j := n - i - 1
            result[i], result[j] = result[j], result[i]
        }
        fmt.Println(result)
        return result
    }
```

Alternative implementation using an array (list) as stack

```
    func PostOrder(root *BinaryTreeNode) []int {
        result := []int{}
        stack := []*BinaryTreeNode{root}
        for len(stack) > 0 {
            root = stack[len(stack)-1]
            stack = stack[:len(stack)-1]
```

```
            if root == nil {
                continue
            }
            result = append(result, root.data)
            stack = append(stack, root.left)
            stack = append(stack, root.right)
        }
        // reverse
        n := len(result)
        for i := 0; i < n/2; i++ {
            j := n - i - 1
            result[i], result[j] = result[j], result[i]
        }
        fmt.Println(result)
        return result
    }
```

Time Complexity: $O(n)$. Space Complexity: $O(n)$.

Level Order Traversal

Level order traversal is defined as follows:

- Visit the root.
- While traversing level l, keep all the elements at level $l + 1$ in queue.
- Go to the next level and visit all the nodes at that level.
- Repeat this until all levels are completed.

The nodes of the tree are visited in the order: [1] [2 3] [4 5 6 7]

```
func LevelOrder(root *BinaryTreeNode) [][]int { // Data from each level is being returned as a separate list
    if root == nil {
        return [][]int{}
    }
    var result [][]int
    queue := []*BinaryTreeNode{root}
    for len(queue) > 0 {
        qlen := len(queue)
        var level []int
        for i := 0; i < qlen; i++ {
            node := queue[0]
            level = append(level, node.data)
            queue = queue[1:]
            if node.left != nil {
                queue = append(queue, node.left)
            }
            if node.right != nil {
                queue = append(queue, node.right)
            }
        }
        result = append(result, level)
    }
    return result
}
```

Time Complexity: $O(n)$.
Space Complexity: $O(n)$. In the worst case, all the nodes on the entire last level could be in the queue.

Binary Trees: Problems & Solutions

Problem-1 Give an algorithm for finding maximum element in binary tree.

Solution: One simple way of solving this problem is: find the maximum element in left subtree, find the maximum element in right sub tree, compare them with root data and select the one which is giving the maximum value. This approach can be easily implemented with recursion.

```
func findMax(root *BinaryTreeNode) int {
```

```
    max := math.MinInt32
    if root != nil {
        root_val := root.data
        left := findMax(root.left)
        right := findMax(root.right)
        // Find the largest of the three values.
        if left > right {
            max = left
        } else {
            max = right
        }
        if root_val > max {
            max = root_val
        }
    }
    return max
}
```

Time Complexity: O(n). Space Complexity: O(n).

Problem-2 Give an algorithm for finding the maximum element in binary tree without recursion.

Solution: Using level order traversal: just observe the element's data while deleting.

```
func findMax(root *BinaryTreeNode) int { // Data from each level is being returned as a separate list
    max := math.MinInt32
    if root == nil {
        return max
    }
    queue := []*BinaryTreeNode{root}
    for len(queue) > 0 {
        qlen := len(queue)
        for i := 0; i < qlen; i++ {
            node := queue[0]
            if node.data > max {
                max = node.data
            }
            queue = queue[1:]
            if node.left != nil {
                queue = append(queue, node.left)
            }
            if node.right != nil {
                queue = append(queue, node.right)
            }
        }
    }
    return max
}
```

Time Complexity: O(n). Space Complexity: O(n).

Problem-3 Give an algorithm for searching an element in binary tree.

Solution: Given a binary tree, return true if a node with data is found in the tree. Recurse down the tree, choose the left or right branch by comparing data with each node's data.

```
func find(root *BinaryTreeNode, data int) *BinaryTreeNode {
    // Base case == empty tree, in that case, the data is not found so return false
    if root == nil {
        return root
    } else {
        //see if found here
        if data == root.data {
            return root
        } else {
            // otherwise recur down the correct subtree
            temp := find(root.left, data)
```

```
            if temp != nil {
                return temp
            } else {
                return find(root.right, data)
            }
        }
    }
}
```

Time Complexity: O(n). Space Complexity: O(n).

Problem-4 Give an algorithm for searching an element in binary tree without recursion.

Solution: We can use level order traversal for solving this problem. The only change required in level order traversal is, instead of printing the data, we just need to check whether the root data is equal to the element we want to search.

```
func find(root *BinaryTreeNode, data int) *BinaryTreeNode {
    if root == nil {
        return root
    }
    queue := []*BinaryTreeNode{root}
    for len(queue) > 0 {
        qlen := len(queue)
        for i := 0; i < qlen; i++ {
            node := queue[0]
            if node.data == data {
                return node
            }
            queue = queue[1:]
            if node.left != nil {
                queue = append(queue, node.left)
            }
            if node.right != nil {
                queue = append(queue, node.right)
            }
        }
    }
    return nil
}
```

Time Complexity: O(n). Space Complexity: O(n).

Problem-5 Give an algorithm for inserting an element into binary tree.

Solution: Since the given tree is a binary tree, we can insert the element wherever we want. To insert an element, we can use the level order traversal and insert the element wherever we find the node whose left or right child is nil.

```
Recursive insert with a random generator
func Insert(root *BinaryTreeNode, v int) *BinaryTreeNode {
    newNode := &BinaryTreeNode{nil, v, nil}
    if root == nil {
        return newNode
    }
    if root.left == nil {
        root.left = Insert(root.left, v)
    } else if root.right == nil {
        root.right = Insert(root.right, v)
    } else {
        randomize := rand.Intn(1)          // select either left or right randomly; It generate 0 or 1
        if randomize == 0 {
            root.left = Insert(root.left, v)
        } else {
            root.right = Insert(root.right, v)
        }
    }
```

```
    return root
}
```

Insert with level order traversal

```
func Insert(root *BinaryTreeNode, v int) *BinaryTreeNode {
    newNode := &BinaryTreeNode{nil, v, nil}
    if root == nil {
        return newNode
    }
    queue := []*BinaryTreeNode{root}
    for len(queue) > 0 {
        qlen := len(queue)
        for i := 0; i < qlen; i++ {
            node := queue[0]
            queue = queue[1:]
            if node.left != nil {
                queue = append(queue, node.left)
            } else {
                node.left = newNode
                return root
            }
            if node.right != nil {
                queue = append(queue, node.right)
            } else {
                node.right = newNode
                return root
            }
        }
    }
    return root
}
```

Time Complexity: O(n). Space Complexity: O(n).

Problem-6 Give an algorithm for finding the size of binary tree.

Solution: Calculate the size of left and right subtrees recursively, add 1 (current node) and return to its parent.

```
func Size(root *BinaryTreeNode) int {    // Compute the number of nodes in a tree
    if root == nil {
        return 0
    } else {
        return Size(root.left) + 1 + Size(root.right)
    }
}
```

Time Complexity: O(n). Space Complexity: O(n).

Problem-7 Can we solve Problem-6 without recursion?

Solution: Yes, using level order traversal.

```
func Size(root *BinaryTreeNode) int {    // Compute the number of nodes in a tree
    if root == nil {
        return 0
    }
    var result int
    queue := []*BinaryTreeNode{root}
    for len(queue) > 0 {
        qlen := len(queue)
        var level []int
        for i := 0; i < qlen; i++ {
            node := queue[0]
            result++
            level = append(level, node.data)
            queue = queue[1:]
            if node.left != nil {
                queue = append(queue, node.left)
```

```
            }
            if node.right != nil {
                queue = append(queue, node.right)
            }
        }

    }
    return result
}
```

Time Complexity: O(n). Space Complexity: O(n).

Problem-8 Give an algorithm for printing the level order data in reverse order. For example, the output for the below tree should be: [[4 5 6 7] [2 3] [1]]

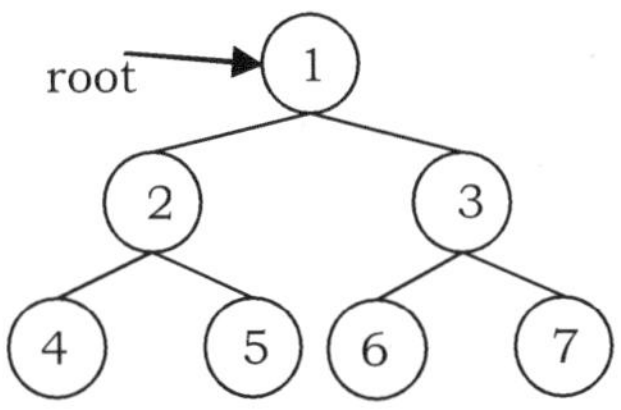

Solution:

```
func LevelOrderBottomUp(root *BinaryTreeNode) [][]int {
    if root == nil {
        return [][]int{}
    }
    var result [][]int
    queue := []*BinaryTreeNode{root}
    stack := NewStack(1)        // Refer Stacks chapter for implementation details
    for len(queue) > 0 {
        qlen := len(queue)
        var level []int
        for i := 0; i < qlen; i++ {
            node := queue[0]
            level = append(level, node.data)
            queue = queue[1:]
            if node.right != nil {
                queue = append(queue, node.right)
            }
            if node.left != nil {
                queue = append(queue, node.left)
            }

        }
        stack.Push(level)
    }
    for !stack.IsEmpty() {
        result = append(result, stack.Pop().([]int))
    }
    return result
}
```

Time Complexity: O(n). Space Complexity: O(n).

Problem-9 Give an algorithm for deleting the tree.

Solution:

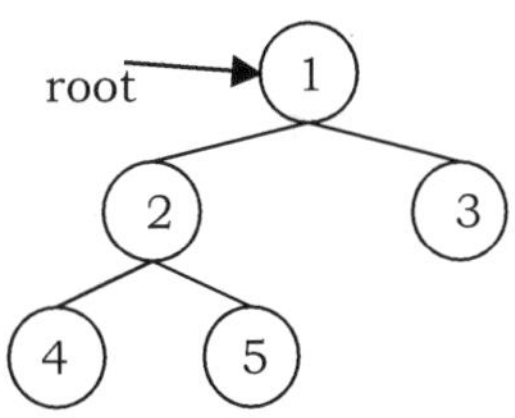

To delete a tree, we must traverse all the nodes of the tree and delete them one by one. So which traversal should we use: InOrder, PreOrder, PostOrder or Level order Traversal?

Before deleting the parent node, we should delete its children nodes first. We can use post order traversal as it does the work without storing anything. We can delete tree with other traversals also with extra space complexity. For the following, tree nodes are deleted in order – 4, 5, 2, 3, 1.

```
func DeleteTree(root *BinaryTreeNode) *BinaryTreeNode {
    if root == nil {
        return nil
    }
    // first delete both subtrees
    root.left = DeleteTree(root.left)
    root.right = DeleteTree(root.right)
    // Delete current node only after deleting subtrees
    root = nil
    return root
}
```

Time Complexity: O(n). Space Complexity: O(n).

Problem-10 Give an algorithm for finding the height (or depth) of the binary tree.

Solution: Recursively calculate height of left and right subtrees of a node and assign height to the node as max of the heights of two children plus 1. This is similar to *PreOrder* tree traversal (and *DFS* of Graph algorithms).

```
// Compute the height (or depth) of a tree
func Height(root *BinaryTreeNode) int {
    if root == nil {
        return 0
    } else {
        // compute the depth of each subtree
        leftheight := Height(root.left)
        rightheight := Height(root.right)
        if leftheight > rightheight {
            return leftheight + 1
        } else {
            return rightheight + 1
        }
    }
}
```

Time Complexity: O(n). Space Complexity: O(n).

Problem-11 Can we solve Problem-10 without recursion?

Solution: Yes, using level order traversal. This is similar to *BFS* of Graph algorithms. End of level is identified with nil.

```
// Compute the height (or depth) of a tree.
func Height(root *BinaryTreeNode) int {
    if root == nil {
        return 0
    }
    count := 0
    queue := []*BinaryTreeNode{root}
    for len(queue) > 0 {
        qlen := len(queue)
        var level []int
        for i := 0; i < qlen; i++ {
            node := queue[0]
            level = append(level, node.data)
            queue = queue[1:]
            if node.left != nil {
                queue = append(queue, node.left)
            }
            if node.right != nil {
                queue = append(queue, node.right)
            }
        }
```

```
        count++
    }
    return count
}
```

Time Complexity: O(n). Space Complexity: O(n).

Problem-12 Give an algorithm for finding the deepest node of the binary tree.

Solution: A node is deepest if it has the largest depth possible among any node in the entire tree. The deepest node is the one that gets deleted last from the queue.

```
// Compute the deepest node of a tree
func Deepest(root *BinaryTreeNode) *BinaryTreeNode {
    if root == nil {
        return nil
    }
    var node *BinaryTreeNode
    queue := []*BinaryTreeNode{root}
    for len(queue) > 0 {
        qlen := len(queue)
        var level []int
        for i := 0; i < qlen; i++ {
            node = queue[0]
            level = append(level, node.data)
            queue = queue[1:]

            if node.left != nil {
                queue = append(queue, node.left)
            }
            if node.right != nil {
                queue = append(queue, node.right)
            }
        }
    }
    return node
}
```

Time Complexity: O(n). Space Complexity: O(n).

Problem-13 Give an algorithm for deleting an element (assuming data is given) from binary tree.

Solution: The deletion of a node in binary tree can be implemented as

- Starting at root, find the node which we want to delete.
- Find the deepest node in the tree.
- Replace the deepest node's data with node to be deleted.
- Then delete the deepest node.

Problem-14 Give an algorithm for finding the number of leaves in the binary tree without using recursion.

Solution: The set of nodes whose both left and right children are *nil* are called leaf nodes.

```
// Compute the number of leaves in a tree
func LeavesCount(root *BinaryTreeNode) int {
    if root == nil {
        return 0
    }
    count := 0
    queue := []*BinaryTreeNode{root}
    for len(queue) > 0 {
        qlen := len(queue)
        var level []int
        for i := 0; i < qlen; i++ {
            node := queue[0]
            level = append(level, node.data)
            queue = queue[1:]
            if node.left == nil && node.right == nil {
                count++
```

```
            }
            if node.left != nil {
                queue = append(queue, node.left)
            }
            if node.right != nil {
                queue = append(queue, node.right)
            }
        }
    }
    return count
}
```

Time Complexity: O(n). Space Complexity: O(n).

Problem-15 Give an algorithm for finding the number of full nodes in the binary tree without using recursion.

Solution: The set of all nodes with both left and right children are called full nodes.

```
// Compute the number of full nodes in a tree
func FullNodesCount(root *BinaryTreeNode) int {
    if root == nil {
        return 0
    }
    count := 0
    queue := []*BinaryTreeNode{root}
    for len(queue) > 0 {
        qlen := len(queue)
        var level []int
        for i := 0; i < qlen; i++ {
            node := queue[0]
            level = append(level, node.data)
            queue = queue[1:]
            if node.left != nil && node.right != nil {
                count++
            }
            if node.left != nil {
                queue = append(queue, node.left)
            }
            if node.right != nil {
                queue = append(queue, node.right)
            }
        }
    }
    return count
}
```

Time Complexity: O(n). Space Complexity: O(n).

Problem-16 Give an algorithm for finding the number of half nodes (nodes with only one child) in the binary tree without using recursion.

Solution: The set of all nodes with either left or right child (but not both) are called half nodes.

```
// Compute the number of nodes in a tree with either left subtree or right subtree but not both
func HalfNodesCount(root *BinaryTreeNode) int {
    if root == nil {
        return 0
    }
    count := 0
    queue := []*BinaryTreeNode{root}
    for len(queue) > 0 {
        qlen := len(queue)
        var level []int
        for i := 0; i < qlen; i++ {
            node := queue[0]
            level = append(level, node.data)
            queue = queue[1:]
            if (node.left != nil && node.right == nil) || (node.right != nil && node.left == nil) {
```

```
                fmt.Println(node.data)
                count++
            }
            if node.left != nil {
                queue = append(queue, node.left)
            }
            if node.right != nil {
                queue = append(queue, node.right)
            }
        }
    }
    return count
}
```

Time Complexity: O(n). Space Complexity: O(n).

Problem-17 Given two binary trees, return true if they are structurally identical.

Solution:

Algorithm:

- If both trees are nil then return true.
- If both trees are not nil, recursively check left and right subtree structures.

```
// Return true if they are structurally identical
func CompareStructures(root1, root2 *BinaryTreeNode) bool {
    // both empty->true
    if root1 == nil && root2 == nil {
        return true
    }
    if root1 == nil || root2 == nil {
        return false
    }
    // both non-empty->compare them
    return compareStructures(root1.left, root2.left) && compareStructures(root1.right, root2.right)
}
```

Time Complexity: O(n). Space Complexity: O(n), for recursive stack.

Problem-18 Give an algorithm for finding the diameter of the binary tree. The diameter of a tree (sometimes called the *width*) is the number of nodes on the longest path between two leaves in the tree.

Solution: There are three cases to consider when trying to find the longest path between two nodes in a binary tree (diameter):

- The longest path passes through the root,
- The longest path is entirely contained in the left sub-tree,
- The longest path is entirely contained in the right sub-tree.

We can find Diameter of the tree with post order traversal logic. At each node calculate diameter of left node and right node, and check if Left+Right+1 is greater than previously found diameter.

```
d = max(left_height + right_height + 1, max(left_diameter, right_diameter))
```

```
func DiameterOfBinaryTree(root *BinaryTreeNode) int {
    if root == nil {
        return 0
    }
    var diameter int
    Diameter(root, &diameter)
    return diameter
}
func Diameter(root *BinaryTreeNode, diameter *int) int {
    if root == nil {
        return 0
    }
    leftDepth := Diameter(root.left, diameter)
    rightDepth := Diameter(root.right, diameter)
    if leftDepth+rightDepth > *diameter {
```

```
        *diameter = leftDepth + rightDepth
    }
    return max(leftDepth, rightDepth) + 1
}
```

Alternative coding

```
func Diameter(root *BinaryTreeNode) int {
    diameter := 0
    var depth func(node *BinaryTreeNode) int
    depth = func(node *BinaryTreeNode) int {
        if node == nil {
            return 0
        }
        leftDepth := depth(node.left)
        rightDepth := depth(node.right)
        diameter = max(diameter, leftDepth+rightDepth)
        return max(leftDepth, rightDepth) + 1
    }
    depth(root)
    return diameter
}
```

Time Complexity: O(n). Space Complexity: O(n).

Problem-19 Give an algorithm for finding the level that has the maximum sum in the binary tree.

Solution: The logic is very much similar to finding the number of levels. The only change is, we need to keep track of the sums as well.

```
func maxLevelSum(root *BinaryTreeNode) (elements []int, maxSum, level int) {
    elements , maxSum, level = []int{}, math.MinInt32, 0
    if root == nil {
        return elements , maxSum, level
    }
    var result [][]int
    levelNumber := 0
    queue := []*BinaryTreeNode{root}
    for len(queue) > 0 {
        qlen := len(queue)
        var currentLevel []int
        sum := 0
        for i := 0; i < qlen; i++ {
            node := queue[0]
            currentLevel = append(currentLevel, node.data)
            sum = sum + node.data
            queue = queue[1:]
            if node.left != nil {
                queue = append(queue, node.left)
            }
            if node.right != nil {
                queue = append(queue, node.right)
            }
        }
        if sum > maxSum {
            maxSum = sum
            elements = currentLevel
            level  = levelNumber
        }
        result = append(result, currentLevel)
        levelNumber++
    }
    return elements , maxSum, level
}
```

Time Complexity: O(n). Space Complexity: O(n).

Problem-20 Given a binary tree, print out all its root-to-leaf paths.

Solution: Refer to comments in functions.

```
func BinaryTreePaths(root *BinaryTreeNode) []string {
    result := make([]string, 0)
    paths(root, "", &result)
    return result
}
func paths(root *BinaryTreeNode, prefix string, result *[]string) {
    if root == nil {
        return
    }
    // append this node to the path array
    if len(prefix) == 0 {
        prefix += strconv.Itoa(root.data)
    } else {
        prefix += "->" + strconv.Itoa(root.data)
    }
    if root.left == nil && root.right == nil { // it's a leaf, so print the path that led to here
        *result = append(*result, prefix+"\n")
        return
    }
    // otherwise try both subtrees
    paths(root.left, prefix, result)
    paths(root.right, prefix, result)
}
```

Time Complexity: O(n). Space Complexity: O(n), for recursive stack.

Problem-21 Give an algorithm for checking the existence of path with given sum. That means, given a sum, check whether there exists a path from root to any of the nodes.

Solution: For this problem, the strategy is: subtract the node value from the sum before calling its children recursively, and check to see if the sum is 0 when we run out of tree.

```
func HasPathSum(root *BinaryTreeNode, sum int) bool {
    allSums := make([]int, 0)
    getAllSums(root, &allSums, 0)
    for _, val := range allSums {
        if sum == val {
            allSums = []int{}
            return true
        }
    }
    allSums = []int{}
    return false
}
func getAllSums(root *BinaryTreeNode, allSums *[]int, currSum int) {
    if root != nil {
        currSum += root.data
        if root.left == nil && root.right == nil {
            *allSums = append(*allSums, currSum)
        } else {
            getAllSums(root.left, allSums, currSum)
            getAllSums(root.right, allSums, currSum)
        }
    }
}
```

Time Complexity: O(n). Space Complexity: O(n).

Problem-22 Give an algorithm for finding the sum of all elements in binary tree.

Solution: Recursively, call left subtree sum, right subtree sum and add their values to current nodes data.

```
func Sum(root *BinaryTreeNode) int {
```

```
    if root == nil {
        return 0
    }
    return (root.data + Sum(root.left) + Sum(root.right))
}
```

Time Complexity: O(n). Space Complexity: O(n).

Problem-23 Can we solve Problem-22 without recursion?

Solution: We can use level order traversal with a simple change. Every time, after deleting an element from queue, add the nodes data to *sum* variable.

```
func Sum(root *BinaryTreeNode) int {
    if root == nil {
        return 0
    }
    var result int
    queue := []*BinaryTreeNode{root}
    for len(queue) > 0 {
        qlen := len(queue)
        var level []int
        for i := 0; i < qlen; i++ {
            node := queue[0]
            result += node.data
            level = append(level, node.data)
            queue = queue[1:]
            if node.left != nil {
                queue = append(queue, node.left)
            }
            if node.right != nil {
                queue = append(queue, node.right)
            }
        }
    }
    return result
}
```

Time Complexity: O(n). Space Complexity: O(n).

Problem-24 Give an algorithm for converting a tree to its mirror (also, called invert tree). Mirror of a tree is another tree with left and right children of all non-leaf nodes interchanged. The trees below are mirrors to each other.

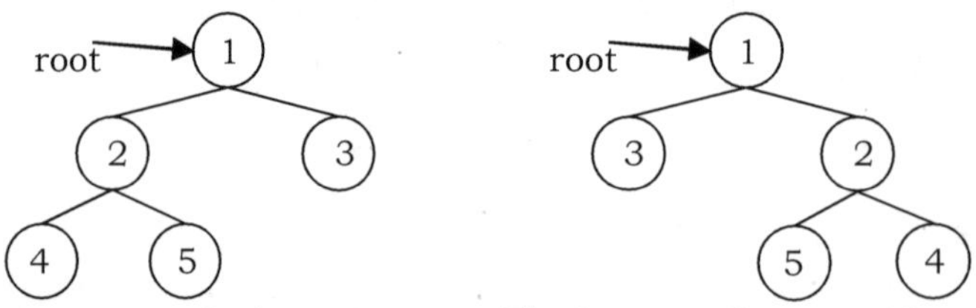

Solution: The inverse of an empty tree is the empty tree. The inverse of a tree with root r, and subtrees right and left, is a tree with root, whose *right* subtree is the inverse of $left$, and whose $left$ subtree is the inverse of $right$.

```
func InvertTree(root *BinaryTreeNode) *BinaryTreeNode {
    if root != nil {
        root.left, root.right = InvertTree(root.right), InvertTree(root.left)
    }
    return root
}
```

Alternative coding

```
func InvertTree(root *BinaryTreeNode) {
    if root == nil {
        return
    }
    root.left, root.right = root.right, root.left      // swap the pointers in this node
    InvertTree(root.left)
    InvertTree(root.right)
    return
```

```
}
```

Time Complexity: O(n). Space Complexity: O(n).

Problem-25 Given two trees, give an algorithm for checking whether they are mirrors of each other.

Solution:

```
func checkMirror(root1, root2 *BinaryTreeNode) bool {
    if root1 == nil && root2 == nil {
        return true
    }
    if root1 == nil || root2 == nil {
        return false
    }
    if root1.data != root2.data {
        return false
    }
    return checkMirror(root1.left, root2.right) && checkMirror(root1.right, root2.left)
}
```

Time Complexity: O(n). Space Complexity: O(n).

Problem-26 Give an algorithm for finding LCA (Least Common Ancestor) of two nodes in a Binary Tree. The lowest common ancestor is defined between two nodes α and β as the lowest node in T that has both α and β as descendants (where we allow a node to be a descendant of itself).

Solution: The approach is pretty intuitive. Traverse the tree in a depth first manner. The moment we encounter either of the nodes α or β, return some boolean flag. The flag helps to determine if we found the required nodes in any of the paths. The least common ancestor would then be the node for which both the subtree recursions return a true flag. It can also be the node which itself is one of α or β and for which one of the subtree recursions returns a true flag.

Algorithm

- Start traversing the tree from the root node.
- If the current node itself is one of α or β, we would mark a variable mid as true and continue the search for the other node in the left and right branches.
- If either of the left or the right branch returns true, this means one of the two nodes was found below.
- If at any point in the traversal, any two of the three flags left, right or mid become true, this means we have found the lowest common ancestor for the nodes α and β.

```
func LCA(root *BinaryTreeNode, α, β int) *BinaryTreeNode {
    if root == nil {
        return root
    }
    if root.data == α || root.data == β {
        return root
    }
    left := LCA(root.left, α, β)
    right := LCA(root.right, α, β)
    if left != nil && right != nil {
        return root
    }
    if left != nil {
        return left
    } else {
        return right
    }
}
```

Time Complexity: O(n). Space Complexity: O(n) for recursion.

Problem-27 Give an algorithm for constructing binary tree from given Inorder and Preorder traversals.

Solution: Let us consider the traversals below:

Inorder sequence: D B E A F C
Preorder sequence: A B D E C F

In a Preorder sequence, leftmost element denotes the root of the tree. So we know 'A' is the root for given sequences. By searching 'A' in Inorder sequence we can find out all elements on the left side of 'A', which come under the left subtree, and elements on the right side of '*A*', which come under the right subtree. So we get the structure as seen below.

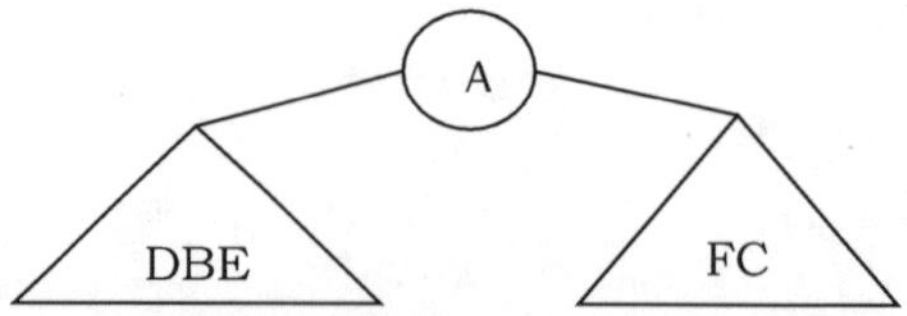

We recursively follow the above steps and get the following tree.

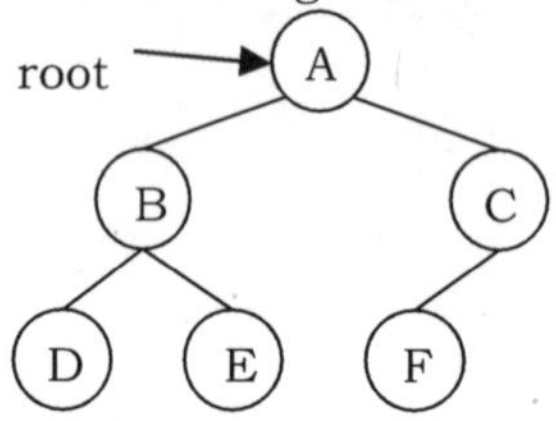

Algorithm: BuildBinaryTree ()

1. Select an element from *Preorder*. Increment a *Preorder* index variable (*preOrderIndex* in code below) to pick next element in next recursive call.
2. Create a new tree node (*newNode*) with the data as selected element.
3. Find the selected element's index in Inorder. Let the index be *inOrderIndex*.
4. Call BuildBinaryTree for elements before *inOrderIndex* and make the built tree as left subtree of *newNode*.
5. Call BuildBinaryTree for elements after *inOrderIndex* and make the built tree as right subtree of *newNode*.
6. return *newNode*.

```
func BuildBinaryree(preOrder []int, inOrder []int) *BinaryTreeNode {
    if len(preOrder) == 0 || len(inOrder) == 0 {
        return nil
    }
    inOrderIndex := find(inOrder, preOrder[0])
    left := BuildBinaryree(preOrder[1:inOrderIndex+1], inOrder[:inOrderIndex])
    right := BuildBinaryree(preOrder[inOrderIndex+1:], inOrder[inOrderIndex+1:])
    return &BinaryTreeNode{
        data:  preOrder[0],
        left:  left,
        right: right,
    }
}
func find(A []int, target int) int {
    for i, x := range A {
        if x == target {
            return i
        }
    }
    return -1
}
```

Time Complexity: O(n). Space Complexity: O(n).

Problem-28 If we are given two traversal sequences, can we construct the binary tree uniquely?

Solution: It depends on what traversals are given. If one of the traversal methods is *Inorder* then the tree can be constructed uniquely, otherwise not.

Therefore, the following combinations can uniquely identify a tree:

- In-order and Pre-order
- In-order and Post-order
- In-order and Level-order

The following combinations do not uniquely identify a tree.

- Post-order and Pre-order
- Pre-order and Level-order
- Post-order and Level-order

For example, Pre-order, Level-order and Post-order traversals are the same for the above trees:

Preorder Traversal = AB   Postorder Traversal = BA   Level-order Traversal = AB

So, even if three of them (PreOrder, Level-Order and PostOrder) are given, the tree cannot be constructed uniquely.

Problem-29 **Zigzag Tree Traversal:** Give an algorithm to traverse a binary tree in Zigzag order. For example, the output for the tree below should be: 1 3 2 4 5 6 7

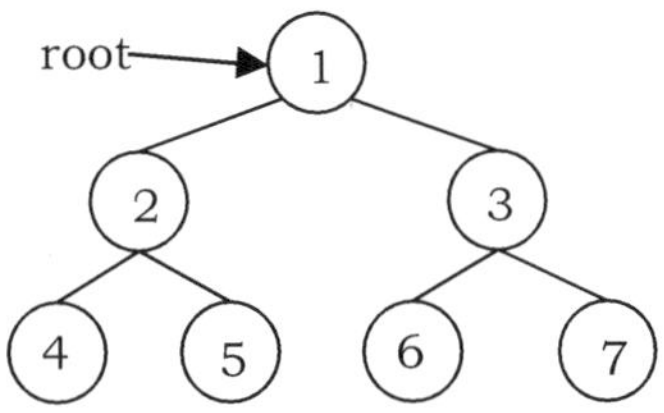

Solution: We can just perform usual level order traversal and once store values at the same height, and then only if we should store them from right to left, reverse the array before storing it to the result.

```
func ZigzagLevelOrder(root *BinaryTreeNode) [][]int {
    if root == nil {
        return [][]int{}
    }
    queue := []*BinaryTreeNode{root}
    var res [][]int
    leftToright := false
    for {
        qlen := len(queue)
        if qlen == 0 {
            break
        }
        var levelData []int
        for i := qlen - 1; i >= 0; i-- {
            node := queue[0]
            levelData = append(levelData, node.data)

            if node.left != nil {
                queue = append(queue, node.left)
            }
            if node.right != nil {
                queue = append(queue, node.right)
            }
            queue = queue[1:]
        }
        if leftToright {
            reverse(levelData)
        }
        res = append(res, levelData)
        leftToright = !leftToright
    }
    return res
}
func reverse(list []int) {
    if len(list) > 0 {
        for i := 0; i < len(list)/2; i++ {
            list[i], list[len(list)-1-i] = list[len(list)-1-i], list[i]
        }
    }
}
```

Time Complexity: O(n). Space Complexity: O(n), for the queue.

Problem-30 Can we solve Problem-29, without reverse function?

Solution: We can just perform usual level order traversal and once store values at the same height, and then only if we should store them from right to left, prepend to the array (current queue data) instead of appending.

```
func ZigzagLevelOrder(root *BinaryTreeNode) [][]int {
    if root == nil {
        return make([][]int, 0)
    }
    queue := []*BinaryTreeNode{}
    queue = append(queue, root)
    var result [][]int
    level := 0
    for len(queue) > 0 {
        size := len(queue)
        if len(result) == level {
            result = append(result, []int{})
        }
        for i := 0; i < size; i++ {
            cur := queue[0]
            if level%2 == 0 { // append data to current queue; left to right
                result[level] = append(result[level], cur.data)
            } else { // append current queue to the data; right to left
                result[level] = append([]int{cur.data}, result[level]...)
            }
            if cur.left != nil {
                queue = append(queue, cur.left)
            }
            if cur.right != nil {
                queue = append(queue, cur.right)
            }
            queue = queue[1:]
        }
        level++
    }
    return result
}
```

Time Complexity: O(n). Space Complexity: O(n), for the queue.

Problem-31 Can we solve Problem-29, without reverse function?

Solution: This problem can be solved easily using two stacks. Assume the two stacks are: *currentLevel* and *nextLevel*. We would also need a variable to keep track of the current level order (whether it is left to right or right to left).

We pop from *currentLevel* stack and print the node's value. Whenever the current level order is from left to right, push the node's left child, then its right child, to stack *nextLevel*. Since a stack is a Last In First Out (*LIFO*) structure, the next time that nodes are popped off nextLevel, it will be in the reverse order.

On the other hand, when the current level order is from right to left, we would push the node's right child first, then its left child. Finally, don't forget to swap those two stacks at the end of each level (*i.e.*, when *currentLevel* is empty).

```
func ZigzagLevelOrder(root *BinaryTreeNode) [][]int {
    if root == nil {
        return [][]int{}
    }
    lqueue, rqueue := []*BinaryTreeNode{root}, []*BinaryTreeNode{root}
    var res [][]int
    leftToRight := true
    for {
        lqlen, rqlen := len(lqueue), len(rqueue)
        if lqlen == 0 || rqlen == 0 {
            break
        }
        var arr []int
```

```
            for i := 0; i < lqlen; i++ {
                lnode, rnode := lqueue[0], rqueue[0]
                if lnode.left != nil {
                    lqueue = append(lqueue, lnode.left)
                }
                if lnode.right != nil {
                    lqueue = append(lqueue, lnode.right)
                }

                if rnode.right != nil {
                    rqueue = append(rqueue, rnode.right)
                }
                if rnode.left != nil {
                    rqueue = append(rqueue, rnode.left)
                }
                lqueue, rqueue = lqueue[1:], rqueue[1:]

                if leftToRight {
                    arr = append(arr, lnode.data)
                } else {
                    arr = append(arr, rnode.data)
                }
            }
            res = append(res, arr)
            leftToRight = !leftToRight
        }
        return res
    }
```

Time Complexity: $O(n)$. Space Complexity: Space for two stacks = $O(n) + O(n) = O(n)$.

Problem-32 Give an algorithm for finding the vertical sum of a binary tree. For example,
The tree has 5 vertical lines

Vertical-1: nodes-4 => vertical sum is 4

Vertical-2: nodes-2 => vertical sum is 2

Vertical-3: nodes-1,5,6 => vertical sum is 1 + 5 + 6 = 12

Vertical-4: nodes-3 => vertical sum is 3

Vertical-5: nodes-7 => vertical sum is 7

We need to output: 4 2 12 3 7

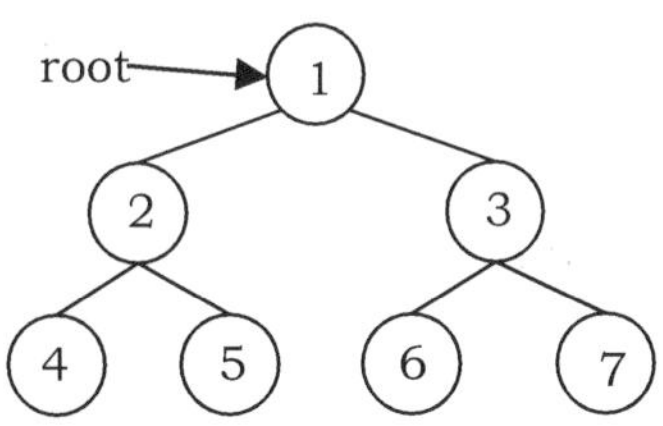

Solution: This problem can be easily solved with the help of hashing tables. The idea is to create an empty map where each key represents the relative horizontal distance of a node from the root node and value in the map maintains sum of all nodes present at same horizontal distance. Then we do a pre-order traversal of the tree and we update the sum for current horizontal distance in the map. For each node, we recur for its left subtree by decreasing horizontal distance by 1 and recur for right subtree by increasing horizontal distance by 1.

```
    func VerticalTraversal(root *BinaryTreeNode) [][]int {
        data := [][]int{}
        preorder(root, 0, 0, &data)
        sort.Slice(data, func(i, j int) bool {
            if data[i][0] == data[j][0] {
                if data[i][1] == data[j][1] {
                    return data[i][2] < data[j][2]
                }
                return data[i][1] > data[j][1]
            }
            return data[i][0] < data[j][0]
        })
        lastX := data[0][0]
```

```
    traversal := [][]int{{}}
    for _, v := range data {
        if v[0] != lastX {
            traversal = append(traversal, []int{})
            lastX = v[0]
        }
        traversal[len(traversal)-1] = append(traversal[len(traversal)-1], v[2])
    }
    return traversal
}
func preorder(node *BinaryTreeNode, x, y int, data *[][]int) {
    if node == nil {
        return
    }
    *data = append(*data, []int{x, y, node.data})
    preorder(node.left, x-1, y-1, data)
    preorder(node.right, x+1, y-1, data)
}
```

Problem-33 How many different binary trees are possible with n nodes?

Solution: For example, consider a tree with 3 nodes ($n = 3$). It will have the maximum combination of 5 different (i.e., $2^3 - 3 = 5$) trees.

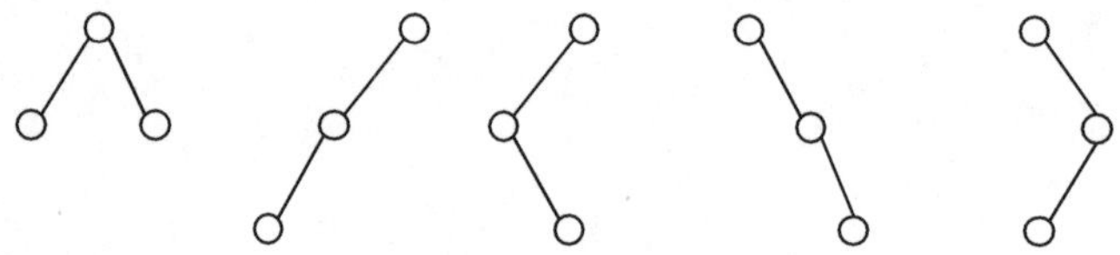

In general, if there are n nodes, there exist $2^n - n$ different trees.

Problem-34 Given a tree with a special property where leaves are represented with 'L' and internal node with 'I'. Also, assume that each node has either 0 or 2 children. Given preorder traversal of this tree, construct the tree. **Example**: Given preorder string => ILILL

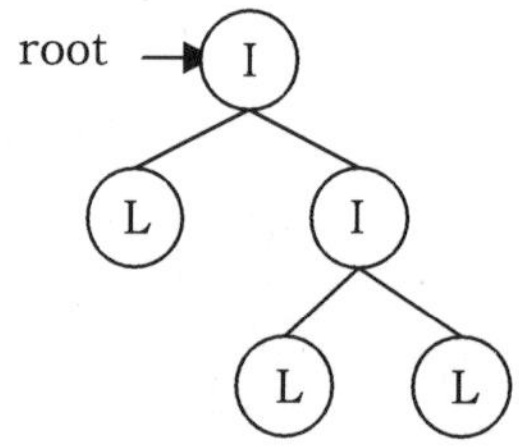

Solution: First, we should see how preorder traversal is arranged. Pre-order traversal means first put root node, then pre-order traversal of left subtree and then pre-order traversal of right subtree. In a normal scenario, it's not possible to detect where left subtree ends and right subtree starts using only pre-order traversal. Since every node has either 2 children or no child, we can surely say that if a node exists then its sibling also exists. So every time when we are computing a subtree, we need to compute its sibling subtree as well.

Secondly, whenever we get 'L' in the input string, that is a leaf and we can stop for a particular subtree at that point. After this 'L' node (left child of its parent 'L'), its sibling starts. If 'L' node is right child of its parent, then we need to go up in the hierarchy to find the next subtree to compute.

Keeping the above invariant in mind, we can easily determine when a subtree ends and the next one starts. It means that we can give any start node to our method and it can easily complete the subtree it generates going outside of its nodes. We just need to take care of passing the correct start nodes to different sub-trees.

```
func BuildTreeFromPreOrder(preOrder string, i *int) *BinaryTreeNode {
    newNode := &BinaryTreeNode{
        data: preOrder[*i],
    }
    if len(preOrder) == 0 {          // boundary Condition
        return nil
    }
    if preOrder[*i] == 'L' {         // on reaching leaf node, return
        return newNode
    }
```

```
        *i = *i + 1                    // populate left sub tree
        newNode.left = BuildTreeFromPreOrder(preOrder, i)
        *i = *i + 1                    // populate right sub tree
        newNode.right = BuildTreeFromPreOrder(preOrder, i)
        return newNode
    }
```

Time Complexity: O(n).

Problem-34 Given a binary tree with three pointers (left, right and nextSibling), give an algorithm for filling the *nextSibling* pointers assuming they are nil initially.

Solution: We can use simple queue (similar to the solution of Problem-11). Let us assume that the structure of binary tree is:

```
func ConnectSiblings(root *BinaryTreeNode) *BinaryTreeNode {
    if root == nil {
        return nil
    }
    queue := []*BinaryTreeNode{root}
    for len(queue) > 0 {
        curr := queue[0]
        queue = queue[1:]
        if curr.left != nil && curr.right != nil {   // connect only if the right child is available
            curr.left.nextSibling = curr.right
            if curr.nextSibling != nil {
                curr.right.nextSibling = curr.nextSibling.left
            }
            queue = append(queue, curr.left)
            queue = append(queue, curr.right)
        }
    }
    return root
}
Recursive solution
func ConnectSiblings(root *BinaryTreeNode) *BinaryTreeNode {
    if root.left != nil && root.right != nil { // connect only if the right child is available
        root.left.nextSibling = root.right
        if root.nextSibling != nil {
            root.right.nextSibling = root.nextSibling.left
        }
        ConnectSiblings(root.left)
        ConnectSiblings(root.right)
    }
    return root
}
```

Time Complexity: O(n). Space Complexity: O(n).

Problem-35 Is there any other way of solving Problem-34?

Solution: Since we are manipulating tree nodes on the same level, it's easy to come up with a very standard level-order (BFS) solution using queue. But because of next pointer, we actually don't need a queue to store the order of tree nodes at each level, we just use a next pointer like it's a link list at each level. In addition, we can borrow the idea used in the binary tree level order traversal problem, which use *cur* and *next* pointer to store first node at each level; we exchange *cur* and *next* every time when *cur* is the last node at each level.

```
func ConnectSiblings(root *BinaryTreeNode) *BinaryTreeNode {
    if root == nil {
        return nil
    }
    cur := root
    next := root.left
    for next != nil {
        cur.left.nextSibling = cur.right
        if cur.nextSibling != nil {
            cur.right.nextSibling = cur.nextSibling.left
```

```
            cur = cur.nextSibling
        } else {
            cur = next
        }
        next = cur.left
    }
    return root
}
```

Time Complexity: O(n). Space Complexity: O(n).

Problem-36 Given a binary tree, find its minimum depth. The minimum depth of a binary tree is the number of nodes along the shortest path from the root node down to the nearest leaf node. For example, minimum depth of the following binary tree is 3.

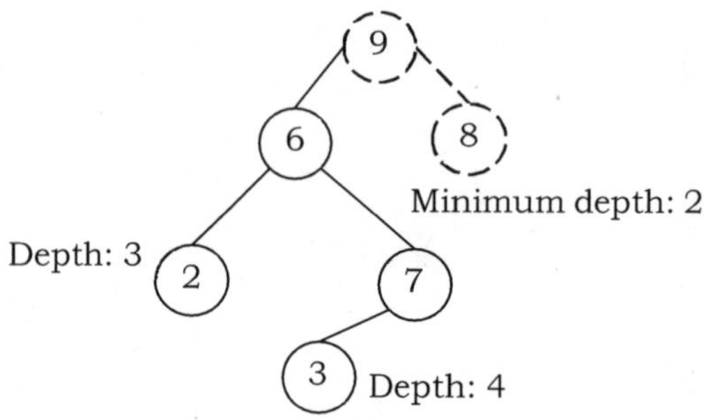

Solution: The algorithm is similar to the algorithm of finding depth (or height) of a binary tree, except here we are finding minimum depth. One simplest approach to solve this problem would be by using recursion. But the question is when do we stop it? We stop the recursive calls when it is a leaf node or *nil*.

Algorithm:

Let *root* be the pointer to the root node of a subtree.

- If the *root* is equal to *nil*, then the minimum depth of the binary tree would be 0.
- If the *root* is a leaf node (*nil*), then the minimum depth of the binary tree would be 1.
- If the *root* is not a leaf node and if left subtree of the *root* is *nil*, then find the minimum depth in the right subtree. Otherwise, find the minimum depth in the left subtree.
- If the *root* is not a leaf node and both left subtree and right subtree of the *root* are not *nil*, then recursively find the minimum depth of left and right subtree. Let it be $leftSubtreeMinDepth$ and $rightSubtreeMinDepth$ respectively. To get the minimum height of the binary tree rooted at root, we will take minimum of $leftSubtreeMinDepth$ and $rightSubtreeMinDepth$ and 1 for the *root* node.

```
func MinDepth(root *BinaryTreeNode) int {
    if root == nil {
        return 0 // If root (tree) is empty, minimum depth would be 0
    }
    if root.left == nil && root.right == nil { // If root is a leaf node, minimum depth would be 1
        return 1
    }
    if root.left == nil { // If left subtree is nil, find minimum depth in right subtree
        return MinDepth(root.right) + 1
    }
    if root.right == nil { // If right subtree is nil, find minimum depth in left subtree
        return MinDepth(root.left) + 1
    }
    // Get the minimum depths of left and right subtrees and add 1 for current level.
    return min(MinDepth(root.left), MinDepth(root.right)) + 1
}
# Approach two
func MinDepth(root *BinaryTreeNode) int {
    if root == nil {
        return 0
    }
    left, right := MinDepth(root.left), MinDepth(root.right)
    if left == 0 || right == 0 {
```

```
            return left + right + 1
        }
        return min(left, right) + 1
    }
```

Time complexity: O(*n*), as we are doing pre order traversal of tree only once. Space complexity: O(*n*), for recursive stack space.

Solution with level order traversal: The above recursive approach may end up with complete traversal of the binary tree even when the minimum depth leaf is close to the root node. A better approach is to use level order traversal. In this algorithm, we will traverse the binary tree by keeping track of the levels of the node and closest leaf node found till now.

Algorithm:

Let *root* be the pointer to the root node of a subtree at level L.

- If root is equal to *NULL*, then the minimum depth of the binary tree would be 0.
- If root is a leaf node, then check if its level(L) is less than the level of closest leaf node found till now. If yes, then update closest leaf node to current node and return.
- Recursively traverse left and right subtree of node at level L + 1.

```
func MinDepth(root *BinaryTreeNode) int {    // Compute the minimum height (or depth) of a tree
    if root == nil {
        return 0
    }
    count := 0
    queue := []*BinaryTreeNode{root}
    for len(queue) > 0 {
        qlen := len(queue)
        var level []int
        for i := 0; i < qlen; i++ {
            node := queue[0]
            level = append(level, node.data)
            queue = queue[1:]
            if node.left == nil && node.right == nil {
                return count+1
            }
            if node.left != nil {
                queue = append(queue, node.left)
            }
            if node.right != nil {
                queue = append(queue, node.right)
            }
        }
        count++
    }
    return count
}
```

Time complexity: O(*n*), as we are doing lever order traversal of the tree only once. Space complexity: O(*n*), for queue.

Symmetric question: Maximum depth of a binary tree: Given a binary tree, find its maximum depth. The maximum depth of a binary tree is the number of nodes along the path from the root node down to the farthest leaf node. For example, maximum depth of following binary tree is 4. Careful observation tells us that it is exactly same as finding the depth (or height) of the tree.

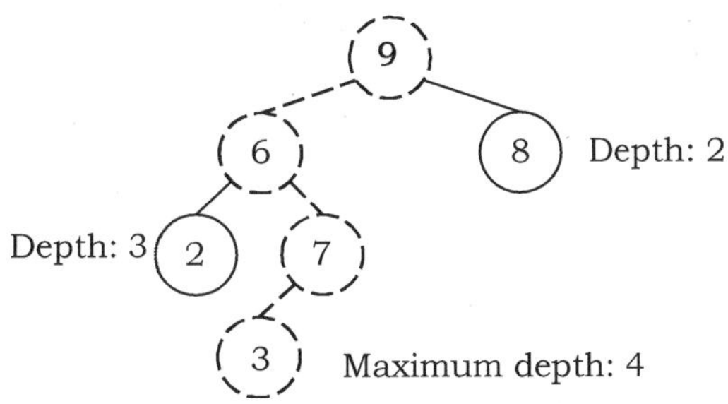

Problem-36 Given a binary tree, how do we check whether it is a complete binary tree?

Solution: A complete binary tree is a binary tree in which all the levels are completely filled except possibly the lowest one, which is filled from the left. A complete binary tree is a binary tree in which every level, except possibly the last, is completely filled, and all nodes are as far left as possible. Whereas, a full binary tree (sometimes proper binary tree or 2-tree) is a tree in which every node other than the leaves has two children.

If we have say, 4 nodes in a row with depth 3 and positions 0, 1, 2, 3; and we want 8 new nodes in a row with depth 4 and positions 0, 1, 2, 3, 4, 5, 6, 7; then we can see that the rule for going from a node to its left child is (depth, position) -> (depth + 1, position * 2), and the rule for going from a node to its right child is (depth, position) -> (depth + 1, position * 2 + 1). Then, our row at depth dd is completely filled if it has 2^{d-1} nodes, and all the nodes in the last level are left-justified when their positions take the form 0, 1, ... in sequence with no gaps.

```
func IsCompleteBinaryTree(root BinaryTreeNode) bool {
    if root == nil {
        return true
    }
    var q DeQueue
    q.PushBack(root)
    for !q.IsEmpty() {
        temp := q.remove()
        if temp == nil { // If a nil is encountered, now no other non nil value could be on the Queue.
            for !q.IsEmpty() {
                temp2 := q.remove()
                if temp2 != nil {
                    return false
                }
            }
            return true
        }
        q.PushBack(temp.left)
        q.PushBack(temp.right)
    }
    return true
}
```

Problem-37 You are given a tree with n nodes numbered from 0 to $n-1$ in the form of a parent array where parent[i] is the parent of node i. The root of the tree is node 0. Give an algorithm to return all ancestors of the given node. If there is no such ancestor, return -1.

Alternative problem statement: Give an algorithm for printing all the ancestors of a node in a Binary tree. For the tree below, for 7 the ancestors are 1 3 7.

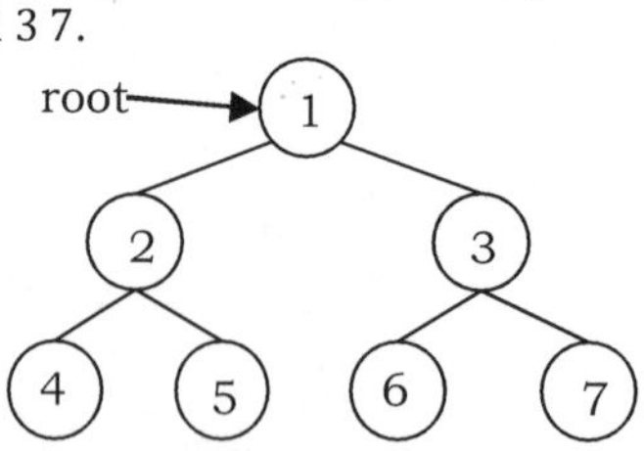

Solution: The idea is to traverse the tree in post order fashion and search for given node in the tree. If the node is found, we return true from the function. So for any node, if the given node is found in either its left subtree or its right subtree, then the current node is an ancestor of it.

```
// Recursive function to print all ancestors of a given node in a binary tree. The
// function returns true if the node is found in the subtree rooted at the given root node
func printAncestors(root *BinaryTreeNode, node int) bool {
    if root == nil {                              // base case
        return false
    }

    if root.data == node {                        // return true if given node is found
        return true
    }

    left := printAncestors(root.left, node)       // search node in left subtree
    right := false                                // search node in right subtree
    if !left {
```

```
        right = printAncestors(root.right, node)
    }
    // if given node is found in either left or right subtree, current node is an ancestor of given node
    if left || right {
        fmt.Printf("%d ", root.data)
    }
    return left || right      // return true if node is found
}
```

Time complexity: O(*n*). Space complexity: O(*h*), for the call stack where *h* is the height of the tree.

Problem-38 You are given a tree with n nodes numbered from 0 to $n-1$ in the form of a parent array where parent[i] is the parent of node i. The root of the tree is node 0. Give an algorithm to return the k-th ancestor of the given node. If there is no such ancestor, return -1.

Solution: In line with the previous solution, the idea is to first find the node and then backtrack to the kth parent. We can achieve this logic, by using recursive preorder traversal without using an extra array. The idea of using preorder traversal is to first find the given node in the tree, and then backtrack k times to reach to kth ancestor, once we have reached to the kth parent, we will simply print the node and return *nil*.

```
// Recursive function to print kth ancestor of a given node in a binary tree.
func kthAncestor(root *BinaryTreeNode, node int, k *int) *BinaryTreeNode {
    if root == nil {                          // base case
        return nil
    }
    if root.data == node || (kthAncestor(root.left, node, k) != nil) || (kthAncestor(root.right, node, k) != nil) {
        if *k > 0 {
            *k--
        } else if *k == 0 {
            fmt.Printf("%d ", root.data)      // print the kth ancestor
            return nil                        // return nil to stop further backtracking
        }
        return root                           // return current node to previous call
    }
    return nil
}
```

Time complexity: O(*n*). Space complexity: O(*h*), for the call stack where *h* is the height of the tree.

6.7 Generic Trees (N-ary Trees)

In the previous section we discussed binary trees where each node can have a maximum of two children and these are represented easily with two pointers. But suppose if we have a tree with many children at every node and also if we do not know how many children a node can have, how do we represent them?

For example, consider the tree shown below.

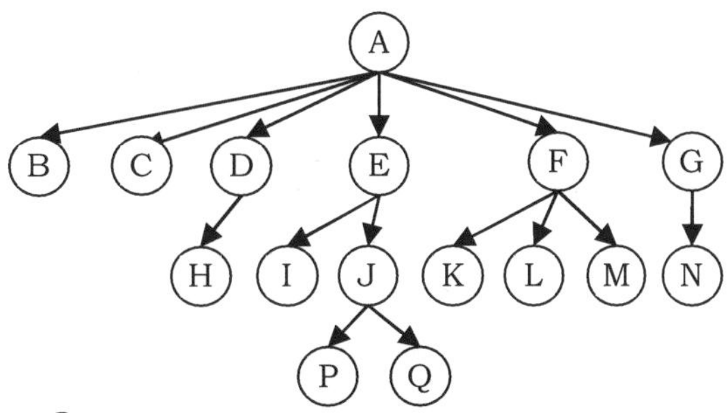

How do we represent the tree?

In the above tree, there are nodes with 6 children, with 3 children, with 2 children, with 1 child, and with zero children (leaves). To present this tree we have to consider the worst case (6 children) and allocate that many child pointers for each node. Based on this, the node representation can be given as:

```
struct TreeNode{
    int data;
    struct TreeNode *firstChild;
```

```
        struct TreeNode *secondChild;
        struct TreeNode *thirdChild;
        struct TreeNode *fourthChild;
        struct TreeNode *fifthChild;
        struct TreeNode *sixthChild;
};
```

Since we are not using all the pointers in all the cases, there is a lot of memory wastage. Another problem is that we do not know the number of children for each node in advance. In order to solve this problem we need a representation that minimizes the wastage and also accepts nodes with any number of children.

Representation of Generic Trees

Since our objective is to reach all nodes of the tree, a possible solution to this is as follows:

- At each node link children of same parent (siblings) from left to right.
- Remove the links from parent to all children except the first child.

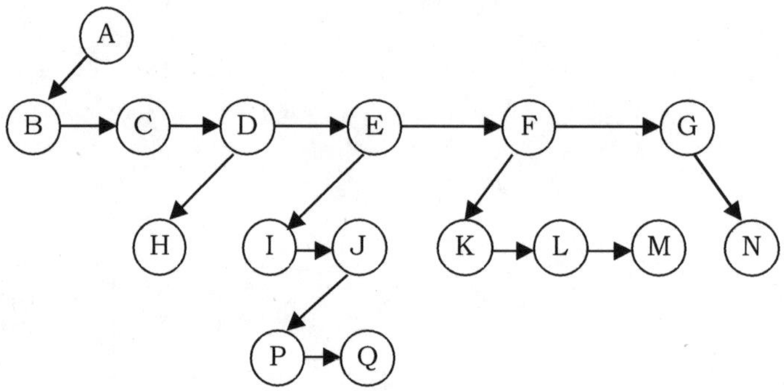

What these above statements say is if we have a link between children then we do not need extra links from parent to all children. This is because we can traverse all the elements by starting at the first child of the parent. So if we have a link between parent and first child and also links between all children of same parent then it solves our problem.

This representation is sometimes called first child/next sibling representation. First child/next sibling representation of the generic tree is shown above. The actual representation for this tree is:

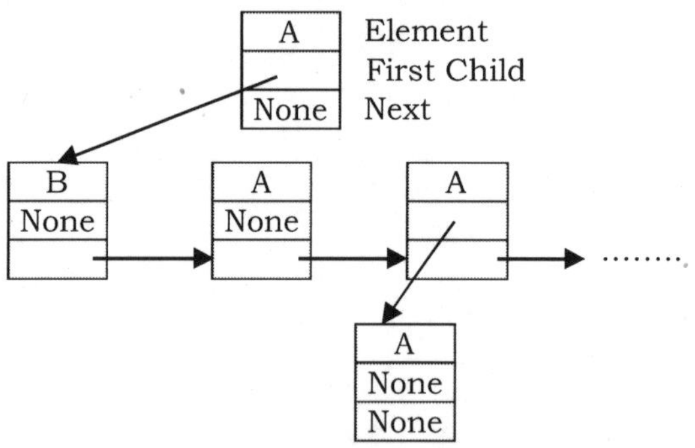

Based on this discussion, the tree node declaration for general tree can be given as:

```
    type TreeNode struct {
        data int
        firstChild *TreeNode
        nextSibling *TreeNode
    }
```

Note: Since we are able to convert any generic tree to binary representation; in practice we use binary trees. We can treat all generic trees with a first child/next sibling representation as binary trees.

Generic Trees: Problems & Solutions

Problem-37 Can you implement a simple N-ary tree?

Solution: Trie is one of the most frequently used N-ary trees. Refer *String Algorithms* chapter for more details.

```
    package main
    import (
        "fmt"
```

```
)
var total = 1      // Total is a fun way to total how many nodes we have
// N-ary
const N = 3        // N-ary
// NaryTreeNode  is a super simple NaryTreeNode  struct that will form the tree
type NaryTreeNode struct {
    parent   *NaryTreeNode
    children []*NaryTreeNode
    depth    int
    data     int
}
// BuildNaryTree will construct the tree for walking.
// total = (N * childrenChildren) + rootChildren + 1
func BuildNaryTree() *NaryTreeNode {
    var root NaryTreeNode
    root.addChildren()
    for _, child := range root.children {
        child.addChildren()
    }
    return &root
}
// addChildren is a convenience to add an arbitrary number of children
func (n *NaryTreeNode) addChildren() {
    for i := 0; i < N; i++ {
        newChild := &NaryTreeNode{
            parent: n,
            depth:  n.depth + 1,
        }
        n.children = append(n.children, newChild)
    }
}
// addChild is a convenience to add an a children
func (n *NaryTreeNode) addChild() {
    newChild := &NaryTreeNode{
        parent: n,
        depth:  n.depth + 1,
    }
    n.children = append(n.children, newChild)
}
// walk is a recursive function that calls itself for every child
func (n *NaryTreeNode) walk() {
    n.visit()
    for _, child := range n.children {
        child.walk()
    }
}
// visit will get called on every NaryTreeNode  in the tree.
func (n *NaryTreeNode) visit() {
    d := "└"
    for i := 0; i <= n.depth; i++ {
        d = d + "───"
    }
    fmt.Printf("%s Visiting NaryTreeNode  with addr %p and parent %p Total (%d)\n", d, n, n.parent, total)
    total = total + 1
}
// main will build and walk the tree
func main() {
    fmt.Println("Building N-ary Tree")
    root := BuildNaryTree()
```

```
        fmt.Println("Walking N-ary Tree")
        root.walk()
}
```

Problem-39 Given a tree, give an algorithm for finding the sum of all the elements of the tree.

Solution: The solution is similar to what we have done for simple binary trees. That means, traverse the complete list and keep on adding the values. We can either use level order traversal or simple recursion.

```
func findSum(root *TreeNode) int {
    if root == nil {
        return 0
    }
    return root.data + findSum(root.firstChild) + findSum(root.nextSibling)
}
```

Time Complexity: $O(n)$. Space Complexity: $O(1)$ (if we do not consider stack space), otherwise $O(n)$.

Note: All problems which we have discussed for binary trees are applicable for generic trees also. Instead of left and right pointers we just need to use firstChild and nextSibling.

Problem-40 For a 4-ary tree (each node can contain maximum of 4 children), what is the maximum possible height with 100 nodes? Assume height of a single node is 0.

Solution: In 4-ary tree each node can contain 0 to 4 children, and to get maximum height, we need to keep only one child for each parent. With 100 nodes, the maximum possible height we can get is 99.

If we have a restriction that at least one node has 4 children, then we keep one node with 4 children and the remaining nodes with 1 child. In this case, the maximum possible height is 96. Similarly, with n nodes the maximum possible height is $n - 4$.

Problem-41 For a 4-ary tree (each node can contain maximum of 4 children), what is the minimum possible height with n nodes?

Solution: Similar to the above discussion, if we want to get minimum height, then we need to fill all nodes with maximum children (in this case 4). Now let's see the following table, which indicates the maximum number of nodes for a given height.

Height, h	Maximum Nodes at height, $h = 4^h$	Total Nodes height $h = \frac{4^{h+1}-1}{3}$
0	1	1
1	4	1+4
2	4 × 4	1+ 4 × 4
3	4 × 4 × 4	1+ 4 × 4 + 4 × 4 × 4

For a given height h the maximum possible nodes are: $\frac{4^{h+1}-1}{3}$. To get minimum height, take logarithm on both sides:

$$n = \frac{4^{h+1}-1}{3} \Rightarrow 4^{h+1} = 3n + 1 \Rightarrow (h+1)log4 = \log(3n+1) \Rightarrow h + 1 = \log_4(3n+1) \Rightarrow h = \log_4(3n+1) - 1$$

Problem-42 Given a node in the generic tree, give an algorithm for counting the number of siblings for that node.

Solution: Since tree is represented with the first child/next sibling method, for a given node in the tree, we just need to traverse all its next siblings.

```
func SiblingCount(root *TreeNode) int {
    count := 0
    current = root
    for current != nil {
        count++
        current = current.nextSibling
    }
    return count
}
```

Time Complexity: $O(n)$. Space Complexity: $O(1)$.

Problem-43 Given a node in the generic tree, give an algorithm for counting the number of children for that node.

Solution: For a given node in the tree, we just need to point to its first child and keep traversing all its next siblings.

```
func ChildCount(root *TreeNode) int {
    count := 0
```

```
        current = root.firstChild
        for current != nil {
            count++
            current = current.nextSibling
        }
        return count
    }
```

Time Complexity: O(n). Space Complexity: O(1).

Problem-44 Given two trees how do we check whether the trees are isomorphic to each other or not?

Solution:

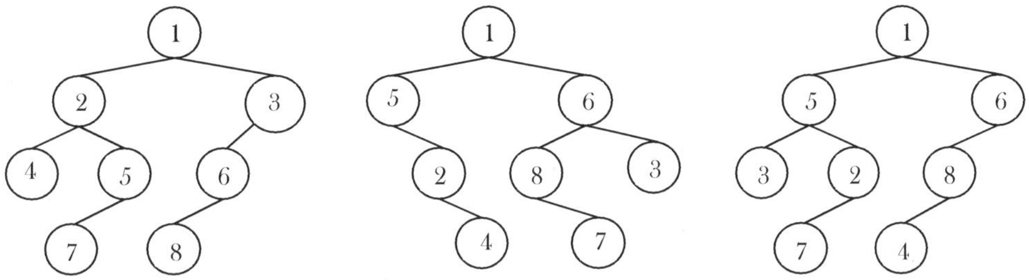

Two binary trees *root*1 and *root*2 are isomorphic if they have the same structure. The values of the nodes does not affect whether two trees are isomorphic or not. In the diagram below, the tree in the middle is not isomorphic to the other trees, but the tree on the right is isomorphic to the tree on the left.

```
    func IsIsomorphic(root1, root2 *BinaryTreeNode) bool {
        if root1 == nil && root2 == nil {
            return true
        }
        if (root1 == nil && root2 != nil) || (root1 != nil && root2 == nil) {
            return false
        }
        return IsIsomorphic(root1.left, root2.left) && IsIsomorphic(root1.right, root2.right)
    }
```

Time Complexity: O(n). Space Complexity: O(n).

Problem-45 Given two trees how do we check whether they are quasi-isomorphic to each other or not?

Solution:

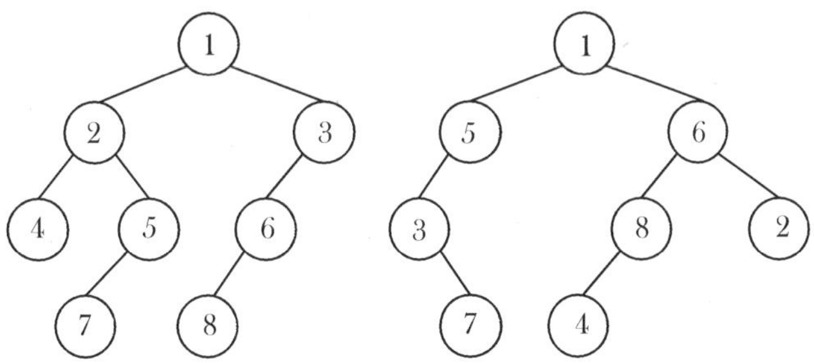

Two trees *root*1 and *root*2 are quasi-isomorphic if *root*1 can be transformed into *root*2 by swapping the left and right children of some of the nodes of *root*1. Data in the nodes are not important in determining quasi-isomorphism; only the shape is important. The trees below are quasi-isomorphic because if the children of the nodes on the left are swapped, the tree on the right is obtained.

```
    func QuasiIsomorphic(root1, root2 *BinaryTreeNode) bool {
        if root1 == nil && root2 == nil {
            return true
        }
        if (root1 == nil && root2 != nil) || (root1 != nil && root2 == nil) {
            return false
        }
        return (QuasiIsomorphic(root1.left, root2.left) && QuasiIsomorphic(root1.right, root2.right)) ||
                        (QuasiIsomorphic(root1.right, root2.left) && QuasiIsomorphic(root1.left, root2.right))
    }
```

Time Complexity: O(n). Space Complexity: O(n).

Problem-46 Given a parent array P, where $P[i]$ indicates the parent of ith node in the tree (assume parent of root node is indicated with -1). Give an algorithm for finding the height or depth of the tree.

Solution: For example: if the P is

-1	0	1	6	6	0	0	2	7
0	1	2	3	4	5	6	7	8

Its corresponding tree is:

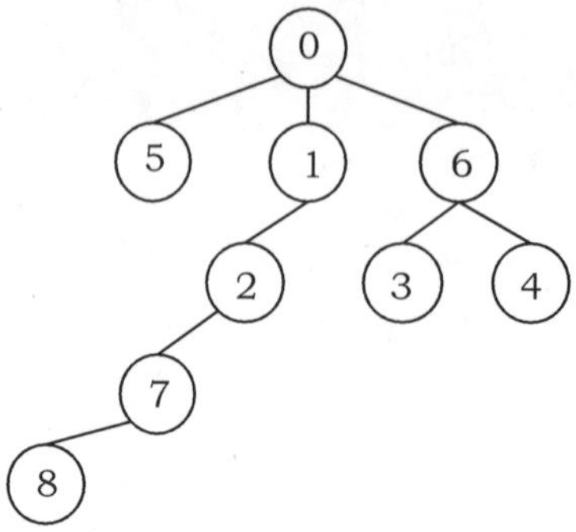

From the problem definition, the given array represents the parent array. That means, we need to consider the tree for that array and find the depth of the tree. The depth of this given tree is 4. If we carefully observe, we just need to start at every node and keep going to its parent until we reach -1 and also keep track of the maximum depth among all nodes.

```
// function to find the height of tree
func findHeight(P []int, n int) int {
    var maxDepth int
    for i := 0; i < n; i++ {
        var j int = i
        var currentDepth int = 1
        for P[j] != -1 {
            currentDepth++
            j = P[j]
        }
        if currentDepth > maxDepth {
            maxDepth = currentDepth
        }
    }
    return maxDepth
}
```

Time Complexity: O(n^2). For skew trees we will be re-calculating the same values. Space Complexity: O(1).

Note: We can optimize the code by storing the previous calculated nodes' depth in some hash table or other array. This reduces the time complexity but uses extra space.

Problem-47 A full n $-$ary tree is a tree where each node has either 0 or n children. Given a n-ary tree, give an algorithm which prints preorder traversal of its nodes' values.

Solution: A binary tree can be traversed in preorder, inorder, postorder or level-order. Among these traversal methods, preorder, postorder and level-order traversal are suitable to be extended to a n-ary tree. In a n-ary tree, preorder means visit the root node first and then traverse the subtree rooted at its children one by one. *Trie* is one of the most frequently used n-ary trees. Refer *String Algorithms* chapter for more details about tries data structure. Let us assume the following as the n-ary tree node structure:

```
type NaryTreeNode struct {
    data     int
    children []*NaryTreeNode
}
```

```
func traverse(root *NaryTreeNode, arr *[]int) {
    if root == nil {
        return
    }
    if root != nil {
        nodes := root.Children
        for _, node := range nodes {
            *arr = append(*arr, node.data)
            traverse(node, arr)
```

```
            }
        }
    }
    func preorder(root *NaryTreeNode) []int {
        preOrder := make([]int, 0)
        if root != nil {
            preOrder = append(preOrder, root.data)
        }
        traverse(root, &preOrder)
        return preOrder
    }
```

Iterative with stack

```
    func preorder(root *NaryTreeNode) []int {
        res := []int{}
        if root == nil {
            return res
        }
        stack := []*NaryTreeNode{root}
        for len(stack) > 0 {
            r := stack[len(stack)-1]
            stack = stack[:len(stack)-1]
            res = append(res, r.data)
            tmp := []*NaryTreeNode{}
            for _, v := range r.Children {
                tmp = append([]*NaryTreeNode{v}, tmp...)
            }
            stack = append(stack, tmp...)
        }
        Return res
    }
```

Problem-48 A full n −ary tree is a tree where each node has either 0 or n children. Given a n-ary tree, find its maximum depth.

Solution: We talked about how to solve tree related problems recursively in the previous sections and problems. In those sections, we focused on binary trees but the idea can also be extended to a n-ary tree. The recursive solutions can be either top-down or bottom-up.

Top-down means that in each recursion level, we will visit the node first to come up with some values, and parse these values to its children when calling the function recursively.

Bottom-up means that in each recursion level, we will firstly call the functions recursively for all the children nodes and then come up with the answer according to the return values and the value of the root node itself.

Let us apply, top down recursive approach for solving this problem.

```
    func MaxDepth(root * NaryTreeNode) int {
        if root == nil {
            return 0
        }
        maxNum := 0
        for _, c := range root.children {
            tmp := MaxDepth(c)
            maxNum = max(maxNum, tmp)
        }
        return maxNum + 1
    }
    func max(a, b int) int {
        if a > b {
            return a
        }
        return b
    }
```

6.8 Threaded Binary Tree Traversals (Stack or Queue-less Traversals)

In earlier sections we have seen that, *preorder, inorder and postorder* binary tree traversals used stacks and *level order* traversals used queues as an auxiliary data structure. In this section we will discuss new traversal algorithms which do not need both stacks and queues. Such traversal algorithms are called *threaded binary tree traversals* or *stack/queue – less traversals*.

Issues with Regular Binary Tree Traversals

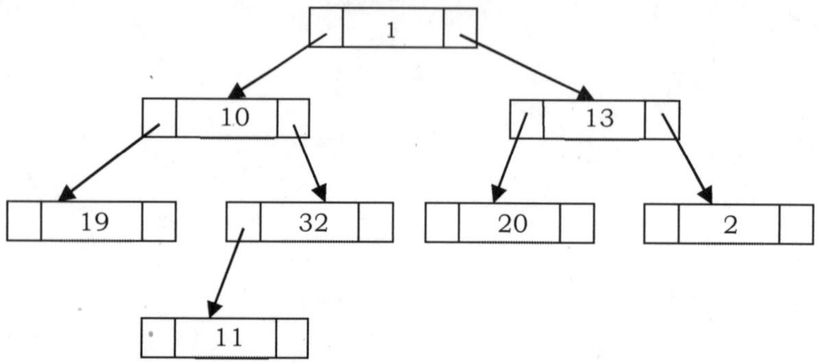

- The storage space required for the stack and queue is large.
- The majority of pointers in any binary tree are nil. For example, a binary tree with n nodes has $n + 1$ nil pointers and these were wasted.
- It is difficult to find successor node (preorder, inorder and postorder successors) for a given node.

Motivation for Threaded Binary Trees

To solve these problems, one idea is to store some useful information in nil pointers. If we observe the previous traversals carefully, stack/queue is required because we have to record the current position in order to move to the right subtree after processing the left subtree. If we store the useful information in nil pointers, then we don't have to store such information in stack/queue.

The binary trees which store such information in nil pointers are called *threaded binary trees*. From the above discussion, let us assume that we want to store some useful information in nil pointers. The next question is what to store?

The common convention is to put predecessor/successor information. That means, if we are dealing with preorder traversals, then for a given node, nil left pointer will contain preorder predecessor information and nil right pointer will contain preorder successor information. These special pointers are called *threads*.

Classifying Threaded Binary Trees

The classification is based on whether we are storing useful information in both nil pointers or only in one of them.

- If we store predecessor information in nil left pointers only, then we can call such binary trees *left threaded binary trees*.
- If we store successor information in nil right pointers only, then we can call such binary trees *right threaded binary trees*.
- If we store predecessor information in nil left pointers and successor information in nil right pointers, then we can call such binary trees *fully threaded binary trees* or simply *threaded binary trees*.

Note: For the remaining discussion we consider only *(fully) threaded binary trees*.

Types of Threaded Binary Trees

Based on above discussion we get three representations for threaded binary trees.

- *Preorder Threaded Binary Trees*: nil left pointer will contain PreOrder predecessor information and nil right pointer will contain PreOrder successor information.
- *Inorder Threaded Binary Trees*: nil left pointer will contain InOrder predecessor information and nil right pointer will contain InOrder successor information.
- *Postorder Threaded Binary Trees*: nil left pointer will contain PostOrder predecessor information and nil right pointer will contain PostOrder successor information.

Note: As the representations are similar, for the remaining discussion we will use InOrder threaded binary trees.

Threaded Binary Tree structure

Any program examining the tree must be able to differentiate between a regular *left/right* pointer and a *thread*. To do this, we use two additional fields in each node, giving us, for threaded trees, nodes of the following form:

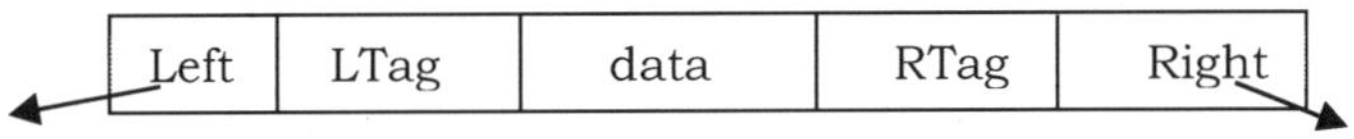


```
type ThreadedBinaryTreeNode struct {
    left *ThreadedBinaryTreeNode
    LTag int
    data int
    RTag int
    right *ThreadedBinaryTreeNode
}
```

Difference between Binary Tree and Threaded Binary Tree Structures

	Regular Binary Trees	Threaded Binary Trees
if LTag == 0	nil	left points to the in-order predecessor
if LTag == 1	left points to the left child	left points to left child
if RTag == 0	nil	right points to the in-order successor
if RTag == 1	right points to the right child	right points to the right child

Note: Similarly, we can define preorder/postorder differences as well.

As an example, let us try representing a tree in inorder threaded binary tree form. The tree below shows what an inorder threaded binary tree will look like. The dotted arrows indicate the threads. If we observe, the left pointer of left most node (2) and right pointer of right most node (31) are hanging.

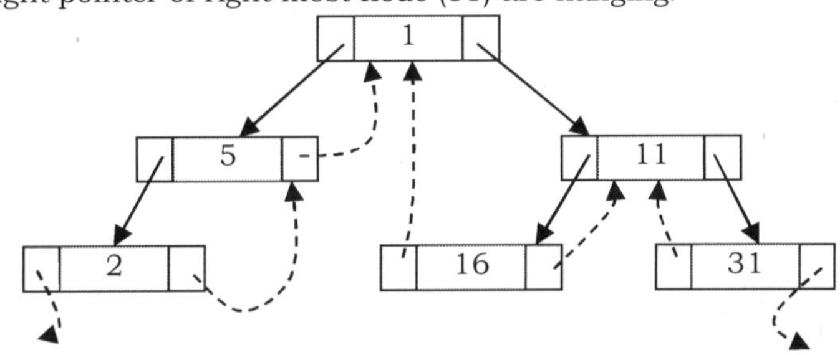

What should leftmost and rightmost pointers point to?

In the representation of a threaded binary tree, it is convenient to use a special node *Dummy* which is always present even for an empty tree. Note that right tag of Dummy node is 1 and its right child points to itself.

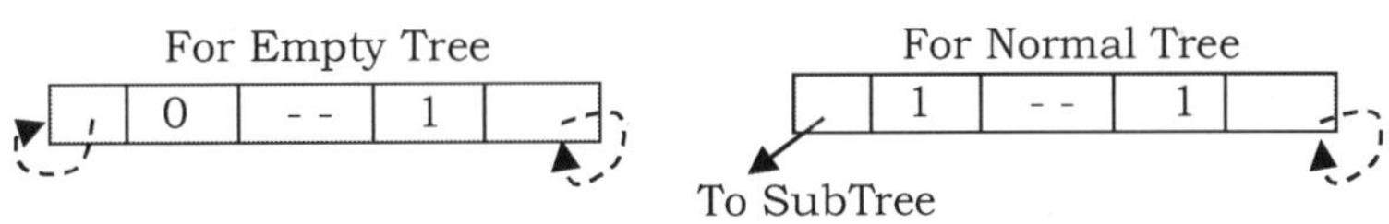

With this convention the above tree can be represented as:

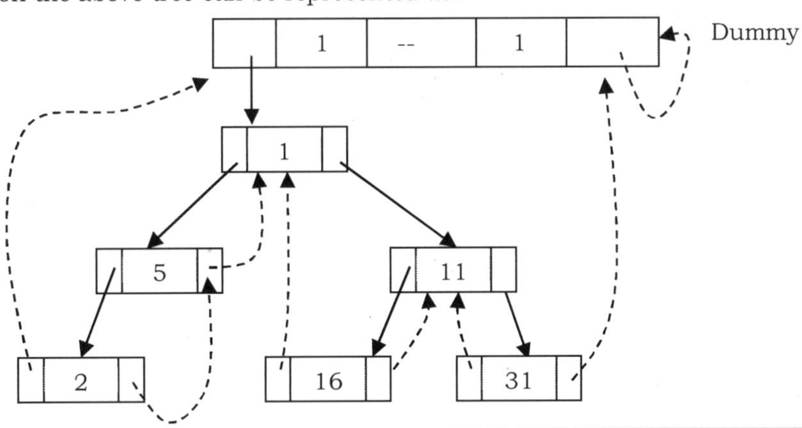

Finding Inorder Successor in Inorder Threaded Binary Tree

To find inorder successor of a given node without using a stack, assume that the node for which we want to find the inorder successor is *P*.

Strategy: If *P* has a no right subtree, then return the right child of *P*. If *P* has right subtree, then return the left of the nearest node whose left subtree contains *P*.

```
func inorderSuccessor(P *ThreadedBinaryTreeNode) *ThreadedBinaryTreeNode {
    if P.RTag == 0 {
        return P.right
    } else {
        position := P.right
        for position.LTag == 1 {
            position = position.left
        }
        return position
    }
}
```

Time Complexity: O(*n*). Space Complexity: O(1).

Inorder Traversal in Inorder Threaded Binary Tree

We can start with *dummy* node and call inorderSuccessor() to visit each node until we reach *dummy* node.

```
func InorderTraversal(root *ThreadedBinaryTreeNode) {
    P := inorderSuccessor(root)
    for P != root {
        P = inorderSuccessor(P)
        fmt.Printf("%d", P.data)
    }
}
```

Alternative coding:

```
func inorderTraversal(root *ThreadedBinaryTreeNode) {
    P := root
    for true {
        P = inorderSuccessor(P)
        if P == root {
            return
        }
        fmt.Printf("%d", P.data)
    }
}
```

Time Complexity: O(*n*). Space Complexity: O(1).

Finding PreOrder Successor in InOrder Threaded Binary Tree

Strategy: If *P* has a left subtree, then return the left child of *P*. If *P* has no left subtree, then return the right child of the nearest node whose right subtree contains *P*.

```
func preorderSuccessor(P *ThreadedBinaryTreeNode) *ThreadedBinaryTreeNode {
    if P.LTag == 1 {
        return P.left
    } else {
        position := P
        for position.RTag == 0 {
            position = position.right
        }
        return position.right
    }
}
```

Time Complexity: O(*n*). Space Complexity: O(1).

PreOrder Traversal of InOrder Threaded Binary Tree

As in inorder traversal, start with *dummy* node and call preorderSuccessor() to visit each node until we get *dummy* node again.

```
func PreorderTraversal(root *ThreadedBinaryTreeNode) {
    P := preorderSuccessor(root)
    for P != root {
        P = preorderSuccessor(P)
        fmt.Printf("%d", P.data)
    }
}
```

Alternative coding:

```
func PreorderTraversal(root *ThreadedBinaryTreeNode) {
    P := root
    for true {
        P = preorderSuccessor(P)
        if P == root {
            return
        }
        fmt.Printf("%d", P.data)
    }
}
```

Time Complexity: O(n). Space Complexity: O(1).

Note: From the above discussion, it should be clear that inorder and preorder successor finding is easy with threaded binary trees. But finding postorder successor is very difficult if we do not use stack.

Insertion of Nodes in InOrder Threaded Binary Trees

For simplicity, let us assume that there are two nodes P and Q and we want to attach Q to right of P. For this we will have two cases.

- Node P does not have right child: In this case we just need to attach Q to P and change its left and right pointers.

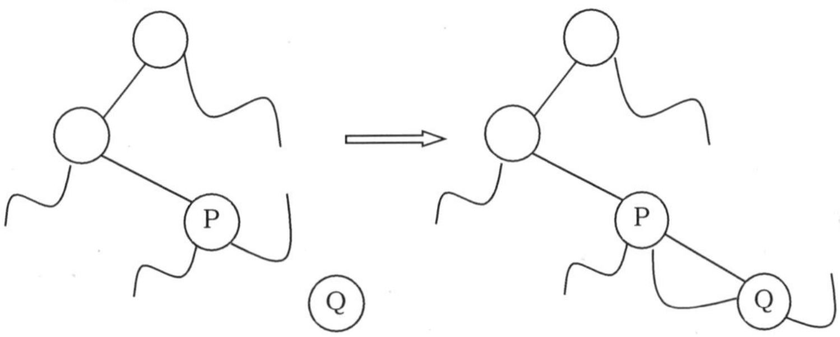

- Node P has right child (say, R): In this case we need to traverse R's left subtree and find the left most node and then update the left and right pointer of that node (as shown below).

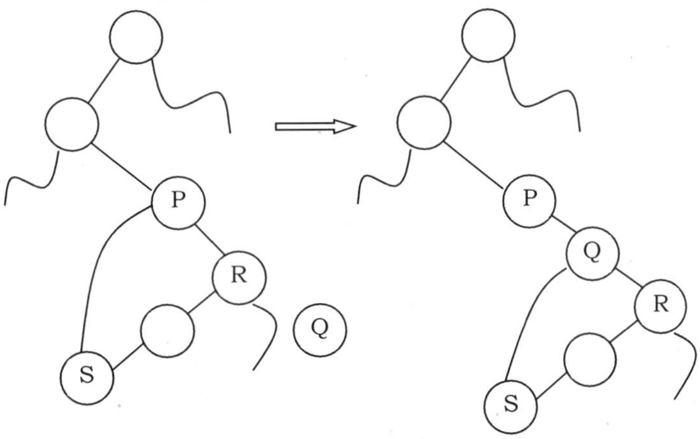


```
func insertRightInInorderTBT(P *ThreadedBinaryTreeNode, Q *ThreadedBinaryTreeNode) {
    var Temp *ThreadedBinaryTreeNode
    Q.right = P.right
    Q.RTag = P.RTag
    Q.left = P
    Q.LTag = 0
    P.right = Q
```

```
    P.RTag = 1
    if Q.RTag == 1 { //Case-2
        Temp = Q.right
        for Temp.LTag == 1 {
            Temp = Temp.left
        }
        Temp.left = Q
    }
}
```

Time Complexity: O(n). Space Complexity: O(1).

Threaded Binary Trees: Problems & Solutions

Problem-49 For a given binary tree (not threaded) how do we find the preorder successor?

Solution: For solving this problem, we need to use an auxiliary stack S. On the first call, the parameter node is a pointer to the head of the tree, and thereafter its value is nil. Since we are simply asking for the successor of the node we got the last time we called the function. It is necessary that the contents of the stack S and the pointer P to the last node "visited" are preserved from one call of the function to the next; they are defined as static variables.

```
// pre-order successor for an unthreaded binary tree
func preorderSuccessor(node *BinaryTreeNode) *BinaryTreeNode {
    var P *BinaryTreeNode
    S := NewStack(1) // Refer Stacks chapter for implementation details of stacks
    if node != nil {
        P = node
    }
    if P.left != nil {
        push(S, P)
        P = P.left
    } else {
        for P.right == nil {
            P = pop(S)
        }
        P = P.right
    }
    return P
}
```

Problem-50 For a given binary tree (not threaded) how do we find the inorder successor?

Solution: Similar to the above discussion, we can find the inorder successor of a node as:

```
// In-order successor for an unthreaded binary tree
func inorderSuccessor(node *BinaryTreeNode) *BinaryTreeNode {
    P * BinaryTreeNode
    S := NewStack(1) // Refer Stacks chapter for implementation details of stacks
    if node != nil {
        P = node
    }
    if P.right == nil {
        P = pop(S)
    } else {
        P = P.right
        for P.left != nil {
            push(S, P)
        }
        P = P.left
    }
    return P
}
```

6.9 Expression Trees

A tree representing an expression is called an *expression tree*. In expression trees, leaf nodes are operands and non-leaf nodes are operators. That means, an expression tree is a binary tree where internal nodes are operators and leaves are operands. An expression tree consists of binary expression. But for a u-nary operator, one subtree will be empty. The figure below shows a simple expression tree for (A + B * C) / D.

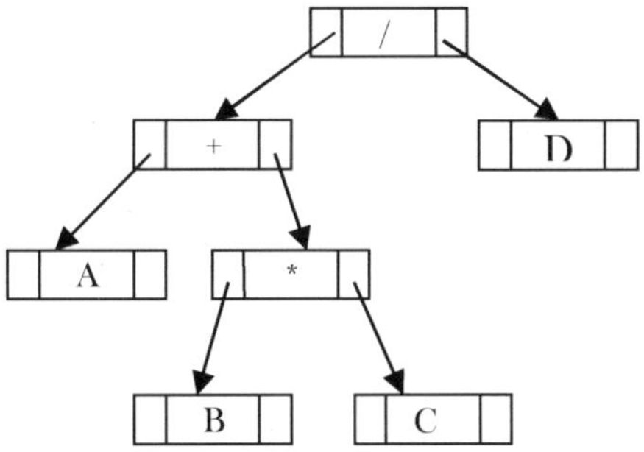

Example: Assume that one symbol is read at a time. If the symbol is an operand, we create a tree node and push a pointer to it onto a stack. If the symbol is an operator, pop pointers to two trees T_1 and T_2 from the stack (T_1 is popped first) and form a new tree whose root is the operator and whose left and right children point to T_2 and T_1 respectively. A pointer to this new tree is then pushed onto the stack.

As an example, assume the input is A B C * + D /. The first three symbols are operands, so create tree nodes and push pointers to them onto a stack as shown below.

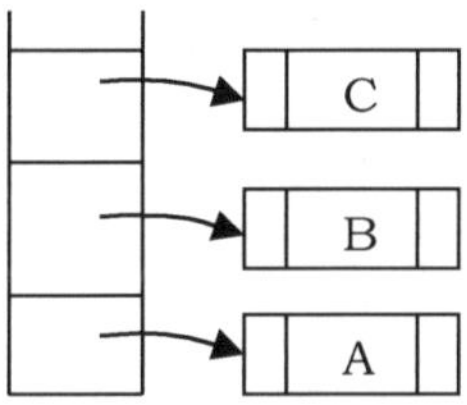

Next, an operator '*' is read, so two pointers to trees are popped, a new tree is formed and a pointer to it is pushed onto the stack.

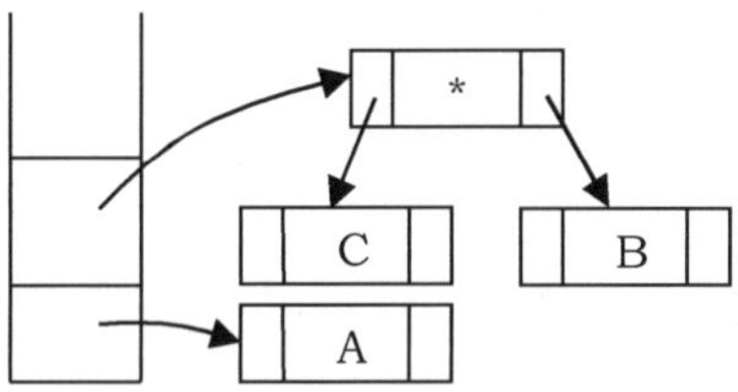

Next, an operator '+' is read, so two pointers to trees are popped, a new tree is formed and a pointer to it is pushed onto the stack.

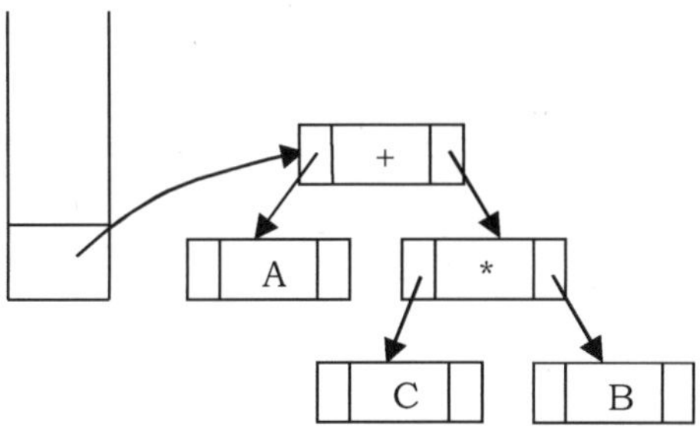

Next, an operand 'D' is read, a one-node tree is created and a pointer to the corresponding tree is pushed onto the stack.

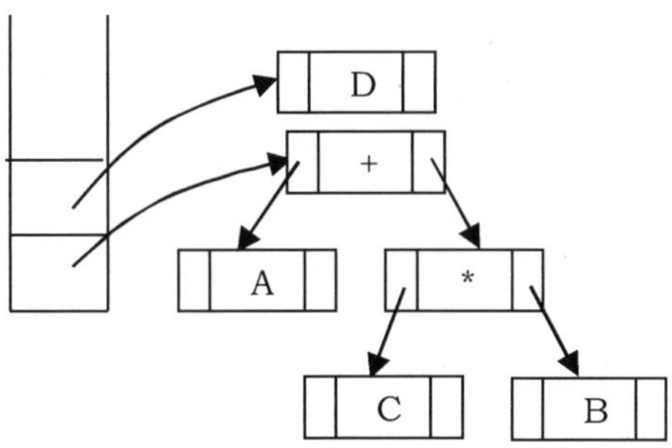

Finally, the last symbol ('/') is read, two trees are merged and a pointer to the final tree is left on the stack.

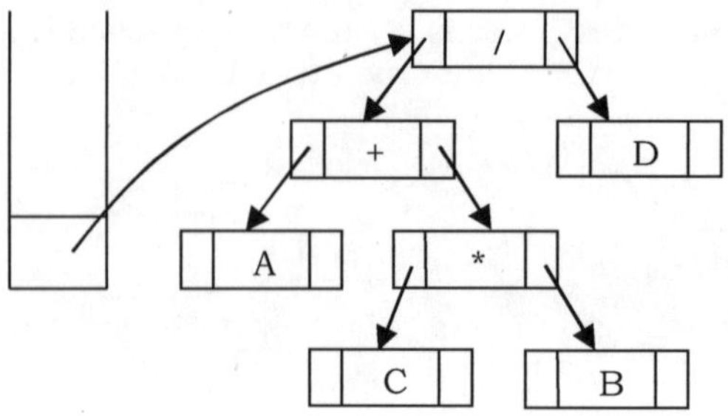

6.10 XOR Trees

This concept is similar to *memory efficient doubly linked lists* of *Linked Lists* chapter. Also, like threaded binary trees this representation does not need stacks or queues for traversing the trees. This representation is used for traversing back (to parent) and forth (to children) using ⊕ operation. To represent the same in XOR trees, for each node below are the rules used for representation:

- Each nodes left will have the ⊕ of its parent and its left children.
- Each nodes right will have the ⊕ of its parent and its right children.
- The root nodes parent is nil and also leaf nodes children are nil nodes.

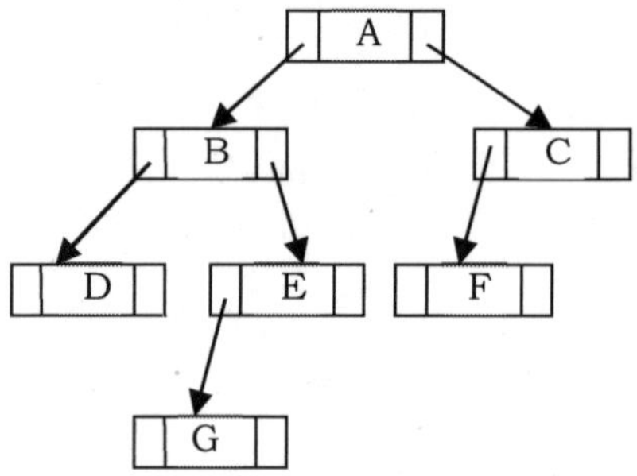

Based on the above rules and discussion, the tree can be represented as:

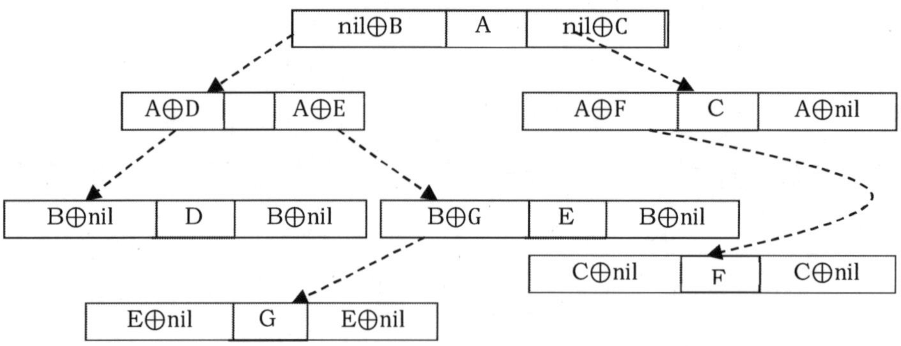

The major objective of this presentation is the ability to move to parent as well to children. Now, let us see how to use this representation for traversing the tree. For example, if we are at node B and want to move to its parent node A, then we just need to perform ⊕ on its left content with its left child address (we can use right child also for going to parent node). Similarly, if we want to move to its child (say, left child D) then we have to perform ⊕ on its left content with its parent node address. One important point that we need to understand about this representation is: When we are at node B, how do we know the address of its children D? Since the traversal starts at node root node, we can apply ⊕ on root's left content with nil. As a result we get its left child, B. When we are at B, we can apply ⊕ on its left content with A address.

6.11 Binary Search Trees (BSTs)

Why Binary Search Trees?

In previous sections we have discussed different tree representations and in all of them we did not impose any restriction on the nodes data. As a result, to search for an element we need to check both in left subtree and in right subtree. Due to this, the worst-case complexity of search operation is $O(n)$. In this section, we will discuss another variant of binary trees: Binary Search Trees (BSTs). As the name suggests, the main use of this representation is for *searching*. In this representation we impose restriction on the kind of data a node can contain. As a result, it reduces the worst-case average search operation to O($logn$).

Binary Search Tree Property

In binary search trees, all the left subtree elements should be less than root data and all the right subtree elements should be greater than root data. This is called binary search tree property. Note that, this property should be satisfied at every node in the tree.

- The left subtree of a node contains only nodes with keys less than the nodes key.
- The right subtree of a node contains only nodes with keys greater than the nodes key.
- Both the left and right subtrees must also be binary search trees.

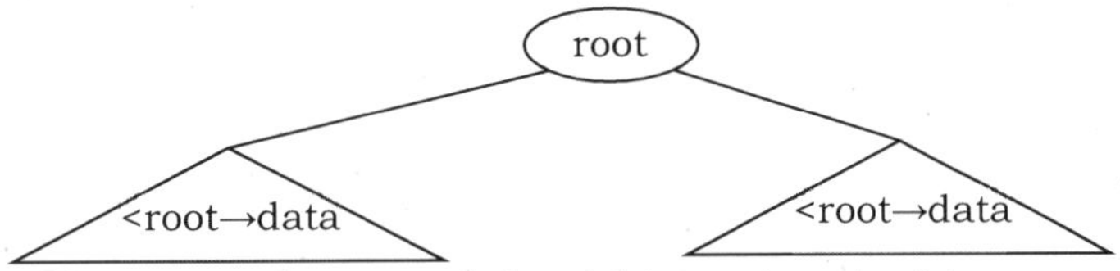

Example: The left tree is a binary search tree and the right tree is not a binary search tree (at node 6 it's not satisfying the binary search tree property).

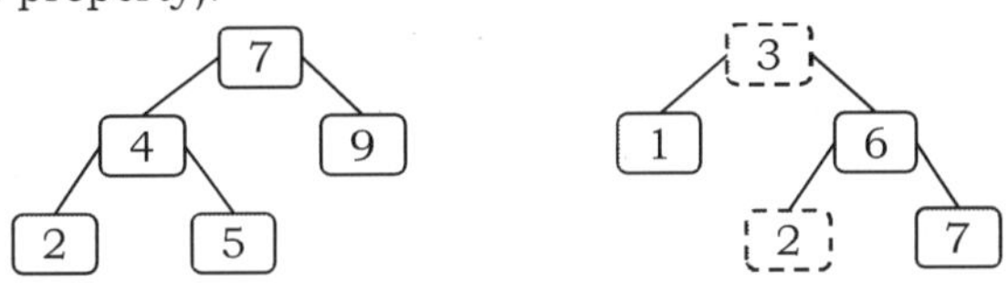

Binary Search Tree Declaration

There is no difference between regular binary tree declaration and binary search tree declaration. The difference is only in data but not in structure. But for our convenience we change the structure name as:

```
type BSTNode struct {
    int  data
    left *BSTNode
    right *BSTNode
}
```

Operations on Binary Search Trees

Main operations: Following are the main operations that are supported by binary search trees:

- Find/ Find Minimum / Find Maximum element in binary search trees
- Inserting an element in binary search trees
- Deleting an element from binary search trees

Auxiliary operations: Checking whether the given tree is a binary search tree or not

- Finding k^{th}-smallest element in tree
- Sorting the elements of binary search tree and many more

Important Notes on Binary Search Trees

- Since root data is always between left subtree data and right subtree data, performing inorder traversal on binary search tree produces a sorted list.
- While solving problems on binary search trees, first we process left subtree, then root data, and finally we process right subtree. This means, depending on the problem, only the intermediate step (processing root data) changes and we do not touch the first and third steps.
- If we are searching for an element and if the left subtree root data is less than the element we want to search, then skip it. The same is the case with the right subtree.. Because of this, binary search trees take less time for searching an element than regular binary trees. In other words, the binary search trees consider either left or right subtrees for searching an element but not both.
- The basic operations that can be performed on binary search tree (BST) are insertion of element, deletion of element, and searching for an element. While performing these operations on BST the height of the tree gets changed each time. Hence there exists variations in time complexities of best case, average case, and worst case.
- The basic operations on a binary search tree take time proportional to the height of the tree. For a complete binary tree with node n, such operations runs in O(logn) worst-case time. If the tree is a linear chain of n nodes (skew-tree), however, the same operations takes O(n) worst-case time.

Finding an Element in Binary Search Trees

Find operation is straightforward in a BST. Start with the root and keep moving left or right using the BST property. If the data we are searching is same as nodes data then we return current node. If the data we are searching is less than nodes data then search left subtree of current node; otherwise search right subtree of current node. If the data is not present, we end up in a nil link.

```
func find(root *BSTNode, data int) *BSTNode {
    if root == nil {
        return nil
    }
    if data < root.data {
        return find(root.left, data)
    } else if data > root.data {
        return find(root.right, data)
    }
    return root
}
```

Time Complexity: O(n), in worst case (when BST is a skew tree). Space Complexity: O(n), for recursive stack.

Non recursive version of the above algorithm can be given as:

```
func find(root *BSTNode, data int) *BSTNode {
    if root == nil {
        return nil
    }
    for root != nil {
        if data == root.data {
            return root
        } else if data > root.data {
            root = root.right
        } else {
            root = root.left
        }
    }
    return nil
}
```

Time Complexity: O(n). Space Complexity: O(1).

Finding Minimum Element in Binary Search Trees

In BSTs, the minimum element is the left-most node, which does not has left child. In the BST below, the minimum element is **4**.

```
func findMin(root *BSTNode) *BSTNode {
    if root == nil {
        return nil
    } else if root.left == nil {
        return root
    } else {
        return findMin(root.left)
    }
}
```

Time Complexity: O(n), in worst case (when BST is a *left skew* tree). Space Complexity: O(n), for recursive stack.

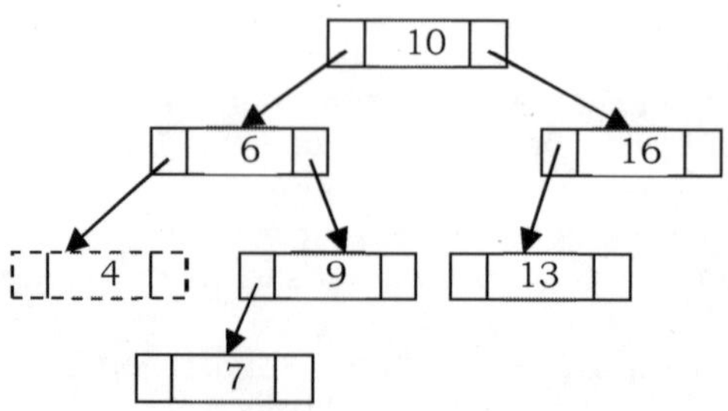

Non recursive version of the above algorithm can be given as:

```
func findMin(root *BSTNode) *BSTNode {
```

```
    if root == nil {
        return nil
    }
    for root.left != nil {
        root = root.left
    }
    return root
}
```

Time Complexity: O(n). Space Complexity: O(1).

Finding Maximum Element in Binary Search Trees

In BSTs, the maximum element is the right-most node, which does not have right child. In the BST below, the maximum element is **16**.

```
func findMax(root *BSTNode) *BSTNode {
    if root == nil {
        return nil
    } else if root.right == nil {
        return root
    } else {
        return findMax(root.right)
    }
}
```

Time Complexity: O(n), in worst case (when BST is a *right skew* tree). Space Complexity: O(n), for recursive stack.

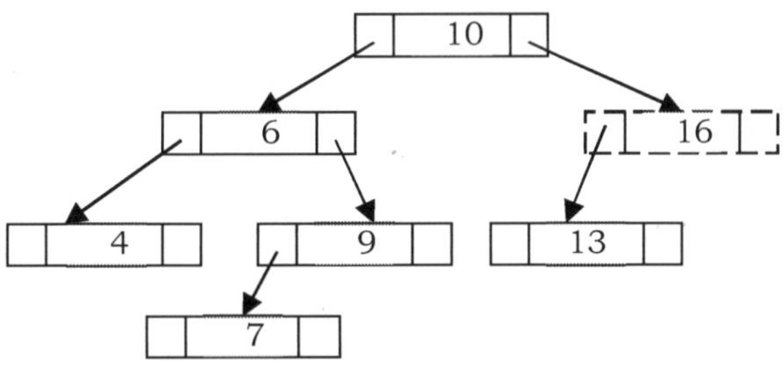

Non recursive version of the above algorithm can be given as:

```
func findMax(root *BSTNode) *BSTNode {
    if root == nil {
        return nil
    }
    for root.right != nil {
        root = root.right
    }
    return root
}
```

Time Complexity: O(n). Space Complexity: O(1).

Where is Inorder Predecessor and Successor?

Where is the inorder predecessor and successor of node X in a binary search tree assuming all keys are distinct?

If X has two children then its inorder predecessor is the maximum value in its left subtree and its inorder successor the minimum value in its right subtree.

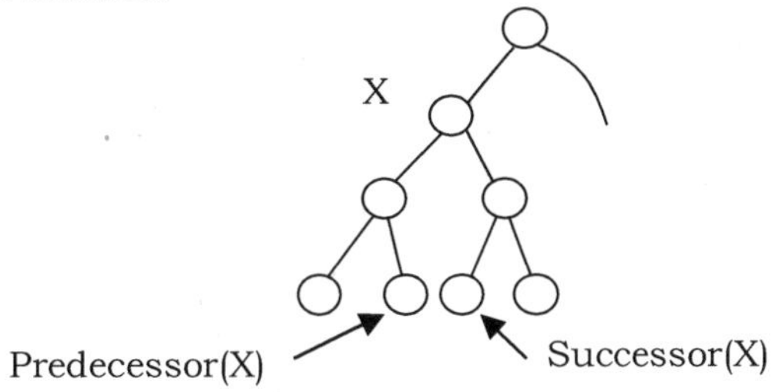

If it does not have a left child, then a node's inorder predecessor is its first left ancestor.

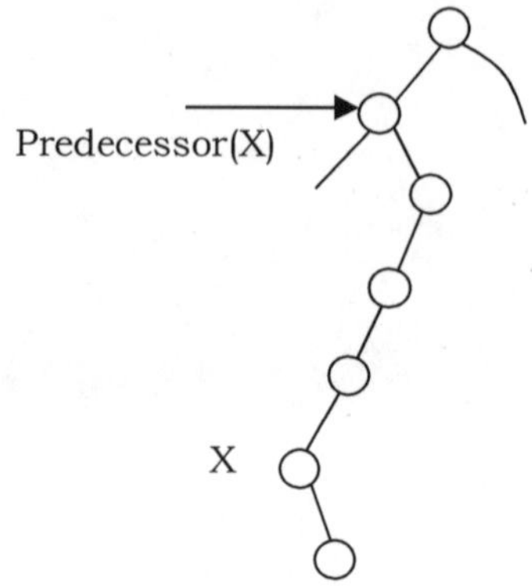

Inserting an Element from Binary Search Tree

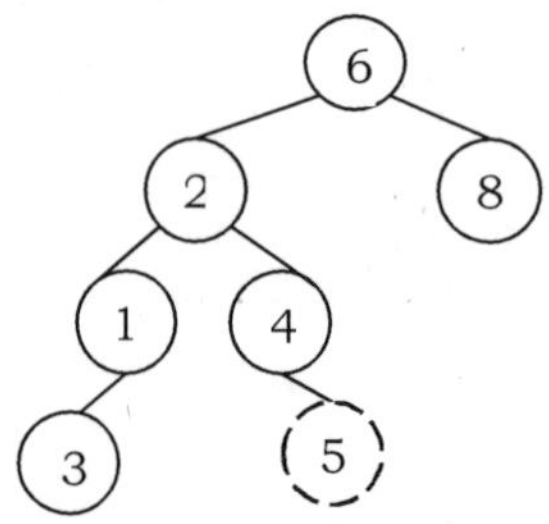

To insert *data* into binary search tree, first we need to find the location for that element. We can find the location of insertion by following the same mechanism as that of *find* operation. While finding the location, if the *data* is already there then we can simply neglect and come out. Otherwise, insert *data* at the last location on the path traversed.

As an example let us consider the following tree. The dotted node indicates the element (5) to be inserted. To insert 5, traverse the tree using *find* function. At node with key 4, we need to go right, but there is no subtree, so 5 is not in the tree, and this is the correct location for insertion.

```
func Insert(root *BSTNode, v int) *BSTNode {
    if root == nil {
        return &BSTNode{nil, v, nil}
    }
    if v < root.data {
        root.left = Insert(root.left, v)
        return root
    }
    root.right = Insert(root.right, v)
    return root
}
```

Note: In the above code, after inserting an element in subtrees, the tree is returned to its parent. As a result, the complete tree will get updated.

Time Complexity: O(n).
Space Complexity: O(n), for recursive stack. For iterative version, space complexity is O(1).

Deleting an Element from Binary Search Tree

The delete operation is more complicated than other operations. This is because the element to be deleted may not be the leaf node. In this operation also, first we need to find the location of the element which we want to delete.

Once we have found the node to be deleted, consider the following cases:

- If the element to be deleted is a leaf node: return *nil* to its parent. That means make the corresponding child pointer *nil*. In the tree below to delete 5, set *nil* to its parent node 2.

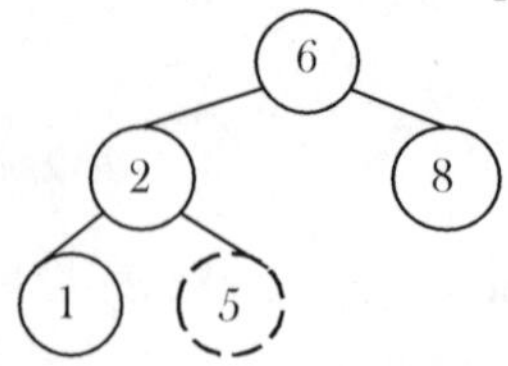

- If the element to be deleted has one child: In this case we just need to send the current node's child to its parent. In the tree below, to delete 4, 4 left subtree is set to its parent node 2.

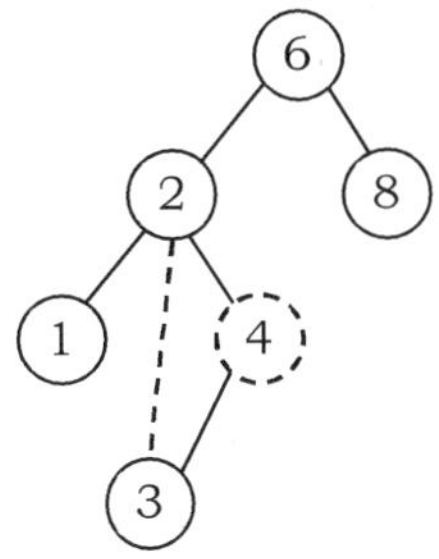

- If the element to be deleted has both children: The general strategy is to replace the key of this node with the largest element of the left subtree and recursively delete that node (which is now empty). The largest node in the left subtree cannot have a right child, so the second *delete* is an easy one. As an example, let us consider the following tree. In the tree below, to delete 8, it is the right child of the root. The key value is 8. It is replaced with the largest key in its left subtree (7), and then that node is deleted as before (second case).

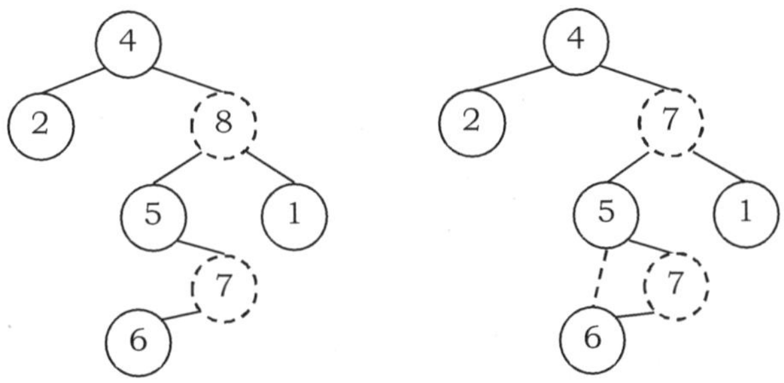

Note: We can replace with minimum element in right subtree also.

```
func Delete(root *BSTNode, data int) *BSTNode {
    if root == nil {
        return nil
    }
    if data < root.data {
        root.left = Delete(root.left, data)
    } else if data > root.data {
        root.right = Delete(root.right, data)
    } else {
        if root.right == nil {
            return root.left
        }
        if root.left == nil {
            return root.right
        }
        t := root
        root = findMin(t.right)
        root.right = deleteMin(t.right)
        root.left = t.left
    }
    return root
}
func deleteMin(root *BSTNode) *BSTNode {
    if root.left == nil {
        return root.right
    }
    root.left = deleteMin(root.left)
    return root
}
```

Time Complexity: $O(n)$. Space Complexity: $O(n)$ for recursive stack.

Binary Search Trees: Problems & Solutions

Note: For ordering related problems with binary search trees and balanced binary search trees, Inorder traversal has advantages over others as it gives the sorted order.

Problem-51 Given two binary search trees, return true if they have same contents.

Solution: Go's concurrency primitives make it easy to express concurrent concepts, such as this binary tree comparison. Trees may be of different shapes, but have the same contents. For example:

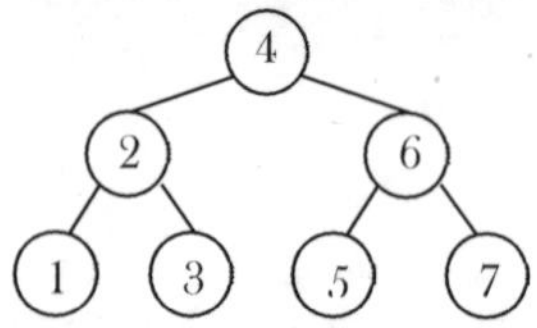

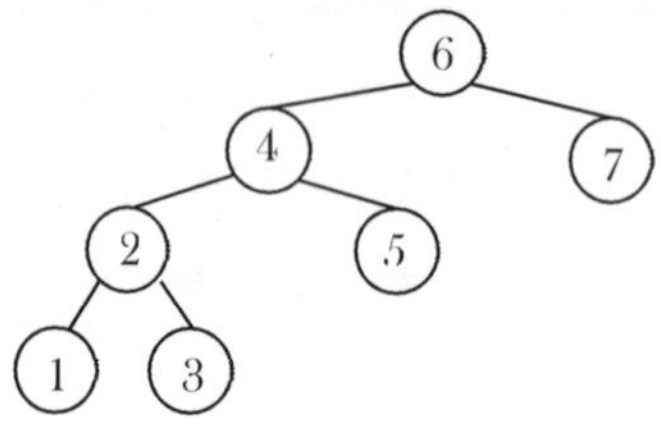

The following code compares a pair of trees by walking each in its own goroutine, sending their contents through a channel to a third goroutine that compares them.

```
// Walk traverses a tree depth-first, sending each data on a channel.
func Walk(root *BinaryTreeNode, ch chan int) {
    if root == nil {
        return
    }
    Walk(root.left, ch)
    ch <- root.data
    Walk(root.right, ch)
}
// Walker launches Walk in a new goroutine, and returns a read-only channel of values.
func Walker(root *BinaryTreeNode) <-chan int {
    ch := make(chan int)
    go func() {
        Walk(root, ch)
        close(ch)
    }()
    return ch
}
// Compare reads values from two Walkers that run simultaneously,
// and returns true if t1 and t2 have the same contents.
func Compare(t1, t2 *BinaryTreeNode) bool {
    c1, c2 := Walker(t1), Walker(t2)
    for {
        v1, ok1 := <-c1
        v2, ok2 := <-c2
        if !ok1 || !ok2 {
            return ok1 == ok2
        }
        if v1 != v2 {
            break
        }
    }
    return false
}
```

Time Complexity: O(n). Space Complexity: O(n) for recursive stacks.

Problem-52 Given pointers to two nodes in a binary search tree, find the lowest common ancestor (LCA). Assume that both values already exist in the tree.

Solution: The main idea of the solution is: while traversing BST from root to bottom, the first node we encounter with value between α and β, i.e., $\alpha < node \rightarrow data < \beta$, is the Least Common Ancestor(LCA) of α and β (where $\alpha < \beta$). So just traverse the BST in pre-order, and if we find a node with value in between α and β, then that node is the LCA. If its value is greater than both α and β, then the LCA lies on the left side of the node, and if its value is smaller than both α and β, then the LCA lies on the right side.

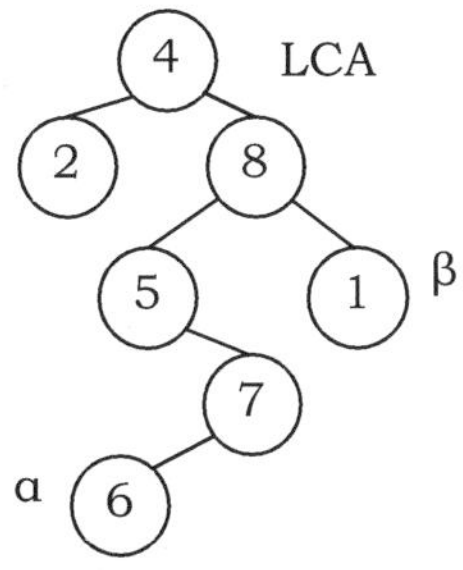


```
func LCA(root *BSTNode, α, β int) *BSTNode {
    cur := root
    for {
        switch {
        case α < cur.data && β < cur.data:
            cur = cur.left
        case α > cur.data && β > cur.data:
            cur = cur.right
        default:
            return cur
        }
    }
    return root
}
```

Time Complexity: O(*n*). Space Complexity: O(*n*), for skew trees.

Problem-53 Give an algorithm for finding the shortest path between two nodes in a BST.

Solution: It's nothing but finding the LCA of two nodes in BST.

Problem-54 Give an algorithm for counting the number of BSTs possible with *n* nodes.

Solution: This is a DP problem. Refer to chapter on *Dynamic Programming* for the algorithm.

Problem-55 Give an algorithm to check whether the given binary tree is a BST or not.

Solution:

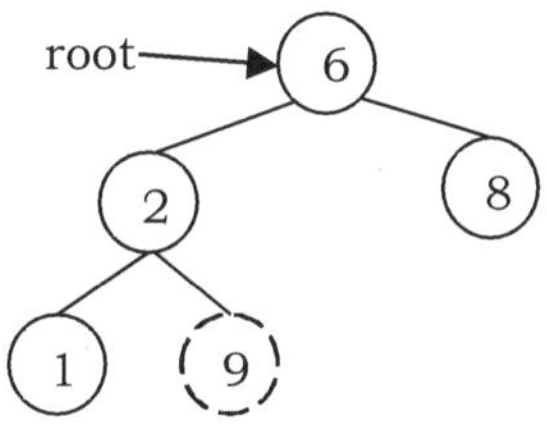

Consider the following simple program. For each node, check if the node on its left is smaller and check if the node on its right is greater. This approach is wrong as this will return true for binary tree below. Checking only at current node is not enough.

```
func IsBST(root *BSTNode) bool {
    if root == nil {
        return true
    }
    // false if left is > than root
    if root.left != nil && root.left.data > root.data {
        return false
    }
    // false if right is < than root
    if root.right != nil && root.right.data < root.data {
        return false
    }
    // false if, recursively, the left or right is not a BST
    if !IsBST(root.left) || !IsBST(root.right) {
        return false
    }
    // passing all that, it's a BST
    return true
```

```
    }
```

Problem-56 Can we think of getting the correct algorithm?

Solution: For each node, check if max value in left subtree is smaller than the current node data and min value in right subtree greater than the node data. It is assumed that we have helper functions *FindMin()* and *FindMax()* that return the min or max integer value from a non-empty tree.

```
// Returns true if a binary tree is a binary search tree
func IsBST (root *BSTNode) bool {
    if root == nil {
        return true
    }
    // false if the max of the left is > than root
    max := findMax(root.left)
    if root.left != nil && (max.data > root.data) {
        return false
    }
    // false if the min of the right is <= than root
    min := findMin(root.right)
    if root.right != nil && (min.data < root.data) {
        return false
    }
    // false if, recursively, the left or right is not a BST
    if !IsBST(root.left) || !IsBST(root.right) {
        return false
    }
    // passing all that, it's a BST
    return true
}
```

Time Complexity: $O(n^2)$. Space Complexity: $O(n)$.

Problem-57 Can we improve the complexity of Problem-56?

Solution: Yes. A better solution is to look at each node only once. The trick is to write a utility helper function isBSTUtil(struct BinaryTreeNode* root, int min, int max) that traverses down the tree keeping track of the narrowing min and max allowed values as it goes, looking at each node only once. The initial values for min and max should be INT_MIN and INT_MAX — they narrow from there.

```
Initial call: IsBST(t1, math.MinInt32, math.MaxInt32)
func IsBST(root *BSTNode, min, max int) bool {
    if root == nil {
        return true
    }
    return (root.data > min && root.data < max && IsBST(root.left, min, root.data) &&
                                                  IsBST(root.right, root.data, max))
}
```

Time Complexity: $O(n)$. Space Complexity: $O(n)$, for stack space.

Problem-58 Can we further improve the complexity of Problem-56?

Solution: Yes, by using inorder traversal. The idea behind this solution is that inorder traversal of BST produces sorted lists. While traversing the BST in inorder, at each node check the condition that its key value should be greater than the key value of its previous visited node. Also, we need to initialize the prev with possible minimum integer value (say, INT_MIN).

```
func IsBST(root *BSTNode, prev *int) bool {
    if root == nil {
        return true
    }
    if !IsBST(root.left, prev) {
        return false
    }
    if root.data < *prev {
        return false
    }
    *prev = root.data
```

```
        return IsBST(root.right, prev)
}
```

Time Complexity: O(n). Space Complexity: O(n), for stack space.

Problem-59 Give an algorithm for converting BST to circular DLL with space complexity O(1).

Solution: Convert left and right subtrees to DLLs and maintain end of those lists. Then, adjust the pointers. The solution for this problem is:

- Convert left subtree into a list;
- Convert right subtree into a list;
- Connect root with leftList.head and then leftList.tail to rightList.head.

The key is to find the head and tail of each converted list. Good news is that head is always root, and we only to figure out how to get the tail. The idea is that if the tail of right subtree is not null, we've got the answer, otherwise, tail of left subtree, or root.

```
func BST2DLL(root *BSTNode) {
    if root == nil || (root.left == nil && root.right == nil) {
        return
    }
    BST2DLL(root.left)
    BST2DLL(root.right)
    currRight := root.right
    root.right = root.left
    root.left = nil
    for root.right != nil {
        root = root.right
    }
    root.right = currRight
}
```

Time Complexity: O(n).

Problem-60 Given a sorted array, give an algorithm for converting the array to BST.

Solution: The important condition that we have to adhere to in this problem is that we have to create a height balanced binary search tree using the set of nodes given to us in the form of a linked list. The good thing is that the nodes in the linked list are sorted in ascending order.

As we know, a binary search tree is essentially a rooted binary tree with a very special property or relationship amongst its nodes. For a given node of the binary search tree, it's value must be ≥ the value of all the nodes in the left subtree and ≤ the value of all the nodes in the right subtree. Since a binary tree has a recursive substructure, so does a BST i.e. all the subtrees are binary search trees in themselves.

The main idea in this approach and the next is that:

The middle element of the given list would form the root of the binary search tree. All the elements to the left of the middle element would form the left subtree recursively. Similarly, all the elements to the right of the middle element will form the right subtree of the binary search tree. This would ensure the height balance required in the resulting binary search tree.

If we have to choose an array element to be the root of a balanced BST, which element should we pick? The root of a balanced BST should be the middle element from the sorted array. We would pick the middle element from the sorted array in each iteration. We then create a node in the tree initialized with this element. After the element is chosen, what is left? Could you identify the sub-problems within the problem?

There are two arrays left — the one on its left and the one on its right. These two arrays are the sub-problems of the original problem, since both of them are sorted. Furthermore, they are subtrees of the current node's left and right child.

The code below creates a balanced BST from the sorted array in O(n) time (n is the number of elements in the array). Compare how similar the code is to a binary search algorithm. Both are using the divide and conquer methodology.

```
func SortedArrayToBST(A []int) *BSTNode {
    if A == nil {
        return nil
    }
    return helper(A, 0, len(A)-1)
}
```

```
func helper(A []int, low int, high int) *BSTNode {
    if low > high { // Done
        return nil
    }
    mid := low + (high-low)/2
    node := new(BSTNode)
    node.data = A[mid]
    node.left = helper(A, low, mid-1)
    node.right = helper(A, mid+1, high)
    return node
}
```

Time Complexity: O(n). Space Complexity: O(n), for stack space.

Problem-61 Given a singly linked list where elements are sorted in ascending order, convert it to a height balanced BST.

Solution: A naive way is to apply the Problem-63 solution directly. Since we are given a linked list and not an array, we don't really have access to the elements of the list using indexes. We want to know the middle element of the linked list.

We can use the two-pointer approach (from *Linked Lists* chapter) for finding out the middle element of a linked list. Essentially, we have two pointers called $slowPointer$ and $fastPointer$. The $slowPointer$ moves one node at a time whereas the $fastPointer$ moves two nodes at a time. By the time the $fastPointer$ reaches the end of the linked list, the $slowPointer$ would have reached the middle element of the linked list. For an even sized list, any of the two middle elements can act as the root of the BST.

Once we have the middle element of the linked list, we disconnect the portion of the list to the left of the middle element. The way we do this is by keeping a $previousPointer$ as well which points to one node before the $slowPointer$ i.e. $previousPointer.next = slowPointer$. For disconnecting the left portion we simply do $fastPointer.next = nil$.

We only need to pass the head of the linked list to the function that converts it to a height balances BST. So, we recurse on the left half of the linked list by passing the original head of the list and on the right half by passing $slowPointer.next$ as the head.

```
func SplitList(head *ListNode) (*ListNode, *ListNode, *ListNode) {
    if head.next == nil {
        return nil, head, nil
    }
    slowPointer := head
    fastPointer := head
    previousPointer := head
    for fastPointer != nil && fastPointer.next != nil {
        previousPointer = slowPointer
        fastPointer = fastPointer.next.next
        slowPointer = slowPointer.next
    }
    previousPointer.next = nil
    return head, slowPointer, slowPointer.next
}
func SortedListToBST(head *ListNode) *BSTNode {
    if head == nil {
        return nil
    }
    left, middle, right := SplitList(head)
    var node BSTNode
    node.data = middle.data
    node.left = SortedListToBST(left)
    node.Right = SortedListToBST(right)
    return &node
}
```

In each recursive call, we would have to traverse half of the list's length to find the middle element. The run time complexity is clearly O($nlogn$), where n is the total number of elements in the list. This is because each level of recursive call requires a total of $n/2$ traversal steps in the list, and there are a total of $logn$ number of levels (ie, the height of the balanced tree).

Problem-62 For Problem-61, can we improve the complexity?

Solution: Hint: How about inserting nodes following the list order? If we can achieve this, we no longer need to find the middle element as we are able to traverse the list while inserting nodes to the tree.

Best Solution: The main problem with the above solution seems to be the middle element computation. That takes up a lot of unnecessary time and this is due to the nature of the linked list data structure. Let's look at the next solution which tries to overcome this.

This approach is a classic example of the time-space tradeoff. We can get the time complexity down by using more space. That's exactly what we're going to do in this approach. Essentially, we will convert the given linked list into an array and then use that array to form our binary search tree. In an array fetching the middle element is a O(1) operation and this will bring down the overall time complexity.

Algorithm

- Convert the given linked list into an array. Let's call the beginning and the end of the array as $left$ and $right$.
- Find the middle element as ($left$ + $right$) / 2. Let's call this element as mid. This is a O(1) time operation and is the only major improvement over the previous algorithm.
- The middle element forms the root of the BST.
- Recursively form binary search trees on the two halves of the array represented by ($left$, mid - 1) and (mid + 1, $right$) respectively.

```
var nums *ListNode
func helper(left, right int) *BSTNode {
    if left > right {
        return nil
    }
    mid := int(left + (right-left)/2)
    leftNode := helper(left, mid-1)
    root := new(TreeNode)
    root.data = nums.data
    root.left = leftNode
    nums = nums.Next
    root.right = helper(mid+1, right)
    return root
}
func SortedListToBST(head *ListNode) *BSTNode {
    nums = head
    n := 0
    for head != nil {
        n++
        head = head.Next
    }
    return helper(0, n-1)
}
```

Problem-63 Given a sorted doubly linked list, give an algorithm for converting it into balanced binary search tree.

Solution: It is same as that of Problem-61. It does not matter whether the list is a singly linked list or doubly linked lists as we use that only for finding the middle node.

Problem-64 Give an algorithm for finding the kth smallest element in BST.

Solution: First, we need to traverse the tree, but how? Looking at the question we can see that it's a BST it a binary search tree. A binary search tree has the following properties:

- All the elements on the left subtree of a node have values less than the current node.
- All the elements on the right subtree of a node have values greater than the current node.
- Performing inorder traversal on a Binary search tree will result in a sorted list.

Since we want to find the kth Smallest node, performing inorder traversal on the tree would make sense since we will get a sorted list and it will be easier to determine the kth smallest element. While traversing the BST in inorder, keep track of the number of elements visited.

```
func kthSmallest(root *BSTNode, k int) *BSTNode {
    counter := 0
    return helper(root, k, &counter)
```

```
}
func helper(root *BSTNode, k int, counter *int) *BSTNode {
    if root == nil {
        return nil
    }
    left := helper(root.left, k, counter)
    if left != nil {
        return left
    }
    *counter += 1
    if *counter == k {
        return root
    }
    return helper(root.right, k, counter)
}
```

Time Complexity: O(n). Space Complexity: O(1).

Problem-65 **Floor and ceiling:** If a given key is less than the key at the root of a BST then the floor of the key (the largest key in the BST less than or equal to the key) must be in the left subtree. If the key is greater than the key at the root, then the floor of the key could be in the right subtree, but only if there is a key smaller than or equal to the key in the right subtree; if not (or if the key is equal to the key at the root) then the key at the root is the floor of the key. Finding the ceiling is similar, with interchanging right and left. For example, if the sorted with input array is {1, 2, 8, 10, 10, 12, 19}, then
For $x = 0$: floor doesn't exist in array, ceil = 1, For $x = 1$: floor = 1, ceil = 1
For $x = 5$: floor = 2, ceil = 8, For $x = 20$: floor = 19, ceil doesn't exist in array

Solution: The idea behind this solution is that, inorder traversal of BST produces sorted lists. While traversing the BST in inorder, keep track of the values being visited. If the roots data is greater than the given value then return the previous value which we have maintained during traversal. If the roots data is equal to the given data then return root data.

```
func FloorInBST(root *BSTNode, key int) *BSTNode {
    if root == nil {
        return root
    }
    if key > root.data {
        r := FloorInBST(root.right, key)
        if r == nil {
            return root
        } else {
            return r
        }
    } else if key < root.data {
        return FloorInBST(root.left, key)
    } else {
        return root
    }
}
```

Time Complexity: O(n). Space Complexity: O(n), for stack space.

For ceiling, we just need to call the right subtree first, followed by left subtree.

```
func CeilInBST(root *BSTNode, key int) *BSTNode {
    if root == nil {
        return root
    }
    if root.data == key {
        return root
    } else if root.data < key {
        return CeilInBST(root.right, key)
    } else {
        l := CeilInBST(root.left, key)
        if l != nil {
            return l
        }
```

```
    }
    return root
}
```

Time Complexity: O(n). Space Complexity: O(n), for stack space.

Problem-66 Give an algorithm for finding the union and intersection of BSTs. Assume parent pointers are available (say threaded binary trees). Also, assume the lengths of two BSTs are m and n respectively.

Solution: If parent pointers are available then the problem is same as merging of two sorted lists. This is because if we call inorder successor each time we get the next highest element. It's just a matter of which inorderSuccessor to call.

Time Complexity: O($m + n$). Space complexity: O(1).

Problem-67 For Problem-66, what if parent pointers are not available?

Solution: If parent pointers are not available, the BSTs can be converted to linked lists and then merged.

1. Convert both the BSTs into sorted doubly linked lists in O($n + m$) time. This produces 2 sorted lists.
2. Merge the two double linked lists into one and also maintain the count of total elements in O($n + m$) time.
3. Convert the sorted doubly linked list into height balanced tree in O($n + m$) time.

Problem-68 For Problem-66, is there any alternative way of solving the problem?

Solution: Yes, by using inorder traversal.

- Perform inorder traversal on one of the BSTs.
- While performing the traversal store them in table (hash table).
- After completion of the traversal of first *BST*, start traversal of second *BST* and compare them with hash table contents.

Time Complexity: O($m + n$). Space Complexity: O($Max(m,n)$).

Problem-69 Given a *BST* and two numbers $K1$ and $K2$, give an algorithm for printing all the elements of *BST* in the range $K1$ and $K2$.

Solution: Traverse the tree in the inorder traversal. If the binary search tree is traversed in inorder traversal the keys are traversed in increasing order. So, while traversing the keys in the inorder traversal. If the key lies in the range print the key else skip the subtree.

```
func RangePrinter(root *BSTNode, K1, K2 int) {
    if root == nil {
        return
    }
    if root.data >= K1 {
        RangePrinter(root.left, K1, K2)
    }
    if root.data >= K1 && root.data <= K2 {
        fmt.Print(" ", root.data)
    }
    if root.data <= K2 {
        RangePrinter(root.right, K1, K2)
    }
}
```

Time Complexity: O(n). Space Complexity: O(n), for stack space.

Problem-70 For Problem-69, is there any alternative way of solving the problem?

Solution: We can use level order traversal: while adding the elements to queue check for the range.

```
func RangePrinter(root *BSTNode, K1, K2 int) {
    if root == nil {
        return
    }
    var result [][]int
    queue := []*BSTNode{root}
    for len(queue) > 0 {
        qlen := len(queue)
        var level []int
        for i := 0; i < qlen; i++ {
            node := queue[0]
            level = append(level, node.data)
```

```
            queue = queue[1:]
            if node.data >= K1 && node.data <= K2 {
                fmt.Print(" ", node.data)
            }
            if node.left != nil && node.data >= K1 {
                queue = append(queue, node.left)
            }
            if node.right != nil && node.data <= K2 {
                queue = append(queue, node.right)
            }
        }
        result = append(result, level)
    }
}
```

Time Complexity: $O(n)$. Space Complexity: $O(n)$, for queue.

Problem-71 For Problem-69, can we still think of an alternative way to solve the problem?

Solution: First locate $K1$ with normal binary search and after that use InOrder successor until we encounter $K2$. For algorithm, refer to problems section of threaded binary trees.

Problem-72 Given root of a Binary Search tree, trim the tree, so that all elements returned in the new tree are between the inputs A and B.

Solution: It's just another way of asking Problem-69.

Problem-73 Given two BSTs, check whether the elements of them are the same or not. For example: two BSTs with data 10 5 20 15 30 and 10 20 15 30 5 should return true and the dataset with 10 5 20 15 30 and 10 15 30 20 5 should return false. **Note:** BSTs data can be in any order.

Solution: One simple way is performing an inorder traversal on first tree and storing its data in hash table. As a second step, perform inorder traversal on second tree and check whether that data is already there in hash table or not (if it exists in hash table then mark it with -1 or some unique value).

During the traversal of second tree if we find any mismatch return false. After traversal of second tree check whether it has all -1s in the hash table or not (this ensures extra data available in second tree).

Time Complexity: $O(max(m, n))$, where m and n are the number of elements in first and second BST.
Space Complexity: $O(max(m, n))$. This depends on the size of the first tree.

Problem-74 For Problem-73, can we reduce the time complexity?

Solution: Instead of performing the traversals one after the other, we can perform $in-order$ traversal of both the trees in parallel. Since the $in-order$ traversal gives the sorted list, we can check whether both the trees are generating the same sequence or not.

Time Complexity: $O(max(m, n))$. Space Complexity: $O(1)$. This depends on the size of the first tree.

Problem-75 For the key values $1 \ldots n$, how many structurally unique BSTs are possible that store those keys.

Solution: Strategy: consider that each value could be the root. Recursively find the size of the left and right subtrees. Let p be the root in the BST with n nodes from 1 to n. The left subtree has p-1 nodes, right tree has n-p nodes.

n	f(n), numbers of unique BST with n nodes
0	f(0) = 1
1	f(0) * f(0) = 1 (right 0 left 0)
2	f(1) * f(0) + f(0) * f(1) = 1 + 1 = 2 (right 1 left 0, right 0 left 1)
3	f(2) * f(0) + f(1) * f(1) + f(0) * f(2) = 2 + 1 + 2 = 5 (right 2 left 0, right 1 left 1, right 0 left 2)
4	f(3) * f(0) + f(2) * f(1) + f(1) * f(2) + f(0) * f(3) = 5 + 2 + 2 + 5 = 14 (right 3 left 0, right 2 left 1, right 1 left 2 , right 0 left 3)
5	f(4) * f(0) + f(3) * f(1) + f(2) * f(2) + f(1) * f(3) + f(0) * f(4) = 14 + 5 + 4 + 5 + 14 = 42 (right 4 left 0, right 3 left 1, right 2 left 2, right 1 left 3, right 0 left 4)
......	.....
n	i from n-1 to 0, j=n-1-i, f(n) init to 0, f(n) += f(i) * f(j)

```
func CountTrees(n int) int {
    if n <= 1 {
        return 1
    } else {
        // there will be one value at the root, with whatever remains on the left and right
```

```
        // each forming their own subtrees. Iterate through all the values that could be the root...
        sum := 0
        for root := 1; root <= n; root++ {
            left := CountTrees(root - 1)
            right := CountTrees(n - root)
            sum += left * right  // number of possible trees with this root == left*right
        }
        return sum
    }
}
```

Problem-72 Given a BST of size n, in which each node r has an additional field $r \rightarrow size$, the number of the keys in the sub-tree rooted at r (including the root node r). Give an O(h) algorithm *GreaterthanConstant*(r, k) to find the number of keys that are strictly greater than k (h is the height of the binary search tree).

Solution:

```
func GreaterthanConstant(root *BSTNode, k int) int {
    keysCount := 0
    for r != nil {
        if k < r.data {
            keysCount = keysCount + r.right.size + 1
            r = r.left
        } else if k > r.data {
            r = r.right
        } else { // k = r.data
            keysCount = keysCount + r.right.size
            break
        }
    }
    return keysCount
}
```

The suggested algorithm works well if the key is a unique value for each node. Otherwise when reaching k=r→$data$, we should start a process of moving to the right until reaching a node y with a key that is bigger then k, and then we should return *keysCount* + y→*size*. Time Complexity: O(h) where h=O(n) in the worst case and O($logn$) in the average case.

6.12 Balanced Binary Search Trees

In earlier sections we have seen different trees whose worst-case complexity is O(n), where n is the number of nodes in the tree. This happens when the trees are skew trees. In this section we will try to reduce this worst-case complexity to O($logn$) by imposing restrictions on the heights.

In general, the height balanced trees are represented with $HB(k)$, where k is the difference between left subtree height and right subtree height. Sometimes k is called balance factor.

Full Balanced Binary Search Trees

In $HB(k)$, if $k = 0$ (if balance factor is zero), then we call such binary search trees as *full* balanced binary search trees. That means, in $HB(0)$ binary search tree, the difference between left subtree height and right subtree height should be at most zero. This ensures that the tree is a full binary tree. For example,

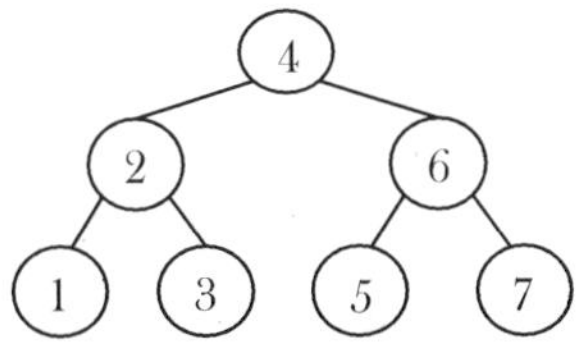

Note: For constructing $HB(0)$ tree refer to *Problems* section.

6.13 AVL (Adelson-Velskii and Landis) Trees

In $HB(k)$, if $k = 1$ (if balance factor is one), such a binary search tree is called an *AVL tree*. That means an AVL tree is a binary search tree with a *balance* condition: the difference between left subtree height and right subtree height is at most 1.

Properties of AVL Trees

A binary tree is said to be an AVL tree, if:

- It is a binary search tree, and
- For any node X, the height of left subtree of X and height of right subtree of X differ by at most 1.

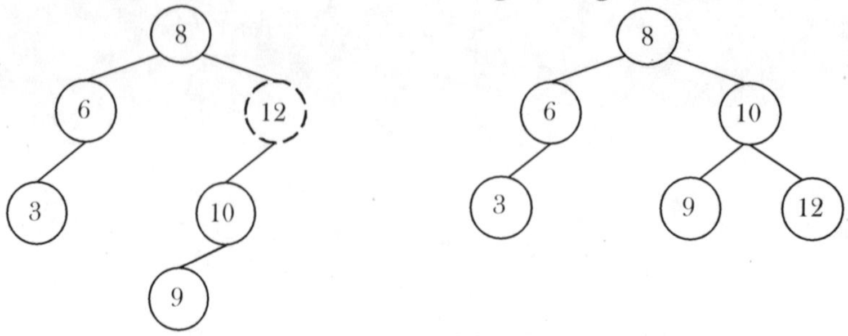

As an example, among the above binary search trees, the left one is not an AVL tree, whereas the right binary search tree is an AVL tree.

Minimum/Maximum Number of Nodes in AVL Tree

For simplicity let us assume that the height of an AVL tree is h and $N(h)$ indicates the number of nodes in AVL tree with height h. To get the minimum number of nodes with height h, we should fill the tree with the minimum number of nodes possible. That means if we fill the left subtree with height $h-1$ then we should fill the right subtree with height $h-2$. As a result, the minimum number of nodes with height h is:

$$N(h) = N(h-1) + N(h-2) + 1$$

In the above equation:

- $N(h-1)$ indicates the minimum number of nodes with height $h-1$.
- $N(h-2)$ indicates the minimum number of nodes with height $h-2$.
- In the above expression, "1" indicates the current node.

We can give $N(h-1)$ either for left subtree or right subtree. Solving the above recurrence gives:

$$N(h) = O(1.618^h) \Longrightarrow h = 1.44logn \approx O(logn)$$

Where n is the number of nodes in AVL tree. Also, the above derivation says that the maximum height in AVL trees is $O(logn)$. Similarly, to get maximum number of nodes, we need to fill both left and right subtrees with height $h-1$. As a result, we get:

$$N(h) = N(h-1) + N(h-1) + 1 = 2N(h-1) + 1$$

The above expression defines the case of full binary tree. Solving the recurrence we get:

$$N(h) = O(2^h) \Longrightarrow h = logn \approx O(logn)$$

$\therefore$ In both the cases, AVL tree property is ensuring that the height of an AVL tree with n nodes is $O(logn)$.

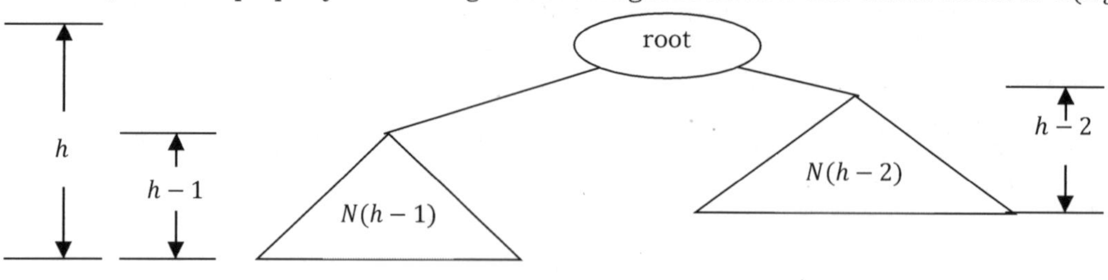

AVL Tree Declaration

Since AVL tree is a BST, the declaration of AVL is similar to that of BST. But just to simplify the operations, we also include the height as part of the declaration.

```
type AVLTreeNode struct {
    data   int
    left   *AVLTreeNode
    right  *AVLTreeNode
    height int
}
```

Finding the Height of an AVL tree

```
func Height(node *AVLTreeNode) int {   // return the height of the node
    if node == nil {
        return -1
    } else {
        return node.height
    }
}
```

Time Complexity: O(1).

Rotations

When the tree structure changes (e.g., with insertion or deletion), we need to modify the tree to restore the AVL tree property. This can be done using single rotations or double rotations. Since an insertion/deletion involves adding/deleting a single node, this can only increase/decrease the height of a subtree by 1.

So, if the AVL tree property is violated at a node X, it means that the heights of left(X) and right(X) differ by exactly 2. This is because, if we balance the AVL tree every time, then at any point, the difference in heights of left(X) and right(X) differ by exactly 2. Rotations is the technique used for restoring the AVL tree property. This means, we need to apply the rotations for the node X.

Observation: One important observation is that, after an insertion, only nodes that are on the path from the insertion point to the root might have their balances altered, because only those nodes have their subtrees altered. To restore the AVL tree property, we start at the insertion point and keep going to the root of the tree.

While moving to the root, we need to consider the first node that is not satisfying the AVL property. From that node onwards, every node on the path to the root will have the issue.

Also, if we fix the issue for that first node, then all other nodes on the path to the root will automatically satisfy the AVL tree property. That means we always need to care for the first node that is not satisfying the AVL property on the path from the insertion point to the root and fix it.

Types of Violations

The tree can be balanced by applying rotations. Rotation is required only if, the balance factor of any node is disturbed upon inserting the new node, otherwise the rotation is not required. Let us assume the node that must be rebalanced is X. Since any node has at most two children, and a height imbalance requires that X's two subtree heights differ by two, we can observe that a violation might occur in four cases:

1. An insertion into the left subtree of the left child of X.
2. An insertion into the right subtree of the left child of X.
3. An insertion into the left subtree of the right child of X.
4. An insertion into the right subtree of the right child of X.

Cases 1 and 4 are symmetric and easily solved with single rotations. Similarly, cases 2 and 3 are also symmetric and can be solved with double rotations (needs two single rotations).

Single Rotations

Left Left Rotation (LL Rotation) [Case-1]: In the case below, node X is not satisfying the AVL tree property. As discussed earlier, the rotation does not have to be done at the root of a tree. In general, we start at the node inserted and travel up the tree, updating the balance information at every node on the path.

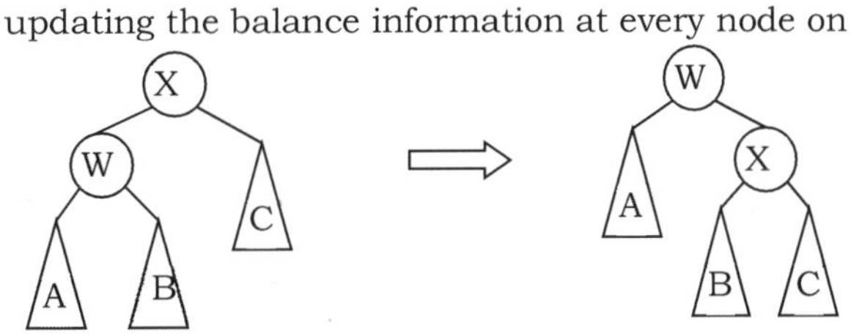

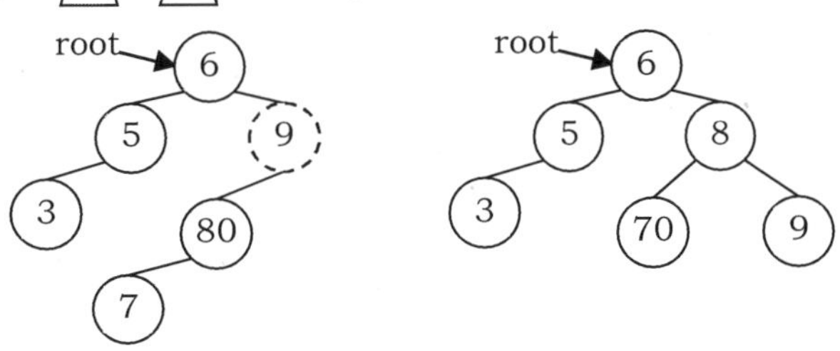

For example, in the figure above, after the insertion of 7 in the original AVL tree on the left, node 9 becomes unbalanced. So, we do a single left-left rotation at 9. As a result we get the tree on the right.

```
// left rotate a root, and update node's height, return the new root
func singleLeftRotate(X *AVLTreeNode) *AVLTreeNode {
    var W *AVLTreeNode
    if X != nil {
        W = X.left
        X.left = W.right
        W.right = X
        // update height
        X.height = max(Height(X.left), Height(X.right)) + 1
        W.height = max(Height(W.left), Height(W.right)) + 1
        X = W
    }
    return X
}
```

Time Complexity: O(1). Space Complexity: O(1).

Right Right Rotation (RR Rotation) [Case-4]: In this case, node *X* is not satisfying the AVL tree property.

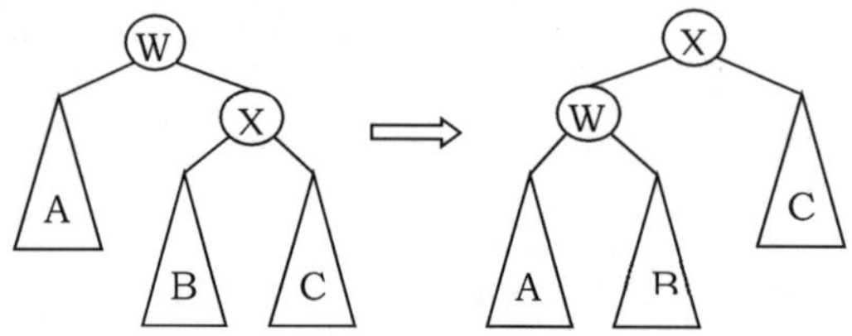

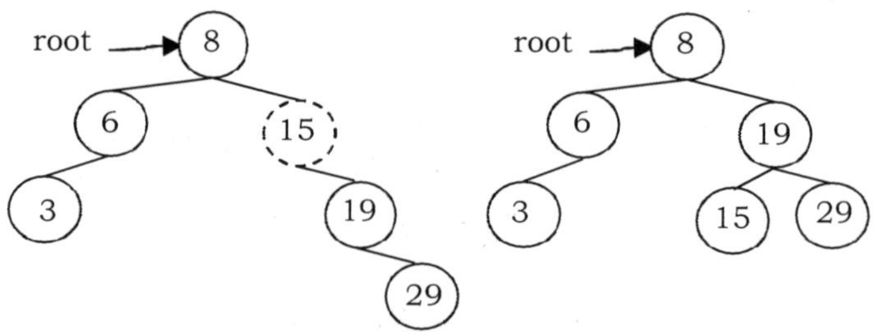

For example, in the above figure, after the insertion of 29 in the original AVL tree on the left, node 15 becomes unbalanced. So, we do a single right-right rotation at 15. As a result we get the tree on the right.

```
// right rotate a root, and update node's height, return the new root
func singleRightRotate(W *AVLTreeNode) *AVLTreeNode {
    var X *AVLTreeNode
    if W != nil {
        X = W.right
        W.right = X.left
        X.left = W
        // update height
        W.height = max(Height(W.left), Height(W.right)) + 1
        X.height = max(Height(X.left), Height(X.right)) + 1
        W = X
    }
    return W
}
```

Time Complexity: O(1). Space Complexity: O(1).

Double Rotations

Left Right Rotation (LR Rotation) [Case-2]: For case-2 and case-3 single rotation does not fix the problem. We need to perform two rotations.

As an example, let us consider the following tree: Insertion of 7 is creating the case-2 scenario and right-side tree is the one after double rotation.

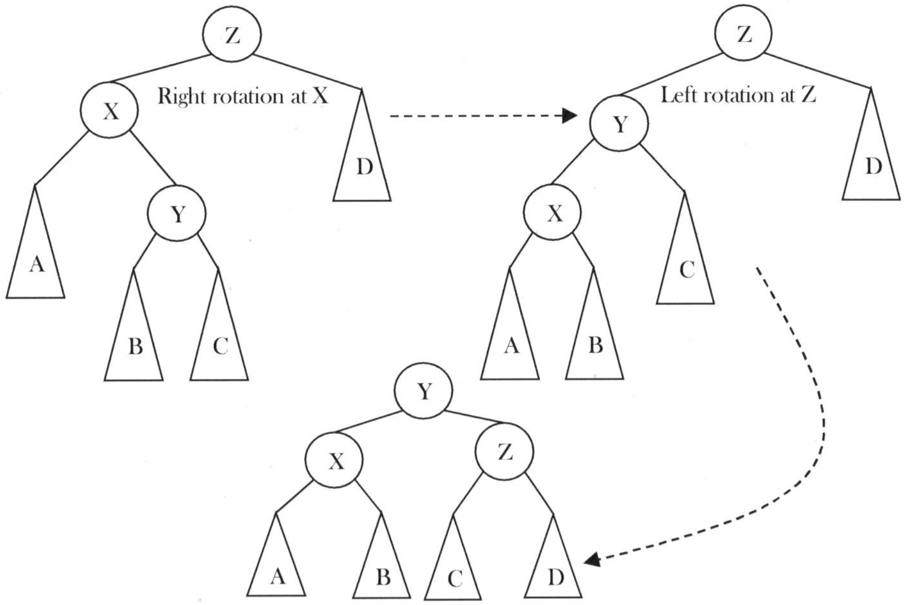

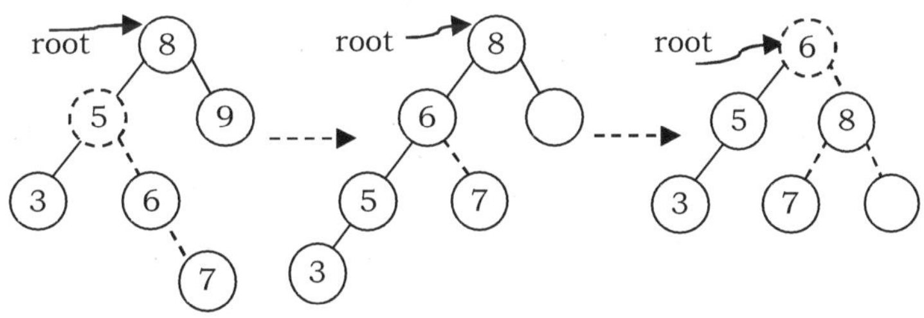

Code for left-right double rotation can be given as:

```
func doubleRotateRightLeft(Z *AVLTreeNode) *AVLTreeNode {
    Z.right = singleLeftRotate(Z.right)
    return singleRightRotate(Z)
}
```

Right Left Rotation (RL Rotation) [Case-3]: Similar to case-2, we need to perform two rotations to fix this scenario.

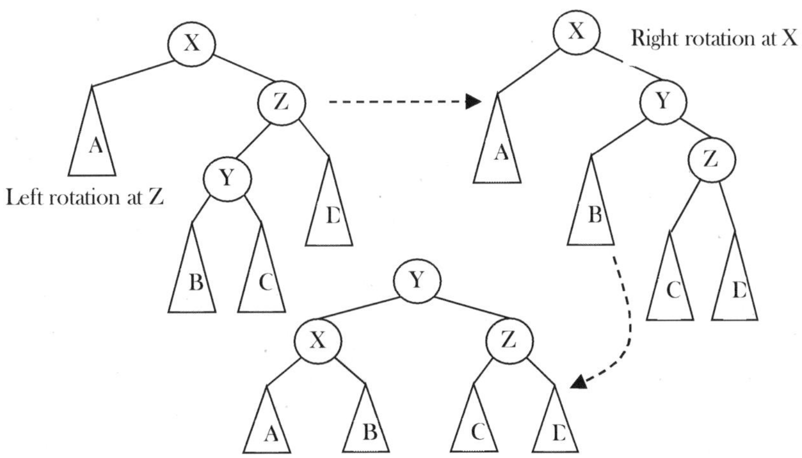

As an example, let us consider the following tree: The insertion of 6 is creating the case-3 scenario and the right-side tree is the one after the double rotation.

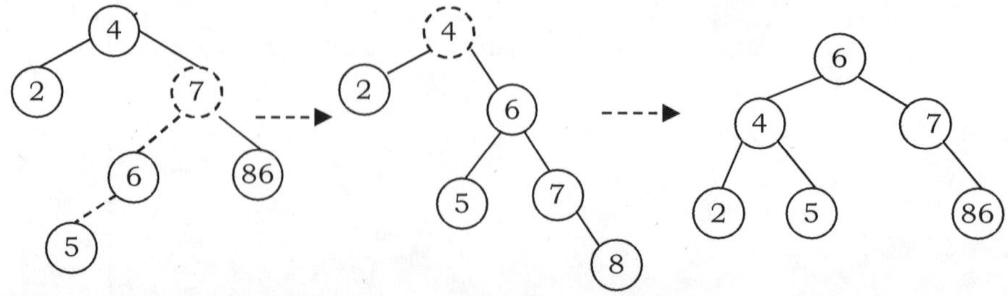


```
func doubleRotateLeftRight(Z *AVLTreeNode) *AVLTreeNode {
    Z.left = singleRightRotate(Z.left)

    return singleLeftRotate(Z)
}
```

Insertion an Element into an AVL tree

Insertion in AVL tree is performed in the same way as it is performed in a binary search tree. After inserting the element, we just need to check whether there is any height imbalance. If there is an imbalance, call the appropriate rotation functions. The new node is added into AVL tree as the leaf node. However, it may lead to violation in the AVL tree property and therefore the tree may need balancing. The tree can be balanced by applying rotations. Rotation is required only if, the balance factor of any node is disturbed upon inserting the new node, otherwise the rotation is not required. As discussed in the previous section, depending upon the type of insertion, the rotations are categorized into four categories.

```
// Insert an element x to AvlTree
func Insert(root *AVLTreeNode, x int) *AVLTreeNode {
    if root == nil {
        root = &AVLTreeNode{
            data:  x,
            height: 0,
        }
    } else if x < root.data {
        root.left = Insert(root.left, x)
        if Height(root.left)-Height(root.right) == 2 {
            if x < root.left.data { //left left
                root = singleLeftRotate(root)
            } else { //left right
                root = doubleRotateLeftRight(root)
            }
        }
    } else if x > root.data {
        root.right = Insert(root.right, x)
        if Height(root.left)-Height(root.right) == 2 {
            if x > root.right.data {
                root = singleRightRotate(root)
            } else {
                root = doubleRotateRightLeft(root)
            }
        }
    } else {
        //x existed, we do nothing.
    }

    root.height = max(Height(root.left), Height(root.right)) + 1

    return root
}
```

Time complexity: O($logn$). Space complexity: O($logn$).

Deleting an Element from AVL tree

Deleting a node from an AVL tree is similar to that in a binary search tree. Deletion may disturb the balance factor of an AVL tree and therefore the tree needs to be rebalanced in order to maintain the AVLness. For this purpose, we need to perform rotations.

```
// Delete an element from AvlTree
func Delete(root *AVLTreeNode, x int) *AVLTreeNode {
    var tmp *AVLTreeNode
    if root != nil {
        if x < root.data {
            root.left = Delete(root.left, x)
            if Height(root.right)-Height(root.left) == 2 {
                if root.right.right != nil {
                    root = singleRightRotate(root)
                } else {
                    root = doubleRotateRightLeft(root)
                }
            } else {
                root.height = max(Height(root.left), Height(root.right)) + 1
            }
        } else if x > root.data {
            root.right = Delete(root.right, x)
            if Height(root.left)-Height(root.right) == 2 {
                if root.left.left != nil {
                    root = singleLeftRotate(root)
                } else {
                    root = doubleRotateLeftRight(root)
                }

            } else {
                root.height = max(Height(root.left), Height(root.right)) + 1
            }
        } else if root.left != nil && root.right != nil {
            tmp = FindMin(root.right)
            root.data = tmp.data
            root.right = Delete(root.right, tmp.data)

        } else {
            if root.left == nil {
                root = root.right
            } else if root.right == nil {
                root = root.left
            }
        }
    }

    return root
}
```

Time complexity: O($logn$). Space complexity: O($logn$).

AVL Trees: Problems & Solutions

Problem-73 Given a height h, give an algorithm for generating the $HB(0)$.

Solution: As we have discussed, $HB(0)$ is nothing but generating full binary tree. In full binary tree the number of nodes with height h is: $2^{h+1} - 1$ (let us assume that the height of a tree with one node is 0). As a result the nodes can be numbered as: 1 to $2^{h+1} - 1$.

```
func BuildHB0(h int) *AVLTreeNode {
    if h == 0 {
        return nil
    }
    newNode := &AVLTreeNode{}
    newNode.left = BuildHB0(h - 1)
    newNode.data = count //assume count is a global variable
    count++
    newNode.right = BuildHB0(h - 1)
    return newNode
}
```

Time Complexity: O(n).
Space Complexity: O($logn$), where $logn$ indicates the maximum stack size which is equal to height of tree.

Problem-74 Is there any alternative way of solving Problem-73?

Solution: Yes, we can solve it following divide and conquer logic. That means, instead of working with height, we can take the range. With this approach, we do not need any global counter to be maintained.

```
func BuildHB0(l, r int) *AVLTreeNode {
    mid := l + (r-l)/2
    if l > r {
        return nil
    }
    newNode := &AVLTreeNode{}
    newNode.data = mid
    newNode.left = BuildHB0(l, mid-1)
    newNode.right = BuildHB0(mid+1, r)
    return newNode
}
```

The initial call to the $BuildHB0$ function could be: $BuildHB0(1, 1 \ll h)$. $1 \ll h$ does the shift operation for calculating the $2^{h+1} - 1$.

Time Complexity: O(n).
Space Complexity: O($logn$). Where $logn$ indicates maximum stack size which is equal to the height of the tree.

Problem-75 Construct minimal AVL trees of height 0, 1, 2, 3, 4, and 5. What is the number of nodes in a minimal AVL tree of height 6?

Solution Let $N(h)$ be the number of nodes in a minimal AVL tree with height h.

$N(0) = 1$

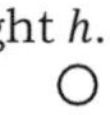

$N(1) = 2$

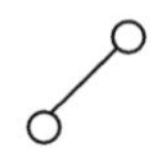

$N(h) = 1 + N(h-1) + N(h-2)$

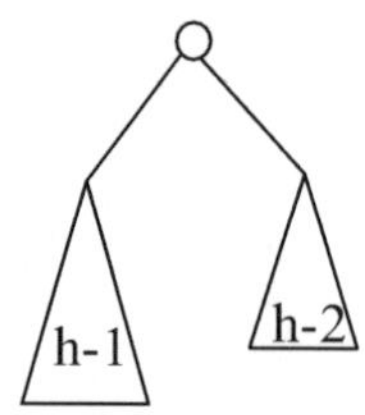

$N(2) = 1 + N(1) + N(0)$
$= 1 + 2 + 1 = 4$

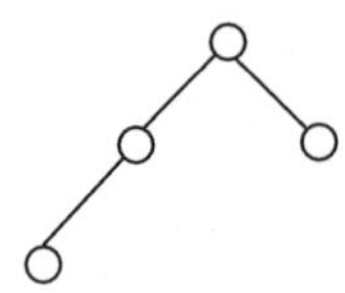

$N(3) = 1 + N(2) + N(1)$
$= 1 + 4 + 2 = 7$

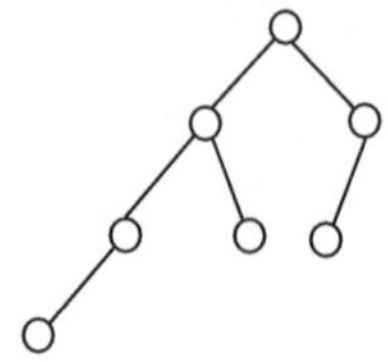

$N(4) = 1 + N(3) + N(2)$
$= 1 + 7 + 4 = 12$

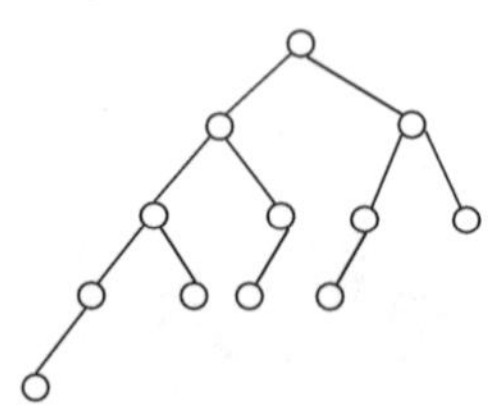

$N(5) = 1 + N(4) + N(3)$
$= 1 + 12 + 7 = 20$

...

Problem-76 For Problem-73, how many different shapes can there be of a minimal AVL tree of height h?

Solution: Let $NS(h)$ be the number of different shapes of a minimal AVL tree of height h.

$NS(0) = 1$

$NS(1) = 2$

$$NS(2) = 2 * NS(1) * NS(0)$$
$$= 2 * 2 * 1 = 4$$

$$NS(3) = 2 * NS(2) * NS(1)$$
$$= 2 * 4 * 1 = 8$$

...

$$NS(h) = 2 * NS(h-1) * NS(h-2)$$

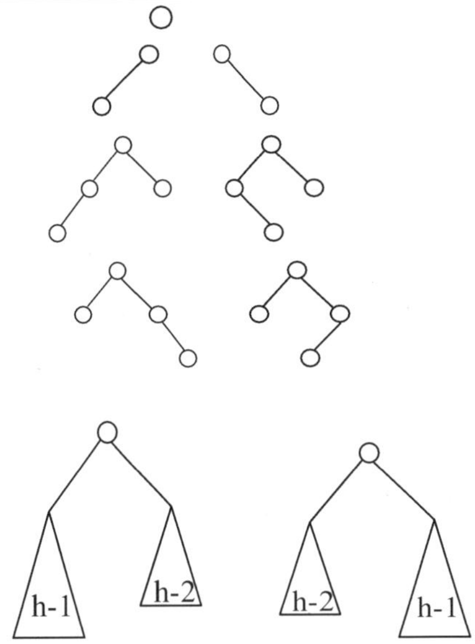

Problem-77 Given a binary search tree, check whether it is an AVL tree or not?

Alternative problem statement: Given a binary tree, determine if it is height-balanced. For this problem, a height-balanced binary tree is defined as: a binary tree in which the left and right subtrees of every node differ in height by no more than 1.

Solution: Simple solution would be to calculate the height of left subtree and right subtree for each node in the tree. If for any node, the absolute difference between the height of its left and right subtree is more than 1, the tree is unbalanced. The time complexity of this solution is $O(n^2)$ as there are n nodes in the tree and for every node we are calculating height of its left subtree and right subtree that takes $O(n)$ time.

We can solve this problem in linear time by doing post-order traversal of the tree. Instead of calculating height of left subtree and right subtree for every node in the tree, we can get the height in constant time. The idea is to start from the bottom of the tree and return height of subtree rooted at given node to its parent node. The height of subtree rooted at any node is equal to 1 plus maximum height of the left subtree or right subtree.

```
const NotBalanced = -1
func isBalanced(root *BSTNode) bool {
    if root == nil {
        return true
    }
    return checkHeight(root) != NotBalanced
}
func checkHeight(root * BSTNode) int {
    if root == nil {
        return 0
    }
    leftHeight := checkHeight(root.left)
    if leftHeight == NotBalanced {
        return NotBalanced
    }
    rightHeight := checkHeight(root.right)
    if rightHeight == NotBalanced {
        return NotBalanced
    }
    if abs(leftHeight-rightHeight) > 1 {
        return false
    }
    return max(leftHeight, rightHeight) + 1
}
```

Time Complexity: $O(n)$. Space Complexity: $O(n)$.

Problem-78 Given a height h, give an algorithm to generate an AVL tree with minimum number of nodes.

Solution: To get minimum number of nodes, fill one level with $h-1$ and the other with $h-2$. This problem is same as that of Problem-73.

```
var count = 1
func GenerateAVLTree(h int) *AVLTreeNode {
    if h == 0 {
        return nil
    }
    newNode := &AVLTreeNode{}
    newNode.left = GenerateAVLTree(h - 1)
    newNode.data = count //assume count is a global variable
    count++
    newNode.right = GenerateAVLTree(h - 1)
    return newNode
}
```

Problem-79 Given an AVL tree with n integer items and two integers a and b, where a and b can be any integers with $a <= b$. Implement an algorithm to count the number of nodes in the range $[a, b]$.

Solution:

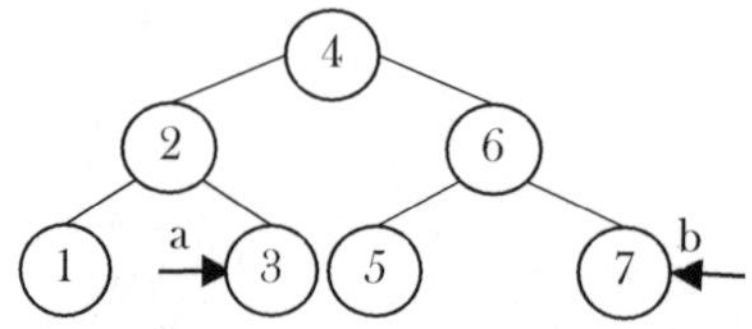

The idea is to make use of the recursive property of binary search trees. There are three cases to consider: whether the current node is in the range $[a, b]$, on the left side of the range $[a, b]$, or on the right side of the range $[a, b]$. Only subtrees that possibly contain the nodes will be processed under each of the three cases.

```
func RangeCount(root *AVLTreeNode, a, b int) int {
    if root == nil {
        return 0
    } else if root.data > b {
        return RangeCount(root.left, a, b)
    } else if root.data < a {
        return RangeCount(root.right, a, b)
    } else if root.data >= a && root.data <= b {
        return RangeCount(root.left, a, b) + RangeCount(root.right, a, b) + 1
    }
    return 0
}
```

The complexity is similar to $in - order$ traversal of the tree but skipping left or right sub-trees when they do not contain any answers. So in the worst case, if the range covers all the nodes in the tree, we need to traverse all the n nodes to get the answer. The worst time complexity is therefore $O(n)$.

If the range is small, which only covers a few elements in a small subtree at the bottom of the tree, the time complexity will be $O(h) = O(logn)$, where h is the height of the tree. This is because only a single path is traversed to reach the small subtree at the bottom and many higher-level subtrees have been pruned along the way.

Note: Refer similar problem in BST.

Problem-80 Given a BST (applicable to AVL trees as well) where each node contains two data elements (its data and also the number of nodes in its subtrees) as shown below. Convert the tree to another BST by replacing the second data element (number of nodes in its subtrees) with previous node data in inorder traversal. Note that each node is merged with *inorder* previous node data. Also make sure that conversion happens in-place.

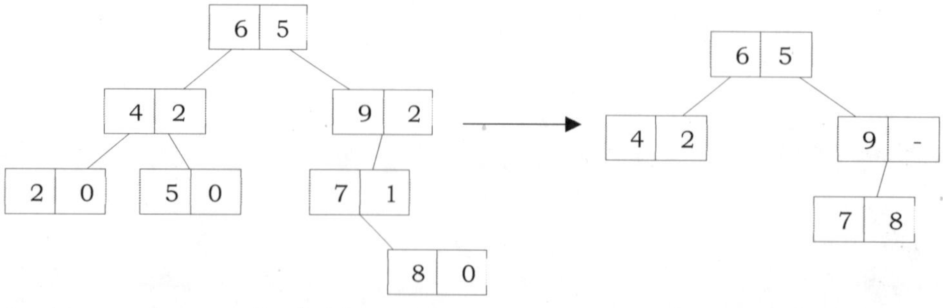

Solution: The simplest way is to use level order traversal. If the number of elements in the left subtree is greater than the number of elements in the right subtree, find the maximum element in the left subtree and replace the current node second data element with it. Similarly, if the number of elements in the left subtree is less than the number of elements in the right subtree, find the minimum element in the right subtree and replace the current node *second* data element with it.

```
type AVLTreeNode struct {
    data1  int
     data1  int
    left     *AVLTreeNode
    right    *AVLTreeNode
}
func TreeCompression(root *AVLTreeNode) *AVLTreeNode {
    if root == nil {
        return nil
    }
    var node, node2 *AVLTreeNode
    queue := []*AVLTreeNode{root}
    for len(queue) > 0 {
        qlen := len(queue)
        var level []int
        for i := 0; i < qlen; i++ {
            node := queue[0]
            level = append(level, node.data)
            queue = queue[1:]
            if node.left != nil && node.right != nil && node.left.data2 > node.right.data2 {
                node2 = FindMax(node)
            } else {
                node2 = FindMin(node)
            }
            node.data2 = node2.data2 //Process current node
            //Remember to delete this node.
            Delete(node2)
            if node.left != nil {
                queue = append(queue, node.left)
            }
            if node.right != nil {
                queue = append(queue, node.right)
            }
        }
        result = append(result, level)

    }
    deleteQueue(Q)
}
```

Time Complexity: O($nlogn$) on average since BST takes O($logn$) on average to find the maximum or minimum element. Space Complexity: O(n). Since, in the worst case, all the nodes on the entire last level could be in the queue simultaneously.

Problem-81 Can we reduce time complexity for the previous problem?

Solution: Let us try using an approach that is similar to what we followed in Problem-64. The idea behind this solution is that inorder traversal of BST produces sorted lists. While traversing the BST in inorder, keep track of the elements visited and merge them.

```
func TreeCompression(root *BinarySearchTreeNode, previousNodeData *int) *AVLTreeNode {
    if root == nil {
        return nil
    }
    TreeCompression(root.left, previousNode)
    if *previousNodeData == math.MinInt32 {
        *previousNodeData = root.data
        root = nil
    }
    if *previousNodeData != math.MinInt32 { // Process current node
        root.data2 = previousNodeData
        *previousNodeData = math.MinInt32
    }
```

```
        return TreeCompression(root.right, previousNode)
    }
```

Time Complexity: O(n). Space Complexity: O(1). Note that, we are still having recursive stack space for inorder traversal.

Problem-82 Given a BST and a key, find the element in the BST which is closest to the given key.

Solution: As a simple solution, we can use level-order traversal and for every element compute the difference between the given key and the element's value. If that difference is less than the previous maintained difference, then update the difference with this new minimum value. With this approach, at the end of the traversal we will get the element which is closest to the given key.

```
func ClosestELement(root *BSTNode, target int) *BSTNode {
    if root == nil {
        return nil
    }
    var result [][]int
    var element *BSTNode
    queue := []*BSTNode{root}
    difference := math.MaxInt32
    for len(queue) > 0 {
        qlen := len(queue)
        var level []int
        for i := 0; i < qlen; i++ {
            node := queue[0]
            level = append(level, node.data)
            queue = queue[1:]
            if difference < abs(node.data-target) {
                difference = abs(node.data - target)
                element = node
            }
            if root.left != nil {
                queue = append(queue, root.left)
            }
            if root.right != nil {
                queue = append(queue, root.right)
            }
        }
        result = append(result, level)
    }
    return element
}
```

Time Complexity: O(n). Space Complexity: O(n).

Problem-83 For Problem-82, can we solve it using the recursive approach?

Solution: The approach is similar to Problem-18. Following is a simple algorithm for finding the closest Value in BST.

1. If the root is *nil*, then the closest value is zero (or *nil*).
2. If the root's data matches the given key, then the closest is the root.
3. Else, consider the root as the closest and do the following:
    a. If the key is smaller than the root data, find the closest on the left side tree of the root recursively and call it temp.
    b. If the key is larger than the root data, find the closest on the right-side tree of the root recursively and call it temp.
4. Return the root or temp depending on whichever is nearer to the given key.

```
func ClosestELement(root *BSTNode, target int) *BSTNode {
    if root == nil {
        return nil
    }
    if root.data == target {
        return root
    }
    if target < root.data {
        if root.left == nil {
            return root
```

```
        }
        temp := ClosestELement(root.left, target)
        if abs(temp.data-target) > abs(root.data-target) {
            return root
        } else {
            return temp
        }
    } else {
        if root.right == nil {
            return root
        }
        temp := ClosestELement(root.right, target)
        if abs(temp.data-target) > abs(root.data-target) {
            return root
        } else {
            return temp
        }
    }
}
```

Time Complexity: $O(n)$ in worst case, and in average case it is $O(logn)$. Space Complexity: $O(n)$.

Problem-84 Median in an infinite series of integers

Solution: Median is the middle number in a sorted list of numbers (if we have odd number of elements). If we have even number of elements, median is the average of two middle numbers in a sorted list of numbers.

For solving this problem we can use a binary search tree with additional information at each node, and the number of children on the left and right subtrees. We also keep the number of total nodes in the tree. Using this additional information we can find the median in $O(logn)$ time, taking the appropriate branch in the tree based on the number of children on the left and right of the current node. But, the insertion complexity is $O(n)$ because a standard binary search tree can degenerate into a linked list if we happen to receive the numbers in sorted order.

So, let's use a balanced binary search tree to avoid worst case behavior of standard binary search trees. For this problem, the balance factor is the number of nodes in the left subtree minus the number of nodes in the right subtree. And only the nodes with a balance factor of +1 or 0 are considered to be balanced.

So, the number of nodes on the left subtree is either equal to or 1 more than the number of nodes on the right subtree, but not less.

If we ensure this balance factor on every node in the tree, then the root of the tree is the median, if the number of elements is odd. In the number of elements is even, the median is the average of the root and its inorder successor, which is the leftmost descendent of its right subtree. So, the complexity of insertion maintaining a balanced condition is $O(logn)$ and finding a median operation is O(1) assuming we calculate the inorder successor of the root at every insertion if the number of nodes is even.

Insertion and balancing is very similar to AVL trees. Instead of updating the heights, we update the number of nodes information. Balanced binary search trees seem to be the most optimal solution, insertion is $O(logn)$ and find median is O(1).

Note: For an efficient algorithm refer to the *Priority Queues and Heaps* chapter.

Problem-85 Given a binary tree, how do you remove all the half nodes (which have only one child)? Note that we should not touch leaves.

Solution: By using post-order traversal we can solve this problem efficiently. We first process the left children, then the right children, and finally the node itself. So we form the new tree bottom up, starting from the leaves towards the root. By the time we process the current node, both its left and right subtrees have already been processed.

```
func RemoveHalfNodes(root *BSTNode) *BSTNode {
    if root == nil {
        return root
    }
    root.left = RemoveHalfNodes(root.left)
    root.right = RemoveHalfNodes(root.right)
    if root.left == nil && root.right == nil {
        return root
    }
    if root.left == nil {
        return root.right
```

```
    }
    if root.right == nil {
        return root.left
    }
    return root
}
```

Time Complexity: O(n).

Problem-86 Given a binary tree, how do you remove its leaves?

Solution: By using post-order traversal we can solve this problem (other traversals would also work).

```
func RemoveLeaves(root *BSTNode) *BSTNode {
    if root == nil {
        return root
    }
    if root.left == nil && root.right == nil {
        root = nil
        return root
    } else {
        root.left = RemoveLeaves(root.left)
        root.right = RemoveLeaves(root.right)
    }
    return root
}
```

Time Complexity: O(n).

Problem-87 Given a BST and two integers (minimum and maximum integers) as parameters, how do you remove (prune) elements that are not within that range?

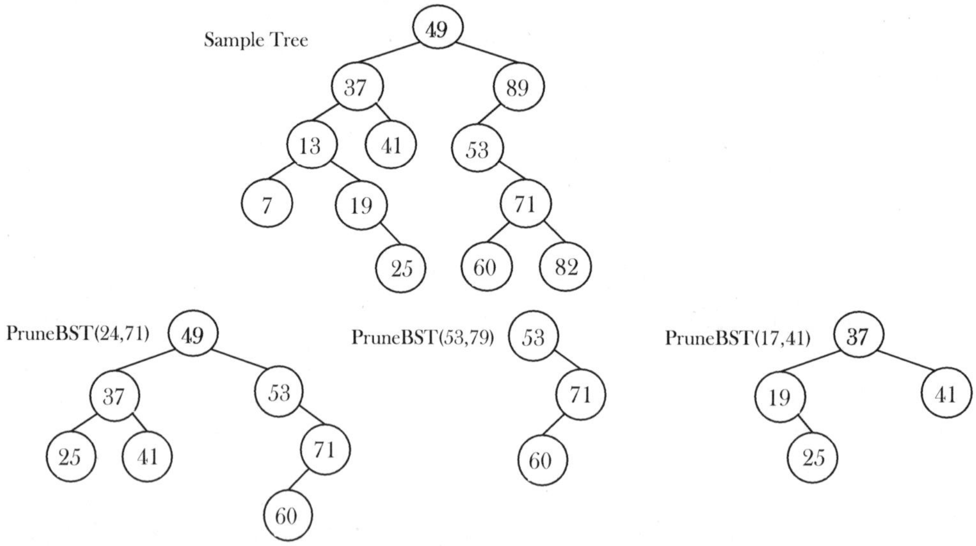

Solution: Observation: Since we need to check each and every element in the tree, and the subtree changes should be reflected in the parent, we can think about using post order traversal. So we process the nodes starting from the leaves towards the root. As a result, while processing the node itself, both its left and right subtrees are valid pruned BSTs. At each node we will return a pointer based on its value, which will then be assigned to its parent's left or right child pointer, depending on whether the current node is the left or right child of the parent. If the current node's value is between A and B ($A <= node's\ data <= B$) then no action needs to be taken, so we return the reference to the node itself.

If the current node's value is less than A, then we return the reference to its right subtree and discard the left subtree. Because if a node's value is less than A, then its left children are definitely less than A since this is a binary search tree. But its right children may or may not be less than A; we can't be sure, so we return the reference to it. Since we're performing bottom-up post-order traversal, its right subtree is already a trimmed valid binary search tree (possibly *nil*), and its left subtree is definitely *nil* because those nodes were surely less than A and they were eliminated during the post-order traversal.

A similar situation occurs when the node's value is greater than B, so we now return the reference to its left subtree. Because if a node's value is greater than B, then its right children are definitely greater than B. But its left children may or may not be greater than B; So we discard the right subtree and return the reference to the already valid left subtree.

```
func PruneBST(root *BSTNode, A, B int) *BSTNode {
    if root == nil {
        return root
    }
    if root.data < A {
        return PruneBST(root.right, A, B)
    }
    if root.data > B {
        return PruneBST(root.left, A, B)
    }
    root.right = PruneBST(root.right, A, B)
    root.left = PruneBST(root.left, A, B)
    return root
}
```

Time Complexity: O(n) in worst case and in average case it is O($logn$).

Note: If the given BST is an AVL tree then O(n) is the average time complexity.

Problem-88 Assume that a set S of n numbers are stored in some form of balanced binary search tree; i.e. the depth of the tree is O($logn$). In addition to the key value and the pointers to children, assume that every node contains the number of nodes in its subtree. Specify a reason(s) why a balanced binary tree can be a better option than a complete binary tree for storing the set S.

Solution: Implementation of a balanced binary tree requires less RAM space as we do not need to keep the complete tree in RAM (since they use pointers).

Problem-89 For the Problem-88, specify a reason (s) why a complete binary tree can be a better option than a balanced binary tree for storing the set S.

Solution: A complete binary tree is more space efficient as we do not need any extra flags. A balanced binary tree usually takes more space since we need to store some flags. For example, in a Red-Black tree we need to store a bit for the color. Also, a complete binary tree can be stored in a RAM as an array without using pointers.

Problem-90 Given a binary tree, find the maximum path sum. The path may start and end at any node in the tree.

Solution: We calculate the maximum path sum rooted at each node and update the max sum during the traversal. Each node can be the root of the final maximum path sum. The root here means the topmost node in a path. We calculate the maximum Path Sum rooted at each node and update the max sum during the traversal.

There can only be four different cases when a particular node is involved in the max path.

- It's the only Node
- Max path through left child + current node
- Max path through right child + current node
- Max path through left child + current node + right child

In this algorithm, we can use post-order traversal and return the maximum sum in the subtree starting from the root. We call it left_result and right_result for left and right subtree

```
func MaxPathSum(root *BinaryTreeNode) int {
    max := math.MinInt64
    var helper func(root *BinaryTreeNode) int
    helper = func(root *BinaryTreeNode) int {
        if root == nil {
            return math.MinInt64
        }
        sums := []int{root.data} // just the current node
        if root.left != nil {   // current node + best path of left subtree
            sums = append(sums, helper(root.left)+root.data)
        }
        if root.right != nil { // current node + best of right subtree
            sums = append(sums, helper(root.right)+root.data)
        }
        // single path connecting best path of left subtree, current node, best path of right subtree
        if len(sums) == 3 {
            sums = append(sums, sums[1]+sums[2]-root.data)
        }
```

```
        localMax := maxIntSlice(sums)
        if localMax > max {
            max = localMax
        }
        returnMax := localMax
        // if the max was the current node + left / right subtrees we can't return it and
        // need to consider the second-best path
        if len(sums) == 4 && returnMax == sums[3] {
            sums = sums[:3]
            returnMax = maxIntSlice(sums)
        }
        return returnMax
    }
    helper(root)
    return max
}
```

Problem-91 Let T be a proper binary tree with root r. Consider the following algorithm.

```
Algorithm
  func TreeTraversal(root *BinaryTreeNode) {
      if r == nil {
          return 1
      } else {
          a = TreeTraversal(r.left)
          b = TreeTraversal(r.right)
          return a + b
      }
  }
```

What does the algorithm do?
A. Always returns the value 1. B. Computes the number of nodes in the tree. C. Computes depth of the nodes.
D. It computes the height of the tree. E. Computes the number of leaves in the tree.

Solution: E.

6.14 Other Variations on Trees

In this section, let us enumerate the other possible representations of trees. In the earlier sections, we have looked at AVL trees, which is a binary search tree (BST) with balancing property. Now, let us look at a few more balanced binary search trees: Red-black Trees and Splay Trees.

6.14.1 Red-Black Trees

In Red-black trees each node is associated with an extra attribute: the color, which is either red or black. To get logarithmic complexity we impose the following restrictions.

Definition: A Red-black tree is a binary search tree that satisfies the following properties:

- Root Property: the root is black
- External Property: every leaf is black
- Internal Property: the children of a red node are black
- Depth Property: all the leaves have the same black

Similar to AVL trees, if the Red-black tree becomes imbalanced, then we perform rotations to reinforce the balancing property. With Red-black trees, we can perform the following operations in $O(logn)$ in worst case, where n is the number of nodes in the trees.

- Insertion, Deletion
- Finding predecessor, successor
- Finding minimum, maximum

6.14.2 Splay Trees

Splay-trees are BSTs with a self-adjusting property. Another interesting property of splay-trees is: starting with an empty tree, any sequence of K operations with maximum of n nodes takes $O(Klogn)$ time complexity in worst case. Splay trees are easier to program and also ensure faster access to recently accessed items. Similar to AVL and Red-Black trees, at any point that the splay tree becomes imbalanced, we can perform rotations to reinforce the balancing property.

Splay-trees cannot guarantee the $O(logn)$ complexity in worst case. But it gives amortized $O(logn)$ complexity. Even though individual operations can be expensive, any sequence of operations gets the complexity of logarithmic behavior. One operation may take more time (a single operation may take $O(n)$ time) but the subsequent operations may not take worst case complexity and on the average *per operation* complexity is $O(logn)$.

6.14.3 B-Trees

B-Tree is like other self-balancing trees such as AVL and Red-black tree such that it maintains its balance of nodes while operations are performed against it. B-Tree has the following properties:

- Minimum degree "t" where, except root node, all other nodes must have no less than $t - 1$ keys
- Each node with n keys has $n + 1$ children
- Keys in each node are lined up where $k_1 < k_2 < .. k_n$
- Each node cannot have more than 2t-1 keys, thus 2t children
- Root node at least must contain one key. There is no root node if the tree is empty.
- Tree grows in depth only when root node is split.

Unlike a binary-tree, each node of a b-tree may have a variable number of keys and children. The keys are stored in non-decreasing order. Each key has an associated child that is the root of a subtree containing all nodes with keys less than or equal to the key but greater than the preceding key. A node also has an additional rightmost child that is the root for a subtree containing all keys greater than any keys in the node.

A b-tree has a minimum number of allowable children for each node known as the *minimization factor*. If t is this *minimization factor*, every node must have at least $t - 1$ keys. Under certain circumstances, the root node is allowed to violate this property by having fewer than $t - 1$ keys. Every node may have at most $2t - 1$ keys or, equivalently, $2t$ children.

Since each node tends to have a large branching factor (a large number of children), it is typically necessary to traverse relatively few nodes before locating the desired key. If access to each node requires a disk access, then a B-tree will minimize the number of disk accesses required. The minimization factor is usually chosen so that the total size of each node corresponds to a multiple of the block size of the underlying storage device. This choice simplifies and optimizes disk access. Consequently, a B-tree is an ideal data structure for situations where all data cannot reside in primary storage and accesses to secondary storage are comparatively expensive (or time consuming).

To *search* the tree, it is similar to binary tree except that the key is compared multiple times in a given node because the node contains more than 1 key. If the key is found in the node, the search terminates. Otherwise, it moves down where at child pointed by ci where key $k < k_i$.

Key *insertions* of a B-tree happens from the bottom fashion. This means that it walk down the tree from root to the target child node first. If the child is not full, the key is simply inserted. If it is full, the child node is split in the middle, the median key moves up to the parent, then the new key is inserted. When inserting and walking down the tree, if the root node is found to be full, it's split first and we have a new root node. Then the normal insertion operation is performed.

Key *deletion* is more complicated as it needs to maintain the number of keys in each node to meet the constraint. If a key is found in leaf node and deleting it still keeps the number of keys in the nodes not too low, it's simply done right away. If it's done to the inner node, the predecessor of the key in the corresponding child node is moved to replace the key in the inner node. If moving the predecessor will cause the child node to violate the node count constraint, the sibling child nodes are combined and the key in the inner node is deleted.

6.14.4 Augmented Trees

In earlier sections, we have seen various problems like finding the Kth – smallest – element in the tree and other similar ones. Of all the problems the worst complexity is $O(n)$, where n is the number of nodes in the tree. To perform such operations in $O(logn)$, augmented trees are useful. In these trees, extra information is added to each node and that extra data depends on the problem we are trying to solve.

For example, to find the K^{th}element in a binary search tree, let us see how augmented trees solve the problem. Let us assume that we are using Red-Black trees as balanced BST (or any balanced BST) and augmenting the size information in the nodes data. For a given node X in Red-Black tree with a field *size*(X) equal to the number of nodes in the subtree and can be calculated as:

$$size(X) = size(X \rightarrow left) + size(X \rightarrow right)) + 1$$

K^{th} – smallest – operation can be defined as:

```
func kthSmallest(X *BinarySearcTreeNode, K int) *BinarySearcTreeNode {
    r := Size(X.left) + 1
    if K == r {
        return X
    }
```

```
        if K < r {
            return kthSmallest(X.left, K)
        }
        if K > r {
            return kthSmallest(X.right, K-r)
        }
    }
```

Time Complexity: O($logn$). Space Complexity: O($logn$).

Example: With the extra size information, the augmented tree will look like:

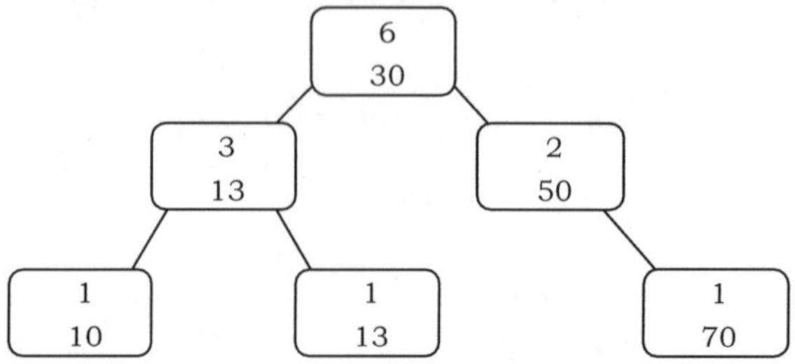

6.14.5 Interval Trees [Segment Trees]

We often face questions that involve queries made in an array based on range. For example, for a given array of integers, what is the maximum number in the range α to β, where α and β are of course within array limits. To iterate over those entries with intervals containing a particular value, we can use a simple array. But if we need more efficient access, we need a more sophisticated data structure.

An array-based storage scheme and a brute-force search through the entire array is acceptable only if a single search is to be performed, or if the number of elements is small. For example, if you know all the array values of interest in advance, you need to make only one pass through the array. However, if you can interactively specify different search operations at different times, the brute-force search becomes impractical because every element in the array must be examined during each search operation.

If you sort the array in ascending order of the array values, you can terminate the sequential search when you reach the object whose low value is greater than the element we are searching. Unfortunately, this technique becomes increasingly ineffective as the low value increases, because fewer search operations are eliminated. That means, what if we have to answer a large number of queries like this? – is brute force still a good option?

Another example is when we need to return a sum in a given range. We can brute force this too, but the problem for a large number of queries still remains. So, what can we do? With a bit of thinking we can come up with an approach like maintaining a separate array of n elements, where n is the size of the original array, where each index stores the sum of all elements from 0 to that index. So essentially we have with a bit of preprocessing brought down the query time from a worst-case O(n) to O(1). Now this is great as far as static arrays are concerned, but, what if we are required to perform updates on the array too?

The first approach gives us an O(n) query time, but an O(1) update time. The second approach, on the other hand, gives us O(1) query time, but an O(n) update time. So, which one do we choose?

Interval trees are also binary search trees and they store interval information in the node structure. That means, we maintain a set of n intervals $[i_1, i_2]$ such that one of the intervals containing a query point Q (if any) can be found efficiently. Interval trees are used for performing range queries efficiently.

A segment tree is a heap-like data structure that can be used for making update/query operations upon array intervals in logarithmical time. We define the segment tree for the interval $[i, j]$ in the following recursive manner:

- The root (first node in the array) node will hold the information for the interval $[i, j]$
- If $i < j$ the left and right children will hold the information for the intervals $[i, \frac{i+j}{2}]$ and $[\frac{i+j}{2}+1, j]$

Segment trees (also called *segtrees* and *interval trees*) is a cool data structure, primarily used for range queries. It is a height balanced binary tree with a static structure. The nodes of a segment tree correspond to various intervals, and can be augmented with appropriate information pertaining to those intervals. It is somewhat less powerful than a balanced binary tree because of its static structure, but due to the recursive nature of operations on the segtree, it is incredibly easy to think about and code.

We can use segment trees to solve range minimum/maximum query problems. The time complexity is T($nlogn$) where O(n) is the time required to build the tree and each query takes O($logn$) time.

Example: Given a set of intervals: S = {[2-5], [6-7], [6-10], [8-9], [12-15], [15-23], [25-30]}. A query with Q = 9 returns [6,10] or [8,9] (assume these are the intervals which contain 9 among all the intervals). A query with Q = 23 returns [15, 23].

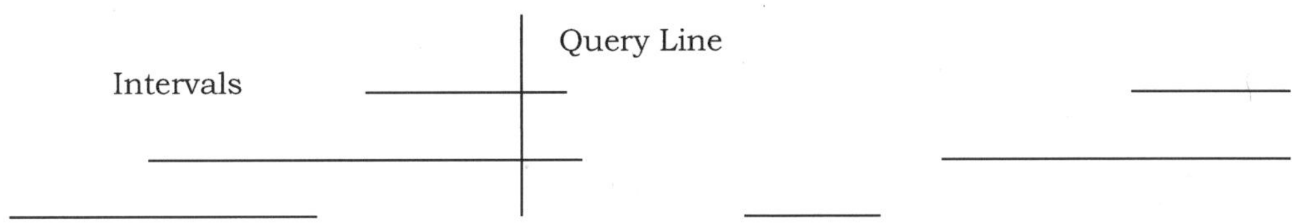

Construction of Interval Trees: Let us assume that we are given a set S of n intervals (called *segments*). These n intervals will have $2n$ endpoints. Now, let us see how to construct the interval tree.

Algorithm: Recursively build tree on interval set S as follows:

- Sort the $2n$ endpoints
- Let X_{mid} be the median point

Time Complexity for building interval trees: O($nlogn$). Since we are choosing the median, Interval Trees will be approximately balanced. This ensures that, we split the set of end points up in half each time. The depth of the tree is O($logn$). To simplify the search process, generally X_{mid} is stored with each node.

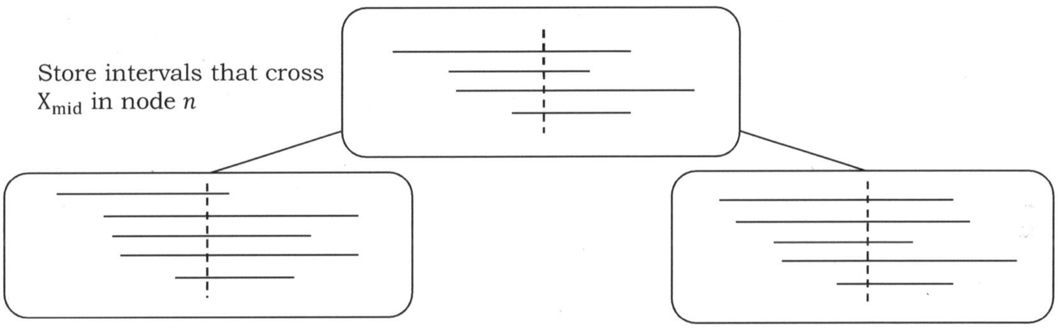

6.14.6 Scapegoat Trees

Scapegoat tree is a self-balancing binary search tree, discovered by Arne Andersson. It provides worst-case O($logn$) search time, and O($logn$) amortized (average) insertion and deletion time.

AVL trees rebalance whenever the height of two sibling subtrees differ by more than one; scapegoat trees rebalance whenever the size of a child exceeds a certain ratio of its parents, a ratio known as a. After inserting the element, we traverse back up the tree. If we find an imbalance where a child's size exceeds the parent's size times alpha, we must rebuild the subtree at the parent, the *scapegoat*.

There might be more than one possible scapegoat, but we only have to pick one. The most optimal scapegoat is actually determined by height balance. When removing it, we see if the total size of the tree is less than alpha of the largest size since the last rebuilding of the tree. If so, we rebuild the entire tree. The alpha for a scapegoat tree can be any number between 0.5 and 1.0. The value 0.5 will force perfect balance, while 1.0 will cause rebalancing to never occur, effectively turning it into a BST.

6.15 Supplementary Questions

Problem-92 A binary tree is univalued if every node in the tree has the same value. Given an algorithm to check whether the given binary tree is univalued or not.

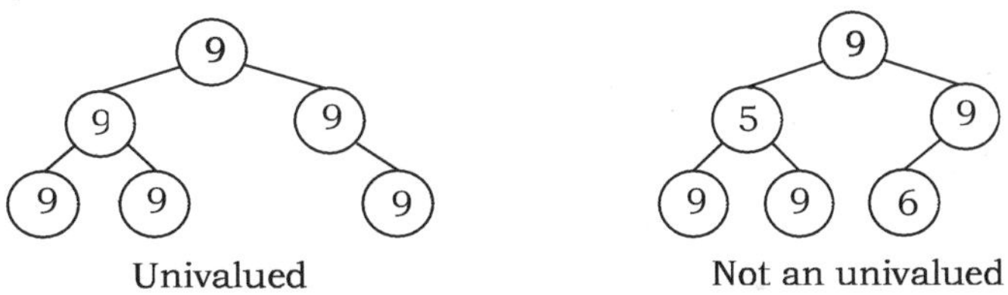

Solution: A tree is univalued if both its children are univalued, plus the root node has the same value as the child nodes. We can write our function recursively. *isLeftUnivalTree* will represent that the left subtree is correct: ie., that it is univalued, and the root value is equal to the left child's value. *isRightUnivalTree* will represent the same thing for the right subtree. We need both of these properties to be true.

```
func IsUnivalTree(root *BinaryTreeNode) bool {
```

```
        isLeftUnivalTree := (root.left == nil || (root.data == root.left.data && IsUnivalTree(root.left)))
        isRightUnivalTree := (root.right == nil || (root.data == root.right.data && IsUnivalTree(root.right)))
        return isLeftUnivalTree && isRightUnivalTree
}
```

Time complexity: O(n), where n is the number of nodes in the given tree.
Space complexity: O(h), where h is the height of the given tree.

CHAPTER 7

PRIORITY QUEUES AND HEAPS

7.1 What is a Priority Queue?

In some situations we may need to find the minimum/maximum element among a collection of elements. We can do this with the help of Priority Queue ADT. A priority queue ADT is a data structure that supports the operations *Insert* and *DeleteMin* (which returns and removes the minimum element) or *DeleteMax* (which returns and removes the maximum element).

These operations are equivalent to *EnQueue* and *DeQueue* operations of a queue. The difference is that, in priority queues, the order in which the elements enter the queue may not be the same in which they were processed. An example application of a priority queue is job scheduling, which is prioritized instead of serving in first come first serve.

A priority queue is called an *ascending – priority* queue, if the item with the smallest key has the highest priority (that means, delete the smallest element always). Similarly, a priority queue is said to be a *descending – priority* queue if the item with the largest key has the highest priority (delete the maximum element always). Since these two types are symmetric, we will be concentrating on one of them: ascending-priority queue.

7.2 Priority Queue ADT

The following operations make priority queues an ADT.

Main Priority Queues Operations

A priority queue is a container of elements, each having an associated key.

- insert (key, data): Inserts data with *key* to the priority queue. Elements are ordered based on key.
- deleteMin/deleteMax: Remove and return the element with the smallest/largest key.
- GetMinimum/getMaximum: Return the element with the smallest/largest key without deleting it.

Auxiliary Priority Queues Operations

- k^{th} – Smallest/k^{th} – Largest: Returns the kth –Smallest/k^{th} –Largest key in priority queue.
- Size: Returns number of elements in priority queue.
- Heap Sort: Sorts the elements in the priority queue based on priority (key).

7.3 Priority Queue Applications

Priority queues have many applications – a few of them are listed below:

- Data compression: Huffman Coding algorithm
- Shortest path algorithms: Dijkstra's algorithm
- Minimum spanning tree algorithms: Prim's algorithm
- Event-driven simulation: customers in a line
- Selection problem: Finding k^{th}- smallest element

7.4 Priority Queue Implementations

Before discussing the actual implementation, let us enumerate the possible options.

Unordered Array Implementation

Elements are inserted into the array without bothering about the order. Deletions (deleteMax) are performed by searching the key and then deleting.

Insertions complexity: O(1). deleteMin complexity: O(n).

Unordered List Implementation

It is very similar to array implementation, but instead of using arrays, linked lists are used.

Insertions complexity: O(1). deleteMin complexity: O(n).

Ordered Array Implementation

Elements are inserted into the array in sorted order based on key field. Deletions are performed at only one end.

Insertions complexity: O(n). deleteMin complexity: O(1).

Ordered List Implementation

Elements are inserted into the list in sorted order based on key field. Deletions are performed at only one end, hence preserving the status of the priority queue. All other functionalities associated with a linked list ADT are performed without modification.

Insertions complexity: O(n). deleteMin complexity: O(1).

Binary Search Trees Implementation

Both insertions and deletions take O($logn$) on average if insertions are random (refer to *Trees* chapter).

Balanced Binary Search Trees Implementation

Both insertions and deletion take O($logn$) in the worst case (refer to *Trees* chapter).

Binary Heap Implementation

In subsequent sections we will discuss this in full detail. For now, assume that binary heap implementation gives O($logn$) complexity for search, insertions and deletions and O(1) for finding the maximum or minimum element.

Comparing Implementations

Implementation	Insertion	Deletion (deleteMax)	Find Min
Unordered array	1	n	n
Unordered list	1	n	n
Ordered array	n	1	1
Ordered list	n	1	1
Binary Search Trees	$logn$ (average)	$logn$ (average)	$logn$ (average)
Balanced Binary Search Trees	$logn$	$logn$	$logn$
Binary Heaps	$logn$	$logn$	1

7.5 Heaps and Binary Heaps

What is a Heap?

A heap is a tree with some special properties. The basic requirement of a heap is that the value of a node must be $\geq$ (or $\leq$) than the values of its children. This is called *heap property*. A heap also has the additional property that all leaves should be at h or $h - 1$ levels (where h is the height of the tree) for some $h > 0$ (*complete binary trees*). That means heap should form a *complete binary tree* (as shown below).

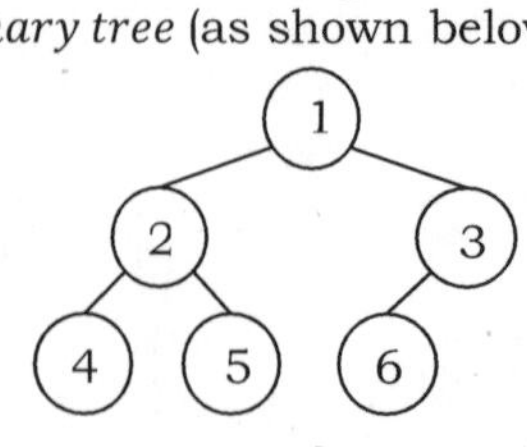

In the examples below, the left tree is a heap (each element is greater than its children) and the right tree is not a heap (since 11 is greater than 2).

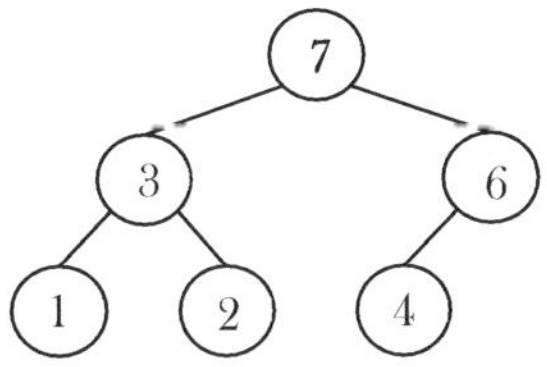

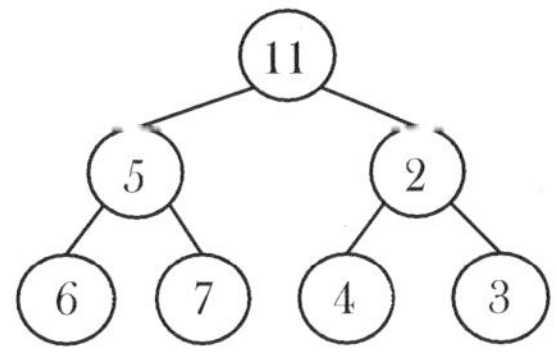

Types of Heaps?

Based on the property of a heap we can classify heaps into two types:

- **Min heap:** The value of a node must be less than or equal to the values of its children

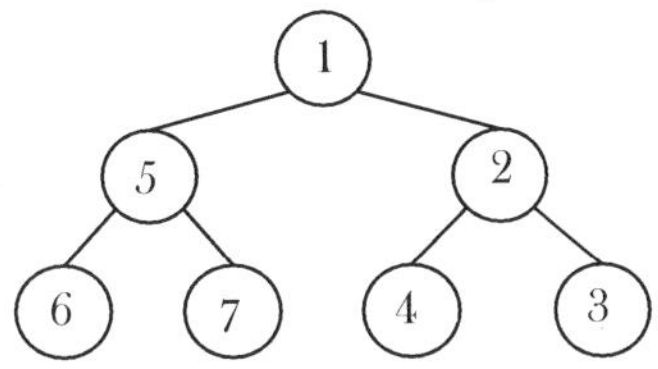

- **Max heap:** The value of a node must be greater than or equal to the values of its children

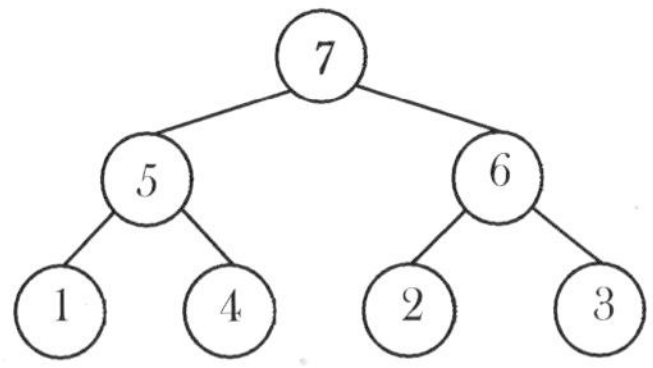

7.6 Binary Heaps

In binary heap each node may have up to two children. In practice, binary heaps are enough and we concentrate on binary min heaps and binary max heaps for the remaining discussion.

Representing Heaps: Before looking at heap operations, let us see how heaps can be represented. One possibility is using arrays. Since heaps are forming complete binary trees, there will not be any wastage of locations. For the discussion below let us assume that elements are stored in arrays, which starts at index 0. The previous max heap can be represented as:

7	5	6	1	4	2	3
0	1	2	3	4	5	6

Note: For the remaining discussion let us assume that we are doing manipulations in max heap.

Declaration of Heap

```
// Item - defines the interface for an element to be held by a Heap instance
type Item interface {
    Less(item Item) bool
}
// Heap - binary heap with support for min heap operations
type Heap struct {
    size int
    data []Item
}
```

Creating Heap

```
// New - returns a pointer to an empty min-heap
func New() *Heap {
    return &Heap{}
}
```

Time Complexity: O(1).

Parent of a Node

For a node at i^{th} location, its parent is at $\frac{i-1}{2}$ location. In the previous example, the element 6 is at second location and its parent is at 0th location.

```
func parent(i int) int {
    return int(math.Floor(float64(i-1) / 2.0))
}
```

Time Complexity: O(1).

Children of a Node

Similar to the above discussion, for a node at i^{th} location, its children are at $2 * i + 1$ and $2 * i + 2$ locations. For example, in the above tree the element 6 is at second location and its children 2 and 5 are at 5 $(2 * i + 1 = 2 * 2 + 1)$ and 6 $(2 * i + 2 = 2 * 2 + 2)$ locations.

```
func leftChild(parent int) int {
    return (2 * parent) + 1
}
```

Time Complexity: O(1).

```
func rightChild(parent int) int {
    return (2 * parent) + 2
}
```

Time Complexity: O(1).

Getting the Maximum Element

Since the maximum element in max heap is always at root, it will be stored at h.array[0].

```
func getMinimum(h *Heap) (Item, error) {
    if h.size == 0 {
        return nil, fmt.Errorf("Unable to get element from empty Heap")
    }
    return h.data[0], nil
}
```

Time Complexity: O(1).

Heapifying an Element

After inserting an element into heap, it may not satisfy the heap property. In that case we need to adjust the locations of the heap to make it heap again. This process is called *heapifying*. In max-heap, to heapify an element, we have to find the maximum of its children and swap it with the current element and continue this process until the heap property is satisfied at every node.

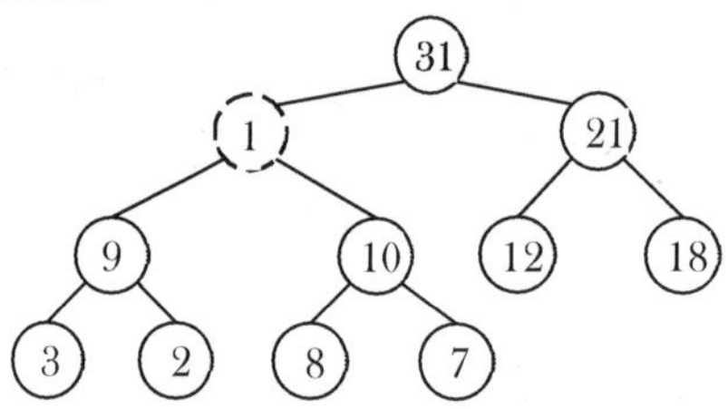

Observation: One important property of heap is that, if an element is not satisfying the heap property, then all the elements from that element to the root will have the same problem. In the example below, element 1 is not satisfying the heap property and its parent 31 is also having the issue.

Similarly, if we heapify an element, then all the elements from that element to the root will also satisfy the heap property automatically. Let us go through an example. In the above heap, the element 1 is not satisfying the heap property. Let us try heapifying this element.

To heapify 1, find the maximum of its children and swap with that.

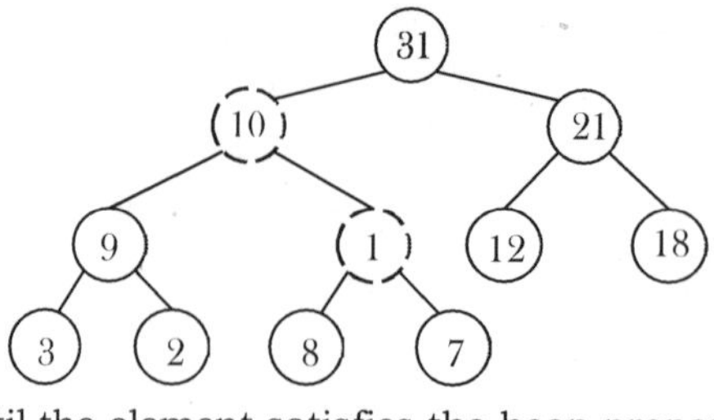

We need to continue this process until the element satisfies the heap properties. Now, swap 1 with 8.

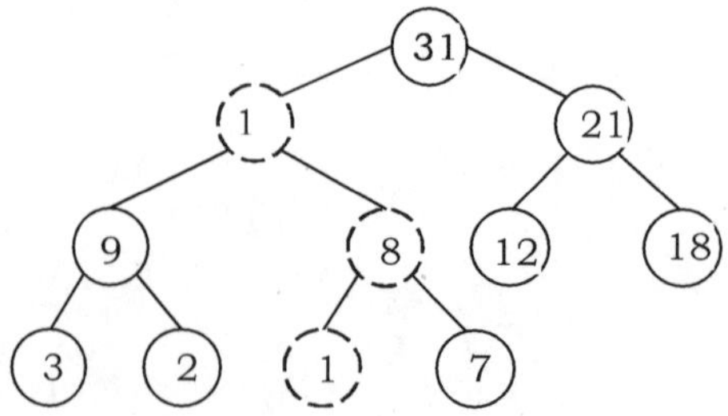

Now the tree is satisfying the heap property. In the above heapifying process, since we are moving from top to bottom, this process is sometimes called *percolate down*. Similarly, if we start heapifying from any other node to root, we can that process *percolate up* as move from bottom to top.

```
func (h *Heap) percolateUp() {
    idx := h.size - 1
    if idx <= 0 {
        return
    }
    for {
        p := parent(idx)
        if p < 0 || h.data[p].Less(h.data[idx]) {
            break
        }
        swap(h, p, idx)
        idx = p
    }
}
func swap(h *Heap, i int, j int) {
    tmp := h.data[i]
    h.data[i] = h.data[j]
    h.data[j] = tmp
}
```

Time Complexity: O($logn$). Heap is a complete binary tree and in the worst case we start at the root and come down to the leaf. This is equal to the height of the complete binary tree. Space Complexity: O(1).

Deleting an Element

To delete an element from heap, we just need to delete the element from the root. This is the only operation (maximum element) supported by standard heap. After deleting the root element, copy the last element of the heap (tree) and delete that last element.

After replacing the last element, the tree may not satisfy the heap property. To make it heap again, call the *percolateDown* function.

- Copy the first element into some variable
- Copy the last element into first element location
- *PercolateDown* the first element

```
func (h *Heap) percolateDown(i int) {
    p := i
    for {
        l := leftChild(p)
        r := rightChild(p)
        s := p
        if l < h.size && h.data[l].Less(h.data[s]) {
            s = l
        }
        if r < h.size && h.data[r].Less(h.data[s]) {
            s = r
        }
        if s == p {
            break
        }
        swap(h, p, s)
        p = s
    }
}
// Extract - removes and returns the 'item' at the top of the heap, maintaining the min-heap invariant
func (h *Heap) Extract() (Item, error) {
    n := h.size
    if n == 0 {
        return nil, fmt.Errorf("Unable to extract from empty Heap")
    }
```

```
        m := h.data[0]
        h.data[0] = h.data[n-1]
        h.data = h.data[:n-1]
        h.size--
        if h.size > 0 {
            h.percolateDown(0)
        } else {
            h.data = nil
        }
        return m, nil
}
```

Note: Deleting an element uses *percolateDown*, and inserting an element uses *percolateUp*.
Time Complexity: same as *percolateUp* function and it is O(*logn*).

Inserting an Element

Insertion of an element is similar to the heapify and deletion process.

- Increase the heap size
- Keep the new element at the end of the heap (tree)
- Heapify the element from bottom to top (root)

Before going through code, let us look at an example. We have inserted the element 19 at the end of the heap and this is not satisfying the heap property.

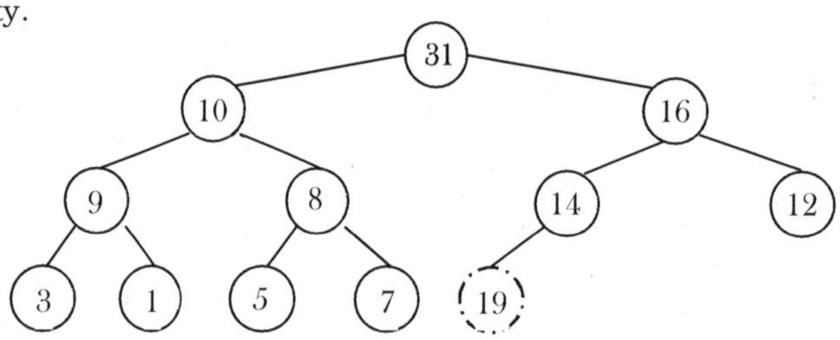

In order to heapify this element (19), we need to compare it with its parent and adjust them. Swapping 19 and 14 gives:

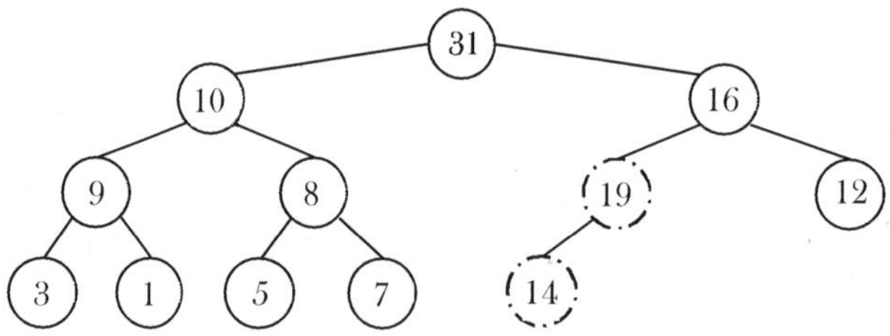

Again, swap 19 and16:

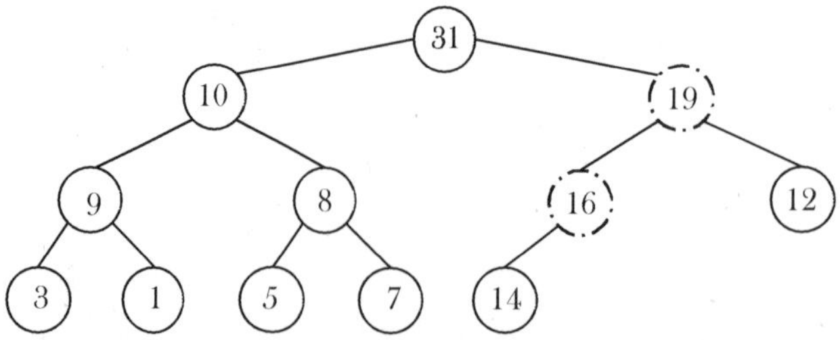

Now the tree is satisfying the heap property. Since we are following the bottom-up approach we sometimes call this process *percolate up*.

```
    func (h *Heap) Insert(item Item) { // Insert - inserts 'item' into the Heap, maintaining the min-heap
        if h.size == 0 {
            h.data = make([]Item, 1)
            h.data[0] = item
        } else {
            h.data = append(h.data, item)
        }
        h.size++
        h.percolateUp()
    }
```

Time Complexity: O(*logn*). The explanation is the same as that of the *heapifying* process.

Destroying Heap

Go has garbage collection. It will scan for data that has no pointer to it and remove it from heap (Garbage collector is running beside your program). The only thing you should do is:

```
h *Heap
........
h = nil
```

Heapifying the Array

One simple approach for building the heap is, take n input items and place them into an empty heap. This can be done with n successive inserts and takes O($nlogn$) in the worst case. This is due to the fact that each insert operation takes O($logn$).

To finish our discussion of binary heaps, we will look at a method to build an entire heap from a list of keys. The first method you might think of may be like the following. Given a list of keys, you could easily build a heap by inserting each key one at a time. Since you are starting with a list of one item, the list is sorted and you could use binary search to find the right position to insert the next key at a cost of approximately O($logn$) operations. However, remember that inserting an item in the middle of the list may require O(n) operations to shift the rest of the list over to make room for the new key. Therefore, to insert n keys into the heap would require a total of O($nlogn$) operations. However, if we start with an entire list then we can build the whole heap in O(n) operations.

Observation: Leaf nodes always satisfy the heap property and do not need to care for them. The leaf elements are always at the end and to heapify the given array it should be enough if we heapify the non-leaf nodes. Now let us concentrate on finding the first non-leaf node. The last element of the heap is at location $h.size - 1$, and to find the first non-leaf node it is enough to find the parent of the last element.

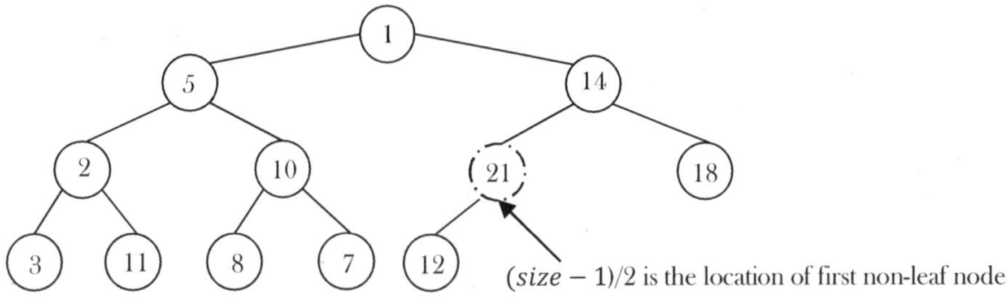


```
// Heapify - returns a pointer to a  min-heap composed of the elements of 'items'
func Heapify(items []Item) *Heap {
    h := New()
    n := len(items)
    h.data = make([]Item, n)
    copy(h.data, items)
    h.size = len(items)
    i := int(n/2)
    for i >= 0 {
        h.percolateDown(i)
        i--
    }
    return h
}
```

Time Complexity: The linear time bound of building heap can be shown by computing the sum of the heights of all the nodes. For a complete binary tree of height h containing $n = 2^{h+1} - 1$ nodes, the sum of the heights of the nodes is $n - h - 1 = n - logn - 1$ (for proof refer to *Problems Section*). That means, building the heap operation can be done in linear time (O(n)) by applying a *PercolateDown* function to the nodes in reverse level order.

Test Code

```
type Int int
func (a Int) Less(b Item) bool {
    val, ok := b.(Int)
    return ok && a <= val
}
```

```
func verifyHeap(h *Heap) bool {
    queue := make([]Int, 1)
    queue[0] = 0
    for len(queue) > 0 {
        p := queue[0]
        queue = queue[1:]
        l := leftChild(int(p))
        r := rightChild(int(p))
        if l < h.size {
            if !h.data[p].Less(h.data[l]) {
                return false
            }
            queue = append(queue, Int(l))
        }
        if r < h.size {
            if !h.data[p].Less(h.data[r]) {
                return false
            }
            queue = append(queue, Int(r))
        }
    }
    return true
}
func verifyStrictlyIncreasing(h *Heap) (bool, []Item) {
    prev, _ := h.Extract()
    order := []Item{prev}
    for h.size > 0 {
        curr, _ := h.Extract()
        order = append(order, curr)
        if curr.Less(prev) {
            return false, order
        }
        prev = curr
        order = append(order, prev)
    }
    return true, order
}
func randomPerm(n int) []Item {
    src := rand.NewSource(time.Now().UnixNano())
    r := rand.New(src)
    ints := r.Perm(n)
    items := make([]Item, n)
    for idx, item := range ints {
        items[idx] = Int(item)
    }
    return items
}
func main() {
    items := randomPerm(20)
    hp := New()
    for _, item := range items {
        fmt.Println("Inserting an element into Heap: ", hp.data)
        hp.Insert(item)
    }
    if !verifyHeap(hp) {
        fmt.Println("invalid Heap: ", hp.data)
        return
    }
    if ok, order := verifyStrictlyIncreasing(hp); !ok {
        fmt.Println("invalid Heap extraction order: ", order)
    }
}
```

7.7 Heapsort

One main application of heap ADT is sorting (heap sort). The heap sort algorithm inserts all elements (from an unsorted array) into a heap, then removes them from the root of a heap until the heap is empty. Note that heap sort can be done in place with the array to be sorted. Instead of deleting an element, exchange the first element (maximum) with the last element and reduce the heap size (array size). Then, we heapify the first element. Continue this process until the number of remaining elements is one.

```
func HeapSort(data []Item) []Item {
    hp := Heapify(data)
    size := len(hp.data)
    for i := size - 1; i > 0; i-- {
        // Move current root to end
        swap(hp, 0, i)
        hp.size--
        hp.percolateDown(0) // heapify the root as it might not satisfy the heap property
    }
    hp.size = size
    return hp.data
}
func main() { // Test code, since the heap is a min-heap, it gives the elements in the descending order
    items := randomPerm(30)
    for i := 0; i < len(items); i++ {
        fmt.Print(items[i].(Int), " ")
    }
    items = HeapSort(items)
    fmt.Print("\n")
    for i := 0; i < len(items); i++ {
        fmt.Print(items[i].(Int), " ")
    }
}
```

Time complexity: As we remove the elements from the heap, the values become sorted (since maximum elements are always *root* only). Since the time complexity of both the insertion algorithm and deletion algorithm is $O(logn)$ (where n is the number of items in the heap), the time complexity of the heap sort algorithm is $O(nlogn)$.

7.8 Priority Queues [Heaps]: Problems & Solutions

Problem-1 What are the minimum and maximum number of elements in a heap of height h?

Solution: Since heap is a complete binary tree (all levels contain full nodes except possibly the lowest level), it has at most $2^{h+1} - 1$ elements (if it is complete). This is because, to get maximum nodes, we need to fill all the h levels completely and the maximum number of nodes is nothing but the sum of all nodes at all h levels.

To get minimum nodes, we should fill the $h - 1$ levels fully and the last level with only one element. As a result, the minimum number of nodes is nothing but the sum of all nodes from $h - 1$ levels plus 1 (for the last level) and we get $2^h - 1 + 1 = 2^h$ elements (if the lowest level has just 1 element and all the other levels are complete).

Problem-2 Is there a min-heap with seven distinct elements so that the preorder traversal of it gives the elements in sorted order?

Solution: **Yes**. For the tree below, preorder traversal produces ascending order.

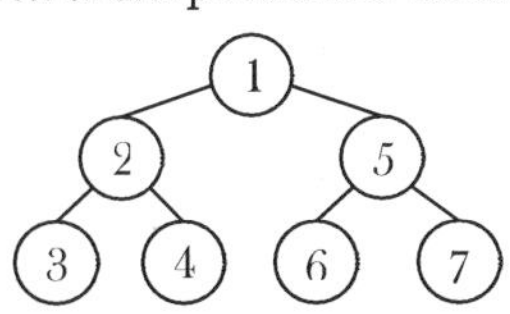

Problem-3 Is there a max-heap with seven distinct elements so that the preorder traversal of it gives the elements in sorted order?

Solution: Yes. For the tree below, preorder traversal produces descending order.

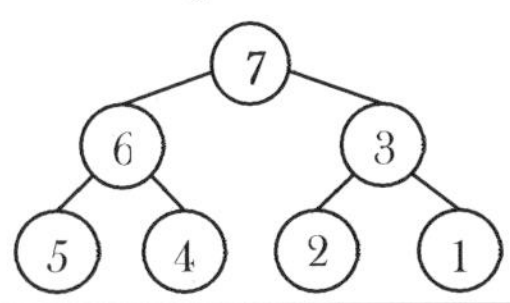

Problem-4 Is there a min-heap/max-heap with seven distinct elements so that the inorder traversal of it gives the elements in sorted order?

Solution: No. Since a heap must be either a min-heap or a max-heap, the root will hold the smallest element or the largest. An inorder traversal will visit the root of the tree as its second step, which is not the appropriate place if the tree's root contains the smallest or largest element.

Problem-5 Is there a min-heap/max-heap with seven distinct elements so that the postorder traversal of it gives the elements in sorted order?

Solution:

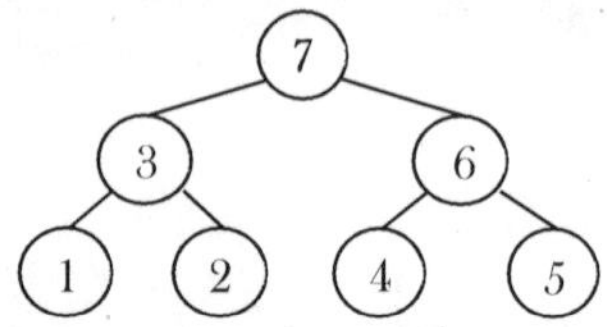

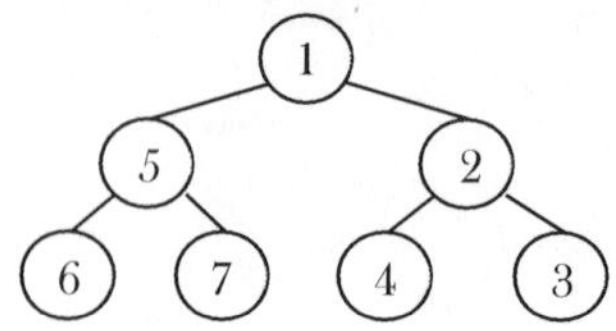

Yes, if the tree is a max-heap and we want descending order (below left), or if the tree is a min-heap and we want ascending order (below right).

Problem-6 Show that the height of a heap with n elements is $logn$?

Solution: A heap is a complete binary tree. All the levels, except the lowest, are completely full. A heap has at least 2^h elements and at most elements $2^h \leq n \leq 2^{h+1} - 1$. This implies, $h \leq logn \leq h + 1$. Since h is an integer, $h = logn$.

Problem-7 Given a min-heap, give an algorithm for finding the maximum element.

Solution: For a given min heap, the maximum element will always be at leaf only. Now, the next question is how to find the leaf nodes in the tree.

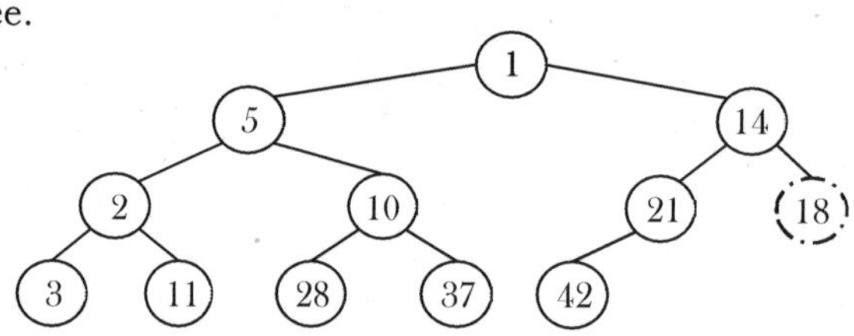

If we carefully observe, the next node of the last element's parent is the first leaf node. Since the last element is always at the $size - 1^{th}$ location, the next node of its parent (parent at location $\frac{size-1}{2}$) can be calculated as:

$$\frac{\text{size} - 1}{2} + 1 \approx \frac{\text{size} + 1}{2}$$

Now, the only step remaining is scanning the leaf nodes and finding the maximum among them.

```
type Int int
func findMaxInMinHeap(h *Heap) Int {
    max := Int(-1)
    for i := (h.size + 1) / 2; i < h.size; i++ {
        if h.data[i].(Int) > max {
            max = h.data[i].(Int)
        }
    }
    return max
}
```

Time Complexity: $O(\frac{n}{2}) \approx O(n)$.

Problem-8 Give an algorithm for deleting an arbitrary element from min heap.

Solution: To delete an element, first we need to search for an element. Let us assume that we are using level order traversal for finding the element. After finding the element we need to follow the deleteMin process.

Time Complexity = Time for finding the element + Time for deleting an element
$= O(n) + O(logn) \approx O(n)$. //Time for searching is dominated.

Problem-9 Give an algorithm for deleting the ith indexed element in a given min-heap.

Solution: The algorithm for this problem is in line with the Extract method. The only difference is that, instead of deleting the root element were going to delete the i^{th}element.

```
func delete(h *Heap, i int) Int {
    if i > h.size {
```

```
            fmt.Println("Wrong position")
            return -1
        }
        key := h.data[i].(Int)
        h.data[i] = h.data[h.size-1]
        h.size--
        h.percolateDown(i)
        return key
    }
    func main() { // Test code
        items := randomPerm(30)
        hp := Heapify(items)
        for i := 0; i < hp.size; i++ {
            fmt.Print(hp.data[i].(Int), " ")
        }
        fmt.Print("\n")
        fmt.Print(delete(hp, 6)) // Delete the element at 6th index
        fmt.Print("\n")
        for i := 0; i < hp.size; i++ {
            fmt.Print(hp.data[i].(Int), " ")
        }
    }
```

Time Complexity = $O(logn)$.

Problem-10 Prove that, for a complete binary tree of height h the sum of the height of all nodes is $O(n - h)$.

Solution: A complete binary tree has 2^i nodes on level i. Also, a node on level i has depth i and height $h - i$. Let us assume that S denotes the sum of the heights of all these nodes and S can be calculated as:

$$S = \sum_{i=0}^{h} 2^i(h-i)$$

$$S = h + 2(h-1) + 4(h-2) + \cdots + 2^{h-1}(1)$$

Multiplying with 2 on both sides gives: $2S = 2h + 4(h-1) + 8(h-2) + \cdots + 2^h(1)$

Now, subtract S from $2S$: $2S - S = -h + 2 + 4 + \cdots + 2^h \Rightarrow S = (2^{h+1} - 1) - (h - 1)$

But, we already know that the total number of nodes n in a complete binary tree with height h is $n = 2^{h+1} - 1$. This gives us: $h = \log(n+1)$.

Finally, replacing $2^{h+1} - 1$ with n, gives: $S = n - (h-1) = O(n - logn) = O(n - h)$.

Problem-11 Give an algorithm to find all elements less than some value of k in a binary heap.

Solution: Start from the root of the heap. If the value of the root is smaller than k then print its value and call recursively once for its left child and once for its right child. If the value of a node is greater or equal than k then the function stops without printing that value.

The complexity of this algorithm is $O(n)$, where n is the total number of nodes in the heap. This bound takes place in the worst case, where the value of every node in the heap will be smaller than k, so the function has to call each node of the heap.

Problem-12 Give an algorithm for merging two binary max-heaps. Let us assume that the size of the first heap is $m + n$ and the size of the second heap is n.

Solution: One simple way of solving this problem is:

- Assume that the elements of the first array (with size $m + n$) are at the beginning. That means, first m cells are filled and remaining n cells are empty.
- Without changing the first heap, just append the second heap and heapify the array.
- Since the total number of elements in the new array is $m + n$, each heapify operation takes $O(log(m + n))$.

The complexity of this algorithm is : $O((m + n)log(m + n))$.

Problem-13 Can we improve the complexity of Problem-12?

Solution: Instead of heapifying all the elements of the $m + n$ array, we can use the technique of "building heap with an array of elements (heapifying array)". We can start with non-leaf nodes and heapify them. The algorithm can be given as:

- Assume that the elements of the first array (with size $m + n$) are at the beginning. That means, the first m cells are filled and the remaining n cells are empty.

- Without changing the first heap, just append the second heap.
- Now, find the first non-leaf node and start heapifying from that element.

In the theory section, we have already seen that building a heap with n elements takes $O(n)$ complexity. The complexity of merging with this technique is: $O(m + n)$.

Problem-14 Is there an efficient algorithm for merging 2 max-heaps (stored as an array)? Assume both arrays have n elements.

Solution: The alternative solution for this problem depends on what type of heap it is. If it's a standard heap where every node has up to two children and which gets filled up so that the leaves are on a maximum of two different rows, we cannot get better than $O(n)$ for the merge.

There is an $O(logm \times logn)$ algorithm for merging two binary heaps with sizes m and n. For $m = n$, this algorithm takes $O(log^2n)$ time complexity. We will be skipping it due to its difficulty and scope.

For better merging performance, we can use another variant of binary heap like a *Fibonacci-Heap* which can merge in O(1) on average (amortized).

Problem-15 Give an algorithm for finding the kth smallest element in min-heap.

Solution: One simple solution to this problem is: perform deletion k times from min-heap.

```
func kThSmallestElement(h *Heap, k int) (Item, error) {
    if k >= h.size {
        return nil, fmt.Errorf("Wrong position")
    }
    for i := 1; i < k; i++ {
        h.Extract()
    }
    return h.Extract()
}
func main() {
    items := randomPerm(30)
    hp := Heapify(items)
    for i := 0; i < hp.size; i++ {
        fmt.Print(hp.data[i].(Int), " ")
    }
    fmt.Print("\n")
    element, _ := kThSmallestElement(hp, 6)
    fmt.Print("Kth Smallest element: ", element)
}
```

Time Complexity: $O(klogn)$. Since we are performing deletion operation k times and each deletion takes $O(logn)$.

Problem-16 For Problem-15, can we improve the time complexity?

Solution: Assume that the original min-heap is called $HOrig$ and the auxiliary min-heap is named $HAux$. Initially, the element at the top of $HOrig$, the minimum one, is inserted into $HAux$. Here we don't do the operation of deleteMin with $HOrig$.

```
func kThSmallestElement(HOrig *Heap, k int) (Item, error) {
    HAux := New()
    element, _ := getMinimum(HOrig)
    count := 0
    HAux.Insert(element)
    for {
        // the minimum element and delete it from the HA heap
        element, _ = HAux.Extract()
        if count == k {
            return element, nil
        } else { //insert the left and right children in HOrig into the HAux
            lc := leftChild(count)
            rc := rightChild(count)
            if lc < HOrig.size {
                HAux.Insert(HOrig.data[lc])
            }
            if rc < HOrig.size {
                HAux.Insert(HOrig.data[rc])
            }
```

```
        }
        count = count + 1
    }
}
```

Every while-loop iteration gives the kth smallest element and we need k loops to get the kth smallest elements. Because the size of the auxiliary heap is always less than k, every while-loop iteration the size of the auxiliary heap increases by one, and the original heap $HOrig$ has no operation during the finding, the running time is O($klogk$).

Note: The above algorithm is useful if the k value is too small compared to n. If the k value is approximately equal to n, then we can simply sort the array (let's say, using *couting* sort or any other linear sorting algorithm) and return k^{th} smallest element from the sorted array. This gives O(n) solution.

Problem-17 Find k max elements from max heap.

Solution: One simple solution to this problem is: build max-heap and perform deletion k times.

$$T(n) = \text{deleteMin from heap } k \text{ times} = \Theta(klogn).$$

Problem-18 For Problem-17, is there any alternative solution?

Solution: We can use the Problem-16 solution. At the end, the auxiliary heap contains the k-largest elements. Without deleting the elements we should keep on adding elements to $HAux$.

Problem-19 How do we implement stack using heap?

Solution: To implement a stack using a priority queue PQ (using min heap), let us assume that we are using one extra integer variable c. Also, assume that c is initialized equal to any known value (e.g., 0). The implementation of the stack ADT is given below. Here c is used as the priority while inserting/deleting the elements from PQ.

```
func (h *Heap) Push(int element) {
    h.Insert(c, element)
    c--
}
func (h *Heap) Pop() int {
    return h.Extract()
}
func (h *Heap) Top() int {
    return h.getMinimum()
}
func (h *Heap) Size() {
    return h.size
}
func (h *Heap) IsEmpty() bool {
    return h.isEmpty()
}
```

We could also increment c back when popping.

Observation: We could use the negative of the current system time instead of c (to avoid overflow). The implementation based on this can be given as:

```
func Push(int element) {
    h.Insert(-gettime(),element)
}
```

Problem-20 How do we implement Queue using heap?

Solution: To implement a queue using a priority queue PQ (using min heap), as similar to stacks simulation, let us assume that we are using one extra integer variable, c. Also, assume that c is initialized equal to any known value (e.g., 0). The implementation of the queue ADT is given below. Here the c is used as the priority while inserting/deleting the elements from PQ.

```
func (h *Heap) EnQueue(element int) {
    h.Insert(c, element)
    c++
}
func (h *Heap) DeQueue() int {
    return h.Extract()
}
func (h *Heap) Front() int {
    return h. getMinimum()
}
```

```
func (h *Heap) Size() int {
    return h.size
}
func (h *Heap) IsEmpty() bool {
    return h.isEmpty()
}
```

Note: We could also decrement c when popping.

Observation: We could use just the current system time instead of c (to avoid overflow). The implementation based on this can be given as:

```
func (h *Heap) EnQueue(element int) {
    h.Insert(gettime(),element)
}
```

Note: The only change is that we need to take a positive c value instead of negative.

Problem-21 Given a big file containing billions of numbers, how can you find the 10 maximum numbers from that file?

Solution: Always remember that when you need to find max n elements, the best data structure to use is priority queues. One solution for this problem is to divide the data in sets of 1000 elements (let's say 1000) and make a heap of them, and then take 10 elements from each heap one by one. Finally heap sort all the sets of 10 elements and take the top 10 among those. But the problem in this approach is where to store 10 elements from each heap. That may require a large amount of memory as we have billions of numbers.

Reusing the top 10 elements (from the earlier heap) in subsequent elements can solve this problem. That means take the first block of 1000 elements and subsequent blocks of 990 elements each. Initially, Heapsort the first set of 1000 numbers, take max 10 elements, and mix them with 990 elements of the 2nd set. Again, Heapsort these 1000 numbers (10 from the first set and 990 from the 2nd set), take 10 max elements, and mix them with 990 elements of the 3rd set. Repeat till the last set of 990 (or less) elements and take max 10 elements from the final heap. These 10 elements will be your answer.

Time Complexity: $O(n) = n/1000 \times$(complexity of Heapsort 1000 elements) Since complexity of heap sorting 1000 elements will be a constant so the $O(n) = n$ i.e. linear complexity.

Problem-22 **Merge k sorted lists with total of n elements:** We are given k sorted lists with total n inputs in all the lists. Give an algorithm to merge them into one single sorted list.

Solution: Since there are k equal size lists with a total of n elements, the size of each list is $\frac{n}{k}$. One simple way of solving this problem is:

- Take the first list and merge it with the second list. Since the size of each list is $\frac{n}{k}$, this step produces a sorted list with size $\frac{2n}{k}$. This is similar to merge sort logic. The time complexity of this step is: $\frac{2n}{k}$. This is because we need to scan all the elements of both the lists.
- Then, merge the second list output with the third list. As a result, this step produces a sorted list with size $\frac{3n}{k}$. The time complexity of this step is: $\frac{3n}{k}$. This is because we need to scan all the elements of both lists (one with size $\frac{2n}{k}$ and the other with size $\frac{n}{k}$).
- Continue this process until all the lists are merged to one list.

Total time complexity: $= \frac{2n}{k} + \frac{3n}{k} + \frac{4n}{k} + \cdots . \frac{kn}{k} = \sum_{i=2}^{n} \frac{in}{k} = \frac{n}{k} \sum_{i=2}^{n} i \approx \frac{n(k^2)}{k} \approx O(nk)$. Space Complexity: $O(1)$.

Problem-23 For Problem-22, can we improve the time complexity?

Solution:

1 Divide the lists into pairs and merge them. That means, first take two lists at a time and merge them so that the total elements parsed for all lists is $O(n)$. This operation gives $k/2$ lists.
2 Repeat step-1 until the number of lists becomes one.

Time complexity: Step-1 executes $logk$ times and each operation parses all n elements in all the lists for making $k/2$ lists. For example, if we have 8 lists, then the first pass would make 4 lists by parsing all n elements. The second pass would make 2 lists by again parsing n elements and the third pass would give 1 list by again parsing n elements. As a result the total time complexity is $O(nlogn)$.
Space Complexity: $O(n)$.

Problem-24 For Problem-23, can we improve the space complexity?

Solution: Let us use heaps for reducing the space complexity.

1. Build the max-heap with all the first elements from each list in $O(k)$.
2. In each step, extract the maximum element of the heap and add it at the end of the output.

3. Add the next element from the list of the one extracted. That means we need to select the next element of the list which contains the extracted element of the previous step.
4. Repeat step-2 and step-3 until all the elements are completed from all the lists.

Time Complexity = $O(nlogk)$. At a time we have k elements max-heap and for all n elements we have to read just the heap in $logk$ time, so total time = $O(nlogk)$. Space Complexity: $O(k)$ [for Max-heap].

Problem-25 Given 2 arrays A and B each with n elements. Give an algorithm for finding largest n pairs $(A[i], B[j])$.

Solution:

Algorithm:

- Heapify A and B. This step takes $O(2n) \approx O(n)$.
- Then keep on deleting the elements from both the heaps. Each step takes $O(2logn) \approx O(logn)$.

Total Time complexity: $O(nlogn)$.

Problem-26 **Min-Max heap:** Give an algorithm that supports min and max in O(1) time, insert, delete min, and delete max in $O(logn)$ time. That means, design a data structure which supports the following operations:

Operation	Complexity
init	$O(n)$, needs heapifying
insert	$O(logn)$
getMin	$O(1)$
getMax	$O(1)$
deleteMin/Extract	$O(logn)$
deleteMax/Extract	$O(logn)$

Solution: This problem can be solved using two heaps. Let us say two heaps are: Minimum-Heap H_{min} and Maximum-Heap H_{max}. Also, assume that elements in both the arrays have mutual pointers. That means, an element in H_{min} will have a pointer to the same element in H_{max} and an element in H_{max} will have a pointer to the same element in H_{min}.

init	Build H_{min} in $O(n)$ and H_{max} in $O(n)$ (Needs heapifying)
insert(x)	Insert x to H_{min} in $O(logn)$. Insert x to H_{max} in $O(logn)$. Update the pointers in O(1)
getMin()	Return root(H_{min}) in O(1)
getMax	Return root(H_{max}) in O(1)
deleteMin/Extract	Delete the minimum from H_{min} in $O(logn)$. Delete the same element from H_{max} by using the mutual pointer in $O(logn)$
deleteMax/Extract	Delete the maximum from H_{max} in $O(logn)$. Delete the same element from H_{min} by using the mutual pointer in $O(logn)$

Problem-27 Dynamic median finding. Design a heap data structure that supports finding the median.

Solution: In a set of n elements, median is the middle element, such that the number of elements lesser than the median is equal to the number of elements larger than the median. If n is odd, we can find the median by sorting the set and taking the middle element. If n is even, the median is usually defined as the average of the two middle elements. This algorithm works even when some of the elements in the list are equal. For example, the median of the multiset {1, 1, 2, 3, 5} is 2, and the median of the multiset {1, 1, 2, 3, 5, 8} is 2.5.

"*Median heaps*" are the variant of heaps that give access to the median element. A median heap can be implemented using two heaps, each containing half the elements. One is a max-heap, containing the smallest elements; the other is a min-heap, containing the largest elements. The size of the max-heap may be equal to the size of the min-heap, if the total number of elements is even. In this case, the median is the average of the maximum element of the max-heap and the minimum element of the min-heap. If there is an odd number of elements, the max-heap will contain one more element than the min-heap. The median in this case is simply the maximum element of the max-heap.

Problem-28 **Maximum sum in sliding window:** Given array A[] with sliding window of size w which is moving from the very left of the array to the very right. Assume that we can only see the w numbers in the window. Each time the sliding window moves rightwards by one position. For example: The array is [1 3 -1 -3 5 3 6 7], and w is 3.

Window position	Max
[1 3 -1] -3 5 3 6 7	3
1 [3 -1 -3] 5 3 6 7	3
1 3 [-1 -3 5] 3 6 7	5
1 3 -1 [-3 5 3] 6 7	5
1 3 -1 -3 [5 3 6] 7	6
1 3 -1 -3 5 [3 6 7]	7

Input: A long array A[], and a window width w.
Output: An array B[], B[i] is the maximum value of from A[i] to A[i+w-1]

Requirement: Find a good optimal way to get B[i]

Solution: Brute force solution is, every time the window is moved we can search for a total of w elements in the window.

Time complexity: $O(nw)$.

Problem-29 For Problem-28, can we reduce the complexity?

Solution: Yes, we can use heap data structure. This reduces the time complexity to $O(nlogw)$. Insert operation takes $O(logw)$ time, where w is the size of the heap. However, getting the maximum value is cheap; it merely takes constant time as the maximum value is always kept in the root (head) of the heap. As the window slides to the right, some elements in the heap might not be valid anymore (range is outside of the current window). How should we remove them? We would need to be somewhat careful here. Since we only remove elements that are out of the window's range, we would need to keep track of the elements' indices too.

Problem-30 For Problem-28, can we further reduce the complexity?

Solution: Yes, The double-ended queue is the perfect data structure for this problem.

This problem can be solved nicely using a deque. A deque is a queue data structure that allows to systematically access and/or remove elements from either the top or the bottom of it. Now, first of all, we will have n-k+1 results as the number of windows. If input has length 3 and k is 1, we'll have 3 - 1 + 1 = 3 windows. Now, for the approach, we use a deque that will store the index of the numbers. We store the index rather than the value to understand if an element is out of the current i-k window.

We loop through the numbers, for each one of them, we remove from the queue the top if it's outside the current window - we do this only once per iteration as the index increases linearly. After that, we remove every element from the deque that is smaller than the current analyzed element. This will leave the current maximum at the top of the queue. We push the current element into the deque for future iterations. Finally, if we reached the first window end, we add our current result, this will be at the top of the deque.

```
type DeQueue struct {
    indexes []int
}
func (d *DeQueue) push(i int) {
    d.indexes = append(d.indexes, i)
}
func (d *DeQueue) getFirst() int {
    return d.indexes[0]
}
func (d *DeQueue) popFirst() {
    d.indexes = d.indexes[1:]
}
func (d *DeQueue) getLast() int {
    return d.indexes[len(d.indexes)-1]
}
func (d *DeQueue) popLast() {
    d.indexes = d.indexes[:len(d.indexes)-1]
}
func (d *DeQueue) empty() bool {
    return 0 == len(d.indexes)
}
func maxSlidingWindow(A []int, k int) []int {
    if len(A) < k || 0 == k {
        return make([]int, 0)
    } else if 1 == k {
        return A
    }
    var (
        // len(A)-k+1 this is the number of windows.
        // If input has length 3 and k is 1, we'll have 3 - 1 + 1 = 3 windows.
        res = make([]int, len(A)-k+1)
        dq  = &DeQueue{}
    )
    for i := range A {
        // we pop the first element if it's outside of the current window.
        if false == dq.empty() && (i-k == dq.getFirst()) {
            dq.popFirst()
```

```
        }
        // we pop all the elements that are smaller than the current one.
        for false == dq.empty() && A[dq.getLast()] < A[i] {
            dq.popLast()
        }
        // we push the current one to the window.
        dq.push(i)
        // if we reached at least the first window end.
        if i >= k-1 {
            // we add the current result that is the first in the DeQueue.
            res[i-k+1] = A[dq.getFirst()]
        }
    }
    return res
}
```

Typically, most people try to maintain the queue size the same as the window's size. Try to break away from this thought and think out of the box. Removing redundant elements and storing only elements that need to be considered in the queue is the key to achieving the efficient O(n) solution below. This is because each element in the list is being inserted and removed at most once. Therefore, the total number of insert + delete operations is $2n$.

Time complexity: O(n). Space complexity: O($n - k + 1$).

Problem-31 A priority queue is a list of items in which each item has associated with it a priority. Items are withdrawn from a priority queue in order of their priorities starting with the highest priority item first. If the maximum priority item is required, then a heap is constructed such than priority of every node is greater than the priority of its children.

Design such a heap where the item with the middle priority is withdrawn first. If there are n items in the heap, then the number of items with the priority smaller than the middle priority is $\frac{n}{2}$ if n is odd, else $\frac{n}{2} \mp 1$.

Explain how withdraw and insert operations work, calculate their complexity, and how the data structure is constructed.

Solution: We can use one min heap and one max heap such that root of the min heap is larger than the root of the max heap. The size of the min heap should be equal or one less than the size of the max heap. So the middle element is always the root of the max heap.

For the insert operation, if the new item is less than the root of max heap, then insert it into the max heap; else insert it into the min heap. After the withdraw or insert operation, if the size of heaps are not as specified above than transfer the root element of the max heap to min heap or vice-versa. With this implementation, insert and withdraw operation will be in O($logn$) time.

Problem-32 Given two heaps, how do you merge (union) them?

Solution: Binary heap supports various operations quickly: Find-min, insert, decrease-key. If we have two min-heaps, H1 and H2, there is no efficient way to combine them into a single min-heap.

For solving this problem efficiently, we can use mergeable heaps. Mergeable heaps support efficient union operation. It is a data structure that supports the following operations:

- create-Heap(): creates an empty heap
- insert(H,X,K) : insert an item x with key K into a heap H
- find-Min(H) : return item with min key
- delete-Min(H) : return and remove
- Union(H1, H2) : merge heaps H1 and H2

Examples of mergeable heaps are:

- Binomial Heaps
- Fibonacci Heaps

Both heaps also support:

- decrease-Key(H,X,K): assign item Y with a smaller key K
- delete(H,X) : remove item X

Binomial Heaps: Unlike binary heap which consists of a single tree, a *binomial* heap consists of a small set of component trees and no need to rebuild everything when union is performed. Each component tree is in a special format, called a *binomial tree*.

A binomial tree of order k, denoted by B_k is defined recursively as follows:

- B_0 is a tree with a single node
- For $k \geq 1$, B_k is formed by joining two B_{k-1}, such that the root of one tree becomes the leftmost child of the root of the other.

Example:

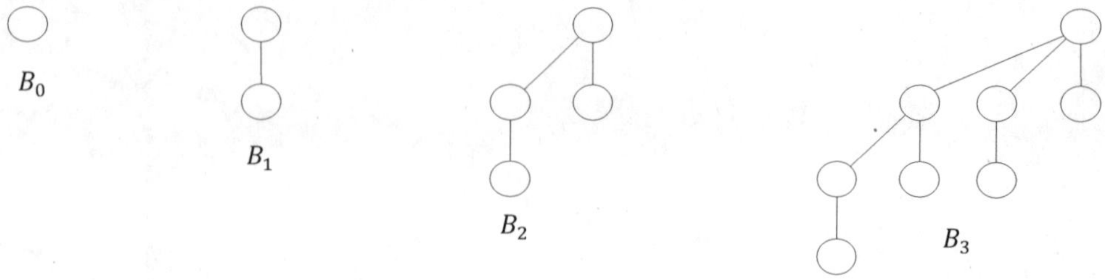

Fibonacci Heaps: Fibonacci heap is another example of mergeable heap. It has no good worst-case guarantee for any operation (except insert/create-Heap). Fibonacci Heaps have excellent amortized cost to perform each operation. Like *binomial* heap, *fibonacci* heap consists of a set of min-heap ordered component trees. However, unlike binomial heap, it has

- No limit on number of trees (up to O(n)), and
- No limit on height of a tree (up to O(n))

Also, *Find-Min, Delete-Min, Union, Decrease-Key, Delete* all have worst-case O(n) running time. However, in the amortized sense, each operation performs very quickly.

Operation	Binary Heap	Binomial Heap	Fibonacci Heap
create-Heap	$\Theta(1)$	$\Theta(1)$	$\Theta(1)$
find-Min	$\Theta(1)$	$\Theta(logn)$	$\Theta(1)$
delete-Min	$\Theta(logn)$	$\Theta(logn)$	$\Theta(logn)$
insert	$\Theta(logn)$	$\Theta(logn)$	$\Theta(1)$
delete	$\Theta(logn)$	$\Theta(logn)$	$\Theta(logn)$
decrease-Key	$\Theta(logn)$	$\Theta(logn)$	$\Theta(1)$
Union	$\Theta(n)$	$\Theta(logn)$	$\Theta(1)$

Problem-33 Median in an infinite series of integers.

Solution: Median is the middle number in a sorted list of numbers (if we have odd number of elements). If we have even number of elements, median is the average of two middle numbers in a sorted list of numbers.

We can solve this problem efficiently by using 2 heaps: One MaxHeap and one MinHeap.

1. MaxHeap contains the smallest half of the received integers
2. MinHeap contains the largest half of the received integers

The integers in MaxHeap are always less than or equal to the integers in MinHeap. Also, the number of elements in MaxHeap is either equal to or 1 more than the number of elements in the MinHeap.

In the stream if we get $2n$ elements (at any point of time), MaxHeap and MinHeap will both contain equal number of elements (in this case, n elements in each heap). Otherwise, if we have received $2n + 1$ elements, MaxHeap will contain $n + 1$ and MinHeap n.

Let us find the Median: If we have $2n + 1$ elements (odd), the Median of received elements will be the largest element in the MaxHeap (nothing but the root of MaxHeap). Otherwise, the Median of received elements will be the average of largest element in the MaxHeap (nothing but the root of MaxHeap) and smallest element in the MinHeap (nothing but the root of MinHeap). This can be calculated in O(1).

Inserting an element into heap can be done in O($logn$). Note that, any heap containing $n + 1$ elements might need one delete operation (and insertion to other heap) as well.

Example:

Insert 1: Insert to MaxHeap.
MaxHeap: {1}, MinHeap:{}
Insert 9: Insert to MinHeap. Since 9 is greater than 1 and MinHeap maintains the maximum elements.
MaxHeap: {1}, MinHeap:{9}
Insert 2: Insert MinHeap. Since 2 is less than all elements of MinHeap.
MaxHeap: {1,2}, MinHeap:{9}
Insert 0: Since MaxHeap already has more than half; we have to drop the max element from MaxHeap and insert it to MinHeap. So, we have to remove 2 and insert into MinHeap. With that it becomes:
MaxHeap: {1}, MinHeap:{2,9}
Now, insert 0 to MaxHeap.

Total Time Complexity: O($logn$).

Problem-34 Suppose the elements 7, 2, 10 and 4 are inserted, in that order, into the valid 3-ary max heap found in the above question, Which one of the following is the sequence of items in the array representing the resultant heap?

(A) 10, 7, 9, 8, 3, 1, 5, 2, 6, 4 (B) 10, 9, 8, 7, 6, 5, 4, 3, 2, 1
(C) 10, 9, 4, 5, 7, 6, 8, 2, 1, 3 (D) 10, 8, 6, 9, 7, 2, 3, 4, 1, 5

Solution: The 3-ary max heap with elements 9, 5, 6, 8, 3, 1 is:

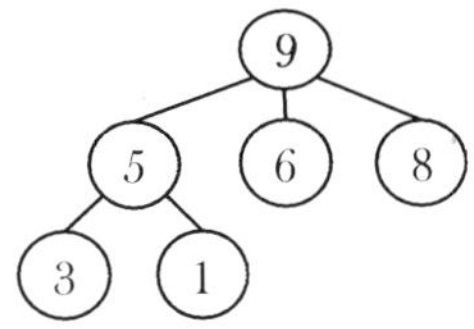

After Insertion of 7:

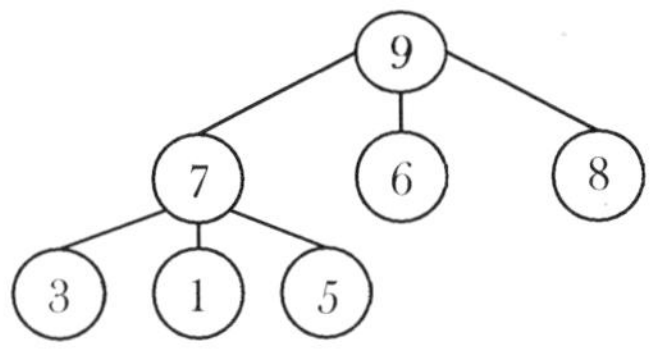

After Insertion of 2:

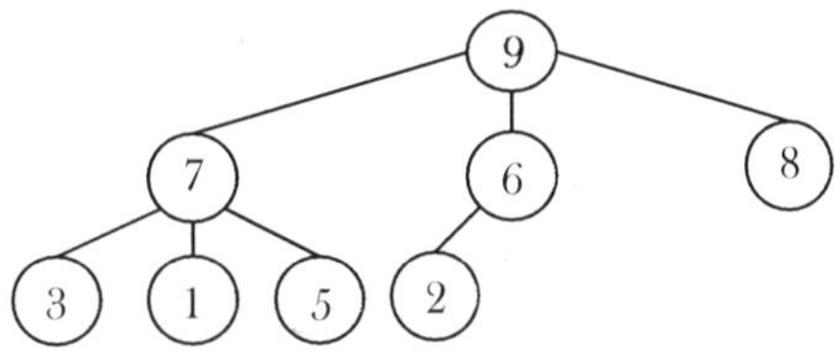

After Insertion of 10:

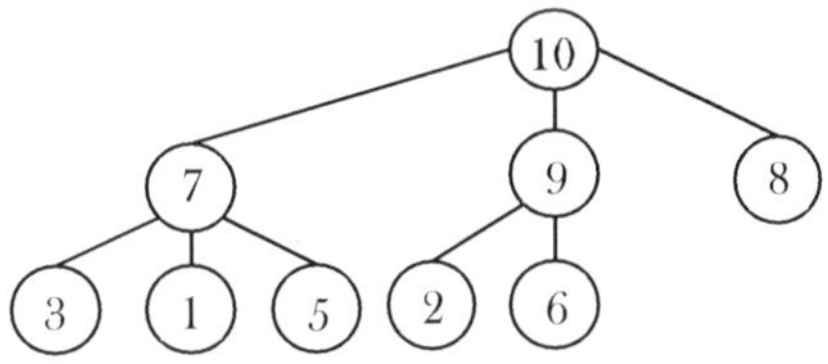

After Insertion of 4:

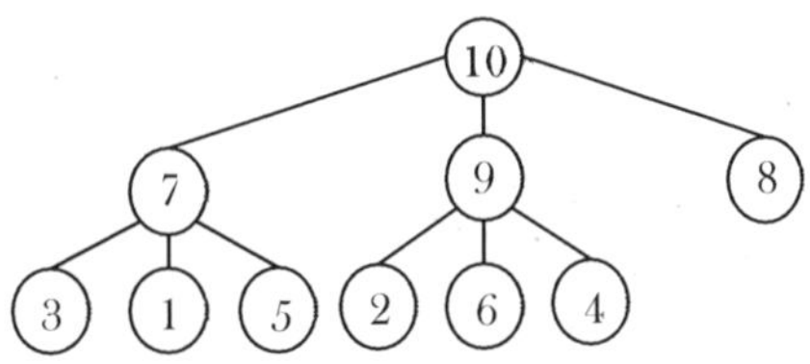

Problem-35 A complete binary min-heap is made by including each integer in [1,1023] exactly once. The depth of a node in the heap is the length of the path from the root of the heap to that node. Thus, the root is at depth 0. The maximum depth at which integer 9 can appear is___.

Solution: As shown in the figure below, for a given number i, we can fix the element i at i^{th} level and arrange the numbers 1 to $i-1$ to the levels above. Since the root is at depth *zero*, the maximum depth of the ith element in a min-heap is $i-1$. Hence, the maximum depth at which integer 9 can appear is 8.

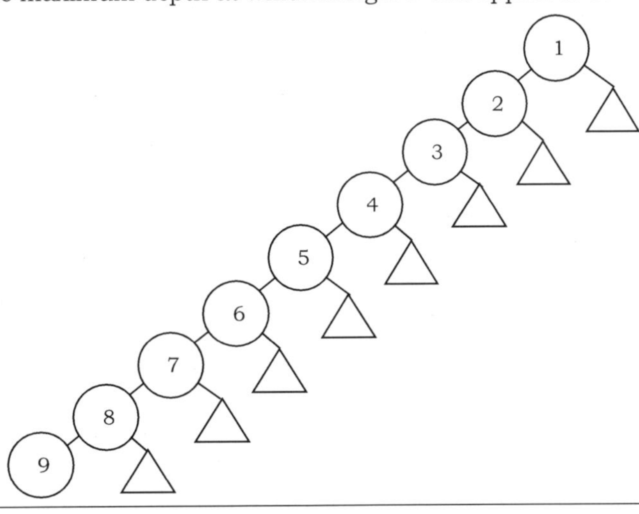

Problem-36 A d-ary heap is like a binary heap, but instead of 2 children, nodes have d children. How would you represent a d-ary heap with n elements in an array? What are the expressions for determining the parent of a given element, $Parent(i)$, and a jth child of a given element, $Child(i, j)$, where $1 \leq j \leq d$?

Solution: The following expressions determine the parent and j^{th} child of element i (where $1 \leq j \leq d$):

$$Parent(i) = \left\lfloor \frac{i + d - 2}{d} \right\rfloor$$

$$Child(i, j) = (i - 1).d + j + 1$$

DISJOINT SETS ADT

CHAPTER 8

8.1 Introduction

In this chapter, we will represent an important mathematics concept: *sets*. This means how to represent a group of elements which do not need any order. The disjoint sets ADT is the one used for this purpose. It is used for solving the equivalence problem. It is very simple to implement. A simple array can be used for the implementation and each function takes only a few lines of code. Disjoint sets ADT acts as an auxiliary data structure for many other algorithms (for example, *Kruskal's* algorithm in graph theory). Before starting our discussion on disjoint sets ADT, let us look at some basic properties of sets.

8.2 Equivalence Relations and Equivalence Classes

For the discussion below let us assume that S is a set containing the elements and a relation R is defined on it. That means for every pair of elements in $a, b \in S$, $a\ R\ b$ is either true or false. If $a\ R\ b$ is true, then we say a is related to b, otherwise a is not related to b. A relation R is called an *equivalence relation* if it satisfies the following properties:

- *Reflexive*: For every element $a \in S$, $a\ R\ a$ is true.
- *Symmetric*: For any two elements $a, b \in S$, if $a\ R\ b$ is true then $b\ R\ a$ is true.
- *Transitive*: For any three elements a, b, c ∈ S, if a R b and $b\ R\ c$ are true then $a\ R\ c$ is true.

As an example, relations ≤ (less than or equal to) and ≥ (greater than or equal to) on a set of integers are not equivalence relations. They are reflexive (since $a \leq a$) and transitive ($a \leq b$ and $b \leq c$ implies $a \leq c$) but not symmetric ($a \leq b$ does not imply $b \leq a$).

Similarly, *rail connectivity* is an equivalence relation. This relation is reflexive because any location is connected to itself. If there is connectivity from city a to city b, then city b also has connectivity to city a, so the relation is symmetric. Finally, if city a is connected to city b and city b is connected to city c, then city a is also connected to city c.

The *equivalence class* of an element $a \in S$ is a subset of S that contains all the elements that are related to a. Equivalence classes create a *partition* of S. Every member of S appears in exactly one equivalence class. To decide if $a\ R\ b$, we just need to check whether a and b are in the same equivalence class (group) or not. In the above example, two cities will be in same equivalence class if they have rail connectivity. If they do not have connectivity then they will be part of different equivalence classes.

Since the intersection of any two equivalence classes is empty (ϕ), the equivalence classes are sometimes called *disjoint sets*. Disjoint-set data structure also called a union–find data structure or merge–find set. It maintains a collection $S = \{S_1, S_2, \ldots, S_n\}$ of disjoint dynamic sets. We identify each set by a representative, which is some member of the set.

Disjoint – set forests are data structures where each set is represented by a tree data structure, in which each node holds a reference to its parent node. In a disjoint-set forest, the representative of each set is the root of that set's tree. Find follows parent nodes until it reaches the root. Union combines two trees into one by attaching the root of one to the root of the other.

In the subsequent sections, we will try to see the operations that can be performed on equivalence classes. The possible operations are:

- Creating an equivalence class (making a set)
- Finding the equivalence class name (set name or representative name) (Find)
- Combining the equivalence classes (Union)

8.3 Disjoint Sets ADT

To manipulate the set elements we need basic operations defined on sets. In this chapter, we concentrate on the following set operations:

- MAKESET(X): Creates a new set containing a single element X.
- UNION(X, Y): Creates a new set containing the elements X and Y in their union and deletes the sets containing the elements X and Y.
- FIND(X): Returns the name of the set containing the element X.

8.4 Applications

Disjoint sets ADT have many applications and a few of them are:

- To represent network connectivity
- Image processing
- To find least common ancestor
- To define equivalence of finite state automata
- Kruskal's minimum spanning tree algorithm (graph theory)
- In game algorithms

8.5 Tradeoffs in Implementing Disjoint Sets ADT

Let us see the possibilities for implementing disjoint set operations. Initially, assume the input elements are a collection of n sets, each with one element. That means, initial representation assumes all relations (except reflexive relations) are false. Each set has a different element, so that $S_i \cap S_j = \phi$. This makes the sets *disjoint*.

To add the relation $a\ R\ b$ (UNION), we first need to check whether a and b are already related or not. This can be verified by performing FINDs on both a and b and checking whether they are in the same equivalence class (set) or not.

If they are not, then we apply UNION. This operation merges the two equivalence classes containing a and b into a new equivalence class by creating a new set $S_k = S_i \cup S_j$ and deletes S_i and S_j. Basically there are two ways to implement the above FIND/UNION operations:

- Fast FIND implementation (also called Quick FIND)
- Fast UNION operation implementation (also called Quick UNION)

8.6 Fast FIND Implementation (Quick FIND)

In this method, we use an array. As an example, in the representation below the array contains the set name for each element. For simplicity, let us assume that all the elements are numbered sequentially from 0 to $n-1$. In the example below, element 0 has the set name 3, element 1 has the set name 5, and so on. With this representation FIND takes only O(1) since for any element we can find the set name by accessing its array location in constant time.

Set Name

3	5	....	2	3
0	1	....	n-2	n-1

In this representation, to perform UNION(a, b) [assuming that a is in set i and b is in set j] we need to scan the complete array and change all $i's$ to j. This takes O(n).

A sequence of $n - 1$ unions take O(n^2) time in the worst case. If there are O(n^2) FIND operations, this performance is fine, as the average time complexity is O(1) for each UNION or FIND operation. If there are fewer FINDs, this complexity is not acceptable.

8.7 Fast UNION Implementation (Quick UNION)

In this and subsequent sections, we will discuss the faster *UNION* implementations and its variants. There are different ways of implementing this approach and the following is a list of a few of them.

- Fast UNION implementations (Slow FIND)
- Fast UNION implementations (Quick FIND)
- Fast UNION implementations with path compression

8.8 Fast UNION Implementation (Slow FIND)

As we have discussed, FIND operation returns the same answer (set name) if and only if they are in the same set. In representing disjoint sets, our main objective is to give a different set name for each group. In general we do not care about the name of the set. One possibility for implementing the set is *tree* as each element has only one *root* and we can use it as the set name.

How are these represented? One possibility is using an array: for each element keep the *root* as its set name. But with this representation, we will have the same problem as that of FIND array implementation. To solve this problem, instead of storing the *root* we can keep the parent of the element. Therefore, using an array which stores the parent of each element solves our problem.

An *Element* represents a single element of a set. Note that, perhaps surprisingly, the package does not expose a corresponding Set data type. Sets exist only implicitly based on the sequence of Union operations performed on their elements. The *Data* field lets a program store arbitrary data within an *Element*. This can be used, for example, to keep track of the total number of elements in the associated set, the set's maximum-valued element, a map of attributes associated with the set's elements, or even a map or slice of all elements in the set. (That last possibility would associate a linear-time cost with each Union operation but would not affect Find's near-constant running time.)

```
type Element struct {
    parent *Element        // Parent element
    Data   interface{}     // Arbitrary user-provided payload
}
```

To differentiate the root node, let us assume its parent is the same as that of the element in the array. Based on this representation, MAKESET, FIND, UNION operations can be defined as:

- Makeset(X): Creates a new set containing a single element X and in the array update the parent of X as X. That means root (set name) of X is X.

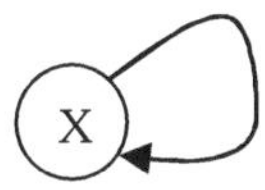

- UNION(X, Y): Replaces the two sets containing X and Y by their union and in the array updates the parent of X as Y.

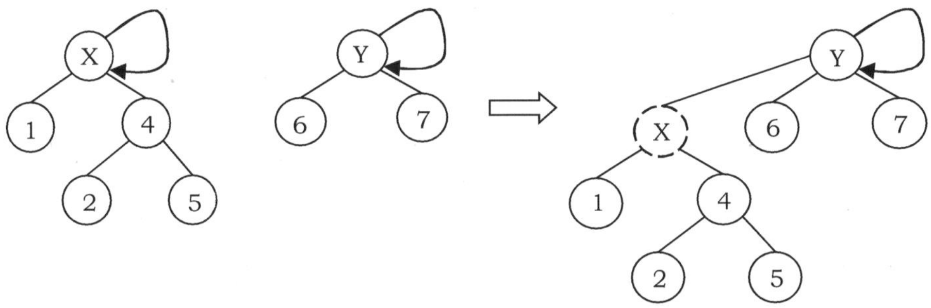

- FIND(X): Returns the name of the set containing the element X. We keep on searching for X's set name until we come to the root of the tree.

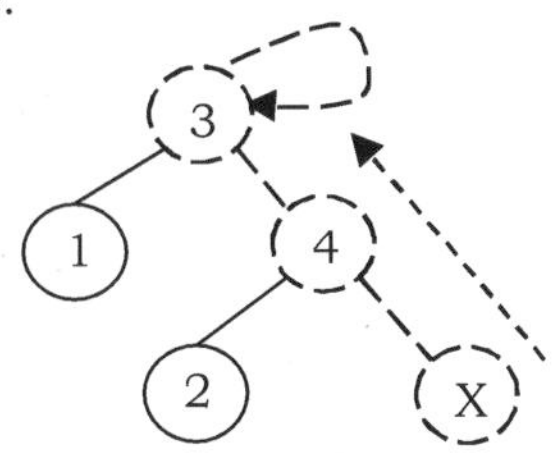

For the elements 0 to $n-1$ the initial representation is:

To perform a UNION on two sets, we merge the two trees by making the root of one tree point to the root of the other.

Initial Configuration for the elements 0 to 6

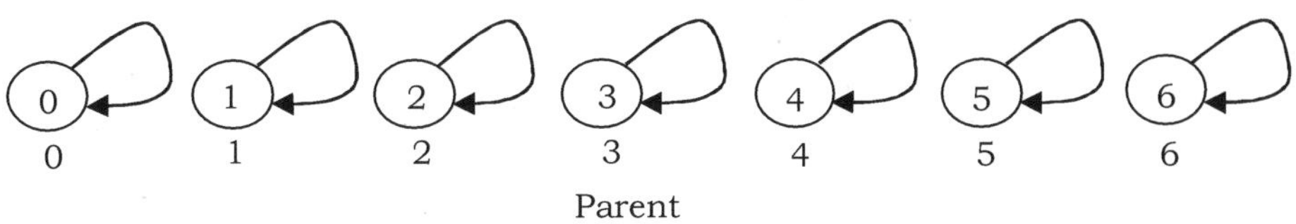

After UNION(5,6)

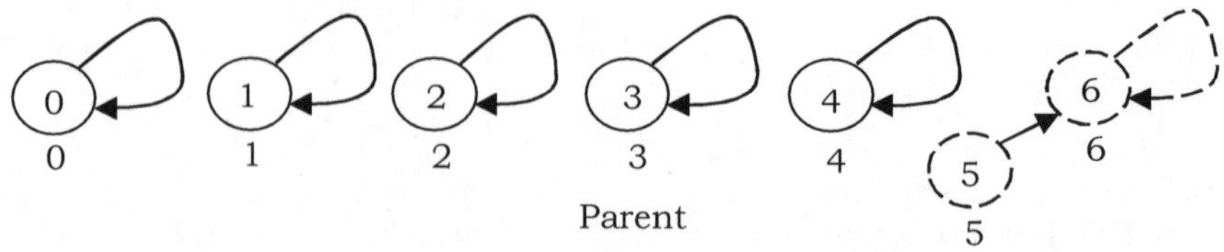

After UNION(1,2)

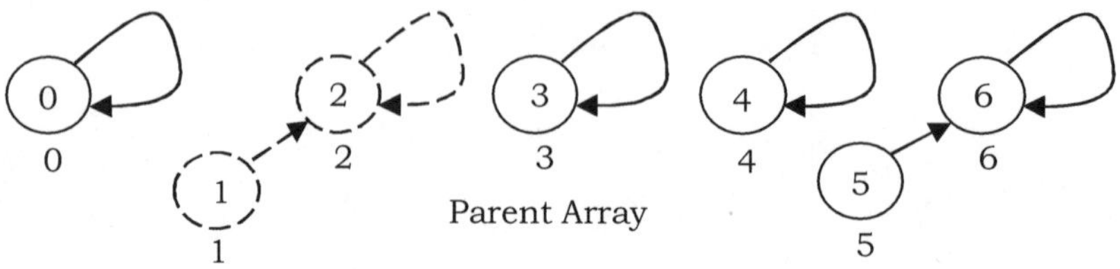

After UNION(0,2)

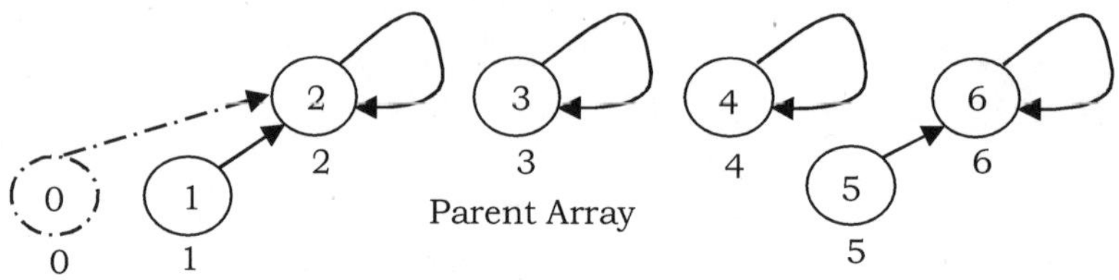

One important thing to observe here is, UNION operation is changing the root's parent only, but not for all the elements in the sets. Due to this, the time complexity of UNION operation is O(1). A FIND(*X*) on element *X* is performed by returning the root of the tree containing *X*.

The time to perform this operation is proportional to the depth of the node representing *X*. Using this method, it is possible to create a tree of depth $n - 1$ (Skew Trees). The worst-case running time of a FIND is O(n) and m consecutive FIND operations take O(mn) time in the worst case.

MAKESET

```
// MakeSet creates a singleton set and returns its sole element.
func MakeSet(Data   interface{}) *Element {
    s := &Element{}
    s.parent = s
    s.Data = Data
    return s
}
```

FIND

Find returns an arbitrary element of a set when invoked on any element of the set. The important feature is that it returns the same value when invoked on any element of the set. Consequently, it can be used to test if two elements belong to the same set.

```
func Find(e *Element) *Element {
    for e.parent != e {
        e = e.parent
    }
    return e
}
```

Recursive

```
func Find(e *Element) *Element {
    if e.parent == e {
        return e
    } else {
        return Find(e.parent)
    }
}
```

UNION

Union establishes the union of two sets when given an element from each set. Afterwards, the original sets no longer exist as separate entities.

```
func Union(e1, e2 *Element) {
    e1.parent = e2
}
```

Test Code

```
func main() {
    aSet := MakeSet("a")
    bSet := MakeSet("b")
    oneSet := MakeSet(1)
    twoSet := MakeSet(2)
    Union(aSet, bSet)
    Union(oneSet, twoSet)
    result := Find(aSet)
    fmt.Println(result.Data)          // prints b
    result = Find(bSet)
    fmt.Println(result.Data)          // prints b
    result = Find(oneSet)
    fmt.Println(result.Data)          // prints 2
    result = Find(twoSet)
    fmt.Println(result.Data)          // prints 2
}
```

8.9 Fast UNION Implementations (Quick FIND)

The main problem with the previous approach is that, in the worst case we are getting the skew trees and as a result the FIND operation is taking $O(n)$ time complexity. There are two ways to improve it:

- UNION by Size (also called UNION by Weight): Make the smaller tree a subtree of the larger tree
- UNION by Height (also called UNION by Rank): Make the tree with less height a subtree of the tree with more height

UNION by Size

In the earlier representation, for each element i we have stored i (in the parent array) for the root element and for other elements we have stored the parent of i. But, in this approach, we add extra property to indicate the size of the tree.

```
type Element struct {
    parent *Element          // Parent element
    size   int               // Size of the subtree with this element as root
    Data   interface{}       // Arbitrary user-provided payload
}
```

MAKESET

```
// MakeSet creates a singleton set and returns its sole element.
func MakeSet(Data interface{}) *Element {
    s := &Element{}
    s.parent = s
    s.size = 1
    s.Data = Data
    return s
}
```

FIND

```
// No change in the find operation
```

UNION by Size

For union operation, the element with higher size would become the root for the new set after the union.

```
func Union(e1, e2 *Element) {
    // Ensure the two Elements aren't already part of the same union.
```

```
        e1SetName := Find(e1)
        e2SetName := Find(e2)
        if e1SetName == e2SetName {
            return
        }
        // Create a union by making the shorter tree point to the root of the larger tree.
        if e1SetName.size < e2SetName.size {
            e1SetName.parent = e2SetName
            e2SetName.size += e1SetName.size
        } else {
            e2SetName.parent = e1SetName
            e1SetName.size += e2SetName.size
        }
}
```

Note: There is no change in FIND operation implementation.

UNION by Height (UNION by Rank)

As in UNION by size, in this method, we store the height of the tree with an extra rank property in the element data structure. We assume the height of a tree with one element set is 1.

```
type Element struct {
    parent *Element    // Parent element
    rank   int         // Rank (approximate depth) of the subtree with this element as root
    Data   interface{} // Arbitrary user-provided payload
}
```

MAKESET

```
// MakeSet creates a singleton set and returns its sole element.
func MakeSet(Data interface{}) *Element {
    s := &Element{}
    s.parent = s
    s.rank = 1
    s.Data = Data
    return s
}
```

UNION by Height

```
func Union(e1, e2 *Element) {
    // Ensure the two Elements aren't already part of the same union.
    e1SetName := Find(e1)
    e2SetName := Find(e2)
    if e1SetName == e2SetName {
        return
    }
    // Create a union by making the shorter tree point to the root of the larger tree.
    switch {
    case e1SetName.rank < e2SetName.rank:
        e1SetName.parent = e2SetName
    case e1SetName.rank > e2SetName.rank:
        e2SetName.parent = e1SetName
    default:
        e2SetName.parent = e1SetName
        e1SetName.rank++
    }
}
```

Note: For FIND operation there is no change in the implementation.

Comparing UNION by Size and UNION by Height

With UNION by size, the depth of any node is never more than $logn$. This is because a node is initially at depth 0. When its depth increases as a result of a UNION, it is placed in a tree that is at least twice as large as before. That means its depth can be increased at most $logn$ times. This means that the running time for a FIND operation is O($logn$), and a sequence of m operations takes O(m $logn$).

Similarly with UNION by height, if we take the UNION of two trees of the same height, the height of the UNION is one larger than the common height, and otherwise equal to the max of the two heights. This will keep the height of tree of n nodes from growing past O($logn$). A sequence of m UNIONs and FINDs can then still cost O(m $logn$).

Path Compression

FIND operation traverses a list of nodes on the way to the root. We can make later FIND operations efficient by making each of these vertices point directly to the root. This process is called *path compression*. For example, in the FIND(X) operation, we travel from X to the root of the tree. The effect of path compression is that every node on the path from X to the root has its parent changed to the root.

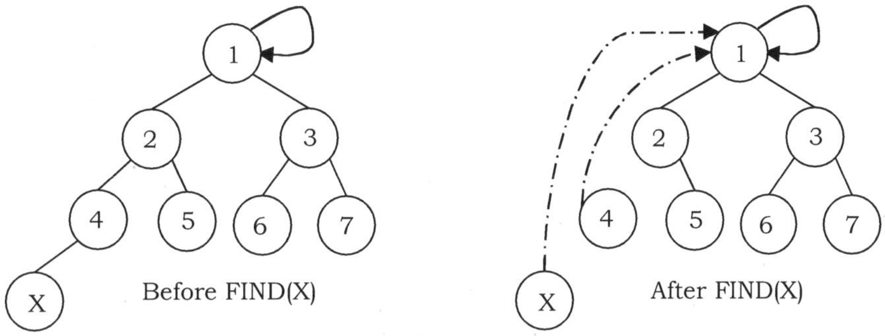

With path compression the only change to the FIND function is that $S[X]$ is made equal to the value returned by FIND. That means, after the root of the set is found recursively, X is made to point directly to it. This happen recursively to every node on the path to the root.

FIND with path compression

```
    func Find(e *Element) *Element {
        for e.parent != e {
            e.parent = e.parent.parent          // Update the parent of current element
            e = e.parent
        }
        return e
    }
Recursive
    func Find(e *Element) *Element {
        if e.parent == e {
            return e
        }
        e.parent = Find(e.parent)               // Update the parent of current element
        return e.parent
    }
```

Note: Path compression is compatible with UNION by size but not with UNION by height as there is no efficient way to change the height of the tree.

8.10 Summary

Performing m union-find operations on a set of n objects.

Algorithm	Worst-case time
Quick-Find	mn
Quick-Union	mn
Quick-Union by Size/Height	$n + m\, logn$
Path compression	$n + m\, logn$
Quick-Union by Size/Height + Path Compression	$(m + n)\, logn$

8.11 Disjoint Sets: Problems & Solutions

Problem-1 Consider a list of cities c_1, c_2,...,c_n. Assume that we have a relation R such that, for any i, j, $R(c_i, c_j)$ is 1 if cities c_i and c_j are in the same state, and 0 otherwise. If R is stored as a table, how much space does it require?

Solution: R must have an entry for every pair of cities. There are $\Theta(n^2)$ of these.

Problem-2 For Problem-1, using a Disjoint sets ADT, give an algorithm that puts each city in a set such that c_i and c_j are in the same set if and only if they are in the same state.

Solution:

```
for i := 1; i <= n; i++ {
    MakeSet(c_i)
    for j := 1; j <= i-1; j++ {
        if R(c_j, c_i) {
            UNION(c_j, c_i)
            break
        }
    }
}
```

Problem-3 For Problem-1, when the cities are stored in the Disjoint sets ADT, if we are given two cities c_i and c_j, how do we check if they are in the same state?

Solution: Cities c_i and c_j are in the same state if and only if Find(c_i) = Find(c_j).

Problem-4 For Problem-1, if we use linked-lists with UNION by size to implement the union-find ADT, how much space do we use to store the cities?

Solution: There is one node per city, so the space is $\Theta(n)$.

Problem-5 For Problem-1, if we use trees with UNION by rank, what is the worst-case running time of the algorithm from Problem-2?

Solution: Whenever we do a UNION in the algorithm from Problem-2, the second argument is a tree of size 1. Therefore, all trees have height 1, so each union takes time O(1). The worst-case running time is then $\Theta(n^2)$.

Problem-6 If we use trees without union-by-rank, what is the worst-case running time of the algorithm from Problem-2? Are there more worst-case scenarios than Problem-5?

Solution: Because of the special case of the unions, union-by-rank does not make a difference for our algorithm. Hence, everything is the same as in Problem-5.

Problem-7 With the quick-union algorithm we know that a sequence of n operations (*unions* and *finds*) can take slightly more than linear time in the worst case. Explain why if all the *finds* are done before all the *unions*, a sequence of n operations is guaranteed to take O(n) time.

Solution: If the *find* operations are performed first, then the *find* operations take O(1) time each because every item is the root of its own tree. No item has a parent, so finding the set an item is in takes a fixed number of operations. Union operations always take O(1) time. Hence, a sequence of n operations with all the *finds* before the *unions* takes O(n) time.

Problem-8 With reference to Problem-7, explain why if all the unions are done before all the finds, a sequence of n operations is guaranteed to take O(n) time.

Solution: This problem requires amortized analysis. *Find* operations can be expensive, but this expensive *find* operation is balanced out by lots of cheap *union* operations.

The accounting is as follows. *Union* operations always take O(1) time, so let's say they have an actual cost of ₹1. Assign each *union* operation an amortized cost of ₹2, so every *union* operation puts ₹1 in the account. Each *union* operation creates a new child. (Some node that was not a child of any other node before is a child now.) When all the union operations are done, there is $1 in the account for every child, or in other words, for every node with a depth of one or greater. Let's say that a *find*(u) operation costs ₹1 if u is a root. For any other node, the *find* operation costs an additional ₹1 for each parent pointer the *find* operation traverses. So the actual cost is ₹(1 + d), where d is the depth of u. Assign each *find* operation an amortized cost of ₹2. This covers the case where u is a root or a child of a root. For each additional parent pointer traversed, ₹1 is withdrawn from the account to pay for it.

Fortunately, path compression changes the parent pointers of all the nodes we pay ₹1 to traverse, so these nodes become children of the root. All of the traversed nodes whose depths are 2 or greater move up, so their depths are now 1. We will never have to pay to traverse these nodes again. Say that a node is a grandchild if its depth is 2 or greater.

Every time *find*(u) visits a grandchild, ₹1 is withdrawn from the account, but the grandchild is no longer a grandchild. So the maximum number of dollars that can ever be withdrawn from the account is the number of grandchildren. But we initially put $1 in the bank for every child, and every grandchild is a child, so the bank balance will never drop below zero. Therefore, the amortization works out. *Union* and *find* operations both have amortized costs of ₹2, so any sequence of n operations where all the unions are done first takes O(n) time.

CHAPTER

GRAPH ALGORITHMS

9

9.1 Introduction

In the real world, many problems are represented in terms of objects and connections between them. For example, in an airline route map, we might be interested in questions like: "What's the fastest way to go from Hyderabad to New York?" *or* "What is the cheapest way to go from Hyderabad to New York?" To answer these questions we need information about connections (airline routes) between objects (towns). Graphs are data structures used for solving these kinds of problems.

As part of this chapter, you will learn several ways to traverse graphs and how you can do useful things while traversing the graph in some order. We will also talk about shortest paths algorithms. We will finish with minimum spanning trees, which are used to plan road, telephone and computer networks and also find applications in clustering and approximate algorithms.

9.2 Glossary

Graph: A graph G is simply a way of encoding pairwise relationships among a set of objects: it consists of a collection V of nodes and a collection E of edges, each of which "joins" two of the nodes. We thus represent an edge e in E as a two-element subset of V: e = {u, v} for some u, v in V, where we call u and v the ends of e.

Edges in a graph indicate a symmetric relationship between their ends. Often we want to encode asymmetric relationships, and for this, we use the closely related notion of a directed graph. A directed graph G' consists of a set of nodes V and a set of directed edges E'. Each e' in E' is an ordered pair (u, v); in other words, the roles of u and v are not interchangeable, and we call u the tail of the edge and v the head. We will also say that edge e' leaves node u and enters node v.

When we want to emphasize that the graph we are considering is *not directed*, we will call it an *undirected graph*; by default, however, the term "graph" will mean an undirected graph. It is also worth mentioning two warnings in our use of graph terminology. First, although an edge e in an undirected graph should properly be written as a set of nodes {u, u}, one will more often see it written in the notation used for ordered pairs: e = (u, v). Second, a node in a graph is also frequently called a vertex; in this context, the two words have exactly the same meaning.

- *Vertices* and *edges* are positions and store elements
- Definitions that we use:
    - *Directed edge*:
        - Ordered pair of vertices (u, v)
        - First vertex u is the origin
        - Second vertex v is the destination
        - Example: one-way road traffic

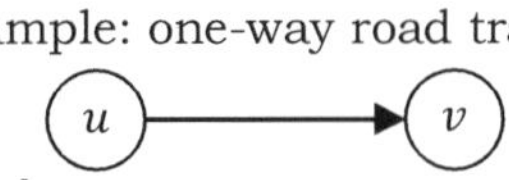

    - *Undirected edge*:
        - Unordered pair of vertices (u, v)
        - Example: railway lines

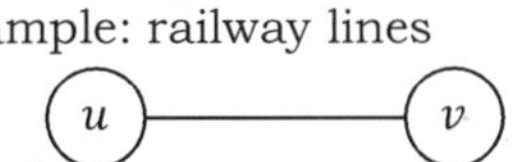

    - *Directed graph*:
        - All the edges are directed
        - Example: route network

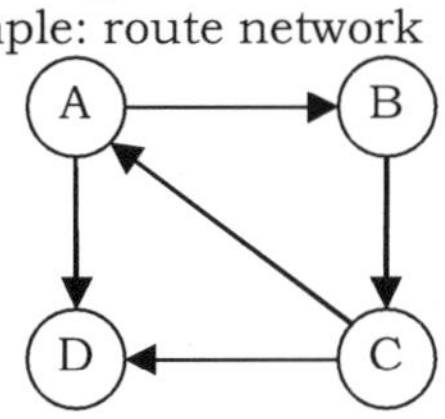

- *Undirected graph*:
    - All the edges are undirected
    - Example: flight network

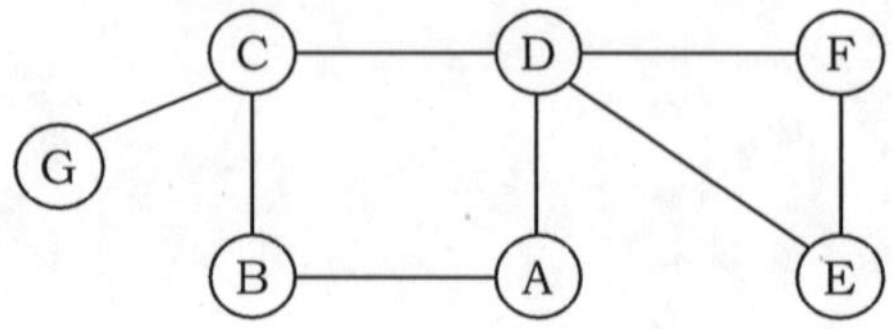

- When an edge connects two vertices, the vertices are said to be adjacent to each other and the edge is incident on both vertices.
- A graph with no cycles is called a *tree*. A tree is an acyclic connected graph.

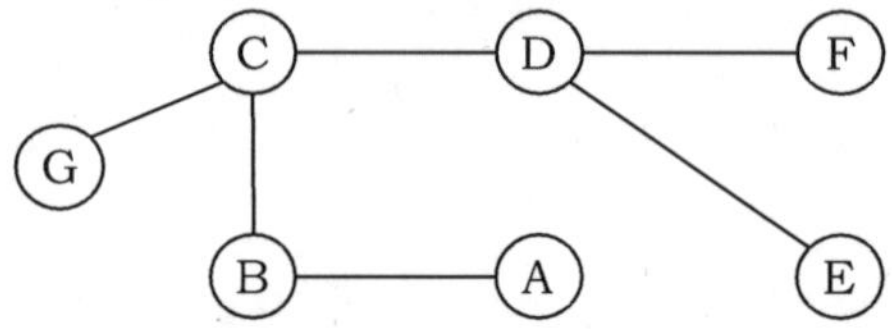

- A self loop is an edge that connects a vertex to itself.

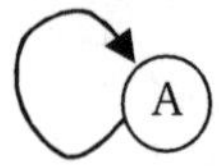

- Two edges are parallel if they connect the same pair of vertices.

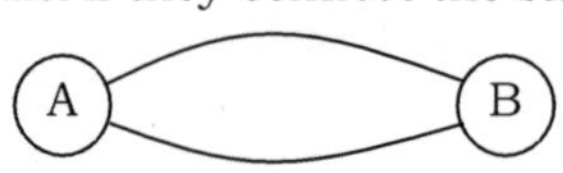

- The *d*egree of a vertex is the number of edges incident on it.
- A subgraph is a subset of a graph's edges (with associated vertices) that form a graph.

One of the fundamental operations in a graph is that of traversing a sequence of nodes connected by edges. We define a path in an undirected graph G = (V, E) to be a sequence P of nodes $v_1, v_2, \ldots, v_{k-1}, v_k$ with the property that each consecutive pair v_i, v_{i+1} is ioined by an edge in G. P is often called a path from v_1 to v_k, or a v_1-v_k path. A path is called *simple* if all its vertices are distinct from one another. A cycle is a path $v_1, v_2, \ldots, v_{k-1}, v_k$ in which $k > 2$, the first $k — 1$ nodes are all distinct, and $v_1 = v_k$. In other words, the sequence of nodes "cycles back" to where it began. All of these definitions carry over naturally to directed graphs, with the following change: in a directed path or cycle, each pair of consecutive nodes has the property that (v_i, v_{i+1}) is an edge. In other words, the sequence of nodes in the path or cycle must respect the directionality of edges.

- A path in a graph is a sequence of adjacent vertices. Simple path is a path with no repeated vertices. In the graph below, the dotted lines represent a path from G to E.

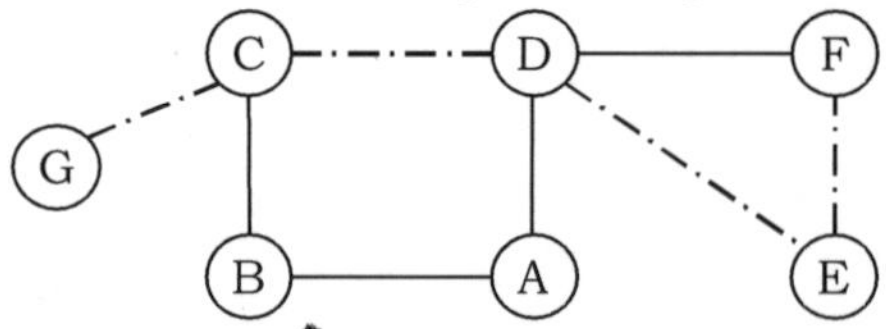

- A cycle is a path where the first and last vertices are the same. A simple cycle is a cycle with no repeated vertices or edges (except the first and last vertices).

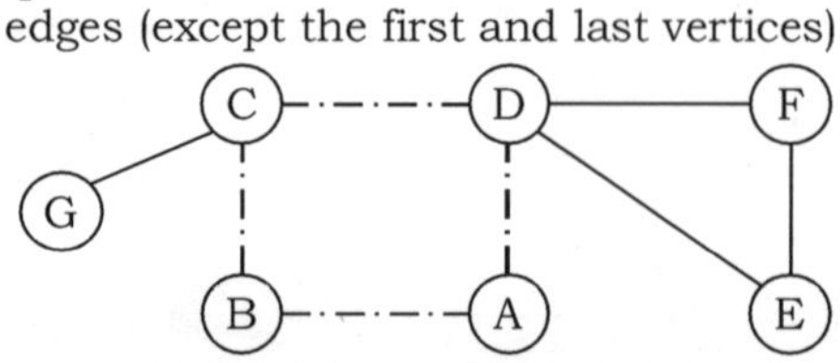

We say that an undirected graph is connected if, for every pair of nodes u and v, there is a path from u to v. Choosing how to define connectivity of a directed graph is a bit more subtle, since it's possible for u to have a path to v while v has no path to u. We say that a directed graph is strongly connected if, for every two nodes u and v, there is a path from u to v and a path from v to u.

- We say that one vertex is connected to another if there is a path that contains both of them.
- A graph is connected if there is a path from *every* vertex to every other vertex.
- If a graph is not connected then it consists of a set of connected components.

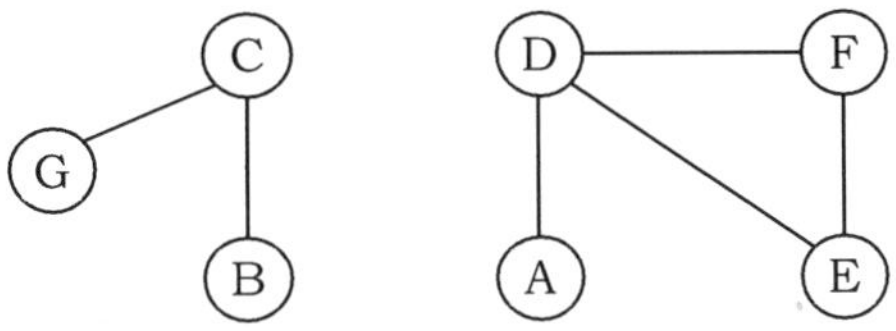

- A *directed acyclic graph* [DAG] is a directed graph with no cycles.

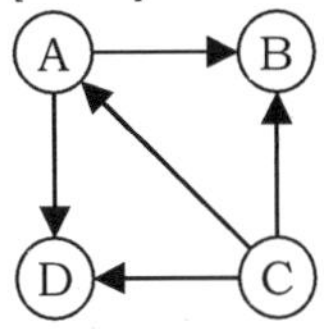

- In *weighted graphs* integers (*weights*) are assigned to each edge to represent (distances or costs).

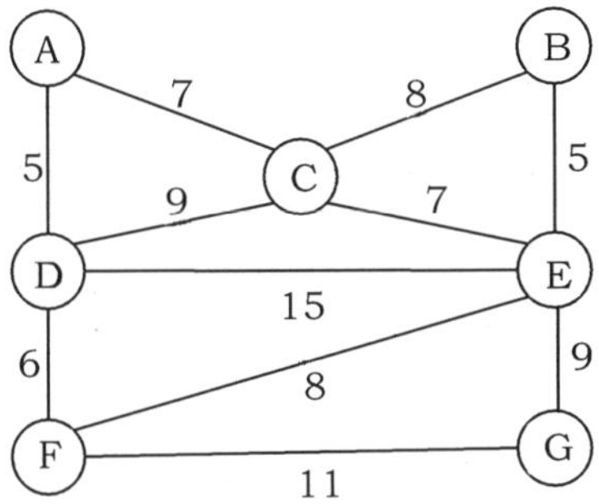

- In addition to simply knowing about the existence of a path between some pair of nodes u and v, we may also want to know whether there is a short path. Thus we define the distance between two nodes u and v to be the minimum number of edges in a u-v path.
- A forest is a disjoint set of trees.
- A spanning tree of a connected graph is a subgraph that contains all of that graph's vertices and is a single tree. A spanning forest of a graph is the union of spanning trees of its connected components.
- A bipartite graph is a graph whose vertices can be divided into two sets such that all edges connect a vertex in one set with a vertex in the other set.

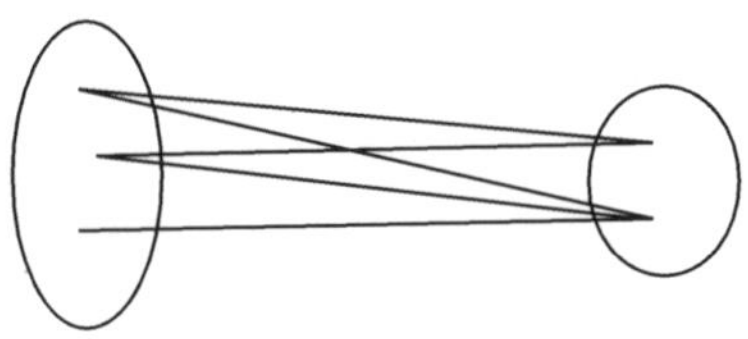

- Graphs with all edges present are called *complete* graphs.

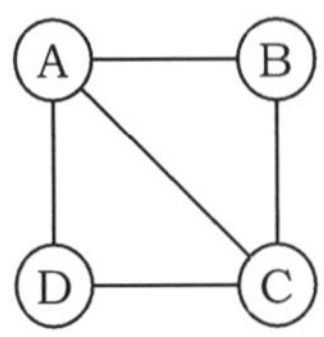

- Graphs with relatively few edges (generally if it edges < $|V| \log |V|$) are called *sparse graphs.*
- Graphs with relatively few of the possible edges missing are called *dense* graphs.
- Directed weighted graphs are sometimes called *network.*
- We will denote the number of vertices in a given graph by $|V|$, and the number of edges by $|E|$. Note that E can range anywhere from 0 to $\frac{|V|(|V|-1)}{2}$ (in undirected graph). This is because each node can connect to every other node.

9.3 Applications of Graphs

- Representing relationships between components in electronic circuits
- Transportation networks: Highway network, Flight network
- Computer networks: Local area network, Internet, Web
- Databases: For representing ER (Entity Relationship) diagrams in databases, for representing dependency of tables in databases

9.4 Graph Representation

As in other ADTs, to manipulate graphs we need to represent them in some useful form. There are several ways to represent graphs, each with its advantages and disadvantages. Some situations, or algorithms that we want to run with graphs as input, call for one representation, and others call for a different representation. Here, we'll see three ways to represent graphs.

- Adjacency Matrix
- Adjacency List
- Adjacency Set

Adjacency Matrix

Graph Declaration for Adjacency Matrix

First, let us look at the components of the graph data structure. To represent graphs, we need the number of vertices, the number of edges and also their interconnections. So, the graph can be declared as:

```
type AdjacencyMatrix struct {
    Vertices  int
    Edges     int
    GraphType GraphType
    AdjMatrix [][]int
}
```

Description

The adjacency matrix of a graph is a square matrix of size $V \times V$. The V is the number of vertices of the graph G. The values of matrix are boolean. Let us assume the matrix is $adjMatrix$. The value $adjMatrix[u, v]$ is set to 1 if there is an edge from vertex u to vertex v and 0 otherwise. In the matrix, each edge is represented by two bits for undirected graphs. That means, an edge from u to v is represented by 1 value in both $adjMatrix[\text{u,v}]$ and $adjMatrix[u, v]$. To save time, we can process only half of this symmetric matrix. Also, we can assume that there is an "edge" from each vertex to itself. So, $adjMatrix[\text{u,u}]$ is set to 1 for all vertices.

If the graph is a directed graph then we need to mark only one entry in the adjacency matrix. As an example, consider the directed graph below.

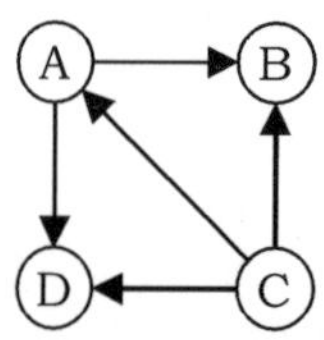

The adjacency matrix for this graph can be given as:

	A	B	C	D
A	0	1	0	1
B	0	0	1	0
C	1	0	0	1
D	0	0	0	0

Now, let us concentrate on the implementation. To read a graph, one way is to first read the vertex names and then read pairs of vertex names (edges). The code below reads an undirected graph.

```
type GraphType string
const (
    DIRECTED   GraphType = "DIRECTED"
    UNDIRECTED GraphType = "UNDIRECTED"
)
type Graph interface {
    Init()
    AddEdge(vertexOne int, vertexTwo int) error
    AddEdgeWithWeight(vertexOne int, vertexTwo int, weight int) error
    RemoveEdge(vertexOne int, vertexTwo int) error
    HasEdge(vertexOne int, vertexTwo int) bool
    GetGraphType() GraphType
    GetAdjacentNodesForVertex(vertex int) map[int]bool
```

```
    GetWeightOfEdge(vertexOne int, vertexTwo int) (int, error)
    GetNumberOfVertices() int
    GetNumberOfEdges() int
    GetIndegreeForVertex(vertex int) int
}
type AdjacencyMatrix struct {
    Vertices  int
    Edges     int
    GraphType GraphType
    AdjMatrix [][]int
}
func (G *AdjacencyMatrix) Init() {
    G.AdjMatrix = make([][]int, G.Vertices)
    G.Edges = 0
    for i := 0; i < G.Vertices; i++ {
        G.AdjMatrix[i] = make([]int, G.Vertices)     // default initialization is 0
    }
}
func (G *AdjacencyMatrix) AddEdge(vertexOne int, vertexTwo int) error {
    if vertexOne >= G.Vertices || vertexTwo >= G.Vertices || vertexOne < 0 || vertexTwo < 0 {
        return errors.New("Index out of bounds")
    }
    G.AdjMatrix[vertexOne][vertexTwo] = 1
    G.Edges++
    if G.GraphType == UNDIRECTED {
        G.AdjMatrix[vertexTwo][vertexOne] = 1
        G.Edges++
    }
    return nil
}
func (G *AdjacencyMatrix) AddEdgeWithWeight(vertexOne int, vertexTwo int, weight int) error {
    if vertexOne >= G.Vertices || vertexTwo >= G.Vertices || vertexOne < 0 || vertexTwo < 0 {
        return errors.New("Index out of bounds")
    }
    G.AdjMatrix[vertexOne][vertexTwo] = weight
    G.Edges++
    if G.GraphType == UNDIRECTED {
        G.AdjMatrix[vertexTwo][vertexOne] = weight
        G.Edges++
    }
    return nil
}
func (G *AdjacencyMatrix) RemoveEdge(vertexOne int, vertexTwo int) error {
    if vertexOne >= G.Vertices || vertexTwo >= G.Vertices || vertexOne < 0 || vertexTwo < 0 {
        return errors.New("Index out of bounds")
    }
    G.AdjMatrix[vertexOne][vertexTwo] = 0
    G.Edges--
    if G.GraphType == UNDIRECTED {
        G.AdjMatrix[vertexTwo][vertexOne] = 0
        G.Edges--
    }
    return nil
}
func (G *AdjacencyMatrix) HasEdge(vertexOne int, vertexTwo int) bool {
    if vertexOne >= G.Vertices || vertexTwo >= G.Vertices || vertexOne < 0 || vertexTwo < 0 {
        return false
    }
    return G.AdjMatrix[vertexOne][vertexTwo] != 0
```

```
}
func (G *AdjacencyMatrix) GetGraphType() GraphType {
    return G.GraphType
}
func (G *AdjacencyMatrix) GetAdjacentNodesForVertex(vertex int) map[int]bool {
    adjacencyMatrixVertices := map[int]bool{}
    if vertex >= G.Vertices || vertex < 0 {
        return adjacencyMatrixVertices
    }
    for i := 0; i < G.Vertices; i++ {
        if G.AdjMatrix[vertex][i] != 0 {
            adjacencyMatrixVertices[i] = (G.AdjMatrix[vertex][i] != 0)
        }
    }
    return adjacencyMatrixVertices
}
func (G *AdjacencyMatrix) GetWeightOfEdge(vertexOne int, vertexTwo int) (int, error) {
    if vertexOne >= G.Vertices || vertexTwo >= G.Vertices || vertexOne < 0 || vertexTwo < 0 {
        return 0, errors.New("Error getting weight for vertex")
    }
    return G.AdjMatrix[vertexOne][vertexTwo], nil
}
func (G *AdjacencyMatrix) GetNumberOfVertices() int {
    return G.Vertices
}
func (G *AdjacencyMatrix) GetNumberOfEdges() int {
    return G.Edges
}
func (G *AdjacencyMatrix) GetIndegreeForVertex(vertex int) int {
    indegree := 0
    adjacentNodes := G.GetAdjacentNodesForVertex(vertex)
    for key := range adjacentNodes {
        if adjacentNodes[key] {
            indegree++
        }
    }
    return indegree
}
func main() {
    var testAdjMatrixDirected = &AdjacencyMatrix{4, 0, DIRECTED, nil}
    testAdjMatrixDirected.Init()
    err := testAdjMatrixDirected.AddEdge(2, 1)
    if err != nil {
        fmt.Printf("Error adding edge")
    }
    if testAdjMatrixDirected.AdjMatrix[2][1] != 1 {
        fmt.Printf("Data not found at index")
    }
    if testAdjMatrixDirected.AdjMatrix[1][2] != 0 {
        fmt.Printf("Data not found at index")
    }
}
```

The adjacency matrix representation is good if the graphs are dense. The matrix requires $O(V^2)$ bits of storage and $O(V^2)$ time for initialization. If the number of edges is proportional to V^2, then there is no problem because V^2 steps are required to read the edges. If the graph is sparse, the initialization of the matrix dominates the running time of the algorithm as it takes takes $O(V^2)$.

The downsides of adjacency matrices are that enumerating the outgoing edges from a vertex takes $O(n)$ time even if there aren't very many, and the $O(V^2)$ space cost is high for sparse graphs, those with much fewer than V^2 edges. The adjacency matrix representation takes $O(V^2)$ amount of space while it is computed. When graph has maximum number of edges or minimum number of edges, in both cases the required space will be same.

Adjacency List

Graph Declaration for Adjacency List

In this representation all the vertices connected to a vertex v are listed on an adjacency list for that vertex v. This can be easily implemented with linked lists. That means, for each vertex v we use a linked list and list nodes represents the connections between v and other vertices to which v has an edge.

The total number of linked lists is equal to the number of vertices in the graph. The graph ADT can be declared as:

```
type AdjacencyList struct {
    Vertices  int
    Edges     int
    GraphType GraphType
    AdjList   []*Node
}
```

Description

Considering the same example as that of the adjacency matrix, the adjacency list representation can be given as:

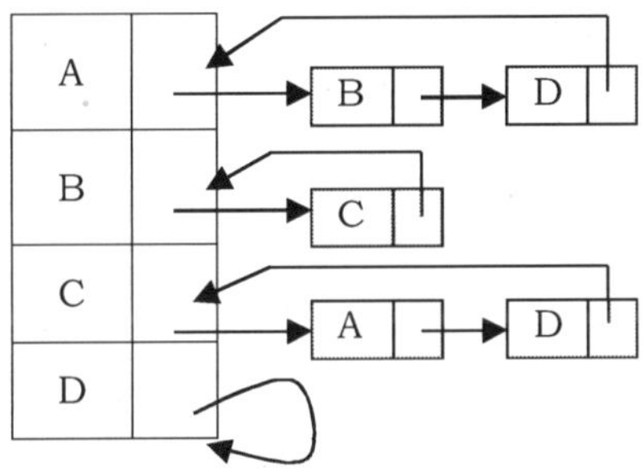

Since vertex A has an edge for B and D, we have added them in the adjacency list for A. The same is the case with other vertices as well.

```
type GraphType string
type AdjacencyList struct {
    Vertices  int
    Edges     int
    GraphType GraphType
    AdjList   []*Node
}
type Node struct {
    Next   *Node
    Weight int
    Key    int
}
// Recursive method to add node to last available slot
func (node Node) AddNode(value int) *Node {
    n := node.Next
    if n == nil {
        newnode := &Node{Next: &Node{}, Key: value}
        return newnode
    }
    nd := n.AddNode(value)
    node.Next = nd
    return &node
}
// Recursive method to append with weight
func (node Node) AddNodeWithWeight(value int, weight int) *Node {
    n := node.Next
    if n == nil {
        newnode := &Node{Next: &Node{}, Key: value, Weight: weight}
        return newnode
    }
```

```
    nd := n.AddNodeWithWeight(value, weight)
    node.Next = nd
    return &node
}
func (node Node) FindNextNode(key int) (*Node, error) {
    n := node
    if n == (Node{}) {
        return &Node{}, errors.New("Node not found")
    }
    if n.Key == key {
        return &n, nil
    }
    nd := n.Next
    return nd.FindNextNode(key)
}
func (G *AdjacencyList) Init() {
    G.AdjList = make([]*Node, G.Vertices)
    G.Edges = 0
    for i := 0; i < G.Vertices; i++ {
        G.AdjList[i] = &Node{}
    }
}
func (G *AdjacencyList) AddEdge(vertexOne int, vertexTwo int) error {
    if vertexOne >= G.Vertices || vertexTwo >= G.Vertices || vertexOne < 0 || vertexTwo < 0 {
        return errors.New("Index out of bounds")
    }
    node := G.AdjList[vertexOne].AddNode(vertexTwo)
    G.AdjList[vertexOne] = node
    G.Edges++
    if G.GraphType == UNDIRECTED {
        node := G.AdjList[vertexTwo].AddNode(vertexOne)
        G.AdjList[vertexTwo] = node
        G.Edges++
    }
    return nil
}
func (G *AdjacencyList) AddEdgeWithWeight(vertexOne int, vertexTwo int, weight int) error {
    if vertexOne >= G.Vertices || vertexTwo >= G.Vertices || vertexOne < 0 || vertexTwo < 0 {
        return errors.New("Index out of bounds")
    }
    node := G.AdjList[vertexOne].AddNodeWithWeight(vertexTwo, weight)
    G.AdjList[vertexOne] = node
    G.Edges++
    if G.GraphType == UNDIRECTED {
        node := G.AdjList[vertexTwo].AddNodeWithWeight(vertexOne, weight)
        G.AdjList[vertexTwo] = node
        G.Edges++
    }
    return nil
}
func (G *AdjacencyList) RemoveEdge(vertexOne int, vertexTwo int) error {
    if vertexOne >= G.Vertices || vertexTwo >= G.Vertices || vertexOne < 0 || vertexTwo < 0 {
        return errors.New("Index out of bounds")
    }
    nodeAdj := G.AdjList[vertexOne]
    if nodeAdj == (&Node{}) {
        return errors.New("Node not found")
    }
    nextNode := nodeAdj
    newNodes := Node{}
    for nextNode != (&Node{}) && nextNode != nil {
        if nextNode.Key != vertexTwo {
```

```
            newNodes.Next = nextNode
            newNodes.Key = nextNode.Key
            newNodes.Weight = nextNode.Weight
            nextNode = nextNode.Next
        } else {
            newNodes.Next = nextNode.Next
            newNodes.Key = nextNode.Next.Key
            newNodes.Weight = nextNode.Next.Weight
            G.AdjList[vertexOne] = &newNodes
            G.Edges--
            return nil
        }
    }
    G.Edges--
    return nil
}
func (G *AdjacencyList) HasEdge(vertexOne int, vertexTwo int) bool {
    if vertexOne >= G.Vertices || vertexTwo >= G.Vertices || vertexOne < 0 || vertexTwo < 0 {
        return false
    }
    nodeAdj := G.AdjList[vertexOne]
    if nodeAdj == (&Node{}) {
        return false
    }
    node, _ := nodeAdj.FindNextNode(vertexTwo)
    if node != nil && node.Key == vertexTwo {
        return true
    }
    return false
}
func (G *AdjacencyList) GetGraphType() GraphType {
    return G.GraphType
}
func (G *AdjacencyList) GetAdjacentNodesForVertex(vertex int) map[int]bool {
    if vertex >= G.Vertices || vertex < 0 {
        return map[int]bool{}
    }
    nodeAdj := G.AdjList[vertex]
    nextNode := nodeAdj
    nodes := map[int]bool{}
    for nextNode != (&Node{}) && nextNode != nil {
        nodes[nextNode.Key] = true
        nextNode = nextNode.Next
    }
    return nodes
}
func (G *AdjacencyList) GetWeightOfEdge(vertexOne int, vertexTwo int) (int, error) {
    if vertexOne >= G.Vertices || vertexTwo >= G.Vertices || vertexOne < 0 || vertexTwo < 0 {
        return 0, errors.New("Error getting weight for vertex")
    }
    nodeAdj := G.AdjList[vertexOne]
    if nodeAdj == (&Node{}) {
        return 0, errors.New("Error getting weight for vertex")
    }
    node, _ := nodeAdj.FindNextNode(vertexTwo)
    if node != nil && node.Key == vertexTwo {
        return nodeAdj.Weight, nil
    }
    return 0, errors.New("Error getting weight for vertex")
}
func (G *AdjacencyList) GetNumberOfVertices() int {
    return G.Vertices
```

```
}
func (G *AdjacencyList) GetNumberOfEdges() int {
    return G.Edges
}
func (G *AdjacencyList) GetIndegreeForVertex(vertex int) int {
    if vertex >= G.Vertices || vertex < 0 {
        return 0
    }
    nodeAdj := G.AdjList[vertex]
    nextNode := nodeAdj.Next
    length := 0
    for nextNode != (&Node{}) && nextNode != nil {
        length += 1
        nextNode = nextNode.Next
    }
    return length
}
func main() {
    var testAdjListDirected = &AdjacencyList{4, 0, DIRECTED, nil}
    var testAdjListUnDirected = &AdjacencyList{4, 0, UNDIRECTED, nil}
    testAdjListDirected.Init()
    testAdjListDirected.AddEdge(2, 1)
    err := testAdjListDirected.AddEdge(2, 3)
    if err != nil {
        fmt.Printf("Error adding edge")
    }
    if testAdjListDirected.AdjList[2].Key != 1 {
        fmt.Printf("Data not found at index")
    }
    if testAdjListDirected.AdjList[2].Next.Key != 3 {
        fmt.Printf("Data not found at index")
    }
}
```

For this representation, the order of edges in the input is *important*. This is because they determine the order of the vertices on the adjacency lists. The same graph can be represented in many different ways in an adjacency list. The order in which edges appear on the adjacency list affects the order in which edges are processed by algorithms.

Disadvantages of Adjacency Lists

Using adjacency list representation we cannot perform some operations efficiently. As an example, consider the case of deleting a node. . In adjacency list representation, it is not enough if we simply delete a node from the list representation. if we delete a node from the adjacency list then that is enough.

For each node on the adjacency list of that node specifies another vertex. We need to search other nodes linked list also for deleting it. This problem can be solved by linking the two list nodes that correspond to a particular edge and making the adjacency lists doubly linked. But all these extra links are risky to process.

Adjacency Set

It is very much similar to adjacency list but instead of using Linked lists, Disjoint Sets [Union-Find] are used. For more details refer to the *Disjoint Sets ADT* chapter.

Adjacency Map

In line with adjacency list and sets representation, we use maps for storing the edges information of the graphs. For more details, refer to the *Dijkstra* algorithm implementation in the problems section of this chapter.

Comparison of Graph Representations

Directed and undirected graphs are represented with the same structures. For directed graphs, everything is the same, except that each edge is represented just once. An edge from x to y is represented by a 1 value in $Adj[x][y]$ in the adjacency matrix, or by adding y on $x's$ adjacency list. For weighted graphs, everything is the same, except fill the adjacency matrix with weights instead of boolean values.

Representation	Space	Checking edge between v and w?	Iterate over edges incident to v?
List of edges	E	E	E
Adj Matrix	V^2	1	V
Adj List	$E+V$	$Degree(v)$	$Degree(v)$
Adj Set	$E+V$	$log(Degree(v))$	$Degree(v)$

9.5 Graph Traversals

To solve problems on graphs, we need a mechanism for traversing the graphs. Graph traversal algorithms are also called *graph search* algorithms. Like trees traversal algorithms (Inorder, Preorder, Postorder and Level-Order traversals), graph search algorithms can be thought of as starting at some source vertex in a graph and "searching" the graph by going through the edges and marking the vertices. Now, we will discuss two such algorithms for traversing the graphs.

- Depth First Search [DFS]
- Breadth First Search [BFS]

A graph can contain cycles, which may bring you to the same node again while traversing the graph. To avoid processing of same node again, use a boolean array which marks the node after it is processed. While visiting the nodes in the layer of a graph, store them in a manner such that you can traverse the corresponding child nodes in a similar order.

Depth First Search [DFS]

Depth-first search (DFS) is a method for exploring a tree or graph. In a DFS, you go as deep as possible down one path before backing up and trying a different one. DFS algorithm works in a manner similar to preorder traversal of the trees. Like preorder traversal, internally this algorithm also uses stack. Let us consider the following example. Suppose a person is trapped inside a maze. To come out from that maze, the person visits each path and each intersection (in the worst case). Let us say the person uses two colors of paint to mark the intersections already passed. When discovering a new intersection, it is marked grey, and he continues to go deeper.

After reaching a "dead end" the person knows that there is no more unexplored path from the grey intersection, which now is completed, and he marks it with black. This "dead end" is either an intersection which has already been marked grey or black, or simply a path that does not lead to an intersection.

The intersections of the maze are the vertices and the paths between the intersections are the edges of the graph. The process of returning from the "dead end" is called *backtracking*. We are trying to go away from the starting vertex into the graph as deep as possible, until we have to backtrack to the preceding grey vertex. In DFS algorithm, we encounter the following types of edges.

Tree edge: encounter new vertex
Back edge: from descendent to ancestor
Forward edge: from ancestor to descendent
Cross edge: between a tree or subtrees

For most algorithms boolean classification, unvisited/visited is enough (for three color implementation refer to problems section). That means, for some problems we need to use three colors, but for our discussion two colors are enough.

false ⟶ Vertex is unvisited

true ⟶ Vertex is visited

Initially all vertices are marked unvisited (false). The DFS algorithm starts at a vertex u in the graph. By starting at vertex u it considers the edges from u to other vertices. If the edge leads to an already visited vertex, then backtrack to current vertex u. If an edge leads to an unvisited vertex, then go to that vertex and start processing from that vertex. That means the new vertex becomes the current vertex. Follow this process until we reach the dead-end. At this point start *backtracking*. The process terminates when backtracking leads back to the start vertex.

As an example, consider the following graph. We can see that sometimes an edge leads to an already discovered vertex. These edges are called *back edges*, and the other edges are called *tree edges* because deleting the back edges from the graph generates a tree.

The final generated tree is called the DFS tree and the order in which the vertices are processed is called *DFS numbers* of the vertices. In the graph below, the gray color indicates that the vertex is visited (there is no other significance). We need to see when the visited table is being updated. In the following example, DFS algorithm traverses from A to B to C to D first, then to E, F, and G and lastly to H. It employs the following rules.

1. Visit the adjacent unvisited vertex. Mark it as visited. Display it (processing). Push it onto a stack.
2. If no adjacent vertex is found, pop up a vertex from the stack. (It will pop up all the vertices from the stack, which do not have adjacent vertices.)
3. Repeat step 1 and step 2 until the stack is empty.

Mark A as visited and put it onto the stack. Explore any unvisited adjacent node from A. We have only one adjacent node B and we can pick that. For this example, we shall take the node in an alphabetical order. Then, mark B as visited and put it onto the stack.

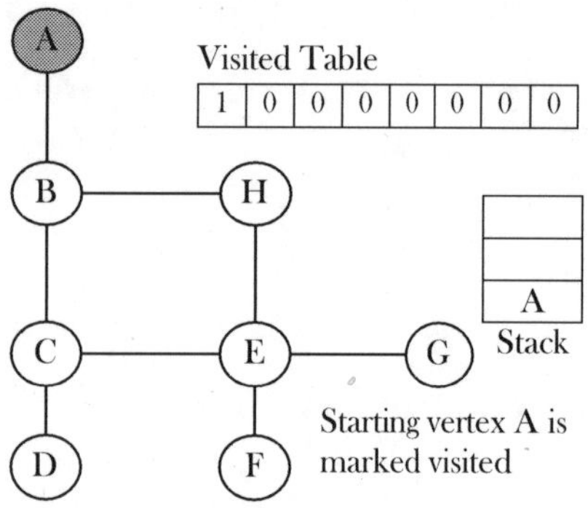

Starting vertex A is marked visited

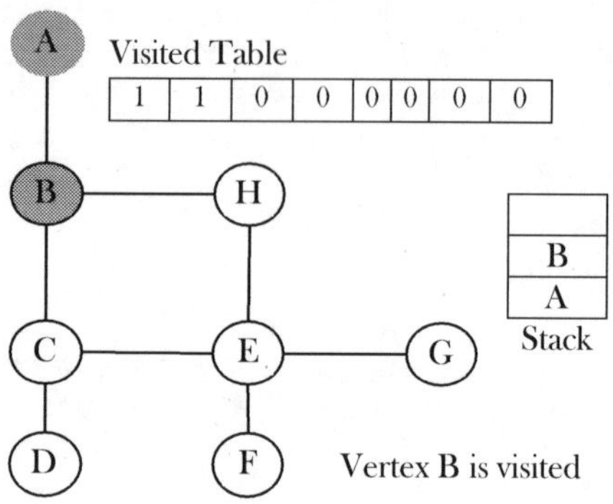

Vertex B is visited

Explore any unvisited adjacent node from B. Both C and H are adjacent to B but we are concerned for unvisited nodes only. Visit C and mark it as visited and put onto the stack. Here, we have B, D, and E nodes, which are adjacent to C and nodes D and E are unvisited. Let us choose one of them; say, D.

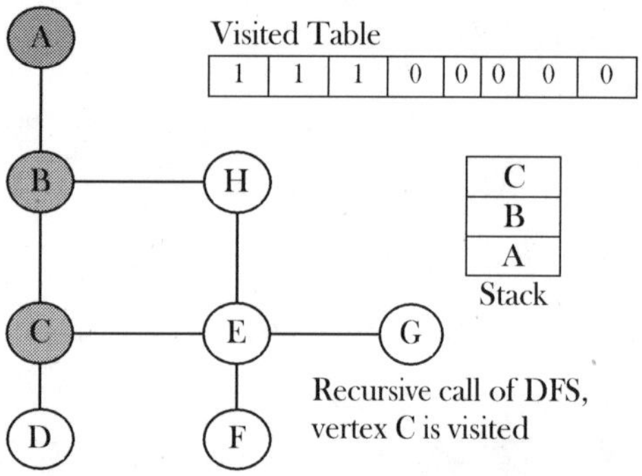

Recursive call of DFS, vertex C is visited

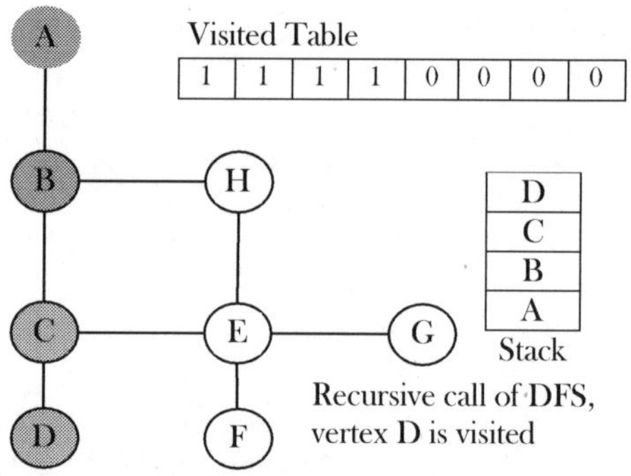

Recursive call of DFS, vertex D is visited

Here D does not have any unvisited adjacent node. So, we pop D from the stack. We check the stack top for return to the previous node and check if it has any unvisited nodes. Here, we find C to be on the top of the stack. Here, we have B, D, and E nodes which are adjacent to C and node E is unvisited.

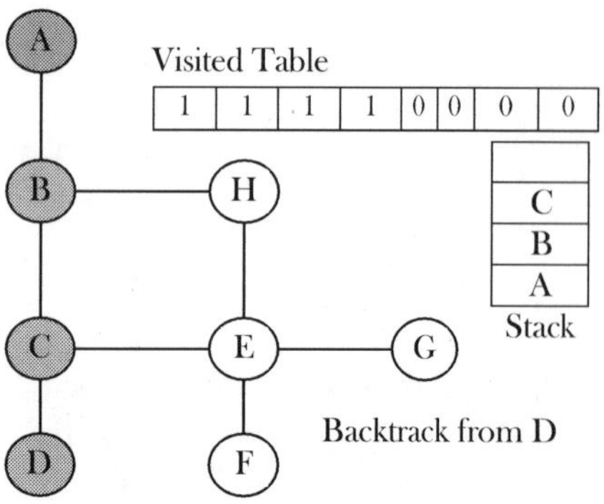

Backtrack from D

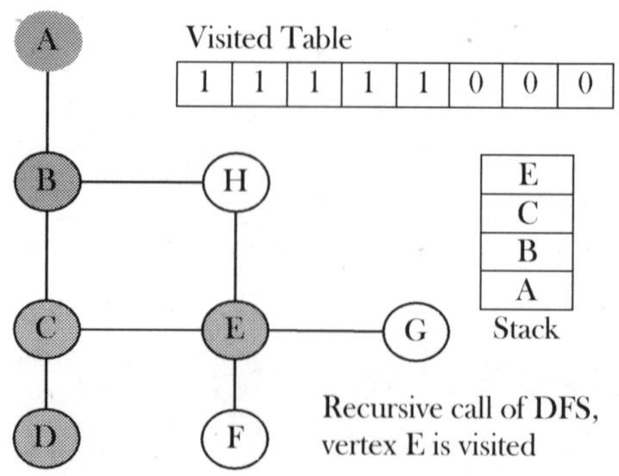

Recursive call of DFS, vertex E is visited

Here, we find E to be on the top of the stack. Here, we have C, F, G, and H nodes which are adjacent to E and nodes F, G, and H are unvisited. Let us choose one of them; say, F. Here node F does not have any unvisited adjacent node. So, we pop F from the stack.

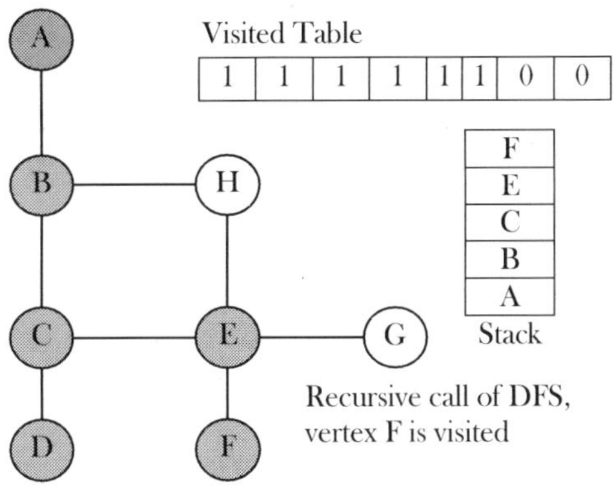

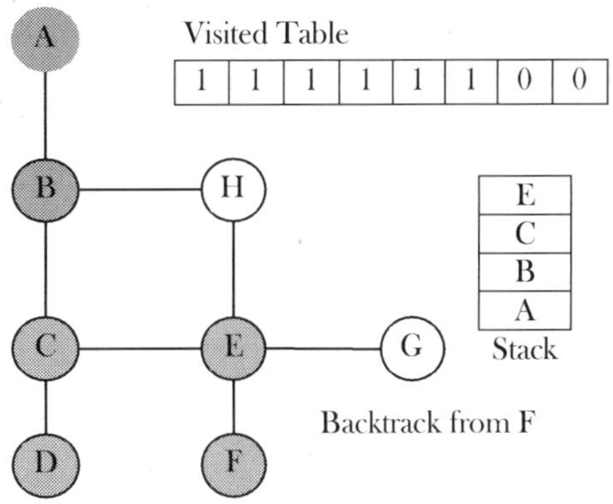

Here, we find E to be on the top of the stack. Here, we have C, F, G, and H nodes which are adjacent to E and nodes G, and H are unvisited. Let us choose one of them; say, G. Here node G does not have any unvisited adjacent node. So, we pop G from the stack.

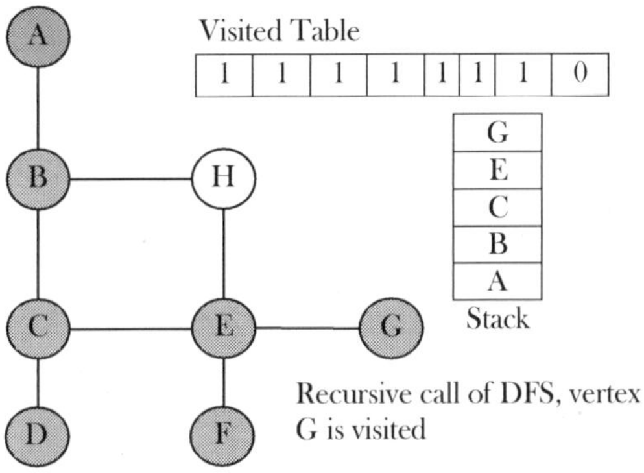

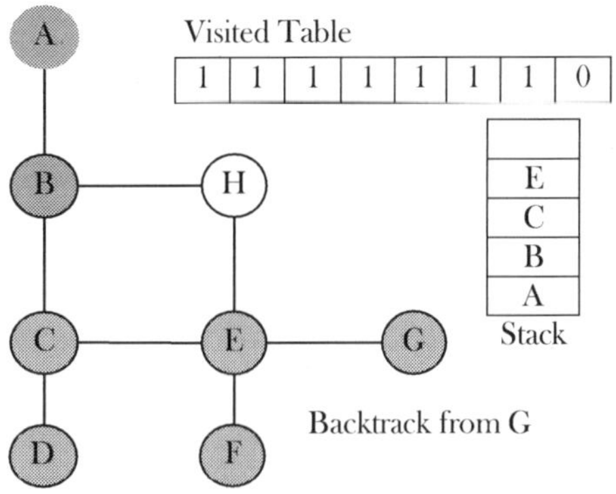

Here, we find E to be on the top of the stack. Here, we have C, F, G, and H nodes which are adjacent to E and node H is unvisited. Let us choose that remaining node H. Here node H does not have any unvisited adjacent node. So, we pop H from the stack.

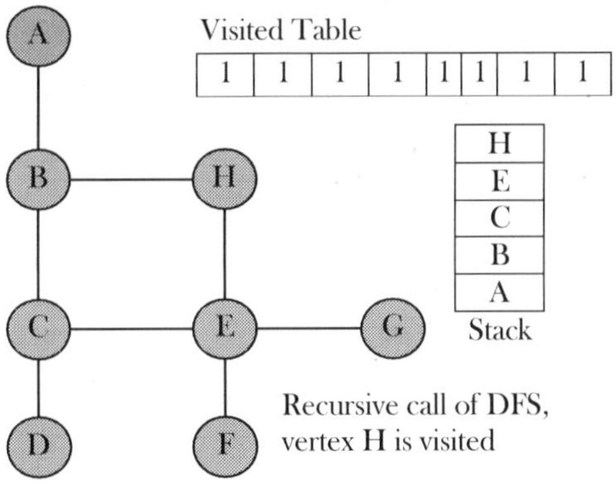

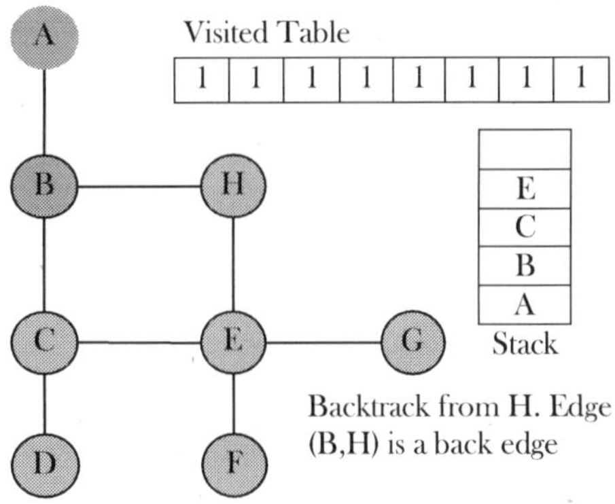

Now, we find E to be on the top of the stack with no unvisited nodes adjacent to it. So, we pop E from the stack. Then, node C becomes the top of the stack. For node C too, there were no adjacent unvisited nodes. Hence, pop node C from the stack.

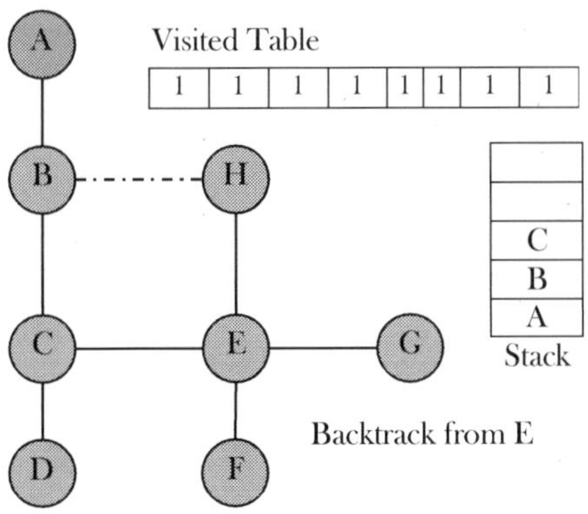

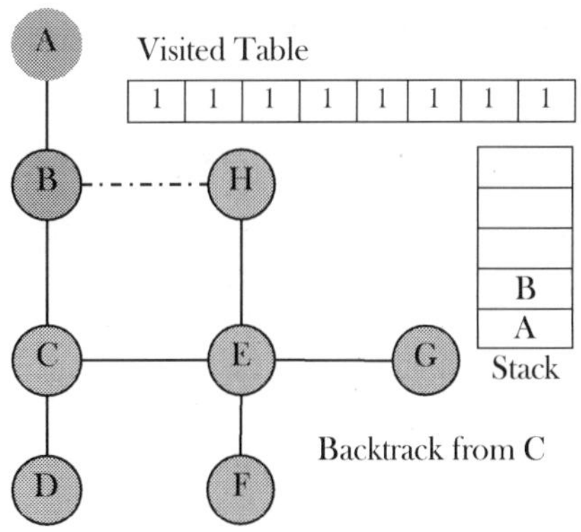

Similarly, we find B to be on the top of the stack with no unvisited nodes adjacent to it. So, we pop B from the stack. Then, node A becomes the top of the stack. For node A too, there were no adjacent unvisited nodes. Hence, pop node A from the stack. With this, the stack is empty.

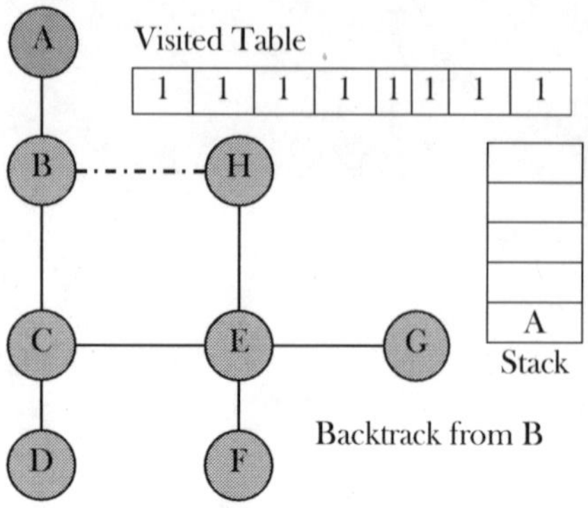

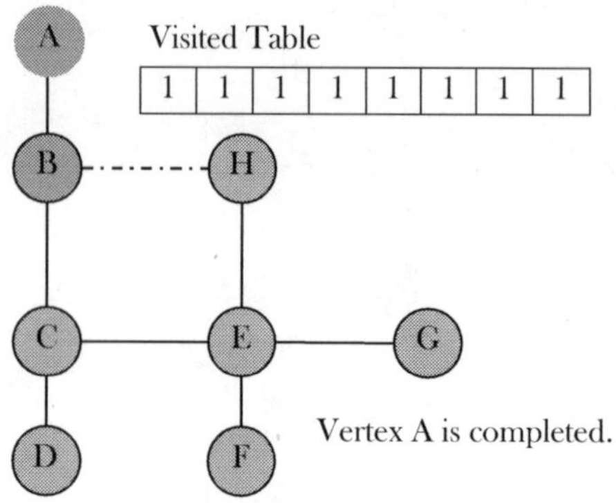

From the above diagrams, it can be seen that the DFS traversal creates a tree (without back edges) and we call such tree a *DFS tree*. In DFS, if we start from a start node it will mark all the nodes connected to the start node as visited. Therefore, if we choose any node in a connected component and run DFS on that node it will mark the whole connected component as visited. The above algorithm works even if the given graph has connected components.

We can see that sometimes an edge leads to an already discovered vertex. These edges are called *back edges*, and the other edges are called *tree edges* because deleting the back edges from the graph generates a tree.

The final generated tree is called the DFS tree and the order in which the vertices are processed is called *DFS numbers* of the vertices. In the graph below, the gray color indicates that the vertex is visited (there is no other significance). We need to see when the visited table is updated.

Advantages

- Depth-first search on a binary tree generally requires less memory than breadth-first.
- Depth-first search can be easily implemented with recursion.

Disadvantages

- A DFS doesn't necessarily find the shortest path to a node, while breadth-first search does.

Applications of DFS

- Topological sorting
- Finding connected components
- Finding articulation points (cut vertices) of the graph
- Finding strongly connected components
- Solving puzzles such as mazes

For algorithms, refer to *Problems Section*.

Implementation

The algorithm based on this mechanism is given below: assume visited[] is a global array.

```
// Refer graph implementation from previous section
func DFS(G *AdjacencyList) []int {
    visited := map[int]bool{}
    var dfsOrdered []int
    for i := 0; i < G.GetNumberOfVertices(); i++ {
        dfs(G, visited, i, &dfsOrdered)
    }
    return dfsOrdered
}
func dfs(G *AdjacencyList, visited map[int]bool, current int, dfsOrdered *[]int) {
    if visited[current] {
        return
    }
    visited[current] = true
    adjNodes := G.GetAdjacentNodesForVertex(current)
```

```
        for key, _ := range adjNodes {
            dfs(G, visited, key, dfsOrdered)
        }
        *dfsOrdered = append(*dfsOrdered, current)
        return
}
func main() {    // Test code
        G := &AdjacencyList{4, 0, DIRECTED, nil}
        G.Init()
        G.AddEdge(2, 1)
        G.AddEdge(3, 2)
        G.AddEdge(2, 0)
        G.AddEdge(1, 0)
        G.AddEdge(1, 1)
        G.AddEdge(2, 3)
        fmt.Printf("Directed Graph with DFS is %v", DFS(G))
}
```

The time complexity of DFS is $O(V + E)$, if we use adjacency lists for representing the graphs. This is because we are starting at a vertex and processing the adjacent nodes only if they are not visited. Similarly, if an adjacency matrix is used for a graph representation, then all edges adjacent to a vertex can't be found efficiently, and this gives $O(V^2)$ complexity.

Breadth First Search [BFS]

Breadth-first search (BFS) is a method for exploring a tree or graph. In a BFS, you first explore all the nodes one step away, then all the nodes two steps away, etc. Breadth-first search is like throwing a stone in the center of a pond. The nodes you explore "ripple out" from the starting point.

The BFS algorithm works similar to *level – order* traversal of the trees. Like *level – order* traversal, BFS also uses queues. In fact, *level – order* traversal got inspired from BFS. BFS works level by level. Initially, BFS starts at a given vertex, which is at level 0. In the first stage it visits all vertices at level 1 (that means, vertices whose distance is 1 from the start vertex of the graph). In the second stage, it visits all vertices at the second level. These new vertices are the ones which are adjacent to level 1 vertices. BFS continues this process until all the levels of the graph are completed.

To make this process easy, use a queue to store the node and mark it as 'visited' once all its neighbors (vertices that are directly connected to it) are marked or added to the queue. The queue follows the First In First Out (FIFO) queuing method, and therefore, the neighbors of the node will be visited in the order in which they were inserted in the node i.e. the node that was inserted first will be visited first, and so on. Generally *queue* data structure is used for storing the vertices of a level.

BFS employs the following rules:

1. Visit the adjacent unvisited vertex. Mark it as visited. Display it. Insert it in a queue.
2. If no adjacent vertex is found, remove the first vertex from the queue.
3. Repeat step 1 and step 2 until the queue is empty.

As similar to DFS, assume that initially all vertices are marked *unvisited* (*false*). Vertices that have been processed and removed from the queue are marked *visited* (*true*). We use a queue to represent the visited set as it will keep the vertices in the order of when they were first visited. As an example, let us consider the same graph as that of the DFS example.

We start from node A (starting node), and add it to the queue. The only element in queue is A. Dequeue the element A and mark it as visited. We then see an unvisited adjacent node B from A. So, enqueue the element B to the queue.

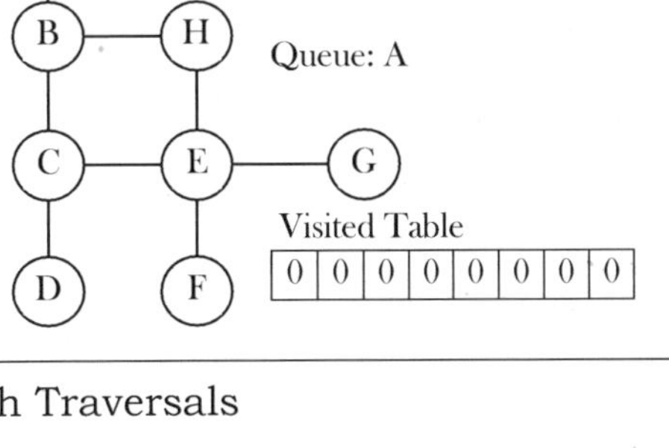

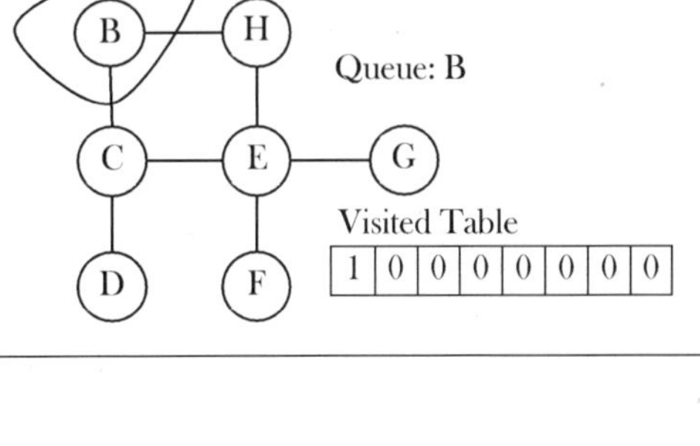

Next, dequeue the element B and mark it as visited. We then see an unvisited adjacent nodes C and H from node B, and enqueue them. Then dequeue the element C, mark it as visited, and enqueue its unvisited adjacent nodes D and E to the queue. Next, dequeue the element H, and mark it as visited. Observe that, node H does not have any unvisited adjacent nodes.

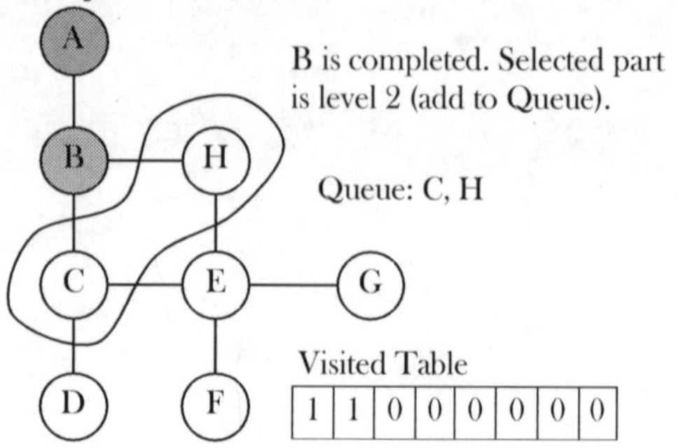

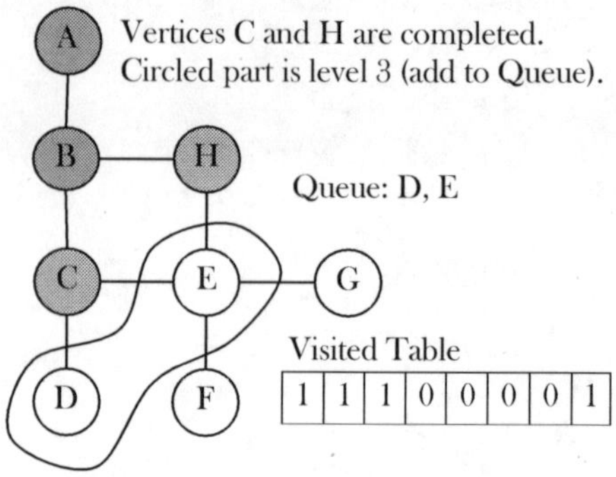

Next, dequeue the element D, and mark it as visited. We see no unvisited adjacent nodes from node D. Then dequeue the element E, mark it as visited, and enqueue its unvisited adjacent nodes F and G to the queue. Next, dequeue the element F, and mark it as visited. Observe that, node G does not have any unvisited adjacent nodes. At this point, queue has only one element G. Dequeue the element and mark it visited. Notice that, node G too does not have any unvisited adjacent nodes.

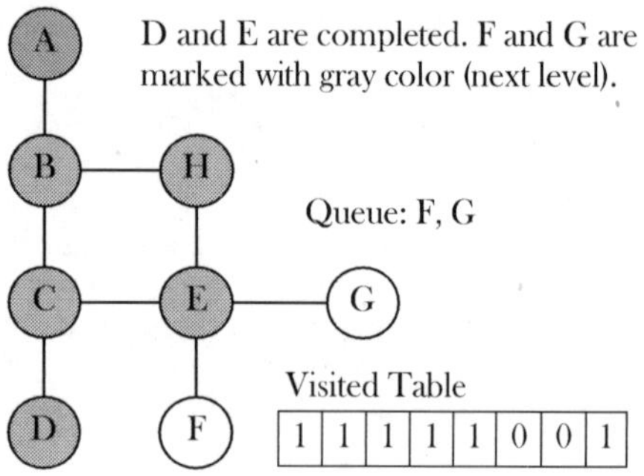

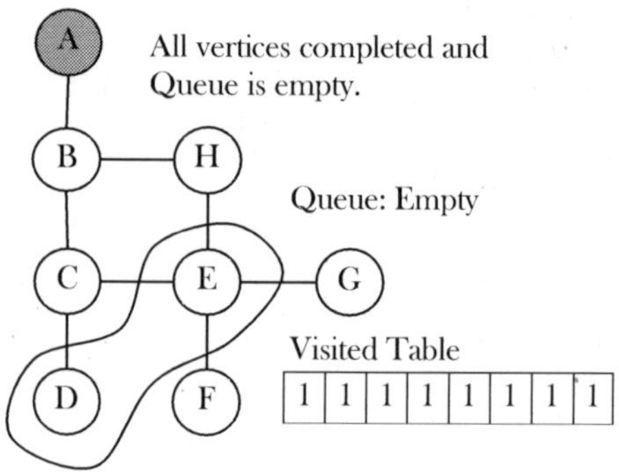

Time complexity of BFS is $O(V + E)$, if we use adjacency lists for representing the graphs, and $O(V^2)$ for adjacency matrix representation.

Advantages

- A BFS will find the shortest path between the starting point and any other reachable node. A depth-first search will not necessarily find the shortest path.

Disadvantages

- A BFS on a binary tree generally requires more memory than a DFS.

Applications of BFS

- Finding all connected components in a graph
- Finding all nodes within one connected component
- Finding the shortest path between two nodes
- Testing a graph for bipartiteness

Implementation

The implementation for the above discussion can be given as:

```
// Refer graph implementation from previous section
func BFS(G *AdjacencyList) []int {
    visited := map[int]bool{}
    var bfsArrayOrdered []int
    for i := 0; i < G.GetNumberOfVertices(); i++ {
        bfsArrayOrdered = bfs(G, visited, i, bfsArrayOrdered)
    }
    return bfsArrayOrdered
```

```
}
func bfs(G *AdjacencyList, visited map[int]bool, node int, bfsArrayOrdered []int) []int {
    queue := make([]int, 0)
    queue = append(queue, node)
    for len(queue) > 0 {
        current := queue[0]
        queue = queue[1:]
        if visited[current] {
            continue
        }
        bfsArrayOrdered = append(bfsArrayOrdered, current)
        visited[current] = true
        adjNodes := G.GetAdjacentNodesForVertex(current)
        for key, _ := range adjNodes {
            queue = append(queue, key)
        }
    }
    return bfsArrayOrdered
}
// Test code
func main() {
    G := &AdjacencyList{4, 0, DIRECTED, nil}
    G.Init()
    G.AddEdge(2, 1)
    G.AddEdge(3, 2)
    G.AddEdge(2, 0)
    G.AddEdge(1, 0)
    G.AddEdge(1, 1)
    G.AddEdge(2, 3)
    fmt.Printf("Directed Graph after BFS is %v", BFS(G))
}
```

Comparing DFS and BFS

Comparing BFS and DFS, the big advantage of DFS is that it has much lower memory requirements than BFS because it's not required to store all of the child pointers at each level. Depending on the data and what we are looking for, either DFS or BFS can be advantageous. For example, in a family tree if we are looking for someone who's still alive and if we assume that person would be at the bottom of the tree, then DFS is a better choice. BFS would take a very long time to reach that last level.

The DFS algorithm finds the goal faster. Now, if we were looking for a family member who died a very long time ago, then that person would be closer to the top of the tree. In this case, BFS finds faster than DFS. So, the advantages of either vary depending on the data and what we are looking for.

DFS is related to preorder traversal of a tree. Like *preorder* traversal, DFS visits each node before its children. The BFS algorithm works similar to $level - order$ traversal of the trees.

If someone asks whether DFS is better or BFS is better, the answer depends on the type of the problem that we are trying to solve. BFS visits each level one at a time, and if we know the solution we are searching for is at a low depth, then BFS is good. DFS is a better choice if the solution is at maximum depth. The below table shows the differences between DFS and BFS in terms of their applications.

Applications	DFS	BFS
Spanning forest, connected components, paths, cycles	Yes	Yes
Shortest paths		Yes
Minimal use of memory space	Yes	

9.6 Topological Sort

Assume that we need to schedule a series of tasks, such as classes or construction jobs, where we cannot start one task until after its prerequisites are completed. We wish to organize the tasks into a linear order that allows us to complete them one at a time without violating any prerequisites. We can model the problem using a DAG. The graph is directed because one task is a prerequisite of another -- the vertices have a directed relationship. It is acyclic because a cycle would indicate a conflicting series of prerequisites that could not be completed without violating at least one prerequisite. The process of laying out the vertices of a DAG in a linear order to meet the prerequisite rules is called a topological sort.

Topological sort is an ordering of vertices in a directed acyclic graph [DAG] in which each node comes before all nodes to which it has outgoing edges. As an example, consider the course prerequisite structure at universities. A directed *edge* (v,w) indicates that course v must be completed before course w. Topological ordering for this example is the sequence which does not violate the prerequisite requirement. Every DAG may have one or more topological orderings. Topological sort is not possible if the graph has a cycle, since for two vertices v and w on the cycle, v precedes w and w precedes v.

Topological sort has an interesting property. All pairs of consecutive vertices in the sorted order are connected by edges; then these edges form a directed Hamiltonian path [refer to *Problems Section*] in the DAG. If a Hamiltonian path exists, the topological sort order is unique. If a topological sort does not form a Hamiltonian path, DAG can have two or more topological orderings. In the graph below: 7, 5, 3, 11, 8, 2, 9, 10 and 3, 5, 7, 8, 11, 2, 9, 10 are both topological orderings.

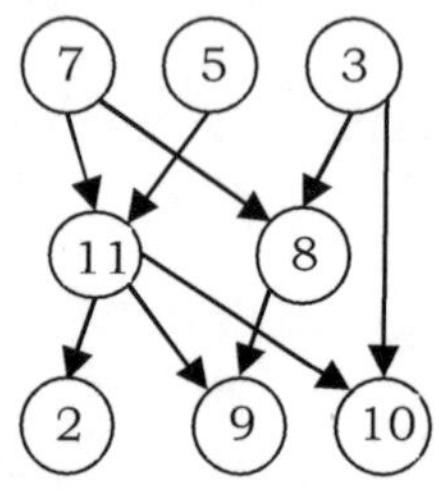

We can implement topological sort using a queue. First visit all edges, counting the number of edges that lead to each vertex (i.e., count the number of prerequisites for each vertex). Initially, *indegree* is computed for all vertices, starting with the vertices which are having indegree 0. That means consider the vertices which do not have any prerequisite. To keep track of vertices with indegree zero we can use a queue.

All vertices with no prerequisites (indegree 0) are placed on the queue. We then begin processing the queue. While the queue is not empty, a vertex v is removed, and all edges adjacent to v have their indegrees decremented. A vertex is put on the queue as soon as its indegree falls to 0. The topological ordering is the order in which the vertices deQueue. If the queue becomes empty without printing all of the vertices, then the graph contains a cycle (i.e., there is no possible ordering for the tasks that does not violate some prerequisite).

The first problem when attempting to create a topographic sort of a graph in any programming language is figuring out how to represent a graph. we can chose a map with an int as a key to simplify the implementation. Each vertex u is represented with a key in the map, each vertex that adjacent to u—v—is stored as a slice in the map referenced by the key u.

```
package main
import "fmt"

// topographicalSort Input: G: a directed acyclic graph with vertices number 1..n
// Output: a linear order of the vertices such that u appears before v
// in the linear order if (u,v) is an edge in the graph.
func topographicalSort(G map[int][]int) []int {
    topoOrder := []int{}

    // 1. Let inDegree[1..n] be a new array, and create an empty linear array of vertices
    inDegree := map[int]int{}

    // 2. Set all values in inDegree to 0
    for u := range G {
        inDegree[u] = 0
    }

    // 3. For each vertex u
    for _, adjacent := range G {
        // A. For each vertex *v* adjacent to *u*:
        for _, v := range adjacent {
            //  i. increment inDegree[v]
            inDegree[v]++
        }
    }

    // 4. Make a list next consisting of all vertices u such that in-degree[u] = 0
    next := []int{}
    for u, v := range inDegree {
        if v != 0 {
            continue
        }
```

```
            next = append(next, u)
        }
        // 5. While next is not empty...
        for len(next) > 0 {
            // A. delete a vertex from next and call it vertex u
            u := next[0]
            next = next[1:]
            // B. Add u to the end of the linear order
            topoOrder = append(topoOrder, u)
            // C. For each vertex v adjacent to u
            for _, v := range G[u] {
                // i. Decrement inDegree[v]
                inDegree[v]--
                // ii. if inDegree[v] = 0, then insert v into next list
                if inDegree[v] == 0 {
                    next = append(next, v)
                }
            }
        }
        // 6. Return the linear order
        return topoOrder
    }
    func main() {
        // Directed Acyclic Graph
        vertices := map[int][]int{
            1:  []int{4},
            2:  []int{3},
            3:  []int{4, 5},
            4:  []int{6},
            5:  []int{6},
            6:  []int{7, 11},
            7:  []int{8},
            8:  []int{14},
            9:  []int{10},
            10: []int{11},
            11: []int{12},
            13: []int{13},
            14: []int{},
        }
        // As yet unimplemented topographicalSort
        fmt.Println(topographicalSort(vertices))
    }
```

The time complexity of this algorithm is $O(|E| + |V|)$ if adjacency lists are used.

Note: The Topological sorting problem can be solved with DFS. Refer to the *Problems Section* for the algorithm.

Applications of Topological Sorting

- Representing course prerequisites
- Detecting deadlocks
- Pipeline of computing jobs
- Checking for symbolic link loop
- Evaluating formulae in spreadsheet

9.7 Shortest Path Algorithms

Shortest path algorithms are a family of algorithms designed to solve the shortest path problem. The shortest path problem is something most people have some intuitive familiarity with: given two points, A and B, what is the shortest path between them? Given a graph $G = (V, E)$ and a distinguished vertex s, we need to find the shortest path from s to every other vertex in G. There are variations in the shortest path algorithms which depends on the type of the input graph and are given below.

Variations of Shortest Path Algorithms

If the edges have weights, the graph is called a weighted graph. Sometimes these edges are bidirectional and the graph is called undirected. Sometimes there can be even be cycles in the graph. Each of these subtle differences are what makes one algorithm work better than another for certain graph type.

There are also different types of shortest path algorithms. Maybe you need to find the shortest path between point A and B, but maybe you need to shortest path between point A and all other points in the graph.

Shortest path in unweighted graph
Shortest path in weighted graph
Shortest path in weighted graph with negative edges

Applications of Shortest Path Algorithms

Shortest path algorithms have many applications. As noted earlier, mapping software like Google or Apple maps makes use of shortest path algorithms. They are also important for road network, operations, and logistics research. Shortest path algorithms are also very important for computer networks, like the Internet.

Any software that helps you choose a route uses some form of a shortest path algorithm. Google Maps, for instance, has you put in a starting point and an ending point and will solve the shortest path problem for you.

- Finding fastest way to go from one place to another
- Finding cheapest way to fly/send data from one city to another

Types of Shortest Path Algorithms

- *Single source shortest path problem*: In a Single Source Shortest Paths Problem, we are given a Graph G = (V, E), we want to find the shortest path from a given source vertex s ∈ V to every vertex v ∈ V.
- *Single destination shortest path problem*: Find the shortest path to a given destination vertex t from every vertex v. By shift the direction of each edge in the graph, we can shorten this problem to a single - source problem.
- *Single pair shortest path problem*: Find the shortest path from u to v for given vertices u and v. If we determine the single - source problem with source vertex u, we clarify this problem also. Furthermore, no algorithms for this problem are known that run asymptotically faster than the best single - source algorithms in the worst case.
- *All pairs shortest path problem*: Find the shortest path from u to v for every pair of vertices u and v. Running a single - source algorithm once from each vertex can clarify this problem; but it can generally be solved faster, and its structure is of interest in the own right.

All these types have algorithms that perform best in their own way. All-pairs algorithms take longer to run because of the added complexity. All shortest path algorithms return values that can be used to find the shortest path, even if those return values vary in type or form from algorithm to algorithm. The most common algorithm for the all-pairs problem is the floyd-warshall algorithm.

Shortest Path in Unweighted Graph

Let *s* be the input vertex from which we want to find the shortest path to all other vertices. Unweighted graph is a special case of the weighted shortest-path problem, with all edges a weight of 1. The algorithm is similar to BFS and we need to use the following data structures:

- A distance table with three columns (each row corresponds to a vertex):
  - Distance from source vertex.
  - Path - contains the name of the vertex through which we get the shortest distance.
- A queue is used to implement breadth-first search. It contains vertices whose distance from the source node has been computed and their adjacent vertices are to be examined.

As an example, consider the following graph and its adjacency list representation.

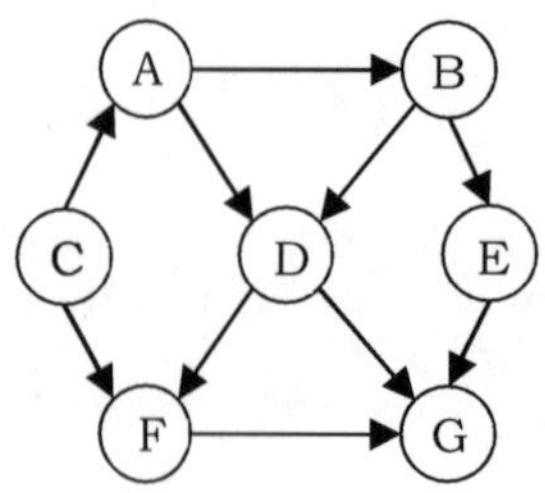

The adjacency list for this graph is:

$A: B \to D$

$\boldsymbol{B}: D \rightarrow E$
$\boldsymbol{C}: A \rightarrow F$
$\boldsymbol{D}: F \rightarrow G$
$\boldsymbol{E}: G$
$\boldsymbol{F}: -$
$\boldsymbol{G}: F$

Let $s = C$. The distance from C to C is 0. Initially, distances to all other nodes are not computed, and we initialize the second column in the distance table for all vertices (except C) with -1 as below.

Vertex	Distance[v]	Previous vertex which gave Distance[v]
A	-1	-
B	-1	-
C	0	-
D	-1	-
E	-1	-
F	-1	-
G	-1	-

Algorithm

```
func UnweightedShortestPath(G *Graph, s int) {
    Q := CreateQueue()
    Q.EnQueue(s)
    for i := 0; i < G.V; i++ {
        Distance[i] = -1
    }
    Distance[s] = 0
    for !Q.IsEmpty(Q) {
        v = Q.DeQueue()
        for true { //for each w adjacent to v        ← Each vertex examined at most once
            if Distance[w] == -1 {
                Distance[w] = Distance[v] + 1
                Path[w] = v
                Q.EnQueue(w)  ←—Each vertex EnQueue'd at most once
            }
        }
        Q.DeleteQueue()
    }
}
```

Running time: $O(|E| + |V|)$, if adjacency lists are used. In for loop, we are checking the outgoing edges for a given vertex and the sum of all examined edges in the while loop is equal to the number of edges which gives $O(|E|)$.

If we use matrix representation the complexity is $O(|V|^2)$, because we need to read an entire row in the matrix of length $|V|$ in order to find the adjacent vertices for a given vertex.

Shortest path in Weighted Graph without Negative Edge Weights [Dijkstra's Algorithm]

A famous solution for the shortest path problem was developed by *Dijkstra*. *Dijkstra's* algorithm is a generalization of the BFS algorithm. The regular BFS algorithm cannot solve the shortest path problem as it cannot guarantee that the vertex at the front of the queue is the vertex closest to source s.

Dijkstra's algorithm makes use of breadth-first search (which is not a single source shortest path algorithm) to solve the single-source problem. It does place one constraint on the graph: there can be no negative weight edges. Dijkstra's algorithm is also sometimes used to solve the all-pairs shortest path problem by simply running it on all vertices in V. Again, this requires all edge weights to be positive.

Before going to code let us understand how the algorithm works. As in unweighted shortest path algorithm, here too we use the distance table. The algorithm works by keeping the shortest distance of vertex v from the source in the *Distance* table. The value *Distance*[v] holds the distance from s to v. The shortest distance of the source to itself is zero. The *Distance* table for all other vertices is set to *math.MaxInt*64 to indicate that those vertices are not already processed.

Vertex	Distance[v]	Previous vertex which gave Distance[v]
A	math.MaxInt64	-1
B	math.MaxInt64	-1
C	0	-
D	math.MaxInt64	-1

E	math.MaxInt64	-1
F	math.MaxInt64	-1
G	math.MaxInt64	-1

After the algorithm finishes, the *Distance* table will have the shortest distance from source s to each other vertex v. To simplify the understanding of *Dijkstra's* algorithm, let us assume that the given vertices are maintained in two sets. Initially the first set contains only the source element and the second set contains all the remaining elements. After the kth iteration, the first set contains k vertices which are closest to the source. These k vertices are the ones for which we have already computed the shortest distances from source.

The *Dijkstra's* algorithm can be better understood through an example, which will explain each step that is taken and how *Distance* is calculated. The weighted graph below has 5 vertices from $A - E$.

The value between the two vertices is known as the edge cost between two vertices. For example, the edge cost between A and C is 1. Dijkstra's algorithm can be used to find the shortest path from source A to the remaining vertices in the graph.

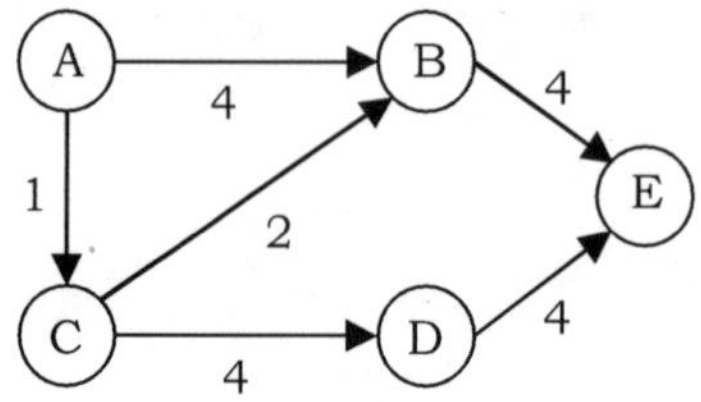

Initially the *Distance* table is:

Vertex	Distance[v]	Previous vertex which gave Distance[v]
A	0	-1
B	math.MaxInt64	-1
C	math.MaxInt64	-1
D	math.MaxInt64	-1
E	math.MaxInt64	-1

After the first step, from vertex A, we can reach B and C. So, in the *Distance* table we update the reachability of B and C with their costs and the same is shown below.

A	0	-
B	4	A
C	1	A
D	math.MaxInt64	-1
E	math.MaxInt64	-1

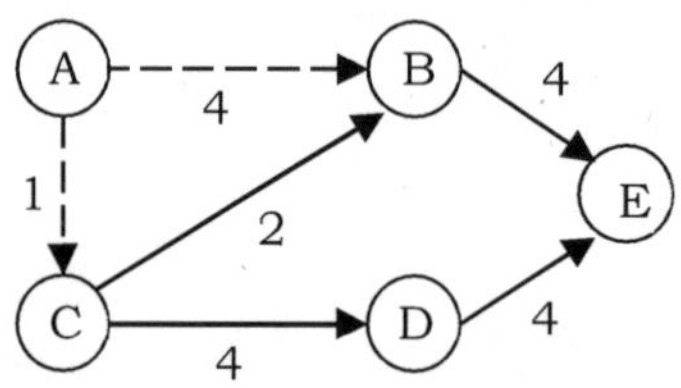

Shortest path from B, C from A

Now, let us select the minimum distance among all. The minimum distance vertex is C. That means, we have to reach other vertices from these two vertices (A and C). For example, B can be reached from A and also from C. In this case we have to select the one which gives the lowest cost. Since reaching B through C is giving the minimum cost (1 + 2), we update the *Distance* table for vertex B with cost 3 and the vertex from which we got this cost as C.

A	0	-
B	3	C
C	1	A
D	5	C
E	math.MaxInt64	-1

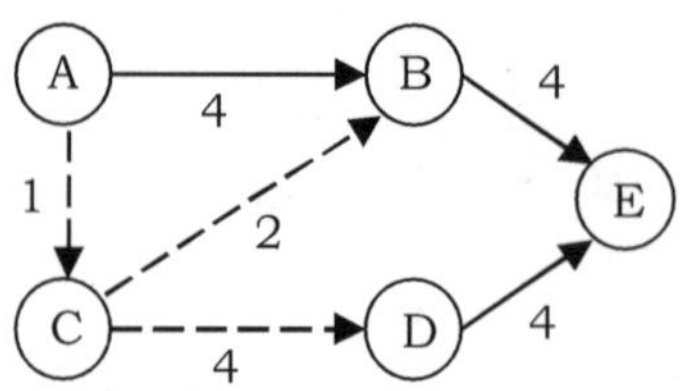

Shortest path to B, D using C as intermediate vertex

The only vertex remaining is E. To reach E, we have to see all the paths through which we can reach E and select the one which gives the minimum cost. We can see that if we use B as the intermediate vertex through C we get the minimum cost.

A	0	-
B	3	C
C	1	A
D	5	C
E	7	B

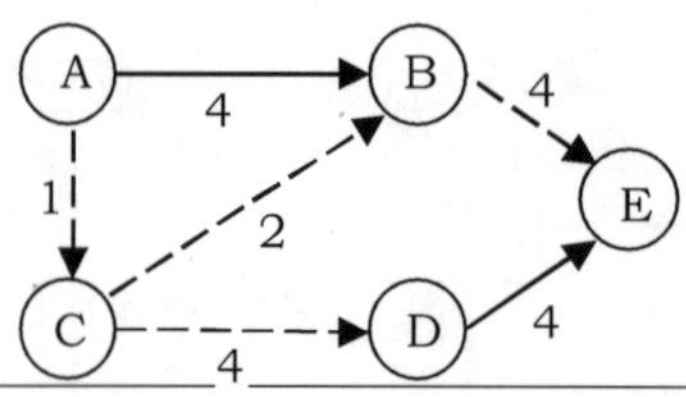

The final minimum cost tree which Dijkstra's algorithm generates is:

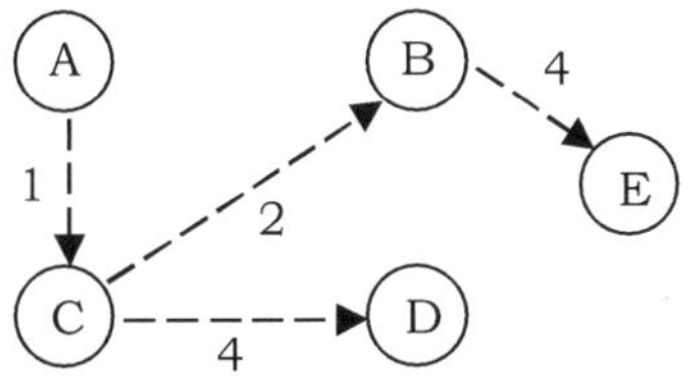


```
package main
import (
	"container/heap"
	"fmt"
)
// Nonnegative integer ID of vertex
type Vertex int
// A Priority Queue implements heap.Interface and holds Items.
type PriorityQueue struct {
	items []Vertex
	// value to index
	m map[Vertex]int
	// value to priority
	pr map[Vertex]int
}
func (pq *PriorityQueue) Len() int          { return len(pq.items) }
func (pq *PriorityQueue) Less(i, j int) bool { return pq.pr[pq.items[i]] < pq.pr[pq.items[j]] }
func (pq *PriorityQueue) Swap(i, j int) {
	pq.items[i], pq.items[j] = pq.items[j], pq.items[i]
	pq.m[pq.items[i]] = i
	pq.m[pq.items[j]] = j
}
func (pq *PriorityQueue) Push(x interface{}) {
	n := len(pq.items)
	item := x.(Vertex)
	pq.m[item] = n
	pq.items = append(pq.items, item)
}
func (pq *PriorityQueue) Pop() interface{} {
	old := pq.items
	n := len(old)
	item := old[n-1]
	pq.m[item] = -1
	pq.items = old[0 : n-1]
	return item
}
// update modifies the priority of an item in the queue.
func (pq *PriorityQueue) update(item Vertex, priority int) {
	pq.pr[item] = priority
	heap.Fix(pq, pq.m[item])
}
func (pq *PriorityQueue) addWithPriority(item Vertex, priority int) {
	heap.Push(pq, item)
	pq.update(item, priority)
}
const (
	Infinity      = int(^uint(0) >> 1)   // maximum integer
	Uninitialized = -1                   // indicates not yet processed the vertex
)
func Dijkstra(G Graph, source Vertex) (distance map[Vertex]int, previous map[Vertex]Vertex) {
	distance = make(map[Vertex]int)
```

```
	previous = make(map[Vertex]Vertex)
	distance[source] = 0
	q := &PriorityQueue{[]Vertex{}, make(map[Vertex]int), make(map[Vertex]int)}
	for _, v := range G.Vertices() {
		if v != source {
			distance[v] = Infinity
		}
		previous[v] = Uninitialized
		q.addWithPriority(v, distance[v])
	}
	for len(q.items) != 0 {
		u := heap.Pop(q).(Vertex)
		for _, v := range G.Neighbors(u) {
			alt := distance[u] + G.Weight(u, v)
			if alt < distance[v] {
				distance[v] = alt
				previous[v] = u
				q.update(v, alt)
			}
		}
	}
	return distance, previous
}
// A Graph is the interface implemented by graphs that this algorithm can run on.
type Graph interface {
	Vertices() []Vertex
	Neighbors(v Vertex) []Vertex
	Weight(u, v Vertex) int
}
// AdjacencyMap is a graph of strings that satisfies the Graph interface.
type AdjacencyMap struct {
	ids   map[string]Vertex
	names map[Vertex]string
	edges map[Vertex]map[Vertex]int
}
func NewGraph(ids map[string]Vertex) AdjacencyMap {
	G := AdjacencyMap{ids: ids}
	G.names = make(map[Vertex]string)
	for k, v := range ids {
		G.names[v] = k
	}
	G.edges = make(map[Vertex]map[Vertex]int)
	return G
}
func (G AdjacencyMap) AddEdge(u, v string, w int) {
	if _, ok := G.edges[G.ids[u]]; !ok {
		G.edges[G.ids[u]] = make(map[Vertex]int)
	}
	G.edges[G.ids[u]][G.ids[v]] = w
}
func (G AdjacencyMap) GetPath(v Vertex, previous map[Vertex]Vertex) (path string) {
	path = G.names[v]
	for previous[v] >= 0 {
		v = previous[v]
		path = G.names[v] + path
	}
	return path
}
func (G AdjacencyMap) Vertices() (vertices []Vertex) {
	for _, v := range G.ids {
		vertices = append(vertices, v)
```

```
	}
	return vertices
}
func (G AdjacencyMap) Neighbors(u Vertex) (vertices []Vertex) {
	for v := range G.edges[u] {
		vertices = append(vertices, v)
	}
	return vertices
}
func (G AdjacencyMap) Weight(u, v Vertex) int { return G.edges[u][v] }
func main() {
	G := NewGraph(map[string]Vertex{
		"a": 1,
		"b": 2,
		"c": 3,
		"d": 4,
		"e": 5,
		"f": 6,
	})
	G.AddEdge("a", "b", 7)
	G.AddEdge("a", "c", 9)
	G.AddEdge("a", "f", 14)
	G.AddEdge("b", "c", 10)
	G.AddEdge("b", "d", 15)
	G.AddEdge("c", "d", 11)
	G.AddEdge("c", "f", 2)
	G.AddEdge("d", "e", 6)
	G.AddEdge("e", "f", 9)
	distance, previous := Dijkstra(G, G.ids["a"])
	fmt.Printf("Distance to %s is %d, Path: %s\n", "e", distance[G.ids["e"]], G.GetPath(G.ids["e"], previous))
	fmt.Printf("Distance to %s is %d, Path: %s\n", "f", distance[G.ids["f"]], G.GetPath(G.ids["f"], previous))
}
```

Performance

In Dijkstra's algorithm, the efficiency depends on the number of deleteMins (V deleteMins) and updates for priority queues (E updates) that are used. If a *standard binary heap* is used then the complexity is $O(ElogV)$. The term $ElogV$ comes from E updates (each update takes $logV$) for the standard heap. If the set used is an array then the complexity is $O(E + V^2)$.

Notes on Dijkstra's Algorithm

- It uses greedy method: Always pick the next closest vertex to the source.
- It uses priority queue to store unvisited vertices by distance from s.
- It does not work with negative weights.

Difference between Unweighted Shortest Path and Dijkstra's Algorithm

1) To represent weights in the adjacency list, each vertex contains the weights of the edges (in addition to their identifier).
2) Instead of ordinary queue we use priority queue [distances are the priorities] and the vertex with the smallest distance is selected for processing.
3) The distance to a vertex is calculated by the sum of the weights of the edges on the path from the source to that vertex.
4) We update the distances in case the newly computed distance is smaller than the old distance which we have already computed.

Disadvantages of Dijkstra's Algorithm

- As discussed above, the major disadvantage of the algorithm is that it does a blind search, thereby wasting time and necessary resources.
- Another disadvantage is that it cannot handle negative edges. This leads to acyclic graphs and most often cannot obtain the right shortest path.

Relatives of Dijkstra's Algorithm

- The *Bellman–Ford* algorithm computes single-source shortest paths in a weighted digraph. It uses the same concept as that of *Dijkstra's* algorithm but can handle negative edges as well. It has more running time than *Dijkstra's* algorithm.
- Prim's algorithm finds a minimum spanning tree for a connected weighted graph. It implies that a subset of edges that form a tree where the total weight of all the edges in the tree is minimized.

Bellman-Ford Algorithm

The Bellman-Ford algorithm is a graph search algorithm that finds the shortest path between a given source vertex and all other vertices in the graph. This algorithm can be used on both weighted and unweighted graphs. Like Dijkstra's shortest path algorithm, the Bellman-Ford algorithm is guaranteed to find the shortest path in a graph. If the graph has negative edge costs, then *Dijkstra's* algorithm does not work.

Though it is slower than Dijkstra's algorithm, Bellman-Ford is capable of handling graphs that contain negative edge weights, so it is more versatile. It is worth noting that if there exists a negative cycle in the graph, then there is no shortest path. Going around the negative cycle an infinite number of times would continue to decrease the cost of the path (even though the path length is increasing). Because of this, Bellman-Ford can also detect negative cycles which is a useful feature. , Bellman-Ford computes shortest paths from a single source vertex to all of the other vertices in a weighted digraph with positive or negative edge weights.

The Bellman-Ford algorithm operates on an input graph, G, with |V| vertices and |E| edges. A single source vertex, s, must be provided as well, as the Bellman-Ford algorithm is a single-source shortest path algorithm. No destination vertex needs to be supplied, however, because Bellman-Ford calculates the shortest distance to all vertices in the graph from the source vertex.

The Bellman-Ford algorithm, like Dijkstra's algorithm, uses the principle of relaxation to find increasingly accurate path length. Bellman-Ford, though, tackles two main issues with this process:

1. If there are negative weight cycles, the search for a shortest path will go on forever.
2. Choosing a bad ordering for relaxations leads to exponential relaxations.

The detection of negative cycles is important, but the main contribution of this algorithm is in its ordering of relaxations. Relaxation is the most important step in Bellman-Ford. It is what increases the accuracy of the distance to any given vertex. Relaxation works by continuously shortening the calculated distance between vertices comparing that distance with other known distances.

Bellman Ford algorithm works by overestimating the length of the path from the starting vertex to all other vertices. Then it iteratively relaxes those estimates by finding new paths that are shorter than the previously overestimated paths. Take the baseball example. Let's say I think the distance to the baseball stadium is 30 miles. However, I know that the distance to the corner right before the stadium is 15 miles, and I know that from the corner to the stadium, the distance is 1 mile. Clearly, the distance from me to the stadium is at most 16 miles. So, I can update my belief to reflect that. That is one cycle of relaxation, and it's done over and over until the shortest paths are found.

The problem with *Dijkstra's* algorithm is that once a vertex u is declared known, it is possible that from some other, unknown vertex v there is a path back to u that is very negative. In such case, taking a path from s to v back to u is better than going from s to u without using v. A combination of Dijkstra's algorithm and unweighted algorithms will solve the problem. Initialize the queue with s. Then, at each stage, we *DeQueue* a vertex v. We find all vertices w adjacent to v such that,

$$distance\ to\ v\ +\ weight(v,w) < \text{old distance to w}$$

We update w old distance and path, and place w on a queue if it is not already there. A bit can be set for each vertex to indicate presence in the queue. We repeat the process until the queue is empty.

```
package main
import "fmt"
import (
    "errors"
)
const inf = int(^uint(0) >> 1)
var ErrNegativeCycle = errors.New("bellman: graph contains negative cycle")
var ErrNoPath = errors.New("bellman: no path to vertex")
type Edges []*Edge
// Pair of vertices.
type Edge struct {
    From, To string
```

```
    Distance int
}
type Vertices map[string]*Vertex
// Vertex with predecessor information.
type Vertex struct {
    Distance int
    From     string // predecessor
}
// ShortestPath finds shortest path from source to destination after calling Search.
func (paths Vertices) ShortestPath(src, dest string) ([]*Vertex, error) {
    if len(paths) == 0 {
        // Did you forget calling Search?
        return nil, ErrNoPath
    }
    var all []*Vertex
    pred := dest
    for pred != src {
        if v := paths[pred]; v != nil {
            pred = v.From
            all = append(all, v)
        } else {
            return nil, ErrNoPath
        }
    }
    return all, nil
}
// AddEdge for search.
func (rt *Edges) AddEdge(from, to string, distance int) {
    *rt = append(*rt, &Edge{From: from, To: to, Distance: distance})
}
// Search for single source shortest path.
func (rt Edges) Search(start string) (Vertices, error) {
    // Resulting table constains vertex name to Vertex struct mapping.
    // Use v.From predecessor to trace the path back.
    distances := make(Vertices)
    for _, p := range rt {
        distances[p.From] = &Vertex{inf, " "}
        distances[p.To] = &Vertex{inf, " "}
    }
    distances[start].Distance = 0
    // As many iterations as there are nodes.
    for i := 0; i < len(distances); i++ {
        var changed bool
        // Iterate over pairs.
        for _, pair := range rt {
            n := distances[pair.From]
            if n.Distance != inf {
                if distances[pair.To].Distance > n.Distance+pair.Distance {
                    distances[pair.To].Distance = n.Distance + pair.Distance
                    distances[pair.To].From = pair.From
                    changed = true
                }
            }
        }
        if !changed {
            // No more changes made. We done.
            break
        }
    }
    for _, pair := range rt {
```

```
        if distances[pair.From].Distance != inf &&
            distances[pair.To].Distance != inf &&
            distances[pair.From].Distance+pair.Distance < distances[pair.To].Distance {
            return nil, ErrNegativeCycle
        }
    }
    return distances, nil
}
```

This algorithm works if there are no negative-cost cycles. Each vertex can deQueue at most $|V|$ times, so the running time is $O(|E|.|V|)$ if adjacency lists are used.

Overview of Shortest Path Algorithms

Shortest path in unweighted graph [*Modified BFS*]	$O(\|E\| + \|V\|)$
Shortest path in weighted graph [*Dijkstra's*]	$O(\|E\| \log \|V\|)$
Shortest path in weighted graph with negative edges [*Bellman – Ford*]	$O(\|E\|.\|V\|)$
Shortest path in weighted acyclic graph	$O(\|E\| + \|V\|)$

9.8 Minimal Spanning Tree

The *spanning tree* of a graph is a subgraph that contains all the vertices and is also a tree. A graph may have many spanning trees. As an example, consider a graph with 4 vertices as shown below. Let us assume that the corners of the graph are vertices.

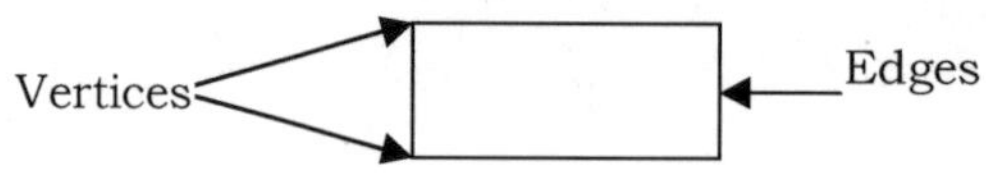

For this simple graph, we can have multiple spanning trees as shown below.

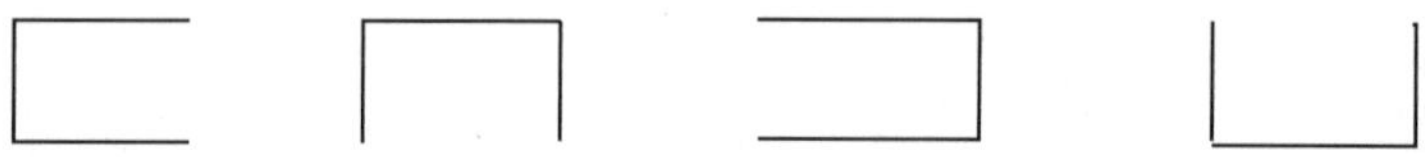

The cost of the spanning tree is the sum of the weights of all the edges in the tree. There can be many spanning trees. Minimum spanning tree is the spanning tree where the cost is minimum among all the spanning trees. There also can be many minimum spanning trees.

The algorithm we will discuss now is *minimum spanning tree* in an undirected graph. We assume that the given graphs are weighted graphs. If the graphs are unweighted graphs then we can still use the weighted graph algorithms by treating all weights as equal. A *minimum spanning tree* of an undirected graph G is a tree formed from graph edges that connect all the vertices of G with minimum total cost (weights). A minimum spanning tree exists only if the graph is connected. There are two famous algorithms for this problem:

- *Prim's* Algorithm
- *Kruskal's* Algorithm

Prim's Algorithm

Prim's algorithm also use *greedy* approach to find the minimum spanning tree. Prim's algorithm shares a similarity with the shortest path first algorithms. In Prim's algorithm we grow the spanning tree from a starting position. Prim's algorithm is almost same as Dijkstra's algorithm. Like in Dijkstra's algorithm, in Prim's algorithm also we keep values *distance* and *paths* in distance table. The only exception is that since the definition of *distance* is different and as a result the updating statement also changes little. The update statement is simpler than before.

In Prim's algorithm, we will start with an arbitrary node (it doesn't matter which one) and mark it. In each iteration we will mark a new vertex that is adjacent to the one that we have already marked. As a greedy algorithm, Prim's algorithm will select the cheapest edge and mark the vertex.

Algorithm

- Maintain two disjoint sets of vertices. One containing vertices that are in the growing spanning tree and other that are not in the growing spanning tree.
- Select the cheapest vertex that is connected to the growing spanning tree and is not in the growing spanning tree and add it into the growing spanning tree. This can be done using priority queues. Insert the vertices, that are connected to growing spanning tree, into the priority queue.
- Check for cycles. To do that, mark the nodes which have been already selected and insert only those nodes in the priority queue that are not marked.

```
func Prims(g *Graph) (*Tree, error) {
```

```
// this is an implementation of Prim's algorithm, which iterates
// through the graph and builds a tree, node by node by choosing the
// next node with the smallest edge that doesn't already exist in the tree.
// requiredNodes returns a map of all of the nodes that are required to build the MST.
requiredNodes := func() map[Node]interface{} {
    nodes := make(map[Node]interface{}, 0)
    iter := func(node Node) bool {
        nodes[node] = struct{}{}
        return true
    }
    g.IterNodes(iter)
    return nodes
}()
// otherNode returns the other node from an Edge; this is useful so we can parse
// the underlying datatype and compose things together as we have done thus far.
otherEdgeNode := func(node Node, e *edge) Node {
    if e.nodes[0] == node {
        return e.nodes[1]
    }
    return e.nodes[0]
}
tree := NewTree()
nodes := make([]Node, 0, len(requiredNodes))
current := func() Node {
    for key, _ := range requiredNodes {
        return key
    }
    // should never be called unless requiredNodes is empty
    return nil
}()
for {
    if len(nodes) == len(requiredNodes)-1 {
        break
    }
    nodeEdges, err := g.Get(current)
    if err != nil {
        return nil, err
    }
    poppedEdges := make([]*edge, 0, nodeEdges.Size())

    for {
        minHeapItem, err := nodeEdges.Pop()
        // if there is nothing to pop from the tree, then that means the algorithm is failing!
        if err != nil {
            return nil, fmt.Errorf("Unable to find a Node to continue building the tree")
        }
        minWeightEdge, ok := minHeapItem.(*edge)
        if !ok {
            log.Fatal("Programming error. Type assertion was attempted which is impossible")
        }
        poppedEdges = append(poppedEdges, minWeightEdge)
        newNode := otherEdgeNode(current, minWeightEdge)
        // if the insertion was successful, then we updated the tree successfully and can exit
        if err := tree.Insert(current, newNode, minWeightEdge); err == nil {
            // update the current iterator to the new node
            current = newNode
            nodes = append(nodes, newNode)
            break
        }
```

```
            }
            // we put all of the popped edges back into the heap, so this doesn't arbitrarily change the underlying
            // heap. Practically speaking, this is a bit of a code smell so this needs a little refactoring.
            for _, poppedEdge := range poppedEdges {
                nodeEdges.Insert(poppedEdge)
            }
        }
        return tree, nil
    }
```

The time complexity of the Prim's algorithm is $O((V + E)logV)$ because each vertex is inserted in the priority queue only once and insertion in priority queue take logarithmic time. The entire implementation of this algorithm is identical to that of Dijkstra's algorithm. The running time is $O(|V|^2)$ without heaps [good for dense graphs], and $O(ElogV)$ using binary heaps [good for sparse graphs].

Kruskal's Algorithm

Kruskal's algorithm is a minimum spanning tree algorithm that uses the *greedy* approach. This algorithm treats the graph as a forest and every node it has as an individual tree. A tree connects to another only and only if, it has the least cost among all available options and does not violate MST properties. Kruskal's Algorithm builds the spanning tree by adding edges one by one into a growing spanning tree.

The algorithm starts with V different trees (V is the vertices in the graph). While constructing the minimum spanning tree, every time Kruskal's algorithm selects an edge that has minimum weight and then adds that edge if it doesn't create a cycle. So, initially, there are |V| single-node trees in the forest. Adding an edge merges two trees into one. When the algorithm is completed, there will be only one tree, and that is the minimum spanning tree.

Algorithm

- Sort the graph edges with respect to their weights.
- Start adding edges to the minimum snapping tree from the edge with the smallest weight until the edge of the largest weight.
- Only add edges which doesn't form a cycle, edges which connect only disconnected components.

The greedy Choice is to put the smallest weight edge that does not because a cycle in the MST constructed so far.

There are two ways of implementing Kruskal's algorithm:

- By using disjoint sets: Using UNION and FIND operations
- By using priority queues: Maintains weights in priority queue

So now the question is how to check if vertices are connected or not?

This could be done using DFS which starts from the first vertex, then check if the second vertex is visited or not. But DFS will make time complexity large as it has an order of O(E+V) where V is the number of vertices, E is the number of edges. Disjoint sets are sets whose intersection is the empty set so it means that they don't have any element in common.

The appropriate data structure is the UNION/FIND algorithm [for implementing forests]. Two vertices belong to the same set if and only if they are connected in the current spanning forest. Each vertex is initially in its own set. If u and v are in the same set, the edge is rejected because it forms a cycle. Otherwise, the edge is accepted, and a UNION is performed on the two sets containing u and v.

As an example, consider the following graph (the edges show the weights).

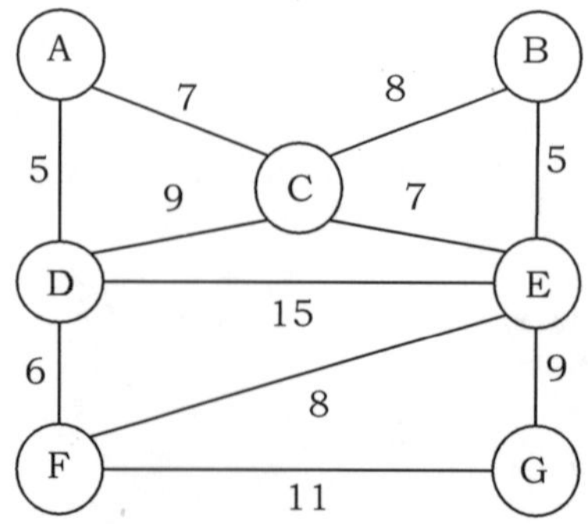

Now let us perform Kruskal's algorithm on this graph. We always select the edge which has minimum weight.

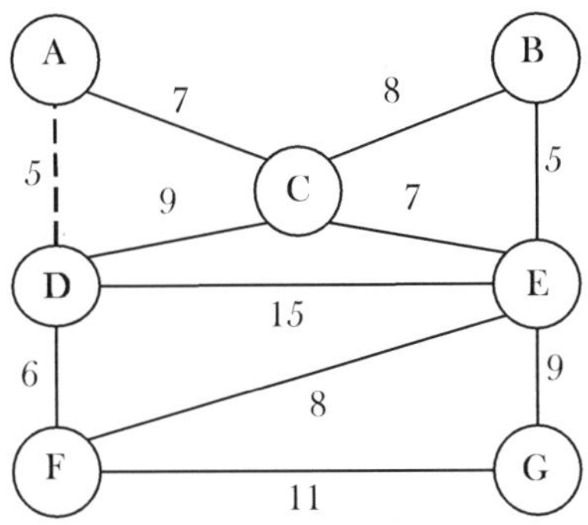

From the above graph, the edges which have minimum weight (cost) are: AD and BE. From these two we can select one of them and let us assume that we select AD (dotted line).

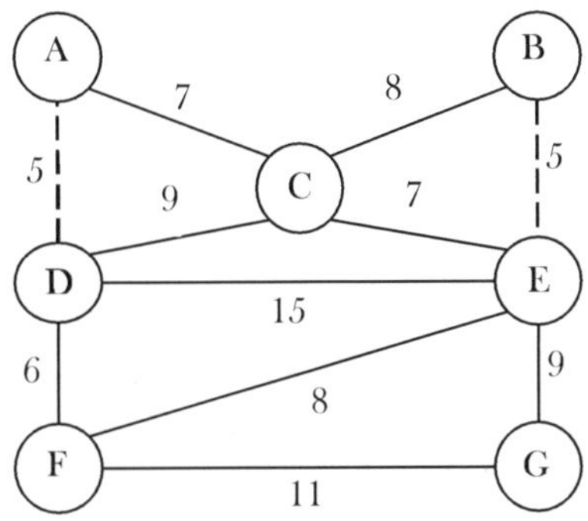

BE now has the lowest cost and we select it (dotted lines indicate selected edges).

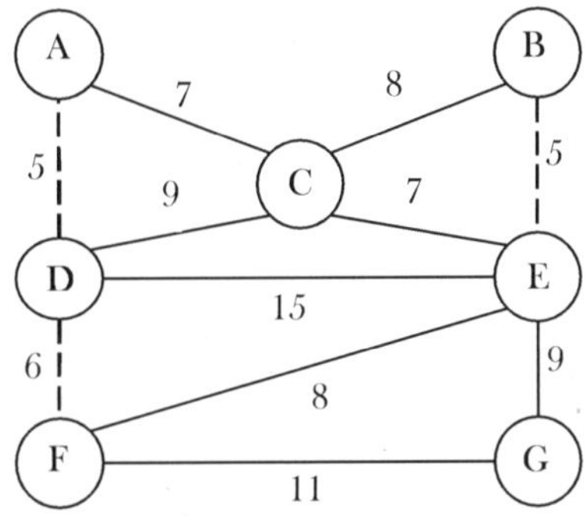

DF is the next edge that has the lowest cost (6).

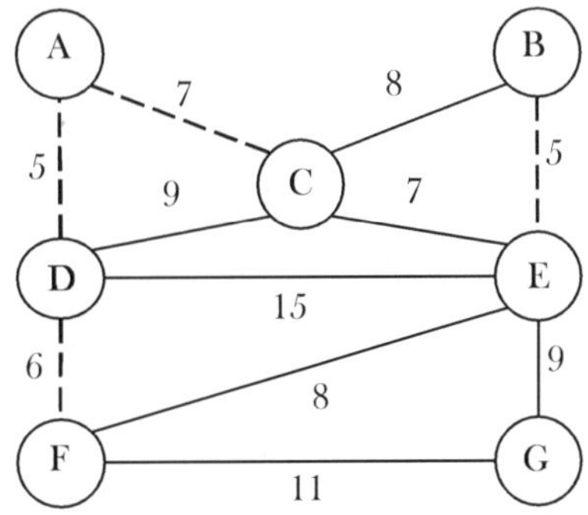

Next, AC and CE have the low cost of 7 and we select AC.

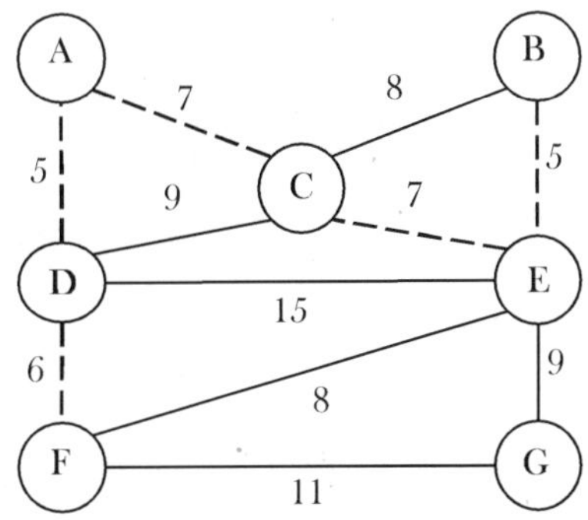

Then we select CE as its cost is 7 and it does not form a cycle.

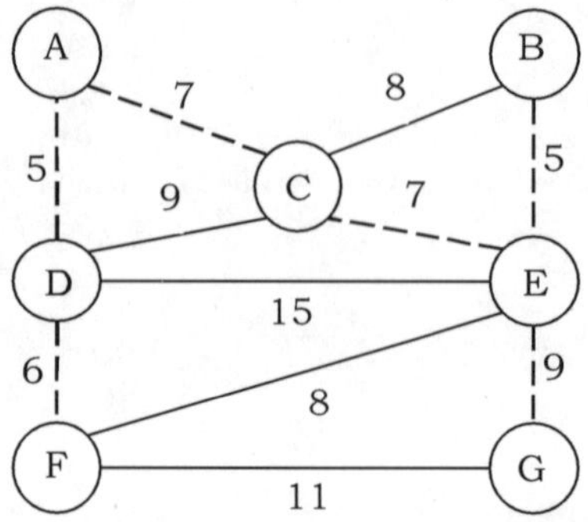

The next lowest cost edges are CB and EF. But if we select CB, then it forms a cycle. So, we discard it. This is also the case with EF. So, we should not select those two. And the next low cost is 9 (DC and EG). Selecting DC forms a cycle so we discard it. Adding EG will not form a cycle and therefore with this edge we complete all vertices of the graph.

```
// Refer Disjoin Sets chapter for implementation of sets
func Kruskals(G *Graph) {
    S = ф // At the end S will contain the edges of a minimum spanning trees
    for v := 0; v < G.V; v++ {
        MakeSet(v)
    }
    Sort edges of E by increasing weights w
    for true { // for each edge (u, v) in E { //from sorted list
        if FIND(u) ≠ FIND(v) {
            S = S ∪ {(u, v)}
            UNION(u, v)
        }
    }
    return S
}
```

Note: For implementation of UNION and FIND operations, refer to the *Disjoint Sets ADT* chapter.

The worst-case running time of this algorithm is $O(ElogE)$, which is dominated by the heap operations. That means, since we are constructing the heap with E edges, we need $O(ElogE)$ time to do that.

9.9 Graph Algorithms: Problems & Solutions

Problem-1 In an undirected simple graph with n vertices, what is the maximum number of edges? Self-loops are not allowed.

Solution: Since every node can connect to all other nodes, the first node can connect to $n-1$ nodes. The second node can connect to $n-2$ nodes [since one edge is already there from the first node]. The total number of edges is: $1 + 2 + 3 + \cdots + n - 1 = \frac{n(n-1)}{2}$ edges.

Problem-2 How many different adjacency matrices does a graph with n vertices and E edges have?

Solution: It's equal to the number of permutations of n elements. i.e., $n!$.

Problem-3 How many different adjacency lists does a graph with n vertices have?

Solution: It's equal to the number of permutations of edges. i.e., $E!$.

Problem-4 Which undirected graph representation is most appropriate for determining whether or not a vertex is isolated (is not connected to any other vertex)?

Solution: Adjacency List. If we use the adjacency matrix, then we need to check the complete row to determine whether that vertex has edges or not. By using the adjacency list, it is very easy to check, and it can be done just by checking whether that vertex has *nil* for next pointer or not [nil indicates that the vertex is not connected to any other vertex].

Problem-5 For checking whether there is a path from source s to target t, which one is best between disjoint sets and DFS?

Solution: The table below shows the comparison between disjoint sets and DFS. The entries in the table represent the case for any pair of nodes (for s and t).

Method	Processing Time	Query Time	Space
Union-Find	$V + E\ logV$	$logV$	V
DFS	$E + V$	1	$E + V$

Problem-6 What is the maximum number of edges a directed graph with n vertices can have and still not contain a directed cycle?

Solution: The number is V (V − 1)/2. Any directed graph can have at most n^2 edges. However, since the graph has no cycles it cannot contain a self-loop, and for any pair x, y of vertices, at most one edge from (x, y) and (y, x) can be included. Therefore the number of edges can be at most $(V^2 - V)/2$ as desired. It is possible to achieve V(V − 1)/2 edges. Label n nodes $1, 2 \ldots n$ and add an edge (x, y) if and only if $x < y$. This graph has the appropriate number of edges and cannot contain a cycle (any path visits an increasing sequence of nodes).

Problem-7 How many simple directed graphs with no parallel edges and self-loops are possible in terms of V?

Solution: (V) × (V − 1). Since, each *vertex can connect to* V − 1 *vertices without* self-loops.

Problem-8 What are the differences between DFS and BFS?

Solution:

DFS	BFS
Backtracking is possible from a dead end.	Backtracking is not possible.
Vertices from which exploration is incomplete are processed in a LIFO order	The vertices to be explored are organized as a FIFO queue.
The search is done in one particular direction	The vertices at the same level are maintained in parallel.

Problem-9 Earlier in this chapter, we discussed minimum spanning tree algorithms. Now, give an algorithm for finding the maximum-weight spanning tree in a graph.

Solution:

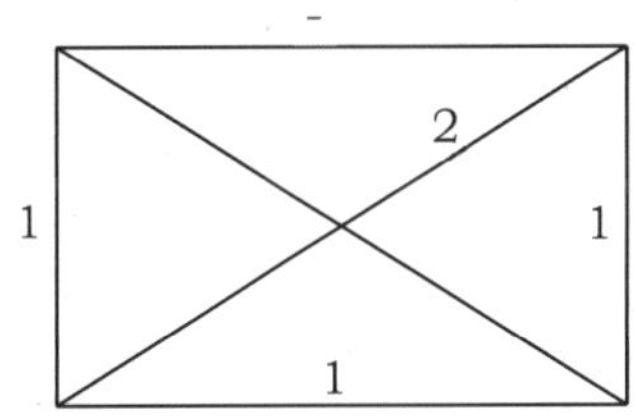

Given graph

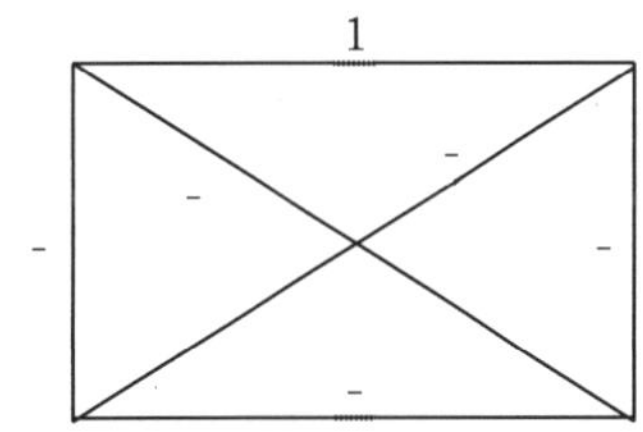

Transformed graph with negative edge

Using the given graph, construct a new graph with the same nodes and edges. But instead of using the same weights, take the negative of their weights. That means, weight of an edge = negative of weight of the corresponding edge in the given graph. Now, we can use existing *minimum spanning tree* algorithms on this new graph. As a result, we will get the maximum-weight spanning tree in the original one.

Problem-10 Give an algorithm for checking whether a given graph G has simple path from source s to destination d. Assume the graph G is represented using the adjacent matrix.

Solution: Let us assume that the structure for the graph is:

```
type Graph struct {
    V         int        //Number of vertices
    E         int        //Number of edges
    adjMatrix **int      //Two-dimensional array for storing the connections
}
```

For each vertex call *DFS* and check whether the current vertex is the same as the destination vertex or not. If they are the same, then return 1. Otherwise, call the *DFS* on its unvisited neighbors. One important thing to note here is that, we are calling the DFS algorithm on vertices which are not yet visited.

```
func HasSimplePath(G *Graph, s, d int) {
    Viisited[s] = true
    if s == d {
        return true
    }
    for t := 0; t < G.V; t++ {
        if G.adjMatrix[s][t] && !Viisited[t] {
            if DFS(G, t, d) {
                return true
            }
        }
    }
    return false
}
```

Time Complexity: O(E). In the above algorithm, for each node, since we are not calling DFS on all of its neighbors (discarding through if condition). Space Complexity: O(V).

Problem-11 Count simple paths for a given graph G has simple path from source s to destination d? Assume the graph is represented using the adjacent matrix.

Solution: Similar to the discussion in Problem-10, start at one node and call DFS on that node. As a result of this call, it visits all the nodes that it can reach in the given graph. That means it visits all the nodes of the connected component of that node. If there are any nodes that have not been visited, then again start at one of those nodes and call DFS.

Before the first DFS in each connected component, increment the connected components $count$. Continue this process until all of the graph nodes are visited. As a result, at the end we will get the total number of connected components. The implementation based on this logic is given below.

```
func CountSimplePaths(G *Graph, s, d int) {
    Viisited[s] = true
    if s == d {
        count++
        Visited[s] = false
        return
    }
    for t := 0; t < G.V; t++ {
        if G.adjMatrix[s][t] && !Viisited[t] {
            DFS(G, t, d)
            Visited[t] = false
        }
    }
}
```

Problem-12 **All pairs shortest path problem:** Find the shortest graph distances between every pair of vertices in a given graph. Let us assume that the given graph does not have negative edges.

Solution: The problem can be solved using n applications of $Dijkstra's$ algorithm. That means we apply $Dijkstra's$ algorithm on each vertex of the given graph. This algorithm does not work if the graph has edges with negative weights.

Problem-13 In Problem-12, how do we solve the all pairs shortest path problem if the graph has edges with negative weights?

Solution: This can be solved by using the $Floyd - Warshall\ algorithm$. This algorithm also works in the case of a weighted graph where the edges have negative weights. This algorithm is an example of Dynamic Programming – refer to the $Dynamic\ Programming$ chapter.

Problem-14 **DFS Application:** $Cut\ Vertex$ or $Articulation\ Points$.

Solution: In an undirected graph, a $cut\ vertex$ (or articulation point) is a vertex, and if we remove it, then the graph splits into two disconnected components. As an example, consider the following figure. Removal of the "D" vertex divides the graph into two connected components ($\{E, F\}$ and $\{A, B, C, G\}$).

Similarly, removal of the "C" vertex divides the graph into ($\{G\}$ and $\{A, B, D, E, F\}$). For this graph, A and C are the cut vertices.

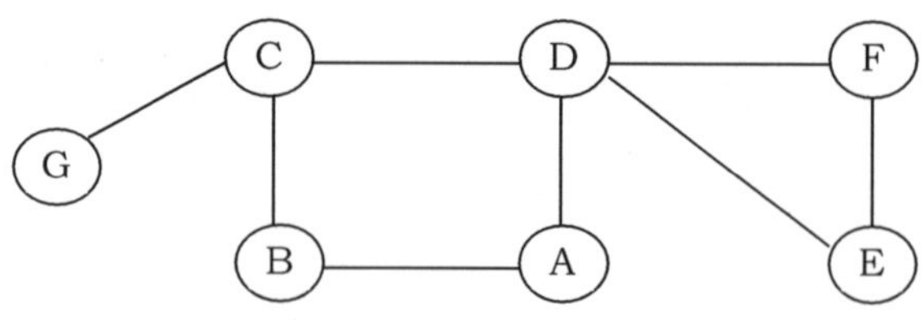

Note: A connected, undirected graph is called $bi - connected$ if the graph is still connected after removing any vertex.

DFS provides a linear-time algorithm (O(n)) to find all cut vertices in a connected graph. Starting at any vertex, call a DFS and number the nodes as they are visited. For each vertex v, we call this DFS number $dfsnum$(v). The tree generated with DFS traversal is called $DFS\ spanning\ tree$. Then, for every vertex v in the DFS spanning tree, we compute the lowest-numbered vertex, which we call $low(v)$, that is reachable from v by taking zero or more tree edges and then possibly one back edge (in that order).

Based on the above discussion, we need the following information for this algorithm: the $dfsnum$ of each vertex in the DFS tree (once it gets visited), and for each vertex v, the lowest depth of neighbors of all descendants of v in the DFS tree, called the low.

The $dfsnum$ can be computed during DFS. The low of v can be computed after visiting all descendants of v (i.e., just before v gets popped off the DFS stack) as the minimum of the $dfsnum$ of all neighbors of v (other than the parent of v in the DFS tree) and the low of all children of v in the DFS tree.

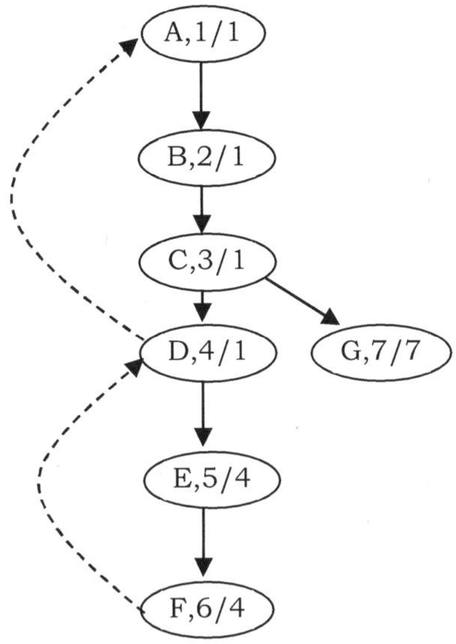

The root vertex is a cut vertex if and only if it has at least two children. A non-root vertex u is a cut vertex if and only if there is a son v of u such that $low(v) \geq dfsnum(u)$. This property can be tested once the DFS is returned from every child of u (that means, just before u gets popped off the DFS stack), and if true, u separates the graph into different bi-connected components. This can be represented by computing one bi-connected component out of every such v (a component which contains v will contain the sub-tree of v, plus u), and then erasing the sub-tree of v from the tree.

For the given graph, the DFS tree with $dfsnum/low$ can be given as shown in the figure below. The implementation for the above discussion is:

```
var dfsnum, low []int
var num int = 0
func CutVertices(u int) {
    low[u], dfsnum[u] = num, num
    num++
    for v := 0; v < 256; v++ {
        if adjMatrix[u][v] && dfsnum[v] == -1 {
            CutVertices(v)
            if low[v] > dfsnum[u] {
                fmt.Printff("Cut Vetex:%d", u)
            }
            low[u] = min(low[u], low[v])
        } else {          // (u,v) is a back edge
            low[u] = min(low[u], dfsnum[v])
        }
    }
}
```

Problem-15 Let G be a connected graph of order n. What is the maximum number of cut-vertices that G can contain?

Solution: $n - 2$. As an example, consider the following graph. In the graph below, except for the vertices 1 and n, all the remaining vertices are cut vertices. This is because removing 1 and n vertices does not split the graph into two. This is a case where we can get the maximum number of cut vertices.

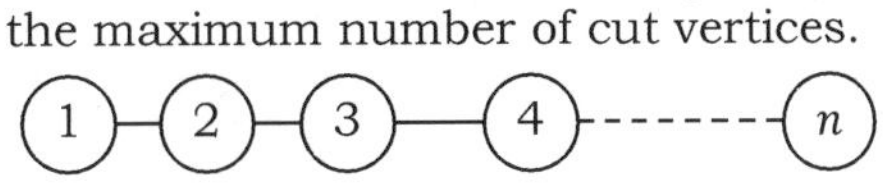

Problem-16 **DFS Application:** *Cut Bridges* or *Cut Edges*

Solution: Definition: Let G be a connected graph. An edge uv in G is called a *bridge* of G if $G - uv$ is disconnected. As an example, consider the following graph.

In the above graph, if we remove the edge uv then the graph splits into two components. For this graph, uv is a bridge. The discussion we had for cut vertices holds good for bridges also. The only change is, instead of printing the vertex, we give the edge. The main observation is that an edge (u, v) cannot be a bridge if it is part of a cycle. If (u, v) is not part of a cycle, then it is a bridge.

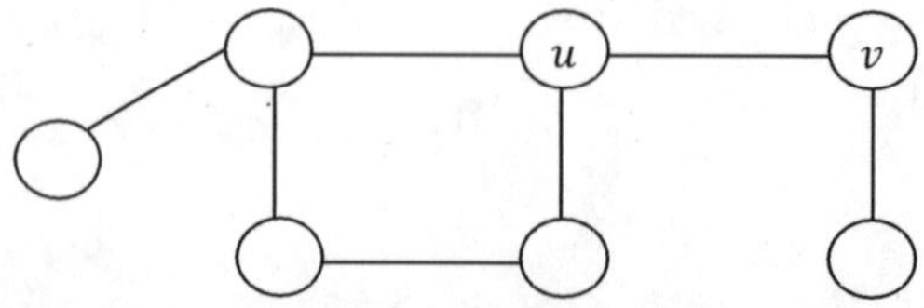

We can detect cycles in *DFS* by the presence of back edges. (u, v) is a bridge if and only if none of v or v's children has a back edge to u or any of u's ancestors. To detect whether any of v's children has a back edge to u's parent, we can use a similar idea as above to see what is the smallest $dfsnum$ reachable from the subtree rooted at v.

```
func Bridges(u int) {
    low[u], dfsnum[u] = num, num
    num++
    for v := 0; v < 256; v++ {
        if adjMatrix[u][v] && dfsnum[v] == -1 {
            Bridges(v)
            if low[v] > dfsnum[u] {
                fmt.Printff("Cut Vetex:%d", u)
            }
            low[u] = min(low[u], low[v])
        } else { // (u,v) is a back edge
            low[u] = min(low[u], dfsnum[v])
        }
    }
}
```

Problem-17 **DFS Application:** Discuss *Euler* Circuits

Solution: Before discussing this problem let us see the terminology:

- *Eulerian tour* – a path that contains all edges without repetition.
- *Eulerian circuit* – a path that contains all edges without repetition and starts and ends in the same vertex.
- *Eulerian graph* – a graph that contains an Eulerian circuit.
- *Even vertex*: a vertex that has an even number of incident edges.
- *Odd vertex*: a vertex that has an odd number of incident edges.

Euler circuit: For a given graph we have to reconstruct the circuits using a pen, drawing each line exactly once. We should not lift the pen from the paper while drawing. That means, we must find a path in the graph that visits every edge exactly once and this problem is called an *Euler path* (also called *Euler tour*) or *Euler circuit problem.* This puzzle has a simple solution based on DFS.

An *Euler* circuit exists if and only if the graph is connected and the number of neighbors of each vertex is even. Start with any node, select any untraversed outgoing edge, and follow it. Repeat until there are no more remaining unselected outgoing edges. For example, consider the following graph: A legal Euler Circuit of this graph is 0 1 3 4 1 2 3 5 4 2 0.

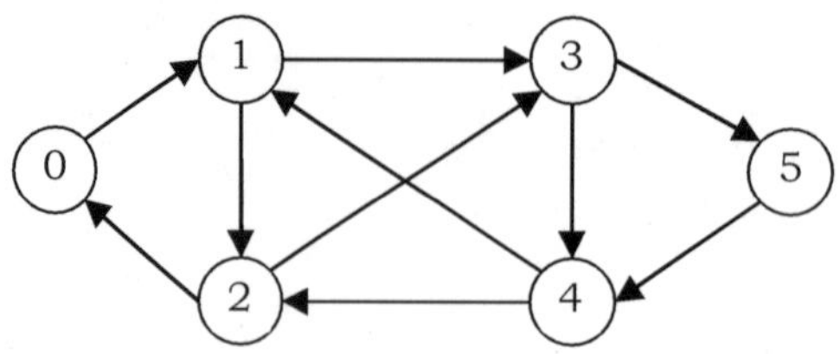

If we start at vertex 0, we can select the edge to vertex 1, then select the edge to vertex 2, then select the edge to vertex 0. There are now no remaining unchosen edges from vertex 0:

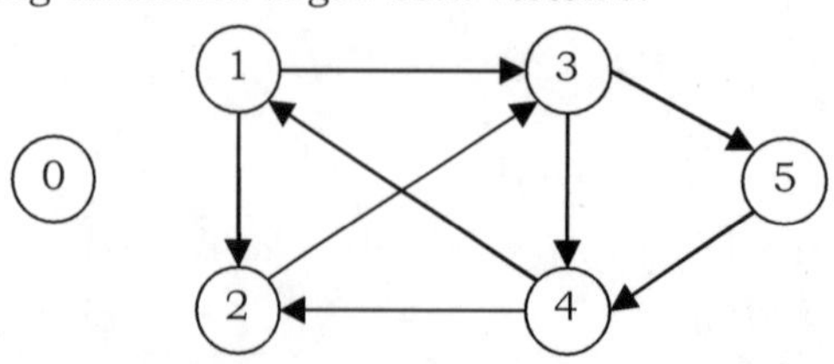

We now have a circuit 0,1,2,0 that does not traverse every edge. So, we pick some other vertex that is on that circuit, say vertex 1. We then do another depth first search of the remaining edges. Say we choose the edge to node 3, then 4, then 1. Again we are stuck. There are no more unchosen edges from node 1. We now splice this path 1,3,4,1 into the old path 0,1,2,0 to get: 0,1,3,4,1,2,0. The unchosen edges now look like this:

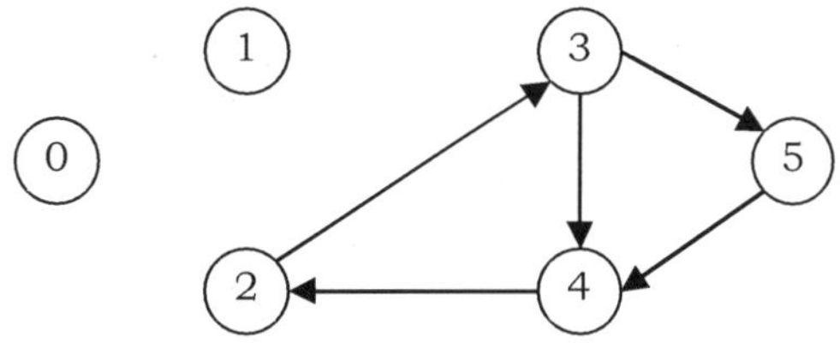

We can pick yet another vertex to start another DFS. If we pick vertex 2, and splice the path 2,3,5,4,2, then we get the final circuit 0,1,3,4,1,2,3,5,4,2,0.

A similar problem is to find a simple cycle in an undirected graph that visits every vertex. This is known as the *Hamiltonian cycle problem*. Although it seems almost identical to the *Euler* circuit problem, no efficient algorithm for it is known.

Notes:

- A connected undirected graph is *Eulerian* if and only if every graph vertex has an even degree, or exactly two vertices with an odd degree.
- A directed graph is *Eulerian* if it is strongly connected and every vertex has an equal *in* and *out* degree.

Application: A postman has to visit a set of streets in order to deliver mails and packages. He needs to find a path that starts and ends at the post-office, and that passes through each street (edge) exactly once. This way the postman will deliver mails and packages to all the necessary streets, and at the same time will spend minimum time/effort on the road.

Problem-18 **DFS Application:** Finding Strongly Connected Components.

Solution: This is another application of DFS. In a directed graph, two vertices u and v are strongly connected if and only if there exists a path from u to v and there exists a path from v to u. The strong connectedness is an equivalence relation.

- A vertex is strongly connected with itself
- If a vertex u is strongly connected to a vertex v, then v is strongly connected to u
- If a vertex u is strongly connected to a vertex v, and v is strongly connected to a vertex x, then u is strongly connected to x

What this says is, for a given directed graph we can divide it into strongly connected components. This problem can be solved by performing two depth-first searches. With two DFS searches we can test whether a given directed graph is strongly connected or not. We can also produce the subsets of vertices that are strongly connected.

Algorithm

- Perform DFS on given graph G.
- Number vertices of given graph G according to a post-order traversal of depth-first spanning forest.
- Construct graph G_r by reversing all edges in G.
- Perform DFS on G_r: Always start a new DFS (initial call to Visit) at the highest-numbered vertex.
- Each tree in the resulting depth-first spanning forest corresponds to a strongly-connected component.

Why this algorithm works?

Let us consider two vertices, v and w. If they are in the same strongly connected component, then there are paths from v to w and from w to v in the original graph G, and hence also in G_r. If two vertices v and w are not in the same depth-first spanning tree of G_r, clearly they cannot be in the same strongly connected component. As an example, consider the graph shown below on the left. Let us assume this graph is G.

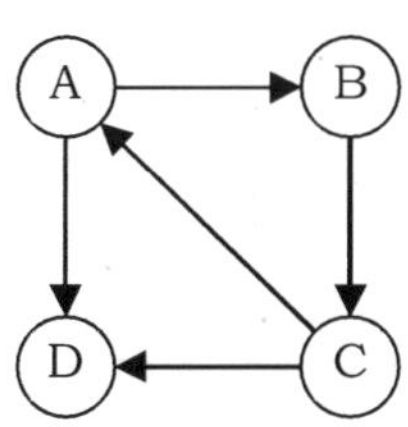

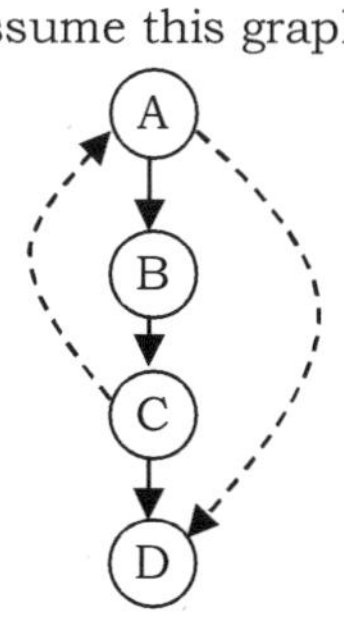

Now, as per the algorithm, performing *DFS* on this G graph gives the following diagram. The dotted line from C to A indicates a back edge.

Now, performing post order traversal on this tree gives: D, C, B and A.

Vertex	Post Order Number
A	4
B	3
C	2
D	1

Now reverse the given graph G and call it G_r and at the same time assign postorder numbers to the vertices. The reversed graph G_r will look like:

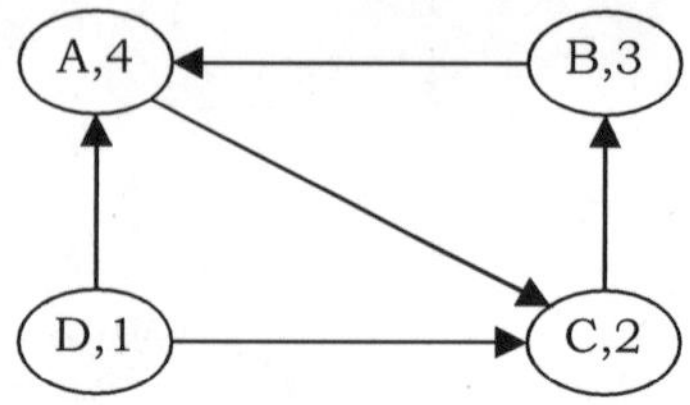

The last step is performing DFS on this reversed graph G_r. While doing DFS, we need to consider the vertex which has the largest DFS number. So, first we start at A and with DFS we go to C and then B. At B, we cannot move further. This says that $\{A, B, C\}$ is a strongly connected component. Now the only remaining element is D and we end our second DFS at D. So the connected components are: $\{A, B, C\}$ and $\{D\}$.

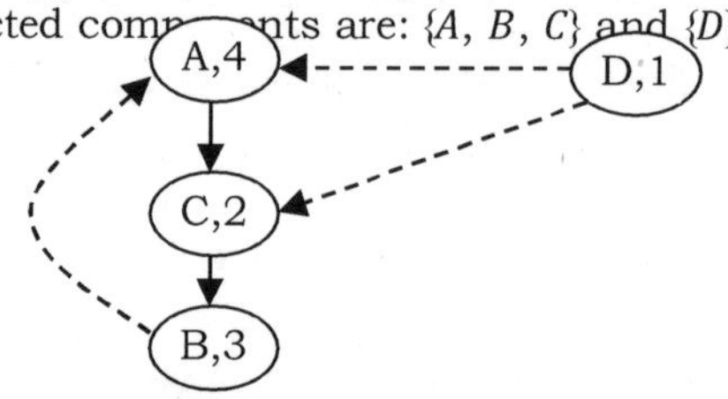

The implementation based on this discussion can be shown as:

```
package main
import (
    "fmt"
)
type Stmt struct {
    Name  string
    After []string
}
func main() {
    dependencies := []Stmt{
        {Name: "A", After: []string{"W"}},
        {Name: "B", After: []string{}},
        {Name: "C", After: []string{"W"}},
        {Name: "D", After: []string{"C", "A"}},
        {Name: "E", After: []string{"C", "L"}},
        {Name: "F", After: []string{"C", "N"}},
        {Name: "G", After: []string{"C", "R"}},
        {Name: "H", After: []string{"C", "T"}},
        {Name: "I", After: []string{"C", "V"}},
        {Name: "J", After: []string{"W"}},
        {Name: "K", After: []string{"C", "T"}},
        {Name: "L", After: []string{"W"}},
        {Name: "M", After: []string{"C", "A"}},
        {Name: "N", After: []string{}},
        {Name: "O", After: []string{"W"}},
        {Name: "P", After: []string{}},
        {Name: "Q", After: []string{}},
        {Name: "O", After: []string{"W"}},
        {Name: "R", After: []string{"W"}},
        {Name: "S", After: []string{}},
        {Name: "T", After: []string{"S"}},
        {Name: "U", After: []string{}},
        {Name: "V", After: []string{"W"}},
        {Name: "W", After: []string{}},
        {Name: "X", After: []string{"W", "Q"}},
```

```
	}
	G := make(Graph)
	for _, s := range dependencies {
		G[s.Name] = after(s.After)
	}
	t := newTarjan(G)
	for _, s := range t.sccs {
		fmt.Println(s)
	}
}
// Graph is an edge list representation of a Graph.
type Graph map[string]set
// set is an integer set.
type set map[string]struct{}
func after(i []string) set {
	if len(i) == 0 {
		return nil
	}
	s := make(set)
	for _, v := range i {
		s[v] = struct{}{}
	}
	return s
}
// tarjan implements Tarjan's strongly connected component finding algorithm.
type tarjan struct {
	G Graph
	index      int
	indexTable map[string]int
	lowLink    map[string]int
	onStack    map[string]bool
	stack []string
	sccs [][]string
}
// newTarjan returns a tarjan with the sccs field filled with the
// strongly connected components of the directed Graph G.
func newTarjan(G Graph) *tarjan {
	t := tarjan{
		G: G,
		indexTable: make(map[string]int, len(G)),
		lowLink:    make(map[string]int, len(G)),
		onStack:    make(map[string]bool, len(G)),
	}
	for v := range t.G {
		if t.indexTable[v] == 0 {
			t.strongconnect(v)
		}
	}
	return &t
}
// strongconnect is the strongconnect function described in the
// wikipedia article.
func (t *tarjan) strongconnect(v string) {
	// Set the depth index for v to the smallest unused index.
	t.index++
	t.indexTable[v] = t.index
	t.lowLink[v] = t.index
	t.stack = append(t.stack, v)
	t.onStack[v] = true
```

```
        // Consider successors of v.
        for w := range t.G[v] {
            if t.indexTable[w] == 0 {
                // Successor w has not yet been visited; recur on it.
                t.strongconnect(w)
                t.lowLink[v] = min(t.lowLink[v], t.lowLink[w])
            } else if t.onStack[w] {
                // Successor w is in stack s and hence in the current SCC.
                t.lowLink[v] = min(t.lowLink[v], t.indexTable[w])
            }
        }
        // If v is a root node, pop the stack and generate an SCC.
        if t.lowLink[v] == t.indexTable[v] {
            // Start a new strongly connected component.
            var (
                scc []string
                w   string
            )
            for {
                w, t.stack = t.stack[len(t.stack)-1], t.stack[:len(t.stack)-1]
                t.onStack[w] = false
                // Add w to current strongly connected component.
                scc = append(scc, w)
                if w == v {
                    break
                }
            }
            // Output the current strongly connected component.
            t.sccs = append(t.sccs, scc)
        }
    }
    func min(a, b int) int {
        if a < b {
            return a
        }
        return b
    }
```

Problem-19 Count the number of connected components of Graph G which is represented in the adjacent matrix.

Solution: This problem can be solved with one extra counter in *DFS*.

```
    // Visited[] is a global array.
    var Visited []bool
    func DFS(G *Graph, u int) {
        Visited[u] = true
        for v := 0; v < G.V; v++ {
            // For example, if the adjacency matrix is used for representing the
            //      graph, then the condition to be used for finding unvisited adjacent
            //      vertex of u  is: if( !Visited[v] && G.Adj[u][v] )
            for each unvisited adjacent node v of u {
                DFS(G, v)
            }
        }
    }
    func DFSTraversal(G *Graph) {
        count := 0
        for i := 0; i < G.V; i++ {
            Visited[i] = false
        }
        //This loop is required if the graph has more than one component
        for i := 0; i < G.V; i++ {
            if !Visited[i] {
                DFS(G, i)
```

```
            count++
        }
    }
    return count
}
```

Time Complexity: Same as that of DFS and it depends on implementation. With adjacency matrix the complexity is $O(|E| + |V|)$ and with adjacency matrix the complexity is $O(|V|^2)$.

Problem-20 Can we solve the Problem-19, using BFS?

Solution: Yes. This problem can be solved with one extra counter in BFS.

```
// Visited[] is a global array.
var Visited []bool
func BFS(G *Graph, u int) {
    Q := CreateQueue()
    Q.EnQueue(Q, u)
    for !Q.IsEmpty(Q) {
        u = Q.DeQueue()
        Process u //For example, print
        Visited[s] = true
        /* For example, if the adjacency matrix is used for representing the
          graph, then the condition be used for finding unvisited adjacent
          vertex of u  is: if( !Visited[v] && G.Adj[u][v] ) */
        for each unvisited adjacent node v of u {
            Q.EnQueue(v)
        }
    }
}
func BFSTraversal(G *Graph) {
    for i := 0; i < G.V; i++ {
        Visited[i] = false
    }
    // This loop is required if the graph has more than one component
    for i := 0; i < G.V; i++ {
        if !Visited[i] {
            BFS(G, i)
        }
    }
}
```

Time Complexity: Same as that of *BFS* and it depends on implementation. With adjacency matrix the complexity is $O(|E| + |V|)$ and with adjacency matrix the complexity is $O(|V|^2)$.

Problem-21 Let us assume that $G(V, E)$ is an undirected graph. Give an algorithm for finding a spanning tree which takes $O(|E|)$ time complexity (not necessarily a minimum spanning tree).

Solution: The test for a cycle can be done in constant time, by marking vertices that have been added to the set S. An edge will introduce a cycle, if both its vertices have already been marked.

Algorithm:

```
S = {}; //Assume S is a set
for each edge e ∈ E {
        if(adding e to S doesn't form a cycle) {
                add e to S
                mark e
        }
}
```

Problem-22 Is there any other way of solving Problem-20?

Solution: Yes. We can run *BFS* and find the *BFS* tree for the graph (level order tree of the graph). Then start at the root element and keep moving to the next levels and at the same time we have to consider the nodes in the next level only once. That means, if we have a node with multiple input edges then we should consider only one of them; otherwise they will form a cycle.

Problem-23 Detecting a cycle in an undirected graph

Solution: An undirected graph is acyclic if and only if a *DFS* yields no back edges, edges (u, v) where v has already been discovered and is an ancestor of u.

- Execute *DFS* on the graph.
- If there is a back edge - the graph has a cycle.

If the graph does not contain a cycle, then $|E| < |V|$ and *DFS* cost $O(|V|)$. If the graph contains a cycle, then a back edge is discovered after $2|V|$ steps at most.

Problem-24 Detecting a cycle in DAG

Solution:

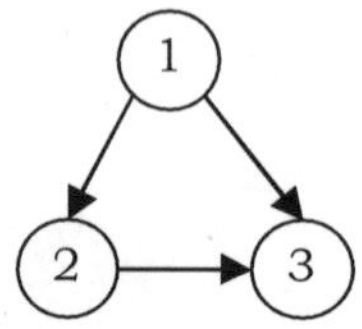

Cycle detection on a graph is different than on a tree. This is because in a graph, a node can have multiple parents. In a tree, the algorithm for detecting a cycle is to do a depth first search, marking nodes as they are encountered. If a previously marked node is seen again, then a cycle exists. This won't work on a graph. Let us consider the graph shown in the figure below. If we use a tree cycle detection algorithm, then it will report the wrong result. That means that this graph has a cycle in it. But the given graph does not have a cycle in it. This is because node 3 will be seen twice in a *DFS* starting at node 1.

The cycle detection algorithm for trees can easily be modified to work for graphs. The key is that in a *DFS* of an acyclic graph, a node whose descendants have all been visited can be seen again without implying a cycle. But, if a node is seen for the second time before all its descendants have been visited, then there must be a cycle. Can you see why this is? Suppose there is a cycle containing node A. This means that A must be reachable from one of its descendants. So when the *DFS* is visiting that descendant, it will see *A* again, before it has finished visiting all of *A's* descendants. So there is a cycle. In order to detect cycles, we can modify the depth first search.

```
func DetectCycle(G *Graph) bool {
    for i := 0; i < G.V; i++ {
        Visited[s] = 0
        Predecessor[i] = 0
    }
    for i := 0; i < G.V; i++ {
        if !Visited[i] && HasCycle(G, i) {
            return true
        }
    }
    return false
}
func HasCycle(G *Graph, u int) bool {
    Visited[u] = 1
    for i := 0; i < G.V; i++ {
        if G.Adj[s][i] {
            if Predecessor[i] != u && Visited[i] {
                return 1
            } else {
                Predecessor[i] = u
                return HasCycle(G, i)
            }
        }
    }
    return 0
}
```

Time Complexity: $O(V + E)$.

Problem-25 Given a directed acyclic graph, give an algorithm for finding its depth.

Solution: If it is an undirected graph, we can use the simple unweighted shortest path algorithm (check *Shortest Path Algorithms* section). We just need to return the highest number among all distances. For directed acyclic graph, we can solve by following the similar approach which we used for finding the depth in trees. In trees, we have solved this problem using level order traversal (with one extra special symbol to indicate the end of the level).

```
func DepthInDAG(G *Graph) int {
    Q := CreateQueue(1) // Refer Queues chapter for implementation details of a Queue
    counter := 0
    for v := 0; v < G.V; v++ {
        if indegree[v] == 0 {
            Q.EnQueue(v)
        }
        Q.EnQueue('$')
    }
    for !Q.IsEmpty() {
        v = Q.DeQueue()
        if v == '$' {
            counter++
            if !Q.IsEmpty() {
                Q.EnQueue('$')
            }
        }
        for each w adjacent to v {
            indegree[w] = indegree[w] - 1
            if indegree[w] == 0 {
                Q.EnQueue(W)
            }
        }
        Q.DeleteQueue()
        return counter
    }
}
```

Total running time is $O(V + E)$.

Problem-26 How many topological sorts of the following dag are there?

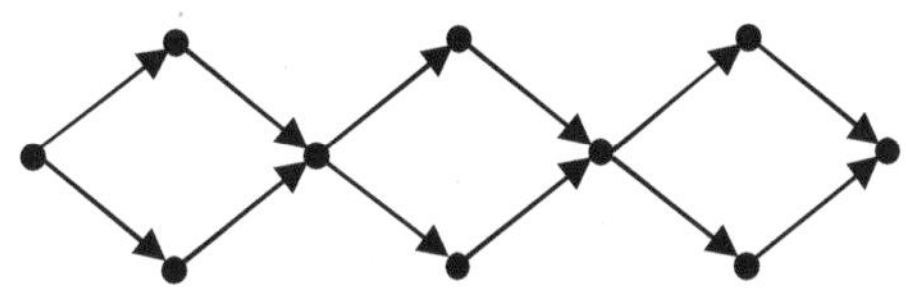

Solution: If we observe the above graph there are three stages with 2 vertices. In the early discussion of this chapter, we saw that topological sort picks the elements with zero indegree at any point of time. At each of the two vertices stages, we can first process either the top vertex or the bottom vertex. As a result, at each of these stages we have two possibilities. So the total number of possibilities is the multiplication of possibilities at each stage and that is, $2 \times 2 \times 2 = 8$.

Problem-27 **Unique topological ordering:** Design an algorithm to determine whether a directed graph has a unique topological ordering.

Solution: A directed graph has a unique topological ordering if and only if there is a directed edge between each pair of consecutive vertices in the topological order. This can also be defined as: a directed graph has a unique topological ordering if and only if it has a Hamiltonian path. If the digraph has multiple topological orderings, then a second topological order can be obtained by swapping a pair of consecutive vertices.

Problem-28 Let us consider the prerequisites for courses at *IIT Bombay*. Suppose that all prerequisites are mandatory, every course is offered every semester, and there is no limit to the number of courses we can take in one semester. We would like to know the minimum number of semesters required to complete the major. Describe the data structure we would use to represent this problem, and outline a linear time algorithm for solving it.

Solution: Use a directed acyclic graph (DAG). The vertices represent courses and the edges represent the prerequisite relation between courses at *IIT Bombay*. It is a DAG, because the prerequisite relation has no cycles.

The number of semesters required to complete the major is one more than the longest path in the dag. This can be calculated on the DFS tree recursively in linear time. The longest path out of a vertex x is 0 if x has outdegree 0, otherwise it is $1 + max\ \{longest\ path\ out\ of\ y \mid (x, y)\ is\ an\ edge\ of\ G\}$.

Problem-29 At a university let's say *IIT Bombay*), there is a list of courses along with their prerequisites. That means, two lists are given:

A - Courses list

B – Prerequisites: B contains couples (x, y) where $x, y \in A$ indicating that course x can't be taken before course y.

Let us consider a student who wants to take only one course in a semester. Design a schedule for this student.

Example: A = {C-Lang, Data Structures, OS, CO, Algorithms, Design Patterns, Programming }. B = { (C-Lang, CO), (OS, CO), (Data Structures, Algorithms), (Design Patterns, Programming) }. *One possible schedule could be*:

Semester 1: Data Structures
Semester 2: Algorithms
Semester 3: C-Lang
Semester 4: OS
Semester 5: CO
Semester 6: Design Patterns
Semester 7: Programming

Solution: The solution to this problem is exactly the same as that of topological sort. Assume that the courses names are integers in the range $[1..n]$, n is known (n is not constant). The relations between the courses will be represented by a directed graph $G = (V, E)$, where V are the set of courses and if course i is prerequisite of course j, E will contain the edge (i, j). Let us assume that the graph will be represented as an Adjacency list.

First, let's observe another algorithm to topologically sort a DAG in O($|V| + |E|$).

- Find in-degree of all the vertices - O($|V| + |E|$)
- Repeat:
  Find a vertex v with in-degree=0 - O($|V|$)
  Output v and remove it from G, along with its edges - O($|V|$)
  Reduce the in-degree of each node u such as (v, u) was an edge in G and keep a list of vertices with in-degree=0 - O($degree(v)$)
  Repeat the process until all the vertices are removed

The time complexity of this algorithm is also the same as that of the topological sort and it is O($|V|$ + $|E|$).

Problem-30 In Problem-29, a student wants to take all the courses in A, in the minimal number of semesters. That means the student is ready to take any number of courses in a semester. Design a schedule for this scenario.
One possible schedule is:
Semester 1: C-Lang, OS, Design Patterns
Semester 2: Data Structures, CO, Programming
Semester 3: Algorithms

Solution: A variation of the above topological sort algorithm with a slight change: In each semester, instead of taking one subject, take all the subjects with zero indegree. That means, execute the algorithm on all the nodes with degree 0 (instead of dealing with one source in each stage, all the sources will be dealt and printed).

Time Complexity: O($|V|$ + $|E|$).

Problem-31 **LCA of a DAG:** Given a DAG and two vertices v and w, find the *lowest common ancestor* (LCA) of v and w. The LCA of v and w is an ancestor of v and w that has no descendants that are also ancestors of v and w.

Hint: Define the height of a vertex v in a DAG to be the length of the longest path from *root* to v. Among the vertices that are ancestors of both v and w, the one with the greatest height is an LCA of v and w.

Problem-32 **Shortest ancestral path:** Given a DAG and two vertices v and w, find the *shortest ancestral path* between v and w. An ancestral path between v and w is a common ancestor x along with a shortest path from v to x and a shortest path from w to x. The shortest ancestral path is the ancestral path whose total length is minimized.

Hint: Run BFS two times. First run from v and second time from w. Find a DAG where the shortest ancestral path goes to a common ancestor x that is not an LCA.

Problem-33 Let us assume that we have two graphs G_1 and G_2. How do we check whether they are isomorphic or not?

Solution: There are many ways of representing the same graph. As an example, consider the following simple graph. It can be seen that all the representations below have the same number of vertices and the same number of edges.

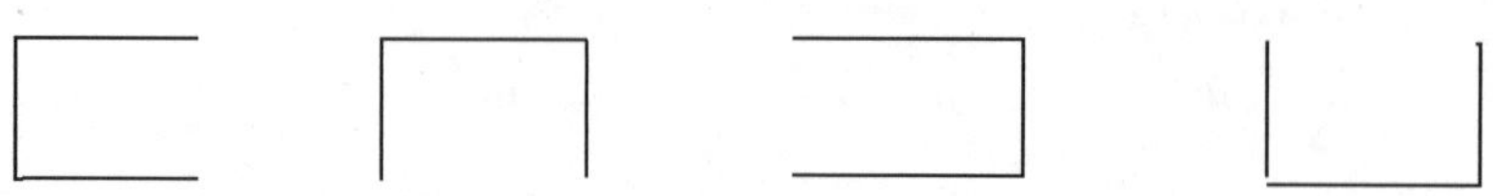

Definition: Graphs $G_1 = \{V_1, E_1\}$ and $G_2 = \{V_2, E_2\}$ are isomorphic if

1) There is a one-to-one correspondence from V_1 to V_2 and
2) There is a one-to-one correspondence from E_1 to E_2 that map each edge of G_1 to G_2.

Now, for the given graphs how do we check whether they are isomorphic or not?

In general, it is not a simple task to prove that two graphs are isomorphic. For that reason we must consider some properties of isomorphic graphs. That means those properties must be satisfied if the graphs are isomorphic. If the given graph does not satisfy these properties then we say they are not isomorphic graphs.

Property: Two graphs are isomorphic if and only if for some ordering of their vertices their adjacency matrices are equal.

Based on the above property we decide whether the given graphs are isomorphic or not. I order to check the property; we need to do some matrix transformation operations.

Problem-34 How many simple undirected non-isomorphic graphs are there with n vertices?

Solution: We will try to answer this question in two steps. First, we count all labeled graphs. Assume all the representations below are labeled with $\{1, 2, 3\}$ as vertices. The set of all such graphs for $n = 3$ are:

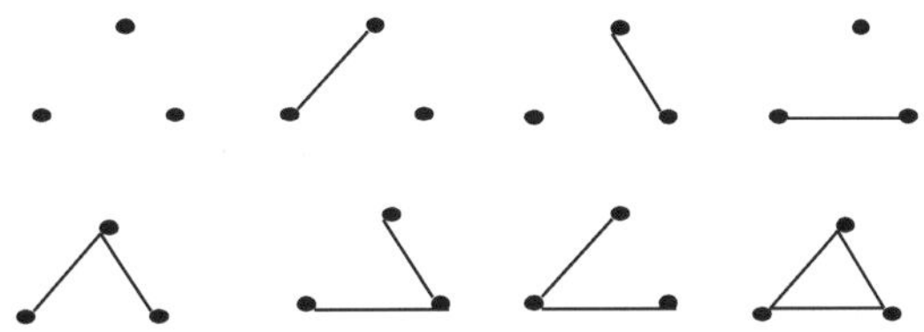

There are only two choices for each edge: it either exists or it does not. Therefore, since the maximum number of edges is $\binom{n}{2}$ *(and since* the maximum number of edges in an undirected graph with n vertices is $\frac{n(n-1)}{2} = n_{c_2} = \binom{n}{2}$*)*, the total number of undirected labeled graphs is $2^{\binom{n}{2}}$.

Problem-35 **Hamiltonian path in DAGs:** Given a DAG, design a linear time algorithm to determine whether there is a path that visits each vertex exactly once.

Solution: The *Hamiltonian* path problem is an NP-Complete problem (for more details ref *Complexity Classes* chapter). To solve this problem, we will try to give the approximation algorithm (which solves the problem, but it may not always produce the optimal solution).

Let us consider the topological sort algorithm for solving this problem. Topological sort has an interesting property: that if all pairs of consecutive vertices in the sorted order are connected by edges, then these edges form a directed *Hamiltonian* path in the DAG. If a *Hamiltonian* path exists, the topological sort order is unique. Also, if a topological sort does not form a *Hamiltonian* path, the DAG will have two or more topological orderings.

Approximation Algorithm: Compute a topological sort and check if there is an edge between each consecutive pair of vertices in the topological order.

In an unweighted graph, find a path from s to t that visits each vertex exactly once. The basic solution based on backtracking is, we start at s and try all of its neighbors recursively, making sure we never visit the same vertex twice. The algorithm based on this implementation can be given as:

```
var seenTable []bool
func HamiltonianPath(G *Graph, u int) {
    if u == t {
        /* Check that we have seen all vertices. */
    } else {
        for v := 0; v < n; v++ {
            if !seenTable[v] && G.AdjMatrix[u][v] {
                seenTable[v] = true
                HamiltonianPath(v)
                seenTable[v] = false
            }
        }
    }
}
```

Note that if we have a partial path from s to u using vertices $s = v_1, v_2, \ldots, v_k = u$, then we don't care about the order in which we visited these vertices so as to figure out which vertex to visit next. All that we need to know is the set of vertices we have seen (the seenTable[] array) and which vertex we are at right now (u).

There are 2^n possible sets of vertices and n choices for u. In other words, there are 2^n possible *seenTable*[ ] arrays and n different parameters to HamiltonianPath(). What HamiltonianPath() does during any particular recursive call is completely determined by the *seenTable*[ ] array and the parameter u.

Problem-36 For a given graph G with n vertices how many trees we can construct?

Solution: There is a simple formula for this problem and it is named after Arthur Cayley. For a given graph with n labeled vertices the formula for finding number of trees on is n^{n-2}. Below, the number of trees with different n values is shown.

n value	Formula value: n^{n-2}	Number of Trees
2	1	1 ——— 2
3	3	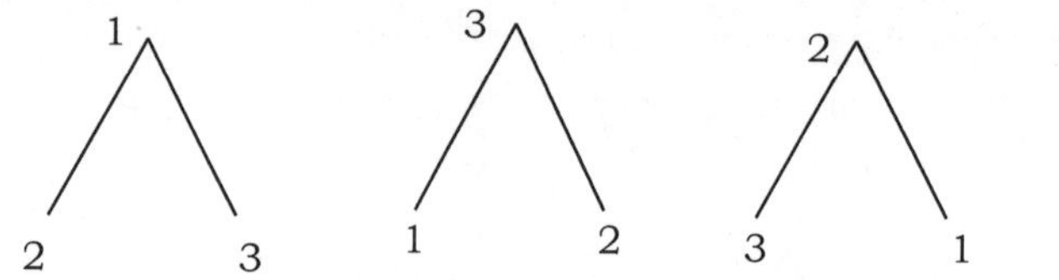

Problem-37 For a given graph G with n vertices how many spanning trees can we construct?

Solution: The solution to this problem is the same as that of Problem-36. It is just another way of asking the same question. Because the number of edges in both regular tree and spanning tree are the same.

Problem-38 The *Hamiltonian cycle* problem: Is it possible to traverse each of the vertices of a graph exactly once, starting and ending at the same vertex?

Solution: Since the *Hamiltonian* path problem is an NP-Complete problem, the *Hamiltonian* cycle problem is an NP-Complete problem. A *Hamiltonian* cycle is a cycle that traverses every vertex of a graph exactly once. There are no known conditions in which are both necessary and sufficient, but there are a few sufficient conditions.

- For a graph to have a *Hamiltonian* cycle the degree of each vertex must be two or more.
- The Petersen graph does not have a *Hamiltonian* cycle and the graph is given below.

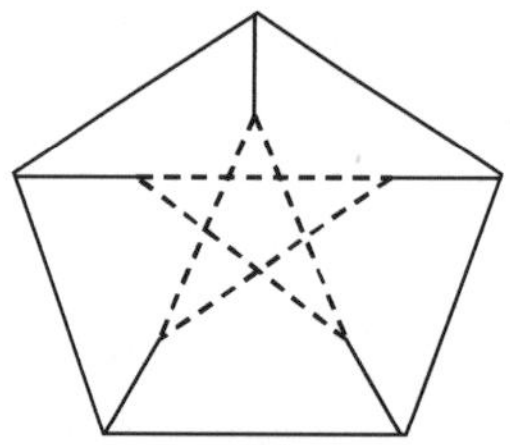

- In general, the more edges a graph has, the more likely it is to have a *Hamiltonian* cycle.
- Let G be a simple graph with n ≥ 3 vertices. If every vertex has a degree of at least $\frac{n}{2}$, then G has a *Hamiltonian* cycle.
- The best-known algorithm for finding a *Hamiltonian* cycle has an exponential worst-case complexity.

Note: For the approximation algorithm of *Hamiltonian* path, refer to the *Dynamic Programming* chapter.

Problem-39 What is the difference between *Dijkstra's* and *Prim's* algorithm?

Solution: *Dijkstra's* algorithm is almost identical to that of *Prim's*. The algorithm begins at a specific vertex and extends outward within the graph until all vertices have been reached. The only distinction is that *Prim's* algorithm stores a minimum cost edge whereas *Dijkstra's* algorithm stores the total cost from a source vertex to the current vertex. More simply, *Dijkstra's* algorithm stores a summation of minimum cost edges whereas *Prim's* algorithm stores at most one minimum cost edge.

Problem-40 **Reversing Graph:** Give an algorithm that returns the reverse of the directed graph (each edge from v to w is replaced by an edge from w to v).

Solution: In graph theory, the reverse (also called *transpose*) of a directed graph G is another directed graph on the same set of vertices with all the edges reversed. That means, if G contains an edge (u, v) then the reverse of G contains an edge (v, u) and vice versa.

Algorithm:

```
func ReverseTheDirectedGraph(G *Graph) Graph{
	Create new graph with name ReversedGraph and
			let us assume that this will contain the reversed graph.
	// The reversed graph also will contain same number of vertices and edges.
```

```
        for each vertex of given graph G {
                for each vertex w adjacent to v {
                     Add the w to v edge in ReversedGraph
                     // That means we just need to reverse the bits in adjacency matrix.
                }
        }
        return ReversedGraph
}
```

Problem-41 **Travelling Sales Person Problem:** Find the shortest path in a graph that visits each vertex at least once, starting and ending at the same vertex.

Solution: The Traveling Salesman Problem (*TSP*) is related to finding a Hamiltonian cycle. Given a weighted graph *G*, we want to find the shortest cycle (may be non-simple) that visits all the vertices.

Approximation algorithm: This algorithm does not solve the problem but gives a solution which is within a factor of 2 of optimal (in the worst-case).

1) Find a Minimal Spanning Tree (MST).
2) Do a DFS of the MST.

For details, refer to the chapter on *Complexity Classes*.

Problem-42 Discuss Bipartite matchings?

Solution: In Bipartite graphs, we divide the graphs in to two disjoint sets, and each edge connects a vertex from one set to a vertex in another subset (as shown in figure).

Definition: A simple graph $G = (V, E)$ is called a *bipartite graph* if its vertices can be divided into two disjoint sets $V = V_1 \cup V_2$, such that every edge has the form $e = (a, b)$ where $a \in V_1$ and $b \in V_2$. One important condition is that no vertices both in V_1 or both in V_2 are connected.

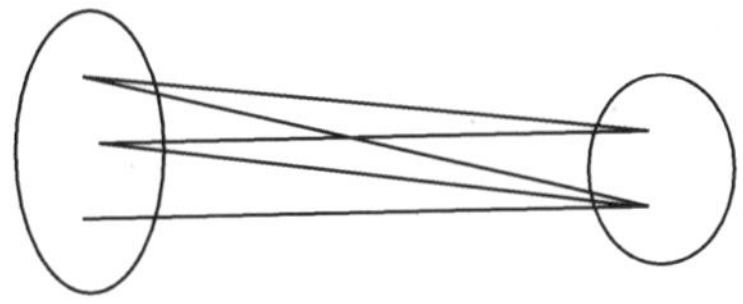

Properties of Bipartite Graphs

- A graph is called bipartite if and only if the given graph does not have an odd length cycle.
- A *complete bipartite graph* $K_{m.n}$ is a bipartite graph that has each vertex from one set adjacent to each vertex from another set.

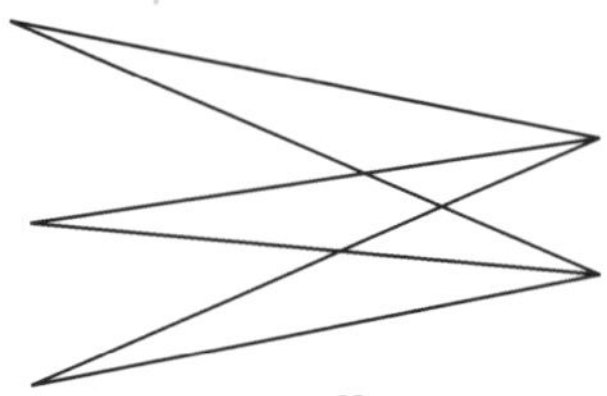

$K_{2,3}$

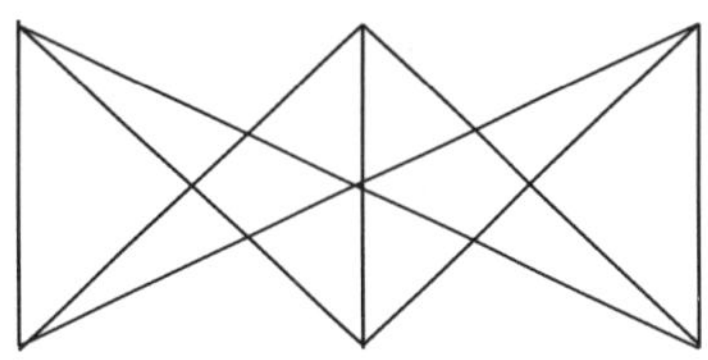

$K_{3,3}$

- A subset of edges $M \subset E$ is a *matching* if no two edges have a common vertex. As an example, matching sets of edges are represented with dotted lines. A matching *M* is called *maximum* if it has the largest number of possible edges. In the graphs, the dotted edges represent the alternative matching for the given graph.

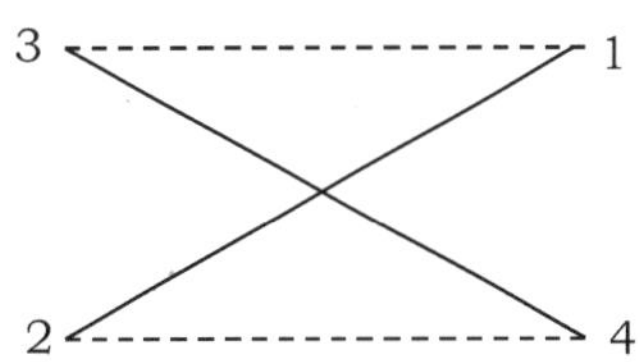

- A matching *M* is *perfect* if it matches all vertices. We must have $V_1 = V_2$ in order to have perfect matching.
- An *alternating path* is a path whose edges alternate between matched and unmatched edges. If we find an alternating path, then we can improve the matching. This is because an alternating path consists of matched and unmatched edges. The number of unmatched edges exceeds the number of matched edges by one. Therefore, an alternating path always increases the matching by one.

The next question is, how do we find a perfect matching? Based on the above theory and definition, we can find the perfect matching with the following approximation algorithm.

Matching Algorithm (Hungarian algorithm)

1) Start at unmatched vertex.
2) Find an alternating path.
3) If it exists, change matching edges to no matching edges and conversely. If it does not exist, choose another unmatched vertex.
4) If the number of edges equals $V/2$, stop. Otherwise proceed to step 1 and repeat, as long as all vertices have been examined without finding any alternating paths.

Time Complexity of the Matching Algorithm: The number of iterations is in $O(V)$. The complexity of finding an alternating path using BFS is $O(E)$. Therefore, the total time complexity is $O(V \times E)$.

Problem-43 Marriage and Personnel Problem?

Marriage Problem: There are X men and Y women who desire to get married. Participants indicate who among the opposite sex could be a potential spouse for them. Every woman can be married to at most one man, and every man to at most one woman. How can we marry everybody to someone they like?

Personnel Problem: You are the boss of a company. The company has M workers and N jobs. Each worker is qualified to do some jobs, but not others. How will you assign jobs to each worker?

Solution: These two cases are just another way of asking about bipartite graphs, and the solution is the same as that of Problem-42.

Problem-44 How many edges will be there in complete bipartite graph $K_{m,n}$?

Solution: $m \times n$. This is because each vertex in the first set can connect all vertices in the second set.

Problem-45 A graph is called regular graph if it has no loops and multiple edges where each vertex has the same number of neighbors; i.e. every vertex has the same degree. Now, if $K_{m,n}$ is a regular graph what is the relation between m and n?

Solution: Since each vertex should have the same degree, the relation should be $m = n$.

Problem-46 What is the maximum number of edges in the maximum matching of a bipartite graph with n vertices?

Solution: From the definition of *matching*, we should not have edges with common vertices. So in a bipartite graph, each vertex can connect to only one vertex. Since we divide the total vertices into two sets, we can get the maximum number of edges if we divide them in half. Finally the answer is $\frac{n}{2}$.

Problem-47 Discuss Planar Graphs. *Planar graph*: Is it possible to draw the edges of a graph in such a way that the edges do not cross?

Solution: A graph G is said to be planar if it can be drawn in the plane in such a way that no two edges meet each other except at a vertex to which they are incident. Any such drawing is called a plane drawing of G. As an example consider the below graph:

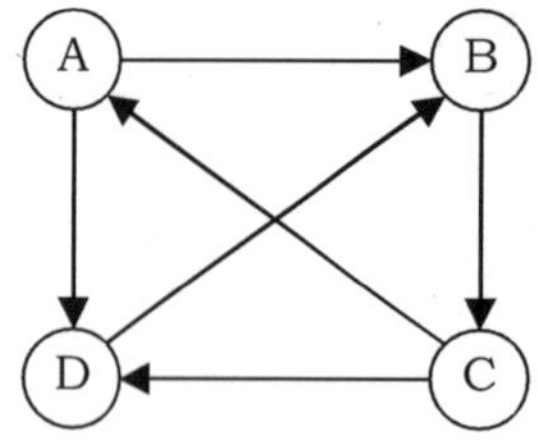

This graph we can easily convert to a planar graph as below (without any crossed edges).

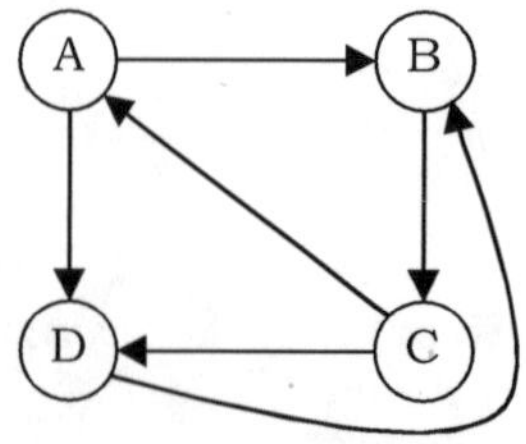

How do we decide whether a given graph is planar or not?

The solution to this problem is not simple, but researchers have found some interesting properties that we can use to decide whether the given graph is a planar graph or not.

Properties of Planar Graphs

- If a graph G is a connected planar simple graph with V vertices, where $V = 3$ and E edges, then $E = 3V - 6$.
- K_5 is non-planar. [K_5 stands for complete graph with 5 vertices].
- If a graph G is a connected planar simple graph with V vertices and E edges, and no triangles, then $E = 2V - 4$.
- $K_{3,3}$ is non-planar. [$K_{3,3}$ stands for bipartite graph with 3 vertices on one side and the other 3 vertices on the other side. $K_{3,3}$ contains 6 vertices].
- If a graph G is a connected planar simple graph, then G contains at least one vertex of 5 degrees or less.
- A graph is planar if and only if it does not contain a subgraph that has K_5 and $K_{3,3}$ as a contraction.
- If a graph G contains a nonplanar graph as a subgraph, then G is non-planar.
- If a graph G is a planar graph, then every subgraph of G is planar.
- For any connected planar graph $G = (V, E)$, the following formula should hold: $V + F - E = 2$, where F stands for the number of faces.
- For any planar graph $G = (V, E)$ with K components, the following formula holds: $V + F - E = 1 + K$.

In order to test the planarity of a given graph, we use these properties and decide whether it is a planar graph or not. Note that all the above properties are only the necessary conditions but not sufficient.

Problem-48 How many faces does $K_{2,3}$ have?

Solution: From the above discussion, we know that $V + F - E = 2$, and from an earlier problem we know that $E = m \times n = 2 \times 3 = 6$ and $V = m + n = 5$. $\therefore$ $5 + F - 6 = 2 \Longrightarrow F = 3$.

Problem-49 Discuss Graph Coloring.

Solution: A k –coloring of a graph G is an assignment of one color to each vertex of G such that no more than k colors are used and no two adjacent vertices receive the same color. A graph is called k –colorable if and only if it has a k –coloring.

Applications of Graph Coloring: The graph coloring problem has many applications such as scheduling, register allocation in compilers, frequency assignment in mobile radios, etc.

Clique: A *clique* in a graph G is the maximum complete subgraph and is denoted by $\omega(G)$.

Chromatic number: The chromatic number of a graph G is the smallest number k such that G is k –colorable, and it is denoted by $X(G)$.

The lower bound for $X(G)$ is $\omega(G)$, and that means $\omega(G) \leq X(G)$.

Properties of Chromatic number: Let G be a graph with n vertices and G′ is its complement. Then,

- $X(G) \leq \Delta(G) + 1$, where Δ (G) is the maximum degree of G.
- $X(G)\,\omega(G') \geq n$
- $X(G) + \omega(G') \leq n + 1$
- $X(G) + (G') \leq n + 1$

K-colorability problem: Given a graph $G = (V, E)$ and a positive integer $k \leq V$. Check whether G is k –colorable?

This problem is NP-complete and will be discussed in detail in the chapter on *Complexity Classes*.

Graph coloring algorithm: As discussed earlier, this problem is *NP*-Complete. So we do not have a polynomial time algorithm to determine $X(G)$. Let us consider the following approximation (no efficient) algorithm.

- Consider a graph G with two non-adjacent vertices a and b. The connection G_1 is obtained by joining the two non-adjacent vertices a and b with an edge. The contraction G_2 is obtained by shrinking $\{a, b\}$ into a single vertex $c(a, b)$ and by joining it to each neighbor in G of vertex a and of vertex b (and eliminating multiple edges).
- A coloring of G in which a and b have the same color yields a coloring of G_1. A coloring of G in which a and b have different colors yields a coloring of G_2.
- Repeat the operations of connection and contraction in each graph generated, until the resulting graphs are all cliques. If the smallest resulting clique is a K –clique, then $(G) = $ K.

Important notes on Graph Coloring

- Any simple planar graph G can be colored with 6 colors.
- Every simple planar graph can be colored with less than or equal to 5 colors.

Problem-50 What is the *four coloring* problem?

Solution: A graph can be constructed from any map. The regions of the map are represented by the vertices of the graph, and two vertices are joined by an edge if the regions corresponding to the vertices are adjacent. The resulting graph is planar. That means it can be drawn in the plane without any edges crossing.

The *Four Color Problem* is whether the vertices of a planar graph can be colored with at most four colors so that no two adjacent vertices use the same color.

History: The *Four Color Problem* was first given by *Francis Guthrie*. He was a student at *University College London* where he studied under *Augusts De Morgan*. After graduating from London he studied law, but some years later his brother Frederick Guthrie had become a student of *De Morgan*. One day Francis asked his brother to discuss this problem with *De Morgan*.

Problem-51 When an adjacency-matrix representation is used, most graph algorithms require time $O(V^2)$. Show that determining whether a directed graph, represented in an adjacency-matrix that contains a sink can be done in time O(V). A sink is a vertex with in-degree $|V| - 1$ and out-degree 0 (Only one can exist in a graph).

Solution: A vertex i is a sink if and only if $M[i,j] = 0$ for all j and $M[j,i] = 1$ for all $j \neq i$. For any pair of vertices i and j:

$$M[i,j] = 1 \rightarrow \text{vertex i can't be a sink}$$
$$M[i,j] = 0 \rightarrow \text{vertex j can't be a sink}$$

Algorithm:

- Start at $i = 1, j = 1$
- If $M[i,j] = 0 \rightarrow i$ wins, $j++$
- If $M[i,j] = 1 \rightarrow j$ wins, $i++$
- Proceed with this process until $j = n$ or $i = n + 1$
- If $i == n + 1$, the graph does not contain a sink
- Otherwise, check row i – it should be all zeros; and check column i – it should be all but $M[i,i]$ ones; – if so, i is a sink.

Time Complexity: O(V), because at most $2|V|$ cells in the matrix are examined.

Problem-52 What is the worst – case memory usage of DFS?

Solution: It occurs when the O(|V|), which happens if the graph is actually a list. So the algorithm is memory efficient on graphs with small diameter.

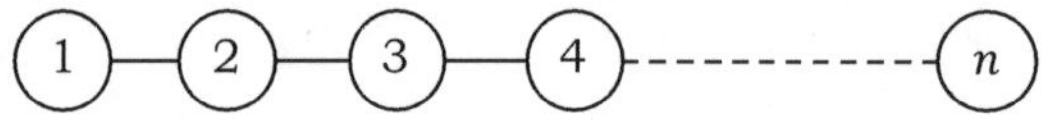

Problem-53 Does DFS find the shortest path from start node to some node w ?

Solution: No. In DFS it is not compulsory to select the smallest weight edge.

Problem-54 True or False: Dijkstra's algorithm does not compute the "all pairs" shortest paths in a directed graph with positive edge weights because, running the algorithm a single time, starting from some single vertex x, it will compute only the min distance from x to y for all nodes y in the graph.

Solution: True.

Problem-55 True or False: Prim's and Kruskal's algorithms may compute different minimum spanning trees when run on the same graph.

Solution: True.

CHAPTER

SORTING

10

10.1 What is Sorting?

Sorting is an algorithm that arranges the elements of a list in a certain order [either *ascending* or *descending*]. The output is a permutation or reordering of the input.

10.2 Why is Sorting Necessary?

Sorting is one of the important categories of algorithms in computer science and a lot of research has gone into this category. Sorting can significantly reduce the complexity of a problem, and is often used for database algorithms and searches.

10.3 Classification of Sorting Algorithms

Sorting algorithms are generally categorized based on the following parameters.

By Number of Comparisons

In this method, sorting algorithms are classified based on the number of comparisons. For comparison based sorting algorithms, best case behavior is $O(nlogn)$ and worst case behavior is $O(n^2)$. Comparison-based sorting algorithms evaluate the elements of the list by key comparison operation and need at least $O(nlogn)$ comparisons for most inputs.

Later in this chapter we will discuss a few *non – comparison* (*linear*) sorting algorithms like Counting sort, Bucket sort, Radix sort, etc. Linear Sorting algorithms impose few restrictions on the inputs to improve the complexity.

By Number of Swaps

In this method, sorting algorithms are categorized by the number of *swaps* (also called *inversions*).

By Memory Usage

Some sorting algorithms are "*in place*" and they need $O(1)$ or $O(logn)$ memory to create auxiliary locations for sorting the data temporarily.

By Recursion

Sorting algorithms are either recursive [quick sort] or non-recursive [selection sort, and insertion sort], and there are some algorithms which use both (merge sort).

By Stability

Sorting algorithm is *stable* if for all indices i and j such that the key $A[i]$ equals key $A[j]$, if record $R[i]$ precedes record $R[j]$ in the original file, record $R[i]$ precedes record $R[j]$ in the sorted list. Few sorting algorithms maintain the relative order of elements with equal keys (equivalent elements retain their relative positions even after sorting).

By Adaptability

With a few sorting algorithms, the complexity changes based on pre-sortedness [quick sort]: pre-sortedness of the input affects the running time. Algorithms that take this into account are known to be adaptive.

10.4 Other Classifications

Another method of classifying sorting algorithms is:

- Internal Sort
- External Sort

Internal Sort

Sort algorithms that use main memory exclusively during the sort are called *internal* sorting algorithms. This kind of algorithm assumes high-speed random access to all memory.

External Sort

Sorting algorithms that use external memory, such as tape or disk, during the sort come under this category.

10.5 Bubble Sort

Bubble sort is the simplest sorting algorithm. Bubble sort, sometimes referred to as sinking sort, is a simple sorting algorithm that repeatedly steps through the list to be sorted, compares each pair of adjacent items and swaps them if they are in the wrong order.

In the bubble sorting, two adjacent elements of a list are first checked and then swapped. In case the adjacent elements are in the incorrect order then the process keeps on repeating until a fully sorted list is obtained. Each pass that goes through the list will place the next largest element value in its proper place. So, in effect, every item bubbles up with an intent of reaching the location wherein it rightfully belongs.

The only significant advantage that bubble sort has over other implementations is that it can detect whether the input list is already sorted or not.

Following table shows the first pass of a bubble sort. The shaded items are being compared to see if they are out of order. If there are n items in the list, then there are $n-1$ pairs of items that need to be compared on the first pass. It is important to note that once the largest value in the list is part of a pair, it will continually be moved along until the pass is complete.

First pass →									Remarks
10	4	43	5	57	91	45	9	7	Swap
4	10	43	5	57	91	45	9	7	No swap
4	10	43	5	57	91	45	9	7	Swap
4	10	5	43	57	91	45	9	7	No swap
4	10	5	43	57	91	45	9	7	No swap
4	10	5	43	57	91	45	9	7	Swap
4	10	5	43	57	45	91	9	7	Swap
4	10	5	43	57	45	9	91	7	Swap
4	10	5	43	57	45	9	7	91	At the end of first pass, 91 is in correct place

At the start of the first pass, the largest value is now in place. There are $n-1$ items left to sort, meaning that there will be $n-2$ pairs. Since each pass places the next largest value in place, the total number of passes necessary will be $n-1$. After completing the $n-1$ passes, the smallest item must be in the correct position with no further processing required.

Implementation

```
func BubbleSort(A []int) []int {
    n := len(A)
    for i := 0; i < n-1; i++ {
        for j := 0; j < n-i-1; j++ {
            if A[j] > A[j+1] {
                A[j], A[j+1] = A[j+1], A[j]
            }
        }
    }
    return A
}
func main() {
    A := []int{3, 4, 5, 2, 1}
```

```
    A = BubbleSort(A)
    fmt.Println("\n After Bubble Sorting")
    for _, val := range A {
        fmt.Println(val)
    }
}
```

Algorithm takes $O(n^2)$ (even in best case). In the above code, all the comparisons are made even if the array is already sorted at some point. It increases the execution time.

The code can be optimized by introducing an extra variable *sorted*. After every pass, if there is no swapping taking place then, there is no need for performing further loops. Variable *sorted* is true if there is no swapping. Thus, we can prevent further iterations. No more swaps indicate the completion of sorting. If the list is already sorted, we can use this flag to skip the remaining passes.

```
func BubbleSort(A []int) []int {
    var sorted bool
    items := len(A)
    for !sorted {  // We run the outer loop until we have sorted all the items.
        // In each iteration we are going to change sorted to true.
        sorted = true
        // Now we're going to range over our slice checking if they're sorted or not.
        for i := 1; i < items; i++ {
            // If they're not sorted we swap them and change sorted to false to loop again.
            if A[i-1] > A[i] {
                A[i-1], A[i] = A[i], A[i-1]
                sorted = false
            }
        }
    }
    return A
}
```

This modified version improves the best case of bubble sort to $O(n)$.

Performance

Worst case complexity	$O(n^2)$
Best case complexity (Improved version)	$O(n)$
Average case complexity (Basic version)	$O(n^2)$
Worst case space complexity	$O(1)$ auxiliary

10.6 Selection Sort

In selection sort, the smallest element is exchanged with the first element of the unsorted list of elements (the exchanged element takes the place where smallest element is initially placed). Then the second smallest element is exchanged with the second element of the unsorted list of elements and so on until all the elements are sorted.

The selection sort improves on the bubble sort by making only one exchange for every pass through the list. In order to do this, a selection sort looks for the smallest (or largest) value as it makes a pass and, after completing the pass, places it in the proper location. As with a bubble sort, after the first pass, the largest item is in the correct place. After the second pass, the next largest is in place. This process continues and requires $n - 1$ passes to sort n items, since the final item must be in place after the $(n-1)^{st}$ pass.

Selection sort is an in-place sorting algorithm. Selection sort works well for small files. It is used for sorting the files with very large values and small keys. This is because selection is made based on keys and swaps are made only when required.

Following table shows the entire sorting process. On each pass, the largest remaining item is selected and then placed in its proper location. The first pass places 91, the second pass places 57, the third places 45, and so on.

→									Remarks: Select largest in each pass
10	4	43	5	57	91	45	9	7	Swap 91 and 7
10	4	43	5	57	7	45	9	91	Swap 57 and 9
10	4	43	5	9	7	45	57	91	45 is the next largest, skip
10	4	43	5	9	7	45	57	91	Swap 43 and 7
10	4	7	5	9	43	45	57	91	Swap 10 amd 9
9	4	7	5	10	43	45	57	91	Swap 9 amd 5

5	4	7	9	10	43	45	57	91	7 is the next largest, skip
5	4	7	9	10	43	45	57	91	Swap 5 amd 4
4	5	7	9	10	43	45	57	91	List is ordered

Alternatively, on each pass, we can select the smallest remaining item and then place in its proper location.

→									Remarks: Select smallest in each pass
10	4	43	5	57	91	45	9	7	Swap 10 and 4
4	10	43	5	57	7	45	9	91	Swap 10 and 5
4	5	43	10	57	7	45	9	91	Swap 43 and 7
4	5	7	10	57	43	45	9	91	Swap 10 and 9
4	5	7	9	57	43	45	10	91	Swap 57 amd 10
4	5	7	9	10	43	45	57	91	43 is the next smallest, skip
5	4	7	9	10	43	45	57	91	45 is the next smallest, skip
5	4	7	9	10	43	45	57	91	57 is the next smallest, skip
4	5	7	9	10	43	45	57	91	List is ordered

Advantages

- Easy to implement
- In-place sort (requires no additional storage space)

Disadvantages

- Doesn't scale well: O(n^2)

Algorithm

1. Find the minimum value in the list
2. Swap it with the value in the current position
3. Repeat this process for all the elements until the entire array is sorted

This algorithm is called *selection sort* since it repeatedly *selects* the smallest element.

Implementation

```
func SelectionSort(A []int) []int {
    var n = len(A)
    for i := 0; i < n; i++ {
        var minIndex = i
        for j := i; j < n; j++ {
            if A[j] < A[minIndex] {
                minIndex = j
            }
        }
        A[i], A[minIndex] = A[minIndex], A[i]
    }
    return A
}
```

Performance

Worst case complexity	O(n^2)
Best case complexity (Improved version)	O(n^2)
Average case complexity (Basic version)	O(n^2)
Worst case space complexity	O(1) auxiliary

10.7 Insertion Sort

Insertion sort algorithm picks elements one by one and places it to the right position where it belongs in the sorted list of elements. Insertion sort is a simple and efficient comparison sort. In this algorithm, each iteration removes an element from the input list and inserts it into the sorted sublist. The choice of the element being removed from the input list is random and this process is repeated until all input elements have gone through.

It always maintains a sorted sublist in the lower positions of the list. Each new item is then "inserted" back into the previous sublist such that the sorted sublist is one item larger.

We begin by assuming that a list with one item (position 0) is already sorted. On each pass, one for each item 1 through $n - 1$, the current item is checked against those in the already sorted sublist. As we look back into the already sorted sublist, we shift those items that are greater to the right. When we reach a smaller item or the end of the sublist, the current item can be inserted.

Advantages

- Easy to implement
- Efficient for small data
- Adaptive: If the input list is presorted [may not be completely] then insertions sort takes $O(n + d)$, where d is the number of inversions
- Practically more efficient than selection and bubble sorts, even though all of them have $O(n^2)$ worst case complexity
- Stable: Maintains relative order of input data if the keys are same
- In-place: It requires only a constant amount O(1) of additional memory space
- Online: Insertion sort can sort the list as it receives it

Algorithm

Every repetition of insertion sort removes an element from the input list, and inserts it into the correct position in the already-sorted list until no input elements remain. Sorting is typically done in-place. The resulting array after k iterations has the property where the first $k + 1$ entries are sorted.

Sorted partial result			Unordered elements
$\leq x$	$> x$	x	...

becomes

Sorted partial result			Unordered elements
$\leq x$	x	$> x$	...

Each element greater than x is copied to the right as it is compared against x.

Implementation

```
func InsertionSort(A []int) []int {
    n := len(A)
    // Run the outer loop n - 1 times, from index 1 to n-1, as first element is already sorted
    // At the end of ith iteration, we have sorted list [0, i]
    for i := 1; i <= n-1; i++ {
        // Pick ith element and keep swapping with i-1th element if A[i] < A[i-1]
        j := i
        for j > 0 {
            // If value at index j is smaller than the one at j-1, swap them
            if A[j] < A[j-1] {
                A[j], A[j-1] = A[j-1], A[j]
            }
            j -= 1
        }
    }
    return A
}
```

Example

Following table shows the sixth pass in detail. At this point in the algorithm, a sorted sublist of six elements consisting of 4, 5, 10, 43, 57 and 91 exists. We want to insert 45 back into the already sorted items. The first comparison against 91 causes 91 to be shifted to the right. 57 is also shifted. When the item 43 is encountered, the shifting process stops and 45 is placed in the open position. Now we have a sorted sublist of seven elements.

→									Remarks: Sixth pass
0	1	2	3	4	5	6	7	8	Hold the current element A[6] in a variable
4	5	10	43	57	91	45	9	7	Need to insert 45 into the sorted list, copy 91 to A[6] as 91> 45
4	5	10	43	57	91	91	9	7	copy 57 to A[5] as 57> 45
4	5	10	43	57	57	91	9	7	45 is the next largest, skip
4	5	10	43	45	57	91	9	7	45>43, so we can insert 45 at A[4], and sublist is sorted

Analysis

The implementation of insertionSort shows that there are again $n-1$ passes to sort n items. The iteration starts at position 1 and moves through position $n-1$, as these are the items that need to be inserted back into the sorted sublists. Notice that this is not a complete swap as was performed in the previous algorithms.

The maximum number of comparisons for an insertion sort is the sum of the first $n-1$ integers. Again, this is $O(n^2)$. However, in the best case, only one comparison needs to be done on each pass. This would be the case for an already sorted list.

One note about shifting versus exchanging is also important. In general, a shift operation requires approximately a third of the processing work of an exchange since only one assignment is performed. In benchmark studies, insertion sort will show very good performance.

Worst case analysis

Worst case occurs when for every i the inner loop has to move all elements $A[1], \ldots, A[i-1]$ (which happens when $A[i]$ = key is smaller than all of them), that takes $\Theta(i-1)$ time.

$$T(n) = \Theta(1) + \Theta(2) + \Theta(2) + \ldots\ldots + \Theta(n-1)$$
$$= \Theta(1 + 2 + 3 + \ldots\ldots + n - 1) = \Theta\left(\frac{n(n-1)}{2}\right) \approx \Theta(n^2)$$

Average case analysis

For the average case, the inner loop will insert $A[i]$ in the middle of $A[1], \ldots, A[i-1]$. This takes $\Theta\left(\frac{i}{2}\right)$ time.

$$T(n) = \sum_{i=1}^{n} \Theta(i/2) \approx \Theta(n^2)$$

Performance

If every element is greater than or equal to every element to its left, the running time of insertion sort is $\Theta(n)$. This situation occurs if the array starts out already sorted, and so an already-sorted array is the best case for insertion sort.

Worst case complexity	$O(n^2)$
Best case complexity (Improved version)	$O(n)$
Average case complexity (Basic version)	$O(n^2)$
Worst case space complexity	$O(n^2)$ total, $O(1)$ auxiliary

Comparisons to Other Sorting Algorithms

Insertion sort is one of the elementary sorting algorithms with $O(n^2)$ worst-case time. Insertion sort is used when the data is nearly sorted (due to its adaptiveness) or when the input size is small (due to its low overhead). For these reasons and due to its stability, insertion sort is used as the recursive base case (when the problem size is small) for higher overhead divide-and-conquer sorting algorithms, such as merge sort or quick sort.

Notes:

- Bubble sort takes $\frac{n^2}{2}$ comparisons and $\frac{n^2}{2}$ swaps (inversions) in both average case and in worst case.
- Selection sort takes $\frac{n^2}{2}$ comparisons and n swaps.
- Insertion sort takes $\frac{n^2}{4}$ comparisons and $\frac{n^2}{8}$ swaps in average case and in the worst case they are double.
- Insertion sort is almost linear for partially sorted input.
- Selection sort is best suits for elements with bigger values and small keys.

10.8 Shell Sort

Shell sort (also called *diminishing increment sort*) was invented by *Donald Shell*. This sorting algorithm is a generalization of insertion sort. Insertion sort works efficiently on input that is already almost sorted. Shell sort is also known as n-gap insertion sort. Instead of comparing only the adjacent pair, shell sort makes several passes and uses various gaps between adjacent elements (ending with the gap of 1 or classical insertion sort).

In insertion sort, comparisons are made between the adjacent elements. At most 1 inversion is eliminated for each comparison done with insertion sort. The variation used in shell sort is to avoid comparing adjacent elements until the last step of the algorithm. So, the last step of shell sort is effectively the insertion sort algorithm. It improves insertion sort by allowing the comparison and exchange of elements that are far away. This is the first algorithm which got less than quadratic complexity among comparison sort algorithms.

Shellsort is actually a simple extension for insertion sort. The primary difference is its capability of exchanging elements that are far apart, making it considerably faster for elements to get to where they should be. For example, if the smallest element happens to be at the end of an array, with insertion sort it will require the full array of steps to put this element at the beginning of the array. However, with shell sort, this element can jump more than one step a time and reach the proper destination in fewer exchanges.

The basic idea in shellsort is to exchange every hth element in the array. Now this can be confusing so we'll talk more about this. h determines how far apart element exchange can happen, say for example take h as 13, the first element (index-0) is exchanged with the 14th element (index-13) if necessary (of course). The second element with the 15th element, and so on. Now if we take h as 1, it is exactly the same as a regular insertion sort.

Shellsort works by starting with big enough (but not larger than the array size) h so as to allow eligible element exchanges that are far apart. Once a sort is complete with a particular h, the array can be said as h-sorted. The next step is to reduce h by a certain sequence, and again perform another complete h-sort. Once h is 1 and h-sorted, the array is completely sorted. Notice that the last sequence for h is 1 so the last sort is always an insertion sort, except by this time the array is already well-formed and easier to sort.

Shell sort uses a sequence $h1, h2, \ldots, ht$ called the *increment sequence*. Any increment sequence is fine as long as $h1 = 1$, and some choices are better than others. Shell sort makes multiple passes through the input list and sorts a number of equally sized sets using the insertion sort. Shell sort improves the efficiency of insertion sort by *quickly* shifting values to their destination.

Implementation

```
func ShellSort(A []int) {
    n := len(A)
    h := 1
    for h < n/3 {
        h = 3*h + 1
    }
    for h >= 1 {
        for i := h; i < n; i++ {
            for j := i; j >= h && A[j] < A[j-h]; j -= h {
                A[j], A[j-h] = A[j-h], A[j]
            }
        }
        h /= 3
    }
}
```

Note that when $h == 1$, the algorithm makes a pass over the entire list, comparing adjacent elements, but doing very few element exchanges. For $h == 1$, shell sort works just like insertion sort, except the number of inversions that have to be eliminated is greatly reduced by the previous steps of the algorithm with $h > 1$.

Analysis

The worse-case time complexity of shell sort depends on the increment sequence. For the increments 1 4 13 40 121..., which is what is used here, the time complexity is $O(n^{3/2})$. For other increments, time complexity is known to be $O(n^{4/3})$ and even $O(n \cdot log_2(n))$. Neither tight upper bounds on time complexity nor the best increment sequence are known.

Shell sort is efficient for medium size lists. For bigger lists, the algorithm is not the best choice. It is the fastest of all $O(n^2)$ sorting algorithms.

The disadvantage of Shell sort is that it is a complex algorithm and not nearly as efficient as the merge, heap, and quick sorts. Shell sort is significantly slower than the merge, heap, and quick sorts, but is a relatively simple algorithm, which makes it a good choice for sorting lists of less than 5000 items unless speed is important. It is also a good choice for repetitive sorting of smaller lists.

The best case in Shell sort is when the array is already sorted in the right order. The number of comparisons is less. The running time of Shell sort depends on the choice of increment sequence.

Because shell sort is based on insertion sort, shell sort inherits insertion sort's adaptive properties. The adapation is not as dramatic because shell sort requires one pass through the data for each increment, but it is significant. For the increment sequence shown above, there are $log_3(n)$ increments, so the time complexity for nearly sorted data is $O(n \cdot log_3(n))$. Because of its low overhead, relatively simple implementation, adaptive properties, and sub-quadratic time complexity, shell sort may be a viable alternative to the $O(n \cdot log(n))$ sorting algorithms for some applications when the data to be sorted is not very large.

Performance

Worst case complexity depends on gap sequence. Best known:	$O(nlog^2n)$
Best case complexity	$O(n)$
Average case complexity depends on gap sequence	
Worst case space complexity	$O(n)$

10.9 Merge Sort

Merge sort is an example of the divide and conquer strategy. Merge sort first divides the array into equal halves and then combines them in a sorted manner. It is a recursive algorithm that continually splits an array in half. If the array is empty or has one element, it is sorted by definition (the base case). If the array has more than one element, we split the array and recursively invoke a merge sort on both halves. Once the two halves are sorted, the fundamental operation, called a merge, is performed. Merging is the process of taking two smaller sorted arrays and combining them together into a single, sorted, new array.

Algorithm

Because we're using divide-and-conquer to sort, we need to decide what our subproblems are going to look like. The full problem is to sort an entire array. Let's say that a subproblem is to sort a subarray. In particular, we'll think of a subproblem as sorting the subarray starting at index $left$ and going through index $right$. It will be convenient to have a notation for a subarray, so let's say that $A[left..right]$ denotes this subarray of array A. In terms of our notation, for an array of n elements, we can say that the original problem is to sort A[0..n-1].

Algorithm Merge-sort(A):

- *Divide* by finding the number *mid* of the position midway between $left$ and $right$. Do this step the same way we found the midpoint in binary search:

$$mid = low + \frac{(high-low)}{2} \text{ or } \frac{low+high}{2}.$$

- *Conquer* by recursively sorting the subarrays in each of the two subproblems created by the divide step. That is, recursively sort the subarray $A[left..mid]$ and recursively sort the subarray $A[mid+1..right]$.
- *Combine* by merging the two sorted subarrays back into the single sorted subarray $A[left..right]$.

We need a base case. The base case is a subarray containing fewer than two elements, that is, when $left \geq right$, since a subarray with no elements or just one element is already sorted. So we'll divide-conquer-combine only when $left < right$.

Example

To understand merge sort, let us walk through an example:

54	26	93	17	77	31	44	55

We know that merge sort first divides the whole array iteratively into equal halves unless the atomic values are achieved. We see here that an array of 8 items is divided into two arrays of size 4.

54	26	93	17

77	31	44	55

This does not change the sequence of appearance of items in the original. Now we divide these two arrays into halves.

54	26

93	17

77	31

44	55

We further divide these arrays and we achieve atomic value which can no more be divided.

54	26	93	17	77	31	44	55

Now, we combine them in exactly the same manner as they were broken down.

We first compare the element for each array and then combine them into another array in a sorted manner. We see that 54 and 26 and in the target array of 2 values we put 26 first, followed by 54.

Similarly, we compare 93 and 17 and in the target array of 2 values we put 17 first, followed by 93. On the similar lines, we change the order of 77 and 31 whereas 44 and 55 are placed sequentially.

26	54

17	93

31	77

44	55

In the next iteration of the combining phase, we compare lists of two data values, and merge them into an array of found data values placing all in a sorted order.

17	26	54	93

31	44	55	77

After the final merging, the array should look like this:

The overall flow of above discussion can be depicted as:

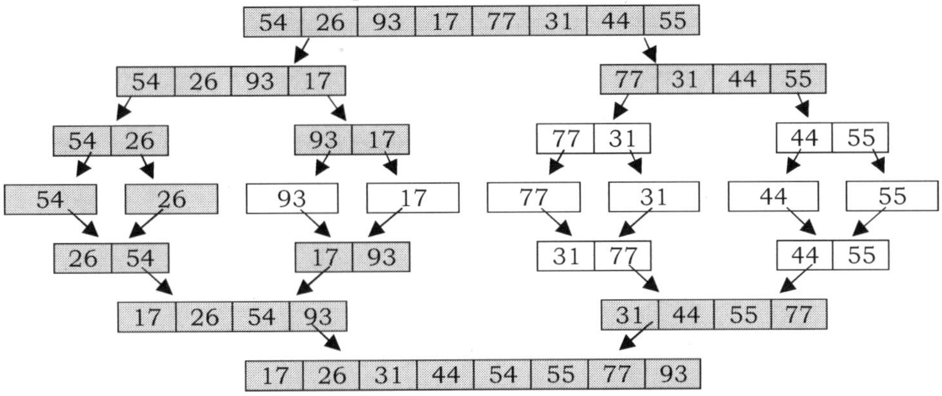

Implementation

```
func MergeSort(A []int) []int {
    if len(A) <= 1 {
        return A
    }
    middle := len(A) / 2
    left := MergeSort(A[:middle])
    right := MergeSort(A[middle:])
    return merge(left, right)
}
func merge(left, right []int) []int {
    result := make([]int, len(left)+len(right))
    for i := 0; len(left) > 0 || len(right) > 0; i++ {
        if len(left) > 0 && len(right) > 0 {
            if left[0] < right[0] {
                result[i] = left[0]
                left = left[1:]
            } else {
                result[i] = right[0]
                right = right[1:]
            }
        } else if len(left) > 0 {
            result[i] = left[0]
            left = left[1:]
        } else if len(right) > 0 {
            result[i] = right[0]
            right = right[1:]
        }
    }
    return result
}
```

Analysis

In merge-sort the input array is divided into two parts and these are solved recursively. After solving the subarrays, they are merged by scanning the resultant subarrays. In merge sort, the comparisons occur during the merging step, when two sorted arrays are combined to output a single sorted array. During the merging step, the first available element of each array is compared and the lower value is appended to the output array. When either array runs out of values, the remaining elements of the opposing array are appended to the output array.

How do determine the complexity of merge-sort? We start by thinking about the three parts of divide-and-conquer and how to account for their running times. We assume that we're sorting a total of n elements in the entire array.

The divide step takes constant time, regardless of the subarray size. After all, the divide step just computes the midpoint *mid* of the indices *left* and *right*. Recall that in big-Θ notation, we indicate constant time by Θ(1).

The conquer step, where we recursively sort two subarrays of approximately $\frac{n}{2}$ elements each, takes some amount of time, but we'll account for that time when we consider the subproblems. The combine step merges a total of n elements, taking $\Theta(n)$ time.

If we think about the divide and combine steps together, the $\Theta(1)$ running time for the divide step is a low-order term when compared with the $\Theta(n)$ running time of the combine step. So let's think of the divide and combine steps together as taking $\Theta(n)$ time. To make things more concrete, let's say that the divide and combine steps together take cn time for some constant c.

Let us assume $T(n)$ is the complexity of merge-sort with n elements. The recurrence for the merge-sort can be defined as:

$$T(n) = 2T(\frac{n}{2}) + \Theta(n)$$

Using Master theorem, we get, $T(n) = \Theta(nlogn)$.

For merge-sort there is no running time difference between best, average and worse cases as the division of input arrays happen irrespective of the order of the elements. Above merge sort algorithm uses an auxiliary space of $O(n)$ for left and right subarrays together. Merge-sort is a recursive algorithm and each recursive step puts another frame on the run time stack. Sorting 32 items will take one more recursive step than 16 items, and it is in fact the size of the stack that is referred to when the space requirement is said to be $O(logn)$.

Worst case complexity	$\Theta(nlogn)$
Best case complexity	$\Theta(nlogn)$
Average case complexity	$\Theta(nlogn)$
Space complexity	$\Theta(logn)$ for runtime stack space and $O(n)$ for the auxiliary space

10.10 Heap Sort

Heapsort is a comparison-based sorting algorithm and is part of the selection sort family. Although somewhat slower in practice on most machines than a good implementation of Quick sort, it has the advantage of a more favorable worst-case $\Theta(nlogn)$ runtime. Heapsort is an in-place algorithm but is not a stable sort.

Performance

Worst case performance	$\Theta(nlogn)$
Best case performance	$\Theta(nlogn)$
Average case performance	$\Theta(nlogn)$
Worst case space complexity	$\Theta(n)$ total, $\Theta(1)$ auxiliary space

For other details on Heapsort refer to the *Priority Queues* chapter.

10.11 Quick Sort

Quick sort is the famous algorithm among comparison-based sorting algorithms. Like merge sort, quick sort uses divide-and-conquer technique, and so it's a recursive algorithm. The way that quick sort uses divide-and-conquer is a little different from how merge sort does. The quick sort uses divide and conquer technique to gain the same advantages as the merge sort, while not using additional storage. As a trade-off, however, it is possible that the list may not be divided into half. When this happens, we will see that the performance is diminished.

It sorts in place and no additional storage is required as well. The slight disadvantage of quick sort is that its worst-case performance is similar to the average performances of the bubble, insertion or selection sorts (i.e., $O(n^2)$).

Divide and conquer strategy

A quick sort first selects an element from the given list, which is called the *pivot* value. Although there are many different ways to choose the pivot value, we will simply use the *first* item in the list. The role of the pivot value is to assist with splitting the list into two sublists. The actual position where the pivot value belongs in the final sorted list, commonly called the *partition* point, will be used to divide the list for subsequent calls to the quick sort.

All elements in the first sublist are arranged to be smaller than the *pivot*, while all elements in the second sublist are arranged to be larger than the *pivot*. The same partitioning and arranging process is performed repeatedly on the resulting sublists until the whole list of items are sorted.

Let us assume that array A is the list of elements to be sorted, and has the lower and upper bounds *low* and *high* respectively. With this information, we can define the divide and conquer strategy as follows:

Divide: The list $A[low ... high]$ is partitioned into two non-empty sublists $A[low ... q]$ and $A[q+1 ... high]$, such that each element of $A[low ... q]$ is less than or equal to each element of $A[q+1 ... high]$. The index q is computed as part of partitioning procedure with the first element as *pivot*.

Conquer: The two sublists $A[low ... q]$ and $A[q+1 ... high]$ are sorted by recursive calls to quick sort.

Algorithm

The recursive algorithm consists of four steps:

1) If there are one or no elements in the list to be sorted, return.
2) Pick an element in the list to serve as the *pivot* point. Usually the first element in the list is used as a *pivot*.
3) Split the list into two parts - one with elements larger than the *pivot* and the other with elements smaller than the *pivot*.
4) Recursively repeat the algorithm for both halves of the original list.

In the above algorithm, the important step is partitioning the list into two sublists. The basic steps to partition a list are:

1. Select the first element as a *pivot* in the list.
2. Start a pointer (the *left* pointer) at the second item in the list.
3. Start a pointer (the *right* pointer) at the last item in the list.
4. While the value at the *left* pointer in the list is lesser than the *pivot* value, move the *left* pointer to the right (add 1). Continue this process until the value at the *left* pointer is greater than or equal to the *pivot* value.
5. While the value at the *right* pointer in the list is greater than the *pivot* value, move the *right* pointer to the left (subtract 1). Continue this process until the value at the *right* pointer is lesser than or equal to the *pivot* value.
6. If the *left* pointer value is greater than or equal to the *right* pointer value, then swap the values at these locations in the list.
7. If the *left* pointer and *right* pointer don't meet, go to step 1.

Example

Following example shows that 50 will serve as our first pivot value. The partition process will happen next. It will find the *partition* point and at the same time move other items to the appropriate side of the list, either lesser than or greater than the *pivot* value.

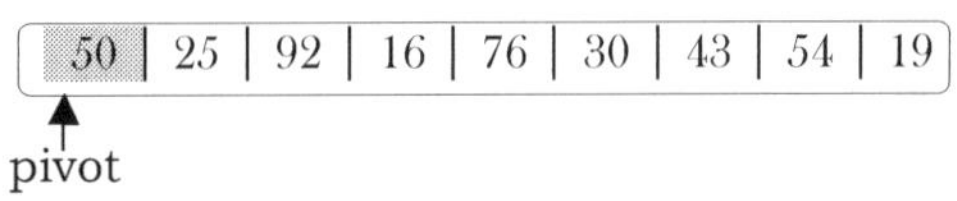

Partitioning begins by locating two position markers—let's call them *left* and *right*—at the beginning and end of the remaining items in the list (positions 1 and 8 in figure). The goal of the partition process is to move items that are on the wrong side with respect to the pivot value while converging on the split point also. The figure given below shows this process as we locate the position of 50.

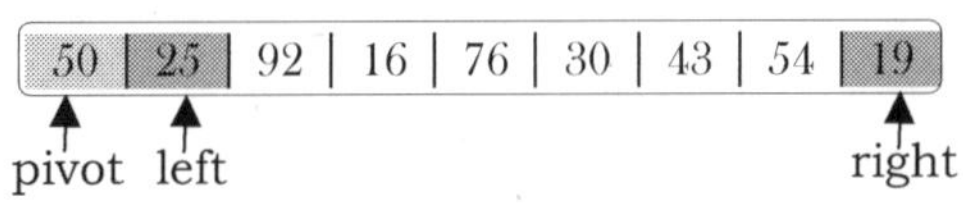

25 < 50, move *left* pointer to right:

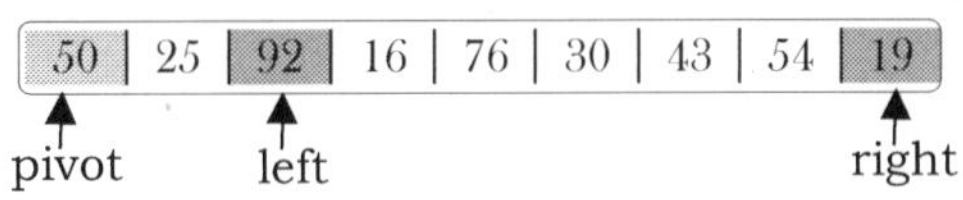

92 > 50, stop from moving *left* pointer:

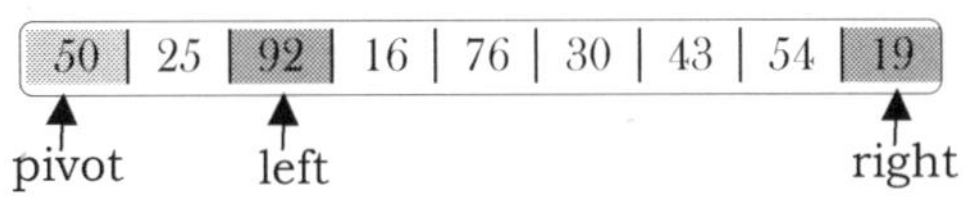

19 < 50, stop from moving *right* pointer:

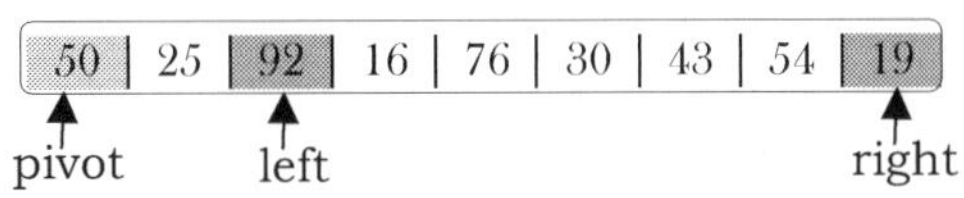

Swap 19 and 92:

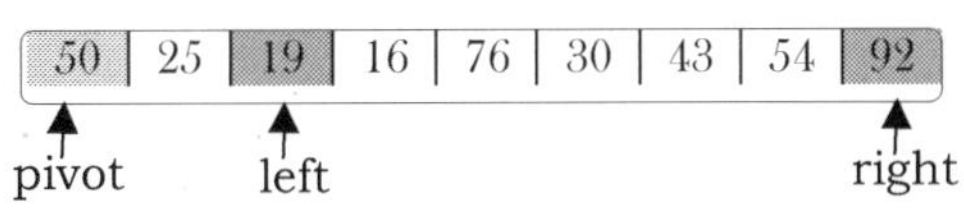

Now, continue moving left and right pointers. 19 < 50, move *left* pointer to right:

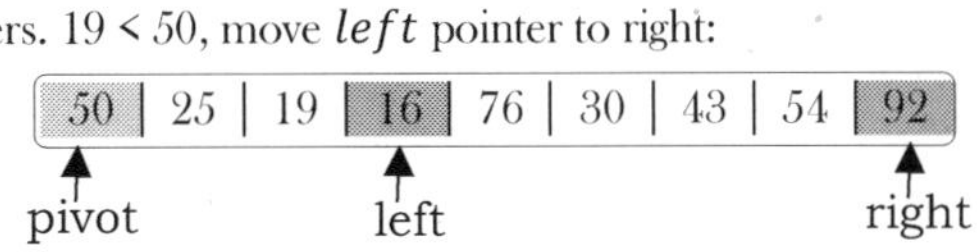

16 < 50, move *left* pointer to right:

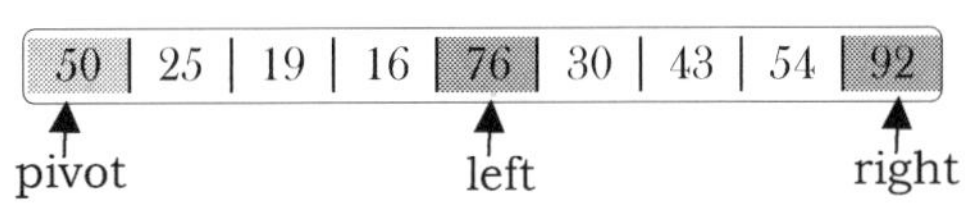

76 > 50, stop from moving *left* pointer:

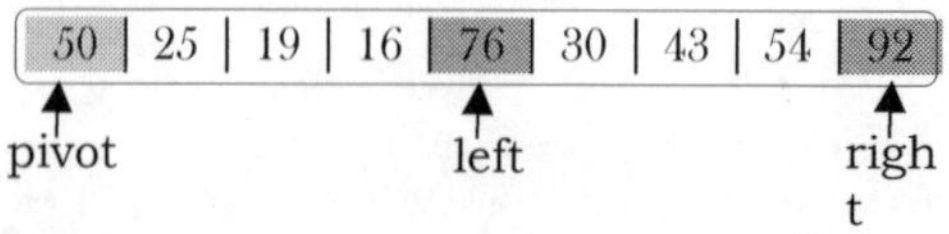

92 > 50, move *right* pointer to left:

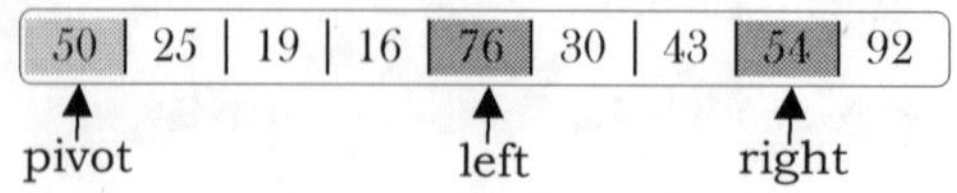

54 > 50, move *right* pointer to left:

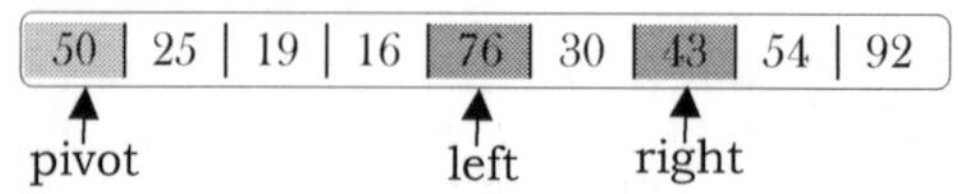

43 < 50, stop from moving *right* pointer:

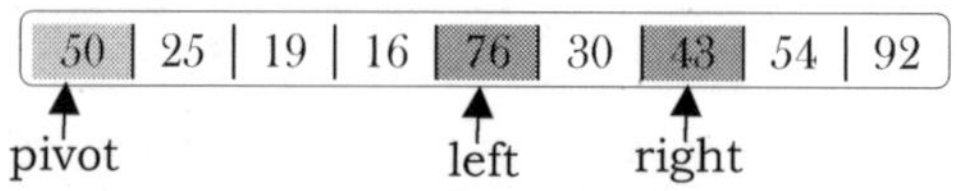

Swap 76 and 43:

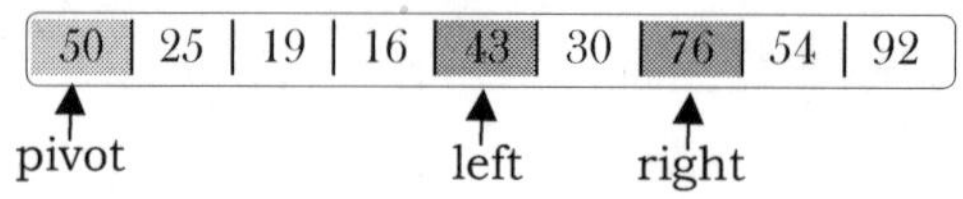

43 < 50, move *left* pointer to right:

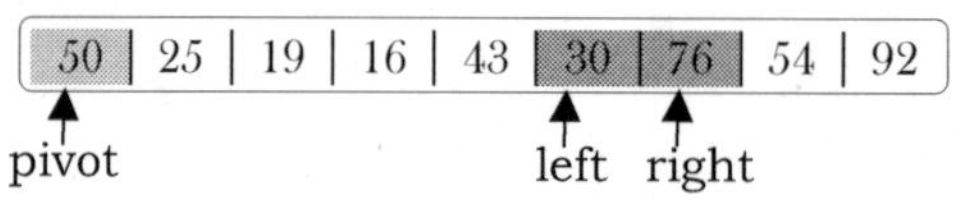

30 < 50, move *left* pointer to right:

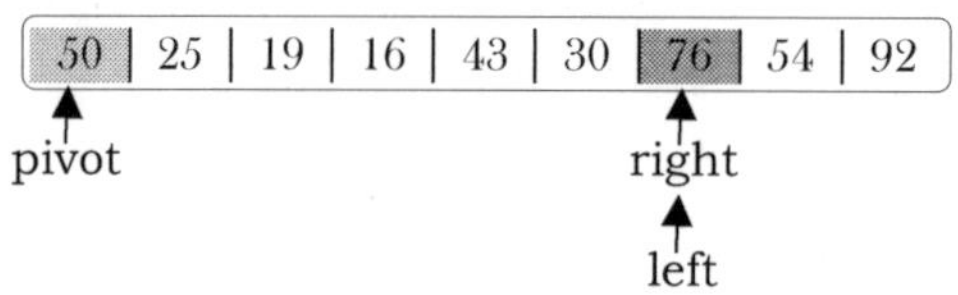

76 > 50, stop from moving *left* pointer:

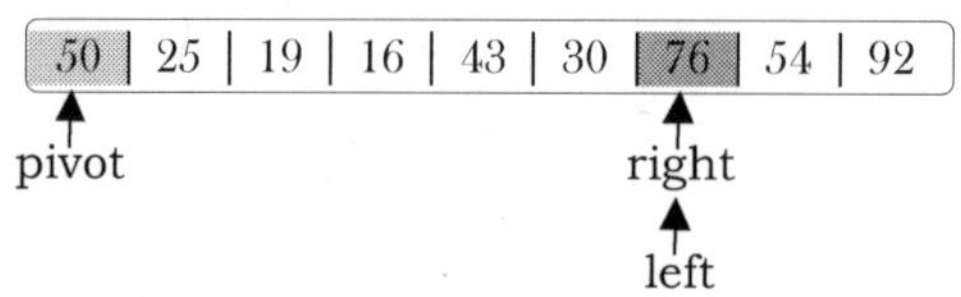

76 > 50, move *right* pointer to left:

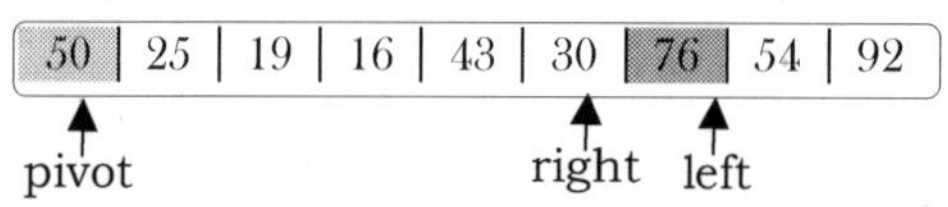

At the point where right becomes less than left, we stop. The position of right is now the *partition* point. The *pivot* value can be exchanged with the contents of the *partition* point. In addition, all the items to the left of the split point are less than the pivot value, and all the items to the right of the split point are greater than the pivot value. Now, we can exchange these two elements 50 and 30. Element 50 is now in correct position.

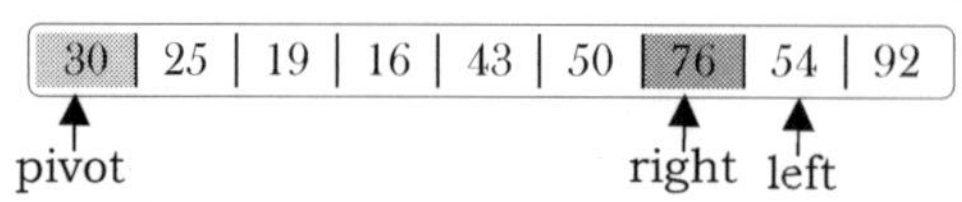

The list can now be divided at the partition point and the quick sort can be invoked recursively on the two halves.

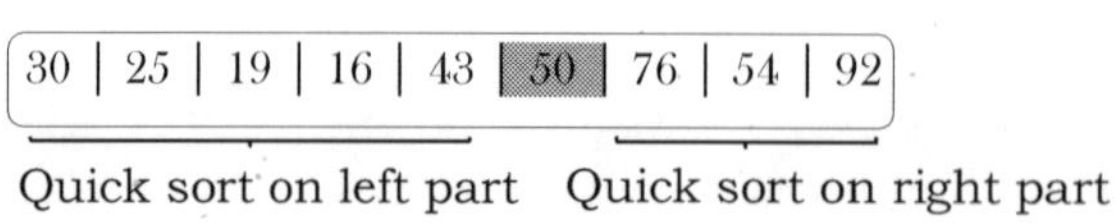

Repeat the process for the two sublists.

Implementation

```
func QuickSort(A []int) {
    recursionSort(A, 0, len(A)-1)
}
func recursionSort(A []int, left int, right int) {
```

```
        if left < right {
            pivot := partition(A, left, right)
            recursionSort(A, left, pivot-1)
            recursionSort(A, pivot+1, right)
        }
    }
    func partition(A []int, left int, right int) int {
        for left < right {
            for left < right && A[left] <= A[right] {
                right--
            }
            if left < right {
                A[left], A[right] = A[right], A[left]
                left++
            }
            for left < right && A[left] <= A[right] {
                left++
            }
            if left < right {
                A[left], A[right] = A[right], A[left]
                right--
            }
        }
        return left
    }
```

Analysis

Let us assume that $T(n)$ be the complexity of Quick sort and also assume that all elements are distinct. Recurrence for $T(n)$ depends on two subproblem sizes which depend on partition element. If pivot is i^{th} smallest element then exactly $(i - 1)$ items will be in left part and $(n - i)$ in right part. Let us call it as i –split. Since each element has equal probability of selecting it as pivot the probability of selecting i^{th} element is $\frac{1}{n}$.

Best Case: Each partition splits array in halves and gives

$$T(n) = 2T(n/2) + \Theta(n) = \Theta(nlogn), \text{ [using } \textit{Divide and Conquer} \text{ master theorem]}$$

Worst Case: Each partition gives unbalanced splits and we get

$$T(n) = T(n - 1) + \Theta(n) = \Theta(n^2)[using\ Subtraction\ and\ Conquer\ master\ theorem]$$

The worst-case occurs when the list is already sorted and last element chosen as pivot.

Average Case: In the average case of Quick sort, we do not know where the split happens. For this reason, we take all possible values of split locations, add all their complexities and divide with n to get the average case complexity.

$$T(n) = \sum_{i=1}^{n} \frac{1}{n}(runtime\ with\ i - split) + n + 1$$

$$= \frac{1}{n}\sum_{i=1}^{N}\left(T(i-1) + T(n-i)\right) + n + 1$$

//since we are dealing with best case we can assume $T(n-i)$ and $T(i-1)$ are equal

$$= \frac{2}{n}\sum_{i=1}^{n} T(i-1) + n + 1$$

$$= \frac{2}{n}\sum_{i=0}^{n-1} T(i) + n + 1$$

Multiply both sides by n.

$$nT(n) = 2\sum_{i=0}^{n-1} T(i) + n^2 + n$$

Same formula for $n - 1$.

$$(n-1)T(n-1) = 2\sum_{i=0}^{n-2} T(i) + (n-1)^2 + (n-1)$$

Subtract the $n-1$ formula from n.

$$nT(n) - (n-1)T(n-1) = 2\sum_{i=0}^{n-1} T(i) + n^2 + n - (2\sum_{i=0}^{n-2} T(i) + (n-1)^2 + (n-1))$$
$$nT(n) - (n-1)T(n-1) = 2T(n-1) + 2n$$
$$nT(n) = (n+1)T(n-1) + 2n$$

Divide with $n(n+1)$.

$$\begin{aligned}\frac{T(n)}{n+1} &= \frac{T(n-1)}{n} + \frac{2}{n+1}\\ &= \frac{T(n-2)}{n-1} + \frac{2}{n} + \frac{2}{n+1}\\ &\;\;\vdots\\ &= O(1) + 2\textstyle\sum_{i=3}^{n}\frac{1}{i}\\ &= O(1) + O\,(2logn)\\ \frac{T(n)}{n+1} &= O\,(logn)\\ T(n) &= O\left((n+1)\,logn\right) = O(nlogn)\end{aligned}$$

Time Complexity, $T(n) = O(nlogn)$.

Performance

Worst case complexity	$O(n^2)$
Best case complexity	$O(nlogn)$
Average case complexity	$O(nlogn)$
Worst case space complexity	$O(1)$

Randomized Quick sort

In average-case behavior of Quick sort, we assume that all permutations of the input numbers are equally likely. However, we cannot always expect it to hold. We can add randomization to an algorithm in order to reduce the probability of getting worst case in Quick sort. There are two ways of adding randomization in Quick sort: either by randomly placing the input data in the array or by randomly choosing an element in the input data for pivot. The second choice is easier to analyze and implement. The change will only be done at the *partition* algorithm.

In normal Quick sort, *pivot* element was always the leftmost element in the list to be sorted. Instead of always using $A[low]$ as *pivot*, we will use a randomly chosen element from the subarray $A[low..high]$ in the randomized version of Quick sort. It is done by exchanging element $A[low]$ with an element chosen at random from $A[low..high]$. This ensures that the *pivot* element is equally likely to be any of the $high - low + 1$ elements in the subarray.

Since the pivot element is randomly chosen, we can expect the split of the input array to be reasonably well balanced on average. This can help in preventing the worst-case behavior of quick sort which occurs in unbalanced partitioning. Even though the randomized version improves the worst-case complexity, its worst-case complexity is still $O(n^2)$. One way to improve $Randomized - Quick\ sort$ is to choose the pivot for partitioning more carefully than by picking a random element from the array. One common approach is to choose the pivot as the median of a set of 3 elements randomly selected from the array.

10.12 Tree Sort

Tree sort uses a binary search tree. It involves scanning each element of the input and placing it into its proper position in a binary search tree. This has two phases:

- First phase is creating a binary search tree using the given array elements.
- Second phase is traversing the given binary search tree in inorder, thus resulting in a sorted array.

Performance

The average number of comparisons for this method is $O(nlogn)$. But in worst case, the number of comparisons is reduced by $O(n^2)$, a case which arises when the sort tree is skew tree.

10.13 Comparison of Sorting Algorithms

Name	Average Case	Worst Case	Auxiliary Memory	Is Stable?	Other Notes
Bubble	$O(n^2)$	$O(n^2)$	1	yes	Small code
Selection	$O(n^2)$	$O(n^2)$	1	no	Stability depends on the implementation.

Insertion	$O(n^2)$	$O(n^2)$	1	yes	Average case is also $O(n + d)$, where d is the number of inversions.
Shell	-	$O(nlog^2n)$	1	no	
Merge sort	$O(nlogn)$	$O(nlogn)$	depends	yes	
Heap sort	$O(nlogn)$	$O(nlogn)$	1	no	
Quick sort	$O(nlogn)$	$O(n^2)$	$O(logn)$	depends	Can be implemented as a stable sort depending on how the pivot is handled.
Tree sort	$O(nlogn)$	$O(n^2)$	$O(n)$	depends	Can be implemented as a stable sort.

Note: n denotes the number of elements in the input.

10.14 Linear Sorting Algorithms

In earlier sections, we have seen many examples of comparison-based sorting algorithms. Among them, the best comparison-based sorting has the complexity $O(nlogn)$. In this section, we will discuss other types of algorithms: Linear Sorting Algorithms. To improve the time complexity of sorting these algorithms, we make some assumptions about the input. A few examples of Linear Sorting Algorithms are:

- Counting Sort
- Bucket Sort
- Radix Sort

10.15 Counting Sort

Counting sort is not a comparison sort algorithm and gives $O(n)$ complexity for sorting. To achieve $O(n)$ complexity, *counting* sort assumes that each of the elements is an integer in the range 1 to K, for some integer K. When $K = O(n)$, the *counting* sort runs in $O(n)$ time. The basic idea of Counting sort is to determine, for each input element X, the number of elements less than X. This information can be used to place it directly into its correct position. For example, if 10 elements are less than X, then X belongs to position 11 in the output.

In the code below, $A[0..n-1]$ is the input array with length n. In Counting sort we need two more arrays: let us assume array $B[0..n-1]$ contains the sorted output and the array $C[0..K-1]$ provides temporary storage.

```
func CountingSort(A []int, K int) []int {
    bucketLen := K + 1
    C := make([]int, bucketLen)
    sortedIndex := 0
    length := len(A)
    for i := 0; i < length; i++ {
        C[A[i]] += 1
    }
    for j := 0; j < bucketLen; j++ {
        for C[j] > 0 {
            A[sortedIndex] = j
            sortedIndex += 1
            C[j] -= 1
        }
    }
    return A
}
```

Total Complexity: $O(K) + O(n) + O(K) + O(n) = O(n)$ if $K = O(n)$. Space Complexity: $O(n)$ if $K = O(n)$.

Note: Counting works well if $K = O(n)$. Otherwise, the complexity will be greater.

10.16 Bucket Sort (or Bin Sort)

Like *Counting* sort, *Bucket* sort also imposes restrictions on the input to improve the performance. In other words, Bucket sort works well if the input is drawn from fixed set. *Bucket* sort is the generalization of *Counting* Sort. For example, assume that all the input elements from $\{0, 1, \ldots, K-1\}$, i.e., the set of integers in the interval $[0, K-1]$. That means, K is the number of distant elements in the input. *Bucket* sort uses K counters. The ith counter keeps track of the number of occurrences of the ith element. Bucket sort with two buckets is effectively a version of Quick sort with two buckets.

For bucket sort, the hash function that is used to partition the elements need to be very good and must produce ordered hash: if i < k then hash(i) < hash(k). Second, the elements to be sorted must be uniformly distributed.

The aforementioned aside, bucket sort is actually very good considering that counting sort is reasonably speaking its upper bound. And counting sort is very fast. The particular distinction for bucket sort is that it uses a hash function to partition the keys of the input array, so that multiple keys may hash to the same bucket. Hence each bucket must effectively be a growable list; similar to radix sort.

In the below code Insertionsort is used to sort each bucket. This is to inculcate that the bucket sort algorithm does not specify which sorting technique to use on the buckets. A programmer may choose to continuously use bucket sort on each bucket until the collection is sorted (in the manner of the radix sort program below). Whichever sorting method is used on the , bucket sort still tends toward $O(n)$.

```
func insertionSort(A []int) {
    for i := 0; i < len(A); i++ {
        temp := A[i]
        j := i - 1
        for ; j >= 0 && A[j] > temp; j-- {
            A[j+1] = A[j]
        }
        A[j+1] = temp
    }
}
func BucketSort(A []int, bucketSize int) []int {
    var max, min int
    for _, n := range A {
        if n < min {
            min = n
        }
        if n > max {
            max = n
        }
    }
    nBuckets := int(max-min)/bucketSize + 1
    buckets := make([][]int, nBuckets)
    for i := 0; i < nBuckets; i++ {
        buckets[i] = make([]int, 0)
    }
    for _, n := range A {
        idx := int(n-min) / bucketSize
        buckets[idx] = append(buckets[idx], n)
    }
    sorted := make([]int, 0)
    for _, bucket := range buckets {
        if len(bucket) > 0 {
            insertionSort(bucket)
            sorted = append(sorted, bucket...)
        }
    }
    return sorted
}
```

Time Complexity: $O(n)$. Space Complexity: $O(n)$.

10.17 Radix Sort

Similar to *Counting* sort and *Bucket* sort, this sorting algorithm also assumes some kind of information about the input elements. Suppose that the input values to be sorted are from base d. That means all numbers are d-digit numbers.

In Radix sort, first sort the elements based on the last digit [the least significant digit]. These results are again sorted by second digit [the next to least significant digit]. Continue this process for all digits until we reach the most significant digits. Use some stable sort to sort them by last digit. Then stable sort them by the second least significant digit, then by the third, etc. If we use Counting sort as the stable sort, the total time is $O(nd) \approx O(n)$.

Algorithm:

1) Take the least significant digit of each element.

2) Sort the list of elements based on that digit, but keep the order of elements with the same digit (this is the definition of a stable sort).
3) Repeat the sort with each more significant digit.

```
func findLargestElement(A []int) int {
    largestElement := 0
    for i := 0; i < len(A); i++ {
        if A[i] > largestElement {
            largestElement = A[i]
        }
    }
    return largestElement
}
func RadixSort(A []int) {
    largestElement := findLargestElement(A)
    size := len(A)
    significantDigit := 1
    semiSorted := make([]int, size, size)
    for largestElement/significantDigit > 0 {
        bucket := [10]int{0}
        for i := 0; i < size; i++ {
            bucket[(A[i]/significantDigit)%10]++
        }
        for i := 1; i < 10; i++ {
            bucket[i] += bucket[i-1]
        }
        for i := size - 1; i >= 0; i-- {
            bucket[(A[i]/significantDigit)%10]--
            semiSorted[bucket[(A[i]/significantDigit)%10]] = A[i]
        }
        for i := 0; i < size; i++ {
            A[i] = semiSorted[i]
        }
        significantDigit *= 10
    }
}
```

The speed of Radix sort depends on the inner basic operations. If the operations are not efficient enough, Radix sort can be slower than other algorithms such as Quick sort and Merge sort. These operations include the insert and delete functions of the sub-lists and the process of isolating the digit we want. If the numbers are not of equal length then a test is needed to check for additional digits that need sorting. This can be one of the slowest parts of Radix sort and also one of the hardest to make efficient.

Since Radix sort depends on the digits or letters, it is less flexible than other sorts. For every different type of data, Radix sort needs to be rewritten, and if the sorting order changes, the sort needs to be rewritten again. In short, Radix sort takes more time to write, and it is very difficult to write a general purpose Radix sort that can handle all kinds of data.

For many programs that need a fast sort, Radix sort is a good choice. Still, there are faster sorts, which is one reason why Radix sort is not used as much as some other sorts.

Time Complexity: $O(nd) \approx O(n)$, if d is small.

10.18 Topological Sort

Refer to *Graph Algorithms* Chapter.

10.19 External Sorting

External sorting is a generic term for a class of sorting algorithms that can handle massive amounts of data. These external sorting algorithms are useful when the files are too big and cannot fit into main memory.

As with internal sorting algorithms, there are a number of algorithms for external sorting. One such algorithm is External Mergesort. In practice, these external sorting algorithms are being supplemented by internal sorts.

Simple External Mergesort

A number of records from each tape are read into main memory, sorted using an internal sort, and then output to the tape. For the sake of clarity, let us assume that 900 megabytes of data needs to be sorted using only 100 megabytes of RAM.

1) Read 100MB of the data into main memory and sort by some conventional method (let us say Quick sort).
2) Write the sorted data to disk.
3) Repeat steps 1 and 2 until all of the data is sorted in chunks of 100MB. Now we need to merge them into one single sorted output file.
4) Read the first 10MB of each sorted chunk (call them input buffers) in main memory (90MB total) and allocate the remaining 10MB for output buffer.
5) Perform a 9-way Mergesort and store the result in the output buffer. If the output buffer is full, write it to the final sorted file. If any of the 9 input buffers gets empty, fill it with the next 10MB of its associated 100MB sorted chunk; or if there is no more data in the sorted chunk, mark it as exhausted and do not use it for merging.

The above algorithm can be generalized by assuming that the amount of data to be sorted exceeds the available memory by a factor of K. Then, K chunks of data need to be sorted and a K -way merge has to be completed.

If X is the amount of main memory available, there will be K input buffers and 1 output buffer of size $X/(K+1)$ each. Depending on various factors (how fast is the hard drive?) better performance can be achieved if the output buffer is made larger (for example, twice as large as one input buffer).

K-Way Mergesort

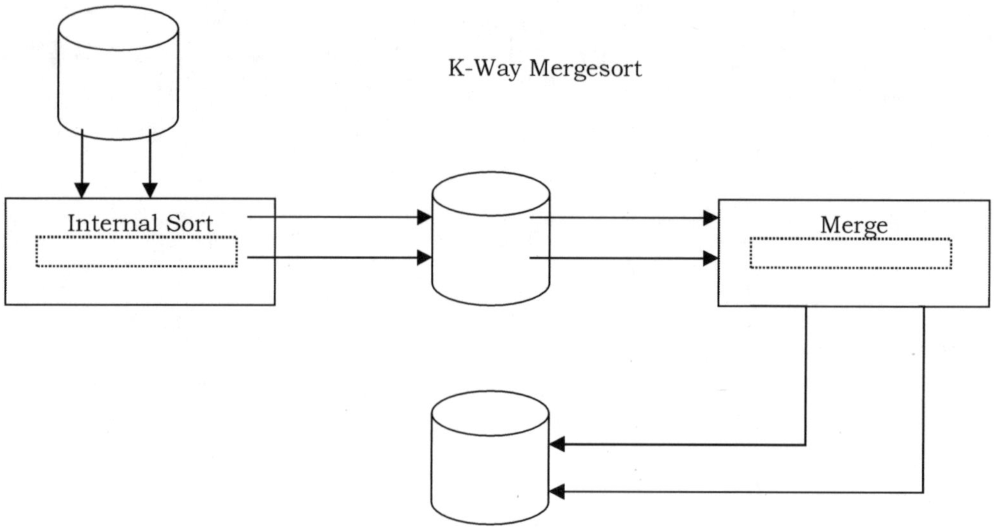

Complexity of the 2-way External Merge sort: In each pass we read + write each page in file. Let us assume that there are n pages in file. That means we need $\lceil logn \rceil + 1$ number of passes. The total cost is $2n(\lceil logn \rceil + 1)$.

10.20 Sorting: Problems & Solutions

Problem-1 Given an array $A[0 \dots n-1]$ of n numbers containing the repetition of some number. Give an algorithm for checking whether there are repeated elements or not. Assume that we are not allowed to use additional space (i.e., we can use a few temporary variables, O(1) storage).

Solution: Since we are not allowed to use extra space, one simple way is to scan the elements one-by-one and for each element check whether that element appears in the remaining elements. If we find a match we return true.

```
func CheckDuplicatesInArray(A []int) bool {
    for i := 0; i < len(A); i++ {
        // Scan slice for a previous element of the same value.
        for v := 0; v < i; v++ {
            if A[v] == A[i] {
                return true
                break
            }
        }
    }
    return false
}
```

Each iteration of the inner, j-indexed loop uses O(1) space, and for a fixed value of i, the j loop executes $n-i$ times. The outer loop executes $n-1$ times, so the entire function uses time proportional to

$$\sum_{i=1}^{n-1} n - i = n(n-1) - \sum_{i=1}^{n-1} i = n(n-1) - \frac{n(n-1)}{2} = \frac{n(n-1)}{2} = O(n^2)$$

Time Complexity: O(n^2). Space Complexity: O(1).

Problem-2 Can we improve the time complexity of Problem-1?

Solution: **Yes**, using sorting technique.

```
func CheckDuplicatesInOrderedArray(A []int) bool {
    sort.Ints(A)
    for i := 0; i < len(A)-1; i++ {
        if A[i] == A[i+1] {
            return true
        }
    }
    return false
}
```

Heapsort function takes O($nlogn$) time, and requires O(1) space. The scan clearly takes $n - 1$ iterations, each iteration using O(1) time. The overall time is O($nlogn + n$) = O($nlogn$).

Time Complexity: O($nlogn$). Space Complexity: O(1).

Note: For variations of this problem, refer to *Searching* chapter.

Problem-3 Given an array $A[0 \dots n-1]$, where each element of the array represents a vote in the election. Assume that each vote is given as an integer representing the ID of the chosen candidate. Give an algorithm for determining who wins the election.

Solution: This problem is nothing but finding the element which repeated the maximum number of times. The solution is similar to the Problem-1 solution: keep track of counter.

```
func checkWhoWinsTheElection(A []int) int {
    maxCounter, counter, candidate := 0, 0, A[0]
    for i := 0; i < len(A); i++ {
        candidate = A[i]
        counter = 0
        for j := i + 1; j < len(A); j++ {
            if A[i] == A[j] {
                counter++
            }
        }
        if counter > maxCounter {
            maxCounter = counter
            candidate = A[i]
        }
    }
    return candidate
}
```

Time Complexity: O(n^2). Space Complexity: O(1).

Note: For variations of this problem, refer to *Searching* chapter.

Problem-4 Can we improve the time complexity of Problem-3? Assume we don't have any extra space.

Solution: Yes. The approach is to sort the votes based on candidate ID, then scan the sorted array and count up which candidate so far has the most votes. Start by sorting the list, which takes O($nlogn$) time. Then move through the list, keeping track of the which candidate has the most votes so far, and how many votes they have received. If the number of votes for the current candidate exceeds the previous maximum, make it the new maximum. The second (counting) stage takes O(n) time, so the whole process takes O($nlogn$) time.

```
func checkWhoWinsTheElection(A []int) int {
    currentCounter, maxCounter, currentCandidate, maxCandidate := 1, 1, A[0], 0
    sort.Ints(A)
    for i := 1; i < len(A); i++ {
        if A[i] == currentCandidate {
            currentCounter++
        } else {
            currentCandidate = A[i]
            currentCounter = 1
        }
        if currentCounter > maxCounter {
            maxCandidate = currentCandidate
```

```
                maxCounter = currentCounter
            }
        }
        return maxCandidate
    }
```

Assuming the sorting algorithm time complexity as $O(nlogn)$ and in-place, it only uses an additional $O(1)$ of storage in addition to the input array. The scan of the sorted array does a constant-time conditional $n - 1$ times, thus using $O(n)$ time. The overall time bound is $O(nlogn)$.

Problem-5 Consider the voting problem from the previous exercise, but now suppose that we know the number k < n of candidates running. Describe an $O(nlogk)$-time algorithm for determining who wins the election.

Solution: In this case, the candidates can be stored in a balanced binary tree (for example, an AVL Tree). Each node should store a candidate ID and the number of votes they have received so far. As each vote in the sequence is processed, search the tree for the candidate ID of the chosen candidate (which takes $O(logk)$ time). If the ID is found, add one to its number of votes. Otherwise, create a new node with this ID and with one vote. At the end, go through all the nodes in the tree to find the one with the most votes. The process could be sped up even further in the average case (though not in the worst case) by replacing the AVL Tree with a Hash Table.

Problem-6 Can we further improve the time complexity of Problem-3?

Solution: In the given problem, number of candidates is less but the number of votes is significantly large. For this problem we can use counting sort.

Time Complexity: $O(n)$, n is the number of votes (elements) in array.
Space Complexity: $O(k)$, k is the number of candidates participated in election.

Problem-7 Given an array A of n elements, each of which is an integer in the range $[1, n^2]$, how do we sort the array in $O(n)$ time?

Solution: If we subtract each number by 1 then we get the range $[0, n^2 - 1]$. If we consider all number as 2 –digit base n. Each digit ranges from 0 to n^2 - 1. Sort this using radix sort. This uses only two calls to counting sort. Finally, add 1 to all the numbers. Since there are 2 calls, the complexity is $O(2n) \approx O(n)$.

Problem-8 For Problem-7, what if the range is $[1...n^3]$?

Solution: If we subtract each number by 1 then we get the range $[0, n^3 - 1]$. Considering all numbers as *3*-digit base n: each digit ranges from 0 to n^3 - 1. Sort this using radix sort. This uses only three calls to counting sort. Finally, add 1 to all the numbers. Since there are 3 calls, the complexity is $O(3n) \approx O(n)$.

Problem-9 Given an array with n integers, each of value less than n^{100}, can it be sorted in linear time?

Solution: Yes. The reasoning is the same as in of Problem-7 and Problem-8.

Problem-10 Let A and B be two arrays of n elements each. Given a number K, give an $O(nlogn)$ time algorithm for determining whether there exists a ∈ A and b ∈ B such that $a + b = K$.

Solution: Since we need $O(nlogn)$, it gives us a pointer that we need to use sorting algorithm. So, we will do that. This is conceptually similar to the hashing approach except that instead of using a hash table, we sort the array elements and use binary search to test if a pair appears.

```
func find(A, B []int, K int) bool {
    sort.Ints(A)                    // O(nlogn)
    for i := 0; i < len(B); i++ {   // O(n)
        c := K - B[i]               // O(1)
        if binarySearch(c, A) {     // O(logn)
            return true
        }
    }
    return false
}
```

The runtime of this algorithm depends on the sorting algorithm used. Using a standard sorting algorithm, this takes time $O(nlogn)$ due to the cost of sorting.

Note: For variations of this problem, refer to *Searching* chapter.

Problem-11 Let A, B and C be three arrays of n elements each. Given a number K, give an $O(nlogn)$ time algorithm for determining whether there exists $a \in A$, $b \in B$ and $c \in C$ such that $a + b + c = K$.

Solution: Refer to *Searching* chapter.

Problem-12 Given an array of n elements, can we output in sorted order the K elements following the median in sorted order in time $O(n + KlogK)$.

Solution: Yes. Find the median and partition the median. With this we can find all the elements greater than it. Now find the Kth largest element in this set and partition it; and get all the elements less than it. Output the sorted list of the final set of elements. Clearly, this operation takes $O(n + KlogK)$ time.

Problem-13 Consider the sorting algorithms: Bubble sort, Insertion sort, Selection sort, Merge sort, Heap sort, and Quick sort. Which of these are stable?

Solution: Let us assume that A is the array to be sorted. Also, let us say R and S have the same key and R appears earlier in the array than S. That means, R is at $A[i]$ and S is at $A[j]$, with $i < j$. To show any stable algorithm, in the sorted output R must precede S.

Bubble sort: Yes. Elements change order only when a smaller record follows a larger. Since S is not smaller than R it cannot precede it.

Selection sort: No. It divides the array into sorted and unsorted portions and iteratively finds the minimum values in the unsorted portion. After finding a minimum x, if the algorithm moves x into the sorted portion of the array by means of a swap, then the element swapped could be R which then could be moved behind S. This would invert the positions of R and S, so in general it is not stable. If swapping is avoided, it could be made stable but the cost in time would probably be very significant.

Insertion sort: Yes. As presented, when S is to be inserted into sorted subarray $A[1..j - 1]$, only records larger than S are shifted. Thus R would not be shifted during $S's$ insertion and hence would always precede it.

Merge sort: Yes, In the case of records with equal keys, the record in the left subarray gets preference. Those are the records that came first in the unsorted array. As a result, they will precede later records with the same key.

Heap sort: No. Suppose $i = 1$ and R and S happen to be the two records with the largest keys in the input. Then R will remain in location 1 after the array is heapified, and will be placed in location n in the first iteration of Heapsort. Thus S will precede R in the output.

Quick sort: No. The partitioning step can swap the location of records many times, and thus two records with equal keys could swap position in the final output.

Problem-14 Consider the same sorting algorithms as that of Problem-13. Which of them are in-place?

Solution:

Bubble sort: Yes, because only two integers are required.

Insertion sort: Yes, since we need to store two integers and a record.

Selection sort: Yes. This algorithm would likely need space for two integers and one record.

Merge sort: No. Arrays need to perform the merge. (If the data is in the form of a linked list, the sorting can be done in-place, but this is a nontrivial modification.)

Heap sort: Yes, since the heap and partially-sorted array occupy opposite ends of the input array.

Quicksort: No, since it is recursive and stores $O(logn)$ activation records on the stack. Modifying it to be non-recursive is feasible but nontrivial.

Problem-15 Among Quick sort, Insertion sort, Selection sort, and Heap sort algorithms, which one needs the minimum number of swaps?

Solution: Selection sort – it needs n swaps only (refer to theory section).

Problem-16 What is the minimum number of comparisons required to determine if an integer appears more than $n/2$ times in a sorted array of n integers?

Solution: Refer to *Searching* chapter.

Problem-17 **Sort an array of 0's, 1's and 2's:** Given an array A[] consisting of 0's, 1's and 2's, give an algorithm for sorting A[]. The algorithm should put all 0's first, then all 1's and all 2's last.
Example: Input = {0,1,1,0,1,2,1,2,0,0,0,1}, Output = {0, 0, 0, 0, 0, 1, 1, 1, 1, 1, 2, 2}

Solution: Use Counting sort. Since there are only three elements and the maximum value is 2, we need a temporary array with 3 elements.

Time Complexity: $O(n)$. Space Complexity: $O(1)$.

Note: For variations of this problem, refer to *Searching* chapter.

Problem-18 Is there any other way of solving Problem-16?

Solution: Using Quick sort. Since we know that there are only 3 elements, 0, 1 and 2 in the array, we can select 1 as a pivot element for Quick sort. Quick sort finds the correct place for 1 by moving all 0's to the left of 1 and all 2's to the right of 1. For doing this it uses only one scan.

Time Complexity: $O(n)$. Space Complexity: $O(1)$.

Note: For efficient algorithm, refer to *Searching* chapter.

Problem-19 How do we find the number that appeared the maximum number of times in an array?

Solution: A simple solution is to run two loops. The outer loop picks all elements one by one. The inner loop finds frequency of the picked element and compares with the maximum so far. Time complexity of this solution is $O(n^2)$. A better approach is to sort the given array and scan the sorted array. While scanning, keep track of the elements that occur the maximum number of times.

Algorithm:
```
func mostFrequent(A []int) int {
    sort.Ints(A)                                    // Sort the array
    currentCounter, maxCounter, res, n := 1, 1, A[0], len(A)
    for i := 1; i < n; i++ {
        if A[i] == A[i-1] {
            currentCounter++
        } else {
            if currentCounter > maxCounter {
                maxCounter = currentCounter
                res = A[i-1]
            }
            currentCounter = 1
        }
    }
    if currentCounter > maxCounter {            // If last element is most frequent
        maxCounter = currentCounter
        res = A[n-1]
    }
    return res
}
```

Time Complexity = Time for Sorting + Time for Scan = $O(nlogn) + O(n) = O(nlogn)$. Space Complexity: O(1).

Note: For variations of this problem, refer to *Searching* chapter.

Problem-20 Is there any other way of solving Problem-19?

Solution: Using Binary Tree. Create a binary tree with an extra field *count* which indicates the number of times an element appeared in the input. Let us say we have created a Binary Search Tree [BST]. Now, do the In-Order traversal of the tree. The In-Order traversal of BST produces the sorted list. While doing the In-Order traversal keep track of the maximum element.

Time Complexity: $O(n) + O(n) \approx O(n)$. The first parameter is for constructing the BST and the second parameter is for Inorder Traversal. Space Complexity: $O(2n) \approx O(n)$, since every node in BST needs two extra pointers.

Problem-21 Is there yet another way of solving Problem-19?

Solution: Using Hash Table. For each element of the given array we use a counter, and for each occurrence of the element we increment the corresponding counter. At the end we can just return the element which has the maximum counter.

Time Complexity: $O(n)$. Space Complexity: $O(n)$. For constructing the hash table we need $O(n)$.

Note: For the efficient algorithm, refer to the *Searching* chapter.

Problem-22 Given a 2 GB file with one string per line, which sorting algorithm would we use to sort the file and why?

Solution: When we have a size limit of 2GB, it means that we cannot bring all the data into the main memory.

Algorithm: How much memory do we have available? Let's assume we have X MB of memory available. Divide the file into K chunks, where $X * K \sim 2\,GB$.

- Bring each chunk into memory and sort the lines as usual (any $O(nlogn)$ algorithm).
- Save the lines back to the file.
- Now bring the next chunk into memory and sort.
- Once we're done, merge them one by one; in the case of one set finishing, bring more data from the particular chunk.

The above algorithm is also known as *external sort*. Step 3 – 4 is known as K-way merge. The idea behind going for an external sort is the size of data. Since the data is huge and we can't bring it to the memory, we need to go for a disk-based sorting algorithm.

Problem-23 **Nearly sorted:** Given an array of n elements, each which is at most K positions from its target position, devise an algorithm that sorts in $O(n\ logK)$ time.

Solution: Divide the elements into n/K groups of size K, and sort each piece in $O(KlogK)$ time, let's say using Mergesort. This preserves the property that no element is more than K elements out of position. Now, merge each block of K elements with the block to its left.

Problem-24 Is there any other way of solving Problem-23?

Solution: Insert the first K elements into a binary heap. Insert the next element from the array into the heap, and delete the minimum element from the heap. Repeat.

Problem-25 **Merging K sorted lists:** Given K sorted lists with a total of n elements, give an $O(nlogK)$ algorithm to produce a sorted list of all n elements.

Solution: Simple Algorithm for merging K sorted lists: Consider groups each having $\frac{n}{K}$ elements. Take the first list and merge it with the second list using a linear-time algorithm for merging two sorted lists, such as the merging algorithm used in merge sort. Then, merge the resulting list of $\frac{2n}{K}$ elements with the third list, and then merge the resulting list of $\frac{3n}{K}$ elements with the fourth list. Repeat this until we end up with a single sorted list of all n elements.

Time Complexity: In each iteration we are merging K elements.

$$T(n) = \frac{2n}{K} + \frac{3n}{K} + \frac{4n}{K} + \cdots \frac{Kn}{K}(n) = \frac{n}{K}\sum_{i=2}^{K} i$$

$$T(n) = \frac{n}{K}\left[\frac{K(K+1)}{2}\right] \approx O(nK)$$

Problem-26 Can we improve the time complexity of Problem-25?

Solution: One method is to repeatedly pair up the lists and then merge each pair. This method can also be seen as a tail component of the execution merge sort, where the analysis is clear. This is called the Tournament Method. The maximum depth of the Tournament Method is $logK$ and in each iteration we are scanning all the n elements.

Time Complexity: O($n$logK).

Problem-27 Is there any other way of solving Problem-25?

Solution: The other method is to use a *min* priority queue for the minimum elements of each of the K lists. At each step, we output the extracted minimum of the priority queue, determine from which of the K lists it came, and insert the next element from that list into the priority queue. Since we are using priority queue, that maximum depth of priority queue is $logK$.

Time Complexity: O($n$logK).

Problem-28 Which sorting method is better for Linked Lists?

Solution: Merge sort is a better choice. At first appearance, merge sort may not be a good selection since the middle node is required to subdivide the given list into two sub-lists of equal length. We can easily solve this problem by finding the middle node in the linked list (refer to *Linked Lists* chapter). Then, sorting these two lists recursively and merging the results into a single list will sort the given one.

```
func sortList(head *ListNode) *ListNode {
    if head == nil || head.next == nil {
        return head
    }
    slow, fast := head, head
    for fast.next != nil && fast.next.next != nil {
        slow, fast = slow.next, fast.next.next
    }
    firstTail := slow
    slow = slow.next
    firstTail.next = nil            // divide the first list and the second
    first, second := sortList(head), sortList(slow)
    return merge(first, second)
}
func merge(head1 *ListNode, head2 *ListNode) *ListNode {
    curHead := &ListNode{}
    tmpHead := curHead
    for head1 != nil && head2 != nil {
        if head1.data < head2.data {
            curHead.next = head1
            head1 = head1.next
            curHead = curHead.next
        } else {
            curHead.next = head2
            head2 = head2.next
```

```
            curHead = curHead.next
        }
    }
    if head1 != nil {
        curHead.next = head1
    } else if head2 != nil {
        curHead.next = head2
    }
    return tmpHead.next
}
```

All external sorting algorithms can be used for sorting linked lists since each involved file can be considered as a linked list that can only be accessed sequentially. We can sort a doubly linked list using its next fields as if it was a singly linked one and reconstruct the prev fields after sorting with an additional scan.

Problem-29 Given an array of $100,000$ pixel color values, each of which is an integer in the range $[0,255]$. Which sorting algorithm is preferable for sorting them?

Solution: Counting Sort. There are only 256 key values, so the auxiliary array would only be of size 256, and there would be only two passes through the data, which would be very efficient in both time and space.

Problem-30 Similar to Problem-29, if we have a telephone directory with 10 million entries, which sorting algorithm is best?

Solution: Bucket Sort. In Bucket Sort the buckets are defined by the last 7 digits. This requires an auxiliary array of size 10 million and has the advantage of requiring only one pass through the data on disk. Each bucket contains all telephone numbers with the same last 7 digits but with different area codes. The buckets can then be sorted by area code with selection or insertion sort; there are only a handful of area codes.

Problem-31 Give an algorithm for merging K-sorted lists.

Solution: Refer to *Priority Queues* chapter.

Problem-32 Given a big file containing billions of numbers. Find maximum 10 numbers from this file.

Solution: Refer to *Priority Queues* chapter.

Problem-33 There are two sorted arrays A and B. The first one is of size $m + n$ containing only m elements. Another one is of size n and contains n elements. Merge these two arrays into the first array of size $m + n$ such that the output is sorted.

Solution: The trick for this problem is to start filling the destination array from the back with the largest elements. We will end up with a merged and sorted destination array.

```
func merge(A []int, m int, B []int, n int) {
    i := m + n - 1
    j, k := m-1, n-1
    for j >= 0 && k >= 0 {
        if A[j] > B[k] {
            A[i] = A[j]
            j--
        } else {
            A[i] = B[k]
            k--
        }
        i--
    }
    if k >= 0 {
        copy(A[:k+1], B[:k+1])
    }
}
```

Time Complexity: O($m + n$). Space Complexity: O(1).

Problem-34 **Nuts and Bolts Problem:** Given a set of n nuts of different sizes and n bolts such that there is a one-to-one correspondence between the nuts and the bolts, find for each nut its corresponding bolt. Assume that we can only compare nuts to bolts: we cannot compare nuts to nuts and bolts to bolts.

Alternative way of framing the question: We are given a box which contains bolts and nuts. Assume there are n nuts and n bolts and that each nut matches exactly one bolt (and vice versa). By trying to match a bolt and a nut we can see which one is bigger, but we cannot compare two bolts or two nuts directly. Design an efficient algorithm for matching the nuts and bolts.

Solution: Brute Force Approach: Start with the first bolt and compare it with each nut until we find a match. In the worst case, we require n comparisons. Repeat this for successive bolts on all remaining gives $O(n^2)$ complexity.

Problem-35 For Problem-34, can we improve the complexity?

Solution: In Problem-34, we got $O(n^2)$ complexity in the worst case (if bolts are in ascending order and nuts are in descending order). Its analysis is the same as that of Quick Sort. The improvement is also along the same lines. To reduce the worst case complexity, instead of selecting the first bolt every time, we can select a random bolt and match it with nuts. This randomized selection reduces the probability of getting the worst case, but still the worst case is $O(n^2)$.

Problem-36 For Problem-34, can we further improve the complexity?

Solution: We can use a divide-and-conquer technique for solving this problem and the solution is very similar to randomized Quick Sort. For simplicity let us assume that bolts and nuts are represented in two arrays B and N.

The algorithm first performs a partition operation as follows: pick a random bolt $B[i]$. Using this bolt, rearrange the array of nuts into three groups of elements:

- First the nuts smaller than $B[i]$
- Then the nut that matches $B[i]$, and
- Finally, the nuts larger than $B[i]$.

Next, using the nut that matches $B[i]$, perform a similar partition on the array of bolts. This pair of partitioning operations can easily be implemented in $O(n)$ time, and it leaves the bolts and nuts nicely partitioned so that the "*pivot*" bolt and nut are aligned with each other and all other bolts and nuts are on the correct side of these pivots – smaller nuts and bolts precede the pivots, and larger nuts and bolts follow the pivots. Our algorithm then completes by recursively applying itself to the subarray to the left and right of the pivot position to match these remaining bolts and nuts. We can assume by induction on n that these recursive calls will properly match the remaining bolts.

To analyze the running time of our algorithm, we can use the same analysis as that of randomized Quick Sort. Therefore, applying the analysis from Quick Sort, the time complexity of our algorithm is $O(nlogn)$.

Alternative Analysis: We can solve this problem by making a small change to Quick Sort. Let us assume that we pick the last element as the pivot, say it is a nut. Compare the nut with only bolts as we walk down the array. This will partition the array for the bolts. Every bolt less than the partition nut will be on the left. And every bolt greater than the partition nut will be on the right.

While traversing down the list, find the matching bolt for the partition nut. Now we do the partition again using the matching bolt. As a result, all the nuts less than the matching bolt will be on the left side and all the nuts greater than the matching bolt will be on the right side. Recursively call on the left and right arrays.

The time complexity is $O(2nlogn) \approx O(nlogn)$.

Problem-37 Given a binary tree, can we print its elements in sorted order in $O(n)$ time by performing an In-order tree traversal?

Solution: Yes, if the tree is a Binary Search Tree [BST]. For more details refer to the *Trees* chapter.

Problem-38 Given an array of elements, convert it into an array such that A < B > C < D > E < F and so on.

Solution: Sort the array, then swap every adjacent element to get the final result.

```
func convertArraytoSawToothWave(A []int) {
    n := len(A)
    sort.Ints(A)
    for i := 1; i < n; i += 2 {
        if i+1 < n {
            A[i], A[i+1] = A[i+1], A[i]
        }
    }
}
```

The time complexity is $O(nlogn + n) \approx O(nlogn)$, for sorting and a scan.

Problem-39 Can we do Problem-39 with O(n) time?

Solution: Make sure all even positioned elements are greater than their adjacent odd elements, and we don't need to worry about odd positioned elements. Traverse all even positioned elements of input array, and do the following:

- If the current element is smaller than the previous odd element, swap previous and current.
- If the current element is smaller than the next odd element, swap next and current.

```
func convertArraytoSawToothWave2(A []int) {
    // Flag true indicates relation "<" is expected, else ">" is expected. The first expected relation is "<"
    flag, n := true, len(A)
```

```
        for i := 0; i <= n-2; i++ {
            if flag {
                if A[i] > A[i+1] {  // If we have a situation like A > B > C, we get A > B < C by swapping B and C
                    A[i], A[i+1] = A[i+1], A[i]
                }
            } else {
                if A[i] < A[i+1] {  // If we have a situation like A < B < C, we get A < C > B by swapping B and C
                    A[i], A[i+1] = A[i+1], A[i]
                }
            }
            if flag {
                flag = false
            } else {
                flag = true
            }
        }
    }
```

The time complexity is $O(n)$.

Problem-40 Merge sort uses

(a) Divide and conquer strategy (b) Backtracking approach (c) Heuristic search (d) Greedy approach

Solution: (a). Refer theory section.

Problem-41 Which of the following algorithm design techniques is used in the quicksort algorithm?

(a) Dynamic programming (b) Backtracking (c) Divide and conquer (d) Greedy method

Solution: (c). Refer theory section.

Problem-42 Sort the linked list elements in O(n), where n is the number of elements in the linked list.

Solution: As stated many times, the lower bound on comparison based sorting for general data is going to be O($nlogn$). So, for general data on a linked list, the best possible sort that will work on any data that can compare two objects is going to be O($nlogn$). However, if you have a more limited domain of things to work in, you can improve the time it takes (at least proportional to n). For instance, if you are working with integers no larger than some value, you could use Counting Sort or Radix Sort, as these use the specific objects you're sorting to reduce the complexity with proportion to n. Be careful, though, these add some other things to the complexity that you may not consider (for instance, Counting Sort and Radix sort both add in factors that are based on the size of the numbers you're sorting, O($n + k$) where k is the size of largest number for Counting Sort, for instance).

Also, if you happen to have objects that have a perfect hash (or at least a hash that maps all values differently), you could try using a counting or radix sort on their hash functions. It is the application of counting sort.

Algorithm:

1) In the given linked list, find the maximum element (k). This would take O(n) time.
2) Create a hash map of the size k. This would need O(k) space.
3) Scan through the linked list elements, set 1 to the corresponding index in the array. Suppose element in the linked is 19, then H[4] = 1. This would take O(n) time.
4) Now the array is sorted as similar to counting sort.
5) Read the elements from the array and add it back to the list with a time complexity of O(k).

Problem-43 For merging two sorted lists of sizes m and n into a sorted list of size m+n, we required comparisons of

(a) O(m) (b) O(n) (c) O($m + n$) (d) O($logm + logn$)

Solution: (c). We can use merge sort logic. Refer theory section.

Problem-44 Quick-sort is run on two inputs shown below to sort in ascending order

(i) 1,2,3 ....n (ii) n, n – 1, n – 2, ... 2, 1

Let C1 and C2 be the number of comparisons made for the inputs (i) and (ii) respectively. Then,

(a) C1 < C2 (b) C1 > C2 (c) C1 = C2 (d) we cannot say anything for arbitrary n.

Solution: (b). Since the given problems needs the output in ascending order, Quicksort on already sorted order gives the worst case (O(n^2)). So, (i) generates worst case and (ii) needs fewer comparisons.

Problem-45 Give the correct matching for the following pairs:

(A) O($logn$) (P) Selection
(B) O(n) (Q) Insertion sort
(C) O($nlogn$) (R) Binary search
(D) O(n^2) (S) Merge sort

(a) A – R B – P C – Q D - S (b) A – R B – P C – S D - Q (c) A – P B – R C – S D - Q (d) A – P B – S C – R D - Q

Solution: (b). Refer theory section.

Problem-46 Let s be a sorted array of n integers. Let t(n) denote the time taken for the most efficient algorithm to determine if there are two elements with sum less than 1000 in s. which of the following statements is true?
a) $t(n)$ is O(1) b) $n < t(n) < nlog_2^n$ c) $nlog_2^n < t(n) < \binom{n}{2}$ d) $t(n) = \binom{n}{2}$

Solution: (a). Since the given array is already sorted it is enough if we check the first two elements of the array.

Problem-47 The usual $\Theta(n^2)$ implementation of Insertion Sort to sort an array uses linear search to identify the position where an element is to be inserted into the already sorted part of the array. If, instead, we use binary search to identify the position, the worst case running time will
(a) remain $\Theta(n^2)$ (b) become $\Theta(n(log\, n)^2)$ (c) become $\Theta(nlogn)$ (d) become $\Theta(n)$

Solution: (a). If we use binary search then there will be $log_2^{n!}$comparisons in the worst case, which is $\Theta(nlogn)$. But the algorithm as a whole will still have a running time of $\Theta(n^2)$ on average because of the series of swaps required for each insertion.

Problem-48 In quick sort, for sorting n elements, the $n/4^{th}$ smallest element is selected as pivot using an O(n) time algorithm. What is the worst case time complexity of the quick sort?
(A) $\Theta(n)$ (B) $\Theta(nLogn)$ (C) $\Theta(n^2)$ (D) $\Theta(n^2 logn)$

Solution: The recursion expression becomes: T(n) = T(n/4) + T(3n/4) + cn. Solving the recursion using *variant* of master theorem, we get $\Theta(nLogn)$.

Problem-49 Consider the Quicksort algorithm. Suppose there is a procedure for finding a pivot element which splits the list into two sub-lists each of which contains at least one-fifth of the elements. Let T(n) be the number of comparisons required to sort n elements. Then
A) T (n) ≤ 2T (n /5) + n B) T (n) ≤ T (n /5) + T (4n /5) + n C) T (n) ≤ 2T (4n /5) + n D) T (n) ≤ 2T (n /2) + n

Solution: (C). For the case where n/5 elements are in one subset, T(n/5) comparisons are needed for the first subset with n/5 elements, T(4n/5) is for the rest 4n/5 elements, and n is for finding the pivot. If there are more than n/5 elements in one set then other set will have less than 4n/5 elements and time complexity will be less than T(n/5) + T(4n/5) + n.

Problem-50 Which of the following sorting algorithms has the lowest worst-case complexity?
(A) Merge sort (B) Bubble sort (C) Quick sort (D) Selection sort

Solution: (A). Refer theory section.

Problem-51 Which one of the following in place sorting algorithms needs the minimum number of swaps?
(A) Quick sort (B) Insertion sort (C) Selection sort (D) Heap sort

Solution: (C). Refer theory section.

Problem-52 You have an array of n elements. Suppose you implement quicksort by always choosing the central element of the array as the pivot. Then the tightest upper bound for the worst case performance is
(A) O(n^2) (B) O($nlogn$) (C) $\Theta(nlogn)$ (D) O(n^3)

Solution: (A). When we choose the first element as the pivot, the worst case of quick sort comes if the input is sorted- either in ascending or descending order.

Problem-53 Let P be a QuickSort Program to sort numbers in ascending order using the first element as pivot. Let t1 and t2 be the number of comparisons made by P for the inputs {1, 2, 3, 4, 5} and {4, 1, 5, 3, 2} respectively. Which one of the following holds?
(A) t1 = 5 (B) t1 < t2 (C) t1 > t2 (D) t1 = t2

Solution: (C). Quick Sort's worst case occurs when first (or last) element is chosen as pivot with sorted arrays.

Problem-54 The minimum number of comparisons required to find the minimum and the maximum of 100 numbers is __

Solution: 147 (Formula for the minimum number of comparisons required is 3n/2 – 3 with n numbers).

Problem-55The number of elements that can be sorted in T($logn$) time using heap sort is
(A) Θ(1) (B) Θ(sqrt(logn)) (C) Θ(log n/(log log n)) (D) Θ(logn)

Solution: (D). Sorting an array with k elements takes time Θ(k log k) as k grows. We want to choose k such that Θ(k log k) = Θ(logn). Choosing k = Θ(logn) doesn't necessarily work, since Θ(k log k) = Θ(logn loglogn) ≠ Θ(logn). On the other hand, if you choose k = T(log n / log log n), then the runtime of the sort will be

= Θ((logn / loglogn) log (logn / loglogn))
= Θ((logn / loglogn) (loglogn - logloglogn))
= Θ(logn - logn logloglogn / loglogn)
= Θ(logn (1 - logloglogn / loglogn))

Notice that 1 - logloglogn / loglogn tends toward 1 as n goes to infinity, so the above expression actually is Θ(log n), as required. Therefore, if you try to sort an array of size Θ(logn / loglogn) using heap sort, as a function of n, the runtime is Θ(logn).

Problem-56 Which one of the following is the tightest upper bound that represents the number of swaps required to sort n numbers using selection sort?

(A) $O(logn)$ (B) $O(n)$ (C) $O(nlogn)$ (D) $O(n^2)$

Solution: (B). Selection sort requires only $O(n)$ swaps.

Problem-57 Which one of the following is the recurrence equation for the worst case time complexity of the Quicksort algorithm for sorting n(≥ 2) numbers? In the recurrence equations given in the options below, c is a constant.

(A)T(n) = 2T (n/2) + cn (B) T(n) = T(n – 1) + T(0) + cn (C) T(n) = 2T (n – 2) + cn (D) T(n) = T(n/2) + cn

Solution: (B). When the pivot is the smallest (or largest) element at partitioning on a block of size n the result yields one empty sub-block, one element (pivot) in the correct place and sub block of size $n - 1$.

Problem-58 True or False. In randomized quicksort, each key is involved in the same number of comparisons.

Solution: False.

Problem-59 True or False: If Quicksort is written so that the partition algorithm always uses the median value of the segment as the pivot, then the worst-case performance is $O(nlogn)$.

Solution: True.

Problem-60 **Squares of a sorted array**: Given an array of numbers A sorted in ascending order, return an array of the squares of each number, also in sorted ascending order. For array = [-6, -4, 1, 2, 3, 5], the output should be [1, 4, 9, 16, 25, 36].

Solution: **Intuitive approach**: One simplest approach to solve this problem is to create an array of the squares of each element, and sort them.

```
func sortedSquares_naive(A []int) []int {
    for i := 0; i < len(A); i++ {
        A[i] = A[i] * A[i]
    }
    sort.Ints(A)
    return A
}
```

Time complexity: $O(nlogn)$, for sorting the array. Space complexity: $O(n)$, for the result array.

Elegant approach: Since the given array A is sorted, it might have some negative elements. The squares of these negative numbers would be in decreasing order. Similarly, the squares of positive numbers would be in increasing order. For example, with [-4, -3, -1, 3, 4, 5], we have the negative part [-4, -3, -1] with squares [16, 9, 1], and the positive part [3, 4, 5] with squares [9, 16, 25]. Our strategy is to iterate over the negative part in reverse, and the positive part in the forward direction.

We can use two pointers to read the positive and negative parts of the array - one pointer i in the positive direction, and another j in the negative direction. Now that we are reading two increasing arrays (the squares of the elements), we can merge these arrays together using a two-pointer technique.

```
func sortedSquares(A []int) []int {
    result := make([]int, len(A))
    left, right := 0, len(A)-1
    for i := len(A) - 1; i >= 0; i-- {
        if abs(A[left]) < abs(A[right]) {
            result[i] = A[right] * A[right]
            right--
        } else {
            result[i] = A[left] * A[left]
            left++
        }
    }
    return result
}
func abs(num int) int {
    if num < 0 {
        return -num
    }
    return num
}
```

Time complexity: $O(n)$. Space complexity: $O(n)$, for the result array.

CHAPTER

11 SEARCHING

11.1 What is Searching?

In computer science, *searching* is the process of finding an item with specified properties from a collection of items. The items may be stored as records in a database, simple data elements in arrays, text in files, nodes in trees, vertices and edges in graphs, or they may be elements of other search spaces.

11.2 Why do we need Searching?

Searching is one of the core computer science algorithms. We know that today's computers store a lot of information. To retrieve this information proficiently we need very efficient searching algorithms. There are certain ways of organizing the data that improves the searching process. That means, if we keep the data in proper order, it is easy to search the required element. Sorting is one of the techniques for making the elements ordered. In this chapter we will see different searching algorithms.

11.3 Types of Searching

Following are the types of searches which we will be discussing in this book.

- Unordered Linear Search
- Sorted/Ordered Linear Search
- Binary Search
- Interpolation search
- Binary Search Trees (operates on trees and refer *Trees* chapter)
- Symbol Tables and Hashing
- String Searching Algorithms: Tries, Ternary Search and Suffix Trees

11.4 Unordered Linear Search

Let us assume we are given an array where the order of the elements is not known. That means the elements of the array are not sorted. In this case, to search for an element we have to scan the complete array and see if the element is there in the given list or not.

```
package main
import "fmt"
func linearSearch(A []int, data int) int {
  for i, item:= range A {
    if(item == data) {
      return i+1
    }
  }
  return 0
}
func main() {
  A := []int {67,68,16,8,5,86,29,21,50}
  a := linearSearch(A, 5)
  fmt.Printf("The Source Array : %v\n", A)
  fmt.Printf("The element %v is found at %v location", 5, a)
}
```

Time complexity: O(n), in the worst case we need to scan the complete array. Space complexity: O(1).

11.5 Sorted/Ordered Linear Search

If the elements of the array are already sorted, then in many cases we don't have to scan the complete array to see if the element is there in the given array or not. In the algorithm below, it can be seen that, at any point if the value at $A[i]$ is greater than the *data* to be searched, then we just return -1 without searching the remaining array.

```
package main
import "fmt"
func  orderedLinearSearch(A []int, data int) int {
  for i, item:= range A {
    if(item == data) {
      return i+1
    } else if (A[i] > data) {
      return 0
    }
  }
  return 0
}
func main() {
  A := []int {67,68,16,8,5,86,29,21,50}
  a := orderedLinearSearch(A, 5)
  fmt.Printf("The Source Array : %v\n", A)
  fmt.Printf("The element %v is found at %v location", 5, a)
}
```

Time complexity of this algorithm is $O(n)$. This is because in the worst case we need to scan the complete array. But in the average case it reduces the complexity even though the growth rate is the same.

Space complexity: O(1).

Note: For the above algorithm we can make further improvement by incrementing the index at a faster rate (say, 2). This will reduce the number of comparisons for searching in the sorted list.

11.6 Binary Search

Let us consider the problem of searching a word in a dictionary. Typically, we directly go to some approximate page [say, middle page] and start searching from that point. If the *name* that we are searching is the same then the search is complete. If the page is before the selected pages then apply the same process for the first half; otherwise apply the same process to the second half. Binary search also works in the same way. The algorithm applying such a strategy is referred to as *binary search* algorithm.

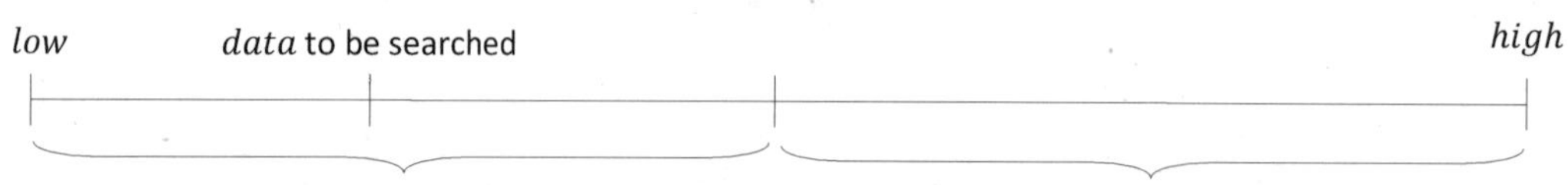

$$mid = low + \frac{(high-low)}{2} \ or \ \frac{low+high}{2}$$

```
// Iterative Binary Search Algorithm
package main
import "fmt"

func binarySearch(data int, A []int) bool {
   low, high := 0, len(A) - 1
   for low <= high{
      mid := (low + high) / 2
      if A[mid] < data {
         low = mid + 1
      }else{
         high = mid - 1
      }
   }
   if low == len(A) || A[low] != data {
      return false
   }
   return true
}
```

```
func main(){
    items := []int{1,2, 9, 10, 11, 45, 73, 80, 200} // should be a sorted array
    fmt.Println(binarySearch(63, items))
    fmt.Println(binarySearch(73, items))
}
// Recursive Binary Search Algorithm
package main
import "fmt"
func binarySearch(data int, A []int) bool {
    low, high := 0, len(A) - 1
    if low <= high {
        mid := ((high + low) / 2)
        if A[mid] > data {
            return binarySearch(data, A[:mid])
        } else if A[mid] < data {
            return binarySearch(data, A[mid+1:])
        } else {
            return true
        }
    }
    return false
}
func main(){
    items := []int{1,2, 9, 10, 11, 45, 73, 80, 200} // should be a sorted array
    fmt.Println(binarySearch(63, items))
    fmt.Println(binarySearch(73, items))
}
```

Recurrence for binary search is $T(n) = T(\frac{n}{2}) + \Theta(1)$. This is because we are always considering only half of the input list and throwing out the other half. Using *Divide and Conquer* master theorem, we get, $T(n) = O(logn)$.

Time Complexity: $O(logn)$. Space Complexity: O(1) [for iterative algorithm].

11.7 Interpolation Search

Undoubtedly binary search is a great algorithm for searching with average running time complexity of *logn*. It always chooses the middle of the remaining search space, discarding one half or the other, again depending on the comparison between the key value found at the estimated (middle) position and the key value sought. The remaining search space is reduced to the part before or after the estimated position.

In the mathematics, interpolation is a process of constructing new data points within the range of a discrete set of known data points. In computer science, one often has a number of data points which represent the values of a function for a limited number of values of the independent variable. It is often required to interpolate (i.e. estimate) the value of that function for an intermediate value of the independent variable.

For example, suppose we have a table like this, which gives some values of an unknown function *f*. Interpolation provides a means of estimating the function at intermediate points, such as $x = 5.5$.

x	$f(x)$
1	10
2	20
3	30
4	40
5	50
6	60
7	70

There are many different interpolation methods, and one of the simplest methods is linear interpolation. Consider the above example of estimating $f(5.5)$. Since 5.5 is midway between 5 and 6, it is reasonable to take $f(5.5)$ midway between $f(5) = 50$ and $f(6) = 60$, which yields 55 ((50+60)/2).

Linear interpolation takes two data points, say (x_1, y_1) and (x_2, y_2), and the interpolant is given by:

$$y = y_1 + (y_2 - y_1)\frac{x - x_1}{x_2 - x_1} \text{ at point } (x, y)$$

With above inputs, what will happen if we don't use the constant ½, but another more accurate constant "K", that can lead us closer to the searched item.

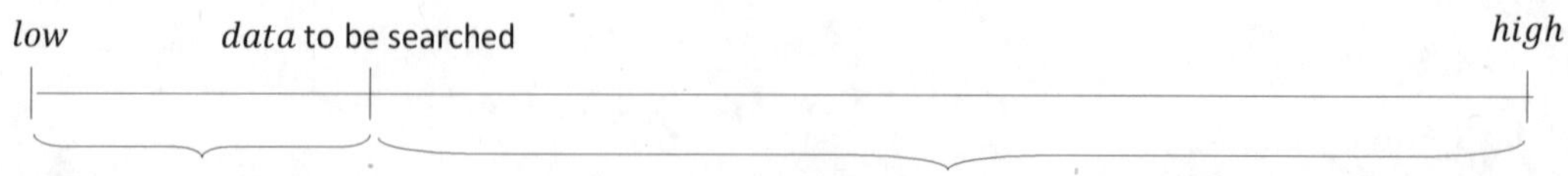

$$K = \frac{data-low}{high-low}$$

This algorithm tries to follow the way we search a name in a phone book, or a word in the dictionary. We, humans, know in advance that in case the name we're searching starts with a "m", like "monk" for instance, we should start searching near the middle of the phone book. Thus if we're searching the word "career" in the dictionary, you know that it should be placed somewhere at the beginning. This is because we know the order of the letters, we know the interval (a-z), and somehow we intuitively know that the words are dispersed equally. These facts are enough to realize that the binary search can be a bad choice. Indeed the binary search algorithm divides the list in two equal sub-lists, which is useless if we know in advance that the searched item is somewhere in the beginning or the end of the list. Yes, we can use also jump search if the item is at the beginning, but not if it is at the end, in that case this algorithm is not so effective.

The interpolation search algorithm tries to improve the binary search. The question is how to find this value? Well, we know bounds of the interval and looking closer to the image above we can define the following formula.

$$K = \frac{data - low}{high - low}$$

This constant K is used to narrow down the search space. For binary search, this constant K is $(low + high)/2$.

Now we can be sure that we're closer to the searched value. On average the interpolation search makes about $log(logn)$ comparisons (if the elements are uniformly distributed), where n is the number of elements to be searched. In the worst case (for instance where the numerical values of the keys increase exponentially) it can make up to O(n) comparisons. In interpolation-sequential search, interpolation is used to find an item near the one being searched for, then linear search is used to find the exact item. For this algorithm to give best results, the dataset should be ordered and uniformly distributed.

```
func interpolationSearch(A []int, data int) int { // Interpolation Search in Golang
    low, high := 0, len(A) - 1
    for low <= high && data >= A[low] && data <= A[high] {
        guessIndex := low + (data-A[low])*(high-low)/(A[high]-A[low])
        if A[guessIndex] == data {
            return guessIndex
        else if A[guessIndex] < data {
            low = guessIndex + 1
        else if A[guessIndex] > data {
            high = guessIndex - 1
        }
    }
    return -1
}
func main(){                    // Test code
    items := []int{1,2, 9, 20, 31, 45, 63, 70, 100}
    fmt.Println(interpolationSearch(items,63))
}
```

11.8 Comparing Basic Searching Algorithms

Implementation	Search-Worst Case	Search-Average Case
Unordered Array	n	$n/2$
Ordered Array (Binary Search)	$logn$	$logn$
Unordered List	n	$n/2$
Ordered List	n	$n/2$
Binary Search Trees (for skew trees)	n	$logn$
Interpolation search	n	$log(logn)$

Note: For discussion on binary search trees refer to *Trees* chapter.

11.9 Symbol Tables and Hashing

Refer to *Symbol Tables* and *Hashing* chapters.

11.10 String Searching Algorithms

Refer to *String Algorithms* chapter.

11.11 Searching: Problems & Solutions

Problem-1 Given an array of n numbers, give an algorithm for checking whether there are any duplicate elements in the array or not?

Solution: This is one of the simplest problems. One obvious answer to this is exhaustively searching for duplicates in the array. That means, for each input element check whether there is any element with the same value. This we can solve just by using two simple *for* loops. The code for this solution can be given as:

```
func checkDuplicatesInArray(A []int) bool {
    for i := 0; i < len(A); i++ {
        for v := 0; v < i; v++ {        // Scan slice for a previous element of the same value.
            if A[v] == A[i] {
                return true
            }
        }
    }
    return false
}
```

Time Complexity: $O(n^2)$, for two nested *for* loops. Space Complexity: O(1).

Problem-2 Can we improve the complexity of Problem-1*'s* solution?

Solution: Yes. Sort the given array. After sorting, all the elements with equal values will be adjacent. Now, do another scan on this sorted array and see if there are elements with the same value and adjacent.

```
func checkDuplicatesInArray(A []int) bool {
    sort.Ints(A)
    for i := 0; i < len(A)-1; i++ {
        if A[i] == A[i+1] {
            return true
        }
    }
    return false
}
```

Time Complexity: $O(nlogn)$, for sorting (assuming $nlogn$ sorting algorithm). Space Complexity: O(1).

Problem-3 Is there any alternative way of solving *Problem-1*?

Solution: Yes, using hash table. Hash tables are a simple and effective method used to implement dictionaries. *Average* time to search for an element is O(1), while worst-case time is $O(n)$. Refer to *Hashing* chapter for more details on hashing algorithms. As an example, consider the array, $A = \{3,2,1,2,2,3\}$.

Scan the input array and insert the elements into the hash. For each inserted element, keep the *counter* as 1 (assume initially all entires are filled with zeros). This indicates that the corresponding element has occurred already. For the given array, the hash table will look like (after inserting the first three elements 3, 2 and 1):

Key		Counter
1	→	1
2	→	1
3	→	1

Now if we try inserting 2, since the counter value of 2 is already 1, we can say the element has appeared twice.

```
func checkDuplicatesInArray(A []int) bool {
    var HT = map[int]bool{}
    for _, num := range A {
        if _, ok := HT[num]; ok {
            return true
        }
        HT[num] = true
    }
    return false
}
```

Time Complexity: $O(n)$. Space Complexity: $O(n)$.

Problem-4 Can we further improve the complexity of Problem-1 solution?

Solution: Let us assume that the array elements are positive numbers and also all the elements are in the range 0 to $n-1$. For each element $A[i]$, go to the array element whose index is $A[i]$. That means select $A[A[i]]$ and mark - $A[A[i]]$ (negate the value at $A[A[i]]$). Continue this process until we encounter the element whose value is already negated. If one such element exists then we say duplicate elements exist in the given array. As an example, consider the array, $A = \{3,2,1,2,2,3\}$.

Initially,

3	2	1	2	2	3
0	1	2	3	4	5

At step-1, negate A[abs(A[0])],

3	2	1	-2	2	3
0	1	2	3	4	5

At step-2, negate A[abs(A[1])],

3	2	-1	-2	2	3
0	1	2	3	4	5

At step-3, negate A[abs(A[2])],

3	-2	-1	-2	2	3
0	1	2	3	4	5

At step-4, negate A[abs(A[3])],

3	-2	-1	-2	2	3
0	1	2	3	4	5

At step-4, observe that $A[abs(A[3])]$ is already negative. That means we have encountered the same value twice.

```
// Abs returns the absolute value of x.
func abs(x int) int {
    if x < 0 {
        return -x
    }
    return x
}
func checkDuplicatesInArray(A []int) bool {
    for i := 0; i < len(A); i++ {
        if A[abs(A[i])] < 0 {
            return true
        } else {
            A[abs(A[i])] = -A[abs(A[i])]
        }
    }
    return false
}
```

Time Complexity: O(n). Since only one scan is required. Space Complexity: O(1).

Notes:

- This solution does not work if the given array is read only.
- This solution will work only if all the array elements are positive.
- If the elements range is not in 0 to $n-1$ then it may give exceptions.

Problem-5 Given an array of n numbers. Give an algorithm for finding the element which appears the maximum number of times in the array.

Brute Force Solution: One simple solution to this is, for each input element check whether there is any element with the same value, and for each such occurrence, increment the counter. Each time, check the current counter with the *max* counter and update it if this value is greater than *max* counter. This we can solve just by using two simple *for* loops.

```
func maxRepetitionsBruteForce(A []int) []int {
    counter, max, maxElement := 0, 0, -1
    for i := 0; i < len(A); i++ {
        counter = 0
        for j := 0; j < len(A); j++ {
            if A[i] == A[j] {
                counter++
            }
        }
```

```
            if counter > max {
                max = counter
                maxElement = A[i]
            }
        }
        return []int{max, maxElement}
    }
```

Time Complexity: O(n^2), for two nested *for* loops. Space Complexity: O(1).

Problem-6 Can we improve the complexity of Problem-5 solution?

Solution: Yes. Sort the given array. After sorting, all the elements with equal values come adjacent. Now, just do another scan on this sorted array and see which element is appearing the maximum number of times.

Time Complexity: O($nlogn$). (for sorting). Space Complexity: O(1).

Problem-7 Is there any other way of solving Problem-5?

Solution: Yes, using hash table. For each element of the input, keep track of how many times that element appeared in the input. That means the counter value represents the number of occurrences for that element.

Time Complexity: O(n). Space Complexity: O(n).

Problem-8 For Problem-5, can we improve the time complexity? Assume that the elements' range is 1 to n. That means all the elements are within this range only.

Solution: Yes. We can solve this problem in two scans. We *cannot* use the negation technique of Problem-3 for this problem because of the number of repetitions. In the first scan, instead of negating, add the value n. That means for each occurrence of an element add the array size to that element. In the second scan, check the element value by dividing it by n and return the element which gives the maximum value. The code based on this method is given below.

```
    func maxRepetitionsBruteForce2(A []int) []int {
        maxCounter, maxElement, n := 0, -1, len(A)
        for i := 0; i < n; i++ {
            A[A[i]%n] += n
        }
        for i := 0; i < n; i++ {
            if A[i]/n > maxCounter {
                maxCounter = A[i] / n
                maxElement = i
            }
        }
        return []int{maxCounter, maxElement}
    }
```

Notes:

- This solution does not work if the given array is read only.
- This solution will work only if the array elements are positive.
- If the elements range is not in 1 to n then it may give exceptions.

Time Complexity: O(n). Since no nested *for* loops are required. Space Complexity: O(1).

Problem-9 Given an array of n numbers, give an algorithm for finding the first element in the array which is repeated. For example, in the array $A = \{3, 2, 1, 2, 2, 3\}$, the first repeated number is 3 (not 2). That means, we need to return the first element among the repeated elements.

Solution: We can use the brute force solution that we used for Problem-1. For each element, since it checks whether there is a duplicate for that element or not, whichever element duplicates first will be returned.

Problem-10 For Problem-9, can we use the sorting technique?

Solution: No. For proving the failed case, let us consider the following array. For example, $A = \{3, 2, 1, 2, 2, 3\}$. After sorting we get $A = \{1, 2, 2, 2, 3, 3\}$. In this sorted array the first repeated element is 2 but the actual answer is 3.

Problem-11 For Problem-9, can we use the hashing technique?

Solution: Yes. But the simple hashing technique which we used for Problem-3 will not work. For example, if we consider the input array as A = {3, 2, 1, 2, 3}, then the first repeated element is 3, but using our simple hashing technique we get the answer as 2. This is because 2 is coming twice before 3. Now let us change the hashing table behavior so that we get the first repeated element. Let us say, instead of storing 1 value, initially we store the position of the element in the array. As a result the hash table will look like (after inserting 3, 2 and 1):

1	→	3
2	→	2
3	→	1

Now, if we see 2 again, we just negate the current value of 2 in the hash table. That means, we make its counter value as −2. The negative value in the hash table indicates that we have seen the same element two times. Similarly, for 3 (the next element in the input) also, we negate the current value of the hash table and finally the hash table will look like:

1	→	3
2	→	-2
3	→	-1

After processing the complete input array, scan the hash table and return the highest negative indexed value from it (i.e., −1 in our case). The highest negative value indicates that we have seen that element first (among repeated elements) and also repeating.

What if the element is repeated more than twice? In this case, just skip the element if the corresponding value i is already negative.

Problem-12 For Problem-9, can we use the technique that we used for Problem-3 (negation technique)?

Solution: No. As an example of contradiction, for the array $A = \{3, 2, 1, 2, 2, 3\}$ the first repeated element is 3. But with negation technique the result is 2.

Problem-13 **Find the Missing Number:** We are given a list of n integers and these integers are in the range of 0 to n. There are no duplicates in the list. One of the integers is missing in the list. Given an algorithm to find the missing integer. **Example**: I/P: $[1, 2, 4, 6, 3, 7, 8]$ O/P: 5

Alternative problem statement: There is an array of numbers. A second array is formed by shuffling the elements of the first array and deleting a random element. Given these two arrays, find which element is missing in the second array.

Alternative problem statement: Given an array containing n distinct numbers taken from 0, 1, 2, ..., n, find the one that is missing from the array.

Brute Force Solution: One naive way to solve this problem is for each number i in the range 0 to n, check whether number i is in the given array or not.

```
func missingNumber(A []int) int {
    for v := 0; v <= len(A); v++ {
        found := false
        for i := 0; i < len(A); i++ {
            if v == A[i] {
                found = true
                break
            }
        }
        if found == false {
            return v
        }
    }
    return -1
}
```

Time Complexity: O(n^2). Space Complexity: O(1).

Problem-14 For Problem-13, can we use the sorting technique?

Solution: Yes. More efficient solution is to sort the first array, so while checking whether an element in the range 1 to n appears in the given array, we can do binary search.

```
func missingNumber2(A []int) int {
    if len(A) == 0 {
        return -1
    }
    sort.Ints(A)
    if A[len(A)-1] != len(A) {
        return len(A)
    }
    for i := 0; i < len(A); i++ {
```

```
            if A[i] != i {
                return i
            }
        }
        return -1
    }
```

Time Complexity: O($nlogn$), for sorting. Space Complexity: O(1).

Problem-15 For Problem-13, can we use the hashing technique?

Solution: Yes. Scan the input array and insert elements into the hash. For inserted elements, keep *value* as *true* (assume initially all entires are filled with false). This indicates that the corresponding element has occurred already. Now, for each element in the range 0 to n check the hash table and return the element which has value false. That is, once we hit an element with false that's the missing element.

```
    func missingNumber3(A []int) int {
        var HT = map[int]bool{}
        for _, num := range A {
            HT[num] = true
        }
        for v := 0; v <= len(A); v++ {
            if _, ok := HT[v]; ok == false {
                return v
            }
        }
        return -1
    }
```

Time Complexity: O(n). Space Complexity: O(n).

Problem-16 For Problem-13, can we improve the complexity?

Solution: Yes. We can use summation formula.

1) Get the sum of numbers, $sum = n \times (n+1)/2$.
2) Subtract all the numbers from *sum* and you will get the missing number.

```
    func missingNumber(A []int) int {
        sum, numsSum := len(A), 0
        for i := range A {
            sum += i
            numsSum += A[i]
        }
        return sum - numsSum
    }
```

Alternative implementation:

```
    func missingNumber(A []int) int {
        n := len(A)
        sum := 0
        for _, num := range A {
            sum += num
        }
        return ((n) * (n + 1) / 2) - sum
    }
```

Time Complexity: O(n), for scanning the complete array.

Problem-17 In Problem-13, if the sum of the numbers goes beyond the maximum allowed integer, then there can be integer overflow and we may not get the correct answer. Can we solve this problem?

Solution:

1) XOR all the array elements, let the result of XOR be X.
2) XOR all numbers from 1 to n, let XOR be Y.
3) XOR of X and Y gives the missing number.

```
    func missingNumber(A []int) int {
        X, Y := 0, 0
        for i := 0; i < len(A); i++ {
```

```
        X ^= A[i]
    }
    for i := 0; i <= len(A); i++ {
        Y ^= i
    }
    return X ^ Y
}
```

Alternative implementation:

```
func missingNumber(A []int) int {
    missing := len(A)
    for i := 0; i < len(A); i++ {
        missing ^= i ^ A[i]
    }
    return missing
}
```

Let's analyze why this approach works. What happens when we XOR two numbers? We should think bitwise, instead of decimal. XORing a 4-bit number with 1101 would flip the first, second, and fourth bits of the number. XORing the result again with 1101 would flip those bits back to their original value. So, if we XOR a number two times with some number nothing will change. We can also XOR with multiple numbers and the order would not matter. For example, say we XOR the number number1 with number2, then XOR the result with number3, then XOR their result with number2, and then with number3. The final result would be the original number number1. Because every XOR operation flips some bits and when we XOR with the same number again, we flip those bits back. So the order of XOR operations is not important. If we XOR a number with some number an odd number of times, there will be no effect.

Above we XOR all the numbers in the given range 1 to n and given array A. All numbers in given array A are from the range 1 to n, but there is an extra number in range 1 to n. So the effect of each XOR from array A is being reset by the corresponding same number in the range 1 to n (remember that the order of XOR is not important). But we can't reset the XOR of the extra number in the range 1 to n, because it doesn't appear in array A. So the result is as if we XOR 0 with that extra number, which is the number itself. Since XOR of a number with 0 is the number. Therefore, in the end we get the missing number in array A. The space complexity of this solution is constant O(1) since we only use one extra variable. Time complexity is O(n) because we perform a single pass from the array A and the range 1 to n.

Time Complexity: O(n), for scanning the complete array. Space Complexity: O(1).

Problem-18 **Find the Number Occurring an Odd Number of Times:** Given an array of positive integers, all numbers occur an even number of times except one number which occurs an odd number of times. Find the number in O(n) time & constant space. **Example**: I/P = [1, 2, 3, 2, 3, 1, 3] O/P = 3

Solution: Do a bitwise XOR of all the elements. We get the number which has odd occurrences. This is because, $A\ XOR\ A = 0$.

```
func singleNumber4(A []int) int {
    result := 0
    for _, n := range A {
        result ^= n
    }
    return result
}
```

Time Complexity: O(n). Space Complexity: O(1).

Problem-19 **Find the two repeating elements in a given array:** Given an array with *size*, all elements of the array are in range 1 to n and also all elements occur only once except two numbers which occur twice. Find those two repeating numbers. For example: if the array is 4, 2, 4, 5, 2, 3, 1 with $size = 7$ and $n = 5$. This input has $n + 2 = 7$ elements with all elements occurring once except 2 and 4 which occur twice. So the output should be 4 2.

Solution: One simple way is to scan the complete array for each element of the input elements. That means use two loops. In the outer loop, select elements one by one and count the number of occurrences of the selected element in the inner loop. For the code below, assume that *PrintRepeatedElements* is called with $n + 2$ to indicate the size.

```
func repeatedElements(A []int) {
    for i := 0; i < len(A); i++ {
        for j := i + 1; j < len(A); j++ {
            if A[i] == A[j] {
```

```
                fmt.Println(A[i])
            }
        }
    }
}
```

Time Complexity: $O(n^2)$. Space Complexity: O(1).

Problem-20 For Problem-19, can we improve the time complexity?

Solution: Sort the array using any comparison sorting algorithm and see if there are any elements which are contiguous with the same value.

Time Complexity: $O(nlogn)$. Space Complexity: O(1).

Problem-21 For Problem-19, can we improve the time complexity?

Solution: Use count array! This solution is like using a hash table. For simplicity we can use array for storing the counts. Traverse the array once and keep track of the count of all elements in the array using a temp array *count*[] of size n. When we see an element whose count is already set, print it as duplicate. For the code below assume that *PrintRepeatedElements* is called with $n + 2$ to indicate the size.

```
func repeatedElementsHashing(A []int) {
    counts := make([]int, len(A))
    for i := 0; i < len(A); i++ {
        counts[A[i]]++
        if counts[A[i]] == 2 {
            fmt.Println(A[i])
        }
    }
}
```

Time Complexity: $O(n)$. Space Complexity: $O(n)$.

Problem-22 Consider Problem-19. Let us assume that the numbers are in the range 1 to n. Is there any other way of solving the problem?

Solution: Yes, by using XOR Operation. Let the repeating numbers be X and Y, if we XOR all the elements in the array and also all integers from 1 to n, then the result will be $X\ XOR\ Y$. The 1's in binary representation of $X\ XOR\ Y$ correspond to the different bits between X and Y. If the kth bit of $X\ XOR\ Y$ is 1, we can XOR all the elements in the array and also all integers from 1 to n whose k^{th} bits are 1. The result will be one of X and Y.

```
func repeatedElementsXOR(A []int) {
    XOR, X, Y, n := 0, 0, 0, len(A)
    for i := 0; i < n; i++ {                  // Compute XOR of all elements in A[]
        XOR ^= A[i]
    }
    for i := 1; i <= n; i++ {                 // Compute XOR of all elements {1, 2 ..n}
        XOR ^= i
    }
    rightMostSetBit := XOR & ^(XOR - 1)   // Get the rightmost set bit in rightMostSetBit
    // Now divide elements in two sets by comparing rightmost set
    for i := 0; i < n; i++ {
        if (A[i] & rightMostSetBit) != 0 {
            X = X ^ A[i]                      // XOR of first set in A[]
        } else {
            Y = Y ^ A[i]
        }
    }
    for i := 1; i <= n; i++ {
        if (i & rightMostSetBit) != 0 {
            X = X ^ i                         // XOR of first set in A[] and {1, 2, ...n }
        } else {
            Y = Y ^ i
        }
    }
    fmt.Println(X, Y)
}
```

Time Complexity: $O(n)$. Space Complexity: O(1).

Problem-23 Consider Problem-19. Let us assume that the numbers are in the range 1 to n. Is there yet other way of solving the problem?

Solution: We can solve this by creating two simple mathematical equations. Let us assume that two numbers we are going to find are X and Y. We know the sum of n numbers is $n(n+1)/2$ and the product is $n!$. Make two equations using these sum and product formulae, and get values of two unknowns using the two equations. Let the summation of all numbers in array be S and product be P and the numbers which are being repeated are X and Y.

$$X + Y = S - \frac{n(n+1)}{2}$$
$$XY = P/n!$$

Using the above two equations, we can find out X and Y. There can be an addition and multiplication overflow problem with this approach.

```
func repeatedElementsMath(A []int) {
    S, P, n := 0, 1, len(A)-2
    for i := 0; i < len(A); i++ {              // Calculate Sum and Product of all elements in A[]
        S = S + A[i]
        P = P * A[i]
    }
    S = S - n*(n+1)/2
    P = P / factorial(n)
    D := int(math.Sqrt(float64(S*S - 4*P)))
    x := (D + S) / 2
    y := (S - D) / 2
    fmt.Println(x, y)
}
func factorial(n int) int {
    factVal := 1
    if n < 0 {
        fmt.Print("Factorial of negative number doesn't exist.")
    } else {
        for i := 1; i <= n; i++ {
            factVal *= i
        }
    }
    return factVal
}
```

Time Complexity: O(n). Space Complexity: O(1).

Problem-24 Can we solve this problem with negation technique?

Solution: This solution works only if array has positive integers and all the elements in the array are in range from 1 to n. The algorithm for this problem involves navigating the array and updating the array for every i^{th}index as $A[abs(A[i])] = A[abs(A[i])] * -1$. If $A[i]$ is already negative, then it means we are visiting it second time, means it is repeated.

```
func repeatedElementsNegationTechnique(A []int) {
    n := len(A)
    for i := 0; i < n; i++ {
        if A[abs(A[i])] < 0 {
            fmt.Println(abs(A[i]))
        } else {
            A[abs(A[i])] = A[abs(A[i])] * -1
        }
    }
}
```

Time Complexity: O(n). Space Complexity: O(1).

Problem-25 Similar to Problem-19, let us assume that the numbers are in the range 1 to n. Also, $n-1$ elements are repeated thrice and the remaining element repeated twice. Find the element which repeated twice.

Solution: If we XOR all the elements in the array and all integers from 1 to n, then all the elements which are repeated thrice will become zero. This is because, since the element is repeating thrice and XOR another time from range makes that element appear four times. As a result, the output of $a\,XOR\,a\,XOR\,a\,XOR\,a = 0$. It is the same case with all elements that are repeated three times.

With the same logic, for the element which repeated twice, if we XOR the input elements and also the range, then the total number of appearances for that element is 3. As a result, the output of $a\,XOR\,a\,XOR\,a = a$. Finally, we get the element which repeated twice.

Time Complexity: O(n). Space Complexity: O(1).

Problem-26 Given an array of n elements. Find two elements in the array such that their sum is equal to given element K.

Brute Force Solution: One simple solution to this is, for each input element, check whether there is any element whose sum is K. This we can solve just by using two simple for loops. The code for this solution can be given as:

```
func twoSum(A []int, target int) []int {
    for i, v := range A {
        for j := i + 1; j < len(A); j++ {
            if A[j] == target-v {
                return []int{i, j}
            }
        }
    }
    panic("should never happen")
}
```

Time Complexity: O(n^2). This is because of two nested for loops. Space Complexity: O(1).

Problem-27 For Problem-26, can we improve the time complexity?

Solution: Yes. Let us assume that we have sorted the given array. This operation takes O($n\,logn$). On the sorted array, maintain indices $loIndex = 0$ and hiIndex = $n-1$ and compute $A[loIndex] + A[hiIndex]$. If the sum equals K, then we are done with the solution. If the sum is less than K, decrement $hiIndex$, if the sum is greater than K, increment $loIndex$.

```
func twoSum(A []int, target int) []int {
    sort.Ints(A)
    fmt.Println(A)
    i, j := 0, len(A)-1
    for i < j {
        sum := A[i] + A[j]
        if sum == target {
            break
        } else if sum < target {
            i++
        } else {
            j--
        }
    }
    return []int{i, j}
}
```

Time Complexity: O($nlogn$). If the given array is already sorted then the complexity is O(n).
Space Complexity: O(1).

Problem-28 Does the solution of Problem-26 work even if the array is not sorted?

Solution: Yes. Since we are checking all possibilities, the algorithm ensures that we get the pair of numbers if they exist.

Problem-29 Is there any other way of solving Problem-26?

Solution: Yes, using hash table. Since our objective is to find two indexes of the array whose sum is K. Let us say those indexes are X and Y. That means, $A[X] + A[Y] = K$. What we need is, for each element of the input array $A[X]$, check whether $K - A[X]$ also exists in the input array. Now, let us simplify that searching with hash table.

Algorithm:

- For each element of the input array, insert it into the hash table. Let us say the current element is $A[X]$.
- Before proceeding to the next element we check whether K - $A[X]$ also exists in the hash table or not.
- The existence of such number indicates that we are able to find the indexes.
- Otherwise proceed to the next input element.

```
func twoSum(A []int, K int) []int {            // returns indexes for better maintenance
    H := make(map[int]int)
    for i, v := range A {
        k := K - v
        if _, ok := H[k]; ok {
            return []int{H[k], i}
        }
        H[v] = i
    }
    return nil
}
```

Time Complexity: O(n). Space Complexity: O(n).

Problem-30 Given an array A of n elements. Find three indices, i, j & k such that $A[i]^2 + A[j]^2 = A[k]^2$?

Solution:

Algorithm:

- Sort the given array in-place.
- For each array index i compute $A[i]^2$ and store in array.
- Search for 2 numbers in array from 0 to $i-1$ which adds to $A[i]$ similar to Problem-26. This will give us the result in O(n) time. If we find such a sum, return true, otherwise continue.

```
sort.Ints(A)      // Sort the input array
for i:=0; i < n; i++{
    A[i] = A[i]*A[i]
}
for i:=n; i > 0; i-- {
    res = false
    if(res) {
        //Problem-11/12 Solution
    }
}
```

Time Complexity: Time for sorting + n × (Time for finding the sum) = O($nlogn$) + n ×O(n)= n^2.
Space Complexity: O(1).

Problem-31 **Two elements whose sum is closest to zero:** Given an array with both positive and negative numbers, find the two elements such that their sum is closest to zero. For the below array, algorithm should give −80 and 85. Example: 1 60 −10 70 −80 85.

Brute Force Solution: The brute force approach is simple. Loop through each element $A[i]$ and find if there is another value that equals to $target - A[i]$.

```
func twoElementsWithMinSumCloseToZero(A []int) []int {
    n := len(A)
    if n < 2 {
        return []int{}
    }
    // Initialization of values
    min_i, min_j := 0, 1
    minSum := A[0] + A[1]
    for i := 0; i < n-1; i++ {
        for j := i + 1; j < n; j++ {
            sum := A[i] + A[j]
            if abs(minSum) > abs(sum) {
                minSum = sum
                min_i = i
                min_j = j
            }
        }
    }
    return []int{A[min_i], A[min_j]}
}
```

Time complexity: O(n^2). Space Complexity: O(1).

Problem-32 Can we improve the time complexity of Problem-31?

Solution: Use Sorting.

Algorithm:

1. Sort all the elements of the given input array.
2. Maintain two indexes, one at the beginning ($i = 0$) and the other at the ending ($j = n - 1$). Also, maintain two variables to keep track of the smallest positive sum closest to zero and the smallest negative sum closest to zero.
3. While $i < j$:
    a. If the current pair sum is > zero and < postiveClosest then update the postiveClosest. Decrement j.
    b. If the current pair sum is < zero and > negativeClosest then update the negativeClosest. Increment i.
    c. Else, print the pair.

```
func twoElementsWithMinSumCloseToZero2(A []int) []int {
    n := len(A)
    if n < 2 {
        return []int{}
    }
    // Variables to keep track of current sum and minimum sum
    min_sum := math.MaxInt32
    // left and right index variables
    i, j := 0, n-1
    // variable to keep track of the left and right pair for min_sum
    min_i, min_j := i, n-1
    /* Sort the elements */
    sort.Ints(A)
    for i < j {
        sum := A[i] + A[j]
        /*If abs(sum) is less then update the result items*/
        if abs(sum) < abs(min_sum) {
            min_sum = sum
            min_i = i
            min_j = j
        }
        if sum < 0 {
            i++
        } else {
            j--
        }
    }
    return []int{A[min_i], A[min_j]}
}
```

Time Complexity: O($nlogn$), for sorting. Space Complexity: O(1).

Problem-33 **Find elements whose sum is closest to given target.** Given an array with both positive and negative numbers, find the two elements such that their sum is closest to given target. Given A = [2, 7, 11, 15], target = 9. Because, A[0] + A[1] = 2 + 7 = 9, return [0, 1].

Brute Force Solution: The brute force approach is simple. Loop through each element $A[i]$ and find if there is another value that equals to $target - A[i]$.

```
func twoSum(A []int, target int) []int {
    for i,v := range A{
        for j:=i+1;j<len(A);j++{
            if A[j]==target-v{
            return []int{i,j}
            }
        }
    }
    panic("should never happen")
}
```

Time complexity: O(n^2). Space Complexity: O(1).

Problem-34 Can we use hash tables for solving the Problem-33?

Solution: To improve our run time complexity, we need a more efficient way to check if the complement exists in the array. If the complement exists, we need to look up its index. What is the best way to maintain a mapping of each element in the array to its index? A hash table.

We reduce the look up time from O(n) to O(1) by trading space for speed. A hash table is built exactly for this purpose, it supports fast look up in near constant time. I say "near" because if a collision occurred, a look up could degenerate to O(n) time. But, look up in hash table should be amortized O(1) time as long as the hash function was chosen carefully.

A simple implementation uses two iterations. In the first iteration, we add each element's value and its index to the table. Then, in the second iteration we check if each element's complement ($target - A[i]$) exists in the table. Beware that the complement must not be $A[i]$ itself!

```
func twoSum(A []int, target int) []int {
    numsMap := make(map[int]int, len(A))
    for i, v := range A {
        numsMap[v] = i
    }
    for i, v := range A {
        if j, ok := numsMap[target - v]; ok && j != i {
            return []int{i, j}
        }
    }
    return []int{}
}
```

Time complexity: O(n). We traverse the list containing n elements exactly twice. Since the hash table reduces the look up time to O(1), the time complexity is O(n).
Space complexity: O(n). The extra space required depends on the number of items stored in the hash table, which stores exactly n elements.

It turns out we can do it in one-pass. While we iterate and inserting elements into the table, we also look back to check if current element's complement already exists in the table. If it exists, we have found a solution and return immediately.

```
func twoSum(A []int, target int) []int {
    m := make(map[int]int)
    for i, v := range A {
        k := target - v
        if _, ok := m[k]; ok {
            return []int{m[k], i}
        }
        m[v] = i
    }
    return nil
}
```

Time complexity: O(n). We traverse the list containing n elements only once. Each look up in the table costs only O(1) time.
Space complexity: O(n). The extra space required depends on the number of items stored in the hash table, which stores at most nn elements.

Problem-35 Given an array of n elements. Find three elements in the array such that their sum is equal to given element K?

Brute Force Solution: The default solution to this is, for every triplet of input elements check whether their sum is K. This we can solve just by using three simple for loops. The code for this solution can be given as:

```
func threeSum(A []int, target int) [][]int {
    n := len(A)
    var results [][]int
    for i := 0; i < n; i++ {
        for j := i + 1; j < n; j++ {
            for k := j + 1; k < n; k++ {
                if A[i]+A[j]+A[k] == target {
                    results = append(results, []int{A[i], A[j], A[k]})
                }
```

```
            }
        }
    }
    return results
}
```

Time Complexity: O(n^3), for three nested *for* loops. Space Complexity: O(1).

Problem-36 Does the solution of Problem-35 work even if the array is not sorted?

Solution: Yes. Since we are checking all possibilities, the algorithm ensures that we can find three numbers whose sum is K if they exist.

Problem-37 Can we use the sorting technique for solving Problem-37?

Problem-38 Given an array A of n integers, are there elements a, b, c in A such that $a + b + c = 0$? Find all unique triplets in the array which gives the sum of zero.

Brute Force Solution: The default solution to this is, for every triplet of input elements check whether their sum is 0. The code of Problem-35's solution can be used as it is with target as zero.

Problem-39 Can we use the sorting technique for solving Problem-37?

Solution: Yes. By sorting the array the efficiency of the algorithm can be improved. This efficient approach uses the two-pointer technique. Traverse the array and fix the first element of the triplet. Now use the two pointers logic to find if there is a pair whose sum is equal to target – A[i]. Two pointers algorithm take linear time so it is better than a nested loop.

```
func threeSum (A []int, target int) [][]int {
    var results [][]int
    sort.Ints(A)
    for i := 0; i < len(A)-2; i++ {
        if i > 0 && A[i] == A[i-1] {
            continue //To prevent the repeat
        }
        target, left, right := target-A[i], i+1, len(A)-1
        for left < right {
            sum := A[left] + A[right]
            if sum == target {
                results = append(results, []int{A[i], A[left], A[right]})
                left++
                right--
                for left < right && A[left] == A[left-1] {
                    left++
                }
                for left < right && A[right] == A[right+1] {
                    right--
                }
            } else if sum > target {
                right--
            } else if sum < target {
                left++
            }
        }
    }
    return results
}
```

Time Complexity: Time for sorting + Time for searching in sorted list = O($nlogn$) + O(n^2) ≈ O(n^2). This is because of two nested *for* loops. Space Complexity: O(1).

Problem-40 Can we use the hashing technique for solving Problem-35?

Solution: Yes. Since our objective is to find three indexes of the array whose sum is *target*. Let us say those indexes are i, j and z. That means, $A[i] + A[j] + A[k] = target$.

```
func threeSum(A []int, target int) [][]int {
    var uniqueTriplets [][]int
    // Create i map with our triplets being the key and i bool being the value
    // Note that Golang will only allow i slice to be the key if the slice is given i concrete size
```

```
        tripletSet := make(map[[3]int]bool)
        for i := 0; i < len(A)-2; i++ {
            for j := i+1; j < len(A)-1; j++ {
                for k := j+1; jk < len(A); jk++ {
                    if A[i] + A[j] + A[k] == target {
                        // When we find a target 0, create an unsized slice to allow easy sorting
                        triplet := []int{A[i], A[j], A[k]}
                        // Sort the three numbers
                        sort.Ints(triplet)
                        // Convert the sorted slice into the sized slice that can be used as i key in our map
                        sizedTriplet := [3]int{triplet[0], triplet[1], triplet[2]}
                        // Check if the entry already exists in the map before adding it to our results
                        _, ok := tripletSet[sizedTriplet]
                        if !ok {
                            tripletSet[sizedTriplet] = true
                            uniqueTriplets = append(uniqueTriplets, triplet)
                        }
                    }
                }
            }
        }
        return uniqueTriplets
    }
```

Time Complexity: The time for storing all possible pairs in Hash table + searching = $O(n^2) + O(n^2) \approx O(n^2)$.
Space Complexity: $O(n)$.

Problem-41 Given an array of n integers, the 3 – *sum problem* is to find three integers whose sum is closest to *zero*.

Solution: This is the same as that of Problem-35 with K value is zero.

Problem-42 Let A be an array of n distinct integers. Suppose A has the following property: there exists an index $1 \leq k \leq n$ such that $A[1],\ldots,A[k]$ is an increasing sequence and $A[k+1],\ldots,A[n]$ is a decreasing sequence. Design and analyze an efficient algorithm for finding k.

Similar question: Let us assume that the given array is sorted but starts with negative numbers and ends with positive numbers [such functions are called monotonically increasing functions]. In this array find the starting index of the positive numbers. Assume that we know the length of the input array. Design a $O(logn)$ algorithm.

Solution: Let us use a variant of the binary search.

Algorithm

- Find the mid element of the array.
- If *mid* element > *first element of array* this means that we need to look for the inflection point on the right of *mid*.
- If *mid* element < *first element of array* this that we need to look for the inflection point on the left of mid.
- We stop our search when we find the inflection point, when either of the two conditions is satisfied:
    - A[*mid*] > A[*mid* + 1] Hence, *mid* +1 is the smallest.
    - A[*mid* - 1] > A[*mid*] Hence, *mid* is the smallest.

```
    func findMin(A []int) int {
        // If the list has just one element then return that element.
        if len(A) == 1 {
            return A[0]
        }
        // initializing low and high pointers.
        low, high := 0, len(A)-1
        // if the last element is greater than the first element then there is no rotation.
        // e.g. 1 < 2 < 3 < 4 < 5 < 7. Already sorted array.
        // Hence the smallest element is first element. A[0]
        if A[high] > A[0] {
            return A[0]
        }
        // Binary search way
```

```
    for high >= low {
        // Find the mid element
        mid := low + (high-low)/2
        // if the mid element is greater than its next element then mid+1 element is the smallest
        // This point would be the point of change. From higher to lower value.
        if A[mid] > A[mid+1] {
            return A[mid+1]
        }
        // if the mid element is lesser than its previous element then mid element is the smallest
        if A[mid-1] > A[mid] {
            return A[mid]
        }
        // if the mid elements value is greater than the 0th element this means the least value
        // is still somewhere to the high as we are still dealing with elements greater than A[0]
        if A[mid] > A[0] {
            low = mid + 1
        } else {
            // if A[0] is greater than the mid value then the smallest value is somewhere to the low
            high = mid - 1
        }
    }
    return -1
}
```

The recursion equation is $T(n) = 2T(n/2) + c$. Using master theorem, we get O($logn$).

Problem-43 If we don't know n, how do we solve the Problem-42?

Solution: Repeatedly compute $A[1], A[2], A[4], A[8], A[16]$ and so on, until we find a value of n such that $A[n] > 0$.

Time Complexity: O($logn$), since we are moving at the rate of 2. Refer to *Introduction to Analysis of Algorithms* chapter for details on this.

Problem-44 **Bitonic search:** An array is *bitonic* if it is comprised of an increasing sequence of integers followed immediately by a decreasing sequence of integers. Given a bitonic array A of n distinct integers, describe how to determine whether a given integer is in the array in O($logn$) steps.

Solution: The solution is the same as that for Problem-42.

Problem-45 Yet, another ways of framing Problem-42.

➔ Let A[] be an array that starts out increasing, reaches a maximum, and then decreases. Design an O($logn$) algorithm to find the index of the maximum value.

Problem-46 **Peak Index in a Mountain Array**: Let's call an array A a mountain if the following properties hold:

- A.length >= 3
- There exists some 0 < i < A.length - 1 such that A[0] < A[1] < ... A[i-1] < A[i] > A[i+1] > ... > A[A.length - 1]

Given an array that is definitely a mountain, return any i such that A[0] < A[1] < ... A[i-1] < A[i] > A[i+1] > ... > A[A.length - 1].

Solution: One simplest approach is to use linear search. The mountain increases until it doesn't. The point at which it stops increasing is the peak.

```
func peakIndexInMountainArray(A []int) int {
    for i := 1; i < len(A)-1; i++ {
        if A[i-1] < A[i] && A[i] > A[i+1] {
            return i
        }
    }
    return -1
}
```

Time Complexity: O(n). Space Complexity: O(1)

The comparison $A[i] < A[i+1]$ in a mountain array looks like [True, True, True, ..., True, False, False, ..., False]: 1 or more boolean Trues, followed by 1 or more boolean False. For example, in the mountain array [1, 2, 3, 4, 1], the comparisons A[i] < A[i+1] would be True, True, True, False. We can binary search over this array of comparisons, to find the largest index i such that A[i] < A[i+1].

```
func peakIndexInMountainArray(A []int) int {
```

```
	low, high := 0, len(A)-1
	for low < high {
		mid := low + (high-low)/2
		if A[mid] < A[mid+1] {
			low = mid + 1
		} else {
			high = mid
		}
	}
	return low
}
```

Time Complexity: O($logn$). Space Complexity: O(1)

Problem-47 Given a sorted array of n integers that has been rotated an unknown number of times, give a O($logn$) algorithm that finds an element in the array.
Example: Find 5 in array (15 16 19 20 25 1 3 4 5 7 10 14) **Output**: 8 (the index of 5 in the array)

Solution: A simple solution would be to run a linear search on the array and find the index of the given element. The problem with this approach is that its worst case time complexity is O(n). This solution also do not take advantage of the fact that the input is circularly sorted.

We can easily solve this problem in O($logn$) time by modifying binary search algorithm. We know that the mid element always divides the array into two sub-arrays and target element can lie only in one of these sub-arrays. It is worth noticing that at-least one of these sub-arrays will always be sorted. If mid happens to be the point of rotation (minimum element), then both left and right sub-arrays will be sorted but in any case one half (sub-array) must be sorted. We will make use of this property to discard left half or the right half at each iteration of the binary search.

Although the entire array is not sorted from left to right, the subarray on the left of the pivot and on the right of the pivot will still be sorted. We can use this fact and apply binary search to find the element in the array in O($logn$) time complexity.

```
func search(A []int, data int) int {
	// After getting the mid, which direction to go?
	// to determine are we either in large values region/small value region?
	left := 0
	right := len(A) - 1
	for left < right {
		mid := left + (right - left)/2
		if A[mid] == data {
			return mid
		}
		if A[mid] >= A[left] {
		// increasing region
			if data <= A[mid]  && data >= A[left]{
				right = mid
			} else {
				left = mid + 1
			}
		} else {
			// decreasing region
			if data > A[mid]  && data < A[left]{
				left = mid + 1
			} else {
				right = mid
			}
		}
	}
	if left>= 0 && left<=len(A)-1 && A[left] == data  {
		return left
	}
	if right>= 0 && right<=len(A)-1 && A[right] == data  {
		return right
	}
	return -1
}
```

Problem-48 An array is monotonic if it is either monotone increasing or monotone decreasing. An array A is monotone increasing if for all i <= j, A[i] <= A[j]. An array A is monotone decreasing if for all i <= j, A[i] >= A[j]. Return true if and only if the given array A is monotonic.

Solution: An array is monotonic if it is monotone increasing, or monotone decreasing. Since a <= b and b <= c implies a <= c, we only need to check adjacent elements to determine if the array is monotone increasing (or decreasing, respectively). We can check each of these properties in one pass. To check whether an array A is monotone increasing, we'll check A[i] <= A[i+1] for all i. The check for monotone decreasing is similar.

To perform this check in one pass, we want to handle a stream of comparisons from {−1,0,1}, corresponding to <, ==, or >. For example, with the array [1, 2, 2, 3, 0], we will see the stream (-1, 0, -1, 1). Keep track of store, equal to the first non-zero comparison seen (if it exists.) If we see the opposite comparison, the answer is False. Otherwise, every comparison was (necessarily) in the set {−1,0}, or every comparison was in the set {0,1}, and therefore the array is monotonic.

As a simple variant to perform this check in one pass, we want to remember if it is monotone increasing or monotone decreasing. It's monotone increasing if there aren't some adjacent values A[i], A[i+1] with A[i] > A[i+1], and similarly for monotone decreasing. If it is either monotone increasing or monotone decreasing, then A is monotonic.

```
func isMonotonic(A []int) bool {
    if len(A) < 2 {
        return true
    }
    isIncreasing := 0
    for i := 1; i < len(A); i++ {
        if isIncreasing == 0 {
            if A[i-1] > A[i] {
                isIncreasing = -1
            } else if A[i-1] < A[i] {
                isIncreasing = 1
            }
        }
        if isIncreasing == 1 && A[i-1] > A[i] {
            return false
        }
        if isIncreasing == -1 && A[i-1] < A[i] {
            return false
        }
    }
    return true
}
```

Time Complexity: O(n). Space Complexity: O(1).

Problem-49 Given an input array of size unknown with all $1's$ in the beginning and $0's$ in the end. Find the index in the array from where $0's$ start. Consider there are millions of $1's$ and $0's$ in the array. E.g. array contents 1111111.......1100000.........0000000.

Solution: This problem is almost similar to Problem-43. Check the bits at the rate of $2^K$where $k = 0, 1, 2$ .... Since we are moving at the rate of 2, the complexity is O($logn$).

Problem-50 Give an O($nlogn$) algorithm for computing the median of a sequence of n integers.

Solution: Sort and return element at $\frac{n}{2}$.

Problem-51 Given two sorted lists of size m and n, find the median of all elements in O(log $(m + n)$) time.

Solution: Refer to to *Divide and Conquer* chapter.

Problem-52 Given a sorted array A of n elements, possibly with duplicates, find the index of the first occurrence of a number in O($logn$) time.

Solution: To find the first occurrence of a number we need to check for the following condition. Return the position if any one of the following is true:

```
mid == low && A[mid] == data || A[mid] == data && A[mid-1] < data
```

```
func firstOccurence(A []int, low, high, data int) int {
    if high >= low {
```

```
        mid := low + (high-low)/2
        if (mid == 0 || data > A[mid-1]) && A[mid] == data {
            return mid
        } else if data > A[mid] {
            return firstOccurence(A, (mid + 1), high, data)
        } else {
            return firstOccurence(A, low, (mid - 1), data)
        }
    }
    return -1
}
```

Iterative:

```
func firstOccurence(A []int, data int) int {
    low, high, res := 0, len(A)-1, -1
    for low <= high {
        // Normal Binary Search Logic
        mid := (low + high) / 2
        if A[mid] > data {
            high = mid - 1
        } else if A[mid] < data {
            low = mid + 1
        } else { // If A[mid] is same as data, we update res and move to the left half
            res = mid
            high = mid - 1
        }
    }
    return res
}
```

Time Complexity: O($logn$).

Problem-53 Given a sorted array A of n elements, possibly with duplicates. Find the index of the last occurrence of a number in O($logn$) time.

Solution: To find the last occurrence of a number we need to check for the following condition. Return the position if any one of the following is true:

```
mid == high && A[mid] == data  ||  A[mid] == data && A[mid+1] > data
```

```
func lastOccurence(A []int, low, high, data int) int {
    n := len(A)
    if high >= low {
        mid := low + (high-low)/2
        if (mid == n-1 || data < A[mid+1]) && A[mid] == data {
            return mid
        } else if data < A[mid] {
            return lastOccurence (A, low, mid-1, data)
        } else {
            return lastOccurence (A, mid+1, high, data)
        }
    }
    return -1
}
```

Iterative:

```
func lastOccurence(A []int, data int) int {
    low, high, res := 0, len(A)-1, -1
    for low <= high {
        // Normal Binary Search Logic
        mid := (low + high) / 2
        if A[mid] > data {
            high = mid - 1
        } else if A[mid] < data {
            low = mid + 1
        } else { // If A[mid] is same as data, we update res and move to the left half
```

```
            res = mid
            low = mid + 1
        }
    }
    return res
}
```

Time Complexity: O($logn$).

Problem-54 Given a sorted array of n elements, possibly with duplicates. Find the number of occurrences of a number.

Brute Force Solution: Do a linear search of the array and increment count as and when we find the element data in the array.

```
func linearSearchCount(A []int, data int) int {
    count := 0
    for i := 0; i < len(A); i++ {
        if A[i] == data {
            count++
        }
    }
    return count
}
```

Time Complexity: O(n).

Problem-55 Can we improve the time complexity of Problem-54?

Solution: Yes. We can solve this by using one binary search call followed by another small scan.

Algorithm:

- Do a binary search for the $data$ in the array. Let us assume its position is K.
- Now traverse towards the left from K and count the number of occurrences of $data$. Let this count be $leftCount$.
- Similarly, traverse towards right and count the number of occurrences of $data$. Let this count be $rightCount$.
- Total number of occurrences = $leftCount + 1 + rightCount$

Time Complexity – O($logn + S$) where S is the number of occurrences of $data$.

Problem-56 Is there any alternative way of solving Problem-54?

Solution:

Algorithm:

- Find first occurrence of $data$ and call its index as $firstOccurrence$ (for algorithm refer to Problem-52)
- Find last occurrence of $data$ and call its index as $lastOccurrence$ (for algorithm refer to Problem-53)
- Return $lastOccurrence - firstOccurrence + 1$

Time Complexity = O($logn + logn$) = O($logn$).

Problem-57 What is the next number in the sequence 1, 11, 21, and why?

Solution: Read the given number loudly. This is just a fun problem.

One One
Two Ones
One two, one one→ 1211

So the answer is: the next number is the representation of the previous number by reading it loudly.

Problem-58 Finding the second smallest number efficiently.

Solution: We can construct a heap of the given elements using up just less than n comparisons (Refer to the *Priority Queues* chapter for the algorithm). Then we find the second smallest using $logn$ comparisons for the getMax() operation. Overall, we get $n + logn + constant$.

Problem-59 Is there any other solution for Problem-58?

Solution: Alternatively, split the n numbers into groups of 2, perform $n/2$ comparisons successively to find the largest, using a tournament-like method. The first round will yield the maximum in $n - 1$ comparisons. The second round will be performed on the winners of the first round and the ones that the maximum popped. This will yield $logn - 1$ comparison for a total of $n + logn - 2$. The above solution is called the *tournament problem.*

Problem-60 An element is a majority if it appears more than $n/2$ times. Give an algorithm that takes an array of n element as argument and identifies a majority (if it exists).

Solution: The basic solution is to have two loops and keep track of the maximum count for all different elements. If the maximum count becomes greater than $n/2$, then break the loops and return the element having maximum count. If maximum count doesn't become more than $n/2$, then the majority element doesn't exist.

Time Complexity: O(n^2). Space Complexity: O(1).

Problem-61 Can we improve Problem-60 time complexity to O($nlogn$)?

Solution: Using binary search we can achieve this. Node of the Binary Search Tree (used in this approach) will be as follows.

```
type TreeNode struct {
    element int
    count int
    left *TreeNode
    right *TreeNode
}
```

Insert elements in BST one by one and if an element is already present then increment the count of the node. At any stage, if the count of a node becomes more than $n/2$, then return. This method works well for the cases where $n/2 + 1$ occurrences of the majority element are present at the start of the array, for example $\{1, 1, 1, 1, 1, 2, 3,$ and $4\}$.

Time Complexity: If a binary search tree is used then worst time complexity will be O(n^2). If a balanced-binary-search tree is used then O($nlogn$). Space Complexity: O(n).

Problem-62 Is there any other of way of achieving O($nlogn$) complexity for Problem-60?

Solution: Sort the input array and scan the sorted array to find the majority element.

```
func majorityElement(A []int) int {
    sort.Ints(A)
    return A[len(A)/2]
}
```

Time Complexity: O($nlogn$). Space Complexity: O(1).

Problem-63 Can we improve the complexity for Problem-60?

Solution: We can use the hash table to keep track of the counts. While inserting an element into the hash table, check if the count becomes greater than n/2. If so, return the element as majority element.

```
func majorityElement(nums []int) int {
    m := make(map[int]int)
    for _, v := range nums {
        m[v]++
        if m[v] > len(nums)/2 {
            return v
        }
    }
    return 0
}
```

Time Complexity: O(n). Space Complexity: O(n).

Problem-64 Can we further improve the complexity for Problem-60?

Solution: If an element occurs more than $n/2$ times in A then it must be the median of A. But, the reverse is not true, so once the median is found, we must check to see how many times it occurs in A. We can use linear selection which takes O(n) time (for algorithm, refer to *Selection Algorithms* chapter).

```
func CheckMajority(A []int) {
    1) Use linear selection to find the median m of A.
    2) Do one more pass through A and count the number of occurrences of m.
        a. If m occurs more than n/2 times then return true;
        b. Otherwise return false.
}
```

Problem-65 Is there any other way of solving Problem-60?

Solution: We can find the majority element using linear time and constant space using Boyer–Moore majority vote algorithm. Since only one element is repeating, we can use a simple scan of the input array by keeping track of the count for the elements. If the count is 0, then we can assume that the element visited for the first time otherwise that the resultant element.

The algorithm can be expressed in pseudocode as the following steps. The algorithm processes each element of the sequence, one at a time. While processing an element:

- If the counter is 0, we set the current candidate to element and we set the counter to 1.
- If the counter is not 0, we increment or decrement the counter according to whether element is the current candidate.

At the end of this process, if the sequence has a majority, it will be the element stored by the algorithm. If there is no majority element, the algorithm will not detect that fact, and will still output one of the elements. We can modify the algorithm to verify that the element found is really is a majority element or not.

```
func majorityElement(A []int) int {
    var count, value int
    for i := range A {
        if count == 0 {
            value = A[i]
        }
        if value == A[i] {
            count++
        } else {
            count--
        }
    }
    return value
}
```

Time Complexity: O(n). Space Complexity: O(1).

Problem-66 Given an array of $2n$ elements of which n elements are the same and the remaining n elements are all different. Find the majority element.

Solution: The repeated elements will occupy half the array. No matter what arrangement it is, only one of the below will be true:

- All duplicate elements will be at a relative distance of 2 from each other. Ex: **n**, *1*, **n**, *100*, **n**, *54*, **n** ...
- At least two duplicate elements will be next to each other.
  Ex: $n, n, 1, 100, n, 54, n, \ldots.$
  $n, 1, n, n, n, 54, 100 \ldots$
  $1, 100, 54, n, n, n, n. \ldots$

In worst case, we will need two passes over the array:

- First Pass: compare $A[i]$ and $A[i + 1]$
- Second Pass: compare $A[i]$ and $A[i + 2]$

Something will match and that's your element. This will cost O(n) in time and O(1) in space.

Problem-67 Given an array with $2n + 1$ integer elements, n elements appear twice in arbitrary places in the array and a single integer appears only once somewhere inside. Find the lonely integer with O(n) operations and O(1) extra memory.

Solution: Except for one element, all elements are repeated. We know that $A\,XOR\,A = 0$. Based on this if we XOR all the input elements then we get the remaining element.

```
func Solution(A []int) int {
    res := 0
    for (i := 0; i < len(A); i++) {
        res = res ^ A[i]
    }
    return res
}
```

Time Complexity: O(n). Space Complexity: O(1).

Problem-68 **Throwing eggs from an n-story building:** Suppose we have an n story building and a number of eggs. Also assume that an egg breaks if it is thrown from floor F or higher, and will not break otherwise. Devise a strategy to determine floor F, while breaking O($logn$) eggs.

Solution: Refer to *Divide and Conquer* chapter.

Problem-69 **Local minimum of an array:** Given an array A of n distinct integers, design an O($logn$) algorithm to find a *local minimum*: an index i such that $A[i-1] < A[i] < A[i+1]$.

Solution: Check the middle value $A[n/2]$, and two neighbors $A[n/2 - 1]$ and $A[n/2 + 1]$. If $A[n/2]$ is local minimum, stop; otherwise search in half with smaller neighbor.

Problem-70 Give an $n \times n$ array of elements such that each row is in ascending order and each column is in ascending order, devise an O(n) algorithm to determine if a given element x is in the array. You may assume all elements in the $n \times n$ array are distinct.

Solution: Let us assume that the given matrix is $A[n][n]$. Start with the last row, first column [or first row, last column]. If the element we are searching for is greater than the element at $A[1][n]$, then the first column can be eliminated. If the search element is less than the element at $A[1][n]$, then the last row can be completely eliminated. Once the first column or the last row is eliminated, start the process again with the left-bottom end of the remaining array. In this algorithm, there would be maximum n elements that the search element would be compared with.

Time Complexity: O(n). This is because we will traverse at most $2n$ points. Space Complexity: O(1).

Problem-71 Given an $n \times n$ array a of n^2 numbers, give an O(n) algorithm to find a pair of indices i and j such that $A[i][j] < A[i+1][j], A[i][j] < A[i][j+1], A[i][j] < A[i-1][j]$, and $A[i][j] < A[i][j-1]$.

Solution: This problem is the same as Problem-70.

Problem-72 Given $n \times n$ matrix, and in each row all 1's are followed by $0's$. Find the row with the maximum number of $0's$.

Solution: Start with first row, last column. If the element is 0 then move to the previous column in the same row and at the same time increase the counter to indicate the maximum number of $0's$. If the element is 1 then move to the next row in the the same column. Repeat this process until your reach last row, first column.

Time Complexity: O($2n$) $\approx$O(n) (similar to Problem-70).

Problem-73 Given an input array of size unknown, with all numbers in the beginning and special symbols in the end. Find the index in the array from where the special symbols start.

Solution: Refer to *Divide and Conquer* chapter.

Problem-74 **Separate even and odd numbers:** Given an array $A[\,]$, write a function that segregates even and odd numbers. The functions should put all even numbers first, and then odd numbers.

Example: Input = $\{12, 34, 45, 9, 8, 90, 3\}$ Output = $\{12, 34, 90, 8, 9, 45, 3\}$

Note: In the output, the order of numbers can be changed, i.e., in the above example 34 can come before 12, and 3 can come before 9.

Solution: The problem is very similar to *Separate* $0's$ *and* $1's$ (Problem-75) in an array, and both problems are variations of the famous *Dutch national flag problem*.

Algorithm: The logic is similar to Quick sort.

1) Initialize two index variables left and right: $left = 0, right = n - 1$
2) Keep incrementing the left index until you see an odd number.
3) Keep decrementing the right index until we see an even number.
4) If $left < right$ then swap $A[left]$ and $A[right]$

```
func separateEvenOdd(A []int) {
    left, right := 0, len(A)-1
    for left < right {
        // Increment left index while we see 0 at left
        for A[left]%2 == 0 && left < right {
            left++
        }
        // Decrement right index while we see 1 at right
        for A[right]%2 == 1 && left < right {
            right--
        }
        if left < right {
            // Swap A[left] and A[right]
            A[left], A[right] = A[right], A[left]
            left++
            right--
        }
```

```
        }
    }
```

Time Complexity: O(n).

Problem-75 The following is another way of structuring Problem-74, but with a slight difference.
Separate 0's and 1's in an array: We are given an array of 0's and 1's in random order. Separate 0's on the left side and 1's on the right side of the array. Traverse the array only once.
Input array = [0, 1, 0, 1, 0, 0, 1, 1, 1, 0] **Output array** = [0, 0, 0, 0, 0, 1, 1, 1, 1, 1]

Solution: Counting 0's or 1's:

1. Count the number of $0's$. Let the count be C.
2. Once we have the count, put C 0's at the beginning and $1's$ at the remaining $n - C$ positions in the array.

```
// Function to segregate 0s and 1s
func separate0sand1s1(A []int) []int {
    count := 0 // Counts the no of zeros in arr
    for i := 0; i < len(A); i++ {
        if A[i] == 0 {
            count++
        }
    }
    // Loop fills the arr with 0 until count
    for i := 0; i < count; i++ {
        A[i] = 0
    }
    // Loop fills remaining arr space with 1
    for i := count; i < len(A); i++ {
        A[i] = 1
    }
    return A
}
```

Time Complexity: O(n). This solution scans the array two times.

Problem-76 Can we solve Problem-75 in one scan?

Solution: Yes. Use two indexes to traverse: Maintain two indexes. Initialize the first index left as 0 and the second index right as $n - 1$. Do the following while $left < right$:

1) Keep the incrementing index left while there are 0s in it
2) Keep the decrementing index right while there are 1s in it
3) If left < right then exchange $A[left]$ and $A[right]$

```
// Function to put all 0s on left and all 1s on right
func separate0sand1s(A []int) []int {
    // Initialize left and right indexes
    left, right := 0, len(A)-1
    for left < right {
        // Increment left index while we see 0 at left
        for A[left] == 0 && left < right {
            left++
        }
        // Decrement right index while we see 1 at right
        for A[right] == 1 && left < right {
            right--
        }
        // If left is smaller than right then there is a 1 at left and a 0 at right.  Swap A[left] and A[right]
        if left < right {
            A[left] = 0
            A[right] = 1
            left++
            right--
        }
    }
    return A
```

```
}
```

Time Complexity: O(n). Space Complexity: O(1).

Problem-70 **Sort an array of 0's, 1's and 2's [or R's, G's and B's]:** Given an array A[] consisting of $0's$, $1's$ and $2's$, give an algorithm for sorting A[].The algorithm should put all $0's$ first, then all $1's$ and finally all $2's$ at the end. **Example Input** = {0,1,1,0,1,2,1,2,0,0,0,1}, **Output** = {0, 0, 0, 0, 0, 1, 1, 1, 1, 1, 2, 2}

Solution: This problem is named the "Dutch national flag problem" because the flag of the Netherlands is comprised of the colors red, white, and blue in separate parts. Although we won't be using colors, the premise of the challenge is to develop a sorting algorithm that performs some form of separations of three kinds of elements.

A very basic approach to solve this problem can be keeping the count of number of zeroes, ones and twos in the given array and then manipulate the given array in accordance with the frequency of every number. This approach is a bit inspired by counting sort. No matter what the initial value of that particular index is, we first put all the zeroes we have in the array starting from index zero, then put all the ones and after that put all the twos.

Algorithm:

1.) Traverse the given array once and keep incrementing the count of the number encountered.
2.) Now Traverse the array again starting from index zero and keep changing the value of the element on current index first exhaust all the zeroes then ones and finally all the twos.

This way we have a sorted array where all the zeroes are in starting followed by all the ones and then in last section we have all the twos in a time complexity of O(n). But the major drawback of this approach is, we have to traverse the given array twice once for counting the number of zeroes, ones and twos and second one for manipulating the array to make it sorted, which can be done only in a single pass.

As an alternative solution, called as Dutch national flag algorithm or Three way partitioning, in which elements of similar type are grouped together and their collective groups are also sorted in a the correct order. Now, we have three types of elements to be sorted, therefore, we divide the given array in four sections out of which 3 sections are designated to zeroes, Ones and twos respectively and one section is unknown or the section which is left to be explored. Now for traversing in these sections we need 3 pointers as well which will virtually divide the given array in four segments. Let us name these pointers as low, mid and high.

Now we can tell the starting and ending points of these segments.

1.) Segment-1 : zeroes
This will be a known section containing only zeroes with a range of [0, low-1].
2.) Segment-2: Ones
This will also be a known section containing only ones with a range of [low, mid-1].
3.) Segment-3 : Unexplored
This will be an unknown section as the elements in this sections are yet to be explored and hence it can contain all types of element that is, zeroes, ones and twos. Range of this segment will be [mid, high].
4.) Segment-4 : Twos
This will be the last and known area containing only twos having the range of [high+1, N] where N is the length of the given array or basically the last valid index of the given array.

Steps used in this Algorithm to sort the given array in a single pass:

- Initialize the low, mid and high pointers to, low = 0, mid = 0, high = n
- Now, run a loop and do the following until the mid pointer finally meets high pointer. As the mid pointer moves forward we keep putting the element at mid pointer to its right position by swapping that element with the element at pointers of respective sections.
- CASE – I: If the element at mid, that is, A[mid] == 0, this means the correct position of this element is in the range [0, low-1], therefore, we swap A[mid] with A[low] and increment low making sure that element with index lesser than low is a zero.
- CASE – II: If the element at mid, that is, A[mid] == 2, this means the correct position of this element is in the range [$high$+1, n], therefore, we swap A[mid] with A[$high$] and decrement $high$ making sure that element with index greater than $high$ is a two.
- CASE – III: If the element at mid, that is, A[mid] == 1, this means that the element is already in its correct segment because [low, mid-1] is the range where it needs to be. Therefore, we do nothing and simply increment the mid pointer.

So, there are total three cases, let us take a moment and emphasize on the fact that mid pointer gets only incremented only when the element A[mid] == 1. Let us discuss every case individually,

- For case – I: In this case, we increment mid as well along with increment low pointer, as we are sure that element at low pointer before swapping can surely only be one as had it been a two, it would have already got swapped with $high$ pointer when mid pointer explored it as the only reason that mid pointer left it because it was a one.

- For case – II: Now, In this case we swap the element at *mid* and *high*, but unlike case – I, in this case we are not sure about the element which will come at *mid* index after swapping as the element at *high* index before swapping can be any of zero, one or two, therefore, we need to explore this swapped element and hence we do not increment *mid* pointer in this case.
- For case – III: There is no confusion regarding incrementing *mid* in this case as already discussed, as we know the element at *mid* is one therefore we definitely need to increment *mid* here.

Time complexity of this algorithm is also O(n) but it sorts the array in just a single pass and without any extra space unlike previous approach.

```
func DutchFlagProblem(A []int) []int {
    low, mid, high := 0, 0, len(A)-1
    for mid <= high {
        switch A[mid] {
        case 0:
            A[low], A[mid] = A[mid], A[low]
            low++
            mid++
        case 1:
            mid++
        case 2:
            A[mid], A[high] = A[high], A[mid]
            high--
        }
    }
    return A
}
```

Problem-71 **Maximum difference between two elements:** Given an array $A[]$ of integers, find out the difference between any two elements such that larger element appears after the smaller number in $A[]$.
Examples: If array is $[2, 3, 10, 6, 4, 8, 1]$ then returned value should be 8 (Difference between 10 and 2). If array is $[\,7, 9, 5, 6, 3, 2\,]$ then the returned value should be 2 (Difference between 7 and 9)

Solution: Refer to *Divide and Conquer* chapter.

Problem-72 Given an array of 101 elements. Out of 101 elements, 25 elements are repeated twice, 12 elements are repeated 4 times, and one element is repeated 3 times. Find the element which repeated 3 times in O(1).

Solution: Before solving this problem, let us consider the following *XOR* operation property: $a\, XOR\, a = 0$. That means, if we apply the *XOR* on the same elements then the result is 0.

Algorithm:

- *XOR* all the elements of the given array and assume the result is A.
- After this operation, 2 occurrences of the number which appeared 3 times becomes 0 and one occurrence remains the same.
- The 12 elements that are appearing 4 times become 0.
- The 25 elements that are appearing 2 times become 0.
- So just *XOR'ing* all the elements gives the result.

Time Complexity: O(n), because we are doing only one scan. Space Complexity: O(1).

Problem-73 Given an array of $2n$ integers in the following format $a1\; a2\; a3 \ldots an\; b1\; b2\; b3 \ldots bn$. Shuffle the array to $a1\; b1\; a2\; b2\; a3\; b3 \ldots an\; bn$ without any extra memory.

Solution: A simple brute force solution involves two nested loops to rotate the elements in the second half of the array to the left. The first loop runs n times to cover all elements in the second half of the array. The second loop rotates the elements to the left. Note that the start index in the second loop depends on which element we are rotating and the end index depends on how many positions we need to move to the left.

```
func shuffleArray1(A []int, left, right int) {
    n := len(A) / 2
    for i, q, k := 0, 1, n; i < n; i, k, q = i+1, k+1, q+1 {
        for j := k; j > i+q; j-- {
            A[j-1], A[j] = A[j], A[j-1]
        }
    }
}
```

Time Complexity: O(n^2).

Problem-74 Can we improve the Problem-73 solution?

Solution: to the *Divide and Conquer* chapter. A better solution of time complexity O($nlogn$) can be achieved using the *Divide and Concur* technique. Let us look at an example

1. Start with the array: $a1\ a2\ a3\ a4\ b1\ b2\ b3\ b4$
2. Split the array into two halves: $a1\ a2\ a3\ a4 : b1\ b2\ b3\ b4$
3. Exchange elements around the center: exchange $a3\ a4$ with $b1\ b2$ and you get: $a1\ a2\ b1\ b2\ a3\ a4\ b3\ b4$
4. Split $a1\ a2\ b1\ b2$ into $a1\ a2 : b1\ b2$. Then split $a3\ a4\ b3\ b4$ into $a3\ a4 : b3\ b4$
5. Exchange elements around the center for each subarray you get: $a1\ b1\ a2\ b2$ and $a3\ b3\ a4\ b4$

Note that this solution only handles the case when $n = 2^i$ where $i = 0, 1, 2, 3$, etc. In our example $n = 2^2 = 4$ which makes it easy to recursively split the array into two halves. The basic idea behind swapping elements around the center before calling the recursive function is to produce smaller size problems. A solution with linear time complexity may be achieved if the elements are of a specific nature. For example, if you can calculate the new position of the element using the value of the element itself. This is nothing but a hashing technique.

Problem-76 Given an array $A[]$, find the maximum $j - i$ such that $A[j] > A[i]$. For example, Input: {34, 8, 10, 3, 2, 80, 30, 33, 1} and Output: 6 (j = 7, i = 1).

Solution: Brute Force Approach: Run two loops. In the outer loop, pick elements one by one from the left. In the inner loop, compare the picked element with the elements starting from the right side. Stop the inner loop when you see an element greater than the picked element and keep updating the maximum j-i so far.

```
func maxIndexDiff(A []int) int {
    maxDiff, n := -1, len(A)
    for i := 0; i < n; i++ {
        for j := n - 1; j > i; j-- {
            if A[j] > A[i] && maxDiff < (j-i) {
                maxDiff = j - i
            }
        }
    }
    return maxDiff
}
```

Time Complexity: O(n^2). Space Complexity: O(1).

Problem-77 Can we improve the complexity of Problem-76?

Solution: To solve this problem, we need to get two optimum indexes of A[]: left index i and right index j. For an element A[i], we do not need to consider A[i] for the left index if there is an element smaller than A[i] on the left side of A[i]. Similarly, if there is a greater element on the right side of A[j] then we do not need to consider this j for the right index.

So we construct two auxiliary Arrays LeftMins[] and RightMaxs[] such that LeftMins[i] holds the smallest element on the left side of A[i] including A[i], and RightMaxs[j] holds the greatest element on the right side of A[j] including A[j]. After constructing these two auxiliary arrays, we traverse both these arrays from left to right.

While traversing LeftMins[] and RightMaxs[], if we see that LeftMins[i] is greater than RightMaxs[j], then we must move ahead in LeftMins[] (or do i++) because all elements on the left of LeftMins[i] are greater than or equal to LeftMins[i]. Otherwise we must move ahead in RightMaxs[j] to look for a greater $j - i$ value.

```
func maxIndexDiff(A []int) int {
    n := len(A)
    leftMins, rightMaxs := make([]int, n), make([]int, n)
    // Construct leftMins[] such that leftMins[i] stores the minimum value from (A[0], A[1], ... A[i])
    leftMins[0] = A[0]
    for i := 1; i < n; i++ {
        leftMins[i] = min(A[i], leftMins[i-1])
    }
    // Construct rightMaxs[] such that rightMaxs[j] stores the maximum value from (A[j], A[j+1], ..A[n-1])
    rightMaxs[n-1] = A[n-1]
    for j := n - 2; j >= 0; j-- {
        rightMaxs[j] = max(A[j], rightMaxs[j+1])
    }
    // Traverse both arrays from left to right to find optimum j - i. This process is similar to merge() of MergeSort.
    i, j, maxDiff := 0, 0, -1
    for j < n && i < n {
        if leftMins[i] < rightMaxs[j] {
```

```
            maxDiff = max(maxDiff, j-i)
            j = j + 1
        } else {
            i = i + 1
        }
    }
    return maxDiff
}
```

Time Complexity: O(n). Space Complexity: O(n).

Problem-78 Given an array of elements, how do you check whether the list is pairwise sorted or not? A list is considered pairwise sorted if each successive pair of numbers is in sorted (non-decreasing) order.

Solution:

```
func checkPairwiseSorted(A []int) bool {
    if len(A) <= 1 {
        return true
    }
    for i := 0; i < len(A)-1; i += 2 {
        if A[i] > A[i+1] {
            return false
        }
    }
    return true
}
```

Time Complexity: O(n). Space Complexity: O(1).

Problem-79 Given an array of n elements, how do you print the frequencies of elements without using extra space. Assume all elements are positive, editable and less than n.

Solution: Use *negation* technique. Array should have numbers in the range $[1, n]$ (where n is the size of the array). The if condition (A[pos] > 0 && A[$expectedPos$] > 0) means that both the numbers at indices pos and $expectedPos$ are actual numbers in the array but not their frequencies. So we will swap them so that the number at the index pos will go to the position where it should have been if the numbers 1, 2, 3, ..., n are kept in 0, 1, 2, ..., $n-1$ indices. In the above example input array, initially $pos = 0$, so 10 at index 0 will go to index 9 after the swap. As this is the first occurrence of 10, make it to -1. Note that we are storing the frequencies as negative numbers to differentiate between actual numbers and frequencies.

The else if condition (A[pos] > 0) means A[pos] is a number and A[$expectedPos$] is its frequency without including the occurrence of A[pos]. So increment the frequency by 1 (that is decrement by 1 in terms of negative numbers). As we count its occurrence we need to move to next pos, so $pos++$, but before moving to that next position we should make the frequency of the number $pos + 1$ which corresponds to index pos of zero, since such a number has not yet occurred.

The final else part means the current index pos already has the frequency of the number $pos + 1$, so move to the next pos, hence $pos++$.

```
// Abs returns the absolute value of x.
func abs(x int) int {
    if x < 0 {
        return -x
    }
    return x
}
func frequencyCounter(A []int) {
    pos, n := 0, len(A)
    for pos < n {
        expectedPos := A[pos] - 1
        if A[pos] > 0 && A[expectedPos] > 0 {
            A[pos], A[expectedPos] = A[expectedPos], A[pos]
            A[expectedPos] = -1
        } else if A[pos] > 0 {
            A[expectedPos]--
            A[pos] = 0
            pos++
        } else {
            pos++
```

```
            }
        }
        for i := 0; i < n; i++ {
            fmt.Println(i+1, " frequency is ", abs(A[i]))
        }
    }
```

Time Complexity: O(*n*). Space Complexity: O(1).

Problem-80 Which one is faster and by how much, a linear search of only 1000 elements on a 5-GHz computer or a binary search of 1 million elements on a 1-GHz computer. Assume that the execution of each instruction on the 5-GHz computer is five times faster than on the 1-GHz computer and that each iteration of the linear search algorithm is twice as fast as each iteration of the binary search algorithm.

Solution: A binary search of 1 million elements would require $log_2^{1,000,000}$ or about 20 iterations at most (i.e., worst case). A linear search of 1000 elements would require 500 iterations on the average (i.e., going halfway through the array). Therefore, binary search would be $\frac{500}{20} = 25$ faster (in terms of iterations) than linear search. However, since linear search iterations are twice as fast, binary search would be $\frac{25}{2}$ or about 12 times faster than linear search overall, on the same machine. Since we run them on different machines, where an instruction on the 5-GhZ machine is 5 times faster than an instruction on a 1-GHz machine, binary search would be $\frac{12}{5}$ or about 2 times faster than linear search! The key idea is that software improvements can make an algorithm run much faster without having to use more powerful software.

Problem-81 Given an array of integers, give an algorithm that returns the *pivot* index of this array. *Pivot* index is the index where the sum of the numbers to the left of the index is equal to the sum of the numbers to the right of the index. If no such index exists, we should return -1. If there are multiple pivot indexes, you should return the left-most pivot index.

Example 1: Input: A = [1, 8, 4, 7, 6, 7], Output: 3
Explanation: The sum of the numbers to the left of index 3 (A[3] = 7) is equal to the sum of numbers to the right of index 3. Also, 3 is the first index where this occurs.

Example 2: Input: A = [2, 3, 4], Output: -1
Explanation: There is no index that satisfies the conditions in the problem statement.

Solution: We need to quickly compute the sum of values to the left and the right of every index. Let's say we knew *totalSum* as the sum of the numbers, and we are at index i. If we knew the sum of numbers leftsum that are to the left of index i, then the other sum to the right of the index would just be $totalSum - A[i] - leftsum$.

As such, we only need to know about $leftsum$ to check whether an index is a pivot index in constant time. Let's do that: as we iterate through candidate indexes i, we will maintain the correct value of leftsum.

```
func pivotIndex(A []int) int {
    sum := 0
    for i := 0; i < len(A); i++ {
        sum += A[i]
    }
    leftsum := 0
    for i := 0; i < len(A); i++ {
        if leftsum == sum - A[i] - leftsum {
            return i
        }
        leftsum += A[i]
    }
    return -1
}
```

Time Complexity: O(*n*), where *n* is the length of array A.
Space Complexity: O(1), the space used by $leftsum$ and *totalSum*.

Problem-82 Given two strings ***s*** and ***t*** which consist of only lowercase letters. String ***t*** is generated by random shuffling string ***s*** and then add one more letter at a random position. Find the letter that was added in ***t***.

Example Input: s = "abcd" t = "abcde" Output: e
Explanation: 'e' is the letter that was added.

Solution: Refer **Other Programming Questions** section in **Hacks on Bitwise Programming** chapter.

Problem-83 Given an array of elements, replace every element with nearest greater element on the right of that element.

Solution: One simple approach would involve scanning the array elements and for each of the elements, scan the remaining elements and find the nearest greater element.

```
func replaceWithNearestGreaterElement(A []int) []int {
    n := len(A)
    for i := 0; i < n; i++ {
        nextNearestGreater := math.MinInt32
        for j := i + 1; j < n; j++ {
            if A[j] > nextNearestGreater {
                nextNearestGreater = A[j]
            }
        }
        A[i] = nextNearestGreater
    }
    return A
}
```

Time Complexity: $O(n^2)$. Space Complexity: O(1).

Problem-84 For Problem-83, can we improve the complexity?

Solution: Replace all elements using one traversal of the array. Start from the rightmost element, move to the left side one by one, and keep track of the maximum element. Replace every element with the maximum element.

```
func replaceWithNearestGreaterElement(A []int) []int {
    greatest := math.MinInt32
    for i := len(A) - 1; i >= 0; i-- {
        temp := greatest
        if A[i] > greatest {
            greatest = A[i]
        }
        A[i] = temp
    }
    return A
}
```

Time Complexity: $O(n)$. Space Complexity: O(1).

CHAPTER

12

SELECTION ALGORITHMS [MEDIANS]

12.1 What are Selection Algorithms?

Selection algorithm is an algorithm for finding the kth smallest/largest number in a list (also called as k^{th} order statistic). This includes finding the minimum, maximum, and median elements. For finding the kth order statistic, there are multiple solutions which provide different complexities, and in this chapter we will enumerate those possibilities.

12.2 Selection by Sorting

A selection problem can be converted to a sorting problem. In this method, we first sort the input elements and then get the desired element. It is efficient if we want to perform many selections.

For example, let us say we want to get the minimum element. After sorting the input elements we can simply return the first element (assuming the array is sorted in ascending order). Now, if we want to find the second smallest element, we can simply return the second element from the sorted list.

That means, for the second smallest element we are not performing the sorting again. The same is also the case with subsequent queries. Even if we want to get k^{th} smallest element, just one scan of the sorted list is enough to find the element (or we can return the kth-indexed value if the elements are in the array).

From the above discussion what we can say is, with the initial sorting we can answer any query in one scan, $O(n)$. In general, this method requires $O(nlogn)$ time (for *sorting*), where n is the length of the input list. Suppose we are performing n queries, then the average cost per operation is just $\frac{n\,logn}{n} \approx O(logn)$. This kind of analysis is called *amortized* analysis.

12.3 Partition-based Selection Algorithm

For the algorithm check Problem-7. This algorithm is similar to Quick sort.

12.4 Linear Selection Algorithm - Median of Medians Algorithm

Worst-case performance	$O(n)$
Best-case performance	$O(n)$
Worst-case space complexity	$O(1)$ auxiliary

Refer to Problem-14.

12.5 Finding the K Smallest Elements in Sorted Order

For the algorithm check Problem-7. This algorithm is similar to Quick sort.

12.6 Selection Algorithms: Problems & Solutions

Problem-1 Find the largest element in an array A of size n.

Solution: Scan the complete array and return the largest element.

```
func findMax(A []int) (max int) {
    max = math.MinInt32
```

```
    for _, value := range A {
        if value > max {
            max = value
        }
    }
    return max
}
```

Time Complexity - O(n). Space Complexity - O(1).

Note: Any deterministic algorithm that can find the smallest of n keys by comparison of keys takes at least $n - 1$ comparisons.

Problem-2 Find the smallest element in an array A of size n.

Solution: Scan the complete array and return the smallest element.

```
func findMin(A []int) (min int) {
    min = math.MaxInt32
    for _, value := range A {
        if value < min {
            min = value
        }
    }
    return min
}
```

Time Complexity - O(n). Space Complexity - O(1).

Problem-3 Find the smallest and largest elements in an array A of size n.

Solution: For this problem, we assign *min* and *max* element to the maximum and minimum integer values from the math library. If the array has zero elements, then *for* loop will not be. If array has elements then *for* loop will get executed. Inside *for* loop, when any element found bigger than *max* element than that element becomes *max*. Similarly happens with *min* also, if any element found lesser than *min* than that element becomes *min*. Finally, *min* and *max* displayed with their position.

```
func findMinAndMax(A []int) (min, max int) {
    min, max = math.MaxInt32, math.MinInt32
    for _, value := range A {
        if value < min {
            min = value
        }
        if value > max {
            max = value
        }
    }
    return min, max
}
```

Time Complexity - O(n). Space Complexity - O(1). The worst-case number of comparisons is $2(n - 1)$.

Problem-4 Can we improve the previous algorithms?

Solution: Yes. We can do this by comparing in pairs. We will have two variables (*min* and *max*), and passthrough the array; each time compare what you get with this two cells (always putting the lowest on *min* and the highest on *max*). With one pass, you will get the minimum and maximum.

```
func findMinMaxWithPairComparison(A []int) (min int, max int) {
    min, max, n := math.MaxInt32, math.MinInt32, len(A)
    var i int
    for i = 0; i < n-1; i = i + 2 { // Increment i by 2.
        if A[i] < A[i+1] {
            if A[i] < min {
                min = A[i]
            }
            if A[i+1] > max {
                max = A[i+1]
            }
        } else {
            if A[i+1] < min {
```

```
                min = A[i+1]
            }
            if A[i] > max {
                max = A[i]
            }
        }
    }
    if n %2 == 1 {          // to deal with odd length array
        if A[i]< min {
            min = A[i]
        }
        if  A[i]> max {
            max = A[i]
        }
    }
    return min, max
}
```

Time Complexity – O(n). Space Complexity – O(1).

Number of comparisons: $\begin{cases} \frac{3n}{2} - 2, if\ n\ is\ even \\ \frac{3n}{2} - \frac{3}{2}\ if\ n\ is\ odd \end{cases}$

Summary

Straightforward comparison – $2(n - 1)$ comparisons
Compare for min only if comparison for max fails
Best case: increasing order – $n - 1$ comparisons
Worst case: decreasing order – $2(n - 1)$ comparisons
Average case: $3n/2 - 1$ comparisons

Note: For divide and conquer techniques refer to the *Divide and Conquer* chapter.

Problem-5 Give an algorithm for finding the second largest element in the given input list of elements.

Solution: Brute Force Method

Algorithm:

- Find the largest element: needs $n - 1$ comparisons
- delete (discard) the largest element
- Again find the largest element: needs $n - 2$ comparisons

Total number of comparisons: $n - 1 + n - 2 = 2n - 3$

Problem-6 Can we reduce the number of comparisons in Problem-5 solution?

Solution: The Tournament method: For simplicity, assume that the numbers are distinct and that n is a power of 2. We pair the keys and compare the pairs in rounds until only one round remains. If the input has eight keys, there are four comparisons in the first round, two in the second, and one in the last. The winner of the last round is the largest key. The figure below shows the method.

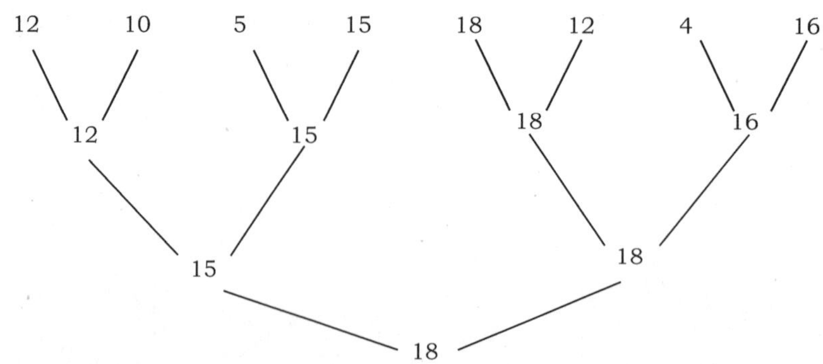

The tournament method directly applies only when n is a power of 2. When this is not the case, we can add enough items to the end of the array to make the array size a power of 2. If the tree is complete then the maximum height of the tree is $logn$. If we construct the complete binary tree, we need $n - 1$ comparisons to find the largest. The second largest key has to be among the ones that were lost in a comparison with the largest one. That means, the second largest element should be one of the opponents of the largest element. The number of keys that are lost to the largest key is the height of the tree, i.e. $logn$ [if the tree is a complete binary tree]. Then, using the selection algorithm to find the largest among them, take $logn - 1$ comparisons. Thus the total number of comparisons to find the largest and second largest keys is $n + logn - 2$.

Problem-7 Can we solve Problem-5 in O(n)?

Solution: Yes. Keep track of the *largest* number and the *second* largest number. If the current number ($A[i]$) is greater than the *largest*, current number becomes the *largest*, *largest* becomes just *second* largest.

```
func findLargestAndSecondLargest(A []int) (largest, second int) {
    largest, second = math.MinInt32, math.MinInt32
    for _, v := range A {
        if v > largest {
            second = largest
            largest = v
        } else if v > second {
            second = v
        }
    }
    return largest, second
}
func main() {
    largest, second := findLargestAndSecondLargest([]int{11, -4, 7, 8, -10})
    fmt.Println("largest: ", largest, "second: ", second)
}
```

Time Complexity – O(n). Space Complexity – O(1).

Problem-8 Find the k-smallest elements in an array S of n elements using the partitioning method.

Solution: Brute Force Approach: Scan through the numbers k times to have the desired element. This method is the one used in bubble sort (and selection sort), every time we find out the smallest element in the whole sequence by comparing every element. In this method, the sequence has to be traversed k times. So the complexity is O($n \times k$).

Problem-9 Can we use the sorting technique for solving Problem-8?

Solution: Yes. Sort and take the first k elements.

1. Sort the numbers.
2. Pick the first k elements.

The time complexity calculation is trivial. Sorting of n numbers is of O($nlogn$) and picking k elements is of O(k). The total complexity is O($nlogn + k$) = O($nlogn$).

Problem-10 Can we use the *tree sorting* technique for solving Problem-8?

Solution: Yes.

1. Insert all the elements in a binary search tree.
2. Do an InOrder traversal and print k elements which will be the smallest ones. So, we have the k smallest elements.

The cost of creation of a binary search tree with n elements is O($nlogn$) and the traversal up to k elements is O(k). Hence the complexity is O($nlogn + k$) = O($nlogn$).

Disadvantage: If the numbers are sorted in descending order, we will be getting a tree which will be skewed towards the left. In that case, the construction of the tree will be $0 + 1 + 2 + \ldots + (n-1) = \frac{n(n-1)}{2}$ which is O(n^2). To escape from this, we can keep the tree balanced, so that the cost of constructing the tree will be only $nlogn$.

Problem-11 Can we improve the *tree sorting* technique for solving Problem-8?

Solution: Yes. Use a smaller tree to give the same result.

1. Take the first k elements of the sequence to create a balanced tree of k nodes (this will cost $klogk$).
2. Take the remaining numbers one by one, and
    a. If the number is larger than the largest element of the tree, return.
    b. If the number is smaller than the largest element of the tree, remove the largest element of the tree and add the new element. This step is to make sure that a smaller element replaces a larger element from the tree. And of course the cost of this operation is $logk$ since the tree is a balanced tree of k elements.

Once Step 2 is over, the balanced tree with k elements will have the smallest k elements. The only remaining task is to print out the largest element of the tree.

Time Complexity:

1. For the first k elements, we make the tree. Hence the cost is $klogk$.
2. For the rest $n - k$ elements, the complexity is $O(logk)$.

Step 2 has a complexity of $(n - k)\,logk$. The total cost is $klogk + (n - k)\,logk = nlogk$ which is $O(nlogk)$. This bound is actually better than the ones provided earlier.

Problem-12 Can we use heaps for solving Problem-8?

Solution: One simplest way of solving this problem is, construct a min-heap with given array and perform deletion (extract-minimum) operation for k-times.

```
func findKSmallest(S []int, k int) []int {
    h := &Heap{items: []int{}}
    heap.Init(h)
    result := []int{}
    for i := 0; i < len(S); i++ {
        heap.Push(h, S[i])
    }

    for i := 0; i < k; i++ {
        result = append(result, heap.Pop(h).(int))
    }
    return result
}
```

Time Complexity – $O(klogn)$.
Space Complexity – $O(n)$. Refer Priority Queues chapter for details on heap data structure.

Problem-13 Can we use the partitioning technique for solving Problem-8?

Solution: Yes.

Algorithm

1. Choose a pivot from the array.
2. Partition the array so that: $A[low...pivotpoint - 1] <= pivotpoint <= A[pivotpoint + 1..high]$.
3. if $k < pivotpoint$ then it must be on the left of the pivot, so do the same method recursively on the left part.
4. if $k = pivotpoint$ then it must be the pivot and print all the elements from low to $pivotpoint$.
5. if $k > pivotpoint$ then it must be on the right of pivot, so do the same method recursively on the right part.

```
func findKSmallest(S []int, k int) []int {
    for start, end := 0, len(S); ; {
        idx := partition(S, start, end)
        if idx == k-1 {
            break
        } else if idx > k-1 {
            end = idx
        } else {
            start = idx + 1
        }
    }
    return S[:k]
}
func partition(S []int, start, end int) int {
    // randomly choose pivot to avoid worst cases
    pivot := start
    S[end-1], S[pivot] = S[pivot], S[end-1]
    // numbers with index less than idx will be greater than pivot
    idx := start
    for i := start; i < end-1; i++ {
        if S[i] < S[end-1] {
            S[i], S[idx] = S[idx], S[i]
            idx++
        }
    }
    S[end-1], S[idx] = S[idx], S[end-1]
    return idx
```

```
    }
    func main() {
        fmt.Println(findKSmallest([]int{11, -4, 7, 8, -10}, 3))
    }
```

Time Complexity: $O(n^2)$ in worst case as similar to Quicksort. Although the worst case is the same as that of Quicksort, this performs much better on the average [$O(nlogk)$ – Average case].

Problem-14 Find the kth-smallest element in an array S of n elements in the best possible way.

Solution: This problem is similar to Problem-8 and all the solutions discussed for Problem-8 are valid for this problem. The only difference is that instead of printing all the k elements, we print only the k^{th}element. We can improve the solution by using the *median of medians* algorithm. Median is a special case of the selection algorithm. The algorithm Selection(A, k) to find the kth smallest element from set A of n elements is as follows:

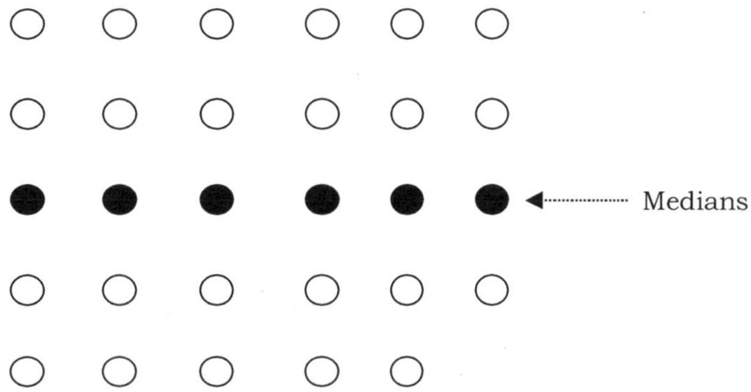

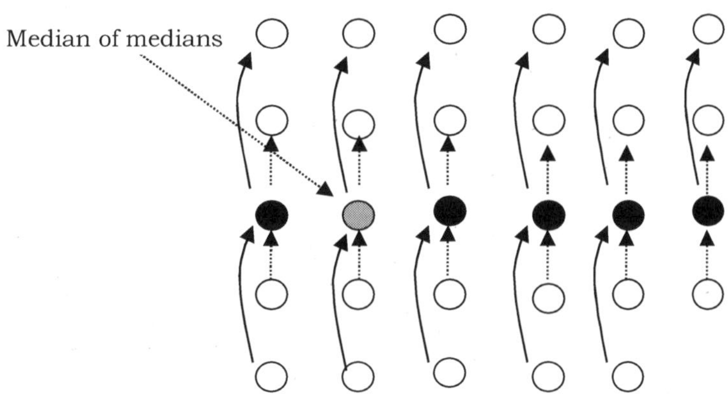

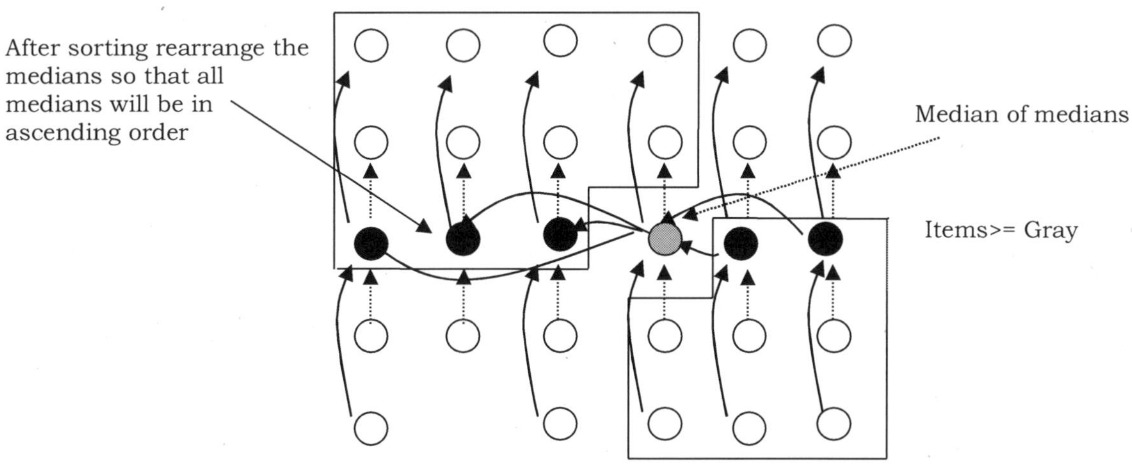

Algorithm: *selection*(A, k)

1. Partition A into $ceil\left(\frac{length(A)}{5}\right)$ groups, with each group having five items (the last group may have fewer items).
2. Sort each group separately (e.g., insertion sort).

3. Find the median of each of the $\frac{n}{5}$ groups and store them in some array (let us say A').
4. Use *Selection* recursively to find the median of A' (median of medians). Let us asay the median of medians is m.

$$m = Selection(A', \frac{\frac{length(A)}{5}}{2});$$

5. Let q = # elements of A smaller than m;
6. If($k == q + 1$)
   return m;
   /* Partition with pivot */
7. Else partition A into X and Y
   - X = {items smaller than m}
   - Y = {items larger than m}

   /* Next,form a subproblem */
8. If($k < q + 1$)
   return Selection(X, k);
9. Else
   return Selection(Y, k – (q+1));

Before developing recurrence, let us consider the representation of the input below. In the figure, each circle is an element and each column is grouped with 5 elements. The black circles indicate the median in each group of 5 elements. As discussed, sort each column using constant time insertion sort.

In the figure above the gray circled item is the median of medians (let us call this m). It can be seen that at least 1/2 of 5 element group medians $\leq m$. Also, these 1/2 of 5 element groups contribute 3 elements that are $\leq m$ except 2 groups [last group which may contain fewer than 5 elements, and other group which contains m]. Similarly, at least 1/2 of 5 element groups contribute 3 elements that are $\geq m$ as shown above. 1/2 of 5 element groups contribute 3 elements, except 2 groups gives: $3(\lceil\frac{1}{2}\lceil\frac{n}{5}\rceil\rceil - 2) \approx \frac{3n}{10} - 6$. The remaining are $n - (\frac{3n}{10} - 6) \approx \frac{7n}{10} + 6$. Since $\frac{7n}{10} + 6$ is greater than $\frac{3n}{10} - 6$ we need to consider $\frac{7n}{10} + 6$ for worst.

Components in recurrence:

- In our selection algorithm, we choose m, which is the median of medians, to be a pivot, and partition A into two sets X and Y. We need to select the set which gives maximum size (to get the worst case).
- The time in function *Selection* when called from procedure *partition.* The number of keys in the input to this call to *Selection* is $\frac{n}{5}$.
- The number of comparisons required to partition the array. This number is $length(S)$, let us say n.

We have established the following recurrence: $T(n) = T\left(\frac{n}{5}\right) + \Theta(n) + Max\{T(X), T(Y)\}$

From the above discussion we have seen that, if we select median of medians m as pivot, the partition sizes are: $\frac{3n}{10} - 6$ and $\frac{7n}{10} + 6$. If we select the maximum of these, then we get:

$$\begin{aligned} T(n) &= T\left(\frac{n}{5}\right) + \Theta(n) + T\left(\frac{7n}{10} + 6\right) \\ &\approx T\left(\frac{n}{5}\right) + \Theta(n) + T\left(\frac{7n}{10}\right) + O(1) \\ &\leq c\frac{7n}{10} + c\frac{n}{5} + \Theta(n) + O(1) \end{aligned}$$

Finally, $T(n) = \Theta(n)$.

Problem-15 In Problem-14, we divided the input array into groups of 5 elements. The constant 5 play an important part in the analysis. Can we divide in groups of 3 which work in linear time?

Solution: In this case the modification causes the routine to take more than linear time. In the worst case, at least half of the $\lceil\frac{n}{3}\rceil$ medians found in the grouping step are greater than the median of medians m, but two of those groups contribute less than two elements larger than m. So as an upper bound, the number of elements larger than the pivotpoint is at least:

$$2(\lceil\frac{1}{2}\lceil\frac{n}{3}\rceil\rceil - 2) \geq \frac{n}{3} - 4$$

Likewise this is a lower bound. Thus up to $n - (\frac{n}{3} - 4) = \frac{2n}{3} + 4$ elements are fed into the recursive call to *Select*. The recursive step that finds the median of medians runs on a problem of size $\lceil\frac{n}{3}\rceil$, and consequently the time recurrence is:

$$T(n) = T(\lceil\frac{n}{3}\rceil) + T(2n/3 + 4) + \Theta(n).$$

Assuming that $T(n)$ is monotonically increasing, we may conclude that $T(\frac{2n}{3} + 4) \geq T(\frac{2n}{3}) \geq 2T(\frac{n}{3})$, and we can say the upper bound for this as $T(n) \geq 3T(\frac{n}{3}) + \Theta(n)$, which is $O(nlogn)$. Therefore, we cannot select 3 as the group size.

Problem-16 As in Problem-15, can we use groups of size 7?

Solution: Following a similar reasoning, we once more modify the routine, now using groups of 7 instead of 5. In the worst case, at least half the $\lceil \frac{n}{7} \rceil$ medians found in the grouping step are greater than the median of medians m, but two of those groups contribute less than four elements larger than m. So as an upper bound, the number of elements larger than the pivotpoint is at least:

$$4(\lceil 1/2 \lceil n/7 \rceil \rceil - 2) \geq \frac{2n}{7} - 8.$$

Likewise this is a lower bound. Thus up to $n - (\frac{2n}{7} - 8) = \frac{5n}{7} + 8$ elements are fed into the recursive call to Select. The recursive step that finds the median of medians runs on a problem of size $\lceil \frac{n}{7} \rceil$, and consequently the time recurrence is

$$T(n) = T(\lceil \frac{n}{7} \rceil) + T(\frac{5n}{7} + 8) + O(n)$$
$$T(n) \leq c\lceil \frac{n}{7} \rceil + c(\frac{5n}{7} + 8) + O(n)$$
$$\leq c\frac{n}{7} + c\frac{5n}{7} + 8c + an, a \text{ is a constant}$$
$$= cn - c\frac{n}{7} + an + 9c$$
$$= (a + c)\, n - (c\frac{n}{7} - 9c).$$

This is bounded above by $(a + c)\, n$ provided that $c\frac{n}{7} - 9c \geq 0$. Therefore, we can select 7 as the group size.

Problem-17 Given two arrays each containing n sorted elements, give an $O(logn)$-time algorithm to find the median of all $2n$ elements.

Solution: The simple solution to this problem is to merge the two lists and then take the average of the middle two elements (note the union always contains an even number of values). But, the merge would be $\Theta(n)$, so that doesn't satisfy the problem statement. To get $logn$ complexity, let $medianA$ and $medianB$ be the medians of the respective lists (which can be easily found since both lists are sorted). If $medianA == medianB$, then that is the overall median of the union and we are done. Otherwise, the median of the union must be between $medianA$ and $medianB$. Suppose that $medianA < medianB$ (the opposite case is entirely similar). Then we need to find the median of the union of the following two sets:

$$\{x \; in \; A \mid x >= medianA\} \; \{x \; in \; B \mid x <= medianB\}$$

The algorithm tracks both arrays (which are sorted) using two indices. These indices are used to access and compare the median of both arrays to find where the overall median lies.

```
func findMedianSortedArrays(A, B []int) float32 {
    m, n := len(A), len(B)
    if m > n { // to ensure m<=n
        A, B = B, A
        m, n = n, m
    }
    iMin, iMax, halfLen := 0, m, (m+n+1)/2
    for iMin <= iMax {
        i := (iMin + iMax) / 2
        j := halfLen - i
        if i < iMax && B[j-1] > A[i] {
            iMin = i + 1 // i is too small
        } else if i > iMin && A[i-1] > B[j] {
            iMax = i - 1 // i is too big
        } else { // i is perfect
            maxLeft := 0
            if i == 0 {
                maxLeft = B[j-1]
            } else if j == 0 {
                maxLeft = A[i-1]
            } else {
                maxLeft = max(A[i-1], B[j-1])
            }
            if (m+n)%2 == 1 {
                return float32(maxLeft)
```

```
            }
            minRight := 0
            if i == m {
                minRight = B[j]
            } else if j == n {
                minRight = A[i]
            } else {
                minRight = min(B[j], A[i])
            }

            return float32((maxLeft + minRight) / 2.0)
        }
    }
    return 0.0
}
```

Time Complexity: O($logn$), since we are reducing the problem size by half every time.

Problem-18 Let A and B be two sorted arrays of n elements each. We can easily find the kth smallest element in A in O(1) time by just outputting $A[k]$. Similarly, we can easily find the kth smallest element in B. Give an O($logk$) time algorithm to find the kth smallest element overall { $i.e.$, the kth smallest in the union of A and B.

Solution: It's just another way of asking Problem-17.

Problem-19 **Find the k smallest elements in sorted order:** Given a set of n elements from a totally-ordered domain, find the k smallest elements, and list them in sorted order. Analyze the worst-case running time of the best implementation of the approach.

Solution: Sort the numbers, and list the k smallest.

$T(n)$ = Time complexity of sort + listing k smallest elements = $\Theta(nlogn) + \Theta(n) = \Theta(nlogn)$.

Problem-20 For Problem-19, if we follow the approach below, then what is the complexity?

Solution: Using the priority queue data structure from heap sort, construct a min-heap over the set, and perform extract-min k times. Refer to the *Priority Queues* (*Heaps*) chapter for more details.

Problem-21 For Problem-19, if we follow the approach below then what is the complexity?
Find the kth-smallest element of the set, partition around this pivot element, and sort the k smallest elements.

Solution:

$$T(n) = Time\ complexity\ of\ kth - smallest + Finding\ pivot + Sorting\ prefix$$
$$= \Theta(n) + \Theta(n) + \Theta(klogk) = \Theta(n + klogk)$$

Since, $k \leq n$, this approach is better than Problem-19 and Problem-20.

Problem-22 Find k nearest neighbors to the median of n distinct numbers in O(n) time.

Solution: Let us assume that the array elements are sorted. Now find the median of n numbers and call its index as X (since array is sorted, median will be at $\frac{n}{2}$ location). All we need to do is select k elements with the smallest absolute differences from the median, moving from $X - 1$ to 0, and $X + 1$ to $n - 1$ when the median is at index m.

Time Complexity: Each step takes $\Theta(n)$. So the total time complexity of the algorithm is $\Theta(n)$.

Problem-23 Is there any other way of solving Problem-22?

Solution: Assume for simplicity that n is odd and k is even. If set A is in sorted order, the median is in position $n/2$ and the k numbers in A that are closest to the median are in positions $(n - k)/2$ through $(n + k)/2$.

We first use linear time selection to find the $(n - k)/2$, $n/2$, and $(n + k)/2$ elements and then pass through set A to find the numbers less than the $(n + k)/2$ element, greater than the $(n - k)/2$ element, and not equal to the $n/2$ element. The algorithm takes O(n) time as we use linear time selection exactly three times and traverse the n numbers in A once.

Problem-24 Given a big file containing billions of numbers, find the maximum 10 numbers from that file.

Solution: Refer to the *Priority Queues* chapter.

Problem-25 Suppose there is a milk company. The company collects milk every day from all its agents. The agents are located at different places. To collect the milk, what is the best place to start so that the least amount of total distance is travelled?

Solution: Starting at the median reduces the total distance travelled because it is the place which is at the center of all the places.

Problem-26 Given (x, y) coordinates of n houses, where should you build a road parallel to x-axis to minimize the construction cost of building driveways?

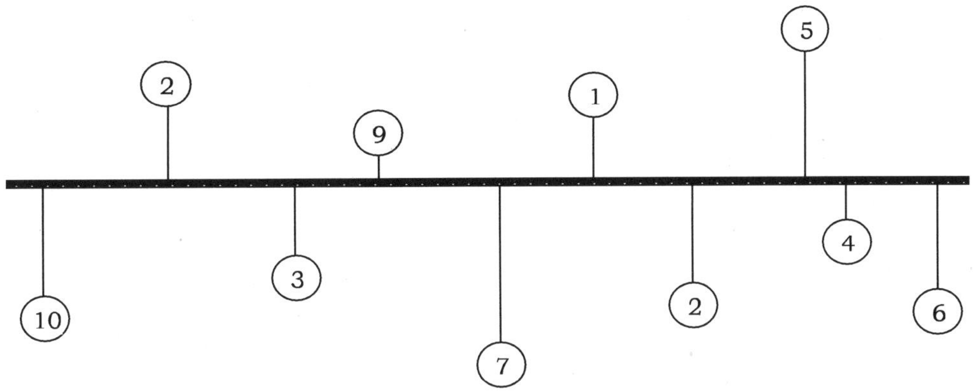

Solution: The road costs nothing to build. It is the driveways that cost money. The driveway cost is proportional to its distance from the road. Obviously, they will be perpendicular. The solution is to put the street at the median of the y coordinates.

CHAPTER

SYMBOL TABLES 13

13.1 Introduction

Since childhood, we all have used a dictionary, and many of us have a word processor (say, Microsoft Word) which comes with a spell checker. The spell checker is also a dictionary but limited in scope. There are many real time examples for dictionaries and a few of them are:

- Spell checker
- The data dictionary found in database management applications
- Symbol tables generated by loaders, assemblers, and compilers
- Routing tables in networking components (DNS lookup)

In computer science, we generally use the term 'symbol table' rather than 'dictionary' when referring to the abstract data type (ADT).

13.2 What are Symbol Tables?

We can define the *symbol table* as a data structure that associates a *value* with a *key*. It supports the following operations:

- Search whether a particular name is in the table
- Get the attributes of that name
- Modify the attributes of that name
- Insert a new name and its attributes
- delete a name and its attributes

There are only three basic operations on symbol tables: searching, inserting, and deleting.

Example: DNS lookup. Let us assume that the key in this case is the URL and the value is an IP address.

- Insert URL with specified IP address
- Given URL, find corresponding IP address

Key[Website]	Value [IP Address]
www.CareerMonks.com	128.112.136.11
www.AuthorsInn.com	128.112.128.15
www.AuthInn.com	130.132.143.21
www.klm.com	128.103.060.55
www.CareerMonk.com	209.052.165.60

13.3 Symbol Table Implementations

Before implementing symbol tables, let us enumerate the possible implementations. Symbol tables can be implemented in many ways and some of them are listed below.

Unordered Array Implementation

With this method, just maintaining an array is enough. It needs O(n) time for searching, insertion and deletion in the worst case.

Ordered [Sorted] Array Implementation

In this we maintain a sorted array of keys and values.

- Store in sorted order by key
- keys[i] = i^{th} largest key
- values[i] = value associated with i^{th} largest key

Since the elements are sorted and stored in arrays, we can use a simple binary search for finding an element. It takes O($logn$) time for searching and O(n) time for insertion and deletion in the worst case.

Unordered Linked List Implementation

Just maintaining a linked list with two data values is enough for this method. It needs O(n) time for searching, insertion and deletion in the worst case.

Ordered Linked List Implementation

In this method, while inserting the keys, maintain the order of keys in the linked list. Even if the list is sorted, in the worst case it needs O(n) time for searching, insertion and deletion.

Binary Search Trees Implementation

Refer to *Trees* chapter. The advantages of this method are: it does not need much code and it has a fast search [O($logn$) on average].

Balanced Binary Search Trees Implementation

Refer to *Trees* chapter. It is an extension of binary search trees implementation and takes O($logn$) in worst case for search, insert and delete operations.

Ternary Search Implementation

Refer to *String Algorithms* chapter. This is one of the important methods used for implementing dictionaries.

Hashing Implementation

This method is important. For a complete discussion, refer to the *Hashing* chapter.

13.4 Comparison Table of Symbols for Implementations

Let us consider the following comparison table for all the implementations.

Implementation	Search	Insert	Delete
Unordered Array	n	n	n
Ordered Array (can be implemented with array binary search)	$logn$	n	n
Unordered List	n	n	n
Ordered List	n	n	n
Binary Search Trees (O($logn$) on average)	$logn$	$logn$	$logn$
Balanced Binary Search Trees (O($logn$) in worst case)	$logn$	$logn$	$logn$
Ternary Search (only change is in logarithms base)	$logn$	$logn$	$logn$
Hashing (O(1) on average)	1	1	1

Notes:

- In the above table, n is the input size.
- Table indicates the possible implementations discussed in this book. But, there could be other implementations.

CHAPTER

HASHING

14

14.1 What is Hashing?

In this chapter we introduce so-called *associative arrays*, that is, data structures that are similar to arrays but are not indexed by integers, but other forms of data such as strings. One popular data structures for the implementation of associative arrays are hash tables. To analyze the asymptotic efficiency of hash tables we have to explore a new point of view, that of average case complexity. Hashing is a technique used for storing and retrieving information as quickly as possible. It is used to perform optimal searches and is useful in implementing symbol tables.

14.2 Why Hashing?

In the *Trees* chapter we saw that balanced binary search trees support operations such as *insert*, *delete* and *search* in O($logn$) time. In applications, if we need these operations in O(1), then hashing provides a way. Remember that worst case complexity of hashing is still O(n), but it gives O(1) on the average.

14.3 Hash Table ADT

The hash table structure is an unordered collection of associations between a key and a data value. The keys in a hash table are all unique so that there is a one-to-one relationship between a key and a value. The operations are given below.

- HashTable: Creates a new hash table
- Get: Searches the hash table with key and return the value if it finds the element with the given key
- Put: Inserts a new key-value pair into hash table
- Delete: Deletes a key-value pair from hash table
- DeleteHashTable: Deletes the hash table

14.4 Understanding Hashing

In simple terms we can treat *array* as a hash table. For understanding the use of hash tables, let us consider the following example: Give an algorithm for printing the first repeated character if there are duplicated elements in it. Let us think about the possible solutions.

The simple and brute force way of solving is: given a string, for each character check whether that character is repeated or not. The time complexity of this approach is O(n^2) with O(1) space complexity.

Now, let us find a better solution for this problem. Since our objective is to find the first repeated character, what if we remember the previous characters in some array?

We know that the number of possible characters is 256 (for simplicity assume *ASCII* characters only). Create an array of size 256 and initialize it with all zeros. For each of the input characters go to the corresponding position and increment its count. Since we are using arrays, it takes constant time for reaching any location. While scanning the input, if we get a character whose counter is already 1 then we can say that the character is the one which is repeating for the first time.

```
func firstRepeatedChar(str string) byte {
    n := len(str)
    counters := [256]int{}
    for i := 0; i < 256; i++ {
        counters[i] = 0
    }
```

```
        for i := 0; i < n; i++ {
            if counters[str[i]] == 1 {
                return str[i]
            }
            counters[str[i]]++
        }
        return byte(0)
    }
    func main() {
        fmt.Printf("%c", firstRepeatedChar("abacd"))
    }
```

Why not Arrays?

Arrays can be seen as a mapping, associating with every integer in a given interval some data item. It is finitary, because its domain, and therefore also its range, is finite. There are many situations when we want to index elements differently than just by integers. Common examples are strings (for dictionaries, phone books, menus, data base records), or structs (for dates, or names together with other identifying information).

In many applications requiring associative arrays, we are storing complex data values and want to access them by a key which is derived from the data. A typical example of keys are strings, which are appropriate for many scenarios. For example, the key might be a student id and the data entry might be a collection of grades, perhaps another associative array where the key is the name of assignment or exam and the data is a score. We make the assumption that keys are unique in the sense that in an associative array there is at most one data item associated with a given key. In some applications we may need to complicate the structure of keys to achieve this uniqueness. This is consistent with ordinary arrays, which have a unique value for every valid index.

In the previous problem, we have used an array of size 256 because we know the number of different possible characters [256] in advance. Now, let us consider a slight variant of the same problem. Suppose the given array has numbers instead of characters, then how do we solve the problem?

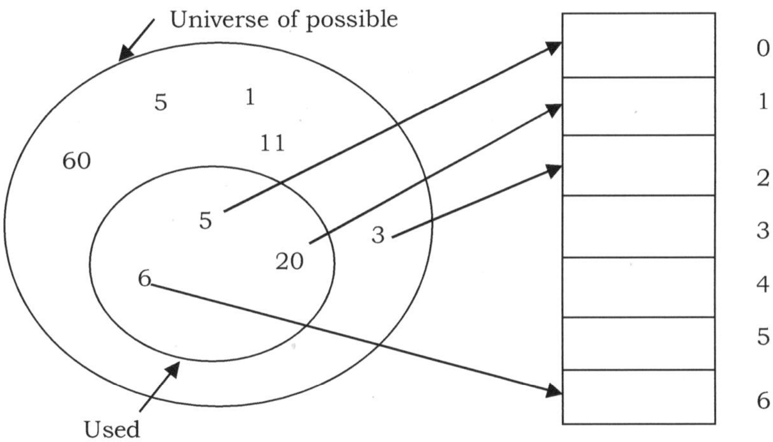

In this case the set of possible values is infinity (or at least very big). Creating a huge array and storing the counters is not possible. That means there are a set of universal keys and limited locations in the main memory. To solve this problem we need to somehow map all these possible keys to the possible memory locations.

From the above discussion and diagram it can be seen that we need a mapping of possible keys to one of the available locations. As a result, using simple arrays is not the correct choice for solving the problems where the possible keys are very big. The process of mapping the keys to available main memory locations is called *hashing*.

Note: For now, do not worry about how the keys are mapped to locations. That depends on the function used for conversions. One such simple function is *key % table size*.

14.5 Components of Hashing

Hashing has four key components:

1) Hash Table
2) Hash Functions
3) Collisions
4) Collision Resolution Techniques

14.6 Hash Table

Hash table is a generalization of array. With an array, we store the element whose key is k at a position k of the array. That means, given a key k, we find the element whose key is k by just looking in the kth position of the array. This is called *direct addressing*.

Direct addressing is applicable when we can afford to allocate an array with one position for every possible key. But if we do not have enough space to allocate a location for each possible key, then we need a mechanism to handle this case. Another way of defining the scenario is: if we have less locations and more possible keys, then simple array implementation is not enough.

In these cases one option is to use hash tables. Hash table or hash map is a data structure that stores the keys and their associated values, and hash table uses a hash function to map keys to their associated values. The general convention is that we use a hash table when the number of keys actually stored is small relative to the number of possible keys.

A hash table is a collection of items which are stored in such a way as to make it easy to find them later. Each position of the hash table, often called a *slot* (or a *bucket*), can hold an item and is named by an integer value starting at 0.

For example, we will have a slot named 0, a slot named 1, a slot named 2, and so on. Initially, the hash table contains no items so every slot is empty. We can implement a hash table by using a list with each element initialized to the special NULL.

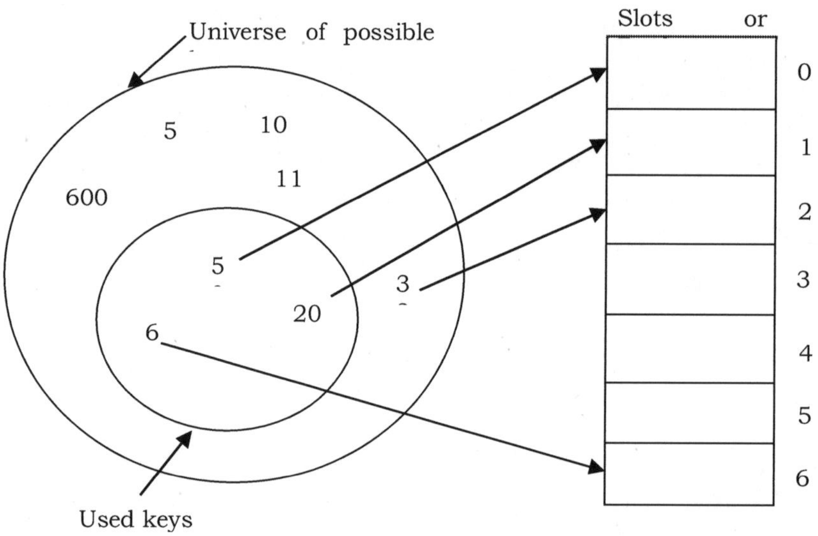

14.7 Hash Function

The first idea behind hash tables is to exploit the efficiency of arrays. So: to map a key to an entry, we first map a key to an integer and then use the integer to index an array A. The first map is called a *hash function*. The hash function is used to transform the key into the slot index (or bucket index). Ideally, the hash function should map each possible key to a unique slot index, but it is difficult to achieve in practice.

Given a collection of elements, a hash function that maps each item into a unique slot is referred to as a *perfect hash function*. If we know the elements and the collection will never change, then it is possible to construct a perfect hash function. Unfortunately, given an arbitrary collection of elements, there is no systematic way to construct a perfect hash function. Luckily, we do not need the hash function to be perfect to still gain performance efficiency.

One way to always have a perfect hash function is to increase the size of the hash table so that each possible value in the element range can be accommodated. This guarantees that each element will have a unique slot. Although this is practical for small numbers of elements, it is not feasible when the number of possible elements is large. For example, if the elements were nine-digit Social Security numbers, this method would require almost one billion slots. If we only want to store data for a class of 25 students, we will be wasting an enormous amount of memory.

Our goal is to create a hash function that minimizes the number of collisions, is easy to compute, and evenly distributes the elements in the hash table. There are a number of common ways to extend the simple remainder method. We will consider a few of them here.

The *folding method* for constructing hash functions begins by dividing the elements into equal-size pieces (the last piece may not be of equal size). These pieces are then added together to give the resulting hash value. For example, if our element was the phone number 436-555-4601, we would take the digits and divide them into groups of 2 (43,65,55,46,01). After the addition, 43+65+55+46+01, we get 210. If we assume our hash table has 11 slots, then we need to perform the extra step of dividing by 11 and keeping the remainder. In this case 210 % 11 is 1, so the phone number 436-555-4601 hashes to slot 1. Some folding methods go one step further and reverse every other piece before the addition. For the above example, we get 43+56+55+64+01=219 which gives 219 % 11=10.

How to Choose Hash Function?

The basic problems associated with the creation of hash tables are:

- An efficient hash function should be designed so that it distributes the index values of inserted objects uniformly across the table.
- An efficient collision resolution algorithm should be designed so that it computes an alternative index for a key whose hash index corresponds to a location previously inserted in the hash table.
- We must choose a hash function which can be calculated quickly, returns values within the range of locations in our table, and minimizes collisions.

Characteristics of Good Hash Functions

A good hash function should have the following characteristics:

- Minimize collisions
- Be easy and quick to compute
- Distribute key values evenly in the hash table
- Use all the information provided in the key
- Have a high load factor for a given set of keys

14.8 Load Factor

The load factor of a non-empty hash table is the number of items stored in the table divided by the size of the table. This is the decision parameter used when we want to rehash *or* expand the existing hash table entries. This also helps us in determining the efficiency of the hashing function. That means, it tells whether the hash function is distributing the keys uniformly or not.

$$Load\ factor = \frac{Number\ of\ elements\ in\ hash\ table}{Hash\ table\ size}$$

14.9 Collisions

Hash functions are used to map each key to a different address space, but practically it is not possible to create such a hash function and the problem is called *collision*. Collision is the condition where two keys are hashed to the same slot.

14.10 Collision Resolution Techniques

Fortunately, there are effective techniques for resolving the conflict created by collisions. The process of finding an alternate location for a key in the case of a collision is called *collision resolution*. Even though hash tables have collision problems, they are more efficient in many cases compared to all other data structures, like search trees. There are a number of collision resolution techniques, and the most popular are direct chaining and open addressing.

- **Direct Chaining (or Closed Addressing):** An array of linked list application
  - Separate chaining (linear chaining)
- **Open Addressing:** Array-based implementation
  - Linear probing (linear search)
  - Quadratic probing (nonlinear search)
  - Double hashing (use multiple hash functions)

Of course, the ideal solution would be to avoid collisions altogether. We might try to achieve this goal by choosing a suitable hash function.

14.11 Separate Chaining

A first idea to explore is to implement the associative array as a linked list, called a chain or a linked list. Separate chaining is one of the most commonly used collision resolution techniques. It is usually implemented using linked lists. Collision resolution by chaining combines linked representation with hash table. When two or more elements hash to the same location, these elements are constituted into a singly-linked list called a *chain*. In chaining, we put all the elements that hash to the same slot in a linked list. If we have a key k and look for it in the linked list, we just traverse it, compute the intrinsic key for each data entry, and compare it with k. If they are equal, we have found our entry, if not we continue the search. If we reach the end of the chain and do not find an entry with key k, then no entry with the given key exists.

In separate chaining, each slot of the hash table is a linked list. To store an element in the hash table you must insert it into a specific linked list. If there is any collision (i.e. two different elements have same hash value) then store both the elements in the same linked list.

As an example, consider the following simple hash function:

$$h(key) = key \ \% \ table \ size$$

In a hash table with size 7, keys 27 and 130 would get 6 and 4 as hash indices respectively.

Slot	
0	
1	
2	
3	
4	→ (130, "John")
5	
6	→ (27, "Ram")

If we insert a new element (18, "Saleem"), that would also go to the fourth index as 18%7 is 4.

Slot		
0		
1		
2		
3		
4	→ (130, "John")	→ (18, "Saleem")
5		
6	→ (27, "Ram")	

The cost of a lookup is that of scanning the entries of the selected linked list for the required key. If the distribution of the keys is sufficiently uniform, then the average cost of a lookup depends only on the average number of keys per linked list. For this reason, chained hash tables remain effective even when the number of table entries (n) is much higher than the number of slots.

For separate chaining, the worst-case scenario is when all the entries are inserted into the same linked list. The lookup procedure may have to scan all its entries, so the worst-case cost is proportional to the number (n) of entries in the table.

The worst-case behavior of hashing with chaining is terrible: all n keys hash to the same slot, creating a list of length n. The worst-case time for searching is thus)(n) plus the time to compute the hash function--no better than if we used one linked list for all the elements. Clearly, hash tables are not used for their worst-case performance.

14.12 Open Addressing

In open addressing all keys are stored in the hash table itself. This approach is also known as *closed hashing*. This procedure is based on probing. A collision is resolved by probing.

Linear Probing

The interval between probes is fixed at 1. In linear probing, we search the hash table sequentially. starting from the original hash location. If a location is occupied, we check the next location. We wrap around from the last table location to the first table location if necessary. The function for rehashing is the following:

$$rehash(key) = (n + 1)\% \ tablesize$$

One of the problems with linear probing is that table items tend to cluster together in the hash table. This means that the table contains groups of consecutively occupied locations that are called *clustering*.

Clusters can get close to one another, and merge into a larger cluster. Thus, the one part of the table might be quite dense, even though another part has relatively few items. Clustering causes long probe searches and therefore decreases the overall efficiency.

The next location to be probed is determined by the step-size, where other step-sizes (more than one) are possible. The step-size should be relatively prime to the table size, i.e. their greatest common divisor should be equal to 1. If we choose the table size to be a prime number, then any step-size is relatively prime to the table size. Clustering cannot be avoided by larger step-sizes.

Quadratic Probing

The interval between probes increases proportionally to the hash value (the interval thus increasing linearly, and the indices are described by a quadratic function). The problem of clustering can be eliminated if we use the quadratic probing method. Quadratic probing is also referred to as *mid – square* method.

In quadratic probing, we start from the original hash location i. If a location is occupied, we check the locations $i + 1^2$, $i + 2^2$, $i + 3^2$, $i + 4^2$... We wrap around from the last table location to the first table location if necessary. The function for rehashing is the following:

$$rehash(key) = (n + k^2)\%\ tablesize$$

Example: Let us assume that the table size is 11 (0..10)

Hash Function: h(key) = key mod 11

Insert keys:

$31\ mod\ 11 = 9$
$19\ mod\ 11 = 8$
$2\ mod\ 11 = 2$
$13\ mod\ 11 = 2 \rightarrow 2 + 1^2 = 3$
$25\ mod\ 11 = 3 \rightarrow 3 + 1^2 = 4$
$24\ mod\ 11 = 2 \rightarrow 2 + 1^2, 2 + 2^2 = 6$
$21\ mod\ 11 = 10$
$9\ mod\ 11 = 9 \rightarrow 9 + 1^2,\ 9 + 2^2\ mod\ 11, 9 + 3^2\ mod\ 11 = 7$

Index	Key
0	
1	
2	2
3	13
4	25
5	5
6	24
7	9
8	19
9	31
10	21

Even though clustering is avoided by quadratic probing, still there are chances of clustering. Clustering is caused by multiple search keys mapped to the same hash key. Thus, the probing sequence for such search keys is prolonged by repeated conflicts along the probing sequence. Both linear and quadratic probing use a probing sequence that is independent of the search key.

Double Hashing

The interval between probes is computed by another hash function. Double hashing reduces clustering in a better way. The increments for the probing sequence are computed by using a second hash function. The second hash function $h2$ should be:

$$h2(key)\ \neq 0 \text{ and } h2\ \neq\ h1$$

We first probe the location $h1(key)$. If the location is occupied, we probe the location $h1(key) + h2(key)$, $h1(key) + 2 * h2(key)$, ...

Example:

Table size is 11 (0..10)
Hash Function: assume $h1(key) = key\ mod\ 11$ and
$h2(key) = 7 - (key\ mod\ 7)$

Insert keys:

$58\ mod\ 11 = 3$
$14\ mod\ 11 = 3 \rightarrow 3 + 7 = 10$
$91\ mod\ 11 = 3 \rightarrow 3 + 7, 3 + 2 * 7\ mod\ 11 = 6$
$25\ mod\ 11 = 3 \rightarrow 3 + 3, 3 + 2 * 3 = 9$

Index	Key
0	
1	
2	
3	58
4	25
5	
6	91
7	
8	
9	25
10	14

14.13 Comparison of Collision Resolution Techniques

Comparisons: Linear Probing vs. Double Hashing

The choice between linear probing and double hashing depends on the cost of computing the hash function and on the load factor [number of elements per slot] of the table. Both use few probes but double hashing take more time because it hashes to compare two hash functions for long keys.

Comparisons: Open Addressing vs. Separate Chaining

It is somewhat complicated because we have to account for the memory usage. Separate chaining uses extra memory for links. Open addressing needs extra memory implicitly within the table to terminate the probe sequence. Open-addressed hash tables cannot be used if the data does not have unique keys. An alternative is to use separate chained hash tables.

Comparisons: Open Addressing methods

Linear Probing	Quadratic Probing	Double hashing
Fastest among three	Easiest to implement and deploy	Makes more efficient use of memory
Uses few probes	Uses extra memory for links and it does not probe all locations in the table	Uses few probes but takes more time
A problem occurs known as primary clustering	A problem occurs known as secondary clustering	More complicated to implement
Interval between probes is fixed - often at 1.	Interval between probes increases proportional to the hash value	Interval between probes is computed by another hash function

14.14 How Hashing Gets O(1) Complexity

We stated earlier that in the best case hashing would provide a O(1), constant time search technique. However, due to collisions, the number of comparisons is typically not so simple. Even though a complete analysis of hashing is beyond the scope of this text, we can state some well-known results that approximate the number of comparisons necessary to search for an item. From the previous discussion, one doubts how hashing gets O(1) if multiple elements map to the same location.

The answer to this problem is simple. By using the load factor we make sure that each block (for example, linked list in separate chaining approach) on the average stores the maximum number of elements less than the *load factor*. Also, in practice this load factor is a constant (generally, 10 or 20). As a result, searching in 20 elements or 10 elements becomes constant.

If the average number of elements in a block is greater than the load factor, we rehash the elements with a bigger hash table size. One thing we should remember is that we consider average occupancy (total number of elements in the hash table divided by table size) when deciding the rehash.

The access time of the table depends on the load factor which in turn depends on the hash function. This is because hash function distributes the elements to the hash table. For this reason, we say hash table gives O(1) complexity on average. Also, we generally use hash tables in cases where searches are more than insertion and deletion operations.

14.15 Hashing Techniques

There are two types of hashing techniques: static hashing and dynamic hashing

Static Hashing

If the data is fixed then static hashing is useful. In static hashing, the set of keys is kept fixed and given in advance, and the number of primary pages in the directory are kept fixed.

Dynamic Hashing

If the data is not fixed, static hashing can give bad performance, in which case dynamic hashing is the alternative, in which case the set of keys can change dynamically.

14.16 Problems for which Hash Tables are not suitable

- Problems for which data ordering is required
- Problems having multidimensional data
- Prefix searching, especially if the keys are long and of variable-lengths
- Problems that have dynamic data
- Problems in which the data does not have unique keys.

14.17 Bloom Filters

A Bloom filter is a probabilistic data structure which was designed to check whether an element is present in a set with memory and time efficiency. It tells us that the element either definitely is *not* in the set or *may* be in the set. The base data structure of a Bloom filter is a *Bit Vector*. The algorithm was invented in 1970 by Burton Bloom and it relies on the use of a number of different hash functions.

How it works?

A Bloom filter starts off with a bit array initialized to zero. To store a data value, we simply apply k different hash functions and treat the resulting k values as indices in the array, and we set each of the k array elements to 1. We repeat this for every element that we encounter.

Now suppose an element turns up and we want to know if we have seen it before. What we do is apply the k hash functions and look up the indicated array elements. If any of them are 0 we can be 100% sure that we have never encountered the element before - if we had, the bit would have been set to 1. However, even if all of them are one, we still can't conclude that we have seen the element before because all of the bits could have been set by the k hash functions applied to multiple other elements. All we can conclude is that it is *likely* that we have encountered the element before.

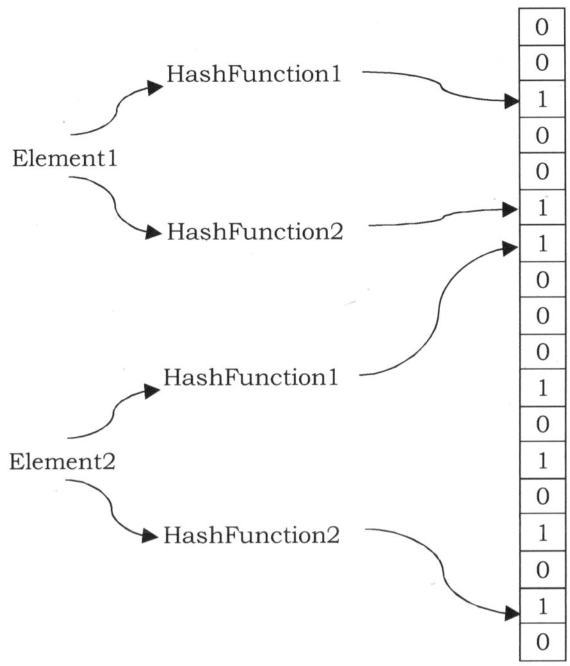

Now that the bits in the bit vector have been set for *Element*1 and *Element*2; we can query the bloom filter to tell us if something has been seen before.

The element is hashed but instead of setting the bits, this time a check is done and if the bits that would have been set are already set the bloom filter will return true that the element has been seen before.

Note that it is not possible to remove an element from a Bloom filter. The reason is simply that we can't unset a bit that appears to belong to an element because it might also be set by another element.

If the bit array is mostly empty, i.e., set to zero, and the k hash functions are independent of one another, then the probability of a false positive (i.e., concluding that we have seen a data item when we actually haven't) is low. For example, if there are only k bits set, we can conclude that the probability of a false positive is very close to zero as the only possibility of error is that we entered a data item that produced the same k hash values - which is unlikely as long as the 'has' functions are independent.

As the bit array fills up, the probability of a false positive slowly increases. Of course when the bit array is full, every element queried is identified as having been seen before. So clearly we can trade space for accuracy as well as for time.

One-time removal of an element from a Bloom filter can be simulated by having a second Bloom filter that contains elements that have been removed. However, false positives in the second filter become false negatives in the composite filter, which may be undesirable. In this approach, re-adding a previously removed item is not possible, as one would have to remove it from the *removed* filter.

Selecting hash functions

The requirement of designing k different independent hash functions can be prohibitive for large k. For a good hash function with a wide output, there should be little if any correlation between different bit-fields of such a hash, so this type of hash can be used to generate multiple $different$ hash functions by slicing its output into multiple bit fields.

Alternatively, one can pass k different initial values (such as 0, 1, ..., k - 1) to a hash function that takes an initial value – or add (or append) these values to the key. For larger m and/or k, independence among the hash functions can be relaxed with negligible increase in the false positive rate.

Selecting size of bit vector

A Bloom filter with 1% error and an optimal value of k, in contrast, requires only about 9.6 bits per element — regardless of the size of the elements. This advantage comes partly from its compactness, inherited from arrays, and partly from its probabilistic nature. The 1% false-positive rate can be reduced by a factor of ten by adding only about 4.8 bits per element.

Space advantages

While risking false positives, Bloom filters have a strong space advantage over other data structures for representing sets, such as self-balancing binary search trees, tries, hash tables, or simple arrays or linked lists of the entries. Most of these require storing at least the data items themselves, which can require anywhere from a small number of bits, for small integers, to an arbitrary number of bits, such as for strings (tries are an exception, since they can share storage between elements with equal prefixes). Linked structures incur an additional linear space overhead for pointers.

However, if the number of potential values is small and many of them can be in the set, the Bloom filter is easily surpassed by the deterministic bit array, which requires only one bit for each potential element.

Time advantages

Bloom filters also have the unusual property that the time needed either to add items or to check whether an item is in the set is a fixed constant, O(k), completely independent of the number of items already in the set. No other constant-space set data structure has this property, but the average access time of sparse hash tables can make them faster in practice than some Bloom filters. In a hardware implementation, however, the Bloom filter shines because its k lookups are independent and can be parallelized.

Implementation

Refer to *Problems Section*.

14.18 Hashing: Problems & Solutions

Problem-1 Implement a separate chaining collision resolution technique. Also, discuss time complexities of each function.

Solution: To create a hash table of given size, say n, we allocate an array of n/L (whose value is usually between 5 and 20) pointers to list, initialized to nil. To perform *get/put/delete* operations, we first compute the index of the table from the given key by using *hashfunction* and then do the corresponding operation in the linear list maintained at that location. To get uniform distribution of keys over a hash table, maintain table size as the prime number.

```
package main
import "fmt"
var (
    minLoadFactor    = 0.25
    maxLoadFactor    = 0.75
    defaultTableSize = 3
)
type Element struct {
    key   int
    value int
    next  *Element
}
type Hash struct {
    buckets []*Element
}
type HashTable struct {
    table *Hash
    size  *int
}
// createHashTable: Called by checkLoadFactorAndUpdate when creating a new hash
func createHashTable(tableSize int) HashTable {
    num := 0
    hash := Hash{make([]*Element, tableSize)}
    return HashTable{table: &hash, size: &num}
}
// CreateHashTable: Called by the user to create a hashtable.
func CreateHashTable() HashTable {
    num := 0
    hash := Hash{make([]*Element, defaultTableSize)}
```

```
    return HashTable{table: &hash, size: &num}
}
// hashFunction: Used to calculate the index of record within the slice
func hashFunction(key int, size int) int {
    return key % size
}
// Display: Print the hashtable in a legible format (publicly callable)
func (h *HashTable) Display() {
    fmt.Printf("----------%d elements-------\n", *h.size)
    for i, node := range h.table.buckets {
        fmt.Printf("%d :", i)
        for node != nil {
            fmt.Printf("[%d, %d]->", node.key, node.value)
            node = node.next
        }
        fmt.Println("nil")
    }
}
// put: inserts a key into the hash table, for internal use only
func (h *HashTable) put(key int, value int) bool {
    index := hashFunction(key, len(h.table.buckets))
    iterator := h.table.buckets[index]
    node := Element{key, value, nil}
    if iterator == nil {
        h.table.buckets[index] = &node
    } else {
        prev := &Element{0, 0, nil}
        for iterator != nil {
            if iterator.key == key { // Key already exists
                iterator.value = value
                return false
            }
            prev = iterator
            iterator = iterator.next
        }
        prev.next = &node
    }
    *h.size += 1
    return true
}
// Put: inserts a key into the hash table (publicly callable)
func (h *HashTable) Put(key int, value int) {
    sizeChanged := h.put(key, value)
    if sizeChanged == true {
        h.checkLoadFactorAndUpdate()
    }
}
// Get: Retrieve a value for a key from the hash table (publicly callable)
func (h *HashTable) Get(key int) (bool, int) {
    index := hashFunction(key, len(h.table.buckets))
    iterator := h.table.buckets[index]
    for iterator != nil {
        if iterator.key == key { // Key already exists
            return true, iterator.value
        }
        iterator = iterator.next
    }
    return false, 0
}
// del: remove a key-value record from the hash table, for internal use only
func (h *HashTable) del(key int) bool {
```

```
    index := hashFunction(key, len(h.table.buckets))
    iterator := h.table.buckets[index]
    if iterator == nil {
        return false
    }
    if iterator.key == key {
        h.table.buckets[index] = iterator.next
        *h.size--
        return true
    } else {
        prev := iterator
        iterator = iterator.next
        for iterator != nil {
            if iterator.key == key {
                prev.next = iterator.next
                *h.size--
                return true
            }
            prev = iterator
            iterator = iterator.next
        }
        return false
    }
}
// Del: remove a key-value record from the hash table (publicly available)
func (h *HashTable) Del(key int) bool {
    sizeChanged := h.del(key)
    if sizeChanged == true {
        h.checkLoadFactorAndUpdate()
    }
    return sizeChanged
}
// getLoadFactor: calculate the loadfactor for the hashtable
// Calculated as: number of buckets stored / length of underlying slice used
func (h *HashTable) getLoadFactor() float64 {
    return float64(*h.size) / float64(len(h.table.buckets))
}
// checkLoadFactorAndUpdate: if 0.25 > loadfactor or 0.75 < loadfactor,
// update the underlying slice to have have loadfactor close to 0.5
func (h *HashTable) checkLoadFactorAndUpdate() {
    if *h.size == 0 {
        return
    } else {
        loadFactor := h.getLoadFactor()
        if loadFactor < minLoadFactor {
            fmt.Println("** Loadfactor below limit, reducing hashtable size **")
            hash := createHashTable(len(h.table.buckets) / 2)
            for _, record := range h.table.buckets {
                for record != nil {
                    hash.put(record.key, record.value)
                    record = record.next
                }
            }
            h.table = hash.table
        } else if loadFactor > maxLoadFactor {
            fmt.Println("** Loadfactor above limit, increasing hashtable size **")
            hash := createHashTable(*h.size * 2)
            for _, record := range h.table.buckets {
                for record != nil {
                    hash.put(record.key, record.value)
                    record = record.next
                }
```

```
            }
            h.table = hash.table
        }
    }
}
func main() {
    h := CreateHashTable()
    h.Display()
    h.Put(1, 2)
    h.Display()
    h.Put(2, 3)
    h.Display()
    h.Put(3, 4)
    h.Display()
    h.Put(4, 5)
    h.Display()
    h.Put(5, 6)
    h.Display()
    h.Del(1)
    h.Display()
    h.Del(2)
    h.Display()
    h.Del(3)
    h.Display()
    h.Put(3, 4)
    h.Display()
    h.Put(4, 5)
    h.Display()
    h.Put(5, 6)
    h.Display()
    h.Del(4)
    h.Display()
    h.Del(5)
    h.Display()
    h.Put(11, 12)
    h.Display()
    h.Put(12, 13)
    h.Display()
    h.Put(13, 14)
    h.Display()
    h.Put(14, 15)
    h.Display()
    h.Put(15, 16)
    h.Display()
}
```

CreatHashTable – O(n). HashSearch – O(1) average. HashInsert – O(1) average. HashDelete – O(1) average.

Problem-2 Implement a linear probing collision resolution technique.

Solution:

```
package main
import "fmt"
type HashTable struct {
    Size   int
    Keys   []interface{}
    Values []interface{}
}
func CreateHashTable() *HashTable {
    h := &HashTable{}
    h.Size = 7
    h.Keys = make([]interface{}, h.Size)
    h.Values = make([]interface{}, h.Size)
    return h
```

```
}
func (h *HashTable) hashFunction(key int) int {
    return key % h.Size
}
func (h *HashTable) Get(key int) int {
    i := h.hashFunction(key)
    for ; h.Keys[i] != nil; i = (i + 1) % h.Size {
        if h.Keys[i] == key {
            return h.Values[i].(int)
        }
    }
    return -1
}
func (h *HashTable) Put(key, value int) {
    i := h.hashFunction(key)
    for ; h.Keys[i] != nil; i = (i + 1) % h.Size {
        if h.Keys[i] == key {
            h.Values[i] = value
            break
        }
    }
    h.Keys[i] = key
    h.Values[i] = value
}
// Display: Print the hashtable in a legible format (publicly callable)
func (h *HashTable) Display() {
    fmt.Printf("----------%d elements-------\n", h.Size)
    for i := 0; i < h.Size; i++ {
        fmt.Println(h.Keys[i], ": ",h.Values[i])
    }
}
func main() {
    h := CreateHashTable()
    h.Display()
    h.Put(1, 2)
    h.Display()
    h.Put(2, 3)
    h.Display()
    h.Put(3, 4)
    h.Display()
    h.Put(4, 5)
    h.Display()
    h.Put(5, 6)
    h.Display()
}
```

Problem-3 Given an array of integers, give an algorithm for removing the duplicates.

Solution: Start with the first character and check whether it appears in the remaining part of the string using a simple linear search. If it does not exists in the remaining string, add that character to the *result* list. Continue this process for character of the given array.

```
func removeDuplicates(str string) string {
    result:= ""
    for i := 0; i < len(str); i++ {
        // Scan slice for a previous element of the same value.
        found := false
        for v := 0; v < i; v++ {
            if str[v] == str[i] {
                found = true
                break
            }
        }
```

```
        // If no previous element found, append this one.
        if !found {
            result = result + string(str[i])
        }
    }
    return result
}
```

Time Complexity: $O(n^2)$. Space Complexity: O(1).

Problem-4 Can we find any other idea to solve this problem in better time than $O(n^2)$? Observe that the order of characters in solutions do not matter.

Solution: Use sorting to bring the repeated characters together. Finally scan through the array to remove duplicates in consecutive positions.

```
type sortRunes []rune
func (s sortRunes) Less(i, j int) bool {
    return s[i] < s[j]
}
func (s sortRunes) Swap(i, j int) {
    s[i], s[j] = s[j], s[i]
}
func (s sortRunes) Len() int {
    return len(s)
}
func SortString(s string) string {
    r := []rune(s)
    sort.Sort(sortRunes(r))
    return string(r)
}
func removeDuplicates2(str string) string {
    if len(str) == 0 {
        return str
    }
    str = SortString(str)
    result := string(str[0])
    for i := 1; i < len(str); i++ {
        if str[i] != str[i-1] {
            result = result + string(str[i])
        }

    }
    return result
}
```

Time Complexity: $\Theta(nlogn)$. Space Complexity: O(1).

Problem-5 Can we solve this problem in a single pass over given array?

Solution: We can use hash table to check whether a character is repeating in the given string or not. If the current character is not available in hash table, then insert it into hash table and keep that character in the given string also. If the current character exists in the hash table then skip that character.

```
func removeDuplicates(str string) string {
    mymap := map[byte]bool{}
    result := ""
    for i := 0; i < len(str); i++ {
        if mymap[str[i]] == true {
        } else {
            mymap[str[i]] = true
            result = result + string(str[i])
        }
    }
    return result
}
```

Time Complexity: $\Theta(n)$ on average. Space Complexity: $O(n)$.

Problem-6 Given two arrays of unordered numbers, check whether both arrays have the same set of numbers?

Solution: Let us assume that two given arrays are A and B. A simple solution to the given problem is: for each element of A, check whether that element is in B or not. A problem arises with this approach if there are duplicates. For example consider the following inputs:

$$A = \{2,5,6,8,10,2,2\}$$
$$B = \{2,5,5,8,10,5,6\}$$

The above algorithm gives the wrong result because for each element of A there is an element in B also. But if we look at the number of occurrences, they are not the same. This problem we can solve by moving the elements which are already compared to the end of the list. That means, if we find an element in B, then we move that element to the end of B, and in the next searching we will not find those elements. But the disadvantage of this is it needs extra swaps. Time Complexity of this approach is $O(n^2)$, since for each element of A we have to scan B.

Problem-7 Can we improve the time complexity of Problem-6?

Solution: Yes. To improve the time complexity, let us assume that we have sorted both the lists. Since the sizes of both arrays are n, we need $O(n \log n)$ time for sorting them. After sorting, we just need to scan both the arrays with two pointers and see whether they point to the same element every time, and keep moving the pointers until we reach the end of the arrays.

Time Complexity of this approach is $O(n \log n)$. This is because we need $O(n \log n)$ for sorting the arrays. After sorting, we need $O(n)$ time for scanning but it is less compared to $O(n \log n)$.

Problem-8 Can we further improve the time complexity of Problem-6?

Solution: Yes, by using a hash table. For this, consider the following algorithm.

Algorithm:

- Construct the hash table with array A elements as keys.
- While inserting the elements, keep track of the number frequency for each number. That means, if there are duplicates, then increment the counter of that corresponding key.
- After constructing the hash table for A's elements, now scan the array B.
- For each occurrence of B's elements reduce the corresponding counter values.
- At the end, check whether all counters are zero or not.
- If all counters are zero, then both arrays are the same otherwise the arrays are different.

Time Complexity: $O(n)$ for scanning the arrays. Space Complexity: $O(n)$ for hash table.

Problem-9 Given a list of number pairs; if $pair(i, j)$ exists, and $pair\,(j, i)$ exists, report all such pairs. For example, in $\{\{1,3\},\{2,6\},\{3,5\},\{7,4\},\{5,3\},\{8,7\}\}$, we see that $\{3,5\}$ and $\{5,3\}$ are present. Report this pair when you encounter $\{5,3\}$. We call such pairs 'symmetric pairs'. So, give an efficient algorithm for finding all such pairs.

Solution: By using hashing, we can solve this problem in just one scan. Consider the following algorithm.

Algorithm:

- Read the pairs of elements one by one and insert them into the hash table. For each pair, consider the first element as key and the second element as value.
- While inserting the elements, check if the hashing of the second element of the current pair is the same as the first number of the current pair.
- If they are the same, then that indicates a symmetric pair exits and output that pair.
- Otherwise, insert that element into that. That means, use the first number of the current pair as key and the second number as value and insert them into the hash table.
- By the time we complete the scanning of all pairs, we have output all the symmetric pairs.

Time Complexity: $O(n)$ for scanning the arrays. Note that we are doing a scan only of the input. Space Complexity: $O(n)$ for hash table.

Problem-10 Given a singly linked list, check whether it has a loop in it or not.

Solution: Using Hash Tables

Algorithm:

- Traverse the linked list nodes one by one.
- Check if the node's address is there in the hash table or not.
- If it is already there in the hash table, that indicates we are visiting a node which was already visited. This is possible only if the given linked list has a loop in it.
- If the address of the node is not there in the hash table. then insert that node's address into the hash table.

- Continue this process until we reach the end of the linked list *or* we find the loop.

Time Complexity: O(n) for scanning the linked list. Note that we are doing a scan only of the input. Space Complexity: O(n) for hash table.

Note: for an efficient solution, refer to the *Linked Lists* chapter.

Problem-11 Given an array of 101 elements. Out of them 50 elements are distinct, 24 elements are repeated 2 times, and one element is repeated 3 times. Find the element that is repeated 3 times in O(1).

Solution: Using Hash Tables

Algorithm:

- Scan the input array one by one.
- Check if the element is already there in the hash table or not.
- If it is already there in the hash table, increment its counter value [this indicates the number of occurrences of the element].
- If the element is not there in the hash table, insert that node into the hash table with counter value 1.
- Continue this process until reaching the end of the array.

Time Complexity: O(n), because we are doing two scans. Space Complexity: O(n), for hash table.

Note: For an efficient solution refer to the *Searching* chapter.

Problem-12 Given m sets of integers that have n elements in them, provide an algorithm to find an element which appeared in the maximum number of sets?

Solution: Using Hash Tables

Algorithm:

- Scan the input sets one by one.
- For each element keep track of the counter. The counter indicates the frequency of occurrences in all the sets.
- After completing the scan of all the sets, select the one which has the maximum counter value.

Time Complexity: O(mn), because we need to scan all the sets. Space Complexity: O(mn), for hash table. Because, in the worst case all the elements may be different.

Problem-13 Given two sets A and B, and a number K, Give an algorithm for finding whether there exists a pair of elements, one from A and one from B, that add up to K.

Solution: For simplicity, let us assume that the size of A is m and the size of B is n.

Algorithm:

- Select the set which has minimum elements.
- For the selected set create a hash table. We can use both key and value as the same.
- Now scan the second array and check whether (*K-selected element*) exists in the hash table or not.
- If it exists then return the pair of elements.
- Otherwise continue until we reach the end of the set.

Time Complexity: O($Max(m, n)$), because we are doing two scans.
Space Complexity: O($Min(m, n)$), for hash table. We can select the small set for creating the hash table.

Problem-14 Give an algorithm to remove the specified characters from a given string which are given in another string?

Solution: First, we create a hash table. Now, scan the characters to be removed, and for each of those characters we set the value to *true*, which indicates that we need to remove that character.

After initialization, scan the input string, and for each of the characters, we check whether that character needs to be deleted or not. If the flag is set to *true* then we simply skip to the next character, otherwise we keep the character in the input string. Continue this process until we reach the end of the input string.

```
func removeChars(str, charsToBeRemoved string) string {
    mymap := map[byte]bool{}
    result := ""
    for i := 0; i < len(charsToBeRemoved); i++ {
        mymap[charsToBeRemoved[i]] = true
    }
    for i := 0; i < len(str); i++ {
        if mymap[str[i]] == false {
            result = result + string(str[i])
        }
```

```
    }
    return result
}
```

Time Complexity: Time for scanning the characters to be removed + Time for scanning the input array= $O(m)$ +$O(n)$ ≈$O(n)$. Where m is the length of the characters to be removed and n is the length of the input string.

Space Complexity: $O(m)$, length of the characters to be removed.

Problem-15 Give an algorithm for finding the first non-repeated character in a string. For example, the first non-repeated character in the string *"abzddab"* is 'z'.

Solution: The solution to this problem is trivial. For each character in the given string, we can scan the remaining string if that character appears in it. If it does not appears then we are done with the solution and we return that character. If the character appears in the remaining string, then go to the next character.

```
func firstUniqChar(str string) rune {
    for i := 0; i < len(str); i++ {
        repeated := false
        for j := 0; j < len(str); j++ {
            if i != j && str[i] == str[j] {
                repeated = true
                break
            }
        }
        if !repeated { // Found the first non-repeated character
            return rune(str[i])
        }
    }
    return rune(0)
}
```

Time Complexity: $O(n^2)$, for two for loops. Space Complexity: $O(1)$.

Problem-16 Can we use sorting technique for solving the Problem-14?

Solution: No. Because, the sorting of string would change the order characters from the original given string.

Problem-17 Can we improve the time complexity of Problem-14?

Solution: Yes. By using hash tables we can reduce the time complexity. Create a hash table by reading all the characters in the input string and keeping count of the number of times each character appears. After creating the hash table, we can read the hash table entries to see which element has a count equal to 1. This approach takes $O(n)$ space but reduces the time complexity also to $O(n)$.

```
func firstUniqChar(str string) rune {
    m := make(map[rune]uint, len(str))        // preallocate the map size
    for _, r := range str {
        m[r]++
    }
    for _, r := range str {
        if m[r] == 1 {
            return r
        }
    }
    return rune(0)
}
```

Time Complexity: We have $O(n)$ to create the hash table and another $O(n)$ to read the entries of hash table. So the total time is $O(n) + O(n) = O(2n) \approx O(n)$. Space Complexity: $O(n)$ for keeping the count values.

Problem-18 Given a string, give an algorithm for finding the first repeating letter in a string?

Solution: The solution to this problem is somewhat similar to Problem-14 and Problem-16. The only difference is, instead of scanning the hash table twice we can give the answer in just one scan. This is because while inserting into the hash table we can see whether that element already exists or not. If it already exists then we just need to return that character.

```
char firstRepeatedCharUsinghash( char * str ) {
    int i, len=strlen(str);
    int count[256]; // additional array
    for(i=0;i<len;++i)
```

```
        count[i] = 0;
    for(i=0; i<len; ++i) {
        if(count[str[i]]==1) {
            printf("%s",str[i]);
            break;
        }
        else count[str[i]]++;
    }
    if(i==len)
    printf("No Repeated Characters");
    return 0;
}
```

Time Complexity: We have $O(n)$ for scanning and creating the hash table. Note that we need only one scan for this problem. So the total time is $O(n)$. Space Complexity: $O(n)$ for keeping the count values.

Problem-19 Given an array of n numbers, create an algorithm which displays all pairs whose sum is S.

Solution: This problem is similar to Problem-13. But instead of using two sets we use only one set.

Algorithm:

- Scan the elements of the input array one by one and create a hash table. Both key and value can be the same.
- After creating the hash table, again scan the input array and check whether $(S - \textit{selected element})$ exits in the hash table *or* not.
- If it exits then return the pair of elements.
- Otherwise continue and read all the elements of the array.

Time Complexity: We have $O(n)$ to create the hash table and another $O(n)$ to read the entries of the hash table. So the total time is $O(n) + O(n) = O(2n) \approx O(n)$. Space Complexity: $O(n)$ for keeping the count values.

Problem-18 Is there any other way of solving Problem-19?

Solution: Yes. The alternative solution to this problem involves sorting. First sort the input array. After sorting, use two pointers, one at the starting and another at the ending. Each time add the values of both the indexes and see if their sum is equal to S. If they are equal then print that pair. Otherwise increase the left pointer if the sum is less than S and decrease the right pointer if the sum is greater than S.

Time Complexity: Time for sorting + Time for scanning = $O(nlogn) + O(n) \approx O(nlogn)$. Space Complexity: $O(1)$.

Problem-19 We have a file with millions of lines of data. Only two lines are identical; the rest are unique. Each line is so long that it may not even fit in the memory. What is the most efficient solution for finding the identical lines?

Solution: Since a complete line may not fit into the main memory, read the line partially and compute the hash from that partial line. Then read the next part of the line and compute the hash. This time use the previous hash also while computing the new hash value. Continue this process until we find the hash for the complete line. Do this for each line and store all the hash values in a file [or maintain a hash table of these hashes]. If at any point you get same hash value, read the corresponding lines part by part and compare.

Note: Refer to *Searching* chapter for related problems.

Problem-20 If h is the hashing function and is used to hash n keys into a table of size s, where $n <= s$, the expected number of collisions involving a particular key X is :

(A) less than 1. (B) less than n. (C) less than s. (D) less than $\frac{n}{2}$.

Solution: A.

Problem-21 Implement Bloom Filters.

Solution: A Bloom filter is a data structure designed to tell, rapidly and memory-efficiently, whether an element is present in a set. It is based on a probabilistic mechanism where false positive retrieval results are possible, but false negatives are not. At the end we will see how to tune the parameters in order to minimize the number of false positive results.

Let's begin with a little bit of theory. The idea behind the Bloom filter is to allocate a bit vector of length m, initially all set to 0, and then choose k independent hash functions, $h_1, h_2, ..., h_k$, each with range $[1..m]$. When an element a is added to the set then the bits at positions $h_1(a)$, h_2(a), ..., h_k(a) in the bit vector are set to 1. Given a query element q we can test whether it is in the set using the bits at positions h_1(q), h_2(q), ..., h_k(q) in the vector. If any of these bits is 0 we report that q is not in the set otherwise we report that q is. The thing we have to care about is that in the first case there remains some probability that q is not in the set which could lead us to a false positive response.

A Bloom filter has two parameters: m, a maximum size (typically a reasonably large multiple of the cardinality of the set to represent) and k, the number of hashing functions on elements of the set. (The actual hashing functions are important, too, but this is not a parameter for this implementation). A Bloom filter is backed by a BitSet; a key is represented in the filter by setting the bits at each value of the hashing functions (modulo m). Set membership is done by testing whether the bits at each value of the hashing functions (again, modulo m) are set. If so, the item is in the set. If the item is actually in the set, a Bloom filter will never fail (the true positive rate is 1.0); but it is susceptible to false positives. The art is to choose k and m correctly.

```
package main
import (
    "crypto/rand"
    "fmt"
    "hash/fnv"
    "math"
)
type BloomFilter struct {
    Capacity          int         // n
    FalsePositiveRate int         // p
    NumHashes         int         // k, Number of hash functions
    BitSize           int64       // m, Size of the bloom filter
    numBuckets        int64
    state             []uint32
}
// You can simulate additional hash functions with two hash functions.
// Furthermore we can simulate 2x32-bit hash functions with one 64-bit hash.
func hashFNV1a(input []byte) (uint32, uint32) {
    hash := fnv.New64a()
    hash.Write(input)
    value64 := hash.Sum64()
    return uint32(value64 & 0xFFFFFFFF), uint32(value64 >> 32)
}
func (set *BloomFilter) setBit(index int64) {
    bucket := (index / 32) % set.numBuckets
    offset := index % 32
    set.state[bucket] = set.state[bucket] | (1 << uint(offset))
}
func (set *BloomFilter) testBit(index int64) int {
    bucket := (index / 32) % set.numBuckets
    offset := index % 32
    if set.state[bucket]&(1<<uint(offset)) != 0 {
        return 1
    } else {
        return 0
    }
}
// Adds a piece of arbitrary data to the set
func (set *BloomFilter) Put(input []byte) {
    hashFn1, hashFn2 := hashFNV1a(input)
    for i := 0; i < set.NumHashes; i++ {
        index := int64((hashFn1 + hashFn2*uint32(i))) % set.BitSize
        set.setBit(index)
    }
}
// Checks the set for a piece of arbitrary data
func (set *BloomFilter) MightContains(input []byte) bool {
    hashFn1, hashFn2 := hashFNV1a(input)
    for i := 0; i < set.NumHashes; i++ {
        index := int64((hashFn1 + hashFn2*uint32(i))) % set.BitSize
        if set.testBit(index) != 1 {
            return false
        }
    }
```

```
        return true
    }
    // Returns a new Bloom filter. Parameters are the expected number of elements
    // in the set and the desired false positive probability. Optimal size and
    // number of hashes are calculated based on these numbers.
    // p = false positive rate of the form 1/p, powers of two preferred
    // optimal number of hashes k = (m/n)ln(2)
    func NewBloomFilter(capacity, probability int) *BloomFilter {
        bitSize := int64(math.Abs(math.Ceil(float64(capacity) *
            math.Log2(math.E) * math.Log2(1/float64(probability)))))
        numHashes := int(math.Floor(float64((bitSize / int64(capacity))) * math.Log(2)))
        numBuckets := bitSize / 32
        return &BloomFilter{
            Capacity:        capacity,
            FalsePositiveRate: probability,
            NumHashes:       numHashes,
            BitSize:         bitSize,
            numBuckets:      numBuckets,
            state:           make([]uint32, uint(numBuckets))}
    }
    func main() {
        trials, rate, counter = 1000, 1000, 0
        // False negatives
        set := NewBloomFilter(trials, rate)
        // Add random data to set
        for i := 0; i < trials; i++ {
            c := 8
            b := make([]byte, c)
            _, err := rand.Read(b)
            if err != nil {
                fmt.Println("Could not generate random string")
                return
            }
            set.Put(b)
            if set.MightContains(b) {
                counter++
            }
        }
        if trials != counter {
            fmt.Println("Lost some random set entries!")
            return
        }
        // False positives
        set = NewBloomFilter(trials, rate)
        // Add random data to set
        for i := 0; i < trials; i++ {
            c := 8
            b := make([]byte, c)
            _, err := rand.Read(b)
            if err != nil {
                fmt.Println("Could not generate random string")
                return
            }
            set.Put(b)
        }
        // Check for different random data
        for i := 0; i < trials; i++ {
            c := 8
            b := make([]byte, c)
            _, err := rand.Read(b)
            if err != nil {
```

```
            fmt.Println("Could not generate random string")
            return
        }
        if set.MightContains(b) {
            counter++
        }
    }
    expected := float64(1) / float64(rate)
    actual := float64(counter) / float64(trials)

    fmt.Println("expected error rate: ", expected)
    fmt.Println("actual error rate: ", actual)
}
```

Problem-22 Given a hash table with size=11 entries and the following hash function h_1 and step function h_2:

$h_1(key) = key \ \% \ size$

$h_2(key) = \{key \ \% \ (size-1)\} + 1$

Insert the keys {22, 1, 13, 11, 24, 33, 18, 42, 31} in the given order (from left to right) to the hash table using each of the following hash methods:

- Chaining with h_1 $[h(key) = h_1(key)]$
- Linear-Probing with h1 --> $h(key,i) = (h_1(key)+i) \ \% \ size]$
- Double-Hashing with h_1 as the hash function and h_2 as the step function $[h(key, i) = (h_1(key) + ih_2(key)) \ \% \ size]$.

Solution:

	Chaining	Linear Probing	Double Hashing
0	33 → 11→ 22	22	22
1	1	1	1
2	24 → 13	13	13
3		11	
4		24	11
5		33	18
6			31
7	18	18	24
8			33
9	31→ 42	42	42
10		31	

String Algorithms

CHAPTER 15

15.1 Introduction

To understand the importance of string algorithms let us consider the case of entering the URL (Uniform Resource Locator) in any browser (say, Internet Explorer, Firefox, or Google Chrome). You will observe that after typing the prefix of the URL, a list of all possible URLs is displayed. That means, the browsers are doing some internal processing and giving us the list of matching URLs. This technique is sometimes called *auto – completion*.

Similarly, consider the case of entering the directory name in the command line interface (in both *Windows* and *UNIX*). After typing the prefix of the directory name, if we press the *tab* button, we get a list of all matched directory names available. This is another example of auto completion.

In order to support these kinds of operations, we need a data structure which stores the string data efficiently. In this chapter, we will look at the data structures that are useful for implementing string algorithms.

We start our discussion with the basic problem of strings: given a string, how do we search a substring (pattern)? This is called a *string matching* problem. After discussing various string matching algorithms, we will look at different data structures for storing strings.

15.2 String Matching Algorithms

In this section, we concentrate on checking whether a pattern P is a substring of another string T (T stands for text) or not. Since we are trying to check a fixed string P, sometimes these algorithms are called *exact string matching* algorithms. To simplify our discussion, let us assume that the length of given text T is n and the length of the pattern P which we are trying to match has the length m. That means, T has the characters from 0 to $n - 1$ ($T[0 \dots n-1]$) and P has the characters from 0 to $m - 1$ ($P[0 \dots m-1]$). This algorithm is implemented in $C++$ as *strstr*().

In the subsequent sections, we start with the brute force method and gradually move towards better algorithms.

- Brute Force Method
- Rabin-Karp String Matching Algorithm
- String Matching with Finite Automata
- KMP Algorithm
- Boyer-Moore Algorithm
- Suffix Trees

15.3 Brute Force Method

In this method, for each possible position in the text T we check whether the pattern P matches or not. Since the length of T is n, we have $n - m + 1$ possible choices for comparisons. This is because we do not need to check the last $m - 1$ locations of T as the pattern length is m. The following algorithm searches for the first occurrence of a pattern string P in a text string T.

Algorithm

```
func strStr(T, P string) int {
   if len(P) == 0 {
      return 0
   }
   i, j := 0, 0
   for i < len(T) {
      if T[i] == P[0] {
         for j = 1; j < len(P); j++ {
```

```
            if i+j >= len(T) || T[i+j] != P[j] {
                break
            }
        }
        if j == len(P) {
            return i
        }
    }
    i++
  }
  return -1
}
```

Alternative Coding: Avoiding inner for loop with slice matching

```
func strStr(T, P string) int {
    if len(P) == 0 {
        return 0
    }
    length := len(P)
    for i := 0; i < len(T)-len(P)+1; i++ {
        if T[i:i+length] == P {
            return i
        }
    }
    return -1
}
```

Time Complexity: $O((n - m + 1) \times m) \approx O(n \times m)$. Space Complexity: $O(1)$.

15.4 Rabin-Karp String Matching Algorithm

Rabin-Karp Algorithm is a string searching algorithm created by Richard M. Karp and Michael O. Rabin that uses hashing to find any one of a set of pattern strings in a text. In this method, we will use the hashing technique and instead of checking for each possible position in T, we check only if the hashing of P and the hashing of m characters of T give the same result.

Initially, apply the hash function to the first m characters of T and check whether this result and P's hashing result is the same or not. If they are not the same, then go to the next character of T and again apply the hash function to m characters (by starting at the second character). If they are the same then we compare those m characters of T with P.

Selecting Hash Function

At each step, since we are finding the hash of m characters of T, we need an efficient hash function. If the hash function takes $O(m)$ complexity in every step, then the total complexity is $O(n \times m)$. This is worse than the brute force method because first we are applying the hash function and also comparing.

Our objective is to select a hash function which takes $O(1)$ complexity for finding the hash of m characters of T every time. Only then can we reduce the total complexity of the algorithm. If the hash function is not good (worst case), the complexity of the Rabin-Karp algorithm is $O(n - m + 1) \times m) \approx O(n \times m)$. If we select a good hash function, the complexity of the Rabin-Karp algorithm complexity is $O(m + n)$. Now let us see how to select a hash function which can compute the hash of m characters of T at each step in $O(1)$.

For simplicity, let's assume that the characters used in string T are only integers. That means, all characters in $T \in \{0, 1, 2, \ldots, 9\}$. Since all of them are integers, we can view a string of m consecutive characters as decimal numbers. For example, string '61815' corresponds to the number 61815. With the above assumption, the pattern P is also a decimal value, and let us assume that the decimal value of P is p. For the given text $T[0..n-1]$, let $t(i)$ denote the decimal value of length–m substring $T[i..i+m-1]$ for $i = 0,1,\ldots,n-m-1$. So, $t(i) == p$ if and only if $T[i..i+m-1] == P[0..m-1]$.

We can compute p in $O(m)$ time using Horner's Rule as:

$$p = P[m-1] + 10(P[m-2] + 10(P[m-3] + \ldots + 10\,(P[1] + 10\,P[0])\ldots))$$

The code for the above assumption is:

```
func hash(s string) uint32 {
    var h uint32
    for i := 0; i < len(s); i++ {
        h = (h*base + uint32(s[i]))
    }
```

```
        return h
    }
```

We can compute all $t(i)$, for $i = 0,1,\ldots,n-m-1$ values in a total of O(n) time. The value of $t(0)$ can be similarly computed from $T[0..m-1]$ in O(m) time. To compute the remaining values $t(0), t(1),\ldots, t\,(n-m-1)$, understand that $t(i+1)$ can be computed from $t(i)$ in constant time.

$$t(i+1) = 10 * (t(i) - 10^{m-1} * T[i]) + T[i + m - 1]$$

For example, if T = "123456" and $m = 3$

$$t(0) = 123$$
$$t(1) = 10 * (123 - 100 * 1) + 4 = 234$$

Step by Step explanation

First : remove the first digit : $123 - 100 * 1 = 23$
Second: Multiply by 10 to shift it : $23 * 10 = 230$
Third: Add last digit : $230 + 4 = 234$

The algorithm runs by comparing, $t(i)$ with p. When $t(i) == p$, then we have found the substring P in T, starting from position i.

```
    const base = 16777619
    func robin_karp(T string, P string) int {
        n, m := len(T), len(P)
        if n < m || len(P) == 0 {
            return 0
        }
        var mult uint32 = 1 // mult = base^(m-1)
        for i := 0; i < m-1; i++ {
            mult = (mult * base)
        }
        hp := hash(P)
        h := hash(T[:m])
        for i := 0; i < n-m+1; i++ {
            if h == hp {
                return i
            }
            if i > 0 {
                h = h - mult*uint32(T[i-1])
                h = h*base + uint32(T[i+m-1])
            }
        }
        return -1
    }
```

15.5 String Matching with Finite Automata

In this method we use the finite automata which is the concept of the Theory of Computation (ToC). Before looking at the algorithm, first let us look at the definition of finite automata.

Finite Automata

A finite automaton F is a 5-tuple $(Q, q_0, A, \sum, \delta)$, where

- Q is a finite set of states
- $q_0 \in Q$ is the start state
- $A \subseteq Q$ is a set of accepting states
- $\sum$ is a finite input alphabet
- δ is the transition function that gives the next state for a given current state and input

How does Finite Automata Work?

- The finite automaton F begins in state q_0
- Reads characters from $\sum$ one at a time
- If F is in state q and reads input character a, F moves to state $\delta(q, a)$
- At the end, if its state is in A, then we say, F accepted the input string read so far
- If the input string is not accepted it is called the rejected string

Example: Let us assume that $Q = \{0,1\}, q_0 = 0, A = \{1\}, \Sigma = \{a,b\}$. $\delta(q,a)$ as shown in the transition table (diagram). This accepts strings that end in an odd number of $a's$; e.g., $abbaaa$ is accepted, aa is rejected.

State	a	b
0	1	0
1	0	0

Input

Transition Function/Table

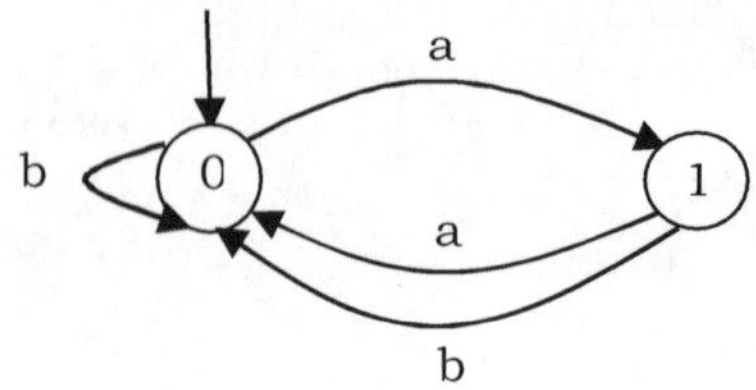

Important Notes for Constructing the Finite Automata

For building the automata, first we start with the initial state. The FA will be in state k if k characters of the pattern have been matched. If the next text character is equal to the pattern character c, we have matched $k+1$ characters and the FA enters state $k+1$. If the next text character is not equal to the pattern character, then the FA go to a state $0, 1, 2, \ldots, or\ k$, depending on how many initial pattern characters match the text characters ending with c

Matching Algorithm

Now, let us concentrate on the matching algorithm.

- For a given pattern $P[0..m-1]$, first we need to build a finite automaton F
  - The state set is $Q = \{0, 1, 2, \ldots, m\}$
  - The start state is 0
  - The only accepting state is m
  - Time to build F can be large if Σ is large
- Scan the text string $T[0..n-1]$ to find all occurrences of the pattern $P[0..m-1]$
- String matching is efficient: $\Theta(n)$
  - Each character is examined exactly once
  - Constant time for each character
  - But the time to compute δ (transition function) is $O(m|\Sigma|)$. This is because δ has $O(m|\Sigma|)$ entries. If we assume $|\Sigma|$ is constant then the complexity becomes $O(m)$.

Algorithm:

```
// Input: Pattern string P[0..m-1], δ and F , Goal: All valid shifts displayed
func finiteAutomataStringMatcher(P []int, m, F, δ int) {
    q := 0
    for i := 0; i < m; i++ {
        q = δ(q, T[i])
        if q == m {
            fmt.Printf("Pattern occurs with shift: %d", i-m)
        }
    }
}
```

Time Complexity: $O(m)$.

15.6 KMP Algorithm

As before, let us assume that T is the string to be searched and P is the pattern to be matched. This algorithm was presented by Knuth, Morris and Pratt. It takes $O(n)$ time complexity for searching a pattern. To get $O(n)$ time complexity, it avoids the comparisons with elements of T that were previously involved in comparison with some element of the pattern P.

The algorithm uses a table and in general we call it *prefix function* or *prefix table* or *fail function* F. First we will see how to fill this table and later how to search for a pattern using this table. The prefix function F for a pattern stores the knowledge about how the pattern matches against shifts of itself. This information can be used to avoid useless shifts of the pattern P. It means that this table can be used for avoiding backtracking on the string T.

Prefix Table

```
// Table building algorithm. Takes pattern P to be analyzed and return prefix table.
func KMP_PrefixTable(P string) (F []int) {
    F = make([]int, len(P))
    pos, cnd := 2, 0
    F[0], F[1] = -1, 0
```

```
    for pos < len(P) {
        if P[pos-1] == P[cnd] {
            cnd++
            F[pos] = cnd
            pos++
        } else if cnd > 0 {
            cnd = F[cnd]
        } else {
            F[pos] = 0
            pos++
        }
    }
    return F
}
```

As an example, assume that $P = a\ b\ a\ b\ a\ c\ a$. For this pattern, let us follow the step-by-step instructions for filling the prefix table F. Initially: $m = length[P] = 7, F[0] = -1$ and $F[1] = 0$.

Step 1: $pos = 2, cnd = 0, \mathrm{F}[2] = 0$

	0	1	2	3	4	5	6
P	a	b	a	b	a	c	a
F	-1	0	0				

Step 2: $\mathrm{pos} = 3, cnd = 0, \mathrm{F}[3] = 1$

	0	1	2	3	4	5	6
P	a	b	a	b	a	c	a
F	-1	0	0	1			

Step 3: $pos = 4, cnd = 1, \mathrm{F}[4] = 2$

	0	1	2	3	4	5	6
P	a	b	a	b	a	c	a
F	-1	0	0	1	2		

Step 4: $pos = 5, cnd = 2, \mathrm{F}[5] = 3$

	0	1	2	3	4	5	6
P	a	b	a	b	a	c	a
F	-1	0	0	1	2	3	

Step 5: $pos = 6, cnd = 1, \mathrm{F}[6] = 0$

	0	1	2	3	4	5	6
P	a	b	a	b	a	c	a
F	-1	0	0	1	2	3	0

At this step the filling of the prefix table is complete.

Matching Algorithm

The KMP algorithm takes pattern *P*, string *T* and prefix function *F* as input, and finds a match of *P* in *T*.

```
// Function KMP performing the Knuth-Morris-Pratt algorithm.
// Prints whether the P(pattern) was found and on what position in the text(T) or not.
// m - current match in T, i - current character in w, c - amount of comparisons.
func KMP(T, P string) {
    m, i, c := 0, 0, 0
    F := KMP_PrefixTable(P)
    for m+i < len(T) {
        fmt.Printf("\ncomparing characters %c %c at positions %d %d", T[m+i], P[i], m+i, i)
        c++
        if P[i] == T[m+i] {
            fmt.Printf(" - match")
            if i == len(P)-1 {
                fmt.Printf("\n\nWord %q was found at position %d in %q with %d comparisons.", P, m, T, c)
                return
            }
            i++
        } else {
            m = m + i - F[i]
            if F[i] > -1 {
                i = F[i]
            } else {
                i = 0
            }
        }
    }
    fmt.Printf("\n\nWord was not found.\n%d comparisons were done.", c)
```

```
        return
    }
```

Time Complexity: O($m+n$), where m is the length of the pattern and n is the length of the text to be searched.
Space Complexity: O(m).

Now, to understand the process let us go through an example. Assume that $T = b\,a\,c\,b\,a\,b\,a\,b\,a\,b\,a\,c\,a\,c\,a$ & $P = a\,b\,a\,b\,a\,c\,a$. Since we have already filled the prefix table, let us use it and go to the matching algorithm. Initially: $n = size\ of\ T\ =\ 15$; $m\ =\ size\ of\ P\ =\ 7$.

Step 1: $i = 0,\ j\ =\ 0$, comparing $P[0]$ with $T[0]$. $P[0]$ does not match with $T[0]$. P will be shifted one position to the right.

T	b	a	c	b	a	b	a	b	a	b	a	c	a	c	a
P	a	b	a	b	a	c	a								

Step 2: $i = 1,\ j\ =\ 0$, comparing $P[0]$ with $T[1]$. $P[0]$ matches with $T[1]$. Since there is a match, P is not shifted.

T	b	a	c	b	a	b	a	b	a	b	a	c	a	c	a
P		a	b	a	b	a	c	a							

Step 3: $i = 2,\ j\ =\ 1$, comparing $P[1]$ with $T[2]$. $P[1]$ does not match with $T[2]$. Backtracking on P, comparing $P[0]$ and $T[2]$.

T	b	a	c	b	a	b	a	b	a	b	a	c	a	c	a
P		a	b	a	b	a	c	a							

Step 4: $i = 3,\ j\ =\ 0$, comparing $P[0]$ with $T[3]$. $P[0]$ does not match with $T[3]$.

T	b	a	c	b	a	b	a	b	a	b	a	c	a	c	a
P				a	b	a	b	a	c	a					

Step 5: $i = 4,\ j\ =\ 0$, comparing $P[0]$ with $T[4]$. $P[0]$ matches with $T[4]$.

T	b	a	c	b	a	b	a	b	a	b	a	c	a	c	a
P					a	b	a	b	a	c	a				

Step 6: $i = 5,\ j\ =\ 1$, comparing $P[1]$ with $T[5]$. $P[1]$ matches with T[5].

T	b	a	c	b	a	b	a	b	a	b	a	c	a	c	a
P					a	b	a	b	a	c	a				

Step 7: $i = 6,\ j\ =\ 2$, comparing $P[2]$ with $T[6]$. $P[2]$ matches with $T[6]$.

T	b	a	c	b	a	b	a	b	a	b	a	c	a	c	a
P					a	b	a	b	a	c	a				

Step 8: $i = 7,\ j\ =\ 3$, comparing $P[3]$ with $T[7]$. $P[3]$ matches with $T[7]$.

T	b	a	c	b	a	b	a	b	a	b	a	c	a	c	a
P					a	b	a	b	a	c	a				

Step 9: $i = 8,\ j\ =\ 4$, comparing $P[4]$ with $T[8]$. $P[4]$ matches with $T[8]$.

T	b	a	c	b	a	b	a	b	a	b	a	c	a	c	a
P					a	b	a	b	a	c	a				

Step 10: $i = 9,\ j\ =\ 5$, comparing $P[5]$ with $T[9]$. $P[5]$ does not match with $T[9]$. Backtracking on P, comparing $P[4]$ with $T[9]$ because after mismatch $j\ =\ F[4]\ =\ 3$.

T	b	a	c	b	a	b	a	b	a	b	a	c	a	c	a
P					a	b	a	b	a	c	a				

Comparing $P[3]$ with $T[9]$.

T	b	a	c	b	a	b	a	b	a	b	a	c	a	c	a
P							a	b	a	b	a	c	a		

Step 11: $i = 10,\ j\ =\ 4$, comparing $P[4]$ with $T[10]$. $P[4]$ matches with $T[10]$.

T	b	a	c	b	a	b	a	b	a	b	a	c	a	c	a
P							a	b	a	b	a	c	a		

Step 12: $i = 11$, $j = 5$, comparing $P[5]$ with $T[11]$. $P[5]$ matches with $T[11]$.

T	b	a	c	b	a	b	a	b	a	b	a	c	a	c	a
P							a	b	a	b	a	c	a		

Step 13: $i = 12$, $j = 6$, comparing $P[6]$ with $T[12]$. $P[6]$ matches with $T[12]$.

T	b	a	c	b	a	b	a	b	a	b	a	c	a	c	a
P							a	b	a	b	a	c	a		

Pattern P has been found to completely occur in string T. The total number of shifts that took place for the match to be found are: $i - m = 13 - 7 = 6$ shifts.

Notes:

- KMP performs the comparisons from left to right
- KMP algorithm needs a preprocessing (prefix function) which takes $O(m)$ space and time complexity
- Searching takes $O(n + m)$ time complexity (does not depend on alphabet size)

15.7 Boyer-Moore Algorithm

Like the KMP algorithm, this also does some pre-processing and we call it *last function*. The algorithm scans the characters of the pattern from right to left beginning with the rightmost character. During the testing of a possible placement of pattern P in T, a mismatch is handled as follows: Let us assume that the current character being matched is $T[i] = c$ and the corresponding pattern character is $P[j]$. If c is not contained anywhere in P, then shift the pattern P completely past $T[i]$. Otherwise, shift P until an occurrence of character c in P gets aligned with $T[i]$. This technique avoids needless comparisons by shifting the pattern relative to the text.

The *last* function takes $O(m + |\Sigma|)$ time and the actual search takes $O(nm)$ time. Therefore the worst case running time of the Boyer-Moore algorithm is $O(nm + |\Sigma|)$. This indicates that the worst-case running time is quadratic, in the case of $n == m$, the same as the brute force algorithm.

- The Boyer-Moore algorithm is very fast on the large alphabet (relative to the length of the pattern).
- For the small alphabet, Boer-Moore is not preferable.
- For binary strings, the KMP algorithm is recommended.
- For the very shortest patterns, the brute force algorithm is better.

15.8 Data Structures for Storing Strings

If we have a set of strings (for example, all the words in the dictionary) and a word which we want to search in that set, in order to perform the search operation faster, we need an efficient way of storing the strings. To store sets of strings we can use any of the following data structures.

- Hashing Tables
- Binary Search Trees
- Tries
- Ternary Search Trees

15.9 Hash Tables for Strings

As seen in the *Hashing* chapter, we can use hash tables for storing the integers or strings. In this case, the keys are nothing but the strings. The problem with hash table implementation is that we lose the ordering information – after applying the hash function, we do not know where it will map to.

As a result, some queries take more time. For example, to find all the words starting with the letter "*K*", with hash table representation we need to scan the complete hash table. This is because the hash function takes the complete key, performs hash on it, and we do not know the location of each word.

15.10 Binary Search Trees for Strings

In this representation, every node is used for sorting the strings alphabetically. This is possible because the strings have a natural ordering: A comes before B, which comes before C, and so on. This is because words can be ordered and we can use a Binary Search Tree (BST) to store and retrieve them.

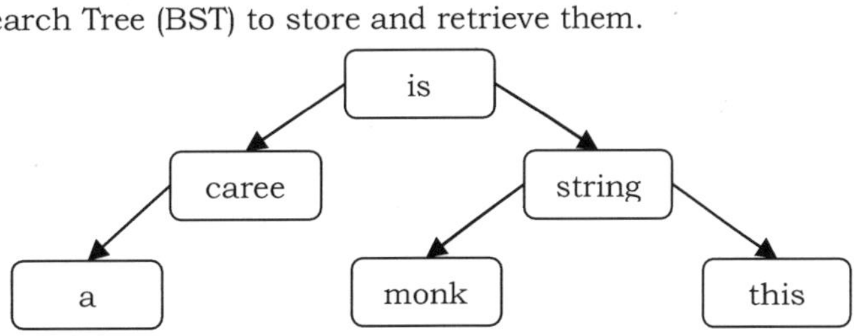

For example, let us assume that we want to store the following strings using BSTs:

this is a career monk string

For the given string there are many ways of representing them in BST. One such possibility is shown in the tree above.

Issues with Binary Search Tree Representation

This method is good in terms of storage efficiency. But the disadvantage of this representation is that, at every node, the search operation performs the complete match of the given key with the node data, and as a result the time complexity of the search operation increases. So, from this we can say that BST representation of strings is good in terms of storage but not in terms of time.

15.11 Tries

Now, let us see the alternative representation that reduces the time complexity of the search operation. The name *trie* is taken from the word re"trie".

What is a Trie?

A *trie* is a tree data structure and each node in it contains a number of pointers equal to the number of characters of the alphabet. For example, if we assume that all the strings are formed with English alphabet characters "*a*" to "*z*" then each node of the trie contains 26 pointers. A trie (also known as a digital tree) and sometimes even radix tree or prefix tree (as they can be searched by prefixes) is an ordered tree structure, which takes advantage of the keys that it stores – usually strings. Suppose we want to store the strings "*a*", "*all*", "*als*", and "*as*"": *trie* for these strings will look like:

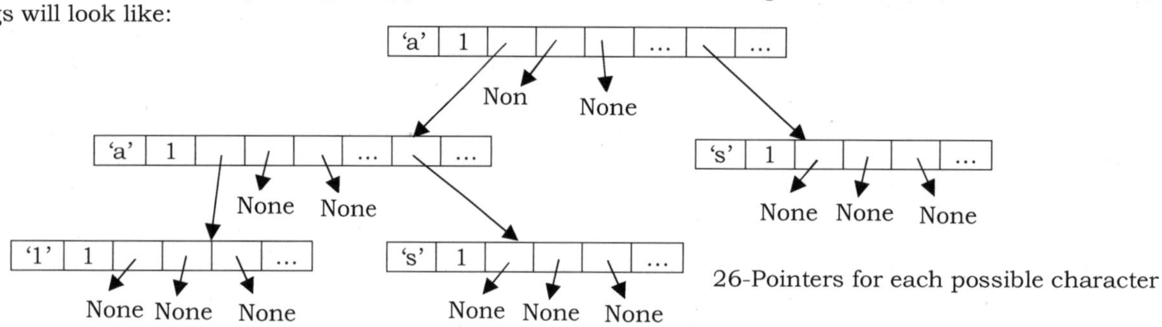

There may be cases when a trie is a binary search tree, but in general, these are different. Both binary search trees and tries are trees, but each node in binary search trees always has two children, whereas tries' nodes, on the other hand, can have more. In a trie, every node (except the root node) stores one character or a digit. By traversing the trie down from the root node to a particular node n, a common prefix of characters or digits can be formed which is shared by other branches of the trie as well.

Why Tries?

The tries can insert and find strings in $O(L)$ time (where L represents the length of a single word). This is much faster than hash table and binary search tree representations.

Trie Declaration

The structure of the *Trie* node has letter (char), isLeaf (boolean), and has a collection of child nodes (Collection of Trie nodes). The basic element – Trie node of a trie data structure looks like this:

```
// Trie node
type Trie struct {
    letter  rune            // Contains the current node character
    children []*Trie        // Pointers to other tri nodes
    meta    map[string]interface{} // meta data for the given word
    isLeaf  bool            // Indicates whether the string formed from root to current node is a string or not
}
```

Now that we have defined our Trie node, let's go ahead and look at the other operations of trie. Fortunately, the trie data structure is simple to implement since it has three major methods: insert, search and delete. Let's look at the elementary implementation of these methods.

Inserting a String in Trie

To insert a string, we just need to start at the root node and follow the corresponding path (path from root indicates the prefix of the given string). Before we start the implementation, it's important to understand the algorithm:

1. Set a current node as a root node
2. Set the current letter as the first letter of the word
3. If the current node has already an existing reference to the current letter (through one of the elements in the "children" field), then set current node to that referenced node. Otherwise, create a new node, set the letter equal to the current letter, and also initialize current node to this new node
4. Repeat step 3 until the key is traversed

```
func (trie *Trie) hasChild(a rune) (bool, *Trie) {
    for _, child := range trie.children {
        if child.letter == a {
            return true, child
        }
    }
    return false, nil
}
func (trie *Trie) addChild(a rune) *Trie {
    nw := NewTrie()
    nw.letter = a
    trie.children = append(trie.children, nw)
    return nw
}
func (trie *Trie) Add(word string) *Trie {          // Add a word to a trie
    letters, node, i := []rune(word), trie, 0
    n := len(letters)
    for i < n {
        if exists, value := node.hasChild(letters[i]); exists {
            node = value
        } else {
            node = node.addChild(letters[i])
        }
        i++
        if i == n {
            node.isLeaf = true
        }
    }
    return node
}
```

Time Complexity: O(L), where L is the length of the string to be inserted.

Searching a String in Trie

Let's now add a method to check whether a particular element is already present in a trie:

1. Get children of the root
2. Iterate through each character of the given string
3. Check whether that character is already a part of a sub-trie. If it isn't present anywhere in the trie, then stop the search and return false
4. Repeat the second and the third step until there isn't any character left in the string. If the end of the string is reached, return true

```
func (trie *Trie) FindNode(word string) *Trie {     // FindNode returns the node whether it is a word or not.
    letters, node, i := []rune(word), trie, 0
    n := len(letters)
    for i < n {
        if exists, value := node.hasChild(letters[i]); exists {
            node = value
        } else {
            return nil
        }
        i++
    }
    return node
}
```

```
func (trie *Trie) Find(word string) *Trie {    // Find returns the node pointing to a word
    node := trie.FindNode(word)
    if node == nil {
        return nil
    }
    if node.isLeaf != true {
        return nil
    }
    return node
}
```

Time Complexity: O(L), where L is the length of the string to be searched.

Deleting an Element in Trie

Aside from inserting and finding an element, it's obvious that we also need to be able to delete elements. For the deletion process, we need to follow the steps:

1. Check whether this element is already part of the trie
2. If the element is found, then remove it from the trie

```
// Remove a word from a trie. This does not free memory; it just marks the node.
func (trie *Trie) Remove(word string) {
    a := trie.Find(word)
    if a != nil {
        a.isLeaf = false
    }
}
```

Time Complexity: O(L), where L is the length of the string to be deleted.

Counting the Number of Strings in Trie

We can simply traverse all the children of every node starting with the root node of the trie recursively.

```
func (trie *Trie) Count() int {       // Count returns the number of words in a trie
    count := 0
    for _, child := range trie.children {
        if child.isLeaf == true {
            count++
        }
        count += child.Count()
    }
    return count
}
```

Setting/Getting the Metadata of a String in Trie

With the following simple code, we can set the meta data. Notice that, it is being stored as a map with the given string as key.

```
func (trie *Trie) Get(key string) (interface{}, bool) {        // Get metadata belonging to a string
    if trie == nil {
        return nil, false
    }
    if _, ok := trie.meta[key]; ok {
        return trie.meta[key], true
    }
    return nil, false
}
func (trie *Trie) Set(key string, value interface{}) {        // Set metadata for a word
    if trie == nil {
        return
    }
    trie.meta[key] = value
}
```

Time Complexity: O(1).

Issues with Tries Representation

The main disadvantage of tries is that they need lot of memory for storing the strings. As we have seen above, for each node we have too many node pointers. In many cases, the occupancy of each node is less. The final conclusion regarding tries data structure is that they are faster but require huge memory for storing the strings.

15.12 Ternary Search Trees

In computer science, a ternary search tree is a type of trie (sometimes called a prefix tree) where nodes are arranged in a manner similar to a binary search tree, but with up to three children rather than the binary tree's limit of two. This representation was initially provided by Jon Bentley and Sedgewick. A ternary search tree takes the advantages of binary search trees (BSTs) and tries. That means, it combines the memory efficiency of BSTs and the time efficiency of tries.

Ternary Search Trees Declaration

```
type (
    TSTNode struct {
        key         byte
        value       interface{}     // Value for the key, if it is the end of the string
        left, eq, right *TSTNode
    }
    TernarySearchTree struct {
        length int
        root   *TSTNode
    }
)
```

Each node of a ternary search tree stores a single character, and pointers to its three children conventionally named equal child, left child and right child. A node may also have a pointer to its parent node as well as an indicator as to whether or not the node marks the end of a word. The left child pointer must point to a node whose character value is less than the current node. The right child pointer must point to a node whose character is greater than the current node. The equal child points to the next character in the word.

Inserting strings in the Ternary Search Tree

Inserting a value into a ternary search can be defined recursively much as lookups are defined. This recursive method is continually called on nodes of the tree given a key which gets progressively shorter by pruning characters off the front of the key. If this method reaches a node that has not been created, it creates the node and assigns it the character value of the first character in the key. Whether a new node is created or not, the method checks to see if the first character in the string is greater than or less than the character value in the node and makes a recursive call on the appropriate node as in the lookup operation. If, however, the key's first character is equal to the node's value then the insertion procedure is called on the *equal* child and the key's first character is pruned away. Like binary search trees and other data structures, ternary search trees can become degenerate depending on the order of the keys.

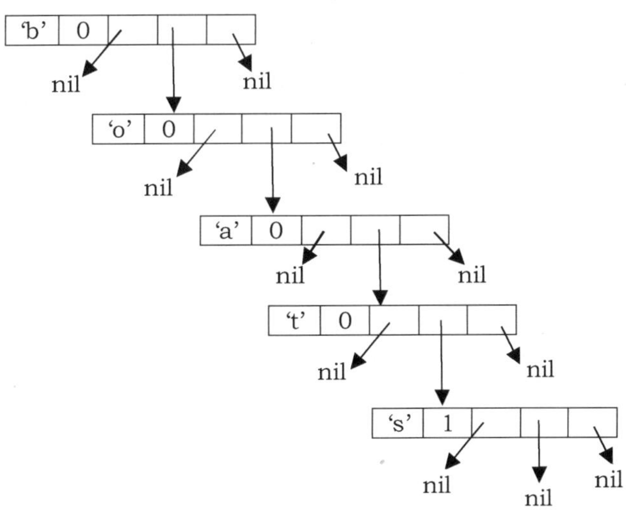

Let us assume that we want to store the following words in TST : ("boats",1), ("*boat*",2), ("*bat*",3) and ("*bats*",4). Initially, let us start with the *boats* string. In the examples, the values 1,2,3, and 4 are the values for the keys "boats", "boat", "bat", and "*bats*" respectively.

Now if we want to insert the string *boat*, then the TST becomes [the only change is setting the *value* flag of "*t*" node to 1]:

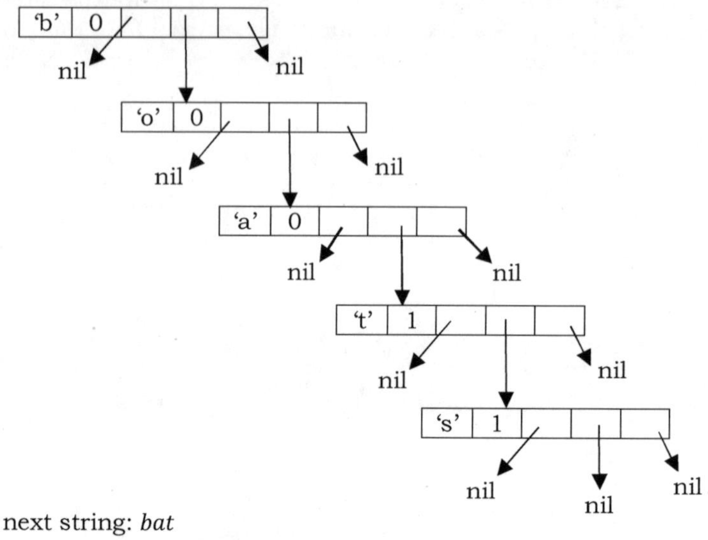

Now, let us insert the next string: *bat*

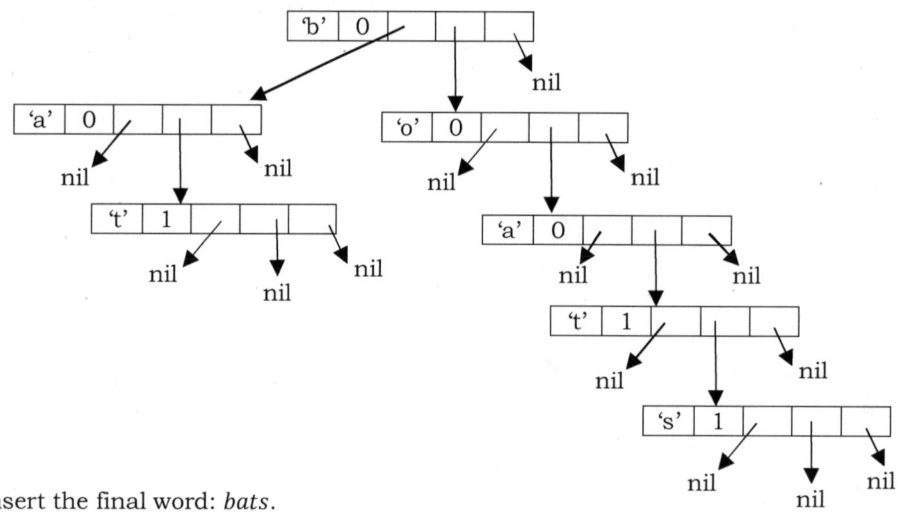

Now, let us insert the final word: *bats*.

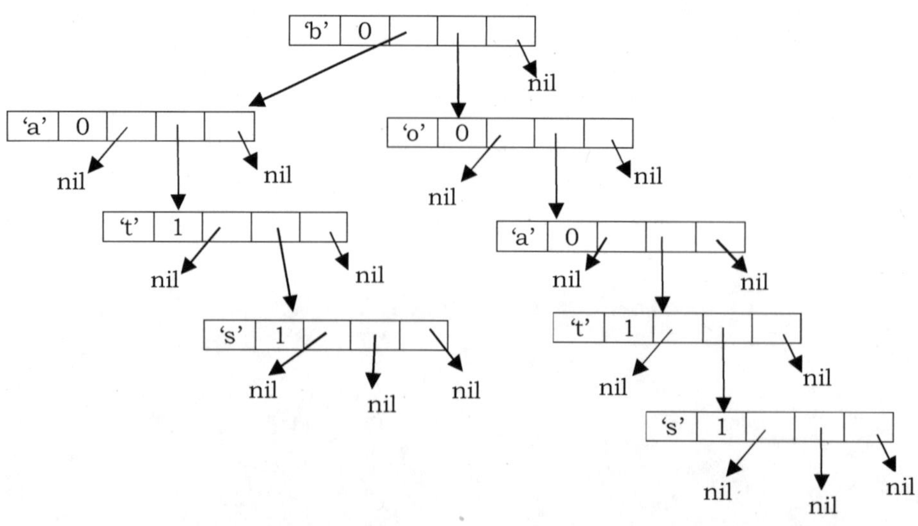

Based on these examples, we can write the insertion algorithm as below. We will combine the insertion operation of BST and tries.

```
// Insert a new key value pair into the collection
func (this *TernarySearchTree) Insert(key string, value interface{}) {
    // If the value is nil then remove this key from the collection
    if value == nil {
        this.Remove(key)
        return
    }
    if this.length == 0 {
        this.root = &TSTNode{0, nil, nil, nil, nil}
    }
    t := this.root
    letters := []byte(key)
    for i := 0; i < len(letters); {
        b := letters[i]
        if b > t.key {
            if t.right == nil {
                t.right = &TSTNode{b, nil, nil, nil, nil}
            }
            t = t.right
        } else if b < t.key {
            if t.left == nil {
                t.left = &TSTNode{b, nil, nil, nil, nil}
            }
            t = t.left
        } else {
            i++
            if i < len(letters) {
                if t.eq == nil {
                    t.eq = &TSTNode{letters[i], nil, nil, nil, nil}
                }
                t = t.eq
            }
        }
    }
    if t.value == nil {
        this.length++
    }
    t.value = value
}
```

Time Complexity: $O(L)$, where L is the length of the string to be inserted.

Searching in Ternary Search Tree

If after inserting the words, we might want to search for them. To search for a string in TST, we have to follow the same rules as that of binary search. The only difference is, in case of match we should check for the remaining characters (in *eq* subtree) instead of return. Also, like BSTs we will see both recursive and non-recursive versions of the search method.

To look up a particular node or the data associated with a node, a string key is needed. A search procedure begins by checking the root node of the TST and determining which of the following conditions has occurred. If the first character of the string is less than the character in the root node, a recursive lookup can be called on the tree whose root is the *left* child of the current root. Similarly, if the first character is greater than the current node in the tree, then a recursive call can be made to the tree whose root is the *right* child of the current node. As a final case, if the first character of the string is equal to the character of the current node then the function returns the node if there are no more characters in the key. If there are more characters in the key then the first character of the key must be removed and a recursive call is made given the *equal* child node and the modified key. This can also be written in a non-recursive way by using a pointer to the current node and a pointer to the current character of the key.

```
// Get the value at the specified key. Returns nil if not found.
func (this *TernarySearchTree) Get(key string) interface{} {
    if this.length == 0 {
        return nil
```

```
    }
    node := this.root
    letters := []byte(key)
    for i := 0; i < len(letters); {
        b := letters[i]
        if b > node.key {
            if node.right == nil {
                return nil
            }
            node = node.right
        } else if b < node.key {
            if node.left == nil {
                return nil
            }
            node = node.left
        } else {
            i++
            if i < len(letters) {
                if node.eq == nil {
                    return nil
                }
                node = node.eq
            } else {
                break
            }
        }
    }
    return node.value
}
```

Time Complexity: O(L), where L is the length of the string to be searched.

Performance

The running time of ternary search trees varies significantly with the input. Ternary search trees run best when given several similar strings, especially when those strings share a common prefix. Alternatively, ternary search trees are effective when storing a large number of relatively short strings.

Operation	Average Case	Worst Case
Search	O($logn$)	O(n)
Insert	O($logn$)	O(n)
Remove	O($logn$)	O(n)

15.13 Comparing BSTs, Tries and TSTs

- Hash table and BST implementation stores complete the string at each node. As a result they take more time for searching. But they are memory efficient.
- TSTs can grow and shrink dynamically but hash tables resize only based on load factor.
- TSTs allow partial search whereas BSTs and hash tables do not support it.
- TSTs can display the words in sorted order, but in hash tables we cannot get the sorted order.
- Tries perform search operations very fast but they take huge memory for storing the string.
- TSTs combine the advantages of BSTs and Tries. That means they combine the memory efficiency of BSTs and the time efficiency of tries.

15.14 Suffix Trees

Suffix trees are an important data structure for strings. With suffix trees we can answer the queries very fast. But this requires some preprocessing and construction of a suffix tree. Even though the construction of a suffix tree is complicated, it solves many other string-related problems in linear time.

Note: Suffix trees use a tree (suffix tree) for one string, whereas Hash tables, BSTs, Tries and TSTs store a set of strings. That means, a suffix tree answers the queries related to one string.

Let us see the terminology we use for this representation.

Prefix and Suffix

Given a string $T = T_1T_2 \ldots T_n$, the *prefix* of T is a string $T_1 \ldots T_i$ where i can take values from 1 to n. For example, if $T = banana$, then the prefixes of T are: $b, ba, ban, bana, banan, banana$. Similarly, given a string $T = T_1T_2 \ldots T_n$, the *suffix* of T is a string $T_i \ldots T_n$ where i can take values from n to 1. For example, if $T = banana$, then the suffixes of T are: $a, na, ana, nana, anana, banana$.

Observation

From the above example, we can easily see that for a given text T and pattern P, the exact string matching problem can also be defined as:

- Find a suffix of T such that P is a prefix of this suffix *or*
- Find a prefix of T such that P is a suffix of this prefix.

Example: Let the text to be searched be $T = accbkkbac$ and the pattern be $P = kkb$. For this example, P is a prefix of the suffix $kkbac$ and also a suffix of the prefix $accbkkb$.

What is a Suffix Tree?

In simple terms, the suffix tree for text T is a Trie-like data structure that represents the suffixes of T. The definition of suffix trees can be given as: A suffix tree for a n character string $T[1 \ldots n]$ is a rooted tree with the following properties.

- A suffix tree will contain n leaves which are numbered from 1 to n
- Each internal node (except root) should have at least 2 children
- Each edge in a tree is labeled by a nonempty substring of T
- No two edges of a node (children edges) begin with the same character
- The paths from the root to the leaves represent all the suffixes of T

The Construction of Suffix Trees

Algorithm

1. Let S be the set of all suffixes of T. Append \$ to each of the suffixes.
2. Sort the suffixes in S based on their first character.
3. For each group S_c $(c \in \sum)$:
   (i) If S_c group has only one element, then create a leaf node.
   (ii) Otherwise, find the longest common prefix of the suffixes in S_c group, create an internal node, and recursively continue with Step 2, S being the set of remaining suffixes from S_c after splitting off the longest common prefix.

For better understanding, let us go through an example. Let the given text be $T = tatat$. For this string, give a number to each of the suffixes.

Index	Suffix
1	\$
2	$t\$$
3	$at\$$
4	$tat\$$
5	$atat\$$
6	$tatat\$$

Now, sort the suffixes based on their initial characters.

Index	**Suffix**	
1	\$	Group S_1 based on a
3	$at\$$	Group S_2 based on a
5	$atat\$$	
2	$t\$$	Group S_3 based on t
4	$tat\$$	
6	$tatat\$$	

In the three groups, the first group has only one element. So, as per the algorithm, create a leaf node for it, as shown below.

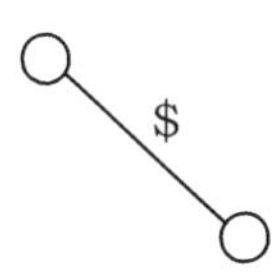

Now, for S_2 and S_3 (as they have more than one element), let us find the longest prefix in the group, and the result is shown below.

Group	Indexes for this group	Longest Prefix of Group Suffixes
S_2	3, 5	*at*
S_3	2, 4, 6	*t*

For S_2 and S_3, create internal nodes, and the edge contains the longest common prefix of those groups.

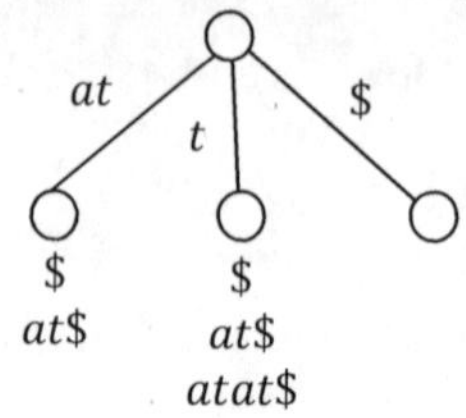

Now we have to remove the longest common prefix from the S_2 and S_3 group elements.

Group	Indexes for this group	Longest Prefix of Group Suffixes	Resultant Suffixes
S_2	3, 5	*at*	$, *at*$
S_3	2, 4, 6	*t*	$, *at*$, *atat*$

Out next step is solving S_2 and S_3 recursively. First let us take S_2. In this group, if we sort them based on their first character, it is easy to see that the first group contains only one element $, and the second group also contains only one element, *at*$. Since both groups have only one element, we can directly create leaf nodes for them.

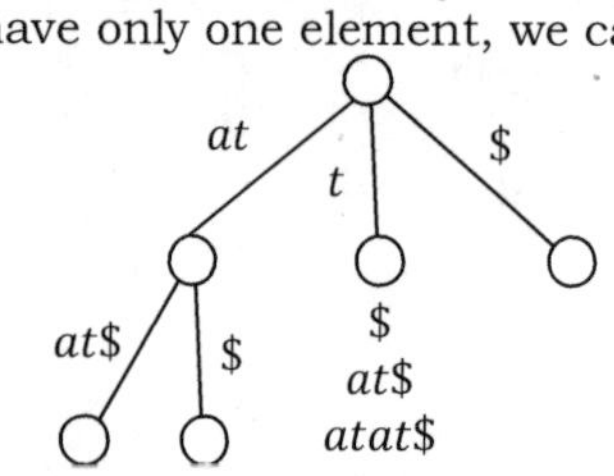

At this step, both S_1 and S_2 elements are done and the only remaining group is S_3. As similar to earlier steps, in the S_3 group, if we sort them based on their first character, it is easy to see that there is only one element in the first group and it is $. For S_3 remaining elements, remove the longest common prefix.

Group	Indexes for this group	Longest Prefix of Group Suffixes	Resultant Suffixes
S_3	4, 6	*at*	$, *at*$

In the S_3 second group, there are two elements: $ and *at*$. We can directly add the leaf nodes for the first group element $. Let us add S_3 subtree as shown below.

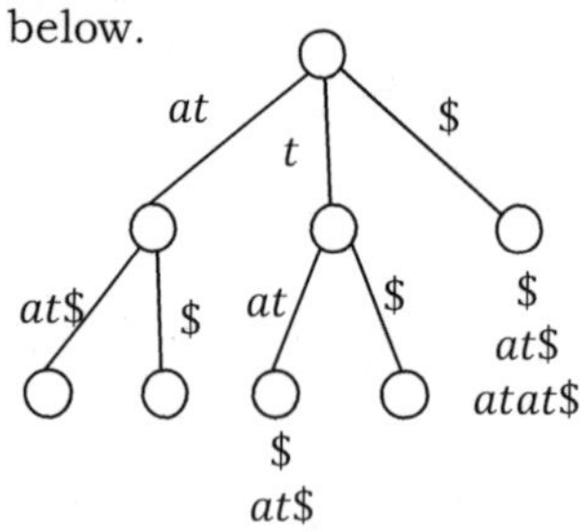

Now, S_3 contains two elements. If we sort them based on their first character, it is easy to see that there are only two elements and among them one is $ and other is *at*$. We can directly add the leaf nodes for them. Let us add S_3 subtree as shown below.

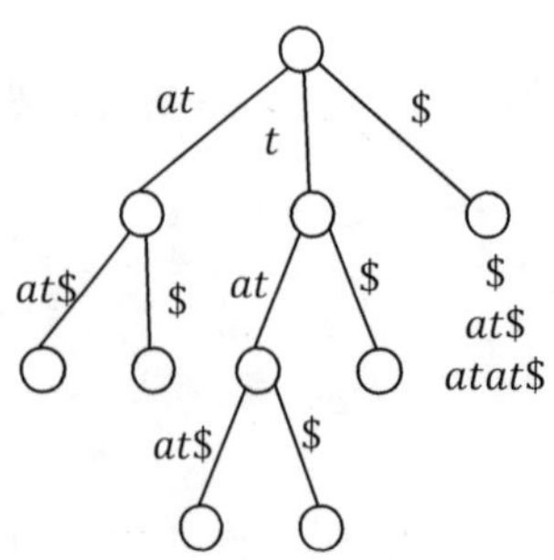

Since there are no more elements, this is the completion of the construction of the suffix tree for string $T = tatat$. The time-complexity of the construction of a suffix tree using the above algorithm is $O(n^2)$ where n is the length of the input string because there are n distinct suffixes. The longest has length n, the second longest has length $n - 1$, and so on.

Note:

- There are $O(n)$ algorithms for constructing suffix trees.
- To improve the complexity, we can use indices instead of string for branches.

Applications of Suffix Trees

All the problems below (but not limited to these) on strings can be solved with suffix trees very efficiently (for algorithms refer to *Problems* section).

- **Exact String Matching:** Given a text T and a pattern P, how do we check whether P appears in T or not?
- **Longest Repeated Substring:** Given a text T how do we find the substring of T that is the maximum repeated substring?
- **Longest Palindrome:** Given a text T how do we find the substring of T that is the longest palindrome of T?
- **Longest Common Substring:** Given two strings, how do we find the longest common substring?
- **Longest Common Prefix:** Given two strings $X[i \ldots n]$ and $Y[j \ldots m]$, how do we find the longest common prefix?
- How do we search for a regular expression in given text T?
- Given a text T and a pattern P, how do we find the first occurrence of P in T?

15.15 String Algorithms: Problems & Solutions

Problem-1 Given a paragraph of words, give an algorithm for finding the word which appears the maximum number of times. If the paragraph is scrolled down (some words disappear from the first frame, some words still appear, and some are new words), give the maximum occurring word. Thus, it should be dynamic.

Solution: For this problem we can use a combination of priority queues and tries. We start by creating a trie in which we insert a word as it appears, and at every leaf of trie. Its node contains that word along with a pointer that points to the node in the heap [priority queue] which we also create. This heap contains nodes whose structure contains a *counter*. This is its frequency and also a pointer to that leaf of trie, which contains that word so that there is no need to store the word twice.

Whenever a new word comes up, we find it in trie. If it is already there, we increase the frequency of that node in the heap corresponding to that word, and we call it heapify. This is done so that at any point of time we can get the word of maximum frequency. While scrolling, when a word goes out of scope, we decrement the counter in heap. If the new frequency is still greater than zero, heapify the heap to incorporate the modification. If the new frequency is zero, delete the node from heap and delete it from trie.

Problem-2 Given two strings, how can we find the longest common substring?

Solution: Let us assume that the given two strings are T_1 and T_2. The longest common substring of two strings, T_1 and T_2, can be found by building a generalized suffix tree for T_1 and T_2. That means we need to build a single suffix tree for both the strings. Each node is marked to indicate if it represents a suffix of T_1 or T_2 or both. This indicates that we need to use different marker symbols for both the strings (for example, we can use $ for the first string and # for the second symbol). After constructing the common suffix tree, the deepest node marked for both T_1 and T_2 represents the longest common substring.

Another way of doing this is: We can build a suffix tree for the string $T_1\$T_2\#$. This is equivalent to building a common suffix tree for both the strings.

Time Complexity: $O(m + n)$, where m and n are the lengths of input strings T_1 and T_2.

Problem-3 **Longest Palindrome:** Given a text T how do we find the substring of T which is the longest palindrome of T?

Solution: The longest palindrome of $T[1..n]$ can be found in $O(n)$ time. The algorithm is: first build a suffix tree for $T\$reverse(T)\#$ or build a generalized suffix tree for T and $reverse(T)$. After building the suffix tree, find the deepest node marked with both $ and #. Basically it means find the longest common substring.

Problem-4 Given a string (word), give an algorithm for finding the next word in the dictionary.

Solution: Let us assume that we are using Trie for storing the dictionary words. To find the next word in Tries we can follow a simple approach as shown below. Starting from the rightmost character, increment the characters one by one. Once we reach Z, move to the next character on the left side.

Whenever we increment, check if the word with the incremented character exists in the dictionary or not. If it exists, then return the word, otherwise increment again. If we use *TST*, then we can find the inorder successor for the current word.

Problem-5 Give an algorithm for reversing a string.

Solution: Golang strings are immutable. So, we cannot perform in-place reversal. Hence, we would need to prepare an output string for returning the reversed string.

```
func reverse(s string) string {
    r := []rune(s)
    for i, j := 0, len(r)-1; i < len(r)/2; i, j = i+1, j-1 {
        r[i], r[j] = r[j], r[i]
    }
    return string(r)
}
```

Time Complexity: $O(\frac{n}{2}) \approx O(n)$, where n is the length of the given string. Space Complexity: $O(n)$.

Problem-6 Can we reverse the string without using any temporary variable?

Solution: Yes, we can use XOR logic for swapping the variables.

```
func reverse(s string) string {
    r := []rune(s)
    for i, j := 0, len(r)-1; i < len(r)/2; i, j = i+1, j-1 {
        r[i] ^= r[j]
        r[j] ^= r[i]
        r[i] ^= r[j]
    }
    return string(r)
}
```

Time Complexity: $O(\frac{n}{2}) \approx O(n)$, where n is the length of the given string. Space Complexity: $O(n)$.

Problem-7 **Wildcard Matching**: Given a text and a pattern, give an algorithm for matching the pattern in the text. Assume ? (single character matcher) and * (multi character matcher) are the wild card characters.

Solution: The following algorithm is very much in line with the brute-force string matching algorithm.

```
func isMatch(text, pattern string) bool {
    prev, now := make([]bool, len(pattern)+1), make([]bool, len(pattern)+1)
    for i := 0; i <= len(text); i++ {
        now, prev = prev, now
        now[0] = i == 0
        for j := 1; j <= len(pattern); j++ {
            if pattern[j-1] == '*' {
                now[j] = prev[j] || prev[j-1] || now[j-1]
            } else {
                now[j] = prev[j-1] && (text[i-1] == pattern[j-1] || pattern[j-1] == '?')
            }
        }
    }
    return now[len(pattern)]
}
func main() {
    fmt.Println(isMatch("CareerMonk Publications", "*ca?ions"))
}
```

Time Complexity: $O(mn)$, where m is the length of the text, and n is the length of the pattern.
Space Complexity: $O(1)$.

Problem-8 Give an algorithm for reversing words in a sentence.
Example: Input: "This is a Career Monk String" Output: "String Monk Career a is This"

Solution: Start from the beginning and keep on reversing the words. The below implementation assumes that ' ' (space) is the delimiter for words in given sentence.

```
func reverseWords(sentence string) string {
    var words []string
    var start, end int
```

```
    for end < len(sentence) {
        for start < len(sentence) && sentence[start] == ' ' {
            start++
        }
        if start == len(sentence) {
            break
        }
        end = start+1
        for end < len(sentence) && sentence[end] != ' ' {
            end++
        }
        words = append(words, sentence[start:end])
        start = end+1
    }
    reverse(words)
    return strings.Join(words, " ")
}
func reverse(words []string) {
    for i, j := 0, len(words)-1; i < j; i, j=i+1, j-1 {
        words[i], words[j] = words[j], words[i]
    }
}
func main() {
    fmt.Println(reverseWords("Hello, world"))
    fmt.Println(reverseWords("CareerMonk Publications"))
}
```

Time Complexity: $O(2n) \approx O(n)$, where n is the length of the string. Space Complexity: O(1).

Problem-9 **Permutations of a string [anagrams]:** Give an algorithm for printing all possible permutations of the characters in a string. Unlike combinations, two permutations are considered distinct if they contain the same characters but in a different order. For simplicity assume that each occurrence of a repeated character is a distinct character. That is, if the input is "aaa", the output should be six repetitions of "aaa". The permutations may be output in any order.

Solution: In Golang string is a sequence of bytes. A string literal actually represents a UTF-8 sequence of bytes. In UTF-8, ASCII characters are single-byte corresponding to the first 128 Unicode characters. All other characters are between 1 to 4 bytes. Due to this, it is not possible to index a character in a string. In Golang, rune data type represents a Unicode point. Once a string is converted to an array of rune then it is possible to index a character in that array of rune. For example, to find all permutations of string abc:

- We will find all perms of the given string based on all perms of its substring
- To find all perms of abc, we need to find all perms of bc, and then add a to those perms
- To find all perms of bc, we need to find all perms of c, and add b to those perms
- To find all perms of c, well we know that is only c
- Now, we can find all perms of bc, insert c at every available space in b: bc $--> bc, cb$
- Now we need to add a to all perms of bc: abc, bac, bca (insert a in bc) -- acb, cab, cba (insert a in cb)

```
// Permute the values at index i to len(str)-1
func permute(str []rune, i int) {
    if i == len(str) {
        fmt.Println(string(str))
    } else {
        for j := i; j < len(str); j++ {
            str[i], str[j] = str[j], str[i]
            permute(str, i+1)
            str[i], str[j] = str[j], str[i]
        }
    }
}
// Perm calls f with each permutation of str
func permutations(str string) {
    permute([]rune(str), 0)
}
```

```
func main() {
    permutations("abc")
}
```

Problem-10 **Combinations of a String:** Unlike permutations, two combinations are considered to be the same if they contain the same characters, but may be in a different order. Give an algorithm that prints all possible combinations of the characters in a string. For example, "*ac*" and "*ab*" are different combinations from the input string "*abc*", but "*ab*" is the same as "*ba*".

Solution: The solution is achieved by generating $n!/r!\,(n-r)!$ strings, each of length between 1 and n where n is the length of the given input string. One simplest algorithm iterates over each number from 1 to $2^{length(input)}$, separating it by binary components and utilizes the true/false interpretation of binary 1's and 0's to extract all unique ordered combinations of the input slice.

For example, a binary number 0011 means selecting the first and second index from the slice and ignoring the third and fourth. For input {"a", "b", "c", "d"} this signifies the combination {"a", "b"}. For input slice {"a", "b", "a", "d"} there are 2^4- 1 = 15 binary combinations, so mapping each bit position to a slice index and selecting the entry for binary 1 and discarding for binary 0 gives the full subset as:

1	=	0001	=>	---a	=>	{"a"}
2	=	0010	=>	--b-	=>	{"b"}
3	=	0011	=>	--ba	=>	{"a", "b"}
4	=	0100	=>	-c--	=>	{"c"}
5	=	0101	=>	-a-a	=>	{"a", "c"}
6	=	0110	=>	-cb-	=>	{"b", "c"}
7	=	0111	=>	-cba	=>	{"a", "b", "c"}
8	=	1000	=>	d---	=>	{"d"}
9	=	1001	=>	d—a	=>	{"d", "d"}
10	=	1010	=>	d-b-	=>	{"b", "d"}
11	=	1011	=>	d-ba	=>	{"a", "b", "d"}
12	=	1100	=>	dc--	=>	{"c", "d"}
13	=	1101	=>	dc-a	=>	{"a", "c", "d"}
14	=	1110	=>	dcb-	=>	{"b", "c", "d"}
15	=	1111	=>	dcba	=>	{"a", "b", "c", "d"}

```
// combinations return all combinations for a given string array.
// This is essentially a powerset of the given set except that the empty set is disregarded.
func combination(set []rune) (subsets []string) {
    length := uint(len(set))
    // Go through all possible combinations of objects
    // from 1 (only first object in subset) to 2^length (all objects in subset)
    for subsetBits := 1; subsetBits < (1 << length); subsetBits++ {
        var subset string
        for object := uint(0); object < length; object++ {
            // checks if object is contained in subset by checking if bit 'object' is set in subsetBits
            if (subsetBits>>object)&1 == 1 {
                subset = subset + string(set[object])       // add object to subset
            }
        }
        subsets = append(subsets, subset)                  // add subset to subsets
    }
    return subsets
}
func combinations(str string) (subsets []string) {
    input := []rune(str)
    return combination(input)
}
func main() {
    fmt.Println(combinations("abc"))
}
```

Problem-11 Given a string "ABCCBCBA", give an algorithm for recursively removing the adjacent characters if they are the same. For example, ABCCBCBA --> ABBCBA-->ACBA

Solution: First we need to check if we have a character pair; if yes, then cancel it. Now check for next character and previous element. Keep canceling the characters until we either reach the start of the array, reach the end of the array, or don't find a pair.

```
func removeAdjacentPairs(str string) string {
    r := []rune(str)
    n, i, j := len(r), 0,0
    for i = 0; i < n; i++ {
        if j > 0 && i < n && (r[i] == r[j-1]) { //Cancel pairs
            j--
        } else {
            r[j] = r[i]
            j++
        }
    }
    return string(r[:j])
}
```

Note: We can solve this problem with stacks too. Refer *Stacks* chapter for algorithm.

Problem-12 Given a set of characters S and a input string T, find the minimum window in S which will contain all the characters in T with complexity $O(n)$. For example, $S = ABBACBAA$ and $T = AAB$ has the minimum window BAA.

Solution: This algorithm is based on the sliding window approach. In this approach, we start from the beginning of the array and move to the right. As soon as we have a window which has all the required elements, try sliding the window as far right as possible with all the required elements. If the current window length is less than the minimum length found until now, update the minimum length. For example, if the input array is $ABBACBAA$ and the minimum window should cover characters AAB, then the sliding window will move like this:

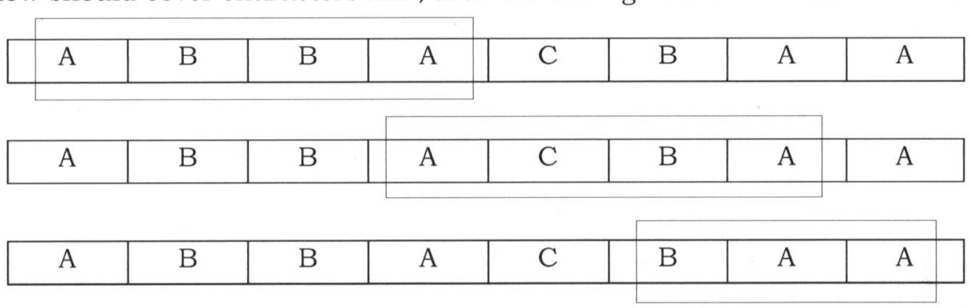

Algorithm:

1 Make an integer array shouldFind[] of len 256. The ith element of this array will have the count of how many times we need to find the element of ASCII value i.
2 Make another array hasFound which will have the count of the required elements found until now.
3 Count <= 0
4 While input[i]
    a. If input[i] element is not to be found→ continue
    b. If input[i] element is required => increase count by 1.
    c. If count is length of chars[] array, slide the window as much right as possible.
    d. If current window length is less than min length found until now, update min length.

```
func minWindow(S string, T string) string {
    rem := 0
    shouldFind := make(map[byte]int)
    for i := range T {
        rem++
        shouldFind[T[i]]++
    }
    if rem > len(S) {
        return ""
    }
    var hasFound = string(make([]byte, len(S)))
    start, end := 0,0
    for end < len(S) {
        if v,ok := shouldFind[S[end]] ;ok {
            if v>0 {
                rem--
```

```
            }
            shouldFind[S[end]]--
        }
        for rem <= 0 {
            if len(hasFound) >= len(S[start:end+1]) {
                hasFound = S[start:end+1]
            }
            if _,ok := shouldFind[S[start]] ;ok {
                shouldFind[S[start]]++
                if shouldFind[S[start]] > 0 {
                    rem++
                }
            }
            start++
        }
        end++
    }

    if hasFound == string(make([]byte, len(S))) {
        return ""
    }
    return hasFound
}
```

Complexity: If we walk through the code, i and j can traverse at most n steps (where n is the input size) in the worst case, adding to a total of $2n$ times. Therefore, time complexity is $O(n)$.

Problem-13 We are given a 2D array of characters and a character pattern. Give an algorithm to find if the pattern is present in the 2D array. The pattern can be in any order (all 8 neighbors to be considered) but we can't use the same character twice while matching. Return 1 if match is found, 0 if not. For example: Find "MICROSOFT" in the below matrix.

A	C	P	**R**	C
X	**S**	**O**	P	**C**
V	**O**	V	N	**I**
W	G	**F**	**M**	N
Q	A	**T**	I	T

Solution: Manually finding the solution of this problem is relatively intuitive; we just need to describe an algorithm for it. Ironically, describing the algorithm is not the easy part.

How do we do it manually? First we match the first element, and when it is matched we match the second element in the 8 neighbors of the first match. We do this process recursively, and when the last character of the input pattern matches, return true.

During the above process, take care not to use any cell in the 2D array twice. For this purpose, you mark every visited cell with some sign. If your pattern matching fails at some point, start matching from the beginning (of the pattern) in the remaining cells. When returning, you unmark the visited cells.

Let's convert the above intuitive method into an algorithm. Since we are doing similar checks for pattern matching every time, a recursive solution is what we need. In a recursive solution, we need to check if the substring passed is matched in the given matrix or not. The condition is not to use the already used cell, and to find the already used cell, we need to add another 2D array to the function (or we can use an unused bit in the input array itself.) Also, we need the current position of the input matrix from where we need to start. Since we need to pass a lot more information than is actually given, we should be having a wrapper function to initialize the extra information to be passed.

Algorithm:

```
If we are past the last character in the pattern
    Return true
If we get a used cell again
    Return false if we got past the 2D matrix
    Return false
If searching for first element and cell doesn't match
    FindMatch with next cell in row-first order (or column-first order)
Otherwise if character matches
    mark this cell as used
```

```
        res = FindMatch with next position of pattern in 8 neighbors
        mark this cell as unused
        Return res
    Otherwise
        Return false
```

```go
func findMatch(board [][]byte, word string) bool {
    visited := make([][]bool, len(board))
    for i := 0; i < len(visited); i++ {
        visited[i] = make([]bool, len(board[0]))
    }
    pos := 0
    for i := 0; i < len(board); i++ {
        for j := 0; j < len(board[0]); j++ {
            if helper(visited, board, i, j, word, pos) {
                return true
            }
        }
    }
    return false
}
func helper(visited [][]bool, board [][]byte, r, c int, word string, pos int) bool {
    if pos == len(word) {
        return true
    }
    if r < 0 || r == len(board) || c < 0 || c == len(board[0]) {
        return false
    }
    if board[r][c] != word[pos] || visited[r][c] {
        return false
    }
    //finding subpattern in 8 neighbors
    visited[r][c] = true
    if helper(visited, board, r-1, c, word, pos+1) {
        return true
    }
    if helper(visited, board, r+1, c, word, pos+1) {
        return true
    }
    if helper(visited, board, r, c-1, word, pos+1) {
        return true
    }
    if helper(visited, board, r, c+1, word, pos+1) {
        return true
    }
    if helper(visited, board, r+1, c+1, word, pos+1) {
        return true
    }
    if helper(visited, board, r+1, c-1, word, pos+1) {
        return true
    }
    if helper(visited, board, r-1, c+1, word, pos+1) {
        return true
    }
    if helper(visited, board, r-1, c-1, word, pos+1) {
        return true
    }
    visited[r][c] = false
    return false
}
func main() {
    board := [][]byte{
        {'A', 'C', 'P', 'R', 'C'},
        {'X', 'S', 'O', 'P', 'C'},
```

```
        {'V', 'O', 'V', 'N', 'I'},
        {'W', 'G', 'F', 'M', 'N'},
        {'Q', 'A', 'T', 'I', 'T'},
    }
    fmt.Println(findMatch(board, "MICROSOFT"))
}
```

Problem-16 Given a matrix with size $n \times n$ containing random integers. Give an algorithm which checks whether rows match with a column(s) or not. For example, if i^{th} row matches with j^{th} column, and i^{th} row contains the elements - [2,6,5,8,9]. Then j^{th} column would also contain the elements - [2,6,5,8,9].

Solution: We can build a trie for the data in the columns (rows would also work). Then we can compare the rows with the trie. This would allow us to exit as soon as the beginning of a row does not match any column (backtracking). Also this would let us check a row against all columns in one pass.

If we do not want to waste memory for empty pointers then we can further improve the solution by constructing a suffix tree.

Problem-17 Write a method to replace all spaces in a string with '%20'. Assume string has sufficient space at end of string to hold additional characters.

Solution: A common approach in string manipulation problems is to edit the string starting from the end and working backwards. This is useful because we have an extra buffer at the end, which allows us to change characters without worrying about what we're overwriting. We will use this approach in this problem. The algorithm employs a two-scan approach. In the first scan, we count the number of spaces. By tripling this number, we can compute how many extra characters we will have in the final string. In the second pass, which is done in reverse order, we actually edit the string. When we see a space, we replace it with %20. If there is no space, then we copy the original character.

```
func urlify(A string) string {
    space, n := 0, len(A)
    for i := 0; i < n; i++ {
        if string(A[i]) == " " {
            space++
        }
    }
    originalLength := space*2 + n
    r := make([]byte, originalLength)
    for i := 0; i < n; i++ {
        r[i] = A[i]
    }
    fmt.Println(string(r))
    for i := n - 1; i >= 0; i-- {
        if r[i] == ' ' {
            r[originalLength-1] = '0'
            r[originalLength-2] = '2'
            r[originalLength-3] = '%'
            originalLength = originalLength - 3
        } else {
            r[originalLength-1] = r[i]
            originalLength--
        }
    }
    return string(r)
}
```

Time Complexity: O(n).
Space Complexity: O(1). Here, we do not have to worry about the space needed for extra characters.

Problem-18 **Running length encoding**: Write an algorithm to compress the given string by using the count of repeated characters and if new com-pressed string length is not smaller than the original string then return the original string. For example, if the input is ["a","a","b","b","c","c","c"], the output would be 6, and the first 6 characters of the input array should be: ["a","2","b","2","c","3"].

Solution: We will use separate pointers *read* and write to mark where we are reading and writing from. Both operations will be done left to right alternately: we will read a contiguous group of characters, then write the compressed version to the array. At the end, the position of the *write* head will be the length of the answer that was written.

Let's maintain *anchor*, the start position of the contiguous group of characters we are currently reading. Now, let's read from left to right. We know that we must be at the end of the block when we are at the last character, or when the next character is different from the current character. When we are at the end of a group, we will write the result of that group down using our *write* head. S[*anchor*] will be the correct character, and the length (if greater than 1) will be $read - anchor + 1$. We will write the digits of that number to the array.

```
func compress(S string) (int, string) {
    n := len(S)
    A := []rune(S)
    anchor := 0        // slow pointer
    read := 0          // fast pointer
    write := 0         // writing head pointer
    for read <= n {
        for (read < n) && (A[anchor] == A[read]) {
            read++
        }
        A[write] = A[anchor]
        write++
        count := read - anchor
        if count > 1 {
            s := strconv.Itoa(count)
            for k := 0; k < len(s); k++ {
                A[write] = rune(s[k])
                write++
            }
        }
        anchor = read
        read++
    }
    return write, string(A)
}
func main() {
    fmt.Println(compress("aabbccc"))         // prints -> 6 a2b2c3c
}
```

Time Complexity: O(n), where n is the length of S.
Space Complexity: O(1), the space used by read, write, and anchor.

ALGORITHMS DESIGN TECHNIQUES

CHAPTER

16

16.1 Introduction

In the previous chapters, we have seen many algorithms for solving different kinds of problems. Before solving a new problem, the general tendency is to look for the similarity of the current problem to other problems for which we have solutions. This helps us in getting the solution easily.

In this chapter, we will see different ways of classifying the algorithms and in subsequent chapters we will focus on a few of them (Greedy, Divide and Conquer, Dynamic Programming).

16.2 Classification

There are many ways of classifying algorithms and a few of them are shown below:

- Implementation Method
- Design Method
- Other Classifications

16.3 Classification by Implementation Method

Recursion or Iteration

A *recursive* algorithm is one that calls itself repeatedly until a base condition is satisfied. It is a common method used in functional programming languages like $C, C++$, etc.

Iterative algorithms use constructs like loops and sometimes other data structures like stacks and queues to solve the problems.

Some problems are suited for recursive and others are suited for iterative. For example, the *Towers of Hanoi* problem can be easily understood in recursive implementation. Every recursive version has an iterative version, and vice versa.

Procedural or Declarative (Non-Procedural)

In *declarative* programming languages, we say what we want without having to say how to do it. With *procedural* programming, we have to specify the exact steps to get the result. For example, SQL is more declarative than procedural, because the queries don't specify the steps to produce the result. Examples of procedural languages include: C, PHP, and PERL.

Serial or Parallel or Distributed

In general, while discussing the algorithms we assume that computers execute one instruction at a time. These are called *serial* algorithms.

Parallel algorithms take advantage of computer architectures to process several instructions at a time. They divide the problem into subproblems and serve them to several processors or threads. Iterative algorithms are generally parallelizable.

If the parallel algorithms are distributed on to different machines then we call such algorithms *distributed* algorithms.

Deterministic or Non-Deterministic

Deterministic algorithms solve the problem with a predefined process, whereas *non – deterministic* algorithms guess the best solution at each step through the use of heuristics.

Exact or Approximate

As we have seen, for many problems we are not able to find the optimal solutions. That means, the algorithms for which we are able to find the optimal solutions are called *exact* algorithms. In computer science, if we do not have the optimal solution, we give approximation algorithms.

Approximation algorithms are generally associated with NP-hard problems (refer to the *Complexity Classes* chapter for more details).

16.4 Classification by Design Method

Another way of classifying algorithms is by their design method.

Greedy Method

Greedy algorithms work in stages. In each stage, a decision is made that is good at that point, without bothering about the future consequences. Generally, this means that some *local best* is chosen. It assumes that the local best selection also makes for the *global* optimal solution.

Divide and Conquer

The D & C strategy solves a problem by:

1) Divide: Breaking the problem into sub problems that are themselves smaller instances of the same type of problem.
2) Recursion: Recursively solving these sub problems.
3) Conquer: Appropriately combining their answers.

Examples: merge sort and binary search algorithms.

Dynamic Programming

Dynamic programming (DP) and memoization work together. The difference between DP and divide and conquer is that in the case of the latter there is no dependency among the sub problems, whereas in DP there will be an overlap of sub-problems. By using memoization [maintaining a table for already solved sub problems], DP reduces the exponential complexity to polynomial complexity ($O(n^2)$, $O(n^3)$, etc.) for many problems.

The difference between dynamic programming and recursion is in the memoization of recursive calls. When sub problems are independent and if there is no repetition, memoization does not help, hence dynamic programming is not a solution for all problems.

By using memoization [maintaining a table of sub problems already solved], dynamic programming reduces the complexity from exponential to polynomial.

Linear Programming

Linear programming is not a programming language like C++, Java, or Visual Basic. Linear programming can be defined as:

> A method to allocate scarce resources to competing activities in an optimal manner when the problem can be expressed using a linear objective function and linear inequality constraints.

A linear program consists of a set of variables, a linear objective function indicating the contribution of each variable to the desired outcome, and a set of linear constraints describing the limits on the values of the variables. The *solution* to a linear program is a set of values for the problem variables that results in the best -- *largest or smallest* -- value of the objective function and yet is consistent with all the constraints. Formulation is the process of translating a real-world problem into a linear program.

Once a problem has been formulated as a linear program, a computer program can be used to solve the problem. In this regard, solving a linear program is relatively easy. The hardest part about applying linear programming is formulating the problem and interpreting the solution. In linear programming, there are inequalities in terms of inputs and *maximizing* (or *minimizing*) some linear function of the inputs. Many problems (example: maximum flow for directed graphs) can be discussed using linear programming.

Reduction [Transform and Conquer]

In this method we solve a difficult problem by transforming it into a known problem for which we have asymptotically optimal algorithms. In this method, the goal is to find a reducing algorithm whose complexity is not dominated by the resulting reduced algorithms. For example, the selection algorithm for finding the median in a list involves first sorting the list and then finding out the middle element in the sorted list. These techniques are also called *transform and conquer*.

16.5 Other Classifications

Classification by Research Area

In computer science each field has its own problems and needs efficient algorithms. Examples: search algorithms, sorting algorithms, merge algorithms, numerical algorithms, graph algorithms, string algorithms, geometric algorithms, combinatorial algorithms, machine learning, cryptography, parallel algorithms, data compression algorithms, parsing techniques, and more.

Classification by Complexity

In this classification, algorithms are classified by the time they take to find a solution based on their input size. Some algorithms take linear time complexity ($O(n)$) and others take exponential time, and some never halt. Note that some problems may have multiple algorithms with different complexities.

Randomized Algorithms

A few algorithms make choices randomly. For some problems, the fastest solutions must involve randomness. Example: Quick Sort.

Branch and Bound Enumeration and Backtracking

These were used in Artificial Intelligence and we do not need to explore these fully. For the Backtracking method refer to the *Recusion and Backtracking* chapter.

Note: In the next few chapters we discuss the Greedy, Divide and Conquer, and Dynamic Programming] design methods. These methods are emphasized because they are used more often than other methods to solve problems.

CHAPTER

GREEDY ALGORITHMS

17

17.1 Introduction

Let us start our discussion with simple theory that will give us an understanding of the Greedy technique. In the game of *Chess*, every time we make a decision about a move, we have to also think about the future consequences. Whereas, in the game of *Tennis* (or *Volleyball*), our action is based on the immediate situation.

This means that in some cases making a decision that looks right at that moment gives the best solution (*Greedy*), but in other cases it doesn't. The Greedy technique is best suited for looking at the immediate situation.

17.2 Greedy Strategy

Greedy algorithms work in stages. In each stage, a decision is made that is good at that point, without bothering about the future. This means that some *local best* is chosen. It assumes that a local good selection makes for a global optimal solution.

17.3 Elements of Greedy Algorithms

The two basic properties of optimal Greedy algorithms are:

1) Greedy choice property
2) Optimal substructure

Greedy choice property

This property says that the globally optimal solution can be obtained by making a locally optimal solution (Greedy). The choice made by a Greedy algorithm may depend on earlier choices but not on the future. It iteratively makes one Greedy choice after another and reduces the given problem to a smaller one.

Optimal substructure

A problem exhibits optimal substructure if an optimal solution to the problem contains optimal solutions to the subproblems. That means we can solve subproblems and build up the solutions to solve larger problems.

17.4 Does Greedy Always Work?

Making locally optimal choices does not always work. Hence, Greedy algorithms will not always give the best solutions. We will see particular examples in the *Problems* section and in the *Dynamic Programming* chapter.

17.5 Advantages and Disadvantages of Greedy Method

The main advantage of the Greedy method is that it is straightforward, easy to understand and easy to code. In Greedy algorithms, once we make a decision, we do not have to spend time re-examining the already computed values. Its main disadvantage is that for many problems there is no greedy algorithm. That means, in many cases there is no guarantee that making locally optimal improvements in a locally optimal solution gives the optimal global solution.

17.6 Greedy Applications

- Sorting: Selection sort, Topological sort
- Priority Queues: Heap sort
- Huffman coding compression algorithm
- Prim's and Kruskal's algorithms
- Shortest path in Weighted Graph without Negative Edge Weights [Dijkstra's Algorithm]

- Coin change problem
- Fractional Knapsack problem
- Disjoint sets-UNION by size and UNION by height (or rank)
- Job scheduling algorithm
- Greedy techniques can be used as an approximation algorithm for complex problems

17.7 Understanding Greedy Technique

For better understanding let us go through an example.

Huffman Coding Algorithm

Definition

Given a set of n characters from the alphabet A [each character c ∈ A] and their associated frequency $freq$(c), find a binary code for each character c ∈ A, such that $\sum_{c \in A} \text{freq(c)}|\text{binarycode(c)}|$ is minimum, where /binarycode(c)/ represents the length of *binary code* of character c. That means the sum of the lengths of all character codes should be minimum [the sum of each character's frequency multiplied by the number of bits in the representation].

The basic idea behind the Huffman coding algorithm is to use fewer bits for more frequently occurring characters. The Huffman coding algorithm compresses the storage of data using variable length codes. We know that each character takes 8 bits for representation. But in general, we do not use all of them. Also, we use some characters more frequently than others. When reading a file, the system generally reads 8 bits at a time to read a single character. But this coding scheme is inefficient. The reason for this is that some characters are more frequently used than other characters. Let's say that the character $'e'$ is used 10 times more frequently than the character $'q'$. It would then be advantageous for us to instead use a 7 bit code for e and a 9 bit code for q because that could reduce our overall message length.

On average, using Huffman coding on standard files can reduce them anywhere from 10% to 30% depending on the character frequencies. The idea behind the character coding is to give longer binary codes for less frequent characters and groups of characters. Also, the character coding is constructed in such a way that no two character codes are prefixes of each other.

An Example

Let's assume that after scanning a file we find the following character frequencies:

Character	Frequency
a	12
b	2
c	7
d	13
e	14
f	85

Given this, create a binary tree for each character that also stores the frequency with which it occurs (as shown below).

The algorithm works as follows: In the list, find the two binary trees that store minimum frequencies at their nodes.

Connect these two nodes at a newly created common node that will store no character but will store the sum of the frequencies of all the nodes connected below it. So our picture looks like this:

Repeat this process until only one tree is left:

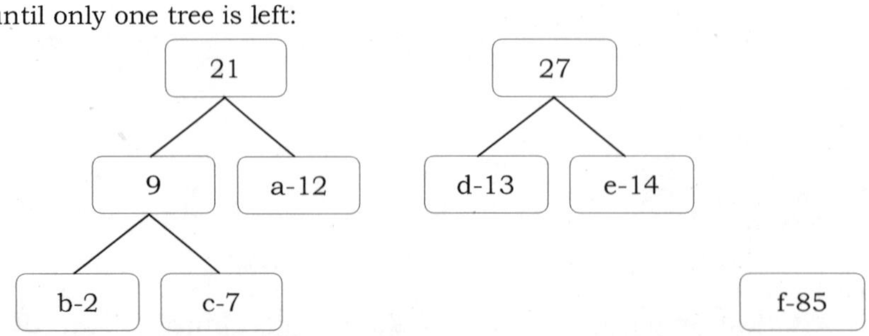

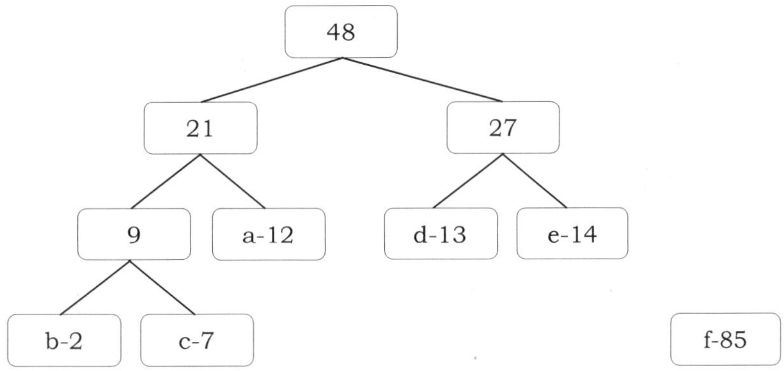

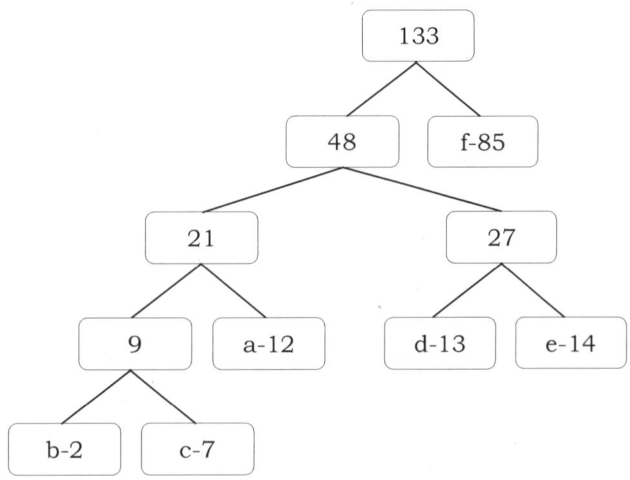

Once the tree is built, each leaf node corresponds to a letter with a code. To determine the code for a particular node, traverse from the root to the leaf node. For each move to the left, append a 0 to the code, and for each move to the right, append a 1. As a result, for the above generated tree, we get the following codes:

Letter	Code
a	001
b	0000
c	0001
d	010
e	011
f	1

Calculating Bits Saved

Now, let us see how many bits that Huffman coding algorithm is saving. All we need to do for this calculation is see how many bits are originally used to store the data and subtract from that the number of bits that are used to store the data using the Huffman code. In the above example, since we have six characters, let's assume each character is stored with a three bit code. Since there are 133 such characters (multiply total frequencies by 3), the total number of bits used is $3 * 133 = 399$. Using the Huffman coding frequencies we can calculate the new total number of bits used:

Letter	Code	Frequency	Total Bits
a	001	12	36
b	0000	2	8
c	0001	7	28
d	010	13	39
e	011	14	42
f	1	85	85
Total			238

Thus, we saved $399 - 238 = 161$ bits, or nearly 40% of the storage space.

```
package main
import (
    "container/heap"
    "fmt"
)
type HuffmanTree interface {
    Freq() int
}
type HuffmanLeaf struct {
    freq  int
    value rune
}
type HuffmanNode struct {
    freq        int
    left, right HuffmanTree
}
func (self HuffmanLeaf) Freq() int {
    return self.freq
}
func (self HuffmanNode) Freq() int {
    return self.freq
}
type treeHeap []HuffmanTree
func (th treeHeap) Len() int {
    return len(th)
}
func (th treeHeap) Less(i, j int) bool {
    return th[i].Freq() < th[j].Freq()
}
func (th *treeHeap) Push(ele interface{}) {
    *th = append(*th, ele.(HuffmanTree))
}
func (th *treeHeap) Pop() (popped interface{}) {
    popped = (*th)[len(*th)-1]
    *th = (*th)[:len(*th)-1]
    return
}
func (th treeHeap) Swap(i, j int) { th[i], th[j] = th[j], th[i] }
func buildTree(frequencies map[rune]int) HuffmanTree {
    var trees treeHeap
    for c, f := range frequencies {
        trees = append(trees, HuffmanLeaf{f, c})
    }
    heap.Init(&trees)
    for trees.Len() > 1 {
        // two trees with least frequency
        a := heap.Pop(&trees).(HuffmanTree)
        b := heap.Pop(&trees).(HuffmanTree)

        // put into new node and re-insert into queue
        heap.Push(&trees, HuffmanNode{a.Freq() + b.Freq(), a, b})
    }
    return heap.Pop(&trees).(HuffmanTree)
}
func printCodes(tree HuffmanTree, prefix []byte) {
    switch i := tree.(type) {
    case HuffmanLeaf:
        // print out symbol, frequency, and code for this leaf (which is just the prefix)
        fmt.Printf("%c\t%d\t%s\n", i.value, i.freq, string(prefix))
    case HuffmanNode:
```

```
            // traverse left
            prefix = append(prefix, '0')
            printCodes(i.left, prefix)
            prefix = prefix[:len(prefix)-1]
            // traverse right
            prefix = append(prefix, '1')
            printCodes(i.right, prefix)
            prefix = prefix[:len(prefix)-1]
        }
    }
    func main() {
        test := "this is an example for huffman encoding and it is working well!"
        frequencies := make(map[rune]int)
        // read each symbol and record the frequencies
        for _, c := range test {
            frequencies[c]++
        }
        tree := buildTree(frequencies) // build Huffman tree
        // print out results
        fmt.Println("SYMBOL\tWEIGHT\tHUFFMAN CODE")
        printCodes(tree, []byte{})
    }
```

Time Complexity: $O(nlogn)$, since there will be *one* build_heap, $2n - 2$ delete_mins, and $n - 2$ inserts, on a priority queue that never has more than n elements. Refer to the *Priority Queues* chapter for details.

17.8 Greedy Algorithms: Problems & Solutions

Problem-1 Given an array F with size n. Assume the array content $F[i]$ indicates the length of the ith file and we want to merge all these files into one single file. Check whether the following algorithm gives the best solution for this problem or not?

Algorithm: Merge the files contiguously. That means select the first two files and merge them. Then select the output of the previous merge and merge with the third file, and keep going...

Note: Given two files A and B with sizes m and n, the complexity of merging is $O(m + n)$.

Solution: This algorithm will not produce the optimal solution. For a counter example, let us consider the following file sizes array.

$$F = \{10,5,100,50,20,15\}$$

As per the above algorithm, we need to merge the first two files (10 and 5 size files), and as a result we get the following list of files. In the list below, 15 indicates the cost of merging two files with sizes 10 and 5.

$$\{15,100,50,20,15\}$$

Similarly, merging 15 with the next file 100 produces: $\{115,50,20,15\}$. For the subsequent steps the list becomes

$$\{165,20,15\}, \{185,15\}$$

Finally, $\{200\}$

The total cost of merging = Cost of all merging operations = $15 + 115 + 165 + 185 + 200 = 680$.

To see whether the above result is optimal or not, consider the order: $\{5, 10, 15, 20, 50,100\}$. For this example, following the same approach, the total cost of merging = $15 + 30 + 50 + 100 + 200 = 395$. So, the given algorithm is not giving the best (optimal) solution.

Problem-2 Similar to Problem-1, does the following algorithm give the optimal solution?

Algorithm: Merge the files in pairs. That means after the first step, the algorithm produces the $n/2$ intermediate files. For the next step, we need to consider these intermediate files and merge them in pairs and keep going.

Note: Sometimes this algorithm is called 2-way merging. Instead of two files at a time, if we merge K files at a time then we call it K-way merging.

Solution: This algorithm will not produce the optimal solution and consider the previous example for a counter example. As per the above algorithm, we need to merge the first pair of files (10 and 5 size files), the second pair of files (100 and 50) and the third pair of files (20 and 15). As a result we get the following list of files.

$$\{15, 150, 35\}$$

Similarly, merge the output in pairs and this step produces [below, the third element does not have a pair element, so keep it the same]:

$$\{165,35\}$$

Finally, $\{200\}$

The total cost of merging = Cost of all merging operations = $15 + 150 + 35 + 165 + 200 = 565$. This is much more than 395 (of the previous problem). So, the given algorithm is not giving the best (optimal) solution.

Problem-3 In Problem-1, what is the best way to merge *all the files* into a single file?

Solution: Using the Greedy algorithm we can reduce the total time for merging the given files. Let us consider the following algorithm.

Algorithm:

1. Store file sizes in a priority queue. The key of elements are file lengths.
2. Repeat the following until there is only one file:
   a. Extract two smallest elements X and Y.
   b. Merge X and Y and insert this new file in the priority queue.

Variant of same algorithm:

1. Sort the file sizes in ascending order.
2. Repeat the following until there is only one file:
   a. Take the first two elements (smallest) X and Y.
   b. Merge X and Y and insert this new file in the sorted list.

To check the above algorithm, let us trace it with the previous example. The given array is:

$$F = \{10,5,100,50,20,15\}$$

As per the above algorithm, after sorting the list it becomes: $\{5, 10, 15, 20, 50, 100\}$. We need to merge the two smallest files (5 and 10 size files) and as a result we get the following list of files. In the list below, 15 indicates the cost of merging two files with sizes 10 and 5.

$$\{15,15,20,50,100\}$$

Similarly, merging the two smallest elements (15 and 15) produces: $\{20,30,50,100\}$. For the subsequent steps the list becomes

$\{50,50,100\}$ //merging 20 and 30
$\{100,100\}$ //merging 20 and 30

Finally, $\{200\}$

The total cost of merging = Cost of all merging operations = $15 + 30 + 50 + 100 + 200 = 395$. So, this algorithm is producing the optimal solution for this merging problem.

Time Complexity: $O(nlogn)$ time using heaps to find best merging pattern plus the optimal cost of merging the files.

Problem-4 **Interval Scheduling Algorithm:** Given a set of n intervals $S = \{(start_i, end_i) | 1 \leq i \leq n\}$. Let us assume that we want to find a maximum subset S' of S such that no pair of intervals in S' overlaps. Check whether the following algorithm works or not.

```
Algorithm: while (S is not empty) {
                Select the interval I that overlaps the least number of other intervals.
                Add I to final solution set S'.
                Remove all intervals from S that overlap with I.
           }
```

Solution: This algorithm does not solve the problem of finding a maximum subset of non-overlapping intervals. Consider the following intervals. The optimal solution is $\{M, O, N, K\}$. However, the interval that overlaps with the fewest others is C, and the given algorithm will select C first.

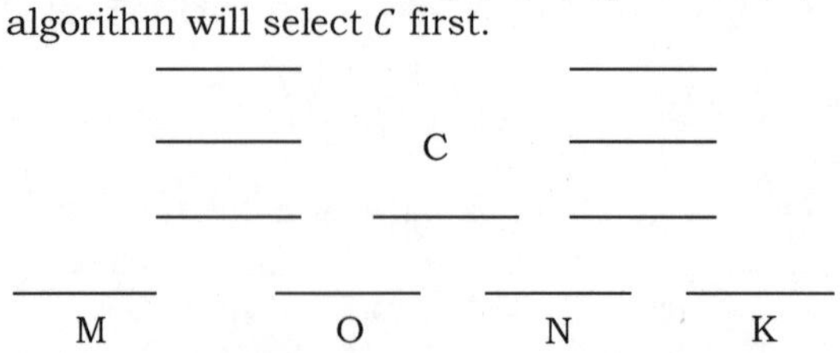

Problem-5 In Problem-4, if we select the interval that starts earliest (also not overlapping with already chosen intervals), does it give the optimal solution?

Solution: No. It will not give the optimal solution. Let us consider the example below. It can be seen that the optimal solution is 4 whereas the given algorithm gives 1.

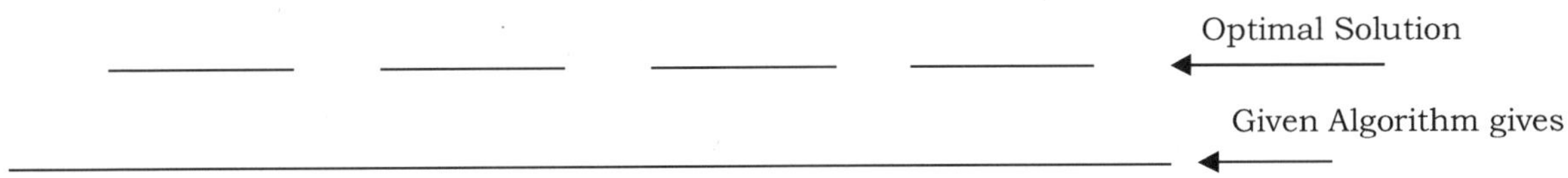

Problem-6 In Problem-4, if we select the shortest interval (but it is not overlapping the already chosen intervals), does it give the optimal solution?

Solution: This also will not give the optimal solution. Let us consider the example below. It can be seen that the optimal solution is 2 whereas the algorithm gives 1.

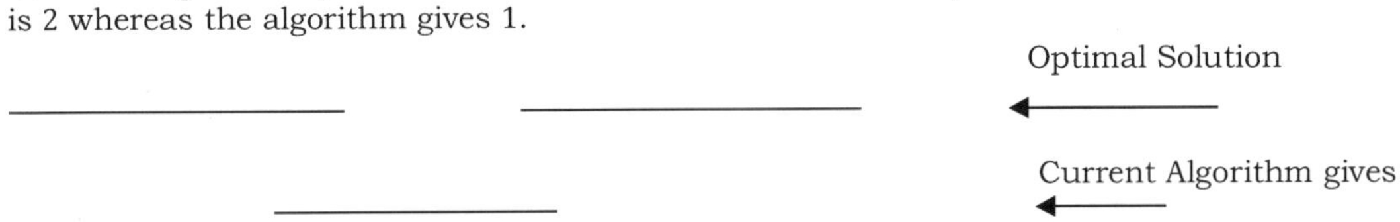

Problem-7 For Problem-4, what is the optimal solution?

Solution: Now, let us concentrate on the optimal greedy solution.

Algorithm:

Sort intervals according to the right-most ends [end times];
for every consecutive interval {
- If the left-most end is after the right-most end of the last selected interval then we select this interval
- Otherwise we skip it and go to the next interval

}

Time complexity = Time for sorting + Time for scanning = $O(nlogn + n) = O(nlogn)$.

Problem-8 Consider the following problem.
Input: $S = \{(start_i, end_i) | 1 \leq i \leq n\}$ of intervals. The interval $(start_i, end_i)$ we can treat as a request for a room for a class with time $start_i$ to time end_i.
Output: Find an assignment of classes to rooms that uses the fewest number of rooms.
Consider the following iterative algorithm. Assign as many classes as possible to the first room, then assign as many classes as possible to the second room, then assign as many classes as possible to the third room, etc. Does this algorithm give the best solution?

Note: In fact, this problem is similar to the interval scheduling algorithm. The only difference is the application.

Solution: This algorithm does not solve the interval-coloring problem. Consider the following intervals:

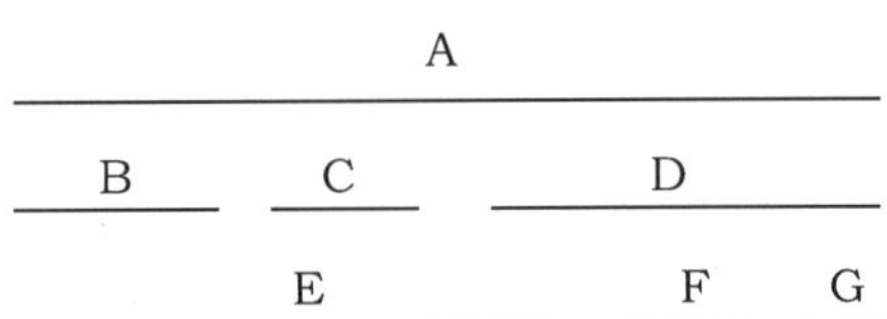

Maximizing the number of classes in the first room results in having $\{B, C, F, G\}$ in one room, and classes $A, D,$ and E each in their own rooms, for a total of 4. The optimal solution is to put A in one room, $\{B, C, D\}$ in another, and $\{E, F, G\}$ in another, for a total of 3 rooms.

Problem-9 For Problem-8, consider the following algorithm. Process the classes in increasing order of start times. Assume that we are processing class C. If there is a room R such that R has been assigned to an earlier class, and C can be assigned to R without overlapping previously assigned classes, then assign C to R. Otherwise, put C in a new room. Does this algorithm solve the problem?

Solution: This algorithm solves the interval-coloring problem. Note that if the greedy algorithm creates a new room for the current class c_i, then because it examines classes in order of start times, c_i start point must intersect with the last class in all of the current rooms. Thus when greedy creates the last room, n, it is because the start time of the current class intersects with $n - 1$ other classes. But we know that for any single point in any class it can only intersect with at most s other class, so it must then be that $n \leq S$. As s is a lower bound on the total number needed, and greedy is feasible, it is thus also optimal.

Note: For optimal solution refer to Problem-7 and for code refer to Problem-10.

Problem-10 Suppose we are given two arrays $Start[1..n]$ and $Finish[1..n]$ listing the start and finish times of each class. Our task is to choose the largest possible subset $X \in \{1,2,...,n\}$ so that for any pair $i,j \in X$, either $Start[i] > Finish[j]$ or $Start[j] > Finish[i]$

Solution: Our aim is to finish the first class as early as possible, because that leaves us with the most remaining classes. We scan through the classes in order of finish time, and whenever we encounter a class that doesn't conflict with the latest class so far, then we take that class.

```
func maxEvents(start, finish []int) int {
    sort.Slice(start, func(i, j int) bool {
        if finish[i] == finish[j] {
            return start[i] < start[j]
        }
        return finish[i] < finish[j]
    })
    m := make(map[int]bool)
    for j := 0; j < len(start); j++ {
        for i := start[j]; i <= finish[j]; i++ {
            if _, ok := m[i]; !ok {
                m[i] = true
                break
            }
        }
    }

    return len(m)
}
```

This algorithm clearly runs in O($nlogn$) time due to sorting.

Problem-11 Consider the making change problem in the country of India. The input to this problem is an integer M. The output should be the minimum number of coins to make M rupees of change. In India, assume the available coins are $1, 5, 10, 20, 25, 50$ rupees. Assume that we have an unlimited number of coins of each type.

For this problem, does the following algorithm produce the optimal solution or not? Take as many coins as possible from the highest denominations. So for example, to make change for 234 rupees the greedy algorithm would take four 50 rupee coins, one 25 rupee coin, one 5 rupee coin, and four 1 rupee coins.

Solution: The greedy algorithm is not optimal for the problem of making change with the minimum number of coins when the denominations are $1, 5, 10, 20, 25$, and 50. In order to make 40 rupees, the greedy algorithm would use three coins of $25, 10$, and 5 rupees. The optimal solution is to use two 20-shilling coins.

Note: For the optimal solution, refer to the *Dynamic Programming* chapter.

Problem-12 Let us assume that we are going for a long drive between cities A and B. In preparation for our trip, we have downloaded a map that contains the distances in miles between all the petrol stations on our route. Assume that our car's tanks can hold petrol for n miles. Assume that the value n is given. Suppose we stop at every point. Does it give the best solution?

Solution: Here the algorithm does not produce optimal solution. Obvious Reason: filling at each petrol station does not produce optimal solution.

Problem-13 For problem Problem-12, stop if and only if you don't have enough petrol to make it to the next gas station, and if you stop, fill the tank up all the way. Prove or disprove that this algorithm correctly solves the problem.

Solution: The greedy approach works: We start our trip from A with a full tank. We check our map to determine the farthest petrol station on our route within n miles. We stop at that petrol station, fill up our tank and check our map again to determine the farthest petrol station on our route within n miles from this stop. Repeat the process until we get to B.

Note: For code, refer to *Dynamic Programming* chapter.

Problem-14 **Fractional Knapsack problem:** Given items $t_1, t_2, ..., t_n$ (items we might want to carry in our backpack) with associated weights $s_1, s_2, ..., s_n$ and benefit values $v_1, v_2, ..., v_n$, how can we maximize the total benefit considering that we are subject to an absolute weight limit C?

Solution:

Algorithm:

1) Compute value per size density for each item $d_i = \frac{v_i}{s_i}$.
2) Sort each item by its value density.
3) Take as much as possible of the density item not already in the bag

```
import (
    "fmt"
    "sort"
)
type item struct {
    item   string
    weight float64
    value  float64
}
type items []item
var all = items{
    {"charger", 3.8, 36},
    {"rice", 5.4, 43},
    {"bread", 3.6, 90},
    {"grapes", 2.4, 45},
    {"apples", 4.0, 30},
    {"shirts", 2.5, 56},
    {"trousers", 3.7, 67},
    {"laptop", 3.0, 95},
    {"sausage", 5.9, 98},
}
// satisfy sort interface
func (z items) Len() int      { return len(z) }
func (z items) Swap(i, j int) { z[i], z[j] = z[j], z[i] }
func (z items) Less(i, j int) bool {
    return z[i].value/z[i].weight > z[j].value/z[j].weight
}
func main() {
    left := 15.
    sort.Sort(all)
    for _, i := range all {
        if i.weight <= left {
            fmt.Println("take all the", i.item)
            if i.weight == left {
                return
            }
            left -= i.weight
        } else {
            fmt.Printf("take %.1fkg %s\n", left, i.item)
            return
        }
    }
}
```

Time Complexity: $O(nlogn)$ for sorting and $O(n)$ for greedy selections.

Note: The items can be entered into a priority queue and retrieved one by one until either the bag is full or all items have been selected. This actually has a better runtime of $O(n + clogn)$ where c is the number of items that actually get selected in the solution. There is a savings in runtime if $c = O(n)$, but otherwise there is no change in the complexity.

Problem-15 **Number of railway-platforms:** At a railway station, we have a time-table with the trains' arrivals and departures. We need to find the minimum number of platforms so that all the trains can be accommodated as per their schedule.

Example: The timetable is as given below, the answer is 3. Otherwise, the railway station will not be able to accommodate all the trains.

Rail	Arrival	Departure
Rail A	0900 hrs	0930 hrs
Rail B	0915 hrs	1300 hrs

Rail C	1030 hrs	1100 hrs
Rail D	1045 hrs	1145 hrs

Solution: Let's take the same example as described above. Calculating the number of platforms is done by determining the maximum number of trains at the railway station at any time.

First, sort all the arrival(A) and departure(D) times in an array. Then, save the corresponding arrivals and departures in the array also. After sorting, our array will look like this:

0900	0915	0930	1030	1045	1100	1145	1300
A	A	D	A	A	D	D	D

Now modify the array by placing 1 for A and -1 for D. The new array will look like this:

1	1	-1	1	1	-1	-1	-1

Finally make a cumulative array out of this:

1	2	1	2	3	2	1	0

Our solution will be the maximum value in this array. Here it is 3.

Note: If we have a train arriving and another departing at the same time, then put the departure time first in the sorted array.

Problem-16 Consider a country with very long roads and houses along the road. Assume that the residents of all houses use cell phones. We want to place cell phone towers along the road, and each cell phone tower covers a range of 7 kilometers. Create an efficient algorithm that allow for the fewest cell phone towers.

Solution:

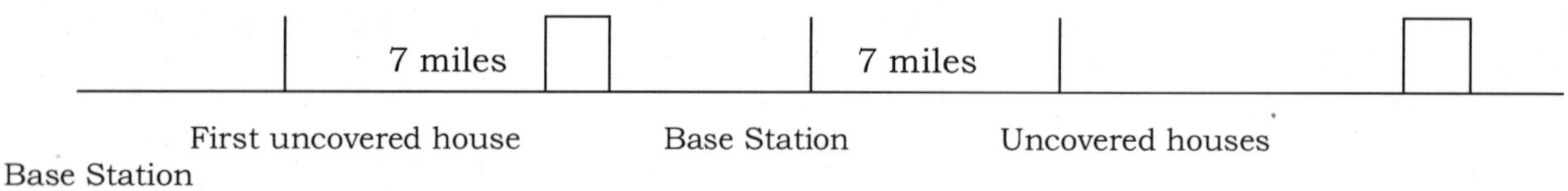

The algorithm to locate the least number of cell phone towers:

1) Start from the beginning of the road
2) Find the first uncovered house on the road
3) If there is no such house, terminate this algorithm. Otherwise, go to next step
4) Locate a cell phone tower 7 miles away after we find this house along the road
5) Go to step 2

Problem-17 **Preparing Songs Cassette:** Suppose we have a set of n songs and want to store these on a tape. In the future, users will want to read those songs from the tape. Reading a song from a tape is not like reading from a disk; first we have to fast-forward past all the other songs, and that takes a significant amount of time. Let $A[1..n]$ be an array listing the lengths of each song, specifically, song i has length $A[i]$. If the songs are stored in order from 1 to n, then the cost of accessing the kth song is:

$$C(k) = \sum_{i=1}^{k} A[i]$$

The cost reflects the fact that before we read song k we must first scan past all the earlier songs on the tape. If we change the order of the songs on the tape, we change the cost of accessing the songs, with the result that some songs become more expensive to read, but others become cheaper. Different song orders are likely to result in different expected costs. If we assume that each song is equally likely to be accessed, which order should we use if we want the expected cost to be as small as possible?

Solution: The answer is simple. We should store the songs in the order from shortest to longest. Storing the short songs at the beginning reduces the forwarding times for the remaining jobs.

Problem-18 Let us consider a set of events at *HITEX* (*Hyderabad Convention Center*). Assume that there are n events where each takes one unit of time. Event i will provide a profit of p_i ($p_i > 0$) if started at or before time t_i, where t_i is an arbitrary number. If an event is not started by t_i then there is no benefit in scheduling it at all. All events can start as early as time 0. Give the efficient algorithm to find a schedule that maximizes the profit.

Solution: This problem can be solved with greedy technique. The setting is that we have n events, each of which takes unit time, and a convention center on which we would like to schedule them in as profitable a manner as possible. Each event has a profit associated with it, as well as a deadline; if the event is not scheduled by the deadline, then we don't get the profit.

Because each event takes the same amount of time, we will think of a *Schedule* E as consisting of a sequence of event "slots" 0, 2, 3, . . . where $E(t)$ is the event scheduled in slot t.

More formally, the input is a sequence (t_0, p_0),(t_1, p_1), (t_2, p_2) $\cdots$,(t_{n-1}, p_{n-1}) where p_i is a nonnegative real number representing the profit obtainable from event i, and t_i is the deadline for event i. Notice that, even if some event deadlines were bigger than n, we can schedule them in a slot less than n as each event takes only one unit of time.

Algorithm:

1. Sort the events according to their profits p_i in the decreasing order.
2. Now, for each of the events:
   - Schedule event i in the latest possible free slot meeting its deadline.
   - If there is no such slot, do not schedule event i.

The sort takes O($nlogn$) and the scheduling take O(n) for n events. So, the overall running time of the algorithm is O($nlogn$) time.

Problem-19 Let us consider a customer-care server (say, mobile customer-care) with n customers to be served in the queue. For simplicity assume that the service time required by each customer is known in advance and it is w_i minutes for customer i. So if, for example, the customers are served in order of increasing i, then the ith customer has to wait: $\sum_{j=1}^{n-1} w_j$ *minutes*. The total waiting time of all customers can be given as = $\sum_{i=1}^{n} \sum_{j=1}^{i-1} w_j$. What is the best way to serve the customers so that the total waiting time can be reduced?

Solution: This problem can be easily solved using greedy technique. Since our objective is to reduce the total waiting time, what we can do is, select the customer whose service time is less. That means, if we process the customers in the increasing order of service time then we can reduce the total waiting time.

Time Complexity: O($nlogn$).

DIVIDE AND CONQUER ALGORITHMS

CHAPTER

18

18.1 Introduction

In the *Greedy* chapter, we have seen that for many problems the Greedy strategy failed to provide optimal solutions. Among those problems, there are some that can be easily solved by using the *Divide and Conquer* (D & C) technique. Divide and Conquer is an important algorithm design technique based on recursion.

The *D & C* algorithm works by recursively breaking down a problem into two or more sub problems of the same type, until they become simple enough to be solved directly. The solutions to the sub problems are then combined to give a solution to the original problem.

18.2 What is the Divide and Conquer Strategy?

The D & C strategy solves a problem by:

1) *Divide*: Breaking the problem into subproblems that are themselves smaller instances of the same type of problem.
2) *Conquer*: Conquer the subproblems by solving them recursively.
3) *Combine*: Combine the solutions to the subproblems into the solution for the original given problem.

18.3 Does Divide and Conquer Always Work?

It's not possible to solve all the problems with the Divide & Conquer technique. As per the definition of D & C, the recursion solves the subproblems which are of the same type. For all problems it is not possible to find the subproblems which are the same size and *D & C* is not a choice for all problems.

18.4 Divide and Conquer Visualization

For better understanding, consider the following visualization. Assume that n is the size of the original problem. As described above, we can see that the problem is divided into sub problems with each of size n/b (for some constant b). We solve the sub problems recursively and combine their solutions to get the solution for the original problem.

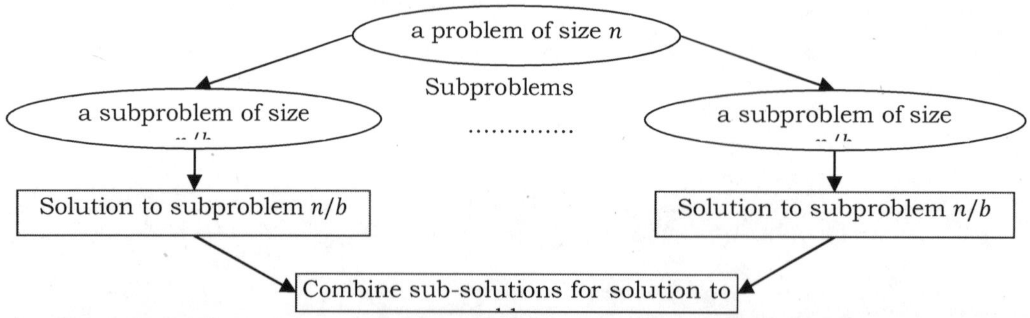


```
func DivideAndConquer ( P ) {
    if( small ( P ) )
        // P is very small so that a solution is obvious
        return solution ( n )
        divide the problem P into k sub problems P1, P2, ..., Pk
```

```
            return (
                Combine (
                DivideAndConquer ( P1 ),
                DivideAndConquer ( P2 ),
                ...
                DivideAndConquer ( Pk )
                )
        )
    }
```

18.5 Understanding Divide and Conquer

For a clear understanding of D & *C*, let us consider a story. There was an old man who was a rich farmer and had seven sons. He was afraid that when he died, his land and his possessions would be divided among his seven sons, and that they would quarrel with one another.

So he gathered them together and showed them seven sticks that he had tied together and told them that anyone who could break the bundle would inherit everything. They all tried, but no one could break the bundle. Then the old man untied the bundle and broke the sticks one by one. The brothers decided that they should stay together and work together and succeed together. The moral for problem solvers is different. If we can't solve the problem, divide it into parts, and solve one part at a time.

In earlier chapters we have already solved many problems based on *D* & *C* strategy: like Binary Search, Merge Sort, Quick Sort, etc.... Refer to those topics to get an idea of how *D* & *C* works. Below are a few other real-time problems which can easily be solved with *D* & *C* strategy. For all these problems we can find the subproblems which are similar to the original problem.

- Looking for a name in a phone book: We have a phone book with names in alphabetical order. Given a name, how do we find whether that name is there in the phone book or not?
- Breaking a stone into dust: We want to convert a stone into dust (very small stones).
- Finding the exit in a hotel: We are at the end of a very long hotel lobby with a long series of doors, with one door next to us. We are looking for the door that leads to the exit.
- Finding our car in a parking lot.

18.6 Advantages of Divide and Conquer

Solving difficult problems: *D* & *C* is a powerful method for solving difficult problems. As an example, consider the Tower of Hanoi problem. This requires breaking the problem into subproblems, solving the trivial cases and combining the subproblems to solve the original problem. Dividing the problem into subproblems so that subproblems can be combined again is a major difficulty in designing a new algorithm. For many such problems D & C provides a simple solution.

Parallelism: Since *D* & *C* allows us to solve the subproblems independently, this allows for execution in multi-processor machines, especially shared-memory systems where the communication of data between processors does not need to be planned in advance, because different subproblems can be executed on different processors.

Memory access: *D* & *C* algorithms naturally tend to make efficient use of memory caches. This is because once a subproblem is small, all its subproblems can be solved within the cache, without accessing the slower main memory.

18.7 Disadvantages of Divide and Conquer

One disadvantage of the *D* & *C* approach is that recursion is slow. This is because of the overhead of the repeated subproblem calls. Also, the *D* & *C* approach needs stack for storing the calls (the state at each point in the recursion). Actually this depends upon the implementation style. With large enough recursive base cases, the overhead of recursion can become negligible for many problems.

Another problem with *D* & *C* is that, for some problems, it may be more complicated than an iterative approach. For example, to add n numbers, a simple loop to add them up in sequence is much easier than a *D* & *C* approach that breaks the set of numbers into two halves, adds them recursively, and then adds the sums.

18.8 Master Theorem

As stated above, in the *D* & *C* method, we solve the sub problems recursively. All problems are generally defined in terms of recursive definitions. These recursive problems can easily be solved using Master theorem. For details on Master theorem, refer to the *Introduction to Analysis of Algorithms* chapter. Just for continuity, let us reconsider the Master theorem.

If the recurrence is of the form $T(n) = aT(\frac{n}{b}) + \Theta(n^k log^p n)$, where $a \geq 1, b > 1, k \geq 0$ and p is a real number, then the complexity can be directly given as:

1) If $a > b^k$, then $T(n) = \Theta(n^{log_b^a})$
2) If $a = b^k$
   a. If $p > -1$, then $T(n) = \Theta(n^{log_b^a} log^{p+1} n)$
   b. If $p = -1$, then $T(n) = \Theta(n^{log_b^a} loglogn)$
   c. If $p < -1$, then $T(n) = \Theta(n^{log_b^a})$
3) If $a < b^k$
   a. If $p \geq 0$, then $T(n) = \Theta(n^k log^p n)$
   b. If $p < 0$, then $T(n) = O(n^k)$

18.9 Divide and Conquer Applications

- Binary Search
- Merge Sort and Quick Sort
- Median Finding
- Min and Max Finding
- Matrix Multiplication
- Closest Pair problem

18.10 Divide and Conquer: Problems & Solutions

Problem-1 Let us consider an algorithm A which solves problems by dividing them into five subproblems of half the size, recursively solving each subproblem, and then combining the solutions in linear time. What is the complexity of this algorithm?

Solution: Let us assume that the input size is n and $T(n)$ defines the solution to the given problem. As per the description, the algorithm divides the problem into 5 sub problems with each of size $\frac{n}{2}$. So we need to solve $5T(\frac{n}{2})$ subproblems. After solving these sub problems, the given array (linear time) is scanned to combine these solutions. The total recurrence algorithm for this problem can be given as: $T(n) = 5T\left(\frac{n}{2}\right) + O(n)$. Using the Master theorem (of D & C), we get the complexity as $O(n^{log_2^5}) \approx O(n^{2+}) \approx O(n^3)$.

Problem-2 Similar to Problem-1, an algorithm B solves problems of size n by recursively solving two subproblems of size $n - 1$ and then combining the solutions in constant time. What is the complexity of this algorithm?

Solution: Let us assume that the input size is n and $T(n)$ defines the solution to the given problem. As per the description of algorithm we divide the problem into 2 sub problems with each of size $n - 1$. So we have to solve $2T(n-1)$ sub problems. After solving these sub problems, the algorithm takes only a constant time to combine these solutions. The total recurrence algorithm for this problem can be given as:

$$T(n) = 2T(n-1) + O(1)$$

Using Master theorem (of *Subtract and Conquer*), we get the complexity as $O\left(n^0 2^{\frac{n}{1}}\right) = O(2^n)$. (Refer to *Introduction* chapter for more details).

Problem-3 Again similar to Problem-1, another algorithm C solves problems of size n by dividing them into nine subproblems of size $\frac{n}{3}$, recursively solving each subproblem, and then combining the solutions in $O(n^2)$ time. What is the complexity of this algorithm?

Solution: Let us assume that input size is n and $T(n)$ defines the solution to the given problem. As per the description of algorithm we divide the problem into 9 sub problems with each of size $\frac{n}{3}$. So we need to solve $9T(\frac{n}{3})$ sub problems. After solving the sub problems, the algorithm takes quadratic time to combine these solutions. The total recurrence algorithm for this problem can be given as: $T(n) = 9T\left(\frac{n}{3}\right) + O(n^2)$. Using D & C Master theorem, we get the complexity as $O(n^2 logn)$.

Problem-4 Write a recurrence and solve it.

```
func function(n int) {
    if n > 1 {
        fmt.Println("*")
        function(n / 2)
        function(n / 2)
    }
}
```

Solution: Let us assume that input size is n and $T(n)$ defines the solution to the given problem. As per the given code, after printing the character and dividing the problem into 2 subproblems with each of size $\frac{n}{2}$ and solving them. So we need to solve $2T(\frac{n}{2})$ subproblems. After solving these subproblems, the algorithm is not doing anything for combining the solutions. The total recurrence algorithm for this problem can be given as:

$$T(n) = 2T\left(\frac{n}{2}\right) + O(1)$$

Using Master theorem (of D & C), we get the complexity as $O\left(n^{log_2^2}\right) \approx O(n^1) = O(n)$.

Problem-5 Given an array, give an algorithm for finding the maximum and minimum.

Solution: Refer to *Selection Algorithms* chapter.

Problem-6 Discuss Binary Search and its complexity.

Solution: Refer to *Searching* chapter for discussion on Binary Search.

Analysis: Let us assume that input size is n and $T(n)$ defines the solution to the given problem. The elements are in sorted order. In binary search we take the middle element and check whether the element to be searched is equal to that element or not. If it is equal then we return that element.

If the element to be searched is less than the middle element then we consider the left sub-array for finding the element and discard the right sub-array. Similarly, if the element to be searched is greater than the middle element then we consider the right sub-array for finding the element and discard the left sub-array.

What this means is, in both the cases we are discarding half of the sub-array and considering the remaining half only. Also, at every iteration we are dividing the elements into two equal halves.

As per the above discussion every time we divide the problem into 2 sub problems with each of size $\frac{n}{2}$ and solve one $T(\frac{n}{2})$ sub problem. The total recurrence algorithm for this problem can be given as:

$$T(n) = 2T\left(\frac{n}{2}\right) + O(1)$$

Using Master theorem (of D & C), we get the complexity as $O(logn)$.

Problem-7 Consider the modified version of binary search. Let us assume that the array is divided into 3 equal parts (ternary search) instead of 2 equal parts. Write the recurrence for this ternary search and find its complexity.

Solution: From the discussion on Problem-5, binary search has the recurrence relation: $T(n) = T\left(\frac{n}{2}\right) + O(1)$. Similar to the Problem-5 discussion, instead of 2 in the recurrence relation we use "3". That indicates that we are dividing the array into 3 sub-arrays with equal size and considering only one of them. So, the recurrence for the ternary search can be given as:

$$T(n) = T\left(\frac{n}{3}\right) + O(1)$$

Using Master theorem (of D & C), we get the complexity as $O(log_3^n) \approx O(logn)$ (we don't have to worry about the base of log as they are constants).

Problem-8 In Problem-5, what if we divide the array into two sets of sizes approximately one-third and two-thirds.

Solution: We now consider a slightly modified version of ternary search in which only one comparison is made, which creates two partitions, one of roughly $\frac{n}{3}$ elements and the other of $\frac{2n}{3}$. Here the worst case comes when the recursive call is on the larger $\frac{2n}{3}$ element part. So the recurrence corresponding to this worst case is:

$$T(n) = T\left(\frac{2n}{3}\right) + O(1)$$

Using Master theorem (of D & C), we get the complexity as $O(logn)$. It is interesting to note that we will get the same results for general k-ary search (as long as k is a fixed constant which does not depend on n) as n approaches infinity.

Problem-9 Discuss Merge Sort and its complexity.

Solution: Refer to *Sorting* chapter for discussion on Merge Sort. In Merge Sort, if the number of elements are greater than 1, then divide them into two equal subsets, the algorithm is recursively invoked on the subsets, and the returned sorted subsets are merged to provide a sorted list of the original set. The recurrence equation of the Merge Sort algorithm is:

$$T(n) = \begin{cases} 2T\left(\frac{n}{2}\right) + O(n), if\ n > 1 \\ 0 \qquad\qquad\qquad ,if n = 1 \end{cases}$$

If we solve this recurrence using D & C Master theorem it gives O(nlogn) complexity.

Problem-10 Discuss Quick Sort and its complexity.

Solution: Refer to *Sorting* chapter for discussion on Quick Sort. For Quick Sort we have different complexities for best case and worst case.

Best Case: In *Quick Sort,* if the number of elements is greater than 1 then they are divided into two equal subsets, and the algorithm is recursively invoked on the subsets. After solving the sub problems we don't need to combine them. This is because in *Quick Sort* they are already in sorted order. But, we need to scan the complete elements to partition the elements. The recurrence equation of *Quick Sort* best case is

$$T(n) = \begin{cases} 2T\left(\frac{n}{2}\right) + O(n), if\ n > 1 \\ 0 \qquad\qquad\qquad , if n = 1 \end{cases}$$

If we solve this recurrence using Master theorem of D & C gives $O(nlogn)$ complexity.

Worst Case: In the worst case, Quick Sort divides the input elements into two sets and one of them contains only one element. That means other set has $n - 1$ elements to be sorted. Let us assume that the input size is n and $T(n)$ defines the solution to the given problem. So we need to solve $T(n - 1)$, $T(1)$ subproblems. But to divide the input into two sets Quick Sort needs one scan of the input elements (this takes $O(n)$).

After solving these sub problems the algorithm takes only a constant time to combine these solutions. The total recurrence algorithm for this problem can be given as:

$$T(n) = T(n - 1) + O(1) + O(n)$$

This is clearly a summation recurrence equation. So, $T(n) = \frac{n(n+1)}{2} = O(n^2)$.

Note: For the average case analysis, refer to *Sorting* chapter.

Problem-11 Given an infinite array in which the first n cells contain integers in sorted order and the rest of the cells are filled with some special symbol (say, $). Assume we do not know the n value. Give an algorithm that takes an integer K as input and finds a position in the array containing K, if such a position exists, in $O(logn)$ time.

Solution: In the infinite array, we don't know the upper bound to apply the binary search. So simple solution we could think to start searching for K linearly from index 0 until you find an element equal to K, then return the index. If you find an element greater than K, then return -1. Let i be the position of the element to be searched, then the time Complexity is O(i), and the space complexity would be O(1).

Since, we know that the array is sorted, we use this info to improve the time complexity, right? If we can track the interval (with the lower and upper bound) where target value reside then we can apply the binary search in that interval. Here we maintain the interval size by constant value C.

Note: In a sorted array, if we check an element at any index j, we could logically know the relative position of element K with respect to A[j].

Algorithm

- Initialize lower and upper index of the interval i.e. left = 0 , right = C.
- Compare the K with the value present at the upper index of the interval.
- if K > A[right] then copy the upper index in the lower index and increase the upper index by C. Keep on doing this until you reach a value that is greater than K.
- If K < A[right], apply binary search in the interval from left to right.
- If found, return the index else return -1.

```
func searchInfiniteArray(A []int, K int) {
    left, right := 0, C
    for A[right] < K {
        left = right
        right = right + C
    }
    return binarySearch(A, left, right, K)
}
```

Let i be the position of the element to be searched, then the number of iterations for finding upper index *right* is equal to $\frac{i}{C}$ in the worst case. Hence, the total time complexity would include the time complexity for finding the upper index *right* of the interval and the binary search in the interval from left to right = $O(\frac{i}{C})$ + $O(logC)$ = $O(i)$.

How should we optimally choose the value of C ? What will happen when we choose a very large arbitrary value? Since we need an $O(logn)$ algorithm, we should not search for all the elements of the given list (which gives $O(n)$ complexity). To get $O(logn)$ complexity one possibility is to use binary search. But in the given scenario, we cannot use binary search as we do not know the end of the list. Our first problem is to find the end of the list. To do that, we can start at the first element and keep searching with doubled index. That means we first search at index 1 then, 2, 4, 8 ... In this approach, we increase the interval size by an exponential order of 2. We call this approach exponential search which helps us to track the upper bound quickly in comparison to the previous approach.

```
func searchInfiniteArray(A []int, K int) {
    left, right := 0, 1
    for A[right] < K {
        left = right
        right = 2 * right
    }
    return binarySearch(A, left, right, K)
}
```

It is clear that, once we have identified a possible interval $A[i,\ldots,2i]$ in which K might be, its length is at most n (since we have only n numbers in the array A), so searching for K using binary search takes $O(logn)$ time.

Problem-12 Given a sorted array of non-repeated integers $A[1..n]$, check whether there is an index i for which $A[i] = i$. Give a divide-and-conquer algorithm that runs in time $O(logn)$.

Solution: We can't use binary search on the array as it is. If we want to keep the $O(logn)$ property of the solution we have to implement our own binary search. If we modify the array (in place or in a copy) and subtract i from A[i], we can then use binary search. The complexity for doing so is $O(n)$.

Problem-13 We are given two sorted lists of size n. Give an algorithm for finding the median element in the union of the two lists.

Solution: We use the Merge Sort process. Use *merge* procedure of merge sort (refer to *Sorting* chapter). Keep track of the count while comparing elements of two arrays. If the count becomes n (since there are $2n$ elements), we have reached the median. Take the average of the elements at indexes $n-1$ and n in the merged array.

Time Complexity: $O(n)$.

Problem-14 Can we give the algorithm if the size of the two lists are not the same?

Solution: The solution is similar to the previous problem. Let us assume that the lengths of two lists are m and n. In this case we need to stop when the counter reaches $\frac{m+n}{2}$.

Time Complexity: $O((m+n)/2)$.

Problem-15 Can we improve the time complexity of Problem-13 to $O(logn)$?

Solution: Yes, using the D & C approach. Let us assume that the given two lists are $L1$ and $L2$.

Algorithm:

1. Find the medians of the given sorted input arrays $L1[]$ and $L2[]$. Assume that those medians are $m1$ and $m2$.
2. If $m1$ and $m2$ are equal then return $m1$ (or $m2$).
3. If $m1$ is greater than $m2$, then the final median will be below two sub arrays.
4. From first element of $L1$ to $m1$.
5. From $m2$ to last element of $L2$.
6. If $m2$ is greater than $m1$, then median is present in one of the two sub arrays below.
7. From $m1$ to last element of $L1$.
8. From first element of $L2$ to $m2$.
9. Repeat the above process until the size of both the sub arrays becomes 2.
10. If size of the two arrays is 2, then use the formula below to get the median.
11. Median = $(max(L1[0], L2[0]) + \frac{min(L1[1], L2[1])}{2}$

Time Complexity: $O(logn)$ since we are considering only half of the input and throwing the remaining half.

Problem-16 Given an input array A. Let us assume that there can be duplicates in the list. Now search for an element in the list in such a way that we get the highest index if there are duplicates.

Solution: Refer to *Searching* chapter.

Problem-17 Discuss Strassen's Matrix Multiplication Algorithm using Divide and Conquer. That means, given two $n \times n$ matrices, A and B, compute the $n \times n$ matrix $C = A \times B$, where the elements of C are given by

$$C_{i,j} = \sum_{k=0}^{n-1} A_{i,k} B_{k,j}$$

Solution: Before Strassen's algorithm, first let us see the basic divide and conquer algorithm. The general approach we follow for solving this problem is given below. To determine, $C[i,j]$ we need to multiply the ith row of A with j^{th} column of B.

```
func multiply(A, B Matrix) (C Matrix, ok bool) {
    rows, cols, extra := len(A), len(B[0]), len(B)
    if len(A[0]) != extra {
        return nil, false
    }
    C = make(Matrix, rows)
    for i := 0; i < rows; i++ {
        C[i] = make([]int, cols)
        for j := 0; j < cols; j++ {
            for k := 0; k < extra; k++ {
                C[i][j] += A[i][k] * B[k][j]
            }
        }
    }
    return C, true
}
```

The matrix multiplication problem can be solved with the D & C technique. To implement a D & C algorithm we need to break the given problem into several subproblems that are similar to the original one. In this instance we view each of the $n \times n$ matrices as a 2×2 matrix, the elements of which are $\frac{n}{2} \times \frac{n}{2}$ submatrices. So, the original matrix multiplication, $C = A \times B$ can be written as:

$$\begin{bmatrix} C_{1,1} & C_{1,2} \\ C_{2,1} & C_{2,2} \end{bmatrix} = \begin{bmatrix} A_{1,1} & A_{1,2} \\ A_{2,1} & A_{2,2} \end{bmatrix} \times \begin{bmatrix} B_{1,1} & B_{1,2} \\ B_{2,1} & B_{2,2} \end{bmatrix}$$

where each $A_{i,j}$, $B_{i,j}$, and $C_{i,j}$ is a $\frac{n}{2} \times \frac{n}{2}$ matrix.

From the given definition o f $C_{i,j}$, we get that the result sub matrices can be computed as follows:

$$\begin{aligned} C_{1,1} &= A_{1,1} \times B_{1,1} + A_{1,2} \times B_{2,1} \\ C_{1,2} &= A_{1,1} \times B_{1,2} + A_{1,2} \times B_{2,2} \\ C_{2,1} &= A_{2,1} \times B_{1,1} + A_{2,2} \times B_{2,1} \\ C_{2,2} &= A_{2,1} \times B_{1,2} + A_{2,2} \times B_{2,2} \end{aligned}$$

Here the symbols + and × are taken to mean addition and multiplication (respectively) of $\frac{n}{2} \times \frac{n}{2}$ matrices.

In order to compute the original $n \times n$ matrix multiplication we must compute eight $\frac{n}{2} \times \frac{n}{2}$ matrix products (*divide*) followed by four $\frac{n}{2} \times \frac{n}{2}$ matrix sums (*conquer*). Since matrix addition is an $O(n^2)$ operation, the total running time for the multiplication operation is given by the recurrence:

$$T(n) = \begin{cases} O(1) & , for\ n = 1 \\ 8T\left(\frac{n}{2}\right) + O(n^2) & , for\ n > 1 \end{cases}$$

Using master theorem, we get $T(n) = O(n^3)$.

Fortunately, it turns out that one of the eight matrix multiplications is redundant (found by Strassen). Consider the following series of seven $\frac{n}{2} \times \frac{n}{2}$ matrices:

$$\begin{aligned} M_0 &= (A_{1,1} + A_{2,2}) \times (B_{1,1} + B_{2,2}) \\ M_1 &= (A_{1,2} - A_{2,2}) \times (B_{2,1} + B_{2,2}) \\ M_2 &= (A_{1,1} - A_{2,1}) \times (B_{1,1} + B_{1,2}) \\ M_3 &= (A_{1,1} + A_{1,2}) \times B_{2,2} \\ M_4 &= A_{1,1} \times (B_{1,2} - B_{2,2}) \\ M_5 &= A_{2,2} \times (B_{2,1} - B_{1,1}) \\ M_6 &= (A_{21} + A_{2,2}) \times B_{1,1} \end{aligned}$$

Each equation above has only one multiplication. Ten additions and seven multiplications are required to compute M_0 through M_6. Given M_0 through M_6, we can compute the elements of the product matrix C as follows:

$$\begin{aligned} C_{1,1} &= M_0 + M_1 - M_3 + M_5 \\ C_{1,2} &= M_3 + M_4 \\ C_{2,1} &= M_5 + M_6 \\ C_{2,2} &= M_0 - M_2 + M_4 - M_6 \end{aligned}$$

This approach requires seven $\frac{n}{2} \times \frac{n}{2}$ matrix multiplications and 18 $\frac{n}{2} \times \frac{n}{2}$ additions. Therefore, the worst-case running time is given by the following recurrence:

$$T(n) = \begin{cases} O(1) & , for\ n = 1 \\ 7T\left(\frac{n}{2}\right) + O(n^2) & , for\ n = 1 \end{cases}$$

Using master theorem, we get, $T(n) = O(n^{log_2^7}) = O(n^{2.81})$.

Problem-18 **Stock Pricing Problem:** Consider the stock price of *CareerMonk.com* in n consecutive days. That means the input consists of an array with stock prices of the company. We know that the stock price will not be the same on all the days. In the input stock prices there may be dates where the stock is high when we can sell the current holdings, and there may be days when we can buy the stock. Now our problem is to find the day on which we can buy the stock and the day on which we can sell the stock so that we can make maximum profit.

Solution: As given in the problem, let us assume that the input is an array with stock prices [integers]. Let us say the given array is $A[1], \ldots, A[n]$. From this array we have to find two days [one for buy and one for sell] in such a way that we can make maximum profit. Also, another point to make is that the buy date should be before sell date. One simple approach is to look at all possible buy and sell dates.

```
func stockStrategy(A []int) []int {
    buyDateIndex, sellDateIndex, profit, n := 0, 0, 0, len(A)
    for i := 0; i < n; i++ {                //indicates buy date
        for j := i + 1; j < n; j++ {        //indicates sell date
            if A[j]-A[i] > profit {
                profit = A[j] - A[i]
                buyDateIndex = i
                sellDateIndex = j
            }
        }
    }
    return []int{profit, buyDateIndex, sellDateIndex}
}
```

The two nested loops take $\frac{n(n+1)}{2}$ computations, so this takes time $\Theta(n^2)$.

Problem-19 For Problem-18, can we improve the time complexity?

Solution: Yes, by opting for the Divide-and-Conquer $\Theta(nlogn)$ solution. Divide the input list into two parts and recursively find the solution in both the parts. Here, we get three cases:

- *buyDateIndex* and *sellDateIndex* both are in the earlier time period.
- *buyDateIndex* and *sellDateIndex* both are in the later time period.
- *buyDateIndex* is in the earlier part and *sellDateIndex* is in the later part of the time period.

The first two cases can be solved with recursion. The third case needs care. This is because *buyDateIndex* is one side and *sellDateIndex* is on other side. In this case we need to find the minimum and maximum prices in the two sub-parts and this we can solve in linear-time.

```
func stockStrategy(prices []int, left, right int) (int, int, int) {
    // If the array has just one element, we return that the profit is zero
    // but the minimum and maximum values are just that array value.
    if left == right {
        return 0, left, right
    }
    mid := left + (right-left)/2
    leftProfit, leftBuyDateIndex, leftSellDateIndex := stockStrategy(prices, left, mid)
    rightProfit, rightBuyDateIndex, rightSellDateIndex := stockStrategy(prices, mid+1, right)
    minIndexLeft := minIndex(prices, left, mid)
    maxIndexRight := maxIndex(prices, mid+1, right)
    centerProfit := prices[maxIndexRight] - prices[minIndexLeft]
    if (centerProfit > leftProfit) && (centerProfit > rightProfit) {
        return centerProfit, minIndexLeft, maxIndexRight
    } else if (leftProfit > centerProfit) && (leftProfit > rightProfit) {
        return leftProfit, leftBuyDateIndex, leftSellDateIndex
    } else {
        return rightProfit, rightBuyDateIndex, rightSellDateIndex
    }
}
```

Algorithm *stockStrategy* is used recursively on two problems of half the size of the input, and in addition $\Theta(n)$ time is spent searching for the maximum and minimum prices. So, the time complexity is characterized by the recurrence $T(n) = 2T(n/2) + \Theta(n)$ and by the Master theorem we get O(nlogn).

Problem-20 We are testing "unbreakable" laptops and our goal is to find out how unbreakable they really are. In particular, we work in an n-story building and want to find out the lowest floor from which we can drop the laptop without breaking it (call this "the ceiling"). Suppose we are given two laptops and want to find the highest ceiling possible. Give an algorithm that minimizes the number of tries we need to make $f(n)$ (hopefully, $f(n)$ is sub-linear, as a linear $f(n)$ yields a trivial solution).

Solution: For the given problem, we cannot use binary search as we cannot divide the problem and solve it recursively. Let us take an example for understanding the scenario. Let us say 14 is the answer. That means we need 14 drops to find the answer. First we drop from height 14, and if it breaks we try all floors from 1 to 13. If it doesn't break then we are left 13 drops, so we will drop it from $14 + 13 + 1 = 28^{th}$ floor. The reason being if it breaks at the 28th floor we can try all the floors from 15 to 27 in 12 drops (total of 14 drops). If it did not break, then we are left with 11 drops and we can try to figure out the floor in 14 drops.

From the above example, it can be seen that we first tried with a gap of 14 floors, and then followed by 13 floors, then 12 and so on. So if the answer is k then we are trying the intervals at $k, k-1, k-2 \ldots .1$. Given that the number of floors is n, we have to relate these two. Since the maximum floor from which we can try is n, the total skips should be less than n. This gives:

$$k + (k-1) + (k-2) + \cdots + 1 \le n$$
$$\frac{k(k+1)}{2} \le n$$
$$k \le \sqrt{n}$$

Complexity of this process is $O(\sqrt{n})$.

Problem-21 Given n numbers, check if any two are equal.

Solution: Refer to *Searching* chapter.

Problem-22 Give an algorithm to find out if an integer is a square? E.g. 16 is, 15 isn't.

Solution: Initially let us say $i = 2$. Compute the value $i \times i$ and see if it is equal to the given number. If it is equal then we are done; otherwise increment the **i** vlaue. Continue this process until we reach $i \times i$ greater than or equal to the given number.

Time Complexity: $O(\sqrt{n})$. Space Complexity: O(1).

Problem-23 Given an array of $2n$ integers in the following format $a1\ a2\ a3 \ldots an\ b1\ b2\ b3 \ldots bn$. Shuffle the array to $a1\ b1\ a2\ b2\ a3\ b3 \ldots an\ bn$ without any extra memory.

Solution: A simple brute force solution involves two nested loops to rotate the elements in the second half of the array to the left. The first loop runs n times to cover all elements in the second half of the array. The second loop rotates the elements to the left. Note that the start index in the second loop depends on which element we are rotating and the end index depends on how many positions we need to move to the left.

```
func shuffleArray1(A []int, left, right int) {
    n := len(A) / 2
    for i, q, k := 0, 1, n; i < n; i, k, q = i+1, k+1, q+1 {
        for j := k; j > i+q; j-- {
            A[j-1], A[j] = A[j], A[j-1]
        }
    }
}
```

A better solution of time complexity O($nlogn$) can be achieved using Divide and Concur technique. Let us take an example:

1. Start with the array: $a1\ a2\ a3\ a4\ b1\ b2\ b3\ b4$
2. Split the array into two halves: $a1\ a2\ a3\ a4 : b1\ b2\ b3\ b4$
3. Exchange elements around the center: exchange $a3\ a4$ with $b1\ b2$ you get: $a1\ a2\ b1\ b2\ a3\ a4\ b3\ b4$
4. Split $a1\ a2\ b1\ b2$ into $a1\ a2 : b1\ b2$ then split $a3\ a4\ b3\ b4$ into $a3\ a4 : b3\ b4$
5. Exchange elements around the center for each subarray you get: $a1\ b1\ a2\ b2$ and $a3\ b3\ a4\ b4$

Note that, this solution only handles the case when $n = 2^i$ where $i = 0, 1, 2, 3$, etc. In our example $n = 2^2 = 4$ which makes it easy to recursively split the array into two halves. The basic idea behind swapping elements around the center before calling the recursive function is to produce smaller size problems. A solution with linear time complexity may be achieved if the elements are of a specific nature. For example you can calculate the new position of the element using the value of the element itself. This is a hashing technique.

```
func shuffleArray2(A []int, left, right int) {
    c := left + (right-left)/2
    q := 1 + left + (c-left)/2
    if left == right {                  //base case when the array has only one element
        return
    }
    k, i := 1, q
    for i <= c {
        //swap elements around the center
        A[i], A[c+k] = A[c+k], A[i]
        i++
        k++
    }
    shuffleArray2(A, left, c)           //Recursively call the function on the left and right
    shuffleArray2(A, c+1, right)        //Recursively call the function on the right
}
```

Time Complexity: $O(nlogn)$.

Problem-24 **Nuts and Bolts Problem:** Given a set of n nuts of different sizes and n bolts such that there is a one-to-one correspondence between the nuts and the bolts, find for each nut its corresponding bolt. Assume that we can only compare nuts to bolts (cannot compare nuts to nuts and bolts to bolts).

Solution: Refer to *Sorting* chapter.

Problem-25 **Maximum Value Contiguous Subsequence:** Given a sequence of n numbers $A(1) \ldots A(n)$, give an algorithm for finding a contiguous subsequence $A(i) \ldots A(j)$ for which the sum of elements in the subsequence is maximum. **Example**: {-2, **11, -4, 13**, -5, 2} → 20 and {1, -3, **4, -2, -1, 6**} → 7.

Solution: Divide this input into two halves. The maximum contiguous subsequence sum can occur in one of 3 ways:

- Case 1: It can be completely in the first half
- Case 2: It can be completely in the second half
- Case 3: It begins in the first half and ends in the second half

We begin by looking at case 3. To avoid the nested loop that results from considering all $n/2$ starting points and $n/2$ ending points independently, replace two nested loops with two consecutive loops. The consecutive loops, each of size $n/2$, combine to require only linear work. Any contiguous subsequence that begins in the first half and ends in the second half must include both the last element of the first half and the first element of the second half. What we can do in cases 1 and 2 is apply the same strategy of dividing into more halves. In summary, we do the following:

1. Recursively compute the maximum contiguous subsequence that resides entirely in the first half.
2. Recursively compute the maximum contiguous subsequence that resides entirely in the second half.
3. Compute, via two consecutive loops, the maximum contiguous subsequence sum that begins in the first half but ends in the second half.
4. Choose the largest of the three sums.

```
func maxSubArray(A []int) int {
    length := len(A)
    low := 0
    high := length - 1
    _, _, sum := findMaxSubArray(A, low, high)
    return sum
}
func findMaxSubArray(A []int, low int, high int) (int, int, int) {
    if high == low {
        return low, high, A[low]
    } else {
        mid := (low + high) / 2
        leftLow, leftHigh, leftSum := findMaxSubArray(A, low, mid)
        rightLow, rightHigh, rightSum := findMaxSubArray(A, mid+1, high)
        crossLow, crossHigh, crossSum := maxCrossingSubArray(A, low, high, mid)
        if (leftSum >= rightSum) && (leftSum >= crossSum) {
            return leftLow, leftHigh, leftSum
        } else if rightSum >= leftSum && rightSum >= crossSum {
```

```
            return rightLow, rightHigh, rightSum
        } else {
            return crossLow, crossHigh, crossSum
        }
    }
}
func maxCrossingSubArray(A []int, low, high, mid int) (int, int, int) {
    leftSum := math.MinInt32
    rightSum := math.MinInt32
    maxLeft, maxRight, sum := 0, 0, 0
    for i := mid; i >= low; i-- {
        sum += A[i]
        if sum > leftSum {
            leftSum = sum
            maxLeft = i
        }
    }
    sum = 0
    for i := mid + 1; i <= high; i++ {
        sum += A[i]
        if sum > rightSum {
            rightSum = sum
            maxRight = i
        }
    }
    return maxLeft, maxRight, (leftSum + rightSum)
}
```

The base case cost is 1. The program performs two recursive calls plus the linear work involved in computing the maximum sum for case 3. The recurrence relation is:

$$T(1) = 1$$
$$T(n) = 2T(n/2) + n$$

Using D & C Master theorem, we get the time complexity as $T(n) = O(nlogn)$.

Note: For an efficient solution refer to *Dynamic Programming* chapter.

Problem-26 **Closest-Pair of Points:** Given a set of n points, $S = \{p_1, p_2, p_3, \dots, p_n\}$, where $p_i = (x_i, y_i)$. Find the pair of points having the smallest distance among all pairs (assume that all points are in one dimension).

Solution: Let us assume that we have sorted the points. Since the points are in one dimension, all the points are in a line after we sort them (either on X-axis or Y-axis). The complexity of sorting is $O(nlogn)$. After sorting we can go through them to find the consecutive points with the least difference. So the problem in one dimension is solved in $O(nlogn)$ time which is mainly dominated by sorting time.

Time Complexity: $O(nlogn)$.

Problem-27 For Problem-26, how do we solve it if the points are in two-dimensional space?

Solution: Before going to the algorithm, let us consider the following mathematical equation:

$$distance(p_1, p_2) = \sqrt{(x_1 - x_2)^2 - (y_1 - y_2)^2}$$

The above equation calculates the distance between two points $p_1 = (x_1, y_1)$ and $p_2 = (x_2, y_2)$.

Brute Force Solution:

- Calculate the distances between all the pairs of points. From n points there are n_{c_2} ways of selecting 2 points. ($n_{c_2} = O(n^2)$).
- After finding distances for all n^2 possibilities, we select the one which is giving the minimum distance and this takes $O(n^2)$.

```
type xy struct {
    x, y float64 // coordinates
}
const n = 1000
// size of bounding box for points. x and y will be random with uniform distribution in the range [0,scale).
const scale = 100.
func d(p1, p2 xy) float64 {
    return math.Hypot(p2.x-p1.x, p2.y-p1.y)
```

```
}
func closestPair(points []xy) (p1, p2 xy) {
    if len(points) < 2 {
        panic("at least two points expected")
    }
    min := 2 * scale
    for i, q1 := range points[:len(points)-1] {
        for _, q2 := range points[i+1:] {
            if dq := d(q1, q2); dq < min {
                p1, p2 = q1, q2
                min = dq
            }
        }
    }
    return
}
func main() {
    rand.Seed(time.Now().Unix())
    points := make([]xy, n)
    for i := range points {
        points[i] = xy{rand.Float64() * scale, rand.Float64() * scale}
    }
    p1, p2 := closestPair(points)
    fmt.Println(p1, p2)
    fmt.Println("distance:", d(p1, p2))
}
```

The overall time complexity is $O(n^2)$.

Problem-28 Give $O(nlogn)$ solution for the *closest pair* problem (Problem-27)?

Solution: To find $O(nlogn)$ solution, we can use the D & C technique. Before starting the divide-and-conquer process let us assume that the points are sorted by increasing x-coordinate. Divide the points into two equal halves based on median of x-coordinates. That means the problem is divided into that of finding the closest pair in each of the two halves. For simplicity let us consider the following algorithm to understand the process.

Algorithm:

1) Sort the given points in S (given set of points) based on their x –coordinates. Partition S into two subsets, S_1 and S_2, about the line l through median of S. This step is the *Divide* part of the D & C technique.
2) Find the closest-pairs in S_1 and S_2 and call them L and R recursively.
3) Now, steps 4 to 8 form the Combining component of the D & C technique.
4) Let us assume that $\delta = min(L, R)$.
5) Eliminate points that are farther than δ apart from l.
6) Consider the remaining points and sort based on their y-coordinates.
7) Scan the remaining points in the y order and compute the distances of each point to all its neighbors that are distanced no more than $2 \times \delta$ (that's the reason for sorting according to y).
8) If any of these distances is less than δ then update δ.

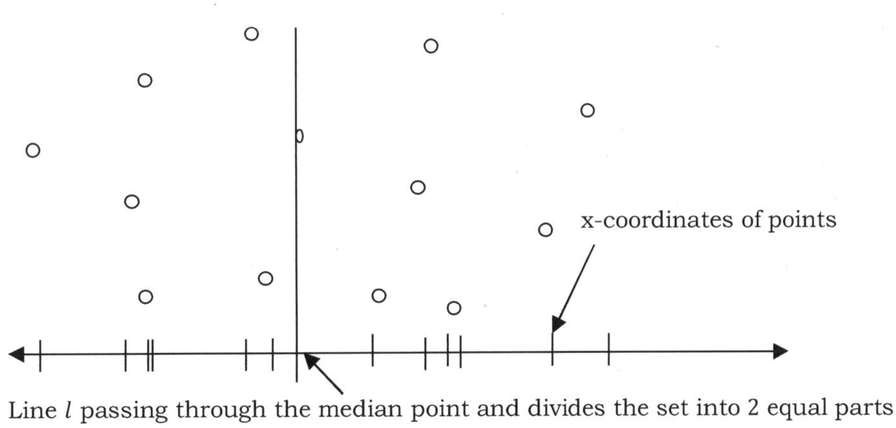

Combining the results in linear time

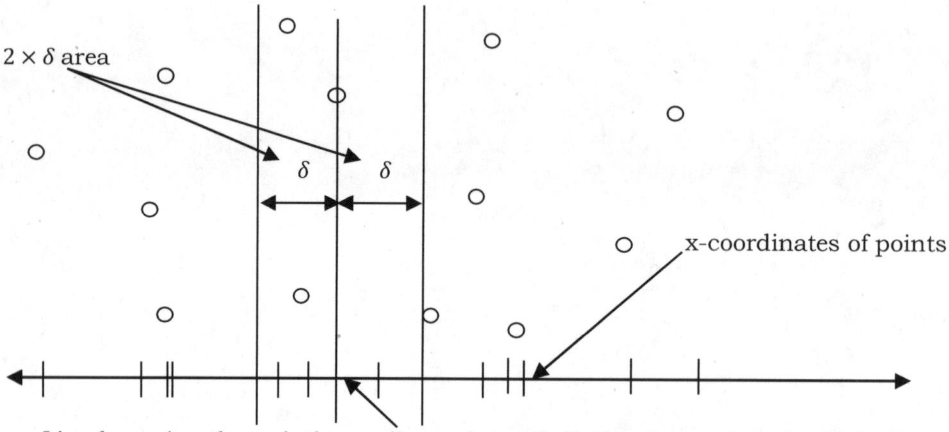

Line l passing through the median point and divides the set into 2 equal parts

Let $\delta = min(L, R)$, where L is the solution to first sub problem and R is the solution to second sub problem. The possible candidates for closest-pair, which are across the dividing line, are those which are less than δ distance from the line. So we need only the points which are inside the 2 × δ area across the dividing line as shown in the figure. Now, to check all points within distance δ from the line, consider the following figure.

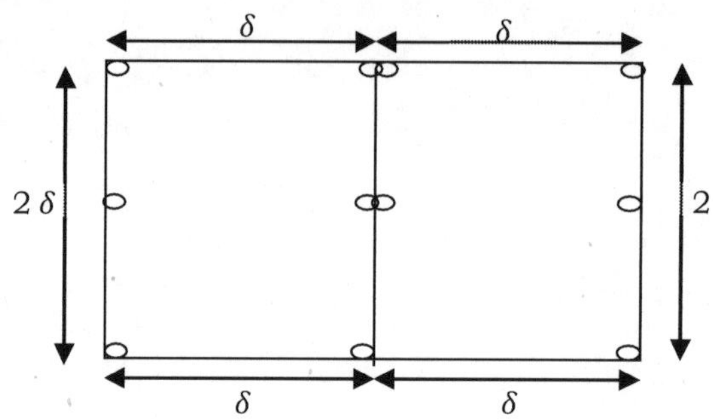

From the above diagram we can see that a maximum of 12 points can be placed inside the square with a distance not less than δ. That means, we need to check only the distances which are within 11 positions in the sorted list. This is similar to the one above, but with the difference that in the above combining of subproblems, there are no vertical bounds. So we can apply the 12-point box tactic over all the possible boxes in the $2 \times \delta$ area with the dividing line as the middle line. As there can be a maximum of n such boxes in the area, the total time for finding the closest pair in the corridor is O(n).

Analysis:

1) Step-1 and Step-2 take O($nlogn$) for sorting and recursively finding the minimum.
2) Step-4 takes O(1).
3) Step-5 takes O(n) for scanning and eliminating.
4) Step-6 takes O($nlogn$) for sorting.
5) Step-7 takes O(n) for scanning.

The total complexity: $T(n) = O(nlogn) + O(1) + O(n) + O(n) + O(n) \approx O(nlogn)$.

```
// number of points to search for closest pair
const n = 1e6

// size of bounding box for points.
// x and y will be random with uniform distribution in the range [0,scale).
const scale = 100.

// point struct
type xy struct {
    x, y float64 // coordinates
    key  int64   // an annotation used in the algorithm
}

func d(p1, p2 xy) float64 {
    return math.Hypot(p2.x-p1.x, p2.y-p1.y)
}
```

```
func closestPair(s []xy) (p1, p2 xy) {
    if len(s) < 2 {
        panic("2 points required")
    }
    var dxi float64
    for s1, i := s, 1; ; i++ {
        // Compute min distance to a random point
        // (for the case of random data, it's enough to just try to pick a different point)
        rp := i % len(s1)
        xi := s1[rp]
        dxi = 2 * scale
        for p, xn := range s1 {
            if p != rp {
                if dq := d(xi, xn); dq < dxi {
                    dxi = dq
                }
            }
        }
        invB := 3 / dxi             // b is size of a mesh cell
        mx := int64(scale*invB) + 1 // mx is number of cells along a side
        // construct map as a histogram: key is index into mesh.  value is count of points in cell
        hm := map[int64]int{}
        for ip, p := range s1 {
            key := int64(p.x*invB)*mx + int64(p.y*invB)
            s1[ip].key = key
            hm[key]++
        }
        // construct s2 = s1 less the points without neighbors
        s2 := make([]xy, 0, len(s1))
        nx := []int64{-mx - 1, -mx, -mx + 1, -1, 0, 1, mx - 1, mx, mx + 1}
        for i, p := range s1 {
            nn := 0
            for _, ofs := range nx {
                nn += hm[p.key+ofs]
                if nn > 1 {
                    s2 = append(s2, s1[i])
                    break
                }
            }
        }
        if len(s2) == 0 {
            break
        }
        s1 = s2
    }
    invB := 1 / dxi
    mx := int64(scale*invB) + 1
    hm := map[int64][]int{}
    for i, p := range s {
        key := int64(p.x*invB)*mx + int64(p.y*invB)
        s[i].key = key
        hm[key] = append(hm[key], i)
    }
    nx := []int64{-mx - 1, -mx, -mx + 1, -1, 0, 1, mx - 1, mx, mx + 1}
    var min = scale * 2
    for ip, p := range s {
        for _, ofs := range nx {
            for _, iq := range hm[p.key+ofs] {
                if ip != iq {
                    if d1 := d(p, s[iq]); d1 < min {
                        min = d1
                        p1, p2 = p, s[iq]
```

```
                    }
                }
            }
        }
    }
    return p1, p2
}
```

Problem-29 To calculate k^n, give the algorithm and discuss its complexity.

Solution: The naive algorithm to compute k^n is: start with 1 and multiply by k until reaching k^n. For this approach; there are $n - 1$ multiplications and each takes constant time giving a $\Theta(n)$ algorithm. But there is a faster way to compute k^n. For example,

$$9^{24} = (9^{12})^2 = ((9^6)^2)^2 = (((9^3)^2)^2)^2 = (((9^2.9)^2)^2)^2$$

Note that taking the square of a number needs only one multiplication; this way, to compute 9^{24} we need only 5 multiplications instead of 23.

```
func exponential(k, n int64) int64{
    if k == 0 {
        return 1
    } else if n == 1 {
        return k
    } else {
        if n%2 == 1 {
            a := exponential(k, n-1)
            return a * k
        } else {
            a := exponential(k, n/2)
            return a * a
        }
    }
}
```

Let T(n) be the number of multiplications required to compute k^n. For simplicity, assume $k = 2^i$ for some $i \geq 1$.

$$T(n) = T(\frac{n}{2}) + 1$$

Using master theorem we get T(n) = O ($logn$).

Problem-30 **The Skyline Problem**: Given the exact locations and shapes of n rectangular buildings in a 2-dimensional city. There is no particular order for these rectangular buildings. Assume that the bottom of all buildings lie on a fixed horizontal line (bottom edges are collinear). The input is a list of triples; one per building. A building B_i is represented by the triple (l_i, h_i, r_i) where l_i denote the x-position of the left edge and r_i denote the x-position of the right edge, and h_i denotes the building's height. Give an algorithm that computes the skyline (in 2 dimensions) of these buildings, eliminating hidden lines. In the diagram below there are 8 buildings, represented from left to right by the triplets (1, 14, 7), (3, 9, 10), (5, 17, 12), (14, 11, 18), (15, 6, 27), (20, 19, 22), (23, 15, 30) and (26, 14, 29).

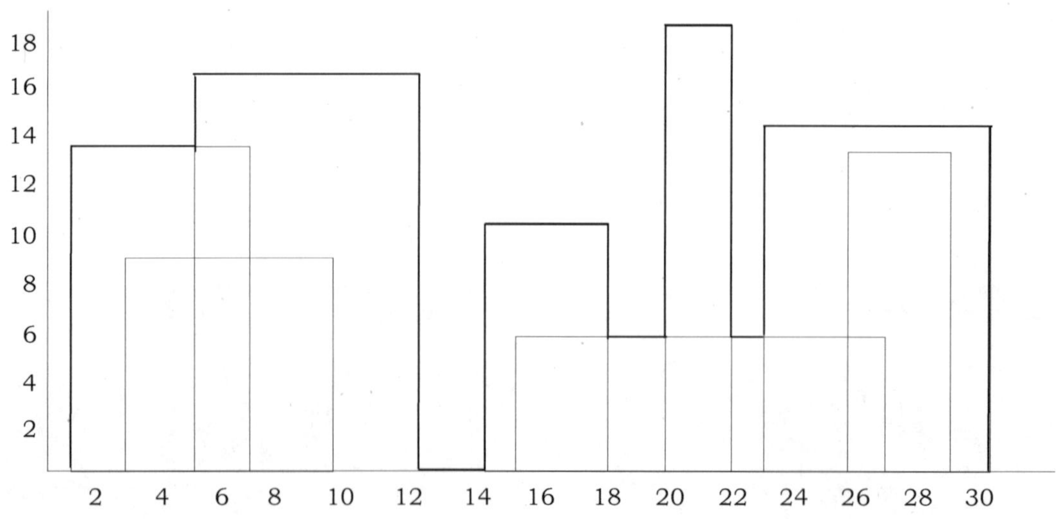

The output is a collection of points which describe the path of the skyline. In some versions of the problem this collection of points is represented by a sequence of numbers $p_1, p_2, ..., p_n$, such that the point p_i represents a horizontal line drawn at height p_i if i is even, and it represents a vertical line drawn at position p_i if i is odd. In our case the collection of points will be a sequence of $p_1, p_2, ..., p_n$ pairs of (x_i, h_i) where $p_i(x_i, h_i)$ represents the h_i height of the skyline at position x_i.

In the diagram above the skyline is drawn with a thick line around the buildings and it is represented by the sequence of position-height pairs (1, 14), (5, 17), (12, 0), (14, 11), (18, 6), (20, 19), (22, 6), (23, 15) and (30, 0). Also, assume that R_i of the right most building can be maximum of 1000. That means, the L_i co-ordinate of left building can be minimum of 1 and R_i of the right most building can be maximum of 1000.

Solution: The most important piece of information is that we know that the left and right coordinates of each and every building are non-negative integers less than 1000. Now why is this important? Because we can assign a height-value to every distinct x_i coordinate where i is between 0 and 9,999.

Algorithm:

- Allocate an array for 1000 elements and initialize all of the elements to 0. Let's call this array *auxHeights*.
- Iterate over all of the buildings and for every B_i building iterate on the range of $[l_i .. r_i)$ where l_i is the left, r_i is the right coordinate of the building B_i.
- For every x_j element of this range check if h_i>*auxHeights*[xj], that is if building B_i is taller than the current height-value at position x_j. If so, replace *auxHeights*$[x_j]$ with h_i.

Once we checked all the buildings, the *auxHeights* array stores the heights of the tallest buildings at every position. There is one more thing to do: convert the *auxHeights* array to the expected output format, that is to a sequence of position-height pairs. It's also easy: just map each and every i index to an (i, *auxHeights*[i]) pair.

```
func skyline(buildings Buildings) (points []KeyPoint) {
    // first determine the width of the skyline
    width := 0
    for _, b := range buildings {
        if b.Right > width {
            width = b.Right
        }
    }
    // determine the maximum height at each point
    auxHeights := make([]int, width+1)
    for _, b := range buildings {
        for i := b.Left; i <= b.Right; i++ {
            if auxHeights[i] < b.Height {
                auxHeights[i] = b.Height
            }
        }
    }
    // read off the critical points from the skyline
    last_height := 0
    for i, h := range auxHeights {
        if h < last_height {
            points = append(points, KeyPoint{X: i - 1, Y: h})
        } else if h > last_height {
            points = append(points, KeyPoint{X: i, Y: h})
        }
        last_height = h
    }
    points = append(points, KeyPoint{X: width, Y: 0})
    return
}
```

Let's have a look at the time complexity of this algorithm. Assume that, n indicates the number of buildings in the input sequence and m indicates the maximum coordinate (right most building r_i). From the above code, it is clear that for every new input building, we are traversing from $left$ (l_i) to $right$ (r_i) to update the heights. In the worst case, with n equal-size buildings, each having $l = 0$ left and $r = m - 1$ right coordinates, that is every building spans over the whole $[0..m)$ interval. Thus the running time of setting the height of every position is $O(n \times m)$. The overall time-complexity is $O(n \times m)$, which is a lot larger than $O(n^2)$ if $m > n$.

Problem-31 Can we improve the solution of the Problem-30?

Solution: It would be a huge speed-up if somehow we could determine the skyline by calculating the height for those coordinates only where it matters, wouldn't it? Intuition tells us that if we can insert a building into an *existing skyline* then instead of all the coordinates the building spans over we only need to check the height at the left and right coordinates of the building plus those coordinates of the skyline the building overlaps with and may modify.

Is merging two skylines substantially different from merging a building with a skyline? The answer is, of course, No. This suggests that we use divide-and-conquer. Divide the input of n buildings into two equal sets. Compute (recursively) the skyline for each set then merge the two skylines. Inserting the buildings one after the other is not the fastest way to solve this problem as we've seen it above. If, however, we first merge pairs of buildings into skylines, then we merge pairs of these skylines into bigger skylines (and not two sets of buildings), and then merge pairs of these bigger skylines into even bigger ones, then - since the problem size is halved in every step - after $logn$ steps we can compute the final skyline.

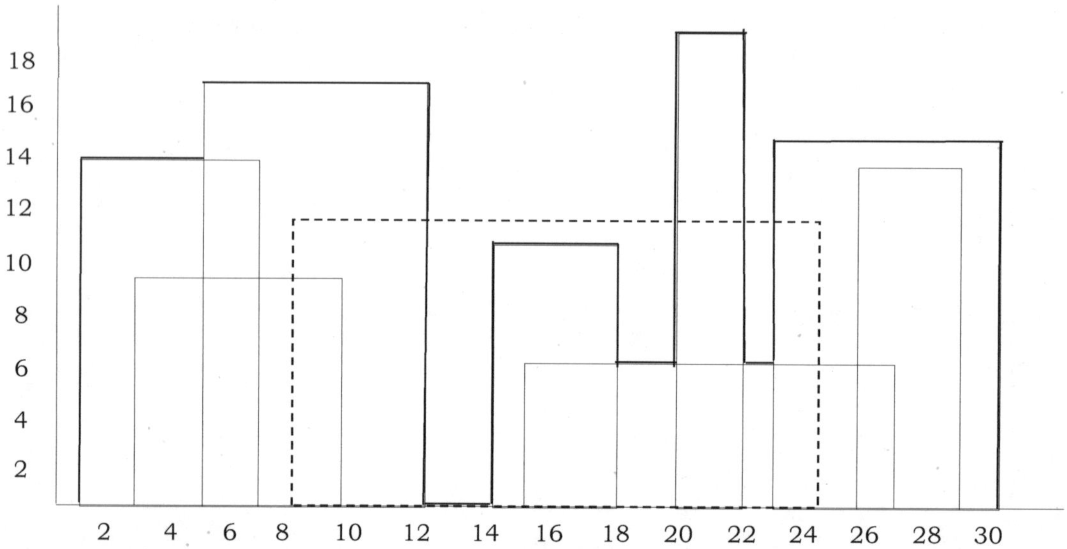


```
func getSkyline(buildings [][]int) [][]int {
    if len(buildings) == 0 {
        return [][]int{}
    }
    if len(buildings) == 1 {
        return [][]int{{buildings[0][0], buildings[0][2]}, {buildings[0][1], 0}}
    }
    mid := len(buildings) / 2
    left := getSkyline(buildings[0 : mid+1])
    right := getSkyline(buildings[mid+1:])
    return merge(left, right)
}
func max(i, j int) int {
    if i > j {
        return i
    }
    return j
}
func merge(left, right [][]int) [][]int {
    i, j := 0, 0
    var h1, h2 int
    result := [][]int{}
    for i < len(left) && j < len(right) {
        if left[i][0] < right[j][0] {
            h1 = left[i][1]
            newB := []int{left[i][0], max(h1, h2)}
            if len(result) == 0 || result[len(result[0])-1][1] != newB[1] {
                result = append(result, newB)
            }
            i += 1
```

```
            } else if left[i][0] > right[j][0] {
                h2 = right[j][1]
                newB := []int{right[j][0], max(h1, h2)}
                if len(result) == 0 || result[len(result[0])-1][1] != newB[1] {
                    result = append(result, newB)
                }
                j += 1
            } else {
                h1 = left[i][1]
                h2 = right[j][1]
                newB := []int{right[j][0], max(h1, h2)}
                if len(result) == 0 || result[len(result[0])-1][1] != newB[1] {
                    result = append(result, newB)
                    result = append(result, []int{right[j][0], max(h1, h2)})
                }
                i += 1
                j += 1
            }
        }
        for i < len(left) {
            if len(result) == 0 || result[len(result[0])-1][1] != left[i][1] {
                result = append(result, left[i][:])
            }
            i += 1
        }
        for j < len(right) {
            if len(result) == 0 || result[len(result[0])-1][1] != right[j][1] {
                result = append(result, right[j][:])
            }
            j += 1
        }
        return result
    }
```

For example, given two skylines A=(a_1, ha_1, a_2, ha_2, ..., a_n, 0) and B=(b_1, hb_1, b_2, hb_2, ..., b_m, 0), we merge these lists as the new list: (c_1, hc_1, c_2, hc_2, ..., c_{n+m}, 0). Clearly, we merge the list of a's and b's just like in the standard Merge algorithm. But, in addition to that, we have to decide on the correct height in between these boundary values. We use two variables $currentHeight1$ and $currentHeight2$ (note that these are the heights prior to encountering the heads of the lists) to store the current height of the first and the second skyline, respectively. When comparing the head entries ($currentHeight1$, $currentHeight2$) of the two skylines, we introduce a new strip (and append to the output skyline) whose x-coordinate is the minimum of the entries' x-coordinates and whose height is the maximum of $currentHeight1$ and $currentHeight2$. This algorithm has a structure similar to Mergesort. So the overall running time of the divide and conquer approach will be O($nlogn$).

CHAPTER

DYNAMIC PROGRAMMING

19

19.1 Introduction

In this chapter, we will try to solve few of the problems for which we failed to get the optimal solutions using other techniques (say, *Greedy* and *Divide & Conquer* approaches). Dynamic Programming is a simple technique but it can be difficult to master. Being able to tackle problems of this type would greatly increase your skill.

Dynamic programming (usually referred to as DP) is a very powerful technique to solve a particular class of problems. It demands very elegant formulation of the approach and simple thinking and the coding part is very easy. The idea is very simple, if you have solved a problem with the given input, then save the result for future reference, so as to avoid solving the same problem again. Simply, we need to remember the past.

One easy way to identify and master DP problems is by solving as many problems as possible. The term DP is not related to coding, but it is from literature, and means filling tables.

19.2 What is Dynamic Programming Strategy?

Dynamic programming is typically applied to *optimization problems*. In such problems there can be many possible solutions. Each solution has a value, and we wish to find a solution with the optimal (minimum or maximum) value. We call such a solution an optimal solution to the problem, as opposed to the optimal solution, since there may be several solutions that achieve the optimal value.

The development of a dynamic-programming algorithm can be broken into a sequence of four steps.

1. Characterize the structure of an optimal solution.
2. Recursively define the value of an optimal solution.
3. Compute the value of an optimal solution in a bottom-up fashion.
4. Construct an optimal solution from computed information.

Steps 1-3 form the basis of a dynamic-programming solution to a problem. Step 4 can be omitted if only the value of an optimal solution is required. When we do perform step 4, we sometimes maintain additional information during the computation in step 3 to ease the construction of an optimal solution.

If the given problem can be broken up into smaller sub-problems and these smaller subproblems are in turn divided into still-smaller ones, and in this process, if you observe some over-lapping subproblems, then it's a big hint for DP. Also, the optimal solutions to the subproblems contribute to the optimal solution of the given problem.

19.3 Properties of Dynamic Programming Strategy

The two dynamic programming properties which can tell whether it can solve the given problem or not are:

- *Optimal substructure*: An optimal solution to a problem contains optimal solutions to sub problems.
- *Overlapping sub problems*: A recursive solution contains a small number of distinct sub problems repeated many times.

19.4 Greedy vs Divide and Conquer vs DP

All algorithmic techniques construct an optimal solution of a subproblem based on optimal solutions of smaller subproblems.

Greedy algorithms are one which finds optimal solution at each and every stage with the hope of finding global optimum at the end. The main difference between DP and greedy is that, the choice made by a greedy algorithm may depend on choices made so far but not on future choices or all the solutions to the sub problem. It iteratively makes one greedy choice after another, reducing each given problem into a smaller one.

In other words, a greedy algorithm never reconsiders its choices. This is the main difference from dynamic programming, which is exhaustive and is guaranteed to find the solution. After every stage, dynamic programming makes decisions based on all the decisions made in the previous stage, and may reconsider the previous stage's algorithmic path to solution.

The main difference between dynamic programming and divide and conquer is that in the case of the latter, sub problems are independent, whereas in DP there can be an overlap of sub problems.

19.5 Can DP solve all problems?

Like greedy and divide and conquer techniques, DP cannot solve every problem. There are problems which cannot be solved by any algorithmic technique [greedy, divide and conquer and DP]. The difference between DP and straightforward recursion is in memoization of recursive calls. If the sub problems are independent and there is no repetition then DP does not help. So, dynamic programming is not a solution for all problems.

19.6 Dynamic Programming Approaches

Dynamic programming is all about ordering computations in a way that we avoid recalculating duplicate work. In dynamic programming, we have a main problem, and subproblems (subtrees). The subproblems typically repeat and overlap. The major components of DP are:

- Overlapping subproblems: Solves sub problems recursively.
- Storage: Store the computed values to avoid recalculating already solved subproblems.

By using extra storage, DP reduces the exponential complexity to polynomial complexity ($O(n^2)$, $O(n^3)$, etc.) for many problems.

Basically, there are two approaches for solving DP problems:

- Top-down approach [Memoization]
- Bottom-up approach [Tabulation]

These approaches were classified based on the way we fill the storage and reuse them.

$$Dynamic\ Programming = Overlapping\ subproblems + \text{Memoization or } Tabulation$$

19.7 Understanding DP Approaches

Top-down Approach [Memoization]

In this method, the problem is broken into sub problems; each of these subproblems is solved; and the solutions remembered, in case they need to be solved. Also, we save each computed value as the final action of the recursive function, and as the first action we check if pre-computed value exists.

Bottom-up Approach [Tabulation]

In this method, we evaluate the function starting with the smallest possible input argument value and then we step through possible values, slowly increasing the input argument value. While computing the values we store all computed values in a table (memory). As larger arguments are evaluated, pre-computed values for smaller arguments can be used.

Example: Fibonacci Series

Let us understand how DP works through an example; Fibonacci series.

In Fibonacci series, the current number is the sum of previous two numbers. The Fibonacci series is defined as follows:

$$\begin{aligned} Fib(\text{n}) &= 0, && for\ n = 0 \\ &= 1, && for\ n = 1 \\ &= Fib(\text{n}-1) + Fib(\text{n}-2), && for\ n > 1 \end{aligned}$$

Calling $fib(5)$ produces a call tree that calls the function on the same value many times:

$fib(5)$
$fib(4) + fib(3)$
$(fib(3) + fib(2)) + (fib(2) + fib(1))$
$((fib(2) + fib(1)) + (fib(1) + fib(0))) + ((fib(1) + fib(0)) + fib(1))$
$(((fib(1) + fib(0)) + fib(1)) + (fib(1) + fib(0))) + ((fib(1) + fib(0)) + fib(1))$

In the above example, $fib(2)$ was calculated three times (overlapping of subproblems). If n is big, then many more values of fib (subproblems) are recalculated, which leads to an exponential time algorithm. Instead of solving the same subproblems again and again we can store the previous calculated values and reduce the complexity.

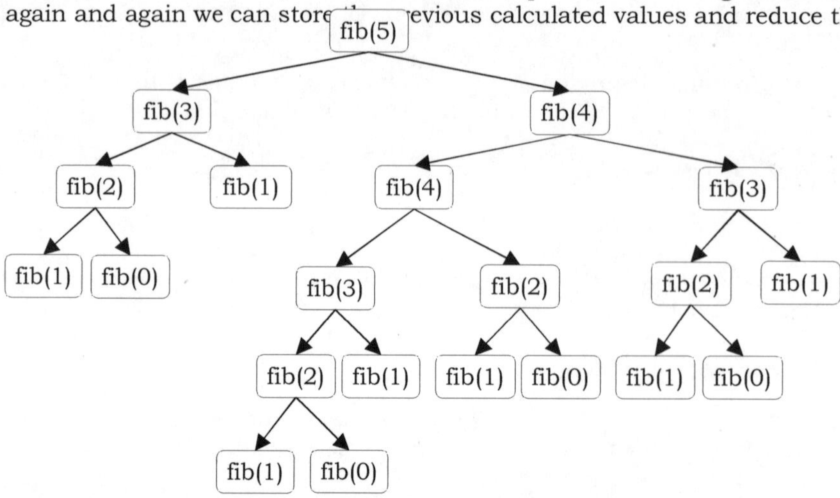

The recursive implementation can be given as:

```
func recursiveFibonacci(n int) int {
    if n == 0 {
        return 0
    }
    if n == 1 {
        return 1
    }
    return recursiveFibonacci(n-1) + recursiveFibonacci(n-2)
}
```

Solving the above recurrence gives:

$$T(n) = T(n-1) + T(n-2) + 1 \approx \left(\frac{1+\sqrt{5}}{2}\right)^n \approx 2^n = O(2^n)$$

Memoization Solution [Top-down]

Memoization works like this: Start with a recursive function and add a table that maps the function's parameter values to the results computed by the function. Then if this function is called twice with the same parameters, we simply look up the answer in the table.

In this method, we preserve the recursive calls and use the values if they are already computed. The implementation for this is given as:

```
func fibonacci(n int) int {
    if n == 0 {
        return 0
    }
    if n == 1 {
        return 1
    }
    if len(fib) == 0 {
        fib = make([]int, n+1)
    }
    if fib[n] != 0 {
        return fib[n]
    }
    fib[n] = fibonacci(n-1) + fibonacci(n-2)
    return fib[n]
}
```

Tabulation Solution [Bottom-up]

The other approach is bottom-up. Now, we see how DP reduces this problem complexity from exponential to polynomial. This method start with lower values of input and keep building the solutions for higher values.

```
func fibonacciDP(n int) int {
```

```
    fib = make([]int, n+1)
    fib[0], fib[1] = 0, 1
    for i := 2; i <= n; i++ {
        fib[i] = fib[i-1] + fib[i-2]
    }
    return fib[n]
}
```

Note: For all problems, it may not be possible to find both top-down and bottom-up programming solutions.

Both versions of the Fibonacci series implementations clearly reduce the problem complexity to $O(n)$. This is because if a value is already computed then we are not calling the subproblems again. Instead, we are directly taking its value from the table.

Time Complexity: $O(n)$. Space Complexity: $O(n)$, for table.

Further Improving

One more observation from the Fibonacci series is: The current value is the sum of the previous two calculations only. This indicates that we don't have to store all the previous values. Instead, if we store just the last two values, we can calculate the current value. The implementation for this is given below:

```
func fibonacciFinal(n int) int {
    a, b, sum := 0, 1, 0
    for i := 1; i < n; i++ {
        sum = a + b
        a = b
        b = sum
    }
    return sum
}
```

Time Complexity: $O(n)$. Space Complexity: $O(1)$.

Note: This method may not be applicable (available) for all problems.

Observations

While solving the problems using DP, try to figure out the following:

- See how the problems are defined in terms of subproblems recursively.
- See if we can use some table [memoization] to avoid the repeated calculations.

Example: Factorial of a Number

As another example, consider the factorial problem: $n!$ is the product of all integers between n and 1. The definition of recursive factorial can be given as:

$$\begin{aligned} n! &= n * (n-1)! \\ 1! &= 1 \\ 0! &= 1 \end{aligned}$$

This definition can easily be converted to implementation. Here the problem is finding the value of $n!$, and the sub-problem is finding the value of $(n - l)!$. In the recursive case, when n is greater than 1, the function calls itself to find the value of $(n - l)!$ and multiplies that with n. In the base case, when n is 0 or 1, the function simply returns 1.

```
func factorial(n int) int {
    if n == 0 || n == 1 {
        return 1
    } else {            // recursive case: multiply n by (n -1) factorial
        return n * factorial(n-1)
    }
}
```

The recurrence for the above implementation can be given as:

$$T(n) = n \times T(n-1) \approx O(n)$$

Time Complexity: $O(n)$. Space Complexity: $O(n)$, recursive calls need a stack of size n.

In the above recurrence relation and implementation, for any n value, there are no repetitive calculations (no overlapping of sub problems) and the factorial function is not getting any benefits with dynamic programming.

Now, let us say we want to compute a series of $m!$ for some arbitrary value m. Using the above algorithm, for each such call we can compute it in $O(m)$. For example, to find both $n!$ and $m!$ we can use the above approach, wherein the total complexity for finding $n!$ and $m!$ is $O(m + n)$.

Time Complexity: $O(n + m)$.
Space Complexity: $O(\max(m, n))$, recursive calls need a stack of size equal to the maximum of m and n.

Improving with Dynamic Programming

Now let us see how DP reduces the complexity. From the above recursive definition it can be seen that $fact(n)$ is calculated from $fact(n-1)$ and n and nothing else. Instead of calling $fact(n)$ every time, we can store the previous calculated values in a table and use these values to calculate a new value. This implementation can be given as:

```
var factorials []int
func factorialDP(n int) int {
    if len(factorials) == 0 {
        factorials = make([]int, n+1)
    }
    if n == 0 || n == 1 {
        return 1
    } else if factorials[n] != 0 {          //Already calculated case
        return factorials[n]
    } else {                                // recursive case: multiply n by (n -1) factorial
        factorials[n] = n * factorialDP(n-1)
        return factorials[n]
    }
}
```

For simplicity, let us assume that we have already calculated $n!$ and want to find $m!$. For finding $m!$, we just need to see the table and use the existing entries if they are already computed. If $m < n$ then we do not have to recalculate $m!$. If $m > n$ then we can use $n!$ and call the factorial on the remaining numbers only.

The above implementation clearly reduces the complexity to $O(max(m, n))$. This is because if the $fact$(n) is already there, then we are not recalculating the value again. If we fill these newly computed values, then the subsequent calls further reduce the complexity.

Time Complexity: $O(max(m, n))$. Space Complexity: $O(max(m, n))$ for table.

Bottom-up versus Top-down Programming

With *tabulation* (bottom-up), we start from smallest instance size of the problem, and *iteratively* solve bigger problems using solutions of the smaller problems (i.e. by reading from the table), until we reach our starting instance.

With *memoization* (top-down) we start right away at original problem instance, and solve it by breaking it down into smaller instances of the same problem (*recursion*). When we have to solve smaller instance, we first check in a look-up table to see if we already solved it. If we did, we just read it up and return value without solving it again and branching into recursion. Otherwise, we solve it recursively, and save result into table for further use.

In bottom-up approach, the programmer has to select values to calculate and decide the order of calculation. In this case, all subproblems that might be needed are solved in advance and then used to build up solutions to larger problems.

In top-down approach, the recursive structure of the original code is preserved, but unnecessary recalculation is avoided. The problem is broken into subproblems, these subproblems are solved and the solutions remembered, in case they need to be solved again.

Recursion with memoization is better whenever the state is sparse space (number of different subproblems are less). In other words, if we don't actually need to solve all smaller subproblems but only some of them. In such cases the recursive implementation can be much faster. Recursion with memoization is also better whenever the state space is irregular, i.e., whenever it is hard to specify an order of evaluation iteratively. Recursion with memoization is faster because only subproblems that are necessary in a given problem instance are solved.

Tabulation methods are better whenever the state space is dense and regular. If we need to compute the solutions to all the subproblems anyway, we may as well do it without all the function calling overhead. An additional advantage of the iterative approach is that we are often able to save memory by forgetting the solutions to subproblems we won't need in the future. For example, if we only need row k of the table to compute row $k + 1$, there is no need to remember row $k - 1$ anymore. On the flip side, in tabulation method, we solve all subproblems in spite of the fact that some subproblems may not be needed for a given problem instance.

19.8 Examples of DP Algorithms

- Many string algorithms including longest common subsequence, longest increasing subsequence, longest common substring, edit distance.
- Algorithms on graphs can be solved efficiently: Bellman-Ford algorithm for finding the shortest distance in a graph, Floyd's All-Pairs shortest path algorithm, etc.
- Chain matrix multiplication
- Subset Sum
- 0/1 Knapsack
- Travelling salesman problem, and many more

19.9 Longest Common Subsequence

Given two strings: string X of length m $[X(1..m)]$, and string Y of length n $[Y(1..n)]$, find the longest common subsequence: the longest sequence of characters that appear left-to-right (but not necessarily in a contiguous block) in both strings. For example, if X = "ABCBDAB" and Y = "BDCABA", the LCS(X, Y) = {"BCBA", "BDAB", "BCAB"}. We can see there are several optimal solutions.

Brute Force Approach: One simple idea is to check every subsequence of $X[1..m]$ (m is the length of sequence X) to see if it is also a subsequence of $Y[1..n]$ (n is the length of sequence Y). Checking takes O(n) time, and there are 2^m subsequences of X. The running time thus is exponential O($n.2^m$) and is not good for large sequences.

Recursive Solution: Before going to DP solution, let us form the recursive solution for this and later we can add memoization to reduce the complexity. Let's start with some simple observations about the LCS problem. If we have two strings, say "ABCBDAB" and "BDCABA", and if we draw lines from the letters in the first string to the corresponding letters in the second, no two lines cross:

```
A  B    C    B D A B
   |    |    |     |
   B D  C A  B     A
```

From the above observation, we can see that the current characters of X and Y may or may not match. That means, suppose that the two first characters differ. Then it is not possible for both of them to be part of a common subsequence - one or the other (or maybe both) will have to be removed. Finally, observe that once we have decided what to do with the first characters of the strings, the remaining sub problem is again a LCS problem, on two shorter strings. Therefore we can solve it recursively.

The solution to LCS should find two sequences in X and Y and let us say the starting index of sequence in X is i and the starting index of sequence in Y is j. Also, assume that $X[i \dots m]$ is a substring of X starting at character i and going until the end of X, and that $Y[j \dots n]$ is a substring of Y starting at character j and going until the end of Y.

Based on the above discussion, here we get the possibilities as described below:

1) If $X[i]$ == $Y[j]$: $1 + LCS(i+1, j+1)$
2) If $X[i] \neq Y[j]$: $LCS(i, j+1)$ // skipping j^{th} character of Y
3) If $X[i] \neq Y[j]$: $LCS(i+1, j)$ // skipping i^{th} character of X

In the first case, if $X[i]$ is equal to $Y[j]$, we get a matching pair and can count it towards the total length of the LCS. Otherwise, we need to skip either i^{th} character of X or j^{th} character of Y and find the longest common subsequence. Now, $LCS(i,j)$ can be defined as:

$$LCS(i,j) = \begin{cases} 0, & if\ i = m\ or\ j = n \\ Max\{LCS(i, j+1), LCS(i+1, j)\}, & if\ X[i] \neq Y[j] \\ 1 + LCS[i+1, j+1], & if\ X[i] == Y[j] \end{cases}$$

LCS has many applications. In web searching, if we find the smallest number of changes that are needed to change one word into another. A *change* here is an insertion, deletion or replacement of a single character.

```
// Initial Call: LCSLengthRecursive(X, 0, m-1, Y, 0, n-1);
func LCSLengthRecursive(X string, i, m int, Y string, j, n int) int {
    if i == m || j == n {
        return 0
    } else if X[i] == Y[j] {
        return 1 + LCSLengthRecursive(X, i+1, m, Y, j+1, n)
    } else {
        return max(LCSLengthRecursive(X, i+1, m, Y, j, n), LCSLengthRecursive(X, i, m, Y, j+1, n))
    }
}
```

```
func LCSLength2(X, Y string) int {
    m, n := len(X), len(Y)
    return LCSLengthRecursive(X, 0, m, Y, 0, n)
}
```

This is a correct solution but it is very time consuming. For example, if the two strings have no matching characters, the last line always gets executed which gives (if $m == n$) close to $O(2^n)$.

DP Solution: Adding Memoization: The problem with the recursive solution is that the same subproblems get called many different times. A subproblem consists of a call to LCSLength, with the arguments being two suffixes of X and Y, so there are exactly $(i + 1)(j + 1)$ possible subproblems (a relatively small number). If there are nearly 2^n recursive calls, some of these subproblems must be being solved over and over.

The DP solution is to check, whenever we want to solve a sub problem, whether we've already done it before. So we look up the solution instead of solving it again. Implemented in the most direct way, we just add some code to our recursive solution. To do this, look up the code. This can be given as:

```
func LCSLength(X, Y string) int {
    m, n := len(X), len(Y)
    LCS := make([][]int, m+1)
    for i := range LCS {
        LCS[i] = make([]int, n+1)                    // defaults to 0
    }
    fmt.Println(LCS)
    for i := m - 1; i >= 0; i-- {
        for j := n - 1; j >= 0; j-- {
            LCS[i][j] = LCS[i+1][j+1]                // matching X[i] to Y[j]
            if X[i] == Y[j] {
                LCS[i][j]++                          // we get a matching pair
            }
            // the other two cases – inserting a gap
            if LCS[i][j+1] > LCS[i][j] {
                LCS[i][j] = LCS[i][j+1]
            }
            if LCS[i+1][j] > LCS[i][j] {
                LCS[i][j] = LCS[i+1][j]
            }
        }
    }
    return LCS[0][0]
}
```

First, take care of the base cases. We have created an LCS table with one row and one column larger than the lengths of the two strings. Then run the iterative DP loops to fill each cell in the table. This is like doing recursion backwards, or bottom up.

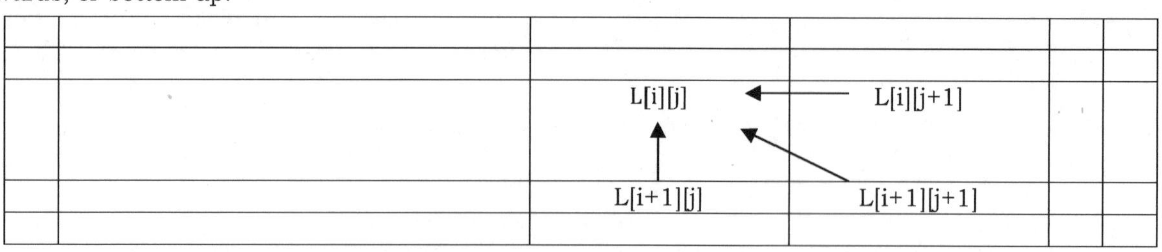

The value of $LCS[i][j]$ depends on 3 other values ($LCS[i + 1][j + 1]$, $LCS[i][j + 1]$ and $LCS[i + 1][j]$), all of which have larger values of i or j. They go through the table in the order of decreasing i and j values. This will guarantee that when we need to fill in the value of $LCS[i][j]$, we already know the values of all the cells on which it depends.

Time Complexity: $O(mn)$, since i takes values from 1 to m and and j takes values from 1 to n.
Space Complexity: $O(mn)$.

Note: In the above discussion, we have assumed $LCS(i, j)$ is the length of the LCS with $X[i \dots m]$ and $Y[j \dots n]$. We can solve the problem by changing the definition as $LCS(i, j)$ is the length of the LCS with $X[1 \dots i]$ and $Y[1 \dots j]$.

Printing the subsequence: The above algorithm can find the length of the longest common subsequence but cannot give the actual longest subsequence. To get the sequence, we trace it through the table. Start at cell $(0, 0)$. We know that the value of $LCS[0][0]$ was the maximum of 3 values of the neighboring cells. So we simply recompute $LCS[0][0]$ and note which cell gave the maximum value. Then we move to that cell (it will be one of $(1,1)$, $(0,1)$ or $(1,0)$) and repeat this until we hit the boundary of the table. Every time we pass through a cell (i,j) where $X[i] == Y[j]$, we have a matching pair and print $X[i]$. At the end, we will have printed the longest common subsequence in $O(mn)$ time.

An alternative way of getting path is to keep a separate table for each cell. This will tell us which direction we came from when computing the value of that cell. At the end, we again start at cell $(0,0)$ and follow these directions until the opposite corner of the table.

From the above examples, I hope you understood the idea behind DP. Now let us see more problems which can be easily solved using the DP technique.

Note: As we have seen above, in DP the main component is recursion. If we know the recurrence then converting that to code is a minimal task. For the problems below, we concentrate on getting the recurrence.

19.10 Dynamic Programming: Problems & Solutions

Problem-1 A child is climbing a stair case. It takes n steps to reach to the top. Each time child can either climb 1 or 2 steps. In how many distinct ways can the child climb to the top?

Solution: This problem is exactly same as that of Fibonacci series. If you see carefully, the answer for n = 1,2,3,4,5 ... form a pattern.

n	Number of ways to climb n^{th} step
1	1
2	2
3	3
4	5
5	8
6	13

This clearly forms a Fibonacci sequence. It is not just a coincidence that the answers to the climbing stair problem form a Fibonacci sequence. Why?

If you want to reach the nth step in the staircase, what will be your last second step? If would be either the $n-1^{th}$ step or the $n-2^{th}$ step, because you can jump only 1 or 2 steps at a time.

Number of ways to reach n^{th}stair = Number of ways to reach $n-1^{th}$ stair + Number of ways to reach $n-2^{th}$ stair

climbStairs(n) = climbStairs(n-1) + climbStairs(n-2)

This is also the relation followed by the Fibonacci sequence. now that we know that our solution follows a Fibonacci sequence and we have a defined recursive relation, we just need to figure out the termination case or base case, i.e., when will the recursion end? The recursion can end if n becomes 0 or 1, the answer in which case will be 1.

```
func climbStairs(n int) int {
    if n < 3 {
        return n
    }
    cache := make([]int, n)
    cache[0], cache[1] = 1, 2
    for i := 2; i < n; i++ {
        cache[i] = cache[i-1] + cache[i-2]
    }
    return cache[n-1]
}
```

Problem-2 A child is climbing up a staircase with n steps, and can hop either 1 step, 2 steps, or 3 steps at a time. Implement a method to count how many possible ways the child can jump up the stairs.

Solution: The solution to this problem is very much similar to the previous problem. If you see carefully, the answer for n = 1,2,4,7,13 ... form a pattern. If you want to reach the nth step in the staircase, what will be your last second step? If would be either the $n-1^{th}$ step, $n-2^{th}$ step or the $n-3^{th}$ step, because you can jump only 1, 2 or 3 steps at a time.

Number of ways to reach n^{th}stair = Number of ways to reach $n-1^{th}$ stair +
Number of ways to reach $n-2^{th}$ stair +
Number of ways to reach $n-3^{th}$ stair

climbStairs(n) = climbStairs(n-1) + climbStairs(n-2) + climbStairs(n-3)

The recursion can end if n becomes 0, 1 or 2, the answer in which case will be 1, 1, and 2.

```
func climbStairs(n int) int {
    cache := make([]int, n)
    cache[0], cache[1], cache[2] = 1, 1, 2
    if n < 3 {
        return cache[n]
    }
    for i := 3; i < n; i++ {
        cache[i] = cache[i-1] + cache[i-2] + cache[i-3]
    }
    return cache[n-1]
}
```

Problem-3 Convert the following recurrence to code.

$$T(0) = T(1) = 2$$

$$T(n) = \sum_{i=1}^{n-1} 2 \times \mathrm{T(i)} \times \mathrm{T(i-1)}\,, \text{for n} > 1$$

Solution: The code for the given recursive formula can be given as:

```
func f(n int) int {
    sum := 0
    if n == 0 || n == 1 {          //base case
        return 2
    }
    for i := 1; i < n; i++ {       //recursive case
        sum += 2 * f(i) * f(i-1)
    }
    return sum
}
```

Problem-4 Can we improve the solution to Problem-1 using memoization of DP?

Solution: Yes. Before finding a solution, let us see how the values are calculated.

$$T(0) = T(1) = 2$$
$$T(2) = 2 * T(1) * T(0)$$
$$T(3) = 2 * T(1) * T(0) + 2 * T(2) * T(1)$$
$$T(4) = 2 * T(1) * T(0) + 2 * T(2) * T(1) + 2 * T(3) * T(2)$$

From the above calculations it is clear that there are lots of repeated calculations with the same input values. Let us use a table for avoiding these repeated calculations, and the implementation can be given as:

```
func f(n int) int {
    T := make([]int, n+1)
    T[0], T[1] = 2, 2
    for i := 2; i <= n; i++ {
        T[i] = 0
        for j := 1; j < i; j++ {
            T[i] += 2 * T[j] * T[j-1]
        }
    }
    return T[n]
}
```

Time Complexity: $O(n^2)$, two *for* loops. Space Complexity: $O(n)$, for table.

Problem-5 Can we further improve the complexity of Problem-4?

Solution: Yes, since all sub-problem calculations are dependent only on previous calculations, the code can be modified as:

```
func f(n int) int {
    T := make([]int, n+1)
    T[0], T[1] = 2, 2
    T[2] = 2 * T[0] * T[1]
    for i := 3; i <= n; i++ {
        T[i] = T[i-1] + 2*T[i-1]*T[i-2]
    }
    return T[n]
}
```

Time Complexity: O(n), since only one for loop. Space Complexity: O(n).

Problem-6 **Maximum Value Contiguous Subsequence:** Given an array of n numbers, give an algorithm for finding a contiguous subsequence $A(i)...A(j)$ for which the sum of elements is maximum.
Example: {-2, **11, -4, 13**, -5, 2} → 20 and {1, -3, **4, -2, -1, 6**} → 7

Solution: Goal: If there are no negative numbers, then the solution is just the sum of all elements in the given array. If negative numbers are there, then our aim is to maximize the sum [there can be a negative number in the contiguous sum]. One simple and brute force approach is to see all possible sums and select the one which has maximum value.

```
func maxContiguousSum(A []int) int {
    maxSum, n := 0, len(A)
    for i := 1; i < n; i++ {          // for each possible start point
        for j := i; j < n; j++ {      // for each possible end point
            currentSum := 0
            for k := i; k <= j; k++ {
                currentSum += A[k]
            }
            if currentSum > maxSum {
                maxSum = currentSum
            }
        }
    }
    return maxSum
}
```

Time Complexity: O(n^3). Space Complexity: O(1).

Problem-5 Can we improve the complexity of Problem-4?

Solution: Yes. One important observation is that, if we have already calculated the sum for the subsequence $i, ..., j-1$, then we need only one more addition to get the sum for the subsequence $i, ..., j$. But, the Problem-4 algorithm ignores this information. If we use this fact, we can get an improved algorithm with the running time O(n^2).

```
func maxContiguousSum(A []int) int {
    maxSum, n := 0, len(A)
    for i := 1; i < n; i++ {
        currentSum := 0
        for j := i; j < n; j++ {
            currentSum += A[j]
            if currentSum > maxSum {
                maxSum = currentSum
            }
        }
    }
    return maxSum
}
```

Time Complexity: O(n^2). Space Complexity: O(1).

Problem-6 Can we solve Problem-4 using divide and conquer technique?

Solution: Yes, refer *Divide and Conquer* chapter for algorithm.

Problem-7 Can we solve Problem-4 using Dynamic Programming?

Solution: Yes. For simplicity, let us say, $M(i)$ indicates maximum sum over all windows ending at i.

Given Array, A: recursive formula considers the case of selecting i^{th} element

	.....	?	
		$A[i]$	

To find maximum sum we have to do one of the following and select maximum among them.

- Either extend the old sum by adding $A[i]$
- or start new window starting with one element $A[i]$

$$M(i) = Max \begin{cases} M(i-1) + A[i] \\ 0 \end{cases}$$

Where, $M(i-1) + A[i]$ indicates the case of extending the previous sum by adding $A[i]$ and 0 indicates the new window starting at $A[i]$.

```
func maxContiguousSum(A []int) int {
    n := len(A)
    M := make([]int, n+1)
    maxSum := 0
    if A[0] > 0 {
        M[0] = A[0]
    } else {
        M[0] = 0
    }
    for i := 1; i < n; i++ {
        if M[i-1]+A[i] > 0 {
            M[i] = M[i-1] + A[i]
        } else {
            M[i] = 0
        }
    }
    for i := 0; i < n; i++ {
        if M[i] > maxSum {
            maxSum = M[i]
        }
    }
    return maxSum
}
```

Time Complexity: O(n). Space Complexity: O(n), for table.

Problem-8 Is there any other way of solving Problem-4?

Solution: Yes. We can solve this problem without DP too (without memory). The algorithm is a little tricky. One simple way is to look for all positive contiguous segments of the array ($sumEndingHere$) and keep track of the maximum sum contiguous segment among all positive segments ($sumSoFar$). Each time we get a positive sum compare it ($sumEndingHere$) with $sumSoFar$ and update $sumSoFar$ if it is greater than $sumSoFar$. Let us consider the following code for the above observation.

```
func maxContiguousSum(A []int) int {
    sumSoFar, sumEndingHere, n := 0, 0, len(A)
    for i := 1; i < n; i++ {
        sumEndingHere = sumEndingHere + A[i]
        if sumEndingHere < 0 {
            sumEndingHere = 0
            continue
        }
        if sumSoFar < sumEndingHere {
            sumSoFar = sumEndingHere
        }
    }
    return sumSoFar
}
```

Note: The algorithm doesn't work if the input contains all negative numbers. It returns 0 if all numbers are negative. To overcome this, we can add an extra check before the actual implementation. The phase will look if all numbers are negative, and if they are it will return maximum of them (or smallest in terms of absolute value).

Time Complexity: O(n), because we are doing only one scan. Space Complexity: O(1), for table.

Problem-9 In the Problem-7 solution, we have assumed that $M(i)$ indicates maximum sum over all windows ending at i. Can we assume $M(i)$ indicates maximum sum over all windows starting at i and ending at n?

Solution: Yes. For simplicity, let us say, $M(i)$ indicates maximum sum over all windows starting at i.

Given Array, A: recursive formula considers the case of selecting i^{th} element

.....	.....	?	
		$A[i]$	

To find maximum window we have to do one of the following and select maximum among them.

- Either extend the old sum by adding $A[i]$

- Or start new window starting with one element A[i]

$$M(i) = Max\begin{cases} M(i+1) + A[i], & if\ M(i+1) + A[i] > 0 \\ 0 \quad\quad , & if\ M(i+1) + A[i] <= 0 \end{cases}$$

Where, $M(i+1) + A[i]$ indicates the case of extending the previous sum by adding $A[i]$, and 0 indicates the new window starting at $A[i]$.

Time Complexity: O(*n*). Space Complexity: O(n), for table.

Note: For O($nlogn$) solution, refer to the *Divide and Conquer* chapter.

Problem-10 Given a sequence of n numbers $A(1) \ldots A(n)$, give an algorithm for finding a contiguous subsequence $A(i) \ldots A(j)$ for which the sum of elements in the subsequence is maximum. Here the condition is we should not select *two* contiguous numbers.

Solution: Let us see how DP solves this problem. Assume that $M(i)$ represents the maximum sum from 1 to i numbers without selecting two contiguous numbers. While computing $M(i)$, the decision we have to make is, whether to select the ith element or not. This gives us two possibilities and based on this we can write the recursive formula as:

$$M(i) = \begin{cases} Max\{A[i] + M(i-2), M(i-1)\}, & if\ i > 2 \\ A[1], & if\ i = 1 \\ Max\{A[1], A[2]\}, & if\ i = 2 \end{cases}$$

- The first case indicates whether we are selecting the ith element or not. If we don't select the ith element then we have to maximize the sum using the elements 1 to $i-1$. If i^{th} element is selected then we should not select $i-1^{th}$ element and need to maximize the sum using 1 to $i-2$ elements.
- In the above representation, the last two cases indicate the base cases.

Given Array, A: recursive formula considers the case of selecting i^{th} element

	.....	.....	?	
	A[i-2]	A[i-1]	A[i]	

```
func maxSumWithNoTwoContinuousNumbers(A []int) int {
	n := len(A)
	M := make([]int, n+1)
	M[0] = A[0]
	if A[0] > A[1] {
		M[1] = A[0]
	} else {
		M[1] = A[1]
	}
	for i := 2; i < n; i++ {
		if M[i-1] > M[i-2]+A[i] {
			M[i] = M[i-1]
		} else {
			M[i] = M[i-2] + A[i]
		}
	}
	return M[n-1]
}
```

Time Complexity: O(n). Space Complexity: O(n).

Problem-11 In Problem-10, we assumed that $M(i)$ represents the maximum sum from 1 to i numbers without selecting two contiguous numbers. Can we solve the same problem by changing the definition as: $M(i)$ represents the maximum sum from i to n numbers without selecting two contiguous numbers?

Solution: Yes. Let us assume that $M(i)$ represents the maximum sum from i to n numbers without selecting two contiguous numbers.

Given Array, A: recursive formula considers the case of selecting i^{th} element

	?	.....	.....	
	A[i]	A[i+1]	A[i+2]	

As similar to Problem-10 solution, we can write the recursive formula as:

$$M(i) = \begin{cases} Max\{A[i] + M(i+2), M(i+1)\}, if\ i > 2 \\ A[1], \qquad\qquad\qquad\qquad\qquad\quad if\ i = 1 \\ Max\{A[1], A[2]\}, \qquad\qquad\qquad if\ i = 2 \end{cases}$$

- The first case indicates whether we are selecting the ith element or not. If we don't select the ith element then we have to maximize the sum using the elements $i+1$ to n. If i^{th} element is selected then we should not select $i+1^{th}$ element need to maximize the sum using $i+2$ to n elements.
- In the above representation, the last two cases indicate the base cases.

Time Complexity: O(n). Space Complexity: O(n).

Problem-12 Given a sequence of n numbers $A(1) \ldots A(n)$, give an algorithm for finding a contiguous subsequence $A(i) \ldots A(j)$ for which the sum of elements in the subsequence is maximum. Here the condition is we should not select *three* continuous numbers.

Solution: Input: Array $A(1) \ldots A(n)$ of n numbers.

Given Array, A: recursive formula considers the case of selecting i^{th} element

	.....	.....	.....	?	
	A[i-3]	A[i-2]	A[i-1]	A[i]	

Assume that $M(i)$ represents the maximum sum from 1 to i numbers without selecting three contiguous numbers. While computing $M(i)$, the decision we have to make is, whether to select i^{th} element or not. This gives us the following possibilities:

$$M(i) = Max \begin{cases} A[i] + A[i-1] + M(i-3) \\ A[i] + M(i-2) \\ M(i-1) \end{cases}$$

- In the given problem the restriction is not to select three continuous numbers, but we can select two elements continuously and skip the third one. That is what the first case says in the above recursive formula. That means we are skipping $A[i-2]$.
- The other possibility is, selecting i^{th} element and skipping second $i-1^{th}$ element. This is the second case (skipping $A[i-1]$).
- The third term defines the case of not selecting i^{th} element and as a result we should solve the problem with $i-1$ elements.

```
func maxSumWithNoTwoContinuousNumbers(A []int) int {
    n := len(A)
    M := make([]int, n+1)
    M[0] = A[0]
    if n >= 1 {
        M[0] = A[0]
    }
    if n >= 2 {
        M[1] = A[0] + A[1]
    }
    if n > 2 {
        M[2] = max(M[1], max(A[1]+A[2], A[0]+A[2]))
    }
    for i := 3; i < n; i++ {
        M[i] = max(max(M[i-1], M[i-2]+A[i]), A[i]+A[i-1]+M[i-3])
    }
    return M[n-1]
}
```

Time Complexity: O(n). Space Complexity: O(n).

Problem-13 In Problem-12, we assumed that $M(i)$ represents the maximum sum from 1 to i numbers without selecting three contiguous numbers. Can we solve the same problem by changing the definition as: $M(i)$ represents the maximum sum from i to n numbers without selecting three contiguous numbers?

Solution: Yes. The reasoning is very much similar. Let us see how DP solves this problem. Assume that $M(i)$ represents the maximum sum from i to n numbers without selecting three contiguous numbers.

Given Array, A: recursive formula considers the case of selecting i^{th} element

	?	.....	.....	.....	
	A[i]	A[i+1]	A[i+2]	A[i+3]	

While computing $M(i)$, the decision we have to make is, whether to select i^{th} element or not. This gives us the following possibilities:

$$M(i) = Max\begin{cases} A[i] + A[i+1] + M(i+3) \\ A[i] + M(i+2) \\ M(i+1) \end{cases}$$

- In the given problem the restriction is to not select three continuous numbers, but we can select two elements continuously and skip the third one. That is what the first case says in the above recursive formula. That means we are skipping $A[i+2]$.
- The other possibility is, selecting i^{th} element and skipping second $i-1^{th}$ element. This is the second case (skipping $A[i+1]$).
- And the third case is not selecting i^{th} element and as a result we should solve the problem with $i+1$ elements.

Time Complexity: O(n). Space Complexity: O(n).

Problem-14 **Catalan Numbers:** How many binary search trees are there with n vertices?

Solution: Binary Search Tree (BST) is a tree where the left subtree elements are less than the root element, and the right subtree elements are greater than the root element. This property should be satisfied at every node in the tree. The number of BSTs with n nodes is called *Catalan Number* and is denoted by C_n. For example, there are 2 BSTs with 2 nodes (2 choices for the root) and 5 BSTs with 3 nodes.

Number of nodes, n	Number of Trees
1	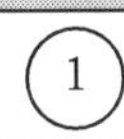
2	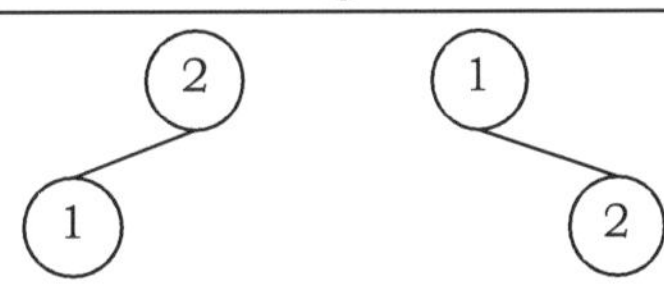
3	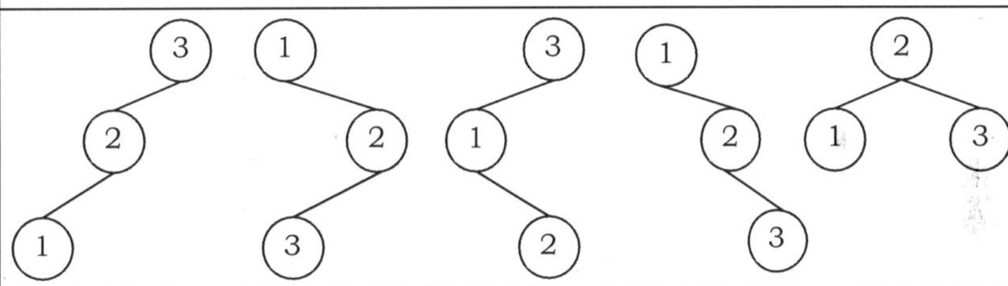

Let us assume that the nodes of the tree are numbered from 1 to n. Among the nodes, we have to select some node as root, and then divide the nodes which are less than root node into left sub tree, and elements greater than root node into right sub tree. Since we have already numbered the vertices, let us assume that the root element we selected is i^{th} element.

If we select i^{th} element as root then we get $i-1$ elements on left sub-tree and $n-i$ elements on right sub tree. Since C_n is the Catalan number for n elements, C_{i-1} represents the Catalan number for left sub tree elements ($i-1$ elements) and C_{n-i} represents the Catalan number for right sub tree elements. The two sub trees are independent of each other, so we simply multiply the two numbers. That means, the Catalan number for a fixed i value is $C_{i-1} \times C_{n-i}$. Since there are n nodes, for i we will get n choices. The total Catalan number with n nodes can be given as:

$$C_n = \sum_{i=1}^{n} C_{i-1} \times C_{n-i}$$

```
func CatalanNumberR(n int) int {
    if n == 0 {
        return 1
    }
    count := 0
    for i := 1; i <= n; i++ {
        count += CatalanNumberR(i-1) * CatalanNumberR(n-i)
    }
    return count
```

```
}
```

Time Complexity: $O(4^n)$. For proof, refer to *Introduction* chapter.

Problem-15 Can we improve the time complexity of Problem-14 using DP?

Solution: The recursive call C_n depends only on the numbers C_0 to C_{n-1} and for any value of i, there are a lot of recalculations. We will keep a table of previously computed values of C_i. If the function *CatalanNumber*() is called with parameter i, and if it has already been computed before, then we can simply avoid recalculating the same subproblem.

```
func CatalanNumber(n int) int {
    C := make([]int, n+1)
    C[0] = 1
    for i := 1; i <= n; i++ {
        for j := 1; j <= i; j++ {
            C[i] += (C[j-1] * C[i-j])
        }
    }
    return C[n]
}
```

The time complexity of this implementation $O(n^2)$, because to compute *CatalanNumber*(n), we need to compute all of the *CatalanNumber*(i) values between 0 and $n-1$, and each one will be computed exactly once, in linear time.

In mathematics, Catalan Number can be represented by direct equation as: $\frac{(2n)!}{n!(n+1)!}$.

Problem-16 **Matrix Product Parenthesizations:** Given a series of matrices: $A_1 \times A_2 \times A_3 \times \ldots \times A_n$ with their dimensions, what is the best way to parenthesize them so that it produces the minimum number of total multiplications. Assume that we are using standard matrix and not Strassen's matrix multiplication algorithm.

Solution: Goal: Parenthesize the given matrices in such a way that it produces the optimal number of multiplications needed to compute $A_1 \times A_2 \times A_3 \times \ldots \times A_n$.

We could write a function which tries all possible parenthesizations. Unfortunately, the number of ways of parenthesizing an expression is very large. If you have just one or two matrices, then there is only one way to parenthesize. If you have n items, then there are $n - 1$ places where you could break the list with the outermost pair of parentheses, namely just after the first item, just after the second item, etc., and just after the $(n - 1)^{st}$ item.

When we split just after the ith item, we create two sublists to be parenthesized, one with i items, and the other with $n - i$ items. Then we could consider all the ways of parenthesizing these. Since these are independent choices, if there are L ways to parenthesize the left sublist and R ways to parenthesize the right sublist, then the total is $L \times R$. This suggests the following recurrence for *P(n)*, the number of different ways of parenthesizing n items:

$$P(n) = \sum_{i=1}^{n} P(i) \times P(n-i)$$

The base case would be $P(1)$, and obviously, the number of ways to parenthesize the two matrices is 1.

$$P(1) = 1$$

This is related to the Catalan numbers (which in turn is related to the number of different binary trees on n nodes). As said above, applying Stirling's formula, we find that *C(n)* is $O\left(\frac{4^n}{n^{\frac{3}{2}}\sqrt{\pi}}\right)$. Since 4^n is exponential and $n^{3/2}$ is just polynomial, the exponential will dominate, implying that function grows very fast. Thus, this will not be practical except for very small n. In summary, brute force is not an option.

```
// Matrix Ai has dimension P[i-1] x P[i] for i = 1..n
func matrixChainOrder(P []int, i, j int) int {
    if i == j {
        return 0
    }
    min := math.MaxInt32
    // place parenthesis at different places between first and last matrix, recursively calculate count of
    // multiplications for each parenthesis placement and return the minimum count
    for k := i; k < j; k++ {
        count := matrixChainOrder(P, i, k) + matrixChainOrder(P, k+1, j) + P[i-1]*P[k]*P[j]
        if count < min {
```

```
            min = count
        }
    }
    return min
}
```

Now let us use DP to improve this time complexity. Assume that, $M[i,j]$ represents the least number of multiplications needed to multiply $A_i \cdots A_j$.

$$M[i,j] = \begin{cases} 0 & ,if\ i = j \\ Min\{M[i,k] + M[k+1,j] + P_{i-1}P_kP_j\}, & if\ i < j \end{cases}$$

The above recursive formula says that we have to find point k such that it produces the minimum number of multiplications. After computing all possible values for k, we have to select the k value which gives minimum value. We can use one more table (say, $S[i,j]$) to reconstruct the optimal parenthesizations. Compute the $M[i,j]$ and $S[i,j]$ in a bottom-up fashion.

```
// Matrix Ai has dimension P[i-1] x P[i] for i = 1..n
func matrixChainOrder(P []int) int {
    // For simplicity of the program, one extra row and one extra column are allocated in M[][].
    // 0th row and 0th column of M[][] are not used
    n := len(P)
    M := make([][]int, n)
    for i := range M {
        M[i] = make([]int, n) // defaults to fa0lse
    }
    // M[i,j] = Minimum number of scalar multiplications needed to compute the
    // matrix A[i]A[i+1]...A[j] = A[i..j] where dimension of A[i] is P[i-1] x P[i]
    // cost is zero when multiplying one matrix.
    for i := 1; i < n; i++ {
        M[i][i] = 0
    }
    // L is chain length.
    for L := 2; L < n; L++ {
        for i := 1; i < n-L+1; i++ {
            j := i + L - 1
            M[i][j] = math.MaxInt32
            for k := i; k <= j-1; k++ {
                q := M[i][k] + M[k+1][j] + P[i-1]*P[k]*P[j]        // q = cost/scalar multiplications
                if q < M[i][j] {
                    M[i][j] = q
                }
            }
        }
    }
    return M[1][n-1]
}
```

How many sub problems are there? In the above formula, i can range from $1\ to\ n$ and j can range from $1\ to\ n$. So there are a total of n^2 subproblems, and also we are doing $n-1$ such operations [since the total number of operations we need for $A_1 \times A_2 \times A_3 \times \ldots \times A_n$ ise $n-1$]. So, the time complexity is $O(n^3)$.
Space Complexity: $O(n^2)$.

Problem-17 For Problem-16, can we use greedy method?

Solution: *Greedy* method is not an optimal way of solving this problem. Let us go through some counter example for this. As we have seen already, *greedy* method makes the decision that is good locally and it does not consider the future optimal solutions. In this case, if we use *Greedy,* then we always do the cheapest multiplication first. Sometimes it returns a parenthesization that is not optimal.

Example: Consider $A_1 \times A_2 \times A_3$ with dimensions 3×100, 100×2 and 2×2. Based on *greedy* we parenthesize them as: $A_1 \times (A_2 \times A_3)$ with $100 \cdot 2 \cdot 2 + 3 \cdot 100 \cdot 2 = 1000$ multiplications. But the optimal solution to this problem is: $(A_1 \times A_2) \times A_3$ with $3 \cdot 100 \cdot 2 + 3 \cdot 2 \cdot 2 = 612$ multiplications. $\therefore$ we cannot use *greedy* for solving this problem.

Problem-18 **Integer Knapsack Problem [Duplicate Items Permitted]:** Given n types of items, where the ith item type has an integer size s_i and a value v_i. We need to fill a knapsack of total capacity C with items of maximum value. We can add multiple items of the same type to the knapsack.

Note: For Fractional Knapsack problem refer to *Greedy Algorithms* chapter.

Solution: Goal: Fill the knapsack with capacity C by using n types of items and with maximum value.

One important note is that it's not compulsory to fill the knapsack completely. That means, filling the knapsack completely [of size C] if we get a value V and without filling the knapsack completely [let us say C – 1] with value U and if V < U then we consider the second one. In this case, we are basically filling the knapsack of size C – 1. If we get the same situation for $C - 1$ also, then we try to fill the knapsack with $C - 2$ size and get the maximum value.

Let us say M(j) denotes the maximum value we can pack into a j size knapsack. We can express M(j) recursively in terms of solutions to sub problems as follows:

$$M(j) = \begin{cases} max\{M(j-1), max_{i=1\ to\ n}(M(j-s_i)) + v_i\}, & if\ j \geq 1 \\ 0, & if\ j \leq 0 \end{cases}$$

For this problem the decision depends on whether we select a particular i^{th} item or not for a knapsack of size j.

- If we select i^{th} item, then we add its value v_i to the optimal solution and decrease the size of the knapsack to be solved to $j - s_i$.
- If we do not select the item then check whether we can get a better solution for the knapsack of size $j - 1$.

The value of $M(C)$ will contain the value of the optimal solution. We can find the list of items in the optimal solution by maintaining and following "back pointers".

Time Complexity: Finding each $M(j)$ value will require $\Theta(n)$ time, and we need to sequentially compute C such values. Therefore, total running time is $\Theta(nC)$.
Space Complexity: $\Theta(C)$.

Problem-19 **0-1 Knapsack Problem:** For Problem-18, how do we solve it if the items are not duplicated (not having an infinite number of items for each type, and each item is allowed to be used for 0 or 1 time)?

Real-time example: Suppose we are going by flight, and we know that there is a limitation on the luggage weight. Also, the items which we are carrying can be of different types (like laptops, etc.). In this case, our objective is to select the items with maximum value. That means, we need to tell the customs officer to select the items which have more weight and less value (profit).

Solution: Input is a set of n items with sizes s_i and values v_i and a Knapsack of size C which we need to fill with a subset of items from the given set. Let us try to find the recursive formula for this problem using DP. Let $M(i,j)$ represent the optimal value we can get for filling up a knapsack of size j with items $1 \ldots i$. The recursive formula can be given as:

$$M(i,j) = Max\ \{\underbrace{M(i-1,j)}_{i^{th}\text{ item is not used}}, \underbrace{M(i-1, j-s_i) + v_i}_{i^{th}\text{ item is used}}\}$$

Time Complexity: O(nC), since there are nC subproblems to be solved and each of them takes O(1) to compute.
Space Complexity: O(nC), where as Integer Knapsack takes only O(C).

Now let us consider the following diagram which helps us in reconstructing the optimal solution and also gives further understanding. Size of below matrix is M.

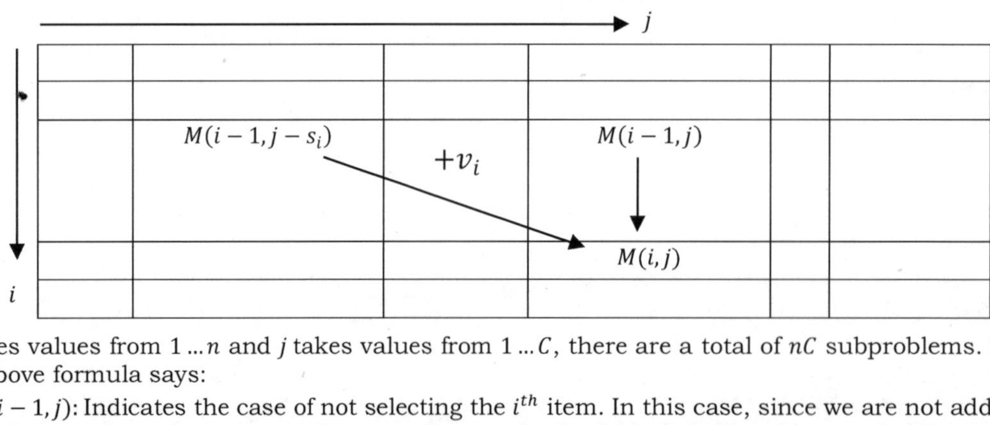

Since i takes values from $1 \ldots n$ and j takes values from $1 \ldots C$, there are a total of nC subproblems. Now let us see what the above formula says:

- $M(i-1,j)$: Indicates the case of not selecting the ith item. In this case, since we are not adding any size to the knapsack we have to use the same knapsack size for subproblems but excluding the ith item. The remaining items are $i - 1$.
- $M(i-1, j-s_i) + v_i$ indicates the case where we have selected the ith item. If we add the ith item then we have to reduce the subproblem knapsack size to $j - s_i$ and at the same time we need to add the value v_i to the optimal solution. The remaining items are $i - 1$.

Now, after finding all $M(i,j)$ values, the optimal objective value can be obtained as: $Max_j\{M(n,j)\}$
This is because we do not know what amount of capacity gives the best solution.

In order to compute some value $M(i,j)$, we take the maximum of $M(i-1,j)$ and $M(i-1,j-s_i)+v_i$. These two values ($M(i,j)$ and $M(i-1,j-s_i)$) appear in the previous row and also in some previous columns. So, $M(i,j)$ can be computed just by looking at two values in the previous row in the table.

Problem-20 **Making Change:** Given n types of coin denominations of values $v_1 < v_2 < \ldots < v_n$ (integers). Assume $v_1 = 1$, so that we can always make change for any amount of money C. Give an algorithm which makes change for an amount of money C with as few coins as possible.

Solution:

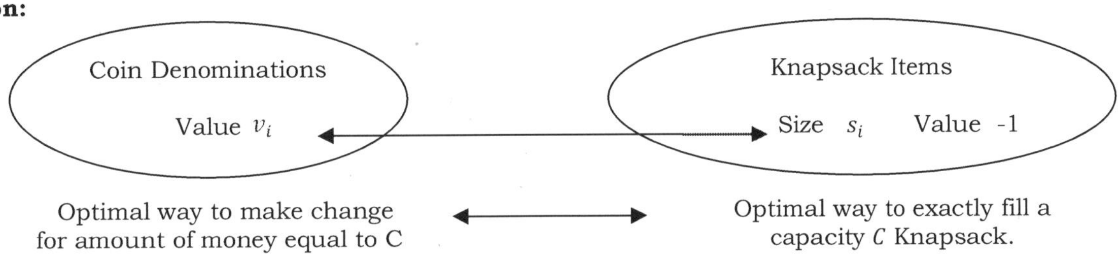

This problem is identical to the Integer Knapsack problem. In our problem, we have coin denominations, each of value v_i. We can construct an instance of a Knapsack problem for each item that has a size s_i, which is equal to the value of v_i coin denomination. In the Knapsack we can give the value of every item as -1.

Now it is easy to understand an optimal way to make money C with the fewest coins is completely equivalent to the optimal way to fill the Knapsack of size C. This is because since every value has a value of -1, and the Knapsack algorithm uses as few items as possible which correspond to as few coins as possible.

Let us try formulating the recurrence. Let $M(j)$ indicate the minimum number of coins required to make change for the amount of money equal to j.

$$M(j) = Min_i\{M(j - v_i)\} + 1$$

What this says is, if coin denomination i was the last denomination coin added to the solution, then the optimal way to finish the solution with that one is to optimally make change for the amount of money $j - v_i$ and then add one extra coin of value v_i.

```
func coinChange(coins []int, C int) int {              // Recursive solution
    if C == 0 {          // base case
        return 0
    }
    const MaxUint = ^uint(0)
    const INT_MAX = int(MaxUint >> 1)
    result := INT_MAX
    // Try every coin that has smaller value than V
    for i := 0; i < len(coins); i++ {
        if coins[i] <= C {
            subRes := coinChange(coins, C-coins[i])
            // Check for INT_MAX to avoid overflow and see if result can minimized
            if subRes != INT_MAX && subRes+1 < result {
                result = subRes + 1
            }
        }
    }
    return result
}
// Dynamic Programming Solution
func coinChange(coins []int, C int) int {
    M := make([]int, C+1)
    const MaxUint = ^uint(0)
    const INT_MAX = int(MaxUint >> 1)
    for i := 1; i <= C; i++ {
        minCoin := INT_MAX
        for _, coin := range coins {
            if i-coin >= 0 && M[i-coin] != -1 {
                minCoin = min(minCoin, M[i-coin]+1)
```

```
            }
        }
        if minCoin == INT_MAX {
            M[i] = -1
        } else {
            M[i] = minCoin
        }
    }
    return M[C]
}
```

Time Complexity: $O(nC)$. Since we are solving **C** sub-problems and each of them requires minimization of n terms. Space Complexity: $O(nC)$.

Problem-21 **Longest Increasing Subsequence (LIS):** Given a sequence of n numbers $A_1 \ldots A_n$, determine a subsequence (not necessarily contiguous) of maximum length in which the values in the subsequence form a strictly increasing sequence.

Solution: Goal: To find a subsequence that is just a subset of elements and does not happen to be contiguous. But the elements in the subsequence should form a strictly increasing sequence and at the same time the subsequence should contain as many elements as possible.

For example, if the sequence is (5,6,2,3,4,1,9,9,8,9,5), then (5,6), (3,5), (1,8,9) are all increasing sub-sequences. The longest one of them is (2, 3, 4, 8, 9), and we want an algorithm for finding it.

First, let us concentrate on the algorithm for finding the longest subsequence. Later, we can try printing the sequence itself by tracing the table. Our first step is finding the recursive formula. First, let us create the base conditions. If there is only one element in the input sequence then we don't have to solve the problem and we just need to return that element. For any sequence we can start with the first element ($A[1]$). Since we know the first number in the LIS, let's find the second number ($A[2]$). If $A[2]$ is larger than $A[1]$ then include $A[2]$ also. Otherwise, we are done – the LIS is the one element sequence ($A[1]$).

Now, let us generalize the discussion and decide about i^{th} element. Let $L(i)$ represent the optimal subsequence which is starting at position $A[1]$ and ending at $A[i]$. The optimal way to obtain a strictly increasing subsequence ending at position i is to extend some subsequence starting at some earlier position j. For this the recursive formula can be written as:

$$L(i) = Max_{j<i \text{ and } A[j]<A[i]}\{L(j)\} + 1$$

The above recurrence says that we have to select some earlier position j which gives the maximum sequence. The 1 in the recursive formula indicates the addition of ith element.

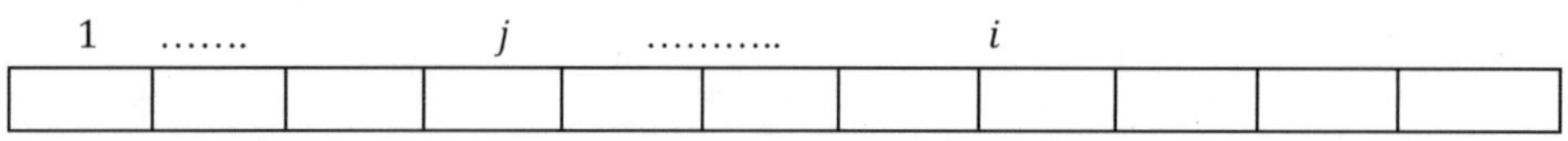

Now after finding the maximum sequence for all positions we have to select the one among all positions which gives the maximum sequence and it is defined as:

$$Max_i\{L(i)\}$$

```
func LIS(A []int) int {
    n := len(A)
    if n == 1 || n == 0 {
        return n
    }
    L := make([]int, n)
    for i := 0; i < n; i++ {
        L[i] = 1
    }
    max := 1
    for i := 1; i < n; i++ {
        for j := 0; j < i; j++ {
            if A[i] > A[j] && L[i] < L[j]+1 {
                L[i] = L[j] + 1
            }
        }
    }
    for i := 0; i < n; i++ {
        if max < L[i] {
```

```
            max = L[i]
        }
    }
    return max
}
```

Time Complexity: O(n^2), since two *for* loops. Space Complexity: O(n), for table.

Problem-22 In Problem-21, we assumed that $L(i)$ represents the optimal subsequence which is starting at position $A[1]$ and ending at $A[i]$. Now, let us change the definition of $L(i)$ as: $L(i)$ represents the optimal subsequence which is starting at position $A[i]$ and ending at $A[n]$. With this approach can we solve the problem?

Solution: Yes.

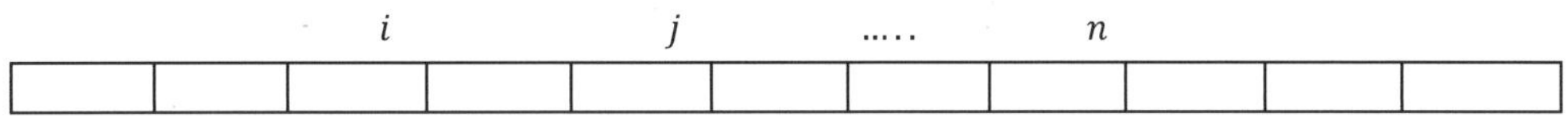

Let $L(i)$ represent the optimal subsequence which is starting at position $A[i]$ and ending at $A[n]$. The optimal way to obtain a strictly increasing subsequence starting at position i is going to be to extend some subsequence starting at some later position j. For this the recursive formula can be written as:

$$L(i) = Max_{i<j \text{ and } A[i]<A[j]}\{L(j)\} + 1$$

We have to select some later position j which gives the maximum sequence. The 1 in the recursive formula is the addition of ith element. After finding the maximum sequence for all positions select the one among all positions which gives the maximum sequence and it is defined as:

$$Max_i\{L(i)\}$$

```
func LIS(A []int) int {
    n := len(A)
    if n == 1 || n == 0 {
        return n
    }
    L := make([]int, n)
    for i := 0; i < n; i++ {
        L[i] = 1
    }
    max := 1
    for i := n-1; i >= 0; i-- {
        for j := i+1; j < n; j++ {
            if A[i] < A[j] && L[i] < L[j]+1 {
                L[i] = L[j] + 1
            }
        }
    }
    for i := 0; i < n; i++ {
        if max < L[i] {
            max = L[i]
        }
    }
    return max
}
```

Time Complexity: O(n^2), since two nested *for* loops. Space Complexity: O(n), for table.

Problem-23 Is there an alternative way of solving Problem-21?

Solution: Yes. The other method is to sort the given sequence and save it into another array and then take out the "Longest Common Subsequence" (LCS) of the two arrays. This method has a complexity of O($nlogn$).

```
func lengthOfLIS(A []int) int {
    if len(A) == 0 {
        return 0
    }
    L := make([]int, len(A))
    L[0], hi = A[0], 0
    for i := 1; i < len(A); i++ {
        idx := binarySearch(L, A[i], 0, hi)
        L[idx] = A[i]
```

```
            if idx == hi+1 {
                hi++
            }
        }
        return hi + 1
    }
    func binarySearch(L []int, data, lo, hi int) int {
        for lo <= hi {
            mid := lo + (hi-lo)/2
            if L[mid] > data {
                hi = mid - 1
            } else if L[mid] < data {
                lo = mid + 1
            } else {
                return mid
            }
        }
    }
```

Problem-24 **Box Stacking:** Assume that we are given a set of n rectangular $3-D$ boxes. The dimensions of ith box are height h_i, width w_i and depth d_i. Now we want to create a stack of boxes which is as tall as possible, but we can only stack a box on top of another box if the dimensions of the $2-D$ base of the lower box are each strictly larger than those of the $2-D$ base of the higher box. We can rotate a box so that any side functions as its base. It is possible to use multiple instances of the same type of box.

Solution: Box stacking problem can be reduced to LIS [Problem-21].

Input: n boxes where i^{th} with height h_i, width w_i and depth d_i. For all n boxes we have to consider all the orientations with respect to rotation. That is, if we have, in the original set, a box with dimensions $1 \times 2 \times 3$, then we consider 3 boxes,

$$1 \times 2 \times 3 \Rightarrow \begin{cases} 1 \times (2 \times 3), with\ height\ 1, base\ 2\ and\ width\ 3 \\ 2 \times (1 \times 3), with\ height\ 2, base\ 1\ and\ width\ 3 \\ 3 \times (1 \times 2), with\ height\ 3, base\ 1\ and\ width\ 2 \end{cases}$$

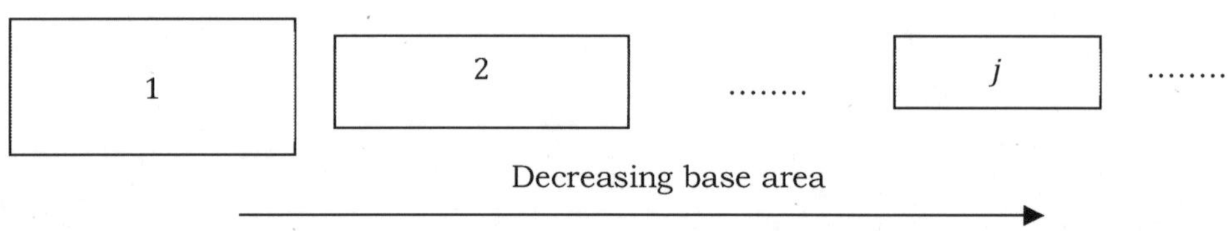

This simplification allows us to forget about the rotations of the boxes and we just focus on the stacking of n boxes with each height as h_i and a base area of $(w_i \times d_i)$. Also assume that $w_i \leq d_i$. Now what we do is, make a stack of boxes that is as tall as possible and has maximum height. We allow a box i on top of box j only if box i is smaller than box j in both the dimensions. That means, if $w_i < w_j$ && $d_i < d_j$. Now let us solve this using DP. First select the boxes in the order of decreasing base area.

Now, let us say $H(j)$ represents the tallest stack of boxes with box j on top. This is very similar to the LIS problem because the stack of n boxes with ending box j is equal to finding a subsequence with the first j boxes due to the sorting by decreasing base area. The order of the boxes on the stack is going to be equal to the order of the sequence.

Now we can write $H(j)$ recursively. In order to form a stack which ends on box j, we need to extend a previous stack ending at i. That means, we need to put j box at the top of the stack [i box is the current top of the stack]. To put j box at the top of the stack we should satisfy the condition $w_i > w_j and\ d_i > d_j$ [this ensures that the low level box has more base than the boxes above it]. Based on this logic, we can write the recursive formula as:

$$H(j) = Max_{i<j\ and\ \mathrm{w_i>w_j and\ d_i>d_j}}\{H(i)\} + h_i$$

Similar to the LIS problem, at the end we have to select the best j over all potential values. This is because we are not sure which box might end up on top.

$$Max_j\{H(j)\}$$

Time Complexity: $O(n^2)$.

Problem-25 **Building Bridges in India:** Consider a very long, straight river which moves from north to south. Assume there are n cities on both sides of the river: n cities on the left of the river and n cities on the right side of the river. Also, assume that these cities are numbered from 1 to n but the order is not known. Now we want to connect as many left-right pairs of cities as possible with bridges such that no two bridges cross. When connecting cities, we can only connect city i on the left side to city i on the right side.

Solution:
Goal: Construct as many bridges as possible without any crosses between the cities on the left side of the river and the cities on the right side.

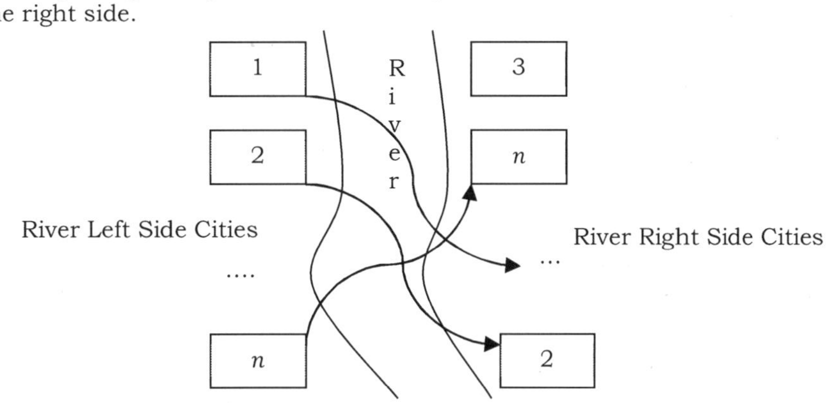

To understand better let us consider the diagram below. In the diagram it can be seen that there are n cities on the left side of river and n cities on the right side of river. Also, note that we are connecting the cities which have the same number [a requirement in the problem]. Our goal is to connect the maximum cities on the left side of river to cities on the right side of the river, without any cross edges. Just to make it simple, let us sort the cities on one side of the river.

If we observe carefully, since the cities on the left side are already sorted, the problem can be simplified to finding the maximum increasing sequence. That means we have to use the LIS solution for finding the maximum increasing sequence on the right side cities of the river.

Time Complexity: $O(n^2)$, (same as LIS).

Problem-26 **Target Sum:** Given a sequence of n positive numbers $A_1 \ldots A_n$, give an algorithm which checks whether there exists a subset of A whose sum of all numbers is T?

Solution: Like all DP problems, the most important and the most challenging part is recognizing the recurrence. This is a variation of the Knapsack problem. As an example, consider the following array:

$$A = [3, 2, 4, 19, 3, 7, 13, 10, 6, 11]$$

Suppose we want to check whether there is any subset whose sum is 17. The answer is yes, because the sum of $4 + 13 = 17$ and therefore $\{4, 13\}$ is such a subset.

```
func targtSum1(A []int, n, T int) bool {
    // Base Cases
    if T == 0 {
        return true
    }
    if n == 0 && T != 0 {
        return false
    }
    // If last element is greater than T, then ignore it
    if A[n-1] > T {
        return targtSum(A, n-1, T)
    }
    return targtSum(A, n-1, T) || targtSum(A, n-1, T-A[n-1])
}
```

Let us try solving this problem using DP in bottom-up manner. In the bottom-up approach, we solve smaller sub-problems first, then solve larger sub-problems from them. The following bottom-up approach computes $M[i][j]$, for each $1 <= i <= n$ and $1 <= j <= T$, which is true if subset with sum j can be found using items up to first i items. It uses value of smaller values i and j already computed. It has the same asymptotic run-time as Memoization but no recursion overhead. We will define $n \times T$ matrix, where n is the number of elements in our input array and T is the sum we want to check.

Let, $M[i,j] = 1$ if it is possible to find a subset of the numbers 1 through i that produce sum j and $M[i,j] = 0$ otherwise.

$$M[i,j] = Max(M[i-1,j], M[i-1, j-A_i])$$

According to the above recursive formula similar to the Knapsack problem, we check if we can get the sum j by not including the element i in our subset, and we check if we can get the sum j by including i and checking if the sum $j - A_i$ exists without the ith element. This is identical to Knapsack, except that we are storing 0/1's instead of values. In the below implementation we can use binary OR operation to get the maximum among $M[i-1,j]$ and $M[i-1,j-A_i]$.

```
func targtSum(A []int, T int) bool {
    n := len(A)
    M := make([][]bool, n+1)
    for i := range M {
        M[i] = make([]bool, T+1)    // defaults to false
    }
    for i := 0; i <= n; i++ {            // If T is 0, then answer is true
        M[i][0] = true
    }
    for i := 1; i <= n; i++ {
        for j := 0; j <= T; j++ {
            if j < A[i-1] {
                M[i][j] = M[i-1][j]
            }
            if j >= A[i-1] {
                M[i][j] = M[i-1][j] || M[i-1][j-A[i-1]]
            }
        }
    }
    return M[n][T]
}
```

How many subproblems are there? In the above formula, i can range from $1\ to\ n$ and j can range from $1\ to\ T$. There are a total of nT subproblems and each one takes O(1). So, the time complexity is O(nT) and this is not polynomial as the running time depends on two variables [n and T], and we can see that they are an exponential function of the other.

Space Complexity: O(nT).

Problem-27 Given a set of n integers and the sum of all numbers is at most K. Find the subset of these n elements whose sum is exactly half of the total sum of n numbers.

Solution: Assume that the numbers are $A_1 \ldots A_n$. Let us use DP to solve this problem. We will create a boolean array T with size equal to $K+1$. Assume that $T[x]$ is 1 if there exists a subset of given n elements whose sum is x. That means, after the algorithm finishes, $T[K]$ will be 1, if and only if there is a subset of the numbers that has sum K. Once we have that value then we just need to return $T[K/2]$. If it is 1, then there is a subset that adds up to half the total sum.

Initially we set all values of T to 0. Then we set $T[0]$ to 1. This is because we can always build 0 by taking an empty set. If we have no numbers in A, then we are done! Otherwise, we pick the first number, $A[0]$. We can either throw it away or take it into our subset. This means that the new $T[]$ should have $T[0]$ and $T[A[0]]$ set to 1. This creates the base case. We continue by taking the next element of A.

Suppose that we have already taken care of the first i – 1 elements of A. Now we take A[i] and look at our table T[]. After processing i – 1 elements, the array T has a 1 in every location that corresponds to a sum that we can make from the numbers we have already processed. Now we add the new number, A[i]. What should the table look like? First of all, we can simply ignore A[i]. That means, no one should disappear from T[] – we can still make all those sums. Now consider some location of T[j] that has a 1 in it. It corresponds to some subset of the previous numbers that add up to j. If we add A[i] to that subset, we will get a new subset with total sum j + A[i]. So we should set T[j + A[i]] to 1 as well. That's all. Based on the above discussion, we can write the algorithm as:

```
func subsetHalfSum(A []int) bool {
    K, n := 0, len(A)
    for i := 0; i < n; i++ {
        K += A[i]
    }
    T := make([]bool, K+1)
    T[0] = true                    // initialize the table
    for i := 1; i <= K; i++ {
        T[i] = false
    }
```

```
    for i := 0; i < n; i++ {         // process the numbers one by one
        for j := K - A[i]; j >= 0; j-- {
            if T[j] {
                T[j+A[i]] = true
            }
        }
    }
    return T[K/2]
}
```

In the above code, j loop moves from right to left. This reduces the double counting problem. That means, if we move from left to right, then we may do the repeated calculations.

Time Complexity: O(nK), for the two *for* loops. Space Complexity: O(K), for the boolean table T.

Problem-28 Can we improve the performance of Problem-27?

Solution: Yes. In the above code what we are doing is, the inner j loop is starting from K and moving left. That means, it is unnecessarily scanning the whole table every time. What we actually want is to find all the 1 entries. At the beginning, only the 0th entry is 1. If we keep the location of the rightmost 1 entry in a variable, we can always start at that spot and go left instead of starting at the right end of the table.

To take full advantage of this, we can sort A[] first. That way, the rightmost 1 entry will move to the right as slowly as possible. Finally, we don't really care about what happens in the right half of the table (after $T[K/2]$) because if $T[x]$ is 1, then $T[Kx]$ must also be 1 eventually – it corresponds to the complement of the subset that gave us x. The code based on above discussion is given below.

```
func subsetHalfSum(A []int) bool {
    K, n, R := 0, len(A), 0
    for i := 0; i < n; i++ {
        K += A[i]
    }
    T := make([]bool, K+1)
    T[0] = true // initialize the table
    for i := 1; i <= K; i++ {
        T[i] = false
    }
    sort.Ints(A)                     // sort the array
    for i := 0; i < n; i++ {         // process the numbers one by one
        for j := R; j >= 0; j-- {
            if T[j] {
                T[j+A[i]] = true
                R = min(K/2, R+A[i])
            }
        }
    }
    return T[K/2]
}
```

After the improvements, the time complexity is still O(nK), but we have removed some useless steps.

Problem-29 The partition problem is to determine whether a given set can be partitioned into two subsets such that the sum of elements in both subsets is the same [the same as the previous problem but a different way of asking]. For example, if A[] = {1, 5, 11, 5}, the array can be partitioned as {1, 5, 5} and {11}. Similarly, if A[] = {1, 5, 3}, the array cannot be partitioned into equal sum sets.

Solution: Let us try solving this problem another way. Following are the two main steps to solve this problem:

1. Calculate the sum of the array. If the sum is odd, there cannot be two subsets with an equal sum, so return false.
2. If the sum of the array elements is even, calculate $sum/2$ and find a subset of the array with a sum equal to $sum/2$.

The first step is simple. The second step is crucial, and it can be solved either using recursion or Dynamic Programming.

Recursive Solution: Following is the recursive property of the second step mentioned above. Let subsetSum(A, n, sum/2) be the function that returns true if there is a subset of A[0..n-1] with sum equal to $sum/2$. The isSubsetSum problem can be divided into two sub problems:

a) *subsetSum*() without considering last element (reducing n to $n-1$)

b) *subsetSum*() considering the last element (reducing sum/2 by A[n-1] and n to $n-1$)

If any of the above sub problems return true, then return true.

$$subsetSum\ (A, n, sum/2)\ =\ isSubsetSum\ (A, n-1, sum/2)\ ||\ subsetSum\ (A, n-1, sum/2\ -\ A[n-1])$$

```
// A utility function that returns true if there is a subset of A[] with sum equal to given sum
func subsetSum(A []int, n, sum int) bool {
    if sum == 0 {
        return true
    }
    if n == 0 && sum != 0 {
        return false
    }
    // If last element is greater than sum, then ignore it
    if A[n-1] > sum {
        return subsetSum(A, n-1, sum)
    }
    return subsetSum(A, n-1, sum) || subsetSum(A, n-1, sum-A[n-1])
}
// Returns true if A[] can be partitioned in two subsets of equal sum, otherwise false
func findPartition(A []int) bool {
    n, sum := len(A), 0
    for i := 0; i < n; i++ {                // Calculate sum of all elements
        sum += A[i]
    }
    // If sum is odd, there cannot be two subsets with equal sum
    if sum%2 != 0 {
        return false
    }
    // Find if there is a subset with a sum equal to half of total sum
    return subsetSum(A, n, sum/2)
}
```

Time Complexity: $O(2^n)$. In worst case, this solution tries two possibilities (whether to include or exclude) for every element.

Dynamic Programming Solution: The problem can be solved using dynamic programming when the sum of the elements is not too big. We can create a 2D array *part*[][] of size $(sum/2)$*$(n+1)$. And we can construct the solution in a bottom-up manner such that every filled entry has a following property

$$part[i][j]\ =\ true\ if\ a\ subset\ of\ \{A[0], A[1], .. A[j-1]\}\ has\ sum\ equal\ to\ sum/2, otherwise\ false$$

```
// Returns true if A[] can be partitioned in two subsets of equal sum, otherwise false
func findPartitionDP(A []int) bool {
    sum, n := 0, len(A)
    // calculate sum of all elements
    for i := 0; i < n; i++ {
        sum += A[i]
    }
    if sum%2 != 0 {                // If sum is odd, there cannot be two subsets with equal sum
        return false
    }
    part := make([][]bool, sum/2+1)
    for i := range part {
        part[i] = make([]bool, n+1) // defaults to 0
    }
    for i := 0; i <= n; i++ {       // initialize top row as true
        part[0][i] = true
    }
    // initialize leftmost column, except part[0][0], as 0
    for i := 1; i <= sum/2; i++ {
        part[i][0] = false
    }
    // Fill the partition table in bottom up manner
```

```
        for i := 1; i <= sum/2; i++ {
            for j := 1; j <= n; j++ {
                part[i][j] = part[i][j-1]
                if i >= A[j-1] {
                    part[i][j] = part[i][j] || part[i-A[j-1]][j-1]
                }
            }
        }
        return part[sum/2][n]
    }
```

Time Complexity: O($sum \times n$). Space Complexity: O($sum \times n$). Notice that this solution will not be feasible for arrays with a big sum.

Problem-30 **Counting Boolean Parenthesizations:** Let us assume that we are given a boolean expression consisting of symbols $'true', 'false', 'and', 'or', and\ 'xor'$. Find the number of ways to parenthesize the expression such that it will evaluate to $true$. For example, there is only 1 way to parenthesize $'true\ and\ false\ xor\ true'$ such that it evaluates to $true$.

Solution: Let the number of symbols be n and between symbols there are boolean operators like and, or, xor, etc. For example, if $n = 4$, $T\ or\ F\ and\ T\ xor\ F$. Our goal is to count the numbers of ways to parenthesize the expression with boolean operators so that it evaluates to $true$. In the above case, if we use $T\ or\ ((F\ and\ T)\ xor\ F)$ then it evaluates to true.

$$T\ or(\ (F\ and\ T)xor\ F) = True$$

Now let us see how DP solves this problem. Let $T(i,j)$ represent the number of ways to parenthesize the sub expression with symbols $i \dots j$ [symbols means only T and F and not the operators] with boolean operators so that it evaluates to $true$. Also, i and j take the values from 1 to n. For example, in the above case, $T(2,4) = 0$ because there is no way to parenthesize the expression $F\ and\ T\ xor\ F$ to make it $true$.

Just for simplicity and similarity, let $F(i,j)$ represent the number of ways to parenthesize the sub expression with symbols $i \dots j$ with boolean operators so that it evaluates to $false$. The base cases are $T(i,i)$ and $F(i,i)$.

Now we are going to compute $T(i,i+1)$ and $F(i,i+1)$ for all values of i. Similarly, $T(i,i+2)$ and $F(i,i+2)$ for all values of i and so on. Now let's generalize the solution.

$$T(i,j) = \sum_{k=i}^{j-1} \begin{cases} T(i,k)T(k+1,j), & for\ "and" \\ Total(i,k)Total(k+1,j) - F(i,k)F(k+1,j), & for\ "or" \\ T(i,k)F(k+1,j) + F(i,k)T(k+1,j), & for\ "xor" \end{cases}$$

Where, $Total(i,k) = T(i,k) + F(i,k)$.

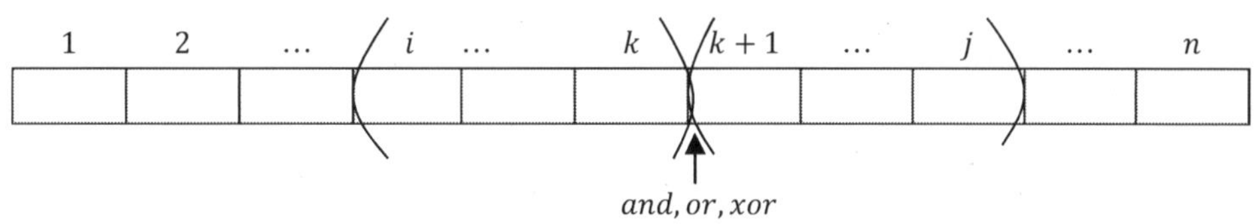

What this above recursive formula says is, $T(i,j)$ indicates the number of ways to parenthesize the expression. Let us assume that we have some sub problems which are ending at k. Then the total number of ways to parenthesize from $i\ to\ j$ is the sum of counts of parenthesizing from $i\ to\ k$ and from $k+1\ to\ j$. To parenthesize between k and $k+1$ there are three ways: "and", "or" and "xor".

- If we use "and" between k and $k+1$, then the final expression becomes $true$ only when both are $true$. If both are $true$ then we can include them to get the final count.
- If we use "or", then if at least one of them is $true$, the result becomes $true$. Instead of including all three possibilities for "or", we are giving one alternative where we are subtracting the "false" cases from total possibilities.
- The same is the case with "xor". The conversation is as in the above two cases.

After finding all the values we have to select the value of k, which produces the maximum count, and for k there are $i\ to\ j-1$ possibilities.

How many subproblems are there? In the above formula, i can range from 1 $to\ n$, and j can range from 1 $to\ n$. So there are a total of n^2 subproblems, and also we are doing summation for all such values. So the time complexity is O(n^3).

Problem-31 **Optimal Binary Search Trees:** Given a set of n (sorted) keys $A[1..n]$, build the best binary search tree for the elements of A. Also assume that each element is associated with $frequency$ which indicates the number of times that a particular item is searched in the binary search trees. That means we need to construct a binary search tree so that the total search time will be reduced.

Solution: Before solving the problem let us understand the problem with an example. Let us assume that the given array is A = [3, 12, 21, 32, 35]. There are many ways to represent these elements, two of which are listed below.

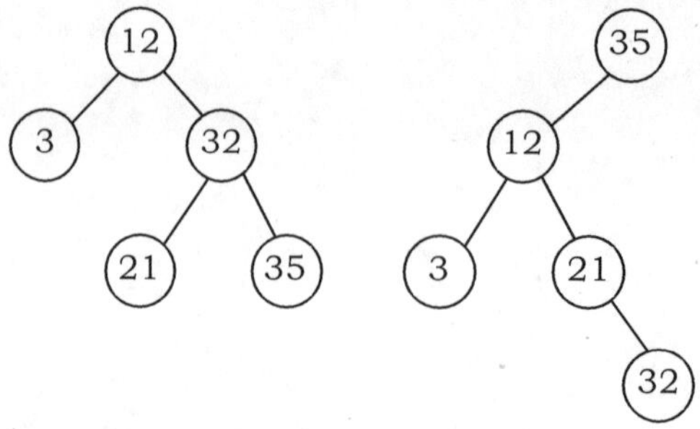

Of the two, which representation is better? The search time for an element depends on the depth of the node. The average number of comparisons for the first tree is: $\frac{1+2+2+3+3}{5} = \frac{11}{5}$ and for the second tree, the average number of comparisons is: $\frac{1+2+3+3+4}{5} = \frac{13}{5}$. Of the two, the first tree gives better results.

If frequencies are not given and if we want to search all elements, then the above simple calculation is enough for deciding the best tree. If the frequencies are given, then the selection depends on the frequencies of the elements and also the depth of the elements. An obvious way to find an optimal binary search tree is to generate each possible binary search tree for the keys, calculate the search time, and keep that tree with the smallest total search time. This search through all possible solutions is not feasible, since the number of such trees grows exponentially with n.

An alternative would be a recursive algorithm. Consider the characteristics of any optimal tree. Of course it has a root and two subtrees. Both subtrees must themselves be optimal binary search trees with respect to their keys and frequencies. First, any subtree of any binary search tree must be a binary search tree. Second, the subtrees must also be optimal.

For simplicity let us assume that, the given array is A and the corresponding frequencies are in array F. $F[i]$ indicates the frequency of ith element $A[i]$. With this, the total search time S(root) of the tree with *root* can be defined as:

$$S(root) = S(r) = \sum_{i=1}^{n} (depth(root, i) + 1) \times F[i])$$

In the above expression, $depth(root, i) + 1$ indicates the number of comparisons for searching the ith element. Since we are trying to create a binary search tree, the left subtree elements are less than root element and the right subtree elements are greater than root element. If we separate the left subtree time and right subtree time, then the above expression can be written as:

$$S(root) = \sum_{i=1}^{r-1} (depth(root, i) + 1) \times F[i] + \sum_{i=1}^{n} F[i] + \sum_{i=r+1}^{n} (depth(root, i) + 1) \times F[i]$$

Where r indicates the position of the root element in the array.

If we replace the left subtree and right subtree times with their corresponding recursive calls, then the expression becomes:

$$S(root) = S(r) = S(root.left) + S(root.right) + \sum_{i=1}^{n} F[i]$$

Since, r can vary from 1 to n, we need to minimize the total search time for the given keys 1 to n considering all possible values for r. Let $OBST(1, n)$ is the optimal binary search tree with keys 1 to n

$$OBST(1, n) = min_{1 \le r \le n}\{S(r)\}$$
$$OBST(i, i) = F[i]$$

On the similar lines, the optimal binary search tree with keys from i to j can be given as:

$$OBST(i, j) = min_{i \le r \le j}\{S(r)\}$$

Implementation:

```
func optimalSearchTree(keys, freq []int, n int) int {
    cost := make([][]int, n)
    for i := range cost {
        cost[i] = make([]int, n)
```

```
    }
    /* cost[i][j] = Optimal cost of binary search tree that can be  formed from
      keys[i] to keys[j]. cost[0][n-1] will store the resultant cost */
    // For a single key, cost is equal to frequency of the key
    for i := 0; i < n; i++ {
        cost[i][i] = freq[i]
    }
    // Now we need to consider chains of length 2, 3, .. L is chain length.
    for L := 2; L <= n; L++ {
        for i := 0; i <= n-L+1; i++ {       // i is row number in cost[][]
            j := i + L - 1                  // Get column number j from row number i and chain length L
            cost[i][j] = math.MaxInt32
            // Try making all keys in interval keys[i..j] as root
            for r := i; r <= j; r++ {
                c := sum(freq, i, j)        // c = cost when keys[r] becomes root of this subtree
                if r > i {
                    c = cost[i][r-1]
                }
                if r < j {
                    c = cost[r+1][j]
                }
                if c < cost[i][j] {
                    cost[i][j] = c
                }
            }
        }
    }
    return cost[0][n-1]
}
```

Problem-32 **Edit Distance:** Given two strings A of length m and B of length n, transform A into B with a minimum number of operations of the following types: delete a character from A, insert a character into A, or change some character in A into a new character. The minimal number of such operations required to transform A into B is called the *edit distance* between A and B.

Solution: Goal of the solution is to convert string A into B with minimal conversions.

Before going to a solution, let us consider the possible operations for converting string A into B.

- If $m > n$, we need to remove some characters of A
- If $m == n$, we may need to convert some characters of A
- If $m < n$, we need to remove some characters from A

So the operations we need are the insertion of a character, the replacement of a character and the deletion of a character, and their corresponding cost codes are defined below.

Costs of operations:

Insertion of a character	c_i
Replacement of a character	c_r
Deletion of a character	c_d

Now let us concentrate on the recursive formulation of the problem. Let, $T(i,j)$ represents the minimum cost required to transform first i characters of A to first j characters of B. That means, $A[1 \ldots i]$ to $B[1 \ldots j]$.

$$T(i,j) = min \begin{cases} c_d + T(i-1,j) \\ T(i,j-1) + c_i \\ \begin{cases} T(i-1,j-1), & if\ A[i] == B[j] \\ T(i-1,j-1) + c_r & if\ A[i] \neq B[j] \end{cases} \end{cases}$$

Based on the above discussion we have the following cases.

- If we delete i^{th} character from A, then we have to convert remaining $i-1$ characters of A to j characters of B
- If we insert i^{th} character in A, then convert these i characters of A to $j-1$ characters of B
- If $A[i] == B[j]$, then we have to convert the remaining $i-1$ characters of A to $j-1$ characters of B
- If $A[i] \neq B[j]$, then we have to replace i^{th} character of A to j^{th} character of B and convert remaining $i-1$ characters of A to $j-1$ characters of B

After calculating all the possibilities we have to select the one which gives the lowest cost.

```
func mins(value int, values ...int) int {
    for _, v := range values {
        if v < value {
            value = v
        }
    }
    return value
}
func minDistance(A string, B string) int {
    T := make([][]int, len(A)+1)
    for i := range T {
        T[i] = make([]int, len(B)+1)
        T[i][0] = i
    }
    for j := range T[0] {
        T[0][j] = j
    }
    for i := 1; i < len(T); i++ {
        for j := 1; j < len(T[0]); j++ {
            offset := 1
            if A[i-1] == B[j-1] {
                offset = 0
            }
            T[i][j] = mins(T[i-1][j]+1, T[i][j-1]+1, T[i-1][j-1]+offset)
        }
    }
    return T[len(T)-1][len(T[0])-1]
}
```

How many subproblems are there? In the above formula, i can range from 1 *to* m and j can range from 1 *to* n. This gives mn subproblems and each one takes O(1) and the time complexity is O(mn). Space Complexity: O(mn) where m is number of rows and n is number of columns in the given matrix.

Problem-33 **All Pairs Shortest Path Problem: Floyd's Algorithm:** Given a weighted directed graph $G = (V, E)$, where $V = \{1, 2, \ldots, n\}$. Find the shortest path between any pair of nodes in the graph. Assume the weights are represented in the matrix $C[V][V]$, where $C[i][j]$ indicates the weight (or cost) between the nodes i and j. Also, $C[i][j] = \infty$ or -1 if there is no path from node i to node j.

Solution: Let us try to find the DP solution (Floyd's algorithm) for this problem. The Floyd's algorithm for all pairs shortest path problem uses matrix $A[1..n][1..n]$ to compute the lengths of the shortest paths. Initially,

$$A[i,j] = C[i,j] \;\; if \;\; i \neq j \\ = 0 \quad if \;\; i = j$$

From the definition, $C[i,j] = \infty$ if there is no path from i to j. The algorithm makes n passes over A. Let $A_0, A_1, \ldots, A_n$ be the values of A on the n passes, with A_0 being the initial value.

Just after the $k-1^{th}$ iteration, $A_{k-1}[i,j]$ = smallest length of any path from vertex i to vertex j that does not pass through the vertices $\{k+1, k+2, \ldots. n\}$. That means, it passes through the vertices possibly through $\{1, 2, 3, \ldots, k-1\}$.

In each iteration, the value $A[i][j]$ is updated with minimum of $A_{k-1}[i,j]$ and $A_{k-1}[i,k] + A_{k-1}[k,j]$.

$$A[i,j] = \min \begin{cases} A_{k-1}[i,j] \\ A_{k-1}[i,k] + A_{k-1}[k,j] \end{cases}$$

The kth pass explores whether the vertex k lies on an optimal path from i to j, for all i, j. The same is shown in the diagram below.

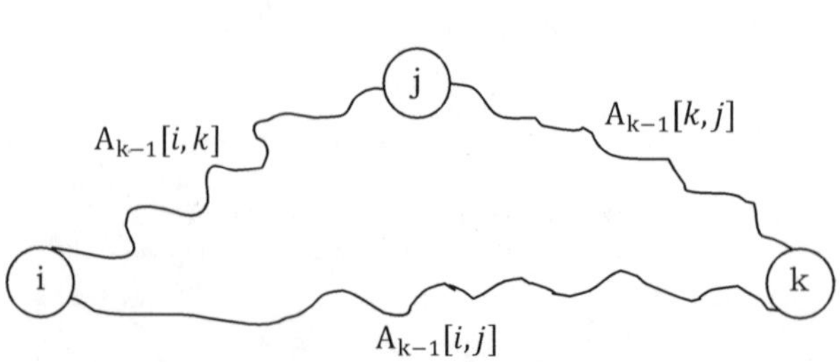

```
func Floyd(C [][]int, A [][]int, int n) {
    for i := 0; i <= n-1; i++ {
        for j := 0; j <= n-1; j++ {
            A[i][j] = C[i][j]
        }
    }
    for i := 0; i <= n-1; i++ {
        A[i][i] = 0
    }
    for k := 0; k <= n-1; k++ {
        for i := 0; i <= n-1; i++ {
            for j := 0; j <= n-1; j++ {
                if A[i][k]+A[k][j] < A[i][j] {
                    A[i][j] = A[i][k] + A[k][j]
                }
            }
        }
    }
    return b
}
```

Time Complexity: O(n^3).

Problem-34 **Optimal Strategy for a Game:** Consider a row of n coins of values v_1 ... v_n, where n is even [since it's a two player game]. We play this game with the opponent. In each turn, a player selects either the first or last coin from the row, removes it from the row permanently, and receives the value of the coin. Determine the maximum possible amount of money we can definitely win if we move first.

Alternative problem statement: Given n pots, each with some number of gold coins, are arranged in a line. You are playing a game against another player. You take turns picking a pot of gold. You may pick a pot from either end of the line, remove the pot, and keep the gold pieces. The player with the most gold at the end wins. Develop a strategy for playing this game.

Alternative problem statement: In this game, which we will call the coins-in-a-line game, an even number, n, of coins, of various denominations from various countries, are placed in a line. Two players, who we will call A and B, take turns removing one of the coins from either end of the remaining line of coins. That is, when it is a player's turn, he or she removes the coin at the left or right end of the line of coins and adds that coin to his or her collection. The player who removes a set of coins with larger total value than the other player wins, where we assume that both A and B know the value of each coin.

Solution: Let us solve the problem using our DP technique. For each turn either we *or* our opponent selects the coin only from the ends of the row. Let us define the subproblems as:

$V(i,j)$: denotes the maximum possible value we can definitely win if it is our turn and the only coins remaining are v_i ... v_j.

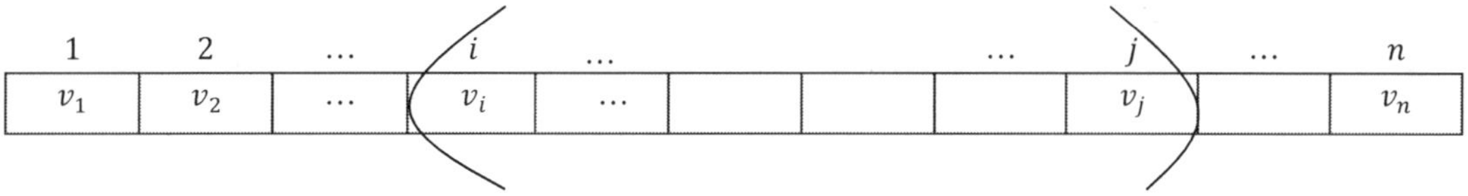

Base Cases: $V(i,i), V(i,i+1)$ for all values of i.
From these values, we can compute $V(i,i+2), V(i,i+3)$ and so on. Now let us define $V(i,j)$ for each sub problem as:

$$V(i,j) = Max\left\{Min\left\{\begin{matrix} V(i+1,j-1) \\ V(i+2,j) \end{matrix}\right\} + v_i, Min\left\{\begin{matrix} V(i,j-2) \\ V(i+1,j-1) \end{matrix}\right\} + v_j\right\}$$

In the recursive call we have to focus on i^{th} coin to j^{th} coin ($v_i \ldots v_j$). Since it is our turn to pick the coin, we have two possibilities: either we can pick v_i or v_j. The first term indicates the case if we select i^{th} coin (v_i) and the second term indicates the case if we select j^{th} coin (v_j). The outer Max indicates that we have to select the coin which gives maximum value. Now let us focus on the terms:

- Selecting i^{th} coin: If we select the ith coin then the remaining range is from $i+1$ to j. Since we selected the ith coin we get the value v_i for that. From the remaining range $i+1$ to j, the opponents can select either $i+1^{th}$ coin or j^{th} coin. But the opponents selection should be minimized as much as possible [the Min term]. The same is described in the below figure.

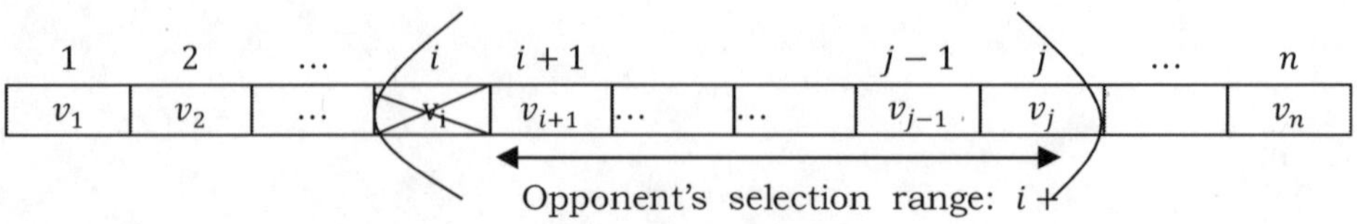

- Selecting the jth coin: Here also the argument is the same as above. If we select the jth coin, then the remaining range is from i *to* $j-1$. Since we selected the jth coin we get the value v_j for that. From the remaining range i *to* $j-1$, the opponent can select either the ith coin or the $j-1^{th}$ coin. But the opponent's selection should be minimized as much as possible [the *Min* term].

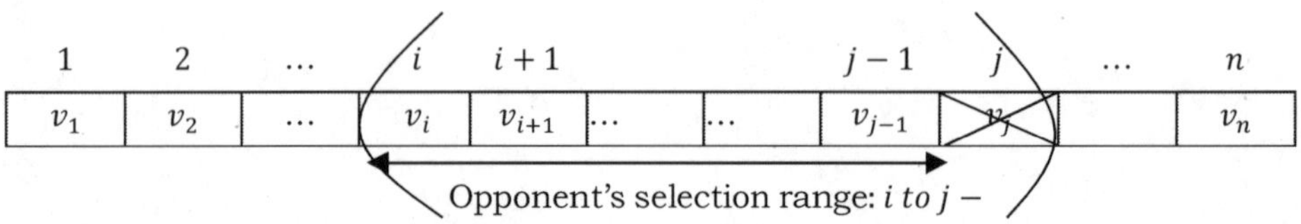


```
func calculate(V [][]int, i, j int) int {
    if i <= j {
        return V[i][j]
    }
    return 0
}
// Function to maximize the number of coins collected by a player,
// assuming that opponent also plays optimally
func optimalStrategy(coins []int) int {
    n := len(coins)
    if n == 1 {          // base case: one pot left, only one choice possible
        return coins[0]
    }
    if n == 2 {          // if we're left with only two pots, choose one with maximum coins
        return max(coins[0], coins[1])
    }
    // create a dynamic 2D matrix to store sub-problem solutions
    V := make([][]int, n)
    for i := range V {
        V[i] = make([]int, n) // defaults to false
    }
    for iteration := 0; iteration < n; iteration++ {
        for i, j := 0, iteration; j < n; i, j = i+1, j+1 {
            start := coins[i] + min(calculate(V, i+2, j), calculate(V, i+1, j-1))
            end := coins[j] + min(calculate(V, i+1, j-1), calculate(V, i, j-2))
            V[i][j] = max(start, end)
        }
    }
    return V[0][n-1]
}
```

How many subproblems are there? In the above formula, i can range from 1 *to* n and j can range from 1 *to* n. There are a total of n^2 subproblems and each takes O(1) and the total time complexity is O(n^2).

Problem-35 **Tiling:** Assume that we use dominoes measuring 2 × 1 to tile an infinite strip of height 2. How many ways can one tile a 2 × n strip of square cells with 1 × 2 dominoes?

Solution: Notice that we can place tiles either vertically or horizontally. For placing vertical tiles, we need a gap of at least 2 × 2. For placing horizontal tiles, we need a gap of 2 × 1. In this manner, the problem is reduced to finding the number of ways to partition n using the numbers 1 and 2 with order considered relevant [1]. For example: 11 = 1 + 2 + 2 + 1 + 2 + 2 + 1.

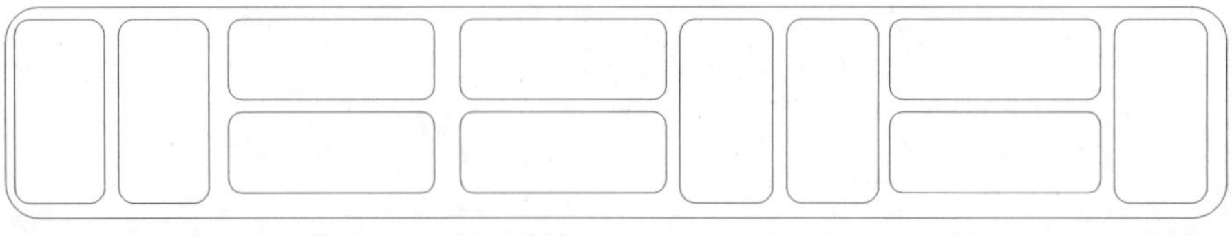

If we have to find such arrangements for 12, we can either place a 1 at the end or we can add 2 in the arrangements possible with 10. Similarly, let us say we have F_n possible arrangements for n. Then for $(n+1)$, we can either place just 1 at the end *or* we can find possible arrangements for $(n-1)$ and put a 2 at the end. Going by the above theory:

$$F_{n+1} = F_n + F_{n-1}$$

Let's verify the above theory for our original problem:

- In how many ways can we fill a 2 × 1 strip: 1 → Only one vertical tile.
- In how many ways can we fill a 2 × 2 strip: 2 → Either 2 horizontal or 2 vertical tiles.
- In how many ways can we fill a 2 × 3 strip: 3 → Either put a vertical tile in the 2 solutions possible for a 2 × 2 strip, or put 2 horizontal tiles in the only solution possible for a 2 × 1 strip. (2 + 1 = 3).
- Similarly, in how many ways can we fill a 2 × n strip: Either put a vertical tile in the solutions possible for 2 X $(n-1)$ strip or put 2 horizontal tiles in the solution possible for a 2 × $(n-2)$ strip. $(F_{n-1} + F_{n-2})$.
- That's how we verified that our final solution is: $F_n = F_{n-1} + F_{n-2}$ with $F_1 = 1$ and $F_2 = 2$.

Problem-36 **Longest Palindrome Subsequence:** A sequence is a palindrome if it reads the same whether we read it left to right or right to left. For example A, C, G, G, G, G, C, A. Given a sequence of length n, devise an algorithm to output the length of the longest palindrome subsequence. For example, the string $A,G,C,T,C,B,M,A,A,C,T,G,G,A,M$ has many palindromes as subsequences, for instance: $A, G, T, C, M, C, T, G, A$ has length 9.

Solution: Let us use DP to solve this problem. If we look at the sub-string A[i,..,j] of the string A, then we can find a palindrome sequence of length at least 2 if A[i] == A[j]. If they are not the same, then we have to find the maximum length palindrome in subsequences A[i + 1,...,j] and A[i,...,j – 1]. Also, every character $A[i]$ is a palindrome of length 1. Therefore the base cases are given by $A[i,i] = 1$. Let us define the maximum length palindrome for the substring A[i,...,j] as L(i, j).

$$L(i,j) = \begin{cases} L(i+1, j-1) + 2, & if\ A[i] == A[j] \\ Max\{L(i+1, j), L(i, j-1)\}, & otherwise \end{cases}$$

$$L(i,i) = 1 \text{ for all } i = 1\ to\ n$$

```
func longestPalindromeSubseq(s string) int {
    L := make([][]int, len(s))
    for i := range L {
        L[i] = make([]int, len(s))
    }
    return helper(s, 0, len(s)-1, L)
}
func helper(s string, lBound, rBound int, L [][]int) int {
    if lBound > rBound {
        return 0
    }
    if L[lBound][rBound] != 0 {
        return L[lBound][rBound]
    }
    if lBound == rBound {
        L[lBound][rBound] = 1
        return 1
    }
    if s[lBound] == s[rBound] {
        L[lBound][rBound] = 2 + helper(s, lBound+1, rBound-1, L)
    } else {
        lMax := helper(s, lBound, rBound-1, L)
        rMax := helper(s, lBound+1, rBound, L)
        if lMax > rMax {
            L[lBound][rBound] = lMax
        } else {
            L[lBound][rBound] = rMax
        }
    }
    return L[lBound][rBound]
}
```

Time Complexity: First *for* loop takes $O(n)$ time while the second 'for' loop takes $O(n-k)$ which is also $O(n)$. Therefore, the total running time of the algorithm is given by $O(n^2)$.

Problem-37 **Longest Palindrome Substring:** Given a string A, we need to find the longest sub-string of A such that the reverse of it is exactly the same.

Solution: The basic difference between the longest palindrome substring and the longest palindrome subsequence is that, in the case of the longest palindrome substring, the output string should be the contiguous characters, which gives the maximum palindrome; and in the case of the longest palindrome subsequence, the output is the sequence of characters where the characters might not be contiguous but they should be in an increasing sequence with respect to their positions in the given string.

Brute-force solution exhaustively checks all $n(n+1)/2$ possible substrings of the given n-length string, tests each one if it's a palindrome, and keeps track of the longest one seen so far. This has worst-case complexity $O(n^3)$, but we can easily do better by realizing that a palindrome is centered on either a letter (for odd-length palindromes) or a space between letters (for even-length palindromes). Therefore we can examine all $n+1$ possible centers and find the longest palindrome for that center, keeping track of the overall longest palindrome. This has worst-case complexity $O(n^2)$.

Let us use DP to solve this problem. It is worth noting that there are no more than $O(n^2)$ substrings in a string of length n (while there are exactly 2^n subsequences). Therefore, we could scan each substring, check for a palindrome, and update the length of the longest palindrome substring discovered so far. Since the palindrome test takes time linear in the length of the substring, this idea takes $O(n^3)$ algorithm. We can use DP to improve this. For $1 \le i \le j \le n$, define

$$L(i,j) = \begin{cases} 1, & if\ A[i] \ldots. A[j] \text{ is a palindrome substring,} \\ 0, & \text{otherwise} \end{cases}$$

$$L[i,i] = 1,$$

$$L[i,j] = L[i,i+1], if\ A[i] == A[i+1], for\ 1 \le i \le j \le n-1$$

Also, for string of length at least 3,

$$L[i,j] = (L[i+1, j-1]\ and\ A[i] = A[j])$$

Note that in order to obtain a well-defined recurrence, we need to explicitly initialize two distinct diagonals of the boolean array $L[i,j]$, since the recurrence for entry $[i,j]$ uses the value $[i-1, j-1]$, which is two diagonals away from $[i,j]$ (that means, for a substring of length k, we need to know the status of a substring of length $k-2$).

```
func longestPalindromeSubstring(A string) int {
    n := len(A)
    L := make([][]bool, n)
    for i := range L {
        L[i] = make([]bool, n)          // defaults to false
    }
    max := 1
    for i := 0; i < n-1; i++ {
        L[i][i] = true
        if A[i] == A[i+1] {
            L[i][i+1] = true
            max = 2
        }
    }
    for k := 3; k <= n; k++ {
        for i := 1; i < n-k+1; i++ {
            j := i + k - 1
            if A[i] == A[j] && L[i+1][j-1] {
                L[i][j] = true
                max = k
            } else {
                L[i][j] = false
            }
        }
    }
    return max
}
```

Time Complexity: First for loop takes $O(n)$ time while the second for loop takes $O(n-k)$ which is also $O(n)$. Therefore the total running time of the algorithm is given by $O(n^2)$.

Problem-38 Given two strings S and T, give an algorithm to find the number of times S appears in T. It's not compulsory that all characters of S should appear contiguous to T. For example, if $S = ab$ and $T = abadcb$ then the solution is 4, because ab is appearing 4 times in $abadcb$.

Solution: **Goal**: Count the number of times that S appears in T.

Assume $L(i, j)$ represents the count of how many times i characters of S are appearing in j characters of T.

$$L(i,j) = Max\begin{cases} 0, & if\ j = 0 \\ 1, & if\ i = 0 \\ L(i-1, j-1) + L(i, j-1), & if\ S[i] == T[j] \\ L(i-1, j), & if\ S[i] \neq T[j] \end{cases}$$

If we concentrate on the components of the above recursive formula,

- If $j = 0$, then since T is empty the count becomes 0.
- If $i = 0$, then we can treat empty string S also appearing in T and we can give the count as 1.
- If S[i] == T[j], it means i^{th} character of S and j^{th} character of T are the same. In this case we have to check the subproblems with $i - 1$ characters of S and $j - 1$ characters of T and also we have to count the result of i characters of S with $j - 1$ characters of T. This is because even all i characters of S might be appearing in $j - 1$ characters of T.
- If S[i] ≠ T[j], then we have to get the result of subproblem with $i - 1$ characters of S and j characters of T.

After computing all the values, we have to select the one which gives the maximum count.

How many subproblems are there? In the above formula, i can range from $1\ to\ m$ and j can range from $1\ to\ n$. There are a total of mn subproblems and each one takes O(1). Time Complexity is O(mn).

Space Complexity: O(mn) where m is number of rows and n is number of columns in the given matrix.

Problem-39 Given a matrix with n rows and m columns ($n \times m$). In each cell there are a number of apples. We start from the upper-left corner of the matrix. We can go down or right one cell. Finally, we need to arrive at the bottom-right corner. Find the maximum number of apples that we can collect. When we pass through a cell, we collect all the apples left there.

Solution: Let us assume that the given matrix is $A[n][m]$. The first thing that must be observed is that there are at most 2 ways we can come to a cell - from the left (if it's not situated on the first column) and from the top (if it's not situated on the most upper row).

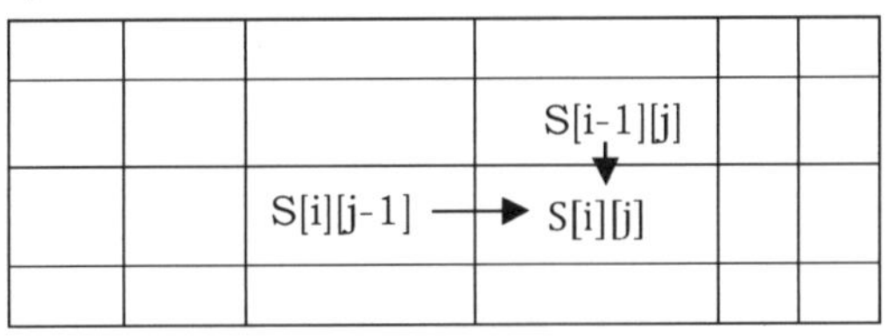

To find the best solution for that cell, we have to have already found the best solutions for all of the cells from which we can arrive to the current cell. From above, a recurrent relation can be easily obtained as:

$$S(i,j) = \left\{ A[i][j] + Max\begin{Bmatrix} S(i, j-1), & if\ j > 0 \\ S(i-1, j), & if\ i > 0 \end{Bmatrix} \right\}$$

$S(i, j)$ must be calculated by going first from left to right in each row and process the rows from top to bottom, or by going first from top to bottom in each column and process the columns from left to right.

```
func findApplesCount(A [][]int) int {
    n, m := len(A), len(A[0])
    S := make([][]int, n)           // computing the vertical prefix sum for columns
    for i := range S {
        S[i] = make([]int, m)       // defaults to 0
    }
    for i := 1; i < n; i++ {
        for j := 1; j < m; j++ {
            S[i][j] = A[i][j]
            if S[i][j] < S[i][j]+S[i][j-1] {
                S[i][j] += S[i][j-1]
            }
            if S[i][j] < S[i][j]+S[i-1][j] {
                S[i][j] += S[i-1][j]
            }
        }
    }
    return S[n-1][m-1]
}
```

How many such subproblems are there? In the above formula, i can range from $1\ to\ n$ and j can range from $1\ to\ m$. There are a total of nm subproblems and each one takes O(1).

Time Complexity is $O(nm)$.
Space Complexity: $O(nm)$, where m is number of rows and n is number of columns in the given matrix.

Problem-40 Similar to Problem-39, assume that we can go down, right one cell, or even in a diagonal direction. We need to arrive at the bottom-right corner. Give DP solution to find the maximum number of apples we can collect.

Solution: Yes. The discussion is very similar to Problem-39. Let us assume that the given matrix is A[n][m]. The first thing that must be observed is that there are at most 3 ways we can come to a cell - from the left, from the top (if it's not situated on the uppermost row) or from the top diagonal. To find the best solution for that cell, we have to have already found the best solutions for all of the cells from which we can arrive to the current cell. From above, a recurrent relation can be easily obtained:

$$S(i,j) = \left\{ A[i][j] + Max \begin{cases} S(i,j-1), & if\ j > 0 \\ S(i-1,j), & if\ i > 0 \\ S(i-1,j-1), if\ i > 0\ and\ j > 0 \end{cases} \right\}$$

$S(i,j)$ must be calculated by going first from left to right in each row and process the rows from top to bottom, or by going first from top to bottom in each column and process the columns from left to right.

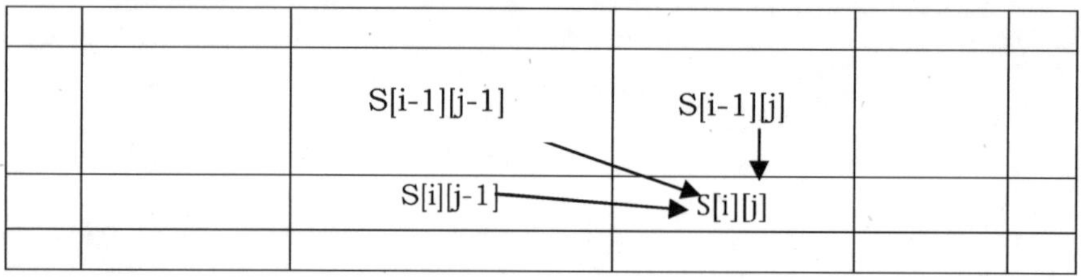

How many such subproblems are there? In the above formula, i can range from 1 to n and j can range from 1 $to\ m$. There are a total of nm subproblems and and each one takes O(1). Time Complexity is $O(nm)$.
Space Complexity: $O(nm)$ where m is number of rows and n is number of columns in the given matrix.

Problem-41 **Maximum size square sub-matrix with all 1's:** Given a matrix with 0's and 1's, give an algorithm for finding the maximum size square sub-matrix with all 1s. For example, consider the binary matrix below.

```
0 1 1 0 1
1 1 0 1 0
0 1 1 1 0
1 1 1 1 0
1 1 1 1 1
0 0 0 0 0
```

The maximum square sub-matrix with all set bits is

```
1 1 1
1 1 1
1 1 1
```

Solution: The simplest approach consists of trying to find out every possible square of 1's that can be formed from within the matrix. The question now is – how to go for it?

We use a variable to contain the size of the largest square found so far and another variable to store the size of the current, both initialized to 0. Starting from the left uppermost point in the matrix, we search for a 1. No operation needs to be done for a 0. Whenever a 1 is found, we try to find out the largest square that can be formed including that 1. For this, we move diagonally (right and downwards), i.e. we increment the row index and column index temporarily and then check whether all the elements of that row and column are 1 or not. If all the elements happen to be 1, we move diagonally further as previously. If even one element turns out to be 0, we stop this diagonal movement and update the size of the largest square. Now we, continue the traversal of the matrix from the element next to the initial 1 found, till all the elements of the matrix have been traversed.

```
func maximalSquare(B [][]byte) int {
    // row column size
    rows, cols, maxSquareLen := len(B), len(B[0]), 0
    for i := 0; i < rows; i++ {
        for j := 0; j < cols; j++ {
            if B[i][j] == 1 {
                sqlen, flag := 1, true
                for sqlen+i < rows && sqlen+j < cols && flag {
                    for k := j; k <= sqlen+j; k++ {
                        if B[i+sqlen][k] == 0 {
                            flag = false
```

```
                        break
                    }
                }
                for k := i; k <= sqlen+i; k++ {
                    if B[k][j+sqlen] == 0 {
                        flag = false
                        break
                    }
                }
                if flag {
                    sqlen++
                }
            }
            if maxSquareLen < sqlen {
                maxSquareLen = sqlen
            }
        }
    }
}
return maxSquareLen * maxSquareLen
}
```

Let us try solving this problem using DP. Let the given binary matrix be $B[m][m]$. The idea of the algorithm is to construct a temporary matrix $L[\,][\,]$ in which each entry $L[i][j]$ represents size of the square sub-matrix with all $1's$ including $B[i][j]$ and $B[i][j]$ is the rightmost and bottom-most entry in the sub-matrix.

Algorithm

1) Construct a sum matrix $L[m][n]$ for the given matrix $B[m][n]$.
    a. Copy first row and first columns as is from $B[\,][\,]$ to $L[\,][\,]$.
    b. For other entries, use the following expressions to construct L[ ][ ]
        if($B[i][j]$)
            $L[i][j] = min(L[i][j-1], L[i-1][j], L[i-1][j-1]) + 1;$
        else $L[i][j] = 0;$
2) Find the maximum entry in $L[m][n]$.
3) Using the value and coordinates of maximum entry in $L[i]$, print sub-matrix of $B[\,][\,]$.

```
func maximalSquareDP(B [][]byte) int {
    if len(B) == 0 || len(B[0]) == 0 {
        return 0
    }
    rows, cols := len(B), len(B[0])
    maxSquareLen := 0
    T := make([][]int, rows+1)
    for i := range T {
        T[i] = make([]int, cols+1)
    }
    for i := 1; i < rows; i++ {
        for j := 1; j < cols; j++ {
            if B[i][j] == 1 {
                T[i][j] = min(T[i-1][j-1], min(T[i][j-1], T[i-1][j])) + 1
            }
            maxSquareLen = max(maxSquareLen, T[i][j])
        }
    }
    return maxSquareLen * maxSquareLen
}
```

How many subproblems are there? In the above formula, i can range from 1 to n and j can range from 1 to m. There are a total of nm subproblems and each one takes O(1). Time Complexity is O(nm). Space Complexity is O(nm), where n is number of rows and m is number of columns in the given matrix.

Problem-42 **Maximum size sub-matrix with all 1's:** Given a matrix with 0's and 1's, give an algorithm for finding the maximum size sub-matrix with all 1s. For example, consider the binary matrix below.

```
1 1 0 0 1 0
0 1 1 1 1 1
1 1 1 1 1 0
```

0 0 1 1 0 0

The maximum sub-matrix with all set bits is

1 1 1 1
1 1 1 1

Solution: If we draw a histogram of all $1's$ cells in the above rows for a particular row, then maximum all $1's$ sub-matrix ending in that row will be equal to maximum area rectangle in that histogram. Below is an example for 3^{rd}row in the above discussed matrix [1]:

1 1 0 0 1 0
0 1 1 1 1 1
1 1 1 1 1 0
0 0 1 1 0 0

If we calculate this area for all the rows, maximum area will be our answer. We can extend our solution very easily to find start and end co-ordinates. For this, we need to generate an auxiliary matrix $S[][]$ where each element represents the number of 1s above and including it, up until the first 0. $S[][]$ for the above matrix will be as shown below:

1 1 0 0 1 0
0 2 1 1 2 1
1 3 2 2 3 0
0 0 3 3 0 0

Now we can simply call our maximum rectangle in histogram on every row in $S[][]$ and update the maximum area every time. Also we don't need any extra space for saving S. We can update original matrix (A) to S and after calculation, we can convert S back to A.

```
func maximalSubMatrix(A [][]int) int {
    max, cur_max, rows, cols := 0, 0, len(A), len(A[0])
    // Calculate Auxilary matrix
    for i := 1; i < rows; i++ {
        for j := 0; j < cols; j++ {
            if A[i][j] == 1 {
                A[i][j] = A[i-1][j] + 1
            }
        }
    }
    // Calculate maximum area in S for each rows
    for i := 0; i < rows; i++ {
        max = maxRectangleArea(A[i], cols) //Refer Stacks Chapter
        if max > cur_max {
            cur_max = max
        }
    }
    // Regenerate Original matrix
    for i := rows - 1; i > 0; i-- {
        for j := 0; j < cols; j++ {
            if A[i][j] == 1 {
                A[i][j] = A[i][j] - A[i-1][j]
            }
        }
    }
    return cur_max
}
```

Problem-43 **Maximum sum sub-matrix:** Given an $n \times n$ matrix M of positive and negative integers, give an algorithm to find the sub-matrix with the largest possible sum.

Solution: Let $Aux[r, c]$ represent the sum of rectangular subarray of M with one corner at entry $[1, 1]$ and the other at $[r, c]$. Since there are n^2 such possibilities, we can compute them in $O(n^2)$ time. After computing all possible sums, the sum of any rectangular subarray of M can be computed in constant time. This gives an $O(n^4)$ algorithm: we simply guess the lower-left and the upper-right corner of the rectangular subarray and use the Aux table to compute its sum.

Problem-44 Can we improve the complexity of Problem-43?

Solution: We can use the Problem-4 solution with little variation, as we have seen that the maximum sum array of a $1 - D$ array algorithm scans the array one entry at a time and keeps a running total of the entries. At any point, if this total becomes negative, then set it to 0. This algorithm is called *Kadane's* algorithm. We use this as an auxiliary function to solve a two-dimensional problem in the following way.

```
func findMaximumSubMatrix(A [][]int) int {
    n := len(A)
    M := make([][]int, n)          // computing the vertical prefix sum for columns
    for i := range M {
        M[i] = make([]int, n)      // defaults to 0
    }
    for i := 0; i < n; i++ {
        for j := 0; j < n; j++ {
            if j == 0 {
                M[j][i] = A[j][i]
            } else {
                M[j][i] = A[j][i] + M[j-1][i]
            }
        }
    }
    maxSoFar := 0
    // iterate over the possible combinations applying Kadane's Alg.
    for i := 0; i < n; i++ {
        for j := i; j < n; j++ {
            min := 0
            subMatrix := 0
            for k := 0; k < n; k++ {
                if i == 0 {
                    subMatrix += M[j][k]
                } else {
                    subMatrix += M[j][k] - M[i-1][k]
                }
                if subMatrix < min {
                    min = subMatrix
                }
                if (subMatrix - min) > maxSoFar {
                    maxSoFar = subMatrix - min
                }
            }
        }
    }
    return maxSoFar
}
```

Time Complexity: $O(n^3)$.

Problem-45 Given a number n, find the minimum number of squares required to sum a given number n.
Examples: min[1] = 1 = 1^2, min[2] = 2 = $1^2 + 1^2$, min[4] = 1 = 2^2, min[13] = 2 = $3^2 + 2^2$.

Solution: This problem can be reduced to a coin change problem. The denominations are 1 to $\sqrt{n}$. Now, we just need to make change for n with a minimum number of denominations.

```
func numSquares(n int) int {
    T := make([]int, n+1)
    T[0], T[1] = 0, 1
    for i := 2; i <= n; i++ {
        T[i] = math.MaxInt32
        for j := 1; i-j*j >= 0; j++ {
            T[i] = min(T[i], T[i-j*j]+1)
        }
    }
    return T[n]
}
```

Problem-46 **Finding Optimal Number of Jumps To Reach Last Element:** Given an array, start from the first element and reach the last by jumping. The jump length can be at most the value at the current position in the array. The optimum result is when you reach the goal in the minimum number of jumps.
Example: Given array A = {2,3,1,1,4}. Possible ways to reach the end (index list) are:

- 0,2,3,4 (jump 2 to index 2, and then jump 1 to index 3, and then jump 1 to index 4)
- 0,1,4 (jump 1 to index 1, and then jump 3 to index 4)

Since second solution has only 2 jumps it is the optimum result.

Solution: This problem is a classic example of Dynamic Programming. Though we can solve this by brute-force, it would be complex. We can use the LIS problem approach for solving this. As soon as we traverse the array, we should find the minimum number of jumps for reaching that position (index) and update our result array. Once we reach the end, we have the optimum solution at last index in result array.

How can we find the optimum number of jumps for every position (index)? For first index, the optimum number of jumps will be zero. Please note that if value at first index is zero, we can't jump to any element and return infinite. For $n + 1^{th}$ element, initialize result[$n + 1$] as infinite. Then we should go through a loop from $0 \ldots n$, and at every index i, we should see if we are able to jump to $n + 1$ from i or not. If possible, then see if total number of jumps (result[i] + 1) is less than result[$n + 1$], then update result[$n + 1$], else just continue to next index.

```
func minimumJumps(A []int) int {
    n, step, start, end := len(A), 0, 0, 0
    for end < n-1 {
        step++
        maxEnd := end + 1
        for i := start; i <= end; i++ {
            if i+A[i] >= n-1 {
                return step
            }
            maxEnd = max(maxEnd, i+A[i])
        }
        start = end + 1
        end = maxEnd
    }
    return step
}
```

The above code will return optimum number of jumps. To find the jump indexes as well, we can very easily modify the code as per requirement.

Time Complexity: Since we are running 2 loops here and iterating from 0 to i in every loop, then total time takes will be $1 + 2 + 3 + 4 + \ldots + n - 1$. So time efficiency $O(n) = O(n * (n-1)/2) = O(n^2)$.
Space Complexity: $O(n)$ space for result array.

Problem-47 Explain what would happen if a dynamic programming algorithm is designed to solve a problem that does not have overlapping sub-problems.

Solution: It will be just a waste of memory, because the answers of sub-problems will never be used again. And the running time will be the same as using the Divide & Conquer algorithm.

Problem-48 Christmas is approaching. You're helping Santa Claus to distribute gifts to children. For ease of delivery, you are asked to divide n gifts into two groups such that the weight difference of these two groups is minimized. The weight of each gift is a positive integer. Please design an algorithm to find an optimal division minimizing the value difference. The algorithm should find the minimal weight difference as well as the groupings in $O(nS)$ time, where S is the total weight of these n gifts. Briefly justify the correctness of your algorithm.

Solution: This problem can be converted into making one set as close to $\frac{S}{2}$ as possible. We consider an equivalent problem of making one set as close to W=$\left\lfloor\frac{S}{2}\right\rfloor$ as possible. Define FD(i, w) to be the minimal gap between the weight of the bag and W when using the first i gifts only. WLOG, we can assume the weight of the bag is always less than or equal to W. Then fill the DP table for $0 \le i \le n$ and $0 \le w \le W$ in which F(0, w) = W for all w, and

$$FD(i,w) = min\{FD(i-1, w-w_i) - w_i, FD(i-1,w)\}\ if\ \{FD(i-1, w-w_i) \geq w_i$$
$$= FD(i-1,w)\ \text{otherwise}$$

This takes $O(nS)$ time. $FD(n, W)$ is the minimum gap. Finally, to reconstruct the answer, we backtrack from (n, W). During backtracking, if $FD(i,j) = FD(i-1,j)$ then i is not selected in the bag and we move to $F(i-1, j)$. Otherwise, i is selected and we move to $F(i-1, j-w_i)$.

Problem-49 A circus is designing a tower routine consisting of people standing atop one another's shoulders. For practical and aesthetic reasons, each person must be both shorter and lighter than the person below him or her. Given the heights and weights of each person in the circus, write a method to compute the largest possible number of people in such a tower.

Solution: It is same as Box stacking and Longest increasing subsequence (LIS) problem.

CHAPTER 20

COMPLEXITY CLASSES

20.1 Introduction

In the previous chapters we have solved problems of different complexities. Some algorithms have lower rates of growth while others have higher rates of growth. The problems with lower rates of growth are called *easy* problems (or *easy solved problems*) and the problems with higher rates of growth are called *hard* problems (or *hard solved problems*). This classification is done based on the running time (or memory) that an algorithm takes for solving the problem.

Time Complexity	Name	Example	Problems
O(1)	Constant	Adding an element to the front of a linked list	Easy solved problems
$O(logn)$	Logarithmic	Finding an element in a binary search tree	
$O(n)$	Linear	Finding an element in an unsorted array	
$O(nlogn)$	Linear Logarithmic	Merge sort	
$O(n^2)$	Quadratic	Shortest path between two nodes in a graph	
$O(n^3)$	Cubic	Matrix Multiplication	
$O(2^n)$	Exponential	The Towers of Hanoi problem	Hard solved problems
$O(n!)$	Factorial	Permutations of a string	

There are lots of problems for which we do not know the solutions. All the problems we have seen so far are the ones which can be solved by computer in deterministic time. Before starting our discussion let us look at the basic terminology we use in this chapter.

20.2 Polynomial/Exponential Time

Exponential time means, in essence, trying every possibility (for example, backtracking algorithms) and they are very slow in nature. Polynomial time means having some clever algorithm to solve a problem, and we don't try every possibility. Mathematically, we can represent these as:

- Polynomial time is $O(n^k)$, for some k.
- Exponential time is $O(k^n)$, for some k.

20.3 What is a Decision Problem?

A decision problem is a question with a *yes/no* answer and the answer depends on the values of input. For example, the problem "Given an array of n numbers, check whether there are any duplicates or not?" is a decision problem. The answer for this problem can be either *yes* or *no* depending on the values of the input array.

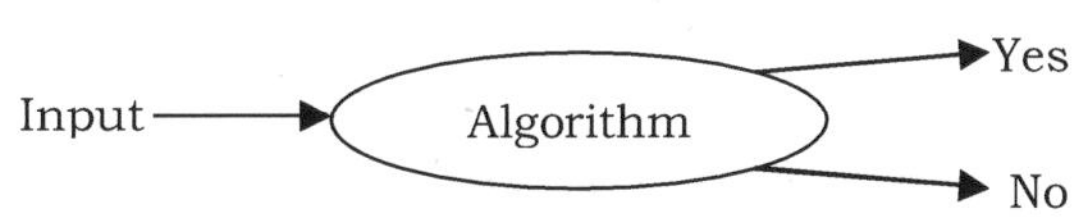

20.4 Decision Procedure

For a given decision problem let us assume we have given some algorithm for solving it. The process of solving a given decision problem in the form of an algorithm is called a *decision procedure* for that problem.

20.5 What is a Complexity Class?

In computer science, in order to understand the problems for which solutions are not there, the problems are divided into classes and we call them as complexity classes. In complexity theory, a *complexity class* is a set of problems with related complexity. It is the branch of theory of computation that studies the resources required during computation to solve a given problem.

The most common resources are time (how much time the algorithm takes to solve a problem) and space (how much memory it takes).

20.6 Types of Complexity Classes

P Class

The complexity class P is the set of decision problems that can be solved by a deterministic machine in polynomial time (P stands for polynomial time). P problems are a set of problems whose solutions are easy to find.

NP Class

The complexity class NP (NP stands for non-deterministic polynomial time) is the set of decision problems that can be solved by a non-deterministic machine in polynomial time. NP class problems refer to a set of problems whose solutions are hard to find, but easy to verify.

For better understanding let us consider a college which has 500 students on its roll. Also, assume that there are 100 rooms available for students. A selection of 100 students must be paired together in rooms, but the dean of students has a list of pairings of certain students who cannot room together for some reason.

The total possible number of pairings is too large. But the solutions (the list of pairings) provided to the dean, are easy to check for errors. If one of the prohibited pairs is on the list, that's an error. In this problem, we can see that checking every possibility is very difficult, but the result is easy to validate.

That means, if someone gives us a solution to the problem, we can tell them whether it is right or not in polynomial time. Based on the above discussion, for NP class problems if the answer is *yes*, then there is a proof of this fact, which can be verified in polynomial time.

Co-NP Class

$Co-NP$ is the opposite of NP (complement of NP). If the answer to a problem in $Co-NP$ is *no*, then there is a proof of this fact that can be checked in polynomial time.

P	Solvable in polynomial time
NP	*Yes* answers can be checked in polynomial time
$Co-NP$	*No* answers can be checked in polynomial time

Relationship between P, NP and Co-NP

Every decision problem in P is also in NP. If a problem is in P, we can verify YES answers in polynomial time. Similarly, any problem in P is also in $Co-NP$.

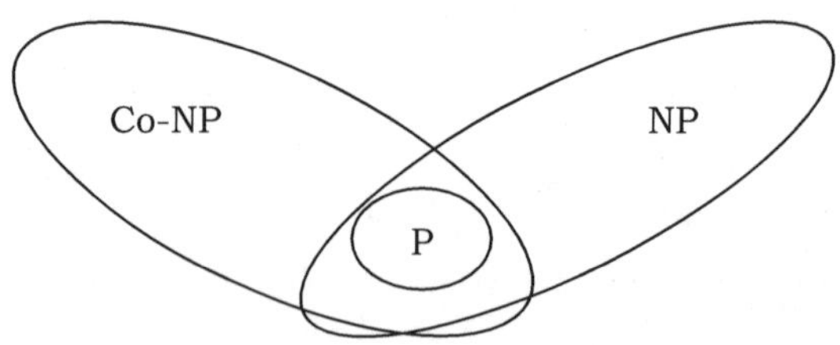

One of the important open questions in theoretical computer science is whether or not $P = NP$. Nobody knows. Intuitively, it should be obvious that $P \neq NP$, but nobody knows how to prove it.

Another open question is whether NP and $Co-NP$ are different. Even if we can verify every YES answer quickly, there's no reason to think that we can also verify NO answers quickly.

It is generally believed that $NP \neq Co-NP$, but again nobody knows how to prove it.

NP-hard Class

It is a class of problems such that every problem in NP reduces to it. All NP-hard problems are not in NP, so it takes a long time to even check them. That means, if someone gives us a solution for NP-hard problem, it takes a long time for us to check whether it is right or not.

A problem K is NP-hard indicates that if a polynomial-time algorithm (solution) exists for K then a polynomial-time algorithm for every problem is NP. Thus:

K is NP-hard implies that if K can be solved in polynomial time, then $P = NP$

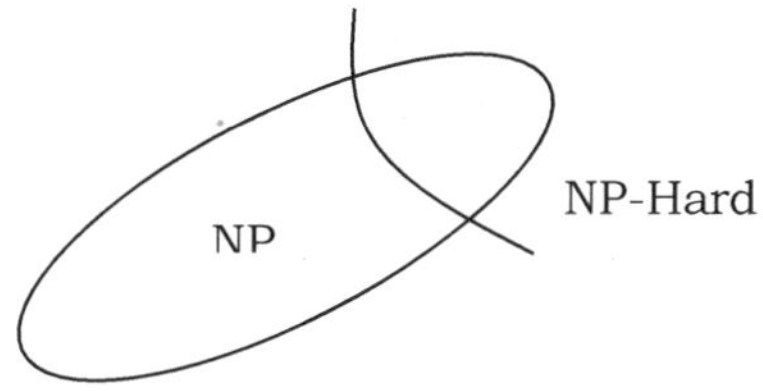

NP-complete Class

Finally, a problem is NP-complete if it is part of both NP-hard and NP. NP-complete problems are the hardest problems in NP. If anyone finds a polynomial-time algorithm for one NP-complete problem, then we can find polynomial-time algorithm for every NP-complete problem. This means that we can check an answer fast and every problem in NP reduces to it.

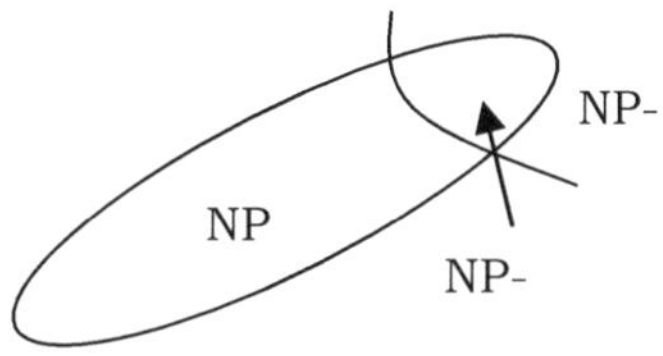

Relationship between P, NP Co-NP, NP-Hard and NP-Complete

From the above discussion, we can write the relationships between different components as shown below (remember, this is just an assumption).

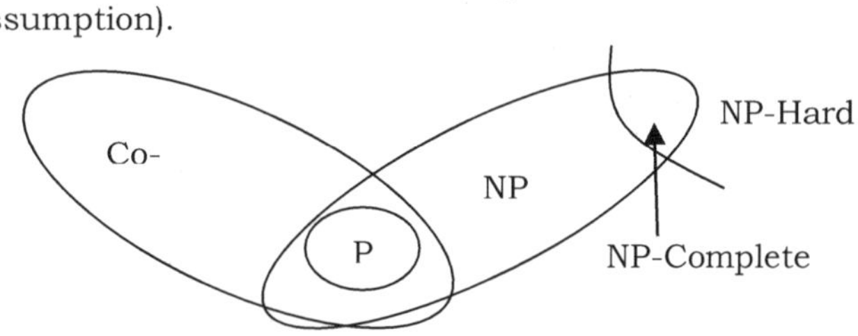

The set of problems that are NP-hard is a strict superset of the problems that are NP-complete. Some problems (like the halting problem) are NP-hard, but not in NP. NP-hard problems might be impossible to solve in general. We can tell the difference in difficulty between NP-hard and NP-complete problems because the class NP includes everything easier than its "toughest" problems – if a problem is not in NP, it is harder than all the problems in NP.

Does P==NP?

If $P = NP$, it means that every problem that can be checked quickly can be solved quickly (remember the difference between checking if an answer is right and actually solving a problem).

This is a big question (and nobody knows the answer), because right now there are lots of NP-complete problems that can't be solved quickly. If $P = NP$, that means there is a way to solve them fast. Remember that "quickly" means not trial-and-error. It could take a billion years, but as long as we didn't use trial and error, it was quick. In future, a computer will be able to change that billion years into a few minutes.

20.7 Reductions

Before discussing reductions, let us consider the following scenario. Assume that we want to solve problem X but feel it's very complicated. In this case what do we do?

The first thing that comes to mind is, if we have a similar problem to that of X (let us say Y), then we try to map X to Y and use $Y's$ solution to solve X also. This process is called reduction.

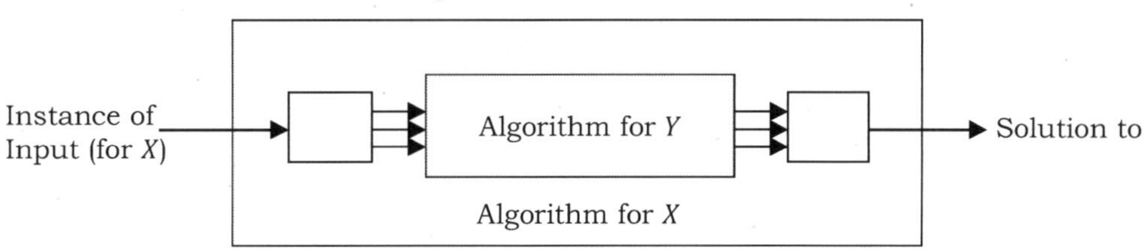

In order to map problem X to problem Y, we need some algorithm and that may take linear time or more. Based on this discussion the cost of solving problem X can be given as:

$$Cost\ of\ solving\ X = Cost\ of\ solving\ Y + Reduction\ time$$

Now, let us consider the other scenario. For solving problem X, sometimes we may need to use $Y's$ algorithm (solution) multiple times. In that case,

$$Cost\ of\ solving\ X = Number\ of\ Times * Cost\ of\ solving\ X + Reduction\ time$$

The main thing in NP-Complete is reducibility. That means, we reduce (or transform) given NP-Complete problems to other known NP-Complete problem. Since the NP-Complete problems are hard to solve and in order to prove that given NP-Complete problem is hard, we take one existing hard problem (which we can prove is hard) and try to map given problem to that and finally we prove that the given problem is hard.

Note: It's not compulsory to reduce the given problem to known hard problem to prove its hardness. Sometimes, we reduce the known hard problem to given problem.

Important NP-Complete Problems (Reductions)

Satisfiability Problem: A boolean formula is in *conjunctive normal form* (CNF) if it is a conjunction (AND) of several clauses, each of which is the disjunction (OR) of several literals, each of which is either a variable or its negation. For example: $(a \lor b \lor c \lor d \lor e) \land (b \lor \sim c \lor \sim d) \land (\sim a \lor c \lor d) \land (a \lor \sim b)$

A 3-CNF formula is a CNF formula with exactly three literals per clause. The previous example is not a 3-CNF formula, since its first clause has five literals and its last clause has only two.

2-SAT Problem: 3-SAT is just SAT restricted to 3-CNF formulas: Given a 3-CNF formula, is there an assignment to the variables so that the formula evaluates to TRUE?

2-SAT Problem: 2-SAT is just SAT restricted to 2-CNF formulas: Given a 2-CNF formula, is there an assignment to the variables so that the formula evaluates to TRUE?

Circuit-Satisfiability Problem: Given a boolean combinational circuit composed of AND, OR and NOT gates, is it satisfiable?. That means, given a boolean circuit consisting of AND, OR and NOT gates properly connected by wires, the Circuit-SAT problem is to decide whether there exists an input assignment for which the output is TRUE.

Hamiltonian Path Problem (Ham-Path): Given an undirected graph, is there a path that visits every vertex exactly once?

Hamiltonian Cycle Problem (Ham-Cycle): Given an undirected graph, is there a cycle (where start and end vertices are same) that visits every vertex exactly once?

Directed Hamiltonian Cycle Problem (Dir-Ham-Cycle): Given a directed graph, is there a cycle (where start and end vertices are same) that visits every vertex exactly once?

Travelling Salesman Problem (TSP): Given a list of cities and their pair-wise distances, the problem is to find the shortest possible tour that visits each city exactly once.

Shortest Path Problem (Shortest-Path): Given a directed graph and two vertices s and t, check whether there is a shortest simple path from s to t.

Graph Coloring: A k-coloring of a graph is to map one of k 'colors' to each vertex, so that every edge has two different colors at its endpoints. The graph coloring problem is to find the smallest possible number of colors in a legal coloring.

3-Color problem: Given a graph, is it possible to color the graph with 3 colors in such a way that every edge has two different colors?

Clique (also called complete graph): Given a graph, the $CLIQUE$ problem is to compute the number of nodes in its largest complete subgraph. That means, we need to find the maximum subgraph which is also a complete graph.

Independent Set Problem (Ind_Set): Let G be an arbitrary graph. An independent set in G is a subset of the vertices of G with no edges between them. The maximum independent set problem is the size of the largest independent set in a given graph.

Vertex Cover Problem (Vertex-Cover): A vertex cover of a graph is a set of vertices that touches every edge in the graph. The vertex cover problem is to find the smallest vertex cover in a given graph.

Subset Sum Problem (Subset-Sum): Given a set S of integers and an integer T, determine whether S has a subset whose elements sum to T.

Integer Programming: Given integers b_i, a_{ij} find 0/1 variables x_i that satisfy a linear system of equations.

$$\sum_{j=1}^{N} a_{ij}x_j = b_i \quad 1 \le i \le M$$
$$x_j \in \{0,1\} \ 1 \le j \le N$$

In the figure, arrows indicate the reductions. For example, Ham-Cycle (Hamiltonian Cycle Problem) can be reduced to CNF-SAT. Same is the case with any pair of problems. For our discussion, we can ignore the reduction process for each of the problems. There is a theorem called *Cook's Theorem* which proves that Circuit satisfiability problem is NP-hard. That means, Circuit satisfiability is a known NP-hard problem.

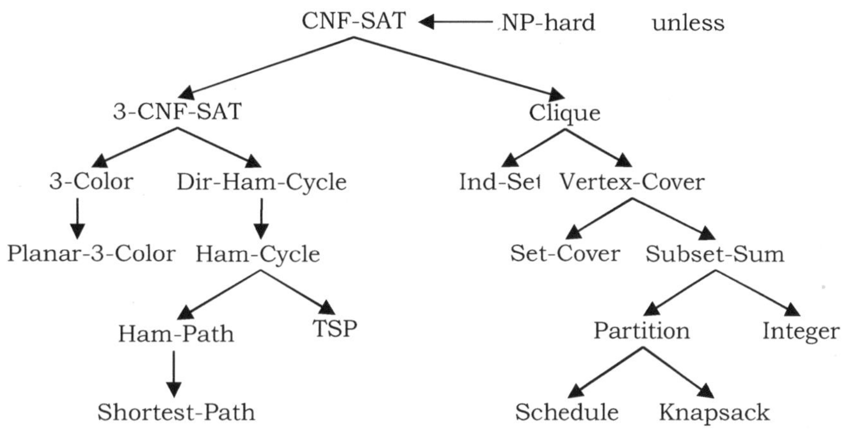

Note: Since the problems below are NP-Complete, they are NP and NP-hard too. For simplicity we can ignore the proofs for these reductions.

20.8 Complexity Classes: Problems & Solutions

Problem-1 What is a quick algorithm?

Solution: A quick algorithm (solution) means not trial-and-error solution. It could take a billion years, but as long as we do not use trial and error, it is efficient. Future computers will change those billion years to a few minutes.

Problem-2 What is an efficient algorithm?

Solution: An algorithm is said to be efficient if it satisfies the following properties:

- Scale with input size.
- Don't care about constants.
- Asymptotic running time: polynomial time.

Problem-3 Can we solve all problems in polynomial time?

Solution: **No**. The answer is trivial because we have seen lots of problems which take more than polynomial time.

Problem-4 Are there any problems which are NP-hard?

Solution: By definition, NP-hard implies that it is very hard. That means it is very hard to prove and to verify that it is hard. Cook's Theorem proves that Circuit satisfiability problem is NP-hard.

Problem-5 For 2-SAT problem, which of the following are applicable?
(a) P (b) NP (c) $CoNP$ (d) NP-Hard
(e) $CoNP$-Hard (f) NP-Complete (g) $CoNP$-Complete

Solution: 2-SAT is solvable in poly-time. So it is P, NP, and $CoNP$.

Problem-6 For 3-SAT problem, which of the following are applicable?
(a) P (b) NP (c) $CoNP$ (d) NP-Hard
(e) $CoNP$-Hard (f) NP-Complete (g) $CoNP$-Complete

Solution: 3-SAT is NP-complete. So it is NP, NP-Hard, and NP-complete.

Problem-7 For 2-Clique problem, which of the following are applicable?
(a) P (b) NP (c) $CoNP$ (d) NP-Hard
(e) $CoNP$-Hard (f) NP-Complete (g) $CoNP$-Complete

Solution: 2-Clique is solvable in poly-time (check for an edge between all vertex-pairs in O(n^2) time). So it is P, NP, and $CoNP$.

Problem-8 For 3-Clique problem, which of the following are applicable?
(a) P (b) NP (c) $CoNP$ (d) NP-Hard
(e) $CoNP$-Hard (f) NP-Complete (g) $CoNP$-Complete

Solution: 3-Clique is solvable in poly-time (check for a triangle between all vertex-triplets in O(n^3) time). So it is P, NP, and $CoNP$.

Problem-9 Consider the problem of determining. For a given boolean formula, check whether every assignment to the variables satisfies it. Which of the following is applicable?
(a) P (b) NP (c) $CoNP$ (d) NP-Hard
(e) CoNP-Hard (f) NP-Complete (g) $CoNP$-Complete

Solution: Tautology is the complimentary problem to Satisfiability, which is NP-complete, so Tautology is $CoNP$-complete. So it is $CoNP$, $CoNP$-hard, and $CoNP$-complete.

Problem-10 Let S be an NP-complete problem and Q and R be two other problems not known to be in NP. Q is polynomial time reducible to S and S is polynomial-time reducible to R. Which one of the following statements is true?
(a) R is NP-complete (b) R is NP-hard (c) Q is NP-complete (d) Q is NP-hard.

Solution: R is NP-hard (b).

Problem-11 Let A be the problem of finding a Hamiltonian cycle in a graph $G = (V, E)$, with $|V|$ divisible by 3 and B the problem of determining if Hamiltonian cycle exists in such graphs. Which one of the following is true?
(a) Both A and B are NP-hard (b) A is NP-hard, but B is not
(c) A is NP-hard, but B is not (d) Neither A nor B is NP-hard

Solution: Both A and B are NP-hard (a).

Problem-12 Let A be a problem that belongs to the class NP. State which of the following is true?
(a) There is no polynomial time algorithm for A.
(b) If A can be solved deterministically in polynomial time, then $P = NP$.
(c) If A is NP-hard, then it is NP-complete.
(d) A may be undecidable.

Solution: If A is NP-hard, then it is NP-complete (c).

Problem-13 Suppose we assume $Vertex - Cover$ is known to be NP-complete. Based on our reduction, can we say $Independent - Set$ is NP-complete?

Solution: Yes. This follows from the two conditions necessary to be NP-complete:

- Independent Set is in NP, as stated in the problem.
- A reduction from a known NP-complete problem.

Problem-14 Suppose *Independent Set* is known to be NP-complete. Based on our reduction, is *Vertex Cover* NP-complete?

Solution: No. By reduction from Vertex-Cover to Independent-Set, we do not know the difficulty of solving Independent-Set. This is because Independent-Set could still be a much harder problem than Vertex-Cover. We have not proved that.

Problem-15 The class of NP is the class of languages that cannot be accepted in polynomial time. Is it true? Explain.

Solution:
- The class of NP is the class of languages that can be *verified* in *polynomial time*.
- The class of P is the class of languages that can be *decided* in *polynomial time*.
- The class of P is the class of languages that can be *accepted* in *polynomial time*.

$P \subseteq NP$ and "languages in P can be accepted in polynomial time", the description "languages in NP cannot be accepted in polynomial time" is wrong.

The term NP comes from nondeterministic polynomial time and is derived from an alternative characterization by using nondeterministic polynomial time Turing machines. It has nothing to do with "cannot be accepted in polynomial time".

Problem-16 Different encodings would cause different time complexity for the same algorithm. Is it true?

Solution: True. The time complexity of the same algorithm is different between unary encoding and binary encoding. But if the two encodings are polynomially related (e.g. base 2 & base 3 encodings), then changing between them will not cause the time complexity to change.

Problem-17 If P = NP, then NPC (NP Complete) ⊆ P. Is it true?

Solution: True. If P = NP, then for any language L ∈ NP C (1) L ∈ NPC (2) L is NP-hard. By the first condition, L ∈ NPC ⊆ NP = P ⇒ NPC ⊆ P.

Problem-18 If NPC ⊆ P, then P = NP. Is it true?

Solution: True. All the NP problem can be reduced to arbitrary NPC problem in polynomial time, and NPC problems can be solved in polynomial time because NPC ⊆ P. ⇒ NP problem solvable in polynomial time ⇒ NP ⊆ P and trivially P ⊆ NP implies NP = P.

CHAPTER

MISCELLANEOUS CONCEPTS

21

21.1 Introduction

In this chapter we will cover the topics which are useful for interviews and exams.

21.2 Hacks on Bit-wise Programming

In C and $C++$ we can work with bits effectively. First let us see the definitions of each bit operation and then move onto different techniques for solving the problems. Basically, there are six operators that C and $C++$ support for bit manipulation:

<table>
<tr><th>Symbol</th><th>Operation</th></tr>
<tr><td>&</td><td>Bitwise AND</td></tr>
<tr><td>|</td><td>Bitwise OR</td></tr>
<tr><td>^</td><td>Bitwise Exclusive-OR</td></tr>
<tr><td><<</td><td>Bitwise left shift</td></tr>
<tr><td>>></td><td>Bitwise right shift</td></tr>
<tr><td>~</td><td>Bitwise complement</td></tr>
</table>

21.2.1 Bitwise AND

The bitwise AND tests two binary numbers and returns bit values of 1 for positions where both numbers had a one, and bit values of 0 where both numbers did not have one:

```
    01001011
&   00010101
    ----------
    00000001
```

21.2.2 Bitwise OR

The bitwise OR tests two binary numbers and returns bit values of 1 for positions where either bit or both bits are one, the result of 0 only happens when both bits are 0:

```
    01001011
|   00010101
    ----------
    01011111
```

21.2.3 Bitwise Exclusive-OR

The bitwise Exclusive-OR tests two binary numbers and returns bit values of 1 for positions where both bits are different; if they are the same then the result is 0:

```
    01001011
^   00010101
    ----------
    01011110
```

21.2.4 Bitwise Left Shift

The bitwise left shift moves all bits in the number to the left and fills vacated bit positions with 0.

```
          01001011
<< 2
          --------
          00101100
```

21.2.5 Bitwise Right Shift

The bitwise right shift moves all bits in the number to the right.

```
        01001011
>> 2
        --------
        ??010010
```

Note the use of ? for the fill bits. Where the left shift filled the vacated positions with 0, a right shift will do the same only when the value is unsigned. If the value is signed then a right shift will fill the vacated bit positions with the sign bit or 0, whichever one is implementation-defined. So the best option is to never right shift signed values.

21.2.6 Bitwise Complement

Golang doesn't have any specified unary Bitwise NOT(~) or we can say Bitwise Complement operator like other programming languages (C/C++, Java, Python, etc.). Here, we have to use Bitwise XOR(^) operator as Bitwise NOT operator. But how?

Here, you can see the result of XOR(A, B) = 1 only if A != B else it will be 0. So here, we will use the XOR operator as a unary operator to implement the one's complement to a number. In Golang, suppose you have a given bit A, so ~A = 1 ^ A which will be equal to one's complement or you can say the Bitwise NOT operator result.

```
        01001011
^       11111111
        ---------
        10110100
```

21.2.7 Checking Whether K-th Bit is Set or Not

Let us assume that the given number is n. Then for checking the Kth bit we can use the expression: $n \,\&\, (1 \ll K - 1)$. If the expression is true then we can say the Kth bit is set (that means, set to 1).

Example:	n	01001011	$K = 4$
	$1 \ll K - 1$	00001000	
	$n \,\&\, (1 \ll K - 1)$	00001000	

21.2.8 Setting K-th Bit

For a given number n, to set the Kth bit we can use the expression: $n \mid 1 \ll (K - 1)$

Example:	n	01001011	$K = 3$
	$1 \ll K - 1$	00000100	
	$n \mid (1 \ll K - 1)$	01001111	

21.2.9 Clearing K-th Bit

To clear K^{th} bit of a given number n, we can use the expression: $n \,\&\, \sim(1 \ll K - 1)$

Example:	n	01001011	$K = 4$
	$1 \ll K - 1$	00001000	
	$\sim(1 \ll K - 1)$	11110111	
	$n \,\&\, \sim(1 \ll K - 1)$	01000011	

21.2.10 Toggling K-th Bit

For a given number n, for toggling the Kth bit we can use the expression: $n \,\hat{}\,(1 \ll K - 1)$

Example:	n	01001011	$K = 3$
	$1 \ll K - 1$	00000100	
	$n \,\hat{}\, (1 \ll K - 1)$	01001111	

21.2.11 Toggling Rightmost One Bit

For a given number n, for toggling rightmost one bit we can use the expression: $n \,\&\, n - 1$

Example:	n	01001011
	$n - 1$	01001010
	$n \,\&\, n - 1$	01001010

21.2.12 Isolating Rightmost One Bit

For a given number n, for isolating rightmost one bit we can use the expression: $n \,\&\, -n$

Example:	n	01001011
	$-n$	10110101
	$n \,\&\, -n$	00000001

Note: For computing $-n$, use two's complement representation. That means, toggle all bits and add 1.

21.2.13 Isolating Rightmost Zero Bit

For a given number n, for isolating rightmost zero bit we can use the expression: $\sim n \,\&\, n+1$

Example:	n	01001011
	$\sim n$	10110100
	$n+1$	01001100
	$\sim n \,\&\, n+1$	00000100

21.2.14 Checking Whether Number is Power of 2 or Not

Given number n, to check whether the number is in 2^n form for not, we can use the expression: $if(n \,\&\, n-1 == 0)$

Example:	n	01001011
	$n-1$	01001010
	$n \,\&\, n-1$	01001010
	$if(n \,\&\, n-1 == 0)$	0

21.2.15 Multiplying Number by Power of 2

For a given number n, to multiply the number with 2^K we can use the expression: $n \ll K$

Example:	n	00001011	$K = 2$
	$n \ll K$	00101100	

21.2.16 Dividing Number by Power of 2

For a given number n, to divide the number with 2^K we can use the expression: $n \gg K$

Example:	n	00001011	$K = 2$
	$n \gg K$	00000010	

21.2.17 Finding Modulo of a Given Number

For a given number n, to find the %8 we can use the expression: $n \,\&\, 0x7$. Similarly, to find %32, use the expression: $n \,\&\, 0x1F$

Note: Similarly, we can find modulo value of any number.

21.2.18 Reversing the Binary Number

For a given number n, to reverse the bits (reverse (mirror) of binary number) we can use the following code snippet:

```
uint n, nReverse = n;
int s = sizeof(n);
for (; n; n >>= 1) {
    nReverse <<= 1;
    nReverse |= n & 1;
    s--;
}
nReverse <<= s;
```

Time Complexity: This requires one iteration per bit and the number of iterations depends on the size of the number.

21.2.19 Counting Number of One's in Number

For a given number n, to count the number of $1's$ in its binary representation we can use any of the following methods.

Method1: Process bit by bit with bitwise and operator

```
func countSetBits(n int) int {
    var count int
    for n != 0 {
        count += n & 1
        n >>= 1
```

```
    }
    return count
}
```

Time Complexity: This approach requires one iteration per bit and the number of iterations depends on system.

Method2: Using modulo approach

```
func countSetBits(n int) int {
    var count int
    for n > 0 {
        if n%2 == 1 {
            count++
        }
        n = n / 2
    }
    return count
}
```

Time Complexity: This requires one iteration per bit and the number of iterations depends on system.

Method3: Using toggling approach: $n \& n - 1$

```
func countSetBits(n int) int {
    var count int
    for n > 0 {
        count++
        n &= n - 1
    }
    return count
}
```

Time Complexity: The number of iterations depends on the number of 1 bits in the number.

Method4: Using preprocessing idea. In this method, we process the bits in groups. For example if we process them in groups of 4 bits at a time, we create a table which indicates the number of one's for each of those possibilities (as shown below).

0000→0	0100→1	1000→1	1100→2
0001→1	0101→2	1001→2	1101→3
0010→1	0110→2	1010→2	1110→3
0011→2	0111→3	1011→3	1111→4

The following code to count the number of 1s in the number with this approach:

```
// Make it as global as it is useful for multiple calls
var Table = []int{0, 1, 1, 2, 1, 2, 2, 3, 1, 2, 2, 3, 2, 3, 3, 4}
func countSetBits(n int) int {
    count := 0
    for ; n > 0; n >>= 4 {
        count = count + Table[n&0xF]
        return count
    }
    return count
}
```

Time Complexity: This approach requires one iteration per 4 bits and the number of iterations depends on system.

21.2.20 Creating Mask for Trailing Zero's

For a given number n, to create a mask for trailing zeros, we can use the expression: $(n \& -n) - 1$

Example: n	01001011
$-n$	10110101
$n \& -n$	00000001
$(n \& -n) - 1$	00000000

Note: In the above case we are getting the mask as all zeros because there are no trailing zeros.

27.2.21 Swap All Odd and Even Bits

Example: n	01001011
Find even bits of given number (evenN) = n & 0xAA	00001010

Find odd bits of given number (oddN) =	n & 0x55	01000001
	evenN >>= 1	00000101
	oddN <<= 1	10000010
Final Expression:	evenN | oddN	10000111

21.2.22 Performing Average without Division

Is there a bit-twiddling algorithm to replace $mid = (low + high) / 2$ (used in Binary Search and Merge Sort) with something much faster?

We can use $mid = (low + high) >> 1$. Note that using $(low + high) / 2$ for midpoint calculations won't work correctly when integer overflow becomes an issue. We can use bit shifting and also overcome a possible overflow issue: $low + ((high - low)/ 2)$ and the bit shifting operation for this is $low + ((high - low) >> 1)$.

21.3 Other Programming Questions

Problem-1 Give an algorithm for printing the matrix elements in spiral order.

Solution: Non-recursive solution involves directions right, left, up, down, and dealing their corresponding indices. Once the first row is printed, direction changes (from right) to down, the row is discarded by incrementing the upper limit. Once the last column is printed, direction changes to left, the column is discarded by decrementing the right hand limit.

```
func spiral(A [][]int) {
    rowStart, rowEnd, columnStart, columnEnd := 0, len(A)-1, 0, len(A[0])-1
    for {
        // Right
        for i := columnStart; i <= columnEnd; i++ {
            fmt.Printf("%d ", A[rowStart][i])
        }
        rowStart++
        if rowStart > rowEnd {
            break
        }
        // Down
        for i := rowStart; i <= rowEnd; i++ {
            fmt.Printf("%d ", A[i][columnEnd])
        }
        columnEnd--
        if columnStart > columnEnd {
            break
        }
        // Left
        for i := columnEnd; i >= columnStart; i-- {
            fmt.Printf("%d ", A[rowEnd][i])
        }
        rowEnd--
        if rowStart > rowEnd {
            break
        }
        // Right
        for i := rowEnd; i >= rowStart; i-- {
            fmt.Printf("%d ", A[i][columnStart])
        }
        columnStart++
        if columnStart > columnEnd {
            break
        }
    }
}
func main() {
    A := [][]int{
        {0, 1, 2, 3},      /* initializers for row indexed by 0 */
        {4, 5, 6, 7},      /* initializers for row indexed by 1 */
        {8, 9, 10, 11},    /* initializers for row indexed by 2 */
```

```
    }
    spiral(A)
}
```

Time Complexity: $O(n^2)$. Space Complexity: O(1).

Problem-2 Give an algorithm for shuffling the deck of cards.

Solution: Assume that we want to shuffle an array of 52 cards, from 0 to 51 with no repeats, such as we might want for a deck of cards. First fill the array with the values in order, then go through the array and exchange each element with a randomly chosen element in the range from itself to the end. It's possible that an element will swap with itself, but there is no problem with that.

```
func shuffle(cards []int, n int) {
    rand.Seed(time.Now().UnixNano())
    for i := len(cards) - 1; i > 0; i-- { // Fisher–Yates shuffle
        j := rand.Intn(i + 1)
        cards[i], cards[j] = cards[j], cards[i]
    }
}
```

Time Complexity: $O(n)$. Space Complexity: O(1).

Problem-3 Reversal algorithm for array rotation: Write a function rotate(A[], d, n) that rotates A[] of size n by d elements. For example, the array $1, 2, 3, 4, 5, 6, 7$ becomes $3, 4, 5, 6, 7, 1, 2$ after 2 rotations.

Solution: Consider the following algorithm.

Algorithm:

```
rotate(Array[], d, n)
reverse(Array[], 1, d) ;
reverse(Array[], d + 1, n);
reverse(Array[], l, n);
```

Let AB be the two parts of the input Arrays where A = Array[0..d-1] and B = Array[d..n-1]. The idea of the algorithm is:

Reverse A to get ArB. /* Ar is reverse of A */
Reverse B to get ArBr. /* Br is reverse of B */
Reverse all to get (ArBr) r = BA.
For example, if Array[] = [1, 2, 3, 4, 5, 6, 7], d =2 and n = 7 then, A = [1, 2] and B = [3, 4, 5, 6, 7]
Reverse A, we get ArB = [2, 1, 3, 4, 5, 6, 7], Reverse B, we get ArBr = [2, 1, 7, 6, 5, 4, 3]
Reverse all, we get (ArBr)r = [3, 4, 5, 6, 7, 1, 2]

Implementation:

```
func leftRotate(arr []int, d int, n int) {
    if d == 0 {
        return
    }
    reverseArray(arr, 0, d-1)
    reverseArray(arr, d, n-1)
    reverseArray(arr, 0, n-1)
}
func printArray(arr []int, size int) {
    var i int
    for i = 0; i < size; i++ {
        fmt.Printf("%d ", arr[i])
    }
}
func reverseArray(arr []int, start int, end int) {
    var temp int
    for start < end {
        //Function to reverse arr[] from index start to end
        temp = arr[start]
        arr[start] = arr[end]
        arr[end] = temp
        start++
        end--
    }
}
```

Problem-4 Suppose you are given an array s[1...n] and a procedure reverse (s,i,j) which reverses the order of elements in between positions i and j (both inclusive). What does the following sequence do, where 1 < k <= n:

```
reverse (s, 1, k);
reverse (s, k + 1, n);
reverse (s, 1, n);
```

a) Rotates s left by k positions b) Leaves s unchanged c) Reverses all elements of s d) None of the above

Solution: (b). Effect of the above 3 reversals for any k is equivalent to left rotation of the array of size n by k [refer to Problem-3].

Problem-5 Finding Anagrams in Dictionary: you are given these 2 files: dictionary.txt and jumbles.txt

The jumbles.txt file contains a bunch of scrambled words. Your job is to print out those jumbles words, 1 word to a line. After each jumbled word, print a list of real dictionary words that could be formed by unscrambling the jumbled word. The dictionary words that you have to choose from are in the dictionary.txt file. Sample content of jumbles.txt:

```
nwae: wean anew wane
eslyep: sleepy
rpeoims: semipro imposer promise
ettniner: renitent
ahicryrhe: hierarchy
dica: acid cadi caid
dobol: blood
......
%
```

Solution: Step-By-Step

Step 1: Initialization

- Open the dictionary.txt file and read the words into an array (before going further verify by echoing out the words back from the array out to the screen).
- Declare a hash table variable.

Step 2: Process the Dictionary for each dictionary word in the array. Do the following:

We now have a hash table where each key is the sorted form of a dictionary word and the value associated to it is a string or array of dictionary words that sort to that same key.

- Remove the newline off the end of each word via chomp($word);
- Make a sorted copy of the word - i.e. rearrange the individual chars in the string to be sorted alphabetically
- Think of the sorted word as the key value and think of the set of all dictionary words that sort to the exact same key word as being the value of the key
- Query the hashtable to see if the sortedWord is already one of the keys
- If it is not already present then insert the sorted word as key and the unsorted original of the word as the value
- Else concat the unsorted word onto the value string already out there (put a space in between)

Step 3: Process the jumbled word file

- Read through the jumbled word file one word at a time. As you read each jumbled word chomp it and make a sorted copy (the sorted copy is your key)
- Print the unsorted jumble word
- Query the hashtable for the sorted copy. If found, print the associated value on same line as key and then a new line.

Step 4: Celebrate, we are all done

Sample code in Perl:

```
#step 1
open("MYFILE",<dictionary.txt>);
while(<MYFILE>){
    $row = $_;
    chomp($row);
    push(@words,$row);
}
my %hashdic = ();
#step 2
foreach $words(@words){
    @not_sorted=split (//, $words);
```

```
    @sorted = sort (@not_sorted);
    $name=join("",@sorted);
    if (exists $hashdic{$name})    {
        $hashdic{$name}.=" $words";
    }
    else {
        $hashdic{$name}=$words;
    }
}
$size=keys %hashdic;
#step 3
open("jumbled",<jumbles.txt>);
while(<jumbled>){
    $jum = $_;
    chomp($jum);
    @not_sorted1=split (//, $jum);
    @sorted1 = sort(@not_sorted1);
    $name1=join("",@sorted1);
    if(length($hashdic{$name1})<1) {
        print "\n$jum : NO MATCHES";
    }
    else {
        @value=split(/ /,$hashdic{$name1});
        print "\n$jum : @values";
    }
}
```

Problem-6 **Pathways:** Given a matrix as shown below, calculate the number of ways for reaching destination *B* from *A*.

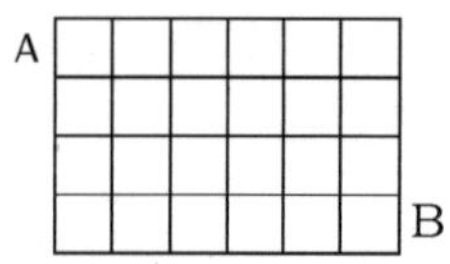

Solution: Before finding the solution, we try to understand the problem with a simpler version. The smallest problem that we can consider is the number of possible routes in a 1×1 grid.

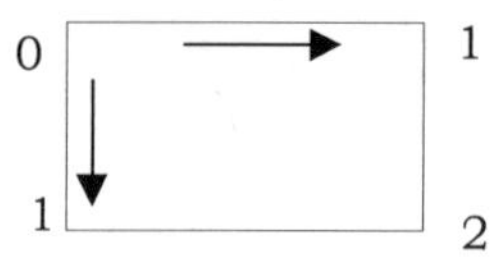

From the above figure, it can be seen that:

- From both the bottom-left and the top-right corners there's only one possible route to the destination.
- From the top-left corner there are trivially two possible routes.

Similarly, for 2*x*2 and 3*x*3 grids, we can fill the matrix as:

0	1
1	**2**

0	1	1
1	2	3
1	3	**6**

From the above discussion, it is clear that to reach the bottom right corner from left top corner, the paths are overlapping. As unique paths could overlap at certain points (grid cells), we could try to alter the previous algorithm, as a way to avoid following the same path again. If we start filling 4*x*4 and 5*x*5, we can easily figure out the solution based on our childhood mathematics concepts.

0	1	1	1
1	2	3	4
1	3	6	10
1	4	10	**20**

0	1	1	1	1
1	2	3	4	5
1	3	6	10	15
1	4	10	20	35
1	5	15	35	**70**

Are you able to figure out the pattern? It is the same as *Pascals* triangle. So, to find the number of ways, we can simply scan through the table and keep counting them while we move from left to right and top to bottom (starting with left-top). We can even solve this problem with mathematical equation of *Pascals* triangle.

Problem-7 Given a string that has a set of words and spaces, write a program to move the spaces to *front* of string. You need to traverse the array only once and you need to adjust the string in place.

Input = "move these spaces to beginning" *Output* =" movethesepacestobeginning"

Solution: Maintain two indices *i* and *j*; traverse from end to beginning. If the current index contains char, swap chars in index *i* with index *j*. This will move all the spaces to beginning of the array.

```
func mySwap(A []rune, i int, j int) {
	var temp rune = A[i]
	A[i] = A[j]
	A[j] = temp
}
func moveSpacesToBegin(A []rune) {
	var i int = len(A) - int(1)
	var j int = i
	for ; j >= 0; j-- {
		if unicode.IsSpace(A[j]) != true {
			mySwap(A, func() int {
				defer func() {
					i--
				}()
				return i
			}(), j)
		}
	}
}
func main() {
	var A []rune = []rune("move these spaces to begi\x00")
	fmt.Println("Value of A is: ", string(A))
	moveSpacesToBegin(sparr)
	fmt.Println("Value of A is: ", string(A))
}
```

Time Complexity: O(*n*) where *n* is the number of characters in input array. Space Complexity: O(1).

Problem-8 For Problem-7, can we improve the complexity?

Solution: We can avoid a swap operation with a simple counter. But, it does not reduce the overall complexity.

```
func moveSpacesToBegin(A []rune) {
	var n int = len(A) - int(1)
	count := n
	var i int = n
	for ; i >= 0; i-- {
		if A[i] != ' ' {
			A[count] = A[i]
			count--
		}
	}
	for count >= 0 {
		A[count] = ' '
		count--
	}
}
func main() {
	var A []rune = []rune("move these spaces to begi\x00")
	fmt.Println("Value of A is: ", string(A))
	moveSpacesToBegin(sparr)
	fmt.Println("Value of A is: ", string(A))
}
```

Time Complexity: O(*n*) where *n* is the number of characters in input array. Space Complexity: O(1).

Problem-9 Given a string that has a set of words and spaces, write a program to move the spaces to *end* of string. You need to traverse the array only once and you need to adjust the string in place.

Input = "move these spaces to end" *Output* = "movethesepacestoend "

Solution: Traverse the array from left to right. While traversing, maintain a counter for non-space elements in array. For every non-space character A[*i*], put the element at A[*count*] and increment *count*. After complete traversal, all non-space elements have already been shifted to front end and *count* is set as index of first 0. Now, all we need to do is run a loop which fills all elements with spaces from *count* till end of the array.

```
func moveSpacesToEnd(A []rune) {
	var n int = len(A) - int(1)
	count := 0
	for i := 0; i <= n; i++ {
		if A[i] != ' ' {
			// Count of non-space elements
			A[count] = A[i]
			count++
		}
	}
func main() {
	var sparr []rune = []rune("move these spaces to end")
	fmt.Println("Input is: ", string(sparr))
	moveSpacesToEnd(sparr)
	fmt.Println("Output is: ", string(sparr))
}
```

```
    for count <= n {
        A[count] = ' '
        count++
    }
}
```

Time Complexity: O(*n*) where *n* is number of characters in input array. Space Complexity: O(1).

Problem-10 Moving Zeros to end: Given an array of *n* integers, move all the zeros of a given array to the end of the array. For example, if the given array is {1, 9, 8, 4, 0, 0, 2, 7, 0, 6, 0}, it should be changed to {1, 9, 8, 4, 2, 7, 6, 0, 0, 0, 0}. The order of all other elements should be same.

Solution: Maintain two variables *i* and *j*; and initialize with 0. For each of the array element *A*[*i*], if *A*[*i*] non-zero element, then replace the element *A*[*j*] with element *A*[*i*]. Variable *i* will always be incremented till *n* - 1 but we will increment *j* only when the element pointed by *i* is non-zero.

```
func moveZerosToEnd(A []int) {
    i := 0
    j := 0
    for i <= len(A)-1 {
        if A[i] != 0 {
            A[j] = A[i]
            j++
        }
        i++
    }
    for j <= len(A)-1 {
        A[j] = 0
        j++
    }
}
```

```
func main() {
    var A []int = []int{1, 9, 8, 4, 0, 0, 2, 7, 0, 6, 0}
    fmt.Println("Input is: ", A)
    moveZerosToEnd(A)
    fmt.Println("Output is: ", A)
}
```

Time Complexity: O(*n*). Space Complexity: O(1).

Problem-11 For Problem-10, can we improve the complexity?

Solution: Using simple swap technique we can avoid the unnecessary second *while* loop from the above code.

```
func moveZerosToEnd(A []int) {
    i := 0
    j := 0
    for ; i < len(A); i++ {
        if A[i] != 0 {
            A[j], A[i] = A[i], A[j]
            j++
        }
    }
}
```

Time Complexity: O(*n*). Space Complexity: O(1).

Problem-12 Variant of Problem-10 and Problem-11: Given an array containing negative and positive numbers; give an algorithm for separating positive and negative numbers in it. Also, maintain the relative order of positive and negative numbers.
Input: -5, 3, 2, -1, 4, -8 Output: -5 -1 -8 3 4 2

Solution: In the *moveZerosToEnd* function, just replace the condition *A*[*i*] !=0 with *A*[*i*] < 0.

Problem-13 Given a number, swap odd and even bits.

Solution:

```
func swap(num int) int {
    even := 0xAAAAAAAA
    odd := 0x55555555
    return (num << 1 & even) | (num >> 1 & odd)
}
```

Problem-14 Count the number of set bits in all numbers from 1 to n

Solution: We can use the technique of section 21.2.19 and iterate through all the numbers from 1 to n.

```
func countSetBits(n int) int {
    count := 0
    i := 0
```

```
    var j int
    for i = 1; i <= n; i++ {
        j = i
        for j > 0 {
            j = j & (j - 1)
            count++
        }
    }
    return count
}
```

Problem-15 **Flower bed**: Suppose you have a long flowerbed in which some of the plots are planted and some are not. However, flowers cannot be planted in adjacent plots - they would compete for water and both would die. Given a flowerbed (represented as an array containing 0 and 1, where 0 means empty and 1 means not empty), and a number *n*, return if n new flowers can be planted in it without violating the no-adjacent-flowers rule.

Example 1: Input: flowerbed = [1,0,0,0,1], n = 1 Output: True
Example 2: Input: flowerbed = [1,0,0,0,1], n = 2 Output: False

Solution: The solution is very simple. We can find out the extra maximum number of flowers, count, that can be planted for the given flowerbed arrangement. To do so, we can traverse over all the elements of the flowerbed and find out those elements which are 0(implying an empty position). For every such element, we check if its both adjacent positions are also empty. If so, we can plant a flower at the current position without violating the no-adjacent-flowers-rule. For the first and last elements, we need not check the previous and the next adjacent positions respectively.

If the count obtained is greater than or equal to *n*, the required number of flowers to be planted, we can plant *n* flowers in the empty spaces, otherwise not.

```
func canPlaceFlowers(flowerbed []int, n int) bool {
    lenF, count := len(flowerbed), 0
    for p := range flowerbed {
        if flowerbed[p] == 0 && (p == 0 || flowerbed[p-1] == 0) && (p == lenF-1 || flowerbed[p+1] == 0) {
            flowerbed[p] = 1
            count++
        }
    }
    return count >= n
}
```

Time complexity: O(*n*). A single scan of the flowerbed array of size *n* is done. Space complexity: O(1).

Problem-16 Given two strings ***s*** and ***t*** which consist of only lowercase letters. String ***t*** is generated by random shuffling string ***s*** and then add one more letter at a random position. Find the letter that was added in ***t***.

Example Input: s = "abcd" t = "abcde" Output: e
Explanation: 'e' is the letter that was added.

Solution: Since there is only character difference between the two given strings, we can simply perform the XOR of all the characters from both the strings to get the difference.

```
func findTheDifference(s string, t string) string {
    var res byte
    for _, b := range []byte(s + t) {
        res ^= b
    }
    return string(res)
}
```

Time Complexity: O(*n*), where *n* is the length of arrays. Space Complexity: O(1).

REFERENCES

[1] Golang tour: https://tour.golang.org/
[2] Alfred V.Aho,J. E. (1983). Data Structures and Algorithms. Addison-Wesley.
[3] Algorithms.Retrieved from cs.princeton.edu/algs4/home
[4] Anderson., S. E. Bit Twiddling Hacks. Retrieved 2010, from Bit Twiddling Hacks: graphics.stanford.edu
[5] Bentley, J. AT&T Bell Laboratories. Retrieved from AT&T Bell Laboratories.
[6] Bondalapati, K. Interview Question Bank. Retrieved 2010, from Interview Question Bank: halcyon.usc.edu/~kiran/msqs.html
[7] Chen. Algorithms hawaii.edu/~chenx.
[8] Database, P.Problem Database. Retrieved 2010, from Problem Database: datastructures.net
[9] Drozdek, A. (1996). Data Structures and Algorithms in C++.
[10] Ellis Horowitz, S. S. Fundamentals of Data Structures.
[11] Gilles Brassard, P. B. (1996). Fundamentals of Algorithmics.
[12] Hunter., J. Introduction to Data Structures and Algorithms. Retrieved 2010, from Introduction to Data Structures and Algorithms.
[13] James F. Korsh, L. J. Data Structures, Algorithms and Program Style Using C.
[14] John Mongan, N. S. (2002). Programming Interviews Exposed. Wiley-India. .
[15] Judges. Comments on Problems and Solutions. http://www.informatik.uni-ulm.de/acm/Locals/2003/html/judge.html.
[16] Kalid. P, NP, and NP-Complete. Retrieved from P, NP, and NP-Complete.: cs.princeton.edu/~kazad
[17] Knuth., D. E. (1973). Fundamental Algorithms, volume 1 of The Art of Computer Programming. Addison-Wesley.
[18] Leon, J. S. Computer Algorithms. Retrieved 2010, from Computer Algorithms : math.uic.edu/~leon
[19] Leon., J. S. Computer Algorithms. math.uic.edu/~leon/cs-mcs401-s08.
[20] OCF. Algorithms. Retrieved 2010, from Algorithms: ocf.berkeley.edu
[21] Parlante., N. Binary Trees. Retrieved 2010, from cslibrary.stanford.edu: cslibrary.stanford.edu
[22] Patil., V. Fundamentals of data structures. Nirali Prakashan.
[23] Poundstone., W. HOW WOULD YOU MOVE MOUNT FUJI? New York Boston.: Little, Brown and Company.
[24] Pryor, M. Tech Interview. Retrieved 2010, from Tech Interview: techinterview.org
[25] Questions, A. C. A Collection of Technical Interview Questions. Retrieved 2010, from A Collection of Technical Interview Questions
[26] S. Dasgupta, C. P. Algorithms cs.berkeley.edu/~vazirani.
[27] Sedgewick., R. (1988). Algorithms. Addison-Wesley.
[28] Sells, C. (2010). Interviewing at Microsoft. Retrieved 2010, from Interviewing at Microsoft
[29] Shene, C.-K. Linked Lists Merge Sort Implementation.
[30] Sinha, P. Linux Journal. Retrieved 2010, from: linuxjournal.com/article/6828.
[31] Structures., d. D. www.math-cs.gordon.edu. Retrieved 2010, from www.math-cs.gordon.edu
[32] T. H. Cormen, C. E. (1997). Introduction to Algorithms. Cambridge: The MIT press.
[33] Tsiombikas, J. Pointers Explained. nuclear.sdf-eu.org.
[34] Warren., H. S. (2003). Hackers Delight. Addison-Wesley.
[35] Weiss., M. A. (1992). Data Structures and Algorithm Analysis in C.
[36] SANDRASI http://sandrasi-sw.blogspot.in/

Made in the USA
Monee, IL
15 September 2026

63245911R00299